黑龙江省艺术科学规划项目阶段性成果（项目编号:2022B099）
黑龙江省博士后科研启动金资助项目（项目编号:2901051671）

STUDY ON THE HISTORY OF HEILONGJIANG IMMIGRATION IN THE LATE QING DYNASTY AND EARLY REPUBLIC OF CHINA

清末民初黑龙江移民史研究

李 朋 魏 影 尹铁超 高龙彬 高振凌◎著
李 靖 张春烨 黄 睿 樊 蓉 龙 瑶 张 伊 刘 慧◎译著

中国经济出版社
CHINA ECONOMIC PUBLISHING HOUSE
·北 京·

图书在版编目（CIP）数据

清末民初黑龙江移民史研究 = Study on the History of Heilongjiang Immigration in the Late Qing Dynasty and Early Republic of China ：汉、英 / 李朋等著；李靖等译著. -- 北京 ：中国经济出版社，2024. 8. -- ISBN 978-7-5136-7897-1

I . D632.4

中国国家版本馆 CIP 数据核字第 20247DC116 号

责任编辑　张　博
责任印制　马小宾
封面设计　任燕飞装帧设计工作室

出版发行　中国经济出版社
印 刷 者　北京建宏印刷有限公司
经 销 者　各地新华书店
开　　本　710mm × 1000mm　1/16
印　　张　27
字　　数　586 千字
版　　次　2024 年 8 月第 1 版
印　　次　2024 年 8 月第 1 次
定　　价　98.00 元
广告经营许可证　京西工商广字第 8179 号

中国经济出版社　**网址** http://epc.sinopec.com/epc/　**社址** 北京市东城区安定门外大街 58 号　**邮编** 100011
本版图书如存在印装质量问题，请与本社销售中心联系调换（联系电话：010-57512564）

译者前言

历史作为一面镜子，记录了人类社会的兴衰成败，也预示着人类的未来。现代历史学家、国学大师钱穆先生曾指出："研究历史，就是要研究此历史背后的民族精神和文化精神。鉴古知今，究往穷来，这才是史学的精神。"

中国历史上出现过的区域移民人数之众、次数之多、距离之长、范围之广、影响之大，遍观整个世界移民史，都是独一无二的存在，而来自不同地域的移民既具有中国移民的整体特征，又有独特的地缘性。因此，开展国内区域移民及其社会影响研究，不仅对移民史料挖掘、个案实证、相关理论建构有深远意义，对推进地方、中国乃至国际移民的相关经济、社会、文化等领域的研究，都将产生不可低估的学术价值，而且对于中国政府善治人口流动问题和创新社会管理，以及国际社会有效管理跨国跨境移民也将起到一定的参考作用。

清末民初的黑龙江移民是中国历史上大规模人口迁徙浪潮之一，对黑龙江流域的历史进程产生了巨大而深远的影响，其所塑造的文明与文化特质及其作用与黑龙江流域外的地方迥然不同。之所以如此，是因为在时空方面它伴随着并促进了中国社会的重大转型——农耕时代迈向工业化时代、封建专制王朝走向共和、封闭的帝国开始拥抱世界。多领域的专家学者在《清末民初黑龙江移民史研究》一书中以同一个主题，全新的方式，结合新的研究成果，初步展示了该时代黑龙江流域社会各方面的全息图景，凸显了那里的经济、政治、文化、军事等诸多领域独特的地位和重要性。《清末民初黑龙江移民史研究》的英译也向世界开启了一扇窗，展示了黑龙江流域文明及其在中华文明转型期里所发挥的作用，堪称是相关研究的里程碑。

传统观念中，黑龙江地处祖国边陲、交通末梢，但是换个思路和角度，边陲就会变中心、末梢就会变前沿——黑龙江作为东北亚的中心，北联俄罗斯，南向广阔的国内市场。"希望黑龙江响应国家'一带一路'倡议，参与'中蒙俄经济走廊'建设，积极扩大对外开放。"这是习近平总书记对黑龙江的殷殷嘱托。《清末民初黑龙江移民史研究》英译的价值在于：①从本土译论出发，传播中国文化的厚重底蕴和价值观念，发展品牌文化，拓宽国际交流渠道，促进中国文化"走出去"；②为政府相关部门制定移民文化旅游实施方案提供依据；③为高等院校、科研机构和学术团体开展中国移民文化研究奠定文献基础；④构建中国移民文化译介模式，减少和规避跨文化交流中的各类错误，为各国人士了解中国多元文化，在哈尔滨投资、经商、旅游提供便利。

该书的英译本出版经历了漫长而曲折的过程：2022 年初张春烨副教授与《清末民初黑龙江移民史研究》的主要作者李朋教授等接洽，商谈翻译事宜；2022 年 12 月李靖教授与中国经济出版社沟通签约出版译著事宜，但由于新冠疫情的影响，2023 年 4 月才完成全部手续正式签约。从 2022 年 2 月开始，李靖教授和张春烨副教授开始组建翻译团队，译者工作组陆续从 5 人扩展至 9 人，700 多个日子里，译者们通过微信、电话、邮件、面谈的方式从祖国各地会聚在一起，研讨译著的点滴细节。译者们首先通读全书，建立术语库，汇总术语溯源，透彻理解源语文本，探究该移民史研究文本的文体特征、语言内涵，总结翻译对策，随后依托变译理论、生态翻译理论、目的论等，提炼适用于历史研究文献的翻译范式。漫长的时光，无常的世事，疫情的反复，家人的安危，一切都无法阻挡我们如火的热情，奋斗的决心！

译著共分五章，前四章为原著译文，第五章为译者们的翻译研究成果汇总。翻译项目组成员分工如下：序言，黄睿（负责 4633 字）、李靖；第一章，张春烨、黄睿（负责 15359 字）、刘明慧（负责 7168 字）；第二章，樊蓉；第三章，李靖、刘慧、樊蓉、龙瑶；第四章，张伊、张春烨；第五章，李靖、刘慧、龙瑶、张伊；附录，张春烨、陆奕婷（负责 6308 字）、刘慧、李靖。全书统稿，由李靖、张春烨完成。

感谢相伴两年的译者团队成员：黄睿、樊蓉、刘慧、龙瑶、张伊、陆奕婷、刘明慧。岁月如梭，流年易逝，感谢你们于滚滚红尘中，与我们携手并肩。聚散寻常事，相聚终有时。期盼有朝一日能与诸君共聚首，把酒祝东风，愿诸位所求皆如愿，所行皆坦途！

特别感谢原著作者李朋教授，译者就一些佶屈聱牙的文言术语深夜打扰的时候，您能不厌其烦地引经据典，一一指点；也要感谢尹铁超教授和高龙彬副教授对原著文化背景的详尽介绍，使译者能够准确把握原著文体风格；还要感谢魏影教授和高振凌先生一直以来的默默鼓励和支持。这一切都让我们深深体会到来自原著作者"天团"的温暖，是他们给了我们砥砺前行的勇气。

在此也要向责任编辑张博表达敬意：疫情时殷切的话语，直抵内心；微信中的上百条回复信息，昭示关注；耐心审阅、细致审查及给予的详尽评注，彰显专业。感谢您一年多来的陪伴与支持，使这本译著能够如期诞生。

历史告诉我们，忘记过去就意味着背弃了自己的根源，而对待历史要既敬畏又审慎。

正如卡尔·马克思所说："历史一再证明，人民可以从他们所选择的道路上解放出来，但他们不能从他们所选择的后果中解放出来。"

因此，追溯历史不仅是对过去的回顾，更是对未来的思考和引导。

谨以此书献给深爱这片沃土，在此耕耘过、奋斗过，流过血、洒过泪的赫赫有名的英雄和默默无闻的百姓！

祝愿家乡黑龙江乘着振兴东北的东风，如天鹅展翅，一飞冲天！

李靖　张春烨

2024年6月于哈尔滨

Preface

As for the topic "immigrants", history research dabbles in various aspects. This book focuses on the issue of "immigrants", not from the view of the macroscopic evolution of civilization, but from the development, transformation, characteristics and other aspects of the culture of this region and the relationship between "the immigrants" who were within the area of today's Heilongjiang Province and the development of that area in the approach of history research. To be more specific, we launched this project for the following practical concerns.

Firstly, in the history of civilization of China and Northeast Asia, the structure of the population around the Heilongjiang River possesses unusual features, and the issue of the distinctive characters, functions and influences of its civilization is one of the central subjects of the civilization study, culture development and harmonious society. It is believed that those distinctive characters made Heilongjiang Province stand out from other areas of China, by which Heilongjiang can identify and cultivate its own cultural characteristics, accordingly, its culture industry is going to thrive on that basis.

Secondly, the wave of immigration in Heilongjiang from the Late Qing Dynasty to the Early Republic of China is one of the largest waves of immigration in the history of China, which has a strong and profound influence on the process of the development of Heilongjiang. As we all know, in the civilization of humanity, whether in the primitive times or the civilized times, the "movement of population" is quite common. However, this wave of immigration is quite special—it is a milestone of the "modernization" of Heilongjiang. In this wave, Heilongjiang shows its unique position and significance in economy, politics, culture, military affairs and other fields. For what has been mentioned above, by identifying its advantages and conditions of development, this project intends to write the "history" for the contributions of people of Heilongjiang and finds a right direction, an easy path and an adequate position for the "Rejuvenation of Heilongjiang" as well in the new era.

Thirdly, this research gives a multi-dimensional insight into various fields in the approach of "dynastic history". It is a comprehensive "interdisciplinary" exploration in the history of immigration, culture, economy, politics and society. Experts and scholars from different fields in this team have made certain new discoveries and offered their unique opinions on the subject through new methods and achievements. "Innovation" is the thread of our work. This research gives a rough panorama of the development of Heilongjiang from the Late Qing Dynasty to the Early Republic of China, which provides a new stage for us to examine the characteristics of the culture and civilization of Heilongjiang from a whole new viewpoint.

I

After two years' thorough study, we understand the issues concerning the subject better and more deeply. We come to find that the problems to be solved are much more complicated than we expected, and thus it takes a great deal of time and toil to finish the project. If we want to solve all the problems once and for all, we are not able to make it within just 30 months or so by only a few people. A more meaningful study requires more talents, tools and time, which can only be successful by wider investigation and research. What is worth expecting is that we will keep going, recruit new talents, raise more funds, and provide statistics in more fields, more specific analyses and testified judgments to our government and different departments of our society. This is our obligatory contribution to Heilongjiang Province at present and in the future.

Nevertheless, what we have achieved is quite satisfying for us, for we have made important accomplishments and pioneering studies in every essential field and direction, all the results laid the foundation and framework of further research. The identification of the paradigm of a discipline is an important prerequisite of its healthy growth. For example:

1. The research of the living conditions of Oroqen people—indigenous people and ethnic minorities.

2. The research of the Manchu people born in Beijing who were dispatched to Northeast China—immigration organized by the government.

3. The research of the Shandong Guild Hall and Shandong Townsmen Association—inter-province immigration within China.

4. The research of the Chinese Eastern Railway Foreign Affairs Office—international factors which influence different aspects of the society of immigrants in Heilongjiang.

5. The research of the Jewish people in Harbin—foreign immigrants to Heilongjiang.

6. The research of the features of Harbin—what roles distinctive domestic and international types of economy and politics played in the formation of the culture of immigrants to Heilongjiang.

7. The research of Li Hongmo—the effects of celebrities on the development process of the immigrants' society.

Those accomplishments are the essential basis on which this project is going to extend, and we also propose the basic framework and the beginning point of the research of "the history of immigrants between areas within China". The further study is made under this framework. The study on the history of Heilongjiang immigration in the Late Qing Dynasty and Early Republic of China will give readers a whole new angle to view the history of Heilongjiang immigration. In reality, besides the above-mentioned wave of immigration, mass waves of government organized immigration with the purpose of building the frontier of China after the victory of the War of Resistance against Japanese Aggression, and mass movement to the major cities in China a few years after the founding of the People's Republic of China also had a significant influence on the formation of the society and the development of economy of Heilongjiang. Those waves are beyond the scope of this project of "the dynastic history research", but they are essential elements which did have "big effects" on the society, economy and politics of today's Heilongjiang, and a number of issues concerning the economy and culture are closely connected with them. As a result, we will probe into the subject step by step, and explore related academic issues for the purpose of solving practical problems.

Ⅱ

Further as we extend into this field, we find it more impossible to make the so called "100% pure research of history". To our surprise, what makes us feel happy and enjoy ourselves are those researches which are not so "pure", namely the researches of culture on the basis of history or the researches of history on the basis of culture. In our viewpoints, they offer us more value and fun of the study. In a word, the history study of immigrants to Heilongjiang more often focuses on culture. The long poem of our memories is a torrent in the river of culture where every piece of the "real history" we describe is soaked, baptized, tailored, wrapped up and sent out.

Nowadays, the development of society, ethnic affairs, politics, economy and culture within Heilongjiang has close links with its distinctive "culture of immigration". The "culture of immigration" and its influences on Heilongjiang have the following major features: ① pluralism; ② continuity and changeability with times; ③ discrepancy in the practical phases of development; ④ compatibility and similarity with the process of modern "Rejuvenation of Heilongjiang".

Based on this research, the main findings are as follows: ① The society of immigrants to Heilongjiang today has its own characteristics—there are distinct discrepancies in the level of development and the features between societies of different communities and ethnic groups. Various models of development, exotic culture and civilization not only "coexist", but "nourish each other". ② Different cultures in Heilongjiang coexist with one another, and they learn from others rather than hold the view that "All his geese are swans". They cherish their own civilization while welcoming good and new things. ③ The genes of ancient cultures flow smoothly in the energetic torrents of coexistence, where exotic cultures turn and merge into a "new culture". People in this area neither feel the pressure from the "culture of the outsiders" nor from the "culture of the insiders". They live and let live harmoniously. ④ In such cultural, economic and political atmosphere, people live with their heart. Furthermore, they create a "new morale of the times" which is widely longed for and accepted by citizens from different status. ⑤ In terms of treating "the culture from another country", they never determine to eradicate the other one, and they appreciate each other while preserving their own characteristics. They consider the existence of others is the survival and "nourishment" of themselves. Every type of culture is not only upheld proudly and confidently but accepted and respected by other cultural units in the symbiosis.

What is more noteworthy is that this type of culture and civilization was widely accepted, admired and praised by people of other regions, and was regarded as the main symbol of the civilization of Heilongjiang and representative characteristics of people of Heilongjiang. During "the Golden Period of Development", people from all walks of life came to Heilongjiang (Harbin was a typical example) from home and abroad: sensitive writers, scholars, politicians, well-informed journalists from Western countries ... They all left their amazed and appreciative comments on this city.

The unique wave of immigration in the history of Heilongjiang and its influences are essential factors in Heilongjiang's thoroughly thriving. It was in the Late Qing Dynasty and Early Republic of China when the features of the civilization of Heilongjiang took shape. Future generations can't avoid those facts no matter in what way they choose to develop. Any distortions and ambiguities will be obstructive and perplex to our endeavor. As the old saying goes, "If we didn't know the past, how can we know the future?"

Ⅲ

Geographically, nowadays the so called "Northeast China" refers to the "three northeastern provinces" (Heilongjiang, Jilin and Liaoning provinces) according to the administrative division, and Heilongjiang is the northmost one. In prehistoric times, Heilongjiang was not wild and uncivilized, but had its own colourful "prehistoric civilization" which was related with other regions. When the Chinese civilization entered agricultural civilization, Heilongjiang couldn't catch up with the development of the inner land though its level of civilization improved a little. As dynasties passing, it gradually lagged behind other inland areas and geographically fell to the "out-of-the-way borderland" and turned into "the edge" of Chinese civilization socially and economically. However, in the times where "the modern culture" led by Western countries and Chinese traditional culture began to blend, it showed a process of the sudden change of "social transformation" because of an "accidental" factor. Its thought-provoking uniqueness is still enigmatic. The most noticing difference of it is that unlike other "forced opening up" (semi-colonial and semi-feudal) areas, in this "wave of modernization", people in Heilongjiang accepted modernization "voluntarily". It is the first "positive modernization" in the history of China. Furthermore, many "accidental factors" resulted in dazzling accomplishments, led by "the construction of the city movement" in Harbin,

Heilongjiang entered "the Golden Period of Development".

The first important feature of "the Golden Period of Development" is "the subjectivity of the event", whether from governmental offices or grass-roots branches, they had "positive" attitudes towards civil affairs and they were "active" in action. That process was without doubt relatively "positive" compared with other cities of the first wave of "modernization". The others were forced to open up mostly because they were defeated by the enemy or burdened with the military pressure from the enemy. The so-called "modernization" was also dominated by imperialist powers, the Qing Government always made concessions and succumbed to them and was reluctant to accept the fact of "modernization", civil officers and citizens also felt the "bitterness" and had mixed feelings toward "modernization". In contrast to what has been mentioned above, this wave of modernization in the northernmost borderland was the "self-salvation" strategy of the Qing Government which was made after weighing the diplomatic pros and cons.

The second important feature is that most of the Northeast cities had already been the centers of economy, culture and politics in the region, which was of considerable scale and local influence before the opened-up, and they were units of traditional Chinese economy system with strong features of traditional civilization. Although most of the land "leased" to imperialist powers was barren land, the adjacent regions are good for the development of commercial business. Before "the modern economic link" with Harbin as the center along the Chinese Eastern Railway turned up, integrated and stable administrative and economic units were yet to form. In addition, the attitudes and expectations of local people were different from those of other regions, at least during "the Golden Period of Development". Whether politicians, businessmen, dignitaries or common people, overseas Chinese immigrants or immigrants from the south of Shanhai Pass, they all considered Harbin as their "second hometown". Since all of them were "immigrants", and they were "equal" at the level of cultural identification, they didn't have the sense of superiority and conservative xenophobia the "native people" sometime had. Instead, they all had the responsibility and courage to be "the builder of the city". That was rare in the "social transformation" of inland areas where the split of social mentalities in the social transformation caused intense cultural conflicts. By comparison, immigrants and their cultures played a positive role in the social transformation in Heilongjiang.

The particularity of the development and transformation in culture and society might relate to these elements: ① "The immigrants" in Heilongjiang were not the same as previous immigrants in other inland areas. In terms of the composition of the immigrants who came to Heilongjiang during the period, most of them didn't come here to do "farming".Instead, the "new trend" of modernization was the main attraction to them. ② The age structure of the immigrant population was relatively young. They tended to seek adventures and try new things, longing for new life and changes of traditions. They were more apt to accept "new things". ③ The economic link flourished because of the construction of the railway, and modern civilization was formed based on the combination of Western and Chinese cultures as modern economic and cultural elements flooded into this area. In the Late Qing Dynasty and Early Republic of China, northeast China, especially the areas along the railway (with Harbin as the center) in Jilin and Heilongjiang, stood out and created "the Butterfly Effect" on the surroundings. ④ "The new trend" in economy and society along the railway areas and "the areas under nobody's jurisdiction" decided the unique model of social transformation in Heilongjiang. In 1917, the Russian shareholders of the Chinese Eastern Railway Company lost their "state-owned" shares, and the company almost became an independent economy entity with no supervision since that time. Russia didn't take back its shares which used to be possessed by the company until the 1930s when the Japanese Puppet Regime (1937—1945) came into power. The Beiyang Government was engaged in the war south of the Shanhai Pass, and the Fengtian Warlord was busy with its own affairs. Therefore, in the politics and administration, the economy and society under the influence of the railway were rarely affected and curbed by the "force of feudalism" as other inland areas had experienced. And before the railway brought modern civilization to Heilongjiang, the impact of feudal economy and culture was quite limited, so there wasn't strong "traditional force". ⑤ Compared with the population, the land was relatively wide. When the railway was under construction, it scarcely confronted protest from local people. As building the roads, buying the land, recruiting workers and other big projects brought "more income" and "employment opportunities" to local people, the conflicts were much rare than those south of the Shanhai Pass. Within Shanhai Pass, such things, however, deprived people of their livelihoods and some people even risked their lives to obstruct the construction and resist everything connected with the railway.

Ⅳ

Although it is not our main concern to make detailed comments, due to the subject which is closely linked to the modern international relations, we are trying to regulate the academic standards of related concepts and logic, and it is also necessary to explain the principles, systems and methods of analysis. From that we can understand better the influences left by the process and learn more information about the stages, features, patterns of development and key factors of the modernization of Heilongjiang. After the 16th century A.D., the world history entered "the modern times", but civilizations around the world didn't do it synchronously. Western countries not only took the lead in the model of their social formation, but gradually formed "principles of modern international relations" and enforced their "principles" and "values" globally as their cultural and material levels advanced rapidly. The center of oriental culture was impacted, and passive transformations occurred in different fields.

The issue to be discussed is how to analyze and evaluate the principles and logic of treaties and cooperation between nations from the national perspective of "nation state". We find three difficult tasks: how to mediate the relationships between domestic struggles between social classes or races and international struggles; how to clarify the interests relationship between dynastic state and nation state and how to deal with the interference of foreign forces in China's domestic and international affairs; what is particularly difficult is that before China had transformed from an ancient country to "a state nation", various conflicts entangled with each other. The problem was so thorny that there couldn't be a solid answer at that time. Accordingly, the answer is as follows: First, according to the situation and the demands of our country, we must assess the international situation and national interests, identify the position of our country, clarify the principal contradictions and secondary contradictions, begin our action from solving problems of principal contradictions and "tell our enemy from our friends" promptly and accurately. Second, we should be aware of the advantages and disadvantages of both sides or every side in the game of the interests, try our best to win our allies ("developing oneself" is the constant while "finding allies" is the variable) and weaken our rivals, "maximizing" our "potential interests". Third, we should know that "there's no free lunch in the world", and thus we must promote any chance to get "potential interests" in the game while weighing pros and cons and obtain skills which we cannot achieve in a short period of time from our allies by sacrificing "relatively small" costs. In the game of many sides, we should uphold that logic whether we judge the history, decide on practical affairs or make future strategies.

Logically, back in the 19th century, Japan, as well as America and Great Britain which intended to make use of Japan to weaken China and curb Russia, "suffered" most from "the purpose for allying" and "the plan of constructing the railway" of *the Sino-Russian Secret Treaty*. Meanwhile, China and Russia benefited from "the alliance cooperation" in the international game in the Far East. In such cooperation, China and Russia were not at war, so China didn't feel military pressure from Russia. After the Sino-Japanese War of 1894—1895 in the Far East, Japan's imperialism threatened the essential interests of China and Russia. Therefore, China and Russia were striving to seek common grounds to fight against Japan, and the construction of the railway was necessary.

As the crisis was looming large, the Qing Government was desperate to contain its biggest enemy Japan by the force of Russia. So, it signed the *Sino-Russian Secret Treaty* (the formal name is *Sino-Russian Defensive Alliance Treaty*) and the *Contract of the Sino-Russian Eastern Railway Company*, which gave birth to "the Chinese Eastern Railway" and started the process of "modernization" and "social transformation" in related areas. Although in the contract the rights and the obligations of both sides were not equal, which was favorable for Russia to control and use the railway, considering the demand of China and the maximum potential interest that China might get, the construction of the railway was "the biggest fruit" the Qing Government could have for it was desperate to get rid of the dilemma of being weak home and abroad and struggle for its life. From the results and the aims of the alliance we can see that rather than China and Russia, Japanese advocated of its invasion of China and those in China who were pro-Japan and the right-wing conservatives in the Qing Government were in disadvantage. The advocates of the invasion explicitly showed their speculations and concerns over "the alliance", which accelerated their pace of preparing the final war with Russia and invading China. In the Late Qing Dynasty and Early Republic of China, almost every aspect of social development of Heilongjiang was related with the context above, so was the issue of immigrants.

The "Heilongjiang Area" which we study (at that time the vast area around the right bank of the Songhua River now becomes a region of Jilin Province) began to step into modern civilization when the "dots(cities)", "lines(roads)" and "surfaces(districts)", representing the "lights of modernization", were linked to each other as a whole by the railway. Under the development of the economy along the railway, "pre-capitalist" villages composed by individual peasants and, even "depopulated zones", quickly grew into "chains of towns" with the social formation of modern society centered around Harbin. Therefore, the research of Harbin is another important field of our project. It seems that the research has become another clue which demonstrate another way in the development of Heilongjiang. Nevertheless, our work keeps reminding us that the ways of development which seem different are related essentially, and that is important characteristic which distinguishes itself from the modernization and transformation of civilization of other areas in China.

"Superficial" as our study may seem, it is aimed at serving as a modest spur to induce more scholars to discuss our topic. Meanwhile, we are also determined to continue the unfinished project and make our own contributions to the research of the history and culture of Heilongjiang and the development of its economy.

Li Peng

Oasis Garden, Heilongjiang University, Year-end of 2019

CONTENTS

Chapter 4 The Role of Celebrities in the Development Process of Immigrant Society

Chapter 5 Study on C-E Translation of Material Concerning Heilongjiang Immigration in the Late Qing Dynasty and Early Republic of China

目 录

第五章 清末民初黑龙江移民文献英译研究

附录

Chapter 1
Government-organized Immigration

In the Late Qing Dynasty and Early Republic of China, another wave of migration in Chinese history formed when people of all walks of life from Hebei and Shandong areas in the south of Shanhai Pass moved north. Previously, after the Qing Dynasty took over, there had been the phenomenon of migrants "making a living in old northeast China", but the scale was not large due to the prohibition of the Qing Government. After the Westernization Movement began, the Qing Government's prohibition in the Northeast was lifted, and the northeastern region, including Heilongjiang, Jilin and Liaoning today, received a large-scale migration wave since the Qing Dynasty. However, the "migration" at that time was only a "shift" of the social form and economic level across Shanhai Pass, so there was no profound change on the "agricultural society" in the Northeast (especially the northernmost Heilongjiang region). Comparing with the inland provinces' changes and the development of productivity levels, the economic and social patterns of the northeast provinces just had limited change.

However, this wave of immigration in the Late Qing Dynasty and Early Republic of China was different from the past waves in terms of nature, scale, and influence. Due to domestic and international reasons after the Sino-Japanese War of 1894—1895, the number of "migrants" across the Shanhai Pass increased, and what was different from the past was the nature, goals and influence of the subjects of "migrant" at this time, which were not only different from the past waves, but also more significant. It is these migrants who are associated with the process of "Chinese path to modernization". From the perspective of migration, it is mainly along the "Dong Qing Railway" (the Chinese name was called "Dong Sheng Railway" after the province was established, and it was renamed the "Chinese Eastern Railway" after the foundation of Republic of China, and the Russian name was not changed). As "destinations", the provinces mainly centered on the hub station "Harbin" of the "Chinese Eastern Railway". Judging from the nature of the migrants, the appeal of this wave was not "farming to make the ends meet", but the attraction of "a modern mode of production", into which people eagerly integrated, that is the "modern industrial civilization" characterizing railroad as the core, and the formation of the first "modern city" social form in the history of China, which is very different from the modern China that was forced to open up and leased the land. As a huge amount of "human resources", these immigrants integrated into the "modern mode of production". This kind of "combination" is neither the first nor rare in modern

China. What is special is that this method of production, which is not originated from China, seems to be the same as the "capitalist invasion" imposed by "imperialist powers" on traditional Chinese society, but there are fundamental differences. The difference is that the construction of this railway originated from the self-preservation of the Qing Dynasty, which was due to its inability to defend its sovereignty and had to take the self-protection action of "confronting foreigners by foreigners" and uniting Russia to contend the Japanese—signing *The Sino-Russian Secret Treaty*.

Immigrants from Shandong and Hebei spontaneously built their own social organizations for survival and development. The "Townsmen Association", a non-governmental organization, is quite common in China through dynasties. It was also one of the forms of non-governmental organizations that was naturally accepted by Shandong immigrants who were spread widely in the northeast. There were big differences among the nature of society, economic characteristics, political structure in Harbin, as well as development trends and cultural customs and other aspects of the city with the mainland. Most migrants were of Shandong and Hebei origin, and they spontaneously organized the social organizations of "Shunzhi and Shandong Guild Hall" and "Shandong People Association in Harbin". The transmutation of the structure and function of this organization reflected the formation of the early immigrant society in Harbin. The textual research and analysis of the historical evolution of these two organizations will help us to deeply understand the life of immigrants in Harbin under the absence of the government and the lack of government functions. It will help us gain a clearer insight into the immigrant society in Harbin and its multicultural background.

1.1 History of "Shunzhi and Shandong Guild Hall" and "Shandong People Association in Harbin"

There are different opinions about the origin and fate of Shandong Guild Hall. As an immigrant organization that existed in Harbin decades ago, it is difficult for the world today to know its true image, functions and role. Even some people who are interested in history can only vaguely outline the image of this organization back then. However, with the development of contemporary economy, culture and even international political and economic relations, today's leaders and people are also keen to reconstruct the "real" image of the history of that period, not only for immediate economic interests, but also for our own history in concern. Contemporary Harbin has set off a wave of "reconstruction". It not only imagines our past and future in thought, but also boldly realizes these demands in form and image, forming a wave of "visual impact". We are delighted to see the history in our memory and our imagination, which is impressively revealed in front of our eyes. However, these "historical reappearances" that embody the emotions of Harbin people always seem to be "not right". The main sticking point here is that in the state of eagerness for instant success, solid and sufficient academic research is ignored, and scientific research is not used as the first basis for "reconstructing" history. The reconstruction of "Shandong Guild Hall" has been included in the work schedule of relevant departments without systematic research. Some media also rendered one-sided information, confusing the cognition about the "Shandong Guild Hall", and reducing the historical significance of the Shandong Guild Hall. From the perspective of textual research, this book tries to restore the reality of the social life of migrants who came from the south of Shanhai Pass and lived in Harbin during this period. This book systematically examines the historical evolution of the Shandong Guild Hall and the reasons for its rise and fall, and provides a relatively complete information to the society, which may provide a reference for people who want to restore historical memory and relevant decision-making departments.

1.1.1 "Free" Harbin Immigrant Society

Before the construction of the Chinese Eastern Railway, Heilongjiang and Jilin were relatively less developed in economy and sparsely populated compared with other inland areas with frequent foreign-related activities. Although it is the birthplace of Qing Dynasty, the Qing Government exercised extensive administrative jurisdiction over this vast territory and had always maintained a relatively low population. At that time, Harbin was just a small village with a population of less than 2,000 people, and economically attached to Acheng and Hulan. The population distribution is as follows: "There are more than 200 households with about 1,200 people around Tianjia Shaoguo; Qinjiagang is a long-uninhabited land with rolling hills, three or five thatched huts, and a limited population; the Butou area is a low-lying river beach with a rugged path, less populated; a village was formed in Fujiadian around 1890, and by 1898 there were two or three hundred households with about 2,000 people. The population in the Harbin area was only three or five thousand people." On June 9th, 1898, The Ship Blagoveshchensk delivered a ship of engineers and technicians and road construction materials through the Chinese Eastern Railway to Harbin (now Xiangfang District). After negotiating with the Chinese authorities, Tsarist Russia designated Harbin as the main station of the Chinese Eastern Railway, which was regarded as the beginning of modern city in the history of Harbin. At this time, the south part of Harbin was governed by Vice Governor Alcuka who came from Shuangcheng Hall and the Binzhou Hall and was under the jurisdiction of General of Jilin Ula and other places. The north part of Harbin was governed by Hulan Hall which was under the jurisdiction of Heilongjiang General. After the Russians came, the Qing Government designated Harbin's old District (Xiangfang), new District (Nangang), Butou area (Daoli), Dockyard in the north of Songhua River and other places totaling 21,000 mu (a unit of area 0.0667 hectares) of land as subsidiary land for the railroad. Since then, China and Russia have sounded the horn of large-scale road construction with an unprecedented scale and vigor. "In June 1898, there were no more than 10,000 people who built roads in China. At the end of this year, it exceeded 25,000, and in 1900, it reached up to 170,000." During the period from 1898 to 1900, nearly 200,000 "working people" were sent from Shandong, Hebei, etc. So far in the modern history, Harbin opened the prelude to a large-scale influx of migrants to this place.

From 1900 to 1906, the Boxer Rebellion and the Russo-Japanese War broke out one after another. Harbin was in a state of war, and road construction was delayed for a period. In 1906, the Russo-Japanese War ended with Japan's victory, and this result had a vital effect on Harbin. As a result of the defeat, the Russian monopoly once established in northeast China was destroyed. At this time, the situation in the Northeast was even more critical because of the entry of Japan, a major power, into the fray, but objectively it increased the opening of the region to the outside world, and in a short time, the originally closed geographical unit of the Northeast was rapidly opened up. With the opening of land and sea routes one after another, the Northeast region has strengthened its land links with European countries such as Tsarist Russia and Britain. The riverside terminals belong to the Chinese Eastern Railway area established shipping networks with domestic and foreign ports such as Dalian, Yantai, Vladivostok, Osaka in Japan and Pusan in Korea. After the war subsided, hundreds of thousands of immigrants from home and abroad poured into the surrounding areas of the Chinese Eastern Railway, and the relatively closed northeast region was included in the world economic circle. The war also aroused the strong interest of political and economic powers in mainland China and other countries, they were all drawn by the Chinese Eastern Railway and its territories. Except for Tsarist Russia, other powers have also become stakeholders in the northern Manchurian region with Harbin as the core. Although Harbin's Chinese Eastern Railway area was not a concession, the situation was similar to that of the concession, and in the short period of time from 1900 to 1906, a "functional urban area" was formed in which "merchants from various countries" were the main inhabitants, and cross-border trade in commodities was the main theme. In this special community, the ultimate result of the maximization of interests and the trade game between great powers is: Relying on the Nationality Law and the general norms of nationality, businessmen from various countries demanded the establishment of "new rules of the game" that "transcend nationality, race, and custom" in this "unified urban functional area" in Harbin.

Japan started to act first, followed by Tsarist Russia, the Qing Government, Britain, America, Germany and France, all of which wanted to expand their power in North Manchuria under the pretext of speculating on the political issue of the municipal administration of Harbin, and Mikado approved the establishment of the "South Manchuria Railway Company" under the full control of the Government on June 7th, 1906, and the chariot of Japan's northward advancement proceeded from the Korean Peninsula to southern part of the Northeast in China. After the Russo-Japanese War, Tsarist Russia's strategy in Northeast Asia also adjusted, from the original policy of resolutely preventing Japan from entering Manchuria and resolutely competing with Japan for the hegemony of Northeast Asia, to the policy of "Russo-Japanese Coordination" and the new line of seeking the interests of Manchuria in conjunction with Japan. On July 30th, 1907, the two sides signed the first *Russo-Japanese Agreement* and the first *Russo-Japanese Secret Agreement*. The *Russo-Japanese Secret Agreement* stipulated that northeast China would be divided into North and South, which would be the separated spheres of influence between Japan and Russia, and that the two sides would promise each other not to hinder each other from seeking more benefits within their spheres of influence and not to expand their own power within other's sphere of influence; and an additional article stipulated the demarcation line between "South Manchuria" and "North Manchuria". From 1906, with the imminent threat of Japan and Russia, the Qing Government has opened the gateway to the Northeast. Starting from a port in Yingkou, successively open Andong, Dadonggou, Fengtian and other places, Japan, the United States, Germany, Britain and other countries sent consular officials to the places. To strengthen the control of the Qing Government in Manchuria, in 1907, the unification of the "three eastern provinces" military and political affairs started by the pro-US faction Xu Shichang as Governor, by Tang Shaoyi, Zhu Jiabao, Duan Zhigui (later changed to Cheng Dequan) served as Governor of Fengtian (Liaoning), Jilin, Heilongjiang. Plans were set up to use U.S. capital to open the Bank of the "Three Provinces of Northeast", to organize the construction of the Northeast in order to build a railroad network to compete with the Russian and Japanese, and also with U.S. capital to stabilize the local currency and build other industries. Facing the competition, Tsarist Russia strengthened its control over the Chinese Eastern Railway territories by sending troops, stationing polices, and seeking to establish self-governing councils.

In 1907, the Chinese Eastern Railway territory became more and more prosperous, and Chinese businessmen poured into the railway territory to look for business opportunities. From 1898 to 1907, the arrival of Chinese and foreign immigrants quickly affected the urban subdivisions of Harbin in terms of economic structure. With the railway as the boundary, Harbin formed a Russian-controlled area and a Chinese-controlled area. The Chinese-controlled area centered on the Fujiadian, Qian Danshili described in June 1903: "The Fujiadian used to be a place with only shabby houses and about 20,000 people living near the dwellings. The Chinese made their living on the railways and lived here." She basically pointed out the reason why Fujiadian has formed an urban functional area. By 1907, Fujiadian had a population of 150,000 people. Compared with road construction workers, the main body of residents at this time has expanded. Not only the "farming laborers" who came to Harbin during the busy farming period and left when it was over, the residents have a certain stability, and the level of immigration was also getting higher and higher. It was mainly composed of the following parts: peasants who went to the villages around Harbin to reclaim wasteland; clerks and apprentices working in shops outside Daowai District; Chinese businessmen (including people from Vladivostok and Russian Far East) who set up shops in Russian-controlled areas; Chinese businessmen from Jilin, Heilongjiang, Shandong, Hebei and even Guangdong who came to Harbin to engage in industrial and commercial activities.

By 1908, the Russians appeared to be aggressive on the issue of Harbin's municipal administration. On January 8th of the same year, the Tsarist Russia implemented the *Harbin Public Governance Local Statute* in Harbin, and immediately set up a public council on the Chinese Eastern Railway Dependencies, which governed the "peoples lived within the Chinese Eastern Railway region". Regarding this, as the interests between Japan and Tsarist Russia in Manchuria were very clear, so concerning this matter, the attitude of Japanese is quite fuzzy, while the United States, Germany, France, China have expressed strong protest from their respective of interests, and they refused to accept Russia's jurisdiction over the expatriates of the host about the municipal administration of Harbin. The political game over Harbin's municipal management is getting hotter by the day.

The boycott of other countries temporarily suppressed the arrogance of Tsarist Russia, which made Harbin's municipal management power on hold for a time. But after a lapse of a year, this stalemate was broken. On January 16th, 1909, the Russian city council established residents' registration within the border. On May 10th, after more than two months of negotiations between Chinese and Russian representatives in Beijing, they finally agreed that under the premise that "China enjoys the sovereignty of the Chinese Eastern Railway", the governments of China and Russia will jointly establish a railway boundary in the East Province. A public council was opened within the city to manage local self-governance, and eighteen articles of the *Outline of Measures For The Public Council* were signed. It was signed by Shi Zhaoji, an official responsible for customs matters (the former one Du Xueying was dismissed in April 1909 for being "decadent, selfish and ignorant of the political system"), Heilongjiang candidate of Vice Governor Yu Sixing, and Holwart, the General Office of the Chinese Eastern Railway Administration. After the official signing of the *Outline of Measures For The Public Council* in Beijing, the positioning of Harbin has undergone a dramatic change—it is legally recognized that China still enjoys the sovereignty of the territory of the Chinese Eastern Railway, but the specific administrative rights have been completely seized by the Tsarist Russia. Since then, Tsarist Russia also set up a "Special Committee" affiliated to the China Eastern Railway Administration to further coordinate the relationship between the Tsarist Russia's various competent departments in Harbin. "The position of the director (general office) is also similar to that of the colonial governor". So far, the Chinese Government in fact completely lost its administrative power over the Chinese Eastern Railway. The territory of the Chinese Eastern Railway was almost reduced to another colony of Tsarist Russia, becoming a "country within a country", but not legally.

The Qing Government, which was much expected to compete with Tsarist Russia and had territorial sovereignty over Harbin, took a compromising stance on the issue of Harbin's municipal administration. This quickly triggered a domino effect. The attitudes of foreign consuls in Harbin softened, and the political balance between the countries and Tsarist Russia quickly shifted in favor of Tsarist Russia.

On May 24th, 1910, U.S. Secretary of State Knox notified U.S. Minister in Beijing Carole Henderson that Americans in Harbin paid the general municipal tax to the Russian authorities, as did all other nationalities. In June 1910, the British and Germans living in Harbin began to pay taxes to the city board. Prior to May 31st, 1910, the Harbin Russian Police Bureau openly implemented the Russian domestic security system, and the Chinese in the field were treated as foreign residents. Registration of servants, affairs, etc, was carried out, and certificates were issued by Russian. So far, the foreign residents of various countries had legally become a member of Harbin, and Harbin had initially become an "immigrant city" in a complete sense. (The Japanese, because of the constraints of the *Russo-Japanese Agreement*, had their sphere of influence mainly in South Manchuria until 1917, and instead declined in Harbin, and therefore began to pay taxes officially as late as 1917.)

In 1909, there were more than 300 ethnic firms in Daoli District, and in 1910, there were 134 ethnic capital and industrial households in Daoli and Nangang District, and the population accounted for nearly 40% of the total population of the entire railway-affiliated area (in 1912, there were 25,458 Chinese in the Russian-controlled area of Harbin, accounting for 37.14% of the total), Chinese businessmen became an important economic force in the Russian-controlled area of Harbin. In 1910, the Chinese government lost the right to manage Harbin, and almost overnight Chinese businessmen became "foreign residents" living in other countries. The pain caused by this contrast was piercing.

As we all know, in the traditional Chinese context, there is no shortage of political concepts such as "foreign residents' groups" and "foreign residents". In Shanghai, Hong Kong and other places that became the area of the lease earlier, people had accumulated the experience, and adapted to the reality of the situation. Compared with Shanghai and other regions with international practices to follow, Harbin, with an alternative Russian "railway dependent territory", was in more complex situation, and the status of residents was quite embarrassing. In 1910, Harbin only had a short period of more than ten years as a modern city. Many Chinese lived there, but it lacked a strong immigrant group such as "Ningbo people in Shanghai", and was short of "Siming Mansion", which was supported by a century-old heritage and great influence of "guild hall culture" in Shanghai. Therefore, how the Qing Government integrated the immigrant forces from Shandong, Hebei and other provinces when the governance was in decline and could not fulfill its administrative and social service functions properly, and how hundreds of thousands of Chinese merchants maintained their own property and life safety in the absence of government, became the most difficult problem in front of the Qing Government and Harbin merchants.

1.1.2 The Political Background Before the Establishment of Townsmen Association

The political game between China and Russia over the municipal management rights of Harbin ended with the victory of Russian side. Government departments such as Jilin Railway Negotiation Department, Heilongjiang Railway Negotiation Department, and Official responsible for Customs Matters, which were previously established by China in Harbin, had been greatly impacted. Under the premise of being unable to stop the Russians from controlling Harbin's municipal management rights, the only remaining government departments in Harbin began to step up integration, actively support the Chinese businessmen, and safeguard the rights and interests of Chinese businessmen.

In October 1909, the Qing Government established the Advisory Parliament, and the three provinces of Feng Tian(now Shenyang), Ji Lin and Heilongjiang established the Provincial Assembly. In July 1910, the Harbin Autonomous Association was established. In December 1908, Chinese merchants established the Harbin General Chamber of Commerce in Daoli District. After the establishment of the Autonomous Association and the Chamber of Commerce, many upper-class migrants in Harbin joined these two organizations one after another, and the leadership core of many hometown associations established in Harbin in the future were all based on this. The establishment of these two organizations was the foundation of the townsman association.

In 1910, Li Hongmo, who was then the chief official of the Heilongjiang Railway Negotiation Department, thought that he should actively negotiate with the Tsarist Russia's administration of the Chinese Eastern Railway to help Chinese merchants to solve the problem of land lease. He believed that "if the Chinese officials ignore this, but let the merchants lease the stores privately, then it will be natural for them to lose the trust of others." Letting the Chinese merchants and the railroads "make ambiguous promises to each other, and if they meet with a dispute, it would be too much for them." He proposed that the Railway Negotiation Department should be responsible for the lease of land in the Chinese Eastern Railway area. He took the *Heilongjiang Railway Negotiations Department General Regulations* as a basis for a note to the Chinese Eastern Railway Administration to "effectively declare" the purpose and authority of the Chinese officials to collect taxes within the border. On September 29th, 1910, the Chinese Eastern Railway Administration announced that "Russian businessmen sign a land lease contract with our company, and the evidence of the signing shall be witnessed by Russian officials. If a Chinese businessmen sign a contract with our company, the signing should be witnessed by the Negotiation Department." This statement formally recognized the right of the Heilongjiang Railway Negotiation Department to lease land within the territories of the Chinese Eastern Railway. The representative power of the Chinese agency was once again recognized by the Russian side. This was the starting point for the return of the lost Chinese power. Substantial progress was made not only in name but also in the defense of the practical interests for the Chinese side.

On this basis, Li Hongmo established a perfect land lease system in combination with the actual situation of the territory of the Chinese Eastern Railway at that time. The regulations were: Specialized personnel were selected in each branch office of the Railway Negotiation Department, "if a Chinese merchant or railway company needs a certificate from the Department, the situation should be checked by the commissioner of the branch office; if it is consistent with the facts, the commissioner of the branch office will sign the rental sticker and declare it for record, and the rental sticker will also be sent by the Department to the Russian side, and after signing it, it will be issued to the other stations to be handled by Russian administrators." So far, if the Chinese merchants within the boundary needed to lease land again, the Railway Negotiation Department would be responsible for the record, and if they encountered disputes with the Russians, the Railway Negotiation Department would be responsible for the negotiation. The right to lease land was also vested in the Railway Negotiation Department.

On November 5th, 1910, Li Hongmo introduced the successful experience of tax collection to Zhou Shumo, the governor of Heilongjiang. Qingshan Railway Station Taxation Bureau in the Chinese Eastern Railway set up a checkpoint outside the railway boundaries of the Chinese Eastern Railway and successfully collected the tax. Li requested Zhou Shumo to allow the "Negotiation Department to do the same thing within the boundaries", and the Railway Negotiation Bureau need to send personnel "to take shifts in the checkpoint". With the support of Zhou Shumo, the railway authorities were able to handle all the tax matters. Under Zhou Shumo's support, from November to December 1910, Li Hongmo noted the Chinese Eastern Railway Administration General Office Holwart and chargé d'affaires Daniel three times, in accordance with the successive Sino-Russian peace treaties, as well as international practice on the "tax collection out-of-boundary" specific details of the negotiation, and finally forced the Chinese Eastern Railway Administration to be "accommodating" and reached a consensus between the two sides.

First, this changed the original donation and tax regulations in Heilongjiang, and imitated the Russian rent and tax system around the Chinese Eastern Railway territories, also abolished the term "donation" on each person, unified name as "tax collection", collected the "tax" from merchants in a unified manner. The tax collection rules were standardized. A new type of tax system was established in the territories of Harbin that "eliminated the excuses of outsiders and facilitated the implementation of the system" and was in line with international practice. Second, in accordance with international practice, combined with the relevant provisions of the "REGULATIONS ON LAND TRANSPORTATION" in the *Renewal of the Sino-Russian Agreement*, the government reasonably argued with the Russian officials stationed along the river. At the ports and customs pass on the Chinese side outside the territory of the Chinese Eastern Railway, officials of the Negotiation Department were stationed, and tax authorities were established. "Import Duties" were uniformly levied on "local products" such as grain, cattle, horses, sheep, grass, hides, etc. Third, a sound tax collection system was established. For merchants who wanted to buy and sell goods within the territory of the China Eastern Railway, and pass through the checkpoints outside the border, the seller must first go to the Railway Negotiation Department to "declare dutiable goods and collect tickets before they are allowed to sell." Fourth, the Russian officials in the territories of the Chinese Eastern Railway were required to bear the corresponding responsibilities and fulfill their obligations to assist the officials of the Railway Negotiation Department to detect tax evaders. It was stipulated that once the Tsarist Russian officials seized the goods sold by the merchants who had no tax receipts issued by the Negotiation Department, they should bring the tax evaders to the Railway Negotiation Department, and the Railway Negotiation Department officials should "punish according to the rules", and Russian officials were not allowed to interfere.

In February 1911, Governor Zhou Shumo informed Li Hongmo that it was decided that the Heilongjiang Railway Negotiation Department would set up a tax bureau on the Chinese side outside the territory of the Chinese Eastern Railway. Jilin Railway Negotiation Department also implemented a new land lease method on the Jilin side outside the territory of the Chinese Eastern Railway in accordance with the method of the Heilongjiang Railway Negotiation Department and set up checkpoints to collect taxes outside the border. In this way, the unsolved issue of collecting taxes in the territory of the Chinese Eastern Railway had finally been solved.

The handling of these two issues had enabled the Heilongjiang Railway Negotiation Department to obtain major rights related to sovereignty such as renting land and paying taxes in the surrounding areas of the Chinese Eastern Railway under the objective framework of "railway as the center". It also marked that the local government in Harbin had realized the tax collection function of "Chinese businessmen in the boundary" and fulfilled an indirect management function. Since then, the Railway Negotiation Department within the land attached to the railway pushed on by using Chinese parliamentarians, chambers of commerce, associations and other social organizations to infiltrate politically and economically, and gradually took the power on taxation, land lease and justice. It had become an independent administrative agency of the Government in the territory of the Chinese Eastern Railway and served as a "shadow government".

1.1.3 Shunzhi and Shandong Guild Hall: Transformation of Traditional Guild Hall

Under the construction of the Railway Negotiation Department, local Chinese government in Harbin gained some limited voice by interpreting International Law and achieved indirect management functions for Chinese businessmen in the Russian-controlled area in Harbin, but this jurisdiction was far from enough. How to establish expatriate organization, how to establish "autonomous organization" in the Russian-controlled area of Harbin, and cooperate with the government to perform management functions such as taxation and administration of justice; How to integrate the Chinese merchants in Daoli, Nangang, and Daowai District to maximize the interests of the Chinese people in the Russian-controlled area of Harbin was still an important issue nagging the wise people of Harbin, and there was no time to lose. These issues were quickly put on the agenda by wise people from all walks of life in Harbin. During 1910—1911, officials in Harbin came up with a compromise solution, which was to set up a "Shunzhi and Shandong Guild Hall" in Harbin, which integrated immigrants from Shandong and Shunzhi. It was hoped that by respecting the historical legacy of the Association as an immigrant organization, and taking advantage of the traditional top-down migrant organization of the Late Ming and Early Qing Dynasties, which was based on the ties of regional nostalgia, the Association would be hoped to integrate the migrants in Harbin from Shandong Province and Shunzhi (Shunzhi is another historical name, roughly equivalent to the region of today's Hebei Province and municipalities of Tianjin and Beijing, in which the Qing Dynasty set up the province directly under the Central Government's control and Shuntian Prefecture, and since then, people had been using the term Shunzhi to refer to this area), and to set up a disguised "expatriate organization" which conformed to the international practice and was suitable for the diversified immigrant society in Harbin.

Objectively speaking, the establishment of the Shunzhi and Shandong Guild Hall was forced by the external political environment, but the incentive for the establishment of the Shunzhi and Shandong Guild Hall depended on the "collective consciousness" triggered by the fact that the Chinese businessmen's rights and interests in Harbin could not be guaranteed by itself. On April 1st, 1911, in Harbin, Yang Jiechen, the deacon of Mobil Foreign Firm, borrowed 2,000 silver dollars from Russia, and upon the proposal of Wang Xiangli from province directly under the Central Government and Zhang Jieshen from Shandong, organized the "Harbin and Shandong People Association". Under the premise of obtaining the start-up funds, there were three other groups involved in Shunzhi and Shandong Guild Hall: Harbin Autonomous Association headed by An Futing from Hebei, Vice Chairman of the Autonomous Association and co-organizer of the Harbin Chamber of Commerce; Harbin Chamber of Commerce headed by Wu Ziqing from Shandong and Gao jiwu; a Government Department in Harbin headed by Zhang Luquan and Lin Xiaoting. So far, the establishment of "Shunzhi and Shandong Guild Hall" had reached the specific operational level. The beginning was good, but the establishment of Shunzhi and Shandong Guild Hall still experienced a series of twists and turns. Shandong, Hebei people in Harbin had never gotten along very well. Both sides argued on the specific management rights. Based on Harbin Autonomous Association and Chamber of Commerce, people from two provinces repeated the arguments on the "real estate issues of Guild Hall", and even fought. Shandong people even proposed to "set up another Shandong Association, not to unite with the Shunzhi people" so that the foundation of Shunzhi and Shandong Guild Hall nearly failed.

Under such circumstances, the Minister of War Zhang Luquan and Ma Xiaoting, and the former Prime Minister of the Harbin Chamber of Commerce Gao Jiwu, actively responded to the issues, and finally made an unbiased ruling against each of the two parties: forbid either party to buy or sell real estate, but instead jointly raise funds. Under the active mediation of the Harbin Government, although there were great differences, both parties gave up their previous demands for the management of Shunzhi and Shandong Guild Hall due to the urgent situation and the fear of the government, and finally reached a consensus. After resolving the differences, the Shunzhi and Shandong Guild Hall finally set up an office in Fujiadian North No.4 Street on September 28th, 1911 to handle all matters. In October 1911, the local government office was requested to issue a license according to the regulations, and the Shunzhi and Shandong Guild Hall was officially established.

After the establishment of Shunzhi and Shandong Guild Hall, the interest difference of Shandong and Hebei Chinese businessmen was not eliminated. In February 1912, Wu Ziqing, a native of Shandong, summoned his fellow villagers to set up "Harbin Savings Bank" in Fujiadian North No.3 Street near Shunzhi and Shandong Guild Hall. In 1912, people from Shandong Province in Harbin opened the "School of Shandong Travelling People in Harbin", and nearly 80 students were all the children of merchants from Shandong in the Shuanghesheng house on Maimai Street in Daowai District. The incidents between the two parties could not be resolved through Shunzhi and Shandong Guild Hall. It can be said that the hastily established Shunzhi and Shandong Guild Hall had no way to gather people from Hebei and Shandong, and its influence was limited to Fujiadian. In this area, Shunzhi and Shandong Guild Hall could not undertake the important task of being an "expatriate organization" in modern times.

1.1.4 Shandong People Association in Harbin: A Quasi-expatriate Organization in the Absence of the Government

In 1914, the Beiyang Government decided to upgrade the diplomatic level of Harbin: this year, the Beiyang Government set up a "Negotiation Officials" system in Harbin, the core city of the Chinese Eastern Railway, and the Central Government directly dispatched professional diplomats to serve as "Harbin Negotiation Officials", stipulating those major issues involving the Chinese Eastern Railway negotiation incidents. Harbin Negotiation Officials would report directly to the Ministry of Foreign Affairs and the Ministry of Transport of the Republic of China. The Railway Negotiation Department was included in the first-level diplomatic system of the Central Government. Since then, important changes had taken place in China's negotiations with Russia.

In this process, Li Hongmo, the then Head of the Heilongjiang Railway Negotiations Department, played a vital role. To cope with the complicated reality that involved Japan, Russia and other powers in the Northeast at that time, on October 1st, 1914, the Beiyang Government of the Republic of China officially decided to retain the establishment of the Jilin and Heilongjiang Railway

Negotiation Department, and Li Hongmo was appointed as the Head of Jilin Railway Negotiation Department, and concurrently as Harbin Negotiator. At the same time, it was expressly stipulated that Ma Zhongjun, the new Head of the Heilongjiang Railway Negotiation Department, was subject to his command. Previously, the General Office of Jilin Railway Negotiation Department had also served as the intendant of Harbin, so Li Hongmo held three positions—Negotiation Officials, Head of Jilin Railway Negotiation Department, and Intendant. He had great autonomy in diplomacy and administration. Since the construction of the Chinese Eastern Railway, in Harbin, the Chinese Eastern Railway subsidiary and its affected areas, for the first time there was a local government head who represented China's national interests, had real power, and was recognized by both China and Russia.

During the First World War, China's national strength increased, while Tsarist Russia was in a more complicated international situation, and its control over the territories in the Chinese Eastern Railway loosened. China's centralization model in Harbin had gained unprecedented favorable living space. The power integrated Jilin Railway Negotiation Department took advantage of the changes in the international situation to challenge the Russian Chinese Eastern Railway Administration in many fields such as diplomacy, military affairs and administration, and achieved many fruitful results.

In this context, the power of Chinese businessmen was also greatly improved. In 1913, there were more than 700 ethnic capital industrial and commercial households in Fujiadian, and more than 700 ethnic industrial and commercial households in Daoli District. In 1914, there were 1,009 Russian and other foreign industrial and commercial enterprises, 800 Chinese-funded industrial and commercial enterprises, and 1,083 Chinese-funded shops in Fujiadian, Harbin. Although there is no population statistics for 1914 and 1915, but in 1916, there were 45,481 Chinese in the Russian-controlled area of Harbin, accounting for 50.67% of the total population, nearly 20 percentage points higher than in 1912. From these two sets of data, we can see that from 1914 to 1915, the power of Chinese businessmen in the Russian-controlled area of Harbin increased significantly, and most of them were new migrants who came from other places to seek fortune. These new immigrants with capital and knowledge would naturally seek the guarantee of maximizing their own interests, and solidarity and mutual assistance were the least wanted choice, which created favorable conditions for the establishment of fellow township organizations. As mentioned above, the Shunzhi and Shandong Guild Hall had geographical differences between Shandong and Hebei at the beginning of its establishment. After its establishment, it did not play the role of integrating migrant forces as expected by Harbin officials. At this time, the arrival of many new migrants accelerated the demise of the Shunzhi and Shandong Guild Hall.

From 1914 to 1915, although the power of the Chinese Government was greatly enhanced after full integration, until 1917, the power of the Government was still unable to reach the Russian-controlled area. The situation had not substantially improved. In the Russian-controlled area of Harbin, foreigners still had the absolute right to speak, and the relative inferior position of the Chinese had not fundamentally changed. But the good news was that within the scope of Harbin, which included the Sino-Russian-controlled area, Chinese businessmen formed a stable migration aggregation from top to bottom. The upper level were mainly the old Chinese businessmen who had been in Harbin for many years, supplemented by the new ones who had flocked to Harbin from other places. The lower level was supplemented by many laborers: immigrants who reclaimed the land, apprentices in shops, and helpers. The government intended to use the power of Chinese businessmen to infiltrate power into the Russian-controlled area of Harbin. Immigrants who had greatly increased their strength also need strong immigrant organizations. With the absence of the government, they would provide administrative functions for people within the border, and effectively solved the problems of education and housing for migrants, security, culture, justice and other practical issues. The common appeal led to the establishment of a new type of immigrant organization—Shandong Guild Hall.

Since the end of the Qing Dynasty, in places where the Chinese Government was weak, such as leased land and railway-affiliated areas, a "Guild Hall and Townsmen Association Culture" appeared. After the establishment of the Republic of China, guild halls were gradually abandoned, and fellow villagers became a new form of immigrant organization. After a lapse of four years, Harbin could finally synchronize with Shanghai and other regions, and had the foundation to form its own Townsmen Association culture. On March 27th, 1915, Intendant of Harbin approved the plan of Shandong People Association in Harbin: The association "aims to promote the friendly feelings of fellow villagers in Harbin, protect their rights, promote public welfare, and readiness for emergencies." The venue of the meeting was the Longevity Palace in Binjiang County (although it was proposed to move from No.4 Street, Daowai District to the Longevity Palace on Taikoo Street in 1915, it was not until April 19th, 1917, that the Townsmen Association officially moved). The meeting consisted of the Appraisal Department, the General Affairs Department, the Secretary Department, the Accounting Department, the Editorial Department, and the Education Department. The Editorial Department published vernacular tabloids and magazines to perform educational function. The Education Department raised funds to organize private primary schools in Harbin to educate the children of fellow villagers, or set up half-day schools to educate the elderly students. In addition, the Shandong People Association was a national organization. The Shandong People Association in Harbin was not an isolated organization, but a branch of the Jilin Shandong Association.

It is not difficult to find from the above documents that, compared with the simple and hasty establishment of Shunzhi and Shandong Guild Hall at the beginning, Shandong People Association had the following characteristics:

First, the plan for the establishment of Shandong People Association in Harbin was approved by Intendant of Harbin, the highest administrator of Harbin, while Shunzhi and Shandong Guild Hall was only approved by the County. In 1914, the management scope of Intendant of Harbin was extended to the territory of the Chinese Eastern Railway, that is, the scope of the Russian-controlled area of Harbin. Intendant's authorization this time signified that he had recognized the absolute dominance of the Shandong Guild Hall over the entire Shandong migrants from a legal point of view. On the other hand, it also shows that Intendant of Harbin regarded Shandong Guild Hall as an alliance consciousness to jointly restore sovereignty and counterbalance the Russians.

Second, Shandong People Association put forward the purpose of "aim to promote the friend feelings of fellow villagers in Harbin, protect their rights, promote public welfare, and readiness for emergencies." The point of "promote the friendly feelings of fellow villagers in Harbin" has no difference from that of traditional guild halls. However, the last three items "protect their rights, promote public welfare, and readiness for emergencies" indicate that compared with traditional guild halls, the upper-level organizers of the Shandong People Association have realized that due to the lack of functionality of the Harbin government, the villagers must be united, and the association must have the consciousness to safeguard their own rights.

Third, the Shandong Association set up the Appraisal Department, the General Affairs Department, the Secretary Department, the Accounting Department, the Editorial Department, and the Education Department. The duties of these departments were clearly defined, and the judicial, educational and cultural functions that originally belonged to the government's service functions had been well grafted by the Townsmen Association. The establishment of these institutions required manpower and material resources and cost much more than the 2000 silver dollars expenditure in the period of Shunzhi and Shandong Guild Hall. These funds were all raised by Chinese businessmen, which can also explain the improvement of social status of Chinese businessmen during 1911—1914.

Although received the approval of Intendant of Harbin, Shunzhi and Shandong Guild Hall was originally invested and established by people from Shandong and Hebei. In addition, "Since the Shunzhi Association had been separated from the Shandong People Association, due to the lack of funds, it only had an undeserved reputation and empty title". For the sake of self-interest, the people of Hebei had always disagreed with the people of Shandong to separate the Association, and they also demanded to divide the real estate and property. People from Hebei requested to hold a "public discussion" many times on the division of property with people from Shandong. It was only in August 1916 that the house for Shandong People Association was finally established, after the house on No.4 Street in Daowai District was given to the Hebei people.

In 1919, Shandong People Association overhauled the Shandong Guild Hall on

Taikoo Street, building more than 120 buildings and spending a total of 200,000 yuan, all of which were donated by their own firms so that even the *Far Eastern Review* at that time marveled with emotion that "the people of Shandong are united". According to later generations, "Shandong Guild Hall was a classical Chinese building, with blue brick and classical gates along the street. The buildings in the hall were of Chinese classical style. The yellow glazed tiles gleamed in the sun. It covered an area of 2,527 square meters." Shandong Guild Hall covered an area from No.4 Taikoo Street in the west to No.12 Taikoo Street in the east. There were boundary markers around the courtyard wall with the inscription "Shandong Guild Hall Boundary", and four major parts of the residential area which were areas for commerce, schools, reception and living districts. The main entrance was on Taikoo Street. Before the demolition, the house number at that time was No.247, Taikoo Street. The main entrance had a gate tower, which was paved with classical green glazed tiles. "Shandong Guild Hall" was written by Wang Shoupeng, the Number One Scholar of the late Qing Dynasty's Imperial examination. On the side of the door, there was a vertical sign of "Private Huimin Primary School in Harbin Special City". The door was a large black iron door with copper nails and a pair of stone drums. There was a Confucian Temple in the Guild Hall area with a height of 8 meters. The Guild Hall held activities such as Confucian worship ceremonies, school opening and graduation ceremonies here every year. There were also basketball courts, sand pits and other sporting facilities in the campus area. There were nearly 20 shops on both sides of the main entrance of Taikoo Street, and behind the shops was the residential area.

In 1915—1916, Harbin embraced the best development opportunities. Harbin Daowai Agriculture and Banking Trust Enterprises were established one after another. Many business tycoons in Daoli District followed the trend and set up branches in Daowai. Chinese people in Daoli and Daowai also jointly negotiated to construct the Sijiazi Markets. Under the supervision of Li Hongmo, the Daoli Chamber of Commerce in the Russian-controlled area of Harbin was renamed as "Jilin Harbin General Chamber of Commerce" and was officially under the jurisdiction of Jilin Government. So far, Chinese businessmen in Daoli had turned to invest in Daowai District, and there was a great momentum of integration of Chinese merchants in Daoli and Daowai. The corresponding situation was: In 1916, Shandong and Hebei were "severely affected by the autumn rain and flood, people there were unable to sustain. Disaster victims from various provinces flocked to Harbin to make a living." The influx of disaster victims led to overcrowding in Harbin, and there was a shortage of housing in Daoli and Daowai, with rents rising from the previous three or four yuan per month to seven, eight or even ten. Many people could not afford to buy train tickets and even came to Harbin on foot from Changchun to make a living. The simultaneous influx of immigrants from the upper and lower classes brought opportunities to Harbin and created a good opportunity for the development of the Association.

Among many new immigrants, the influx of merchants from Shandong was the most striking part. Since ancient times, the Jiaodong region of Shandong had formed the folk custom of "Undertaking Commercial Activity in Vladivostok" and "Undertaking Commercial Activity in Siberia", and every year tens of thousands of people went to the territory of Russia to engage in business. After 1916, on the one hand, the sea and land between Vladivostok and Yantai were gradually blocked. On the other hand, the Jilin Railway Negotiation Department negotiated with the Russian side, making the Department the only organization qualified to issue passports to Chinese, which further strengthened Harbin's status as an important transit point for Shandong businessmen to Russia. Therefore, many Shandong merchants who were originally in Dalian, Yingkou, Yantai and North Korea came to Harbin. For example, Yantai's Xiemao, Yonghengxiang and other merchants appointed counter staffs to bring money to Harbin to organize branch offices. There were also Shandong businessmen who returned to Harbin from Vladivostok to set up canning factories and mushroom factories. According to statistics, since the New Year of 1917, more than 200 companies from Shandong in Dalian, Yantai, Yingkou, and Incheon, Korea had opened branches in Harbin.

The Shandong People Association located outside Daowai. Whether it was Huashang in Daoli or a large bank such as Yantai Xiemao, they all faced the problem of renting land, the responsibility of children's schooling and connecting with fellow villagers. As for the lower-class immigrants who were renting shelters in Harbin, providing necessary assistance to them was key to maintain social order and the stability of Harbin, and furthermore, these immigrants could provide Harbin with more stable labor force. This allowed the Shandong People Association to play its own "social service function" and promoted the integration of these two groups of new migrants into Harbin as soon as possible.

In 1915, "promoting public welfare" was mentioned in the Association's guiding principles. In fact, the Association did play an important role in replacing the government with social service functions. As mentioned above, in 1912, Shandong fellows set up the "School of Shandong People in Harbin" in the "Backyard of Shuanghesheng". In 1912, the school was changed to a national public school and named "Guangyi School". In 1916, the school developed into a Middle School and High School which contained two classes, limited by the house size, it could no longer expand. Since "as more and more of migrants traveled to Harbin and brought more and more children with them, there were often no classes available for those who wished to enroll in the class", the Shandong People Association invested in the construction of another school building in the western part of the Jilin Railway Negotiation Department (Harbin No.1 Senior High School). The organization imitated the single-level system, accepted children whose parents came from Shandong, and solved the problem of children's schooling for the newcomers. In terms of medical treatment, in April 1916, with the support of the Jilin Shandong Association, the Shandong People Association in Harbin proposed to use the rental income from the deposit of coffins over the years as funds to establish a hospital within the association hall to treat fellow townsmen. On August 25th, 1917, the hospital was inaugurated in the Shandong People Association at the eastern end of Taikoo Street.

In 1915, the article "promoting the friendly feelings of fellow villagers in Harbin" was also mentioned in the guiding principles of the Association, and the Association promoted this article. Every year, Shandong People Association organized a group visit to "deepen the fellowship among compatriots". In March 1918 Prosecutor Peng at the Harbin District Prosecutor's Office came to Harbin to serve. After receiving the news, Shandong fellow townsmen in Harbin immediately organized a welcome party for Prosecutor Peng in the Guild Hall.

The Association's guiding principles also mentioned "emergency readiness". In 1916, Yuan Shikai restored the monarchy. As the owner of Harbin Eastern Frontier News Agency, Wang Muguang sold *Shanghai Chinese Times* on which printed slogan against Yuan, and then was arrested by the police and detained in the newly built model prison for a few days and was about to be escorted into the province. It was the president of the Shandong People Association, Fu Juchuan, who met with the Intendant to plead for his release, and made sure that Wang Muguang was released on bail, and was able to regain his freedom. It was also with the financial support of the Association that the funds of the Harbin Eastern Frontier News Agency were secured, which made Wang reorganize the newspaper office after a lapse of one year and changed the newspaper's name into *Eastern Frontier Commercial Daily*.

In addition to the social service function for new immigrants, "giving back to hometown" is also an important responsibility of the Association. As mentioned earlier, there was a drought in Shandong from 1916 to 1917, and many victims flooded into Harbin. Shandong fellows felt that "the very survival of the people in hometown can't be ignored" and they called the fellow villagers to discuss immediately, trying to donate everything to relief the refugees in Shandong. In the end, eight articles were set, and advertisements were placed in newspapers to raise funds for charity. In 1918, when floods occurred in Jinan, Tai'an and other places in Shandong Province, the Shandong People Association joined the two major chambers of commerce in Daoli and Daowai Districts to form the Shandong Flood Rescue Association. Supervising Hou Xuefang was elected as the Main Chairman, Fu Juchuan, Zhang Xiangting, and Ma Xisheng were the Vice-chairmen, Wang Xiyuan and other forty-seven persons were selected as officers to prepare donations. He also sent letters to fellow villagers in Hulan and Suihua, requesting assistance. This move was strongly approved by Li Hongmo, who was the then Intendant of Harbin. Less than a month after the announcement was issued, by October 5th, 1918, a donation of 80,000 rubles had been received in Daoli alone. By December 15th, 1918, Daoli alone had raised 136,000 rubles. This showed the great appeal of the association.

In 1919, the Chinese representatives failed to negotiate on the recovery of Qingdao at the Paris Peace Conference. The news made the fellow villagers in Harbin extremely indignant. On May 23rd, the Shandong People Association, together with the Chambers of Commerce from Daowai and Daoli, called the Shandong Provincial Council and proposed, "We will fight together to protect our sovereignty ... If it fails, we will lead hundreds of thousands of brothers and sisters in Harbin to return to hometown, and we will fight together to ensure our sovereignty." On May 24th, they called the Central Committee, requesting strongly adhere to Qingdao's sovereignty. After learning that Shandong Province would send 80 representatives to petition in Beijing at their own expense, the Shandong People Association raised funds to remit to Beijing to fulfill the obligations to their hometown. These people also organized the National Salvation Group and issued a declaration to the compatriots in Harbin that read: "Better be a headless ghost than a slave of a defeated country".

After 1919, the government of the Republic of China gradually strengthened its influence in Harbin, intervened frequently in Harbin's municipal management, and the phenomenon of government's absence was changed fundamentally. The association, which was originally a supplement to government functions, also weakened. In 1919, the funds for the school in Harbin were in a shortage, and all payments for the teachers and the staffs were paused for several months. Due to the gradual improvement of government functions, the management functions on Chinese businessmen was strengthened, and the dependence of Chinese businessmen on migrants' organizations such as Townsmen Association was also weakened. There was no Chinese businessman willing to donate money to the Association, and without financial resources, the Association would no longer function, and it would naturally face the fate of decline. In 1920, Public School for Shandong immigrants (Guangyi School) was placed under the Chamber of Commerce and was no longer under the responsibility of the Shandong People Association. Soon it was placed under Binjiang County and became a county school. In 1920, the Shandong Jiaodong area had a bad harvest. As usual, the Shandong People Association should actively organize disaster relief. At this time, under the strong manner of the government, the Shandong People Association was no longer able to perform the function of organizing disaster relief on behalf of the government. In the past, the "collective disaster relief" organized by the Association became the "individual disaster relief action" of Chinese businessmen. As a result, Wang Weiqing, the deacon of the East Asia Mill, a giant businessman in Harbin, and Cui Jingchen, an auspicious foreign trader, bought grain from Yingkou and transported them to their homes, to help and benefit the townsmen.

In 1940, Fu Juchuan, Mu Pingren, the chairman of the Shandong People Association, died in Harbin after served as the chairman for 26 years. The successor president of Shandong Guild Hall inherited the regulated management regulations, and with the continuous help of Shandong fellows, he maintained it until 1946.

Later, due to the continuous strengthening of the local government in Harbin, the functions of government became increasingly better, and there was no need for the existence of the association. Therefore, in 1946, the Shandong People Association was temporarily closed, and eventually disintegrated.

Conclusion

Here we use four steps to systematically elucidate the formation process of Harbin's early immigrant society from the perspectives of international relations and immigration history. Harbin Townsmen Associations are placed in the context of immigrant society, and the author find that the function of guild hall can be considered as an expatriate association. Through extensive reading of historical materials, the historical origin of Shunzhi and Shandong Guild Hall and the Shandong People Association in Harbin are systematically examined. Along with the Chinese government's functionality changing from weak to perfect in Harbin, the historical responsibility, and the background of the Townsmen Association (Guild) have been re-introduced to the world. This chapter is not only an examination of this historical product, but also a rethinking of the formation and development of Harbin's diverse immigrant society.

1.2 | Origin of the Jing Bannermen's Reclamation Policy

This chapter will discuss the relevant context of the Qing Government's formulation of the Jing Bannermen's Reclamation. First, it focuses on the situation in the Northeast after the Qing Government seized the power in China, and the two economic-related policies implemented in the Northeast: Cultivation and Reclamation policies and The Prohibition Policy; Second, it goes to the livelihood problems of the Bannermen and the relevant measures taken by the Qing Government for this purpose are discussed. Finally, it will discuss the thought of the Jing Bannermen's Reclamation.

1.2.1 The Situation in Northeast before the Jing Bannermen's Reclamation

(1) The situation in northeast China after the entry of Qing Dynasty

In the Qing Dynasty, the territory of the Northeast region changed greatly. In the early and middle of Qing Dynasty, the Northeast region mainly referred to the north of Shanhai Pass, the south of the Outer Hinggan Mountains, and the Liao River east of Lake Baikal, Songhua River, Heilongjiang, and Ussuri river basins as well as the basins of Binhai and Kuan. The vast area, including the island, had a geographical concept far beyond today's Northeast. After entering Shanhai Pass, the Northeast region, mainly the Manchurian Plain, has undergone great changes.

In the 4th lunar month of 1644 (the 1st year of Shunzhi's reign), the Qing army entered Shanhai Pass in a large scale. In the 8th lunar month of that year, the capital was officially settled in Beijing. Most of the Manchurian nobles, the Eight Banners and their families who originally lived in the northeast China mostly followed the emperor to enter Shanhai Pass. To "make the soldiers lose all hope of returning to their hometowns", the Qing Government did not hesitate to burn down villages in Liaodong. This showed that the migration was so determined and strictly ordered. In the same year, several Japanese who drifted to China saw "a continuous stream of Tatars moving to Beijing". Until the 3rd year of Shunzhi (1646), "men and women supporting each other, and the hubs of the car hitting each other" were seen on the road into Shanhai Pass. This great migration started in the 8th lunar month of 1644 (the 1st year of Shunzhi's reign), continued to the 2nd lunar month of 1646 at least (the 3rd year of Shunzhi's reign), lasted for one and a half years. In addition, before the Qing army entered Shanhai Pass, there were many imperials and noblemen's country estate, and official villages in Liaodong. According to the Records of *the Shunzhi Period of Shengjing Internal Affairs Office*, there were only more than 30 imperial and noblemen country estate in Liaodong at that time. Obviously, most of them moved to the capital city and its environs. Not only that, during the Shunzhi period, because the war for the ruling power of China was not over yet, the Eight Banners were successively transferred to south of Shanhai Pass as reinforcements. When the capital was about to set in Beijing for the 1st year of Shunzhi (1644), there were 83 Colonels originally scheduled to stay in Liaoshen's 15 cities, but in the 16th year of Shunzhi (1659), there were only 25 cavalry officers left, and more than 1,100 armored soldiers stayed in the 6 cities of Shengjing, Xingjing, Niuzhuang, Gaizhou, Fenghuang, and Guangning. This movement to the south of Shanhai Pass in the Shunzhi Dynasty was not just a simple relocation of the capital, but a relocation of a whole nation. It was a complete relocation of the state apparatus and almost all population, it was a movement from the Northeast region to the capital city and its environs.

The large-scale exodus made the sparsely populated Northeast even more desolate. At that time, according to Zhang Shangxian, the Governor of Fengtian Prefecture, the Liaodong area was depicted as "The cities are desolate, the castles are decaying, and even though there are thousands of miles of fertile land, no one cultivates the land, and there is absolutely nothing to fall back on." The economic and cultural prosperity of the past had long disappeared. Until the 10th year of Emperor Kangxi (1671), when Nan Huairen, a foreign missionary, accompanied Emperor Kangxi to the east of Shengjing on a tour, the villagers were still "seldom seen", "the villages and towns were all deserted." At this time, it had been nearly thirty years since the Qing army entered Shanhai Pass, and the treatment of war wounds still had no obvious effect.

As for the vast area from Jilin to Heilongjiang in the north of Liaodong, it was originally relatively desolate. After the Qing Dynasty entered Shanhai Pass, many places even returned to their original situation. In Jilin region, only Jilin City began to "build city with woods" in the 10th year of Kangxi (1671), and "thousands of families belonging to other provinces migrated to live here", and there were only 2,000 Manchurian recruits and veterans. The situation in Heilongjiang at that time was even more desperate, it was "tens of thousands of miles away, and no neighbor can be seen on the barren land".

Many of the above-mentioned materials have clearly shown that: after the Qing Dynasty entered Shanhai Pass, the ruling center moved away from the Northeast, which had a significant impact on the Northeast, the population dropped sharply, there were no merchants on the road, "the households were depressed, and the fields were uncultivated". Abandoned villages and withered economy greatly delayed the development process of Northeast history.

(2) The Qing Government's ruling policy on the northeast region

During the Qing Dynasty, northeast China, which was considered as the "birthplace of the Manchu royal family" and the gateway to the eastern and northern borders, had always been a special region compared to the rest of the country. This was determined by the nature of its border areas, but more importantly by its special relationship with the Qing Court and the Qing Court's special needs for northeast China. Therefore, the Qing Government imposed a special management system in the Northeast and implemented a governance system focusing on administrative construction and border defense construction, supplemented by economic development. In terms of administration, before the Qing Dynasty entered Shanhai Pass, it implemented the Eight Banners system integrating military and government. After entering the Shanhai Pass, Qing Government began to establish a management system called "Three Generals" in the Northeast. There were Lieutenant Generals under the general, four Lieutenant Generals in Shengjing, five in Jilin, and four in Heilongjiang, but the number was changing over the years. In terms of frontier defense construction, Ebo and Kalun were established in the northeastern region, especially in the China-Russia border area, Qing Government established a regular border patrol system and the Heilongjiang Navy Division to strengthen the land and sea defense in the northern frontier. At the same time, a post road connecting the capital was opened to strengthen the connection between the northern frontier and the inland.

The main discussion here is the two main economic policies implemented by the Qing Government in the northeast before the Jing Bannermen's Reclamation: Cultivation and Reclamation Policies and the Prohibition Policy.

① Cultivation and Reclamation policies

In the Early Qing Dynasty, the war was still in full swing, and the unification and control of the whole country had not yet been completed. If the base that had been in operation for many years was abandoned, it would inevitably affect the stability of the regime. Therefore, shortly after entering the Shanhai Pass, the Qing Court began to focus on the reconstruction of the Northeast economy to consolidate the base. From an economic point of view, economic development mainly depends on two factors, one is the smooth natural growth; the other is the promotion of national policies. Due to the continuous large-scale population loss in the Northeast in the Early Qing Dynasty, the area's population was lower than the minimum requirement, and the natural economic growth rate must be quite slow, and the promotion of national policies was of great significance. To stabilize the Central Plains and enrich the Northeast. The Shunzhi Government adopted an open policy to guide population flow back to the northeast.

In the 6th year of Shunzhi (1649), the Qing Government first issued a decree to allow the Han people to go out of the Shanhai Pass to reclaim the uncultivated land: "There are many uncultivated land outside Shanhai Pass, and the people who are willing to go out of the Shanhai Pass to reclaim the uncultivated land will be registered by Shanhai Pass Officials to create a record and live in separate areas." The ethnic oppression of the Manchu rulers was still fresh in Han people's memory at that time, and reclamation in the "birthplace of the Manchu royal family" was often regarded as a dangerous road to take. In addition, the Northeast is in remote areas and the climate is harsh. Under the circumstance that there was still uncultivated land for reclamation outside the Shanhai Pass, the Han nationality farmers were not very enthusiastic about "going out the Shanhai Pass", so this imperial edict had little effect.

The decisive decree for the Han people to go out of the Shanhai Pass and reclaim land was the "Liaodong Recruitment and Reclamation Order" promulgated in the 10th year of Shunzhi (1653). This decree said: "Liaodong recruits people to reclaim the land, recruiting up to 100 people, those who is good at literacy will be appointed the county magistrate, and those who is good at marshal art will be appointed Lieutenant Colonel; those who have less than 100 people and more than 60 will be appointed the prefecture, and the captain accordingly. Those with more than 50 names will be granted the county chief or the chief registrar, and the First Lieutenant; accordingly, for those with many recruits, every 100 persons recruited will raise the recruiter one rank. All registration book and number of recruits will be submitted to the Treasure Department and the recruits will be led out the Shanhai Pass, checked and received by the Liaodong provincial and county government, and then, recruiters will be given official certificates to selected positions for the government and military." It also stipulated: "In accordance with the convention of reclamation in the province, each person recruited by Liaodong will be given a monthly grain ration, which was to be repaid in autumn. Each shang (a land measure equal to fifteen mu in most parts of the Northeast and three or five mu in the Northwest, the same below) of land was given six liters of seed, and 20 cattle were given for every 100 people." From the contents of the recruitment order, we can see that the Qing Government not only rewarded the Han people, but also gave them a very high official position. Moreover, to encourage the head of the recruitment of Han Chinese people, the Qing Court continued to promulgate a favorable decree to supplement the effectiveness of the original order.

In the 12th year of Shunzhi (1655), it was stipulated: "Those who recruit hundreds of people in Liaodong will be divided into three grades, and if they were proficient in the literature and doctrine, they would be granted the official position of a magistrate; otherwise, if they could not be proficient, they would be consulted and sent to the Ministry of the Defense."

In the 15th year of Shunzhi (1658), it was stipulated: "More than 50 qing (a unit of area =6.6667 hectares, the same below) of land have been reclaimed by the civil and military squires. The incumbents will record them, and those new officials will be awarded with honorable plaques."

In the 16th year of the Shunzhi reign (1659), it was stipulated: "If the people reclaim uncultivated land more than 2,000 mu (a unit of area =0.0667 hectares, the same below), they will be appointed as a commander of 1000 men, Those who cultivate more than 2,000 mu of land with a military position will have their official position increased by one rank, as a reserve for managing the general affairs of the army."

In the 2nd year of Emperor Kangxi (1663), it was stipulated: "Those who may recruit 100 people from Liaodong do not need to take examinations, and they will all be hired as magistrates of the county."

In the 6th year of Kangxi (1667), it was stipulated: "When recruiting a hundred households of residents in Liaodong, officials will henceforth cease the previous selection process and instead proceed to select and appoint individuals in order of age."

The basic contents of the five materials above were to supplement the reward regulations of the "Liaodong Recruitment and Reclamation Order" in the 10th year of Shunzhi (1653), which showed the urgency of the Qing Court to develop the Liaodong area.

However, the question was whether the Qing Court could implement such generous incentives seriously?

From the analysis of historical materials, we know that the 2nd year after the promulgation of this decree, that is, the 11th year of Shunzhi(1654), Chen Dade, a native of Yiwu, Zhejiang, "touted 140 households to serve the affairs of Liaoyang County." Chen died of illness, and his minions, Zhao Lianjing, and others requested a letter from Shengjing, Angbangzhang, Jingye, and asked Dade's son, Zhanyuan, to inherit his father's official position. The related records can be found in *Records of the Qing Dynasty's Ancestors Records* and *Notes on Classical Poetry in Xueqiao*. The passage in *Records of the Qing Dynasty's Ancestors Records* is as follows: "This issue had been discussed; Chen Dade was the first to recruit people to go out the Shanhai Pass when Liaoyang was established. He was appointed as the county magistrate for recruiting people, he passed away today and the people wanted to support his son, and let his son to continue the work of recruiting, therefore, people were willing to work with his son, and the request was granted." *Notes on Classical Poetry in Xueqiao* contains: "The well-respected Chen Dade who comes from Yiwu, together with Wu Yangru and other notables, formed the 'Bayong Pavilion Poets Society' and were renowned for their poetry and calligraphy. At the beginning of the founding of the Qing Dynasty, a county was established in Liaoyang. The imperial court ordered that whoever could recruit a hundred people to go to Liaoyang would be appointed as the Magistrate of Liaoyang County. The trustworthy Chen Dade answered the call and led the hundred men to leave Shanhai Pass and head east and was thus granted the post of Liaoyang County Magistrate. He was diligent in reclamation, developing commerce and revitalizing culture, and eventually died in his position, and his son Zhanyuan inherited his title." Although according to the historical materials the author has mastered, only Chen Dade and his son were granted officials for recruiting people, but being rewarded for resettling immigrants undoubtedly played a guiding role in the behavior of local officials. Similarly, for the Han people who recruited to cultivate, they were also honored according to the established incentive measures. "When recruiting new people, the Ministry of Treasury will send the same county officials to the city, and each recruit will be given a 15m long and 8m wide land as the foundation, so that the people can cultivate on it. Each person will be given 50 mu of field, which will be the people's property forever. If six settlers can be recruited, the headman receives a cooking pot, a vat, an ox, a full set of farm implements, and each person is given one bucket of corn per month until the autumn harvest."

Under the encouragement of the policy of recruiting people to reclaim the uncultivated land, the Han people in Shanxi, Hebei, Shandong, and Henan provinces who were stricken and impoverished by the disaster had left the borders and had stayed, all these recruits were basic labors for economical development, and they cultivated Liaodong's barren land. Here is a poetry as proof: "In the past, the grain in the country was transported back and forth, and famine often occurred in Liaodong. Now, the fields in Shenyang have been cultivated, and the grain transportation reaches to the west of Shanhai Pass. We cannot waste the people's labor or fail to make good use of the land. There is no better strategy for planning border defense, which is that agriculture and war should complement each other." But poetry is a kind of perceptual description after all. To clarify the effectiveness of the policy of recruiting people to reclaim uncultivated land in Liaodong, the key lies in the growth of population and arable land in this region. The following table shows the increase in population and cultivated land in Shengjing from the promulgation of the *Reclamation Order* to the 17th year of Kangxi (1668):

Era	Area	Population increases	Growth of cultivated land
The 17th year of Shunzhi	Liaoyang, Haicheng	3723 people	48165 mu
The 18th year of Shunzhi	Jinzhou	299 people	7169 mu
The 7th year of Kangxi	Chengde and other six counties	2643 people	6737 mu

Source of data: Volume 23 of the *Annals of Shengjing,* the edition of the First Year of Qianlong

The data in the table above shows that from the end of Shunzhi to the beginning of Kangxi, the population and land growth in Shengjing increased significantly. This is by no means the result of natural growth, but the result of migration. It also fully illustrates the recruitment of people for reclamation is effective in Eastern Liaoning. In line with this, the dual political structure with the Eight Banners garrisoned and the prefectures and counties as the main body was gradually established. By the 4th year of Kangxi (1665), there were 2 prefectures, 2 states and 7 counties. Moreover, "states and counties are all new, and households' registered residence is also new. There are few original residents in the local area, and they are all new residents". The farmland was also "no original land", and they were "all newly reclaimed land". Although the scale of prefecture, state and county was very small at that time, it became the base for the people to relocate and reclaimed later.

In this way, the social and economic system and political structure of the Northeast as a frontier area was formed, and the urgency and necessity of implementing special policies to promote the development of the frontier area was not strong as before. Therefore, in the 2nd year of Emperor Kangxi's assuming the reins of government (1668), this active migration and reclamation policy—*The Liaodong Recruitment and Reclamation Order*, was abolished.

② The Prohibition Policy

The so-called "Prohibition" means that the Qing Government built a border wall to isolate the Shengjing area from the rest of the Northeast. This was also a basic national policy implemented by the Qing Dynasty in the Northeast for a long time. However, there are still different opinions in the historian circle regarding the timing of this policy. There are roughly four versions about the starting point: from the 16th year of Shunzhi (1649), the 7th year of Kangxi (1668), the last years of Shunzhi or the 5th year of Qianlong (1740).

However, through the research, the author found that the Prohibition Policy cannot be precisely set for a specific time. Because Prohibition Policy, at its core, is nothing more than a means for the ruling Manchus to safeguard their own interests, but at the same time they are the representatives of the interests of the entire Qing Empire. Therefore, when formulating and implementing this policy, it must weigh the pros and cons in the conflict of state and ethnic interests, and even make some kind of compromise in a specific period. It can be said that in the Northeast region in the early Qing Dynasty, the Qing Court never practiced a complete prohibition, but always showed that there was relaxation in the prohibition, and there was prohibition in the relaxation, and the relaxation was always accompanied by the prohibition.

As mentioned above, in the 6th year of Shunzhi (1649), the Qing Government first issued a decree to allow the Han people to go outside the Shanhai Pass to reclaim the uncultivated land and prohibit Han and Mongolian people from entering the uncultivated land for grazing. In the First Historical Archives of China, the author found such a historical material: In the 11th year of Shunzhi (1654), Shanhai Pass prefectural magistrate Bai Hui submitted a letter reporting that seventy households of newly recruited Han people were now requesting to settle on the land previously chosen for reclamation, along with thirty other families, including Zhao Jingming, who went out of Shanhai Pass in the same year with the official dispatch. However, the Qing Court did not allow them to live in the selected place. If they wished to cultivate in Liaoyang, they had to go to the place designated by the court. If they were unwilling to go, they could also live in the inland. From this, we know that even when *The Liaodong Recruitment and Reclamation Order* was actively promoted to recruit people to reclaim land, the Qing Court did not allow Han people to go outside the Shanhai Pass freely. The land policy granted for cultivation was not applicable to the entire Northeast, and even in the restricted Liaodong region, it was limited to certain areas.

In the 16th year of Emperor Kangxi (1677), the Qing Government designated the Changbai Mountain area as the "Holy Land of Birthplace", and stipulated that "the east of Shengjing, the south of Yitong Prefecture, and the north of Tumen River are all prohibited. There were prohibitions on the residence of migrants, the reclamation of land, lumbering and mining, and the harvesting of ginseng and pearls." Therefore, within the territory of more than a thousand miles around Changbai Mountain, it became a "forbidden area within a forbidden area". However, at the same time, it was stipulated that Han people entering Liaodong only needed to "request the Ministry of Defense or go to the government office to issue a Han People's Pass. After arriving at Shanhai Pass ... go to the prefectural magistrate for filing and inspection. If there are Han people accompanying the Manchus as laborers, they can still be granted passing." In the 18th year of Kangxi (1679), he ordered the uncultivated land of his own to be returned and the state and county officials to persuade the people to cultivate. The next year, another order was issued: "Newcomers to Fengtian will be settled in the village, and they will cultivate crops around it." In this case, the Han population flowing outside Shanhai Pass was increasing. What he prohibited was not the whole northeast, but only his most treasured feng shui (geomantic) place-the Changbai Mountain area.

During the reign of Emperor Yongzheng, there was only much said but little done, and no one was severely punished for violating the prohibition. For example, in the 4th lunar month of 1724 (the 2nd year of Yongzheng's reign), he addressed the old practice of privately harvesting ginseng regardless of whether it was obtained or not and sent it to the Punishment Department. "I consider that you are poor people who are apprehended in spring and summer for a small profit, and the case can only be concluded in the 9th and 10th lunar month, which will take several months and days. During this period, you will suffer from cold and heat, most of you will get sick or even die, which is pitiful. There are generals and office supervisors in Ningguta, generals and Ministry of Punishment in Shengjing, in the future, people who have been apprehended for illegally digging ginseng in various places will be trialed by them, and the case will be concluded as soon as possible. At the end of the year, the reports will be collected and sent to me together. From now on, the officials who take charge of trials for illegally harvesting ginseng may not have to go again. In this way, the people related to the case will not be detained for a long time and suffer from cold and hunger." Yongzheng regarded illegally harvesting of ginseng as a trivial matter, and even sheltered the sufferers who violated the prohibition.

Even in the Qianlong Period, which is known for the strictest prohibition, there were frequent alternations between prohibitions and relaxations. In the 3rd year of Qianlong (1738), to strengthen the defense capability of border crossings in the three eastern provinces, the clerks in six important strongholds including Weiyuanbao, were transferred to military positions; In 1734, Qianlong ordered that the Bannermen who went through the Shanhai Pass must be check strictly. In the 5th year of Qianlong's reign (1740), the Qing Government ordered that the domestic refugees in Fengtian must obtain citizenship. However, just after this, the Qing Court immediately wrote a letter to the province: "They are not all unemployed refugees who go out of Shanhai Pass alone. If they are all banned, it will be inconvenient." For the refugees who went out of Shanhai Pass alone, they should "obtain a road guide and an official licence from the place where they are located and go to Shanhai Pass for inspection and then let them pass." In the 8th year of Qianlong's reign (1743), the drought occurred in Tianjin and Hejian. When the victims heard that the weather outside the Shanhai Pass was quite mild, they wanted to go out of Shanhai Pass, but the officials at the Pass still blocked them as usual and did not allow them to leave. Faced with the plight of the impoverished migrants who were unemployed and left their hometown, and the Shanhai Pass did not allow them to leave, Emperor Qianlong, who reigned over the whole country, worried that "if the inspection is too strict, these disaster victims may have no way to survive." So, he had to secretly instruct the officials of Shanhai Pass, "If there are poor people who want to pass, they should not be blocked. Let them go immediately." At the same time, he emphasized that "my orders should not be announced to the public. If my orders are made known to the public, I am afraid that more people will want to leave." The next year, when the floods occurred in Henan and Shandong, for the flood victims who wanted to go outside of the Shanhai Pass, Qianlong still followed the previous year's practice and ordered the local officials to "make some changes and inquiries. If they are really impoverished people, let them leave immediately without too many questions. You must handle it well to show my original intention of caring about the people." The above-mentioned historical materials clearly show the contradictory mind of the Qing Court towards northeast China, which is both prohibited and relaxed.

In addition, this contradiction is also reflected in the issue of clearing up the registration of refugees in Liaoning Province. The clean-up began in the 5th year of Qianlong (1740), and the initial period was half a year. By the 11th year of Qianlong (1746), not only did all the victims in Fengtian fail to register, but the number of victims who went outside the Shanhai Pass increased by tens of thousands. The Qing Court had no choice but to extend the limitation to ten years, and in the 15th year of Qianlong (1750), among the people of Liaoning Province, "there are people who have owned properties and neither wanted to return to their native place nor were willing to be incorporated into Liaoning's region." Faced with this reality, the Qing Court had no choice but to "extend this policy for another ten years". This repeated compromise on the issue also reflects the phenomenon of relaxation in the implementation of the prohibition policy.

Another noteworthy phenomenon is that the loose and tight of the prohibition policy was related to the migration and station of Jing Banner. Before each relocation, there was always a strict prohibition policy introduced. In the 5th lunar month of 1741 (the 6th year of Qianlong's reign), the great scholar Chalanga and the Assistant Minister Arigon went to Fengtian area to measure the terrain in order to restation the loafers of Jing Banner. However, in the 5th (1740), 6th (1741), and 7th (1742) years of Qianlong, the Qing Government issued a prohibition on Fengtian, Jilin, and Heilongjiang respectively, prohibiting refugees from entering. In the 42nd year of Qianlong's reign (1777), the Qing Court pointed out, "The rich and beautiful Xingshan Mountains and Songshan Mountains in the northwest of the Daling River can be used as the relocated places for member of the imperial clan. Relocated people will be given three qing of land, half-official reclamation, half self-cultivation, to built houses and arrange villages, and be offered seeds and tools", so the member of the imperial clan could cultivate their fields to solve their livelihood problems. Just the year before this, in the 41st year of Qianlong (1776), the prohibition was strictly implemented again, and in the following year, local officials who didn't execute the prohibition were downgraded. After that, Emperor Qianlong tried every means to force the existing refugees to give up the land they had occupied by adding tax and other measures and tried to solve the livelihood of the Eight Banners by withdrawing the cultivated land. Judging from the above historical facts, it is quite obvious that the original intention of Emperor Qianlong is to ensure that the land in the Northeast is not occupied by the common people by strict prohibition, thus providing convenient conditions for his relocation of member of the imperial clan.

1.2.2 The Livelihood of the Eight Banners

(1) Preferential treatment for banners after entering Shanhai Pass

With a backward culture and a small number of people, it is conceivable that the Manchus faced difficulties after they conquered the Central Plains. To consolidate the regime, the Qing rulers stipulated that the soldiers of the Eight Banners must be fully engaged in military affairs and become professional soldiers, trying to maintain the dominion of the Qing Dynasty with the force of the whole clan. At the same time, measures were taken in political, economic, legal and other aspects to establish and maintain the superior social status of the banner people, resulting in a form of governance under the clan, in order to enhance the cohesion of Manchu and the entire banner society.

Politically, Manchus owned the priority of official appointment, they had the top position in the organization with the most power, and the seal belonged to Manchu officials. A fixed number of positions were set aside for Manchu officials, which gave priorities for Manchus over other ethnic groups. This created more opportunities for Manchu people to enter government service and ensured that the Manchu people held a legally advantageous position in the regime.

Economically, to ensure the stability and high combat effectiveness of the Eight Banners troops, the Qing Government prohibited the banner people from engaging in agriculture, industry, and commerce. Being a soldier became the only legitimate occupation for the banner people, and their living needs were all provided by the state. The land system and the grain and salary system were established successively.

From the 1st year to the 4th year of Shunzhi (1644-1647), the Qing Government forcibly encircled and occupied civilian land within hundreds of miles around Beijing three times and distributed the encircled fields within the Eight Banners according to grades. In addition, according to the different ranks of the soldiers in the Eight Banners, different amounts of food and salaries, commonly known as "money and food" were distributed, including monthly salaries and quarterly rice. Rules made in the Kangxi Dynasty: four taels of silver for the frontmen, guards, and leaders of banners, three taels of silver for horsemen, 2300 liters rice per year; three taels of silver and for the leaders of the infantry, 1.5 taels of silver for the infantrymen, 1100 liters rice per year, which is the so-called "Monthly fixed rations". During the expedition, there was another "food supply", two taels of silver per person per month, and 0.83 liters of millet per month. Garrison officers and soldiers can borrow money when they are on business trips or have wedding or funeral at home. In addition, to reduce the economic burden of the soldiers of the Eight Banners, the Qing Court stipulated that in addition to military service, the soldiers of each banner would never offer compulsory service, grain and grass, and cloth to the government. The reason for adopting such a policy of "Welfare System for the Eight-banners" had nothing but one purpose, that is, to ensure the soldiers of the Eight Banners to live a secure life and to devote themselves to military operations, to ensure the stability of the Qing Empire's regime.

Legally, bannermen enjoyed different legal privileges from ordinary people. "Where bannermen commit crimes, instead of being beaten by clubs, they will be lashed with multiple whips. They will be put on shackles and shown in public instead of being exiled."

However, while granting various preferential treatments to the Bannermen, various restrictions were also imposed on them, such as forbidding them to trade property, get intermarriage, live together, prohibiting them from going out for long distances, and engaging in other industries such as business and acting, and prohibiting them from borrowing money from others, in order to maintain the dignity of the Bannermen and consolidate the Eight Banners system.

It should be said that series of regulations and systems formulated by the Qing Government to maintain the noble status of the bannermen did help the bannermen to establish their self-esteem and self-confidence when the situation, the regime was unstable, and strong force was still needed to consolidate the new regime. This also contributed to the enhancement of Narrow-minded national consciousness, however, with the gradual cessation of the war and the progress of the times, the various privileges and restraints enjoyed by the bannermen or constraining them have increasingly constituted the obstacle for the further development of the bannermen, especially the Manchu bannermen, as later history has proved.

(2) The poverty-stricken livelihood of the Eight Banners

If the national financial resources allowed, the Qing Government could still implement these measures to support the bannermen with provisions. However, when the national financial resources were limited, but the population of the bannermen was rising, the sale and lease of bannermen's land began to increase, and the corruption of the banner officers and soldiers was worsening, the livelihood of the bannermen increasingly became a burden to the imperial court and a burden on society.

As early as the middle of Kangxi's reign, some families of the bannermen in the capital experienced problems in their livelihoods, the most direct cause of which was the increase in population and the lack of thrift among the bannermen.

When discussing the livelihood of the Eight Banners, population is a factor that must be listed in the Qing Court's decrees and ministers' memorials. After the establishment of the Qing Dynasty, especially after the end of the Revolt of the Three Vassal Kings in the 20th year of Kangxi (1681), the population of the Eight Banners grew rapidly after several decades of recuperation. According to the official statistics of Qing Dynasty, in the 5th year of Shunzhi (1648), the number of men in the Eight Banners was 346,931, and it rose to 696,681 in the 60th year of Kangxi (1721). In more than 70 years, the population of the Eight Banners doubled. For the bannermen, only those who serves in the army can receive a fixed amount of food. However, there is a quota for soldiers. Although the Qing Government had adopted the method of expanding the number of soldiers to absorb some of the increased men, it still could not solve the problem. With the increase in the population of the bannermen, the number of idle people is increasing, which will inevitably increase the difficulties of family livelihood.

The luxury and corruption of the bannermen are another important reason for the livelihood problems of the Eight Banners. In the 5th year of Yongzheng (1727), a decree reflected the specific situation of the luxury and corruption of the Eight Banners' soldiers: "In recent years, the Manchu people have not been good at making a living, relying only on the silver and grain distributed by the government to survive, indulging in extravagance and luxury ... It seems that most Manchu people do not know how to practice thrift, selling their property to satisfy their desires for food and drink. Some soldiers, for example, must have meat at every meal. The price of one jin of meat in the market can buy several days' vegetables and grains, but they still choose to buy the more expensive meat. As a result, the monthly income from the silver and grain is all spent on just a few meals of meat. After getting tired of eating pork, they start to crave other delicious foods. Without calculating their income and expenses each month, they spend all their money as soon as they get it. Moreover, they do not know how to save their grain each season; in order to buy meat for a few days, they violate the ban and sell their grain at a low price to buy wine and meat in the market. As a result, they end up with nothing saved." In another edict, Yongzheng criticized the Bannermen: "In their daily lives, they compete in living a luxurious life, with extravagant furniture, clothing, and food. They indulge in luxurious pleasures and vie with each other in splendor. Some even indulge in the opera and gambling. They forget the hardships of past accumulation, nor do they consider how to live in the future. They squander their money and enjoy the present moment." By the reign of Emperor Qianlong, this corruption phenomenon had become even more serious. There were even dishonest soldiers who "were not allowed to wear satin boots, but instead used satin as the inside material to make boots."

To maintain this luxurious lifestyle, there must be sufficient income. However, the income of the bannermen was fixed. At that time, it was stipulated that the quota of grain and rice for the banner men was distributed quarterly through the Eight Banners system. This system of supplying provisions on a regular and fixed basis was designed to provide for the basic livelihood of the bannermen and their families, ensuring that they would not suffer from hunger. But starting from the mid-period of Kangxi's reign, most bannermen sold their grain and rice as soon as they received them. Kangxi once issued an edict pointing out this issue: "The rice distributed by the government to the Eight Banners' officers and soldiers has not been brought home but sold for profit. The number of taels of silver obtained is particularly small. When the taels of silver are spent and the price of rice increases, everyone regrets it." Not only did they sell their provisions, but many bannermen used their unpaid military pay as collateral to borrow high-interest loans, which were called "usury" at that time. These high-interest loans required interest rates of five or six percent. At that time, most of the people who lent money on interest were bannermen and cavalry officers. Yongzheng once furiously criticized them: "Some bannermen and cavalry officers only consider their own interests and collude with others to lend money on interest. They use other people's names to lend money on interest, and some soldiers have their salaries deducted in ten or twelve months. When they receive their monthly salary, they are forced to repay it without delay. As a result, the interest is used as capital, and interest is added on top of interest. This often leads to a lack of income for the soldiers." This kind of exploitation by high-interest loans inevitably impoverished some banner soldiers and made them suffer from debt stress. Therefore, the Qing Government repeatedly emphasized that "except for the behavior of banner soldiers borrowing from each other, all other bannermen officers who lend money on interest or deduct salaries will be banned, and anyone who violates this will be punished."

Secondly, the livelihood of the bannermen is also in a critical situation, as the income from the Banner land was gradually decreasing, and they had lost their fixed source of income. At the beginning of the Qing's entry into Shanhai Pass, the bannermen generally received farmland and had it cultivated by hired farmers. They could sit back and collect the rent, which was called "supporting each other with land and living in peace with each other". The income from the Banner land was sufficient to support themselves. However, after the mid-period of Kangxi's reign, the population of the bannermen increased rapidly, while the number of military salaries was limited. Many bannermen found it difficult to support the doubled population with their original income. When they could not manage their finances, they often sold most of their farmland and houses to others. According to Qing laws, the sale of Banner land was generally only allowed within the Banner system. Under special circumstances, it was allowed to sell to other Banners. The trade of farmland and houses between bannermen and non-bannermen was strictly prohibited. However, the illegal purchase of Banner land between bannermen and non-bannermen had already occurred. As a result, the land of the bannermen was transferred to the hands of civilians. By the early years of Qianlong's reign, "Most of the land within 500 miles of Beijing belonged to the bannermen. Most of the land was pawned than redeemed." A considerable number of middle and lower level bannermen had already fallen into a situation where they had "no grain or property to live on." This situation indicates that the livelihood of the bannermen had worsened to a very serious level.

(3) Various measures taken by the Qing Government to solve the problem of "Eight Banner Livelihood"

The increasingly serious livelihood problems of the Eight Banners not only brought a crisis to the Eight Banners system, but also directly affected the govern of the Qing Court, causing the rulers to feel uneasy. Continuing to maintain and rely on the Eight Banners system requires painstaking efforts to find a solution to this problem. For this reason, since the Kangxi Dynasty, from Yongzheng to Qianlong, the Qing Court had spent a lot on the establishment of a system for the Hans and Manchu who was not original Bannerman to discharge from the army. The Qing Government also set up fields for cultivating, given pension, redeem the bannermen's land and provide for the soldiers who has no family member and nothing to support themselves.

① The Hans in Manchu army's return to the countryside

Among the various measures taken by the Qing Government to solve the livelihood of the Eight Banners, the effect of the Hans in Manchu Army's discharge to the countryside was the most significant one. The so-called Han Army refers to the Eight Banner Army formed by Han people who joined the banner for various reasons. At the beginning, in order to win over these people, the Qing Government always emphasized that there were only differences between banners and common people, not between the Manchus and Han. However, when the Eight Banners faced a crisis of livelihood, the first thought of the Qing rulers was how to make these meritorious Hans army to discharge. This policy was first decided in Qianlong's 7th year (1742). The edict said:

The bannermen of the Han army have been increasing in number since they followed the Qing Dynasty in pacifying Central Plains. Some of them have joined the government and received salaries and provisions, which are sufficient for their daily needs. However, as time passes, an increasing number of them become loafers, and their livelihoods become increasingly difficult. Also, due to the restrictions of the existing regulations, those who serve in positions outside the capital cannot purchase property or live separately. The loafers, even if they have relatives or friends in other provinces or can engage in craftsmanship or other work to make a living, are also restricted by the regulations and cannot leave. As a result, I am deeply concerned that they sit idly by and live from hand to mouth, trapped in one place. I think that the Han army in the Banner system originally were Hans. Some joined the Banner system when they followed the emperor into the capital, some surrendered and joined the Banner system after the founding of the capital, some joined due to crimes, and some joined from the families of the Three Vessal Kings who surrendered. Some were transferred from the Princes and Dukes and family born servants of the Ministry of Internal Order, and some were recruited as artillerymen or adopted as stepchildren. They joined the Banner system at different times for different reasons, with different backgrounds. Among them, only the descendants of those who joined the Banner system at the beginning have old military achievements and have been in the system for generations, so there is no need to discuss changing their status. The others may have houses and property in their home provinces or may have relatives and in-laws in other provinces. I want to make some changes to broaden their ways of making a living. Those who wish to return to their original provinces are allowed to be registered in the Baojia with the local civilians. Those who do not wish to return to their original provinces but can live in other provinces are allowed to move there without restrictions on distance or direction. If there are hereditary positions among them, they are allowed to take them along. Those who have no support in their original provinces and cannot live in other provinces are allowed to stay in the Banner system and continue to serve as before. All those who wish to change their status to that of civilians or move to other provinces are allowed to do so within one year, whether they are officials or soldiers or loafers. This is a special favor from me to provide long-term security for the Hans in the Banner system. It is not meant to expel them from the Banner system and make them civilians, nor is it meant to stop providing them with grain and provisions. I order that the generals of Han army in the Banner system and others should explain this clearly to the soldiers and ask if they have any wishes or concerns. They should report this to me in a written report.

Although the imperial edict issued to the Han army was very tactful and took the livelihood of the Han army into consideration, but the true purpose is to let the Han banner people to discharge from the Eight Banners and return to Han nationality. After the expiration of one year, a total of 1,396 officers and soldiers in the Han army of the Eight Banners in the capital were willing to withdraw from the banner and return to civilian life, including 140 officials, 23 incumbent officials, and the rest were cavalrymen and infantries, deacons, officials who had been dismissed and loafers.

In addition, the imperial edict stated that this was "a special measure and will not be repeated", which seemed to indicate that this was a temporary measure. However, the development of the situation was sufficient to show that this was not an expedient measure, because once the decision to transfer the Han army to civilian status was implemented, it would never stop. The emperor, that is, the court, repeatedly and clearly proposed a series of policies, principles, and specific requirements for transferring the Han army to civilian status in the form of "edicts", "imperial decrees", or "approved resolutions" and "approved proposals" and continued to promote the realization of this decision. And step by step, the scope was gradually expanded.

In the 19th year of Qianlong's reign (1754), the scope of the Hans in Manchu Army's return to the countryside was expanded from the capital to all garrisons. "If there is a personnel shortage in local garrisons, the Manchus in the capital can be sent, and the capital's crowded garrisons can be relieved a little." This reveals that the Han Army's discharge was a sacrifice to protect the state, the true intention was to preserve Manchuria at the expense of Han soldiers. With one order, from the 19th year(1754), the Han Army's discharge in various garrisons began to unfold. By the 44th year(1779), almost all the Han Army's garrisons in various places had been ordered to discharge their troops.

In the 27th year of Qianlong's reign (1762), it was proposed and approved that "the Han members of the Eight Banners who followed the Qing Court before the conquest of central plains are allowed to leave, if they have places to rely on in other provinces." This breakthrough ended the rule that the descendants of the Han members who joined the Qing Court before the conquest of central plains could stay in the Eight Banners without being expelled. The descendants of the Han members who had been highly favored and enjoyed an excellent status in the Eight Banners were shaken. These Han members were those who were recruited into the Eight Banners before the conquest of inland China, and they were the foundation of the Eight Banners. Now allowing their descendants to leave the Eight Banners and become civilians was equivalent to shaking the foundation. This was a significant change, not only for the Han members, but also for the Eight Banners as a whole. In the same year, it was also proposed and approved that "the Han members who hold official positions below the rank of 6th degree, as well as all officials on reserve, candidates, retired, dismissed and discharged officials and soldiers, if they want to change their status to civilians", can be registered as civilians after submitting applications and reporting. Although there was a condition of "voluntarily", it was just a gobbledygook. The phenomenon of "one size fits all approach" inevitably existed.

In any case, after discharged from the Eight Banners system, this group of Han members showed their survival ability. They indeed partially solved the livelihood problems of bannermen, which is also the reason why this measure could work.

② Establishment of the Hashtag-shaped-field System

The establishment of Hashtag-shaped-field System was an attempt by the Qing Government to reintegrate the loafers of the Eight Banners with the land. Although it ended in failure, it can be said to be the forerunner of the Jing Bannermen's Reclamation.

In the 2nd year of Yongzheng (1724), Seide, the Vice Censor-in-chief of the Court of Censors, petitioned for the establishment of Hashtag-shaped-field System. The method was "From the remaining land in the Internal Affairs Office and the official land collected by the Ministry of Treasury, 116 qing of land was allocated to the new county of Xincheng, and 125 qing 89 mu of land was allocated to Guan County. These lands were made into the Hashtag-shaped-field System Ownership and ordered to be cultivated by 50 Manchu households, 10 Mongolian households, and 40 Han military households that were selected from among the Eight Banners. Each household was given 100 mu of farmland, surrounded by 800 mu private farmland, and the middle 100 mu was public farmland. The public farmland produced grain, which was taxed after three years. No cultivated land was built in the villages, and 400 houses were constructed. Each person was issued 50 taels of silver as their yearly allowance for food, livestock, seeds, and farming tools. There were two administrators and advisors. If they were successful, they could report to the court." It is the practice of turning these bannermen back into state-owned serfs. However, from the perspective of solving the Eight Banners soldiers' property problem, this method of solving the bannermen loafers' livelihood was affirmed by Emperor Yongzheng. In his edict on June 23rd of the same year, he instructed: "The proposal is very good, and anywhere else will be implemented according to it." He ordered this task to be specifically supervised over by Prince Yunxiang and others.

In the 5th year of Yongzheng's reign (1727), because some reformed officials and soldiers of the Eight Banners who were punished for crimes spent their days idly in the capital, depending on relatives for their livelihoods. The court worried that these people would do illegal deeds because they had nothing to do. Therefore, the court ordered, "The Manchus and Mongolians in the Eight Banners who have no grain and have been kicked out of army for breaking the law, will be sent to work on the Hashtag-shaped-field as well as their wives and children. Each household will be given 30 mu of farmland, with 5 households sharing 3 cows. Each household will be given 15 silver taels of silver to purchase cow harness, seeds, and other items, as well as annual provisions. They will be handed over to the officials managing the Hashtag-shaped-field to build houses according to the number of people and let them live there. Strict discipline will be implemented. If anyone continues to do illegal things and causes trouble, their punishment will be doubled after reporting to the court." At the same time, "if someone is sentenced to penal servitude after being removed from their positions, they will be sent to the Hashtag-shaped-field for labor."

This law was implemented for more than ten years. By the first year of Qianlong's reign (1736), "All of the 180 households working on the well-delineated farmland have been recalled for various reasons, with more than 90 households returned. Therefore, rotation is necessary. The Eight Banners who were sent to work on the land are mostly unskilled and unable to serve as officials. After arriving at the Well Field farmland, they still cannot cultivate crops and live properly." As it did not work effectively, the Qing Court had to change the remaining people into tenant farmers. They were required to pay grain tax according to the amount of land they cultivated, and those who could not provide for themselves were sent back to their own Banners and their allocations were stopped. The experiment with the Hashtag-shaped-field System farmland failed.

③ Taels of silver reward

Taels of silver reward was a common method used by the three emperors, Kangxi, Yongzheng and Qianlong, to solve the livelihood problems of the Eight Banners. Emperor Kangxi issued two large sums of money, the first time more than 5,415,000 taels of silver, and the average banner person received hundreds of taels of silver per household; in the 42nd year of Kangxi (1703), more than 6,554,000 taels of silver were awarded to soldiers and others. When Emperor Yongzheng came to the throne, he also rewarded the soldiers of the Eight Banners with money and grain several times, each time about 356,000 taels of silver. In the 8th year of Qianlong's reign (1743), "Each eight bannerman will be rewarded 10,000 taels of silver, 5,000 taels of silver to Manchuria, 2,000 taels of silver to Mongolia, and 3,000 taels of silver to the Han army, each flag should identify those who are really poor, regardless of whether they are Jiala (a team of soldiers) or cavalry officers, count the population, and reward each with two or three taels of silver of silver, and together with the generals and other officials, these reward mustn't be used extravagantly, and everyone shall benefit from the reward. There are also three banners of the Internal Affairs office, each will be rewarded 10,000 taels of silver. The ministers of the Imperial Household Office, etc., shall supervise the process together. All the tales of silver reward will be distributed by the Imperial Household Office and delivered for rewarding immediately." However, the soldiers and others did not use the rewards to buy property. "These taels of silver were only used for food and wines and were all spent in less than ten days", this extravagant consumption made their livelihood even more embarrassing than before.

In addition to the reward of taels of silver, in the mid-Yongzheng period, each banner was also distributed 100,000 the treasury's money for the expenses of weddings and funerals. In the 1st year of Qianlong's reign (1736), soldiers from the Eight Banners, the Imperial Household Office, Manchuria, Mongolia, and Han, received a total of one million taels of silver. In times of difficulty, the order was changed to real estate, pawnshop, or land renting business. According to the *Bordered Red Banner File*, "On the 14th of the 3rd lunar month of 1729 (the 7th year of Yongzheng's reign), the quasi-Imperial Household Office said: 'I hereby enjoin: I will take care of the livelihood of the soldiers and people of the Eight Banners in the capital. When it comes to wedding and funeral in the family, the consumption is quite unaffordable for you, and it is hard and pitiful. The silver in the inner treasury will be delivered to the princes and ministers to accrue interest, the interests can be used by the soldiers for the unexpected needs ... General Shemude and others reported that: from the first of the 11th lunar month of 1731 (the 9th year of Yongzheng's reign) to the 29th of the 11th lunar month of 1732 (the 10th year of Yongzheng's reign), altogether 13 months and a year, including intercalary month, twenty thousand taels of silver would be invested in cloth, rice, dress, money, pawnshops and other shops, and then the amount of silver as interest, the amount of silver for various expenses, and the amount of silver for the expense of wedding and funeral in the homes of soldiers, all these financial records were bound into 36 volumes written in Manchu and Han language, and then delivered to the emperor." From the above address of Imperial Household Office, it can be known that the interest is mainly used for the wedding and funeral affairs of the soldiers in the capital.

④ Redemption of the land sold by the Manchu people to the civilians

The so-called redemption of the land sold by the Manchu people to the civilians means that the banner land sold by the banners to the people will be redeemed by the state. This measure began in the Yongzheng time. In the 13th year of Yongzheng (1735), it was stipulated that all the banner land sold by the red contract (with official seals) could be redeemed with full price; while the banner land sold by the white contract (with civilian seals) could be redeemed with half price or nothing. In the 9th year of Qianlong's reign (1744), the above-mentioned method was revised and changed to: "Regardless of the duration of the deed, the rate of ten years shall be used for the land of the civil code. Deduct one-tenth of the original price; if it is more than 50 years old, it will be redeemed at half price." There is no red or white contract in this revision, but the duration is the basis. In the following year, it was stipulated: "The rate should be ten years. Those beyond ten years shall be reduced every year, and those beyond fifty years shall be redeemed at half price." The redemption policy at this time has been changed from simply protecting the banners' interests, turn to "strike a balance", that is, to protect the interests of the seller (banners) and the interests of the buyer (non-banners). After the 34th year of Qianlong (1769), the "new land price policy" was implemented, which stated that "no matter the time of the contract, the current rent interest will be the standard. The price is based on the amount of rent." There were four large-scale "redemptions" of banner land in the Qianlong Period, and a total of 37,611 qing of banner land were recovered before and after. However, the redemption of the banner land did not solve the livelihood problem of the Eight Banners as expected. The poor banner people were unable to buy the banner land "redeemed" by the government, while the nobles, bureaucrats and wealthy banner people took the opportunity to buy cheap land. Finally, even Emperor Qianlong thought that "the redemption of land may not be beneficial to the poor banners".

⑤ Reservist for Manchu's army

The so-called Reservist for Manchu's Army refers to selecting idle young men who had nothing to do from those Manchu families with many people and surplus labor or living in straitened circumstances due to the inability to fill the quota of soldiers. This was a relief measure to train them to be reserve force, with the aim of accommodating idle Manchus and the Eight Banners who were so poor that cannot support their wives and children.

In the 3rd year of Qianlong's reign (1738), an additional 17,700 reservists for Manchu's Army were raised, and in the 18th year (1753), another 18,800 Reservists for Manchu's Army were added. Initially, the reservists for Manchu's Army received a relatively high salary, but as the number increased, the salary was gradually reduced. At the very beginning, each reservist received a monthly salary of 3 taels of silver, which was reduced to 2 taels of silver in the 2nd year of Qianlong's reign(1737), and further reduced to 1.5 taels of silver in the 18th year of Qianlong's reign (1753). Besides the salary, the reservists could also receive three types of rice (harvested in different years) in spring and autumn, totaling 1.88 dan per year. However, because most of the reservists were young who could not come and fetch the rice by themselves, the team leaders will fetch the rice for them. These team leaders would sell the rice, converting it into taels of silver. This practice had the disadvantage of selling at a high price but giving less money to the reservists. In the 8th lunar month of 1767 (the 32nd year of Qianlong's reign), it was stipulated that in the future, "The three types of rice that the reservists should receive each year should all be converted to ration rice, and the rice should all be delivered in one season, which should be distributed in the 2nd lunar month each year. The head of the banner should come to pick them up by themselves. If the reservists are too young to fetch the rice by themselves, the rice should be fetched by the team leaders under the cavalry officers. If the team leaders sell the rice with discount, they will be punished severely."

As for the origin of the reservist for Manchu's Army, it is stipulated that the soldiers must be tested for infantry skills and archery when they reach the age of twenty-five, if they pass the test, they can choose to be cavalry; if not, they can be infantry. However, if "a father or brother is killed in battle, or a child is orphaned, weak or disabled, the cavalry officer will be given a memorial and a report, and the original salary of the father or brother will be left to the reservist" Although the establishment of the reservist for Manchu's Army did relieve some poor banners, it produced serious adverse consequences. This is because the main source of funds to support these soldiers is to reduce the number of war horses and war ships. The money originally used to buy fodder for war horses or to manufacture and repair warship was used to relieve the soldiers' families, and even the cavalry troops with relatively strong combat effectiveness were disarmed and moved out. The money was used to support more reservists which makes the Eight Banners army full of redundant personnel with low combat effectiveness or even no combat ability at all, thus seriously affecting the combat effectiveness of the Eight Banners Army.

Although the Qing Government took various measures to protect the interests of the officers and soldiers of the Eight Banners and alleviate the livelihood problems of them, most of the measures were palliative measures, with little effect and to no avail. What is more serious is that these measures also brewed the laziness of the Eight Banners officers and soldiers, and further fostered the parasitic and extravagant sentiments of the Eight Banners soldiers.

1.2.3 The Preliminary Construction of the Jing Bannermen's Reclamation

In the early years of Qianlong's reign, within 500 miles of Beijing the bannermen had lost most of their land, while the population of the Eight Banners had soared, and the livelihood issues of the Jing Banners had become increasingly serious. The court was eager to seek more fundamental and long-term solutions to this problem. Under this background, the idea of Jing Bannermen's Reclamation emerged. The most famous representatives were Shu Hede, Fan Xian, Liang Shizheng, He Tai, Chai Chaosheng and others. Their ideas were mainly reflected in the memorials they submitted to the court. Later, they were collected by He Changling and Wei Yuan in the *Royal Classic Selection*. Although their names were different, the solutions they proposed were similar. They all believed that to plan for the long-term future of the Eight Banners members, they must have "land and property" and replace "official support" with "self-support". However, the problem was that by this time, the Manchu rulers had already established a stable rule system in China. The practice of seizing land through "enclosure" and redistributing it to Manchus in the early days of the dynasty was no longer suitable. Because for the Manchu rulers, giving priority to their own clan is understandable, but at the same time, they are also the supreme rulers of the whole country. This forces them to consider the long-term and fundamental interests of the whole country, especially the interests of the Han people who make up the absolute majority of the population. Therefore, they cannot destroy the stable land system that has already been established in the central plains region. In this case, to make these Jing Banners self-reliant and return to farming, there is only one way to go—to develop large-scale undeveloped border areas for agriculture.

However, the ministers at this time were quite aware that the bannermen in Beijing had lost the ability to engage in productive labor, and they could not be expected to devote themselves to work in the fields peacefully. Therefore, after careful consideration, these ministers had planned one solution after another, the main point of which was that the state would organize everything on its behalf, "To give generous rewards, so that everyone will be willing to go, this will ease the pain of migration." They hoped that by giving real estate to them, they would settle down there for a long time, and over time, they would naturally "teach from frugality and return to their original style".

However, the key to the problem lies in the fact that land and funding can be provided by the state, but land reclamation and house construction require labors. But where can the labor come from? The ministers who had become accustomed to the privileged life in the inner provinces naturally thought of the Han people. Shu Hede suggested "recruiting Han people to choose and cultivate land". When the land was cultivated, the bannermen would be sent there, and the cultivated land would be distributed to each household or still be farmed and let the farmer pay rent. Sun Jiagan's suggestion was to distinguish between public and private farmland, and to "order Han people to cultivate and plant in Xinghe, Kai Ping and other places. The cultivated land near the city will be designated as public farmland, and the rest will be private farmland. For every two qing of cultivated private farmland, one qing of public farmland must be cultivated. The private farmland can be used as one's own farmland, and the public farmland will be allocated to bannermen. An appropriate amount of rice will be determined, plus a monthly salary for bannermen" so that the bannermen's "clothing and food will be more abundant". For this "two for Han, one for banners" proposal, He Tai held different views. He believed that "the banners are not originally good at farming. If they want to open up uncultivated land, they must recruit Han people to cultivate it. If three qing are cultivated, two qing will be farmland for Han people and one qing will be public farmland for banners. There won't be enough farmland to feed the banners, and for there is also farmland for Han people, as the banners are not good at farming, and the border of bannermen's and Han people's farmlands are mixed up, within twenty years, the trend of Han people buying banners' land will be no different from that within 500 miles of Beijing." It should be said that He Tai had seen the crux of this issue, but as long as the banners could not participate in productive labor themselves, this contradiction could not be solved. He Tai could not propose a better solution. His suggestion was still to recruit Han people to cultivate land. After several years of accumulating grain, the banners would be sent to live on the already cultivated land. "If they want to farm by themselves, they can do so. Those who cannot farm will rent land to Han people, receive rent from their tenants, and support themselves", which was no different from Shu Hede's suggestion. The essence was still to let Han people serve as laborers without giving them land. As for what would happen to these cultivated lands after they were assigned to banners, they did not say, probably did not think about it. That is why there exist some differences between Han and Manchu officials in considering this issue.

In fact, since the Kangxi period, the Qing Court had considered relocating the bannermen to northeast China to cultivate land. In the 8th year of Kangxi(1669), the Ministry of Revenue, Mi Sihan, wrote in a report, "The bannermen living near Beijing now have a large population. If they were not relocated to the frontier, there will be a population overflow in the future." He also planned to send bannermen who had no positions or property in Beijing to the frontier for defense and cows, seeds, and farmland will be distributed to them. However, few people were willing to go, so the plan was scrapped. In the early years of Yongzheng, there was also an intention to relocate the bannermen in Beijing back to northeast China. The *Records* accounted that in the 2nd year of Yongzheng (1724), the deputy capital Tian Xiangkun submitted a report on cultivating farmland in Boduna, Changzhou, and other places. Because both Boduna and Changzhou were major transportation hubs, cultivating farmland along the roads seems to have no benefits. However, "The places of La Lin and Alcuka are vast and suitable for cultivating farmland, and they are close to Changzhou and Boduna. It is necessary to transfer the cultivated farmland to Changzhou and let the commander of Changzhou check and report on it." In the 2nd lunar month of 1728 (the 6th year of Yongzheng's reign), Yongzheng sent General La Xin and the Lieutenant General Fo Bao to Lai Lin to inspect water and grassland for establishing herds and settlements. On 10th of the 8th lunar month, General La Xin and others reported: "We have carefully inspected the areas from eastern Shuangcheng in Lai Lin to the Eqi'er ferry crossing, which is 155 miles wide and has fertile soil, suitable for settlement and cultivation. From both banks of Lai Lin River to the crossing of the Songhua River, 200 miles away, there is abundant water and grassland, suitable for herding." However, what happened later was not recorded in the historical documents, so it was possible that this matter was dropped. However, in the *Political Documents of Bin Zhou County* compiled in the Xuantong period, it was recorded that "In 1725 (the 3rd year of Yongzheng), 3000 idle Manchu people were relocated from Beijing to Alcuka," and "a commander and troops were stationed there." According to other historical references, this record might be inaccurate.

By the 7th year of Qianlong's reign (1742), under the discussions of the ministers, the Qing Court finally put the consideration of relocation into practice. However, in practice, the Qing rulers were persistent in two aspects. First, it must not hinder the security of the capital's defense, and only those who had no money and food to support were relocated, not those who wore armor. However, this point also varied in specific implementation; Second, it must not undermine the Northeast blockade, and it was absolutely impossible to recruit Han people, because they were indeed deeply cautioned about the phenomenon of civilians taking possession of banner land, which was no different situation from those within 500 miles of the capital.

Although Manchu and Han ministers proposed multiple locations for the relocation of the Jing Banner to the border areas, such as Gansu, Inner Mongolia, and the outer reaches of the Great Wall in the northwest, the final chosen location was their "imperial power rising ground" in northeast China, which was carefully considered. Firstly, in the early years of Qianlong, in northeast China, especially in the vast closed areas of Jilin and Heilongjiang, there was not enough advanced Han political, economic, and cultural infiltration. Most Manchu people still retained their original simple customs. The rulers believed that returning to this native land would be easy to restore the old system of governing the Jing Banner in Liaoyang, and these backup forces of the Jing Banner army would also reappear with the simple habits of "becoming soldiers when going out and farmers when returning home." Secondly, the vast Manchu people in the border areas had never give up productive labor. "The soldiers in the four cities of Changzhou (now Jilin City in Jilin Province, where the Ningguta General Yamun was located at that time) all cultivated land for a living and lived one or two hundred miles away from the city," they could serve as laborers for cultivating farmland and building houses for the Jing Banners in Beijing. The rulers subjectively believed that this would avoid the phenomenon of "Han people purchasing banners' land" from happening again on the land of northeast China. Thirdly, the rulers were afraid that if they scattered the banner soldiers, they would lose their power of leverage. The Three Northeast Provinces were their birthplace and an important base for their military strength. "Although the Jing Banner cannot be scattered in other places, it is necessary to scatter them in this fundamental place. It is not only that the troops in Beijing are not weakened, but also strengthened the defence in fundamental place with more powerful soldiers. This is convenient for both sides." In addition, at that time, there were still large uncultivated fertile soils outside the fence around the fundamental place, with more suitable natural conditions for farming than Mongolia and the Northwest.

1.3 | The Whole Story of the Jing Bannermen's Reclamation Policy

In the Qing Dynasty, although there were many proposals from officials to relocate the Jing Banners to the Northeast for reclamation, only three were implemented. The first was during the Qianlong Period, when the Jing Banners was relocated to Lalin and Alcuka. The second was during the Jiaqing and Daoguang Periods, when the Jing Banners were relocated to Shuangchengpu. Although there was also a plan for the Jing banners' reclamation to Bodune during this period, no Jing Banner households were relocated until the end of the Qing Dynasty. The third was during the late Qing Dynasty, when the Jing Banner was relocated to Hulan during the Guangxu period. What we want to discuss here is the specific process of three times of Jing Bannermen's Reclamation.

1.3.1 The Twice Reclamation of Jing Bannermen to Lalin and Alcuka in Qianlong's Reign

In the early years of Qianlong's reign, the Qing Dynasty was in the heyday of the Kangxi-Qianlong Period, and the country's strength reached its peak under the original framework system. Therefore, the Qing Government showed great courage in dealing with the issue of Jing Bannermen's Reclamation. From the official preparation of Jing Bannermen's Reclamation to in the 6th year of Qianlong (1741) to the last relocation of the Beijing Banner in the 23rd year (1758), it took 17 years and over 10,000 people and relocated 3,000 households to finish Jing Bannermen's Reclamation. If we add in Jilin soldiers, courier station laborers, family slaves, etc. who cultivated land and built houses for the Jing Banners, the number would be even larger. It can be said that this was quite a large-scale settlement activity.

As for the specific process of this reclamation, apart from the fragmentary edicts in the *Records* and some recounts in the minister's petitions of the reclamation of Shuangchengpu during the reigns of Jiaqing and Daoguang, there were almost no complete materials available. One of the most important archives of Qianlong Dynasty, *Qianlong's Imperial Red Seal Comments*, did not mention it at all. When it comes to this reclamation, people can only say that the country spent millions of funds and gave generous treatment to the Jing Banner, but after the Jing Banner spent all the money they were given, they fled back to Beijing, so this reclamation was completely ineffective.

After unsuccessful search for Chinese materials, the author found a batch of detailed Manchu archives about this reclamation in the First National Archives of China. Why was the Jing Banner's reclamation recorded in Manchu? By referring to the history of Qianlong Period, we can know that Manchu was the main common language used both in the civil and official sectors in the Northeast at that time. It is particularly important to note that although the Jing Banner returning to the Northeast was an economic activity carried out by the Qing Government to solve the livelihood of the Jing Banner, from another perspective, it was also an important military operation. Because all participants in this reclamation were reservists—the idle Bannermen, and the organizers were the highest military institutions of the country—the Ministry of Defense. In the archives, we can also frequently see the military style words, such as "relocate". Under the historical conditions at that time, for such a military operation that belonged to state secrets, it was understandable that all official documents were written in Manchu. Though these Manchu archives that have been preserved and have not been published before, we can see many problems of this reclamation and put forward our own views on conventional views.

(1) The introduction of the Jing Bannermen's Reclamation

After Emperor Qianlong ascended the throne, facing the increasingly serious livelihood problems of the Eight Banners left by his father and grandfather, he took various measures, "repeatedly rewarding soldiers with money and grain, and issuing edicts to investigate and exempt their debts", "appointing officials to investigate and reward the land as property", and allocating special funds to "establish a public treasury" and lend money to the Banners. It can be said that "whatever is beneficial to the support of the Banners is fully implemented". However, "the soldiers idle away, enjoying the luxury of clothing and food, and squandering their money", and there has been no improvement in their livelihood. In desperation, Emperor Qianlong decided to seek advice from all sides and asked, "the Eight Banners ministers may express their views and plan for their management". Against this background, in the 2nd year of Qianlong (1737), the Office General Shu Hede submitted the famous "Report on Reclaiming the Borderland by the Eight Banners". In the memorial, Shu Hede discussed what was the way of supporting people. He believed that "the way of supporting people lies in benefiting from the natural advantages and must make people self-reliant". Although the Court "has made every effort to support them, it is only a temporary plan, not a long-term strategy". Nowadays, "the only thing that the Banners rely on for their livelihood is their real estate, nothing else. The houses in the capital are still available for accommodation, but the land that was once known as being within 250 kilometers of the capital half belonged to the Han people now. Therefore, it is necessary to seek new land for the Banners. Shengjing, Heilongjiang, and Ningguta are prosperous places in our dynasty. The soil is fertile, and the ground is rich. It is heard that there are many vacant places that can be reclaimed. Although the Eight Banners cannot be scattered in other places, it seems that they can be relocated here as their basic survival." In the memorial, Shu Hede also imagined how to select loyal and capable officials to handle the matter in time, how to secretly instruct three generals to inspect their respective areas, how to recruit people to choose land for reclamation, etc. When the Jing Banners arrive there, they may be allocated land according to households or still let the Han people to cultivate land and pay rent to them. In this way, "the Banners will only have one-way labor of going there, but compared to being in Beijing, they will have permanent property for generations."

Three years later, in the 5th year of Qianlong's reign (1740), Fan Xian also submitted a palace memorial "Records of Eight Banner Reclamation", the content of which was roughly the same as that of Shu Hede. He thought that "Nothing is more urgent at the moment than the fund raising for the real estate of the Eight Banners of Manchuria." However, in addition to the Northeast, he suggested that the location of the farmland could be placed in Northwest area as well, because he was once posted in Shaanxi. It was suggested that after the Bannermen were moved to the Northwest, "they may work on the farm for three seasons, and the other time will be taught martial arts. In the future, not only will the Northwest military camp need troops transported from other places, but also the soldiers will engage in agriculture as well as military, and the frontier defense will be reinforced conveniently."

These two records can be said to be the prelude to the introduction of the Jing Bannermen's Reclamation policy. Since we could not find the original archives, we cannot know the direct attitude of the Qing Court at that time. We can infer that these two records were rejected for the reason that "Jilin is a place for producing ginseng, if the Bannermen are moved there, they are not familiar with agriculture and they will hire Han people to do the agricultural work, the Han people will inevitably harvest the ginseng illegally. Heilongjiang's custom and climate are totally different from the Capital, Bannermen cannot farm the land with the locals there or hunt animals, endure hard work, and cannot be alleviated in the event of a bad harvest; Fengtian also has no virgin soil to cultivate too." Although there is some truth in this, it is because the matter involves sensitive issues such as the "imperial power's rising ground" in the Qing Dynasty. In the absence of precedent, it is not easy to draw a conclusion, which is why "Manchu and Chinese officials dare not speak out lightly, because they see the matter as too important. This is why this issue is often talked than implemented."

The direct cause of the introduction of Jing Bannermen's reclamation to the border was a memorial submitted by Liang Shizheng in the 6th year of Qianlong's reign (1741), entitled "Please timely adapt the policy for the Eight Banners' idle people, and it is best to send them to the border to expand their livelihoods". At that time, Liang Shizheng's official position was the Left Assistant Minister of the Ministry of Treasury, in charge of agriculture. In a large agricultural country like the Qing Dynasty, agricultural taxes were the main source of national finance. Liang Shizheng was quite clear about this, so after carefully investigating the amount of annual expenditure, he found that there were significant loopholes in the national finances. "Every year, two appropriations of silver are issued separately in spring and autumn, with a maximum of seven or eight million taels of silver and a minimum of four or five million teals. However, the expenses for various items in Beijing totaled 11.2 million taels of silver, which was not enough to cover the expenses. This situation occurred every year." The reason for this situation, he believed, was that "the Eight Banners' salaries were too high, so the court spent more; the green banner soldiers' salaries in various provinces were increasing too, so the money sent to the Ministry of Treasury was less than before. The soldiers' salaries accounted for 60% to 70% of the country's total expenses. These ordinary expenses were not enough. If there were additional expenses, it would inevitably lead to financial difficulties." Therefore, he proposed a solution to replace "official support" with "self-support", and the specific measures were the same as those proposed by the previous officials. The relocation of the Eight Banners to border areas where there was arable land, especially in the country's fundamental areas, would enable them to "enjoy the benefits of farming and herding for generations, while paying attention to military training and enhance border defense. In this way, the surplus would become elite troops, and Beijing would have more support from its surrounding areas. The foreign states would also respect and fear its power. With the Eight Banners having their own plans for survival, there state funds will never be empty." Although Liang Shizheng's proposed solution was like those of the previous two people, and the opinions of the Prince Regent and Ministers still remained the same as before, this time Liang Shizheng's reason for excessive military expenditure causing financial difficulties in Beijing deeply touched the sensitive nerves of Emperor Qianlong. Therefore, he made up his mind to implement the plan of relocating the Eight Banners to the border. However, when instructing the Ministry of Finance to reply, his attitude remained cautiously, "The matter of the Eight Banners stationing at the border and doing agricultural work should be discussed after the Senior Scholar Chalaang and the Assistant Minister Arigon have inspected the local situation in Fengtian."

The above all illustrate a problem, that is, the Jing Bannermen's Reclamation is a major political decision taken by the Qing Government to solve the livelihood problem of the Eight Banners. Its introduction has its profound historical and practical reasons, and it is not the result of someone's hotheadedness.

(2) The first time Jing Banners returned to Lalin

In the 9th year (1744) and 10th year (1745) of Qianlong's reign, the Jing Bannermen's reclamation started for the first time. Because there was no precedent, both the assessment of terrain, the formulation of pre-planning matters and their implementation, as well as the specific relocation of the thousand households of the Jing Banners were carried out in a tentative manner, and inevitably leading to unsatisfactory results. However, both successful experiences and lessons learned from failures served as references for later generations.

① Terrain survey of Chalaang and Arigon

To ensure the progress of the Jing Bannermen's Reclamation, first, it is necessary to choose a location, which is the premise of accomplishing the process. This has been the case for all subsequent reclamations. In the 5th lunar month of 1741 (the 6th year of Qianlong's reign), the Senior Scholar Chalaang and the Assistant Minister Arigon were ordered to go to Fengtian area to assess the terrain. In this case, based on the *Record*, previous scholars mostly believed that Chalaang directly requested after assessing the terrain to take Lalin (now Lalin Town, Wuchang City, Heilongjiang Province) and Alcuka (now A' cheng District, Harbin City, Heilongjiang Province) in Jilin as the reclamation land for the Jing Banner Sula. At the National Archives of China, I found four memorials submitted by the two individuals to Emperor Qianlong on this matter. Based on this, we can know some details.

On the 19th of the 9th lunar month of 1741 (the 6th year of Qianlong's reign), Chalaang and Arigon arrived in Fengtian. On the 8th day of the 10th lunar month, they submitted their first memorial, mainly reporting the situation of arable land along the road from the capital to Fengtian, "From the east of Weiyuanbao's side gate, there is a piece of land in the southeast of Hersu Station, which is 5 kilometers to 15 kilometers wide and about 2,500 kilometers to 3,000 kilometers long." From Heersu Station to the north of Yitong River, there is a piece of land, which is 3.5 kilometers or 4 kilometers wide to 20 kilometers long, about 50 kilometers long. In the southwest of Shuayan Station, there is a piece of land, which is 7.5 kilometers to 15 kilometers wide and about 25 kilometers to 30 kilometers long. In the northeast of Shuayan Station, there is a piece of land, which is 10 kilometers to 20 kilometers wide and about 30 kilometers to 35 kilometers long. And in these four areas, there are already places where the banner people have cultivated the lands. According to the established plan, after arriving in Fengtian, Chalaang and others should first investigate the arable land in Shengjing. However, since in the 5th year of Yongzheng's reign (1727), a survey was conducted on this area of uncultivated land. At that time, there were more than 1.09 million shang (a land measure equal to fifteen mu in most parts of the Northeast and three or five mu in the Northwest, the same below) of uncultivated land. Now, except for those that have been cultivated, there are still more than 940,000 shang. Therefore, they decided to take advantage of the fact that it has not yet snowed, so the first place they headed should be Jilin Wula and Heilongjiang. At the same time, they ordered the Ministry of Treasury in Shengjing and the Prefectural Governor in Fengtian to make a detailed statistical survey on all cultivated and uncultivated land areas and bind them into volume and make a booklet for review on the way. After returning to Fengtian, they will copy it and conduct an inspection according to the land. This detailed memorial was praised by Emperor Qianlong, who thought that "all reports are quite detailed".

After surveying Jilin Wula and Heilongjiang, Chalaang and Arigon submitted their second memorial to Emperor Qianlong in the 12th lunar month of the same year, arguing that in addition to the lack of good farmland in Sanxing, Qiqihar and other places in the two provinces, coupled with the cold weather, early frost fall, difficulty in crops planting, and unsuitability for reclamation, there were "a section of land in Lalin and Alcuka, with a circumference of more than 400 kilometers; a section of land in Feiketu, with a circumference of more than 125 kilometers; a section of land in Hulan, with a circumference of more than 250 kilometers; and a section of land in Fotexisusu, with a circumference of more than 100 kilometers". The four sections of land were fertile, and now there were some areas where the bannermen had already reclaimed, and all had good harvest.

Three months later, On the 20th of the 2nd lunar month of 1742 (the 7th year of Qianlong's reign), Chalaang and Arigon submitted two memorials on the same day. One of the memorials reported that after completing the survey of the terrain in Wula, Jilin, and Heilongjiang, they should comply with the order to return to Fengtian to conduct further surveys. However, "after reading the records of the Ministry of Treasury in Shengjing and the Prefectural Governor in Fengtian, they found that during the 5th year of Emperor Yongzheng's reign (1727), the total area of arable land in 14 cities and 9 counties in the area around Fengtian was over 1,092,900 shang, excluding the land originally owned by the bannermen. Since the 6th year of Emperor Yongzheng's reign (1728), the bannermen had cultivated more than 119,200 shang, and the Han people had cultivated more than 24,500 shang. In total, over 143,800 shang of arable land had been cultivated. There are still more than 949,000 shang of uncultivated land. The two men believed that these lands were scattered among various villages and towns in 7 cities and 5 counties and could not be cultivated in large sections. If they were used to relocate Jing Banners, it would be very difficult to manage. Moreover, the Eight Banners' population in Shengjing was increasing rapidly. It would be more beneficial to leave this land to the local bannermen to cultivate gradually. For this proposal, Emperor Qianlong strongly agreed and believed that "since there is no arable land, there is no need to conduct further surveys."

In another memorial on the same day, Chalaang and Arigon comprehensively summarized the situation of the terrain survey, and classified the various soil according to the standards of whether the terrain is flat, whether rivers are flowing through it, and whether it is convenient to lumber in the mountain area. Three places, including Lalin Alcuka, Feiketu and Hulan, were listed as superior; four places, including Nanjiazi in the south of Hersu Station, the north of the river channel from Hersu Station to Yitong, and the southwest and northeast of Shuayan Station, were listed as inferior. Here, Lalin and Alcuka were listed as the superior, which had a great influence on the specific location of the first batch for Jing Bannermen's reclamation in the Qing Dynasty.

Just as the work of surveying the terrain was about to end, Wuchala, the Deputy Capital of Jilin Wula, also submitted a very ambitious plan to relocate 10,000 people from Beijing. He requested that the existing people of Jilin Wula could be relocated within Weiyuanpu, and that 2,000 Manchus from Beijing could be resettled in Jilin Wula, 4,000 in Lalin and Alcukha, and 4,000 in Hulan and Fotexisusu of Heilongjiang. For this memorial, the Qing Court copied it to Chalaang, Arigon and Ningguta General Emida in the Northeast, and Heilongjiang General Bodie, asking them to conduct field investigations to verify its feasibility.

On the 12th of the 3rd lunar month, Emida and others comprehensively refuted the unrealistic plan of moving Jing Banners to Wuchala in their memorial to the Court. Firstly, they refuted the proposal to move the existing people of Jilin Wula to Weiyuanpu, because "according to the records of Yongji Prefecture, there are 3,780 households of people who pay taxes, and according to the records of Bodune, there are 394 households of people who pay taxes, totaling 15,498 people, including more than 40 people consisted of tribute students who passed imperial examination, civil and military students, and donors. In addition, there are 18,532 people who are merchants and craftsmen without households excluded in the records." These people had lived here for many years and had established their own businesses and family, becoming "indigenous people". If they were expelled at the same time, many people would lose their livelihoods. In addition, the border area of Fengtian had been inhabited for many years, and there were many people who had grown up here. Except for Adunsulu, there was no arable land left. Therefore, it was not feasible to move the existing people of Jilin Wula to Weiyuanpu.

In response to the proposal in the Wuchala's memorial that 2,000 Manchus would be relocated from the capital to Jilin Wula, and that the existing houses and land of the Yongji Prefecture's people who paid taxes in grain would be appropriated and allocated to bannermen, and the bannermen would also be given two years' rations, Emida and others found that "Jilin Wula's grain storage only has 70,000 dan (a unit of dry measure for grain, the same below), which is not enough for 2,000 Manchus to consume in one year." Since the Han people could not then move into the border, it was impossible to allocate the 2,000 Manchu houses and land for reclamation. Therefore, it was impossible to relocate at once.

In Wuchala's memorial, it was suggested that the fertile land of Alcuka and Lalin were suitable for the stationing of 500 soldiers, and that the area was vast and rich in animals and plants. There were already 500 soldiers stationed in Alcuka, while never stationed in Lalin. Each area should be stationed with 2,000 soldiers from Manchuria. Jilin Wula currently had 500 soldiers, and it was suggested that another 500 soldiers should be stationed there to make up a total of 1,000. The farmland allocated to bannermen, and the land owned by Han people could be cultivated together. The housing for the soldiers should be built by 1,500 soldiers from the Sanxing and Bodune garrisons. Emida and others believed that "4,000 soldiers from the capital will be transferred to Lalin and Alcuka and the 2,000 soldiers from the capital will be transferred to Jilin Wula, these 6,000 soldiers who are stationed there to cultivate the land should be given rations, but there is no stored grain there. there is no way to provide them. Therefore, it is necessary to store 200,000 or 300,000 dan of grain in Lalin and Alcuka before handling the matter of stationing unemployed bannermen from Beijing. Without the grain, now it is impossible to carry out the plan."

In addition, Hulan and Fotexisusu areas belonged to Heilongjiang Province, and after consultation with Bodie, Chalaang, Arigon and others, it was considered "unsuitable to include in the current report". Since then, the unrealistic plan of Jing Bannermen's reclamation by Wuchala was completely rejected.

Although Chalaang and others in the northeast surveyed as many as seven parts of arable lands, it would be quite difficult to handle all the bannermen stationed there at the same time for a while, and it would also cost a lot. Therefore, the Qing Court finally selected a place around Lalin and Alcuka, which located more than 150 kilometers northeast of Wula in Jilin Province, as the place for relocating the Jing Banners. Compared with other locations, there were four advantages here: First, it was close to the shipyard, which was convenient for management; Second, it was a flat and fertile land, suitable for planting all kinds of crops; Third, the river surrounded it and the river ran through it, so it could take advantage of the water conservancy of Songhua River and Lalin River; Fourth, there were dense forests, which can solve the problems of building houses and collecting firewood. At the same time, it was decided to move 1000 Manchu people to this place to cultivate the land first. If it had any effect, they would be relocated from near to far accordingly. This laid a foundation for the later reclamation of Jing Bannermen.

② Preparation in advance for the Jing Bannermen's Reclamation

In the 10th lunar month of 1742 (the 7th year of Qianlong's reign), after repeated discussions, the ministers in charge of government affairs formulated a very detailed plan for the preparation in advance for the Jing Bannermen's Reclamation. This included three items: the selection and appointment of the banner people to be relocated; the allocation of funds for relocation; and the treatment of the minister in charge of suppressing them. The three items that should be prepared in advance by the local government were: setting boundaries and establishing villages; pre-stocking grain and stones; and setting up local supervisory personnel.

In the selection of migrants from the banner people, "those who are sent to cultivate the land must be selected from those who are disciplined and diligent in managing their families," and it was required that all banners take care of publicity. "The Manchu capital of the Eight Banners and all cavalry officers should select 1,000 people who are married or remained single, regardless of whether they are soldiers or not, and hand them over to the cavalry officers. If they go to Lalin and other places with fertile land, they can live a prosperous life and always protect their family. Please try to guide them and explain the situation." Although the policy was formulated in this way, the specific implementation was quite different. Therefore, the selection of Jing Bannermen was not entirely voluntary.

In terms of the funds for dispatch, it was stipulated that the treatment for the relocation of the Jing Banners should be determined according to the usual practice of relocating garrison soldiers and sending the idle people of the Eight Banners to cultivate land. Due to the long distance between Lalin and Alcuka, their due items must be generous to avoid the hardship of relocation. "Before setting off, each household should be rewarded with fifty taels of silver for clothes; when setting off, in addition to the usual allocation of rice and horse supplies, two carts should be provided; after arriving, each household should be rewarded with another thirty taels of silver for setting up a household." In this way, each household of Jing Banner could receive eighty taels of silver, which was extremely generous.

In terms of the remuneration of the dispatched officials, it was stipulated that Balinga, the Deputy Generals who went to Lalin and Alcuka to handle land matters, and Sanhe, the Assistant Minister, were awarded with horses of the courier station as usual. In addition, they were "rewarded with two taels of silver for daily expenses" when they worked there. Later, when Balinga led the banner people to relocate, their due salaries, guards, money and grain should be "in accordance with the example of the Deputy General stationed in Ningguta".

In terms of setting the boundaries of cultivated land, building houses, and establishing villages, there only allocated 1,000 Manchu households on the land covering more than 400 kilometers. It could be said that the land was vast, and the population was sparse. Therefore, it was stipulated that "houses must be divided into villages and connected to each other for ease of farming". It was also envisaged that when the land was vast and the population was small, if it was not clearly divided, disputes over land occupation would inevitably occur in the long run. This was a well-thought-out consideration. As for the relocated Manchu idle people, "each household should be allocated five houses and three qing of land. In the future, if they are familiar with farming and have surplus capacity for cultivation, they will also be allowed to cultivate beyond the originally allocated land." At the same time, Sanhe, the Imperial Envoy, the Assistant Minister of Ningguta, would establish eight townships according to the relocated Eight Jing Banners. "The allocated land will be inspected and measured, and boundaries will be set up. A clear-boundary register will be prepared for inspection by the Ministry. The houses should be built separately according to the banners, and the Deputy General's government office should be built in the middle of the eight banners for ease of management." How to start construction should be left to the Imperial Envoy Sanhe when he arrives, together with the General Emida, to examine the terrain with and discuss in detail before reporting for construction.

Before the arrival of the Jing Banners, due to the lack of stored rice in the local area, it was necessary to send people in advance to reclaim land and accumulate grain. This could not be done by the Jing Banners, as both Lalin and Alcuka were then barren lands. These Jing Banners who grew up in the capital city were not familiar with the methods of cutting grass and reclaiming land, making it difficult for them to personally participate in the reclamation. It was also difficult to hire civilians to reclaim land. On the one hand, Jilin had just established the Baojia System, which strictly prohibited Han people from wandering outside the border. On the other hand, it was feared that the Manchus would not want to work hard and would be content with their comfort, which was not the original intention of reclaiming land. In fact, the main concern was that "the Han people would take advantage of this land and go to reclaim it, resulting in self-settlement plans and abandoning their original homes." The final result of the discussion was to send idle underage people from Jilin and station personnel from courier station, but specific matters such as how to reclaim land; how to store the required rations; how to provide cattle, tools, and seeds needed for reclaiming land; and how to replace cattle and tools that were lost or damaged during future relocation of Manchus from the capital were handed over to Deputy General Balinga and General Emida for detailed discussion.

In terms of the appointing of local supervisory personnel, due to the large population of the land-owning Banner families and the scattered establishment of villages, it was advisable to set up supervisory inspectors. "Each Banner has two tuns (The larger administrative region than the village, the same below), each tun selects one person who is honest and sincere as the head and is given a rank of seventh grade. They inspect the household registration of each tun. Each Banner selects one person who is clear-minded and good at management as a nominal cavalry officer and is given a rank of sixth grade. They manage two tuns of each Banner and direct the heads of tun to inspect the daily affairs." These officials' fields and other needs should be addressed by the appointed ministers. In addition, a detailed method for selecting and filling vacancies in these management positions had been formulated. "When the position of the nominal cavalry officer is vacant, it shall be filled by selecting people from the tun heads. The vacancy of the tun head shall be filled by selecting people from the idle personnel. The vacant fields originally added to the person shall be allocated to the person who fills the vacancy". In addition, "in Alcuka, there was originally one assistant leader, eight cavalry officers and other officers, five hundred soldiers, and a deputy general, they were all under the command of a general. Now, there are only two kinds of management positions for Manchus in Alcuka, namely, the nominal officer and the head of tun. If they are not appointed concurrently, the banners management will be in chaos in the future. Alcuka currently has eight cavalry officers, so it is advisable to send Manchus to join them according to their banners. The people who are willing to go as soldiers should be selected according to the soldier vacancy. If the nominal cavalry officers' managing and training works are excellent, equestrianism and archery are outstanding, then whether to select them to fill the vacancies in these positions can be carefully discussed with Balinga and other generals. Furthermore, there was only one commander in the Alcuka area. Now that the Banner people have been assigned to reclaim the area, under the jurisdiction of the cavalry officer and the command of general, with only one depute cavalry officer, it is difficult to manage and inconsistent with the regulations. Therefore, in addition to the original position, it is advisable to add another depute cavalry officer to assist. The additional depute cavalry officer can be appointed when the relocation begins".

The final provision goes like this, "All the above-mentioned items shall be discussed in detail by Deputy General Balinga and Assistant Minister Sanhe, together with General Emida. After clarifying the situation and reporting to the emperor, Balinga shall be instructed to organize the 1,000 Manchu households into four groups and start the journey gradually."

This pre-planning document should be regarded as a programmatic document, which not only provided macro guidance for the Jing Bannermen's reclamation, but also left sufficient room for local organizers to operate. It involved aspects such as the selection of personnel for the relocation of the Jing Bannermen, the handling of vacancies after the relocation, the source of funding for the relocation, the setting up of officials, the delimitation of villages and tuns, the remuneration of officials and soldiers during the relocation, and the storage of grain before the relocation. It was extremely detailed. This report was submitted to the emperor on the 7th of the 5th lunar month of 1742 (the 7th year of Qianlong's reign), and three days later, Emperor Qianlong issued a written order: "Follow the proposal". This shows the importance attached to this matter. In this way, the Qing Court set a tone for this reclamation on a macro systematical level.

Following the principles of this plan, the Imperial Envoy, the Assistant Minister Sanhe, the Lieutenant General Balinga, and the General of Ningguta Emida went to Lalin and Alcuka for detailed investigations. On the 9th of the 10th lunar month of that year, they listed eight items of all the necessary matters and made a detailed report to the Qing Court.

First, after the investigation, it was found that the area on the east bank of the Lalin River was wide, with fertile land, dense forests, numerous wild animals, abundant fish and shrimp. Therefore, it was decided to set up 1,000 Manchu banners in the east bank of the Lalin River, with the fording as the center and divided the left and right wings along the river. "The four banners on the left wing were divided into eight tuns from the south of fording, and the four banners on the right wing were divided into eight tuns from the north of fording. It was estimated that it would take about two years to save one year's rice and build houses for these 1,000 Manchus. Therefore, it was decided to move to Manchuria in the autumn of the 9th year (1744). When they arrived, they would be given land, cattle, tools, etc. and divide the two years' cultivated land equally. The silver used was distributed from the reserve silver of the general's government treasury."

Second, regarding the reclamation of land and the construction of houses, "The land that should be given to resettle in Manchuria should be measured and allocated in each tun." As for the residence of the Deputy Lieutenant General of the General Manager, it should be in the middle of the two villages and tuns, built on high ground. "There are 21 public offices, 36 houses for the Lieutenant General, 12 qing of land; 18 houses for the Commanders, eight qing of land; 5,000 houses for the 1000 Manchurian settlers from Beijing." The construction of the houses should be accompanied by 300 soldiers from Bodune and 300 soldiers from Sanxing, these soldiers will be charged with building walls and other chores. Two Commanders and nine High-ranking officials will be appointed to supervise the construction. The cost of building doors and windows, covering roofs, payments for carpenters and other craftsmen "should be 3.3 taels of silver when the word begins. When the work is completed, the actual cost will be recorded by the General's Government and reported to the Ministry for verification."

The third task was to prepare the wood and thatch required for housing construction. This task should be assigned to 300 soldiers from Sanxing and 300 soldiers from Bodune, and they would be sent to the source of the Lalin River in October this year to collect timber. When the ice melted next year, they could be transported along the Lalin River to the place where the houses were built, and the thatch would be cut in the area around the Lalin River fording. As for the remuneration of these personnel, it was stipulated that "no grain or rice will be paid, and each person will be given two taels of silver for salt and vegetables per month; each soldier will be given three-tenths of a tael in equivalent to daily consumption of salt, vegetables and rice."

The fourth was the dispatch of people to reclaim the land. The ministers of state originally planned to send underage loafers from Jilin and courier station personnel to reclaim the land. After inspection, it was found that "although there are underage loafers in Jilin and other places, they are too young to cultivate the land, and the soldiers who has slaves and maidservants are few, they will plant, collect timber, feed horses and raise their families all by themselves. If courier station personnel send underage loafers to reclaim the land, their own land will not be cultivated, which may lead to their inability to support their wives and children." Therefore, it was decided to reclaim this land, and it was appropriate to send "800 soldiers from Jilin Wula, 200 soldiers from Alcuka, 500 courier station personnel, a total of 1500 people to go." Each person was given "0.4 taels of silver in equivalent to daily rice, salt and vegetables". In addition, five people who were familiar with farming were selected from the officials of Jilin, and 30 leaders were responsible for management. Their treatment was that the officials "were given two taels of silver in equivalent to monthly consumption of salt, vegetables and rice; each leader was given 0.3 taels of silver in equivalent to daily consumption of salt, vegetables and rice".

Fifth, the cattle for land reclamation should be purchased in advance. Since 1,500 soldiers and courier station personnel had been dispatched to reclaim land, 1,500 cattle were needed. To ensure timely reclamation and cultivation, it was necessary to prepare more cattle. Therefore, it was advisable to purchase an additional 100 cattle. If there were any injured or sick animals, they should be replenished in time to avoid any delays in reclamation and cultivation. It was difficult to purchase all the cattle in a short time, so it was advisable to "purchase cattle according to the established regulations from the 1st day of the 12th lunar month this year to the 30th day of the 1st lunar month next year, with each cattle for seven taels of silver." Take 3 cattle as a unit, and 1,500 cattle in total, making a total of 500 cattle units. Each unit needed seeds, ploughs, replacement agricultural tools and vehicles, etc., which should be purchased in sufficient quantities according to the number. When the cattle units arrived in Manchuria, each person would be allocated one two-cattle unit, and the cultivated land would be divided equally.

Sixth, incentive measures were made. Each of the Eight Banners was provided with one title of nominal cavalry officer and five qing of land; each tun was provided with one village head of the seventh grade and four qing of land. After three years, if there were people who were sincere in their services and good at equestrianism and archery, "the title of nominal cavalry officer should be considered as the cavalry officer vacancy of this Banner, and be selected, introduced and recommended together with the leader. If the title of nominal officer was vacant, it should be filled from among the village heads of the seventh grade. If the village head was vacant, it should be filled from among those who had moved to Manchuria and were honest and diligent in their fields. If there were people who wanted to serve in Manchuria for another three years, they should be considered as the candidates of the reserved officers and be selected together with the underage loafers of Alcuka." It could be seen that after the idle Manchurian migrants moved out from Beijing, they could also have a place for living, which was also one of the intentions.

Seventh, the grain harvested from the cultivated land should be stored in warehouses. It was estimated that in the first year of farming with 500 cattle units, "roughly 40,000 to 50,000 dan of grain would be harvested. In the second year, when the cultivated land was ready for farming, another 80,000 to 90,000 dan of grain would be harvested. Adding another 600 people to cultivate the land would yield about 20,000 dan of grain. In these two years, about 130,000 to 140,000 dan of grain would be harvested. Based on this capacity, according to the example of Jilin Wula Yongning Warehouse, after deducting the price of buying wood and transporting it, it was recommended to build 126 warehouses in Lianmen. When construction completed, the actual cost of silver would be made into a detailed list by the General's Government and sent to the Ministry for verification."

Finally, it was stipulated that it was advisable to give Manchuria a reward of silver as a permanent benefit. Now the Jing Bannermen were planning to move to Manchuria, although they were granted silver and land, could live a prosperous life, but in the first two or three years after arrival, it was still impossible to establish a stable life. Once there was a marriage and funeral events, the household would be stricken by poverty immediately. Therefore, "With order, 10,000 taels of silver from the reserve silver of Jilin Wula national treasury could be given to the wealthy and wise person to invest. The interest rate would be one point five percent per month. The total silver would be stored in the warehouse. When Manchuria was relocated with people, the principal and interest would be handed over to the Deputy General for distribution." The interests would be used as reward according to the example of Jilin Wula and other places. The silver left after yearly rewarding would be saved. In case of a good harvest, when it was difficult to sell the surplus grain, this silver could be used to purchase and store at the current price. In case of a poor harvest, it would be convenient to be used as relief. If it was not used, it would be useful for later relocation to Manchuria, that would be quite beneficial.

This matter formulated the specific details of the relocation. The two reclamation issues of the central and local governments were the guiding ideology for the Jing Bannermen's reclamation. According to this, the theoretical preparation for the reclamation had been basically completed.

③ Implementation of preparation

In the implementation process of the above-mentioned preparatory issues, the most important ones were land reclamation and house construction, because if the Jing Bannermen wanted to survive in the uncultivated land, houses and arable land were essential prerequisites. This required not only sufficient financial supports, but also sufficient manpower, all these would make it difficult to implement. Therefore, from the 8th year (1743) to the 9th year (1744) of Qianlong's reign, several generals of Ningguta and Lieutenant Generals of Lalin and Alcuka reported to the Qing Court mainly about land reclamation and house construction.

According to the original plan, the 1,000 households of the Jing Bannermen would have 3000 qing of cultivated land and 1,500 soldiers from Jilin would be dispatched to cultivate the land in advance. This plan began in the 8th year of Qianlong's reign (1743), "cultivating 1,200 qing in the first year and 500 qing in the second year". However, the actual amount of cultivated land was far less than required. One year later, only 751 qing and 21 mu (a unit of area =0.0667 hectares, the same below) were cultivated. On average, each person cultivated only half qing. Emperor Qianlong was extremely angry about this, believing that it was due to the poor performance of General Emida. He dismissed him and had him investigated. It was probably unique in the history of the Qing Dynasty that the high-ranking officials were dismissed for the mere reason of cultivating 500 qing of land. At the same time, we can see Emperor Qianlong attached the Jing Bannermen's reclamation with great importance. However, if we carefully analyze the treatment of the soldiers from Jilin, we can see the cause of the problem. In the original plan, it was stipulated that these 1,500 soldiers from Jilin would receive 0.4 taels of silver in equivalent to daily consumption of salt, vegetables and rice. The soldiers who did lumber work and built houses would receive 0.3 taels of silver in equivalent to daily consumption of salt, vegetables and rice. In addition, there were no other benefits. These soldiers all had their own private land, and their only task was to come here temporarily for the reclamation. Based on the above analysis, these soldiers left their own land to cultivate these lands that did not belong to them. After they had finished their work, they had to turn them over to the government. In addition to daily rations, they received nothing else. Doing a good job and doing a bad job received the same thing. Without any incentives, nothing could motivate their enthusiasm. According to Jilin General Fu Jun's calculation, if one soldier and one cattle worked hard, they could cultivate ten shang of land, which was one qing. These soldiers from Lalin were also working with one cattle, so it was obvious that they did not work hard enough. For the successor general Bo Ce, Emperor Qianlong demanded that he "must follow the original plan to cultivate land". With this rigid requirement, coupled with Emida's previous bad example, Bo Ce adjusted manpower and improved the speed of cultivation while also requesting another 600 soldiers for assistant. However, the Qing Government believed that it was unnecessary and only asked him to "make a reasonable allocation among the original 1,500 soldiers and cultivate as much land as possible. The remaining force should be used to cultivate the remaining 250 qing of land that had not been cultivated in last year ... This year all the land must be cultivated". Although the order was tough, in fact, the Qing Court had lowered the standard for land reclamation. As much as 1,000 qing of land were required to be reclaimed within two years, 700 qing less than the original plan. According to this requirement, 1,000 qing of land were finally reclaimed and cultivated in the second year.

Building houses was not as expected as land reclamation. Although in the 8th year of Qianlong (1743), 600 soldiers dispatched from the places of Bodune and Sanxing had already "collected the timber for the construction of the lieutenant general's office and housing, housing for commanders, and 5,810 houses for 16 villages and tuns in Manchuria, of which the woods for the construction for seven villages and tuns had already been pulled from the mountains to the construction site, and two villages had their houses built with thatch". However, due to the cold weather, it was not possible to start construction. Therefore, all projects were suspended from the first day of the 9th lunar month. In the following year, due to the fact that all troops were assigned to land reclamation, the request for additional troops was rejected. Thus, only the Lieutenant General's office and housing, and housing for Commander's were completed within the 8th lunar month, and 750 households in 12 villages and tuns of six banners were completed in the early 9th lunar month. As a result, there were not enough houses for the original 1,000 households to live in, so only 750 households from six banners could be relocated in the 9th year of Qianlong (1744). It can be said that housing is the reason why 750 households from six banners were relocated in the 9th year of Qianlong (1744), which is not recorded in existing official documents.

④ The migration process of thousands of Jing Bannermen

In the past, official records only mentioned that the first batch of 750 idle households of the Jing Bannermen arrived in Lalin in the 9th lunar month of 1744 (the 9th year of Qianlong's reign), and 250 households were transferred in the following year, totaling 1,000 households were relocated in two years. However, due to the lack of historical materials, it is unknown how the specific situation was. Now, after reading the Manchu archives, some details may be understood as follows:

On the 20th of the 9th lunar month of 1744 (the 9th year of Qianlong's reign), the Lieutenant General of the Lalin and Alcuka, Balpin, returned to the capital and, together with the Ministers of the various Banners, first inspected the selected untitled nominal cavalry officer and seven-grade heads of tuns. Then, they formed six teams of 750 Manchus from the six banners that should be relocated. Balpin personally led the team to start their journey before the cold weather set in on the 20th of the 8th lunar month of 1744. According to the existing genealogy of the descendants of Jing Banner who moved to Lalin Heilongjiang Province, the Eight Banners who were relocated generally lived in "Wanping and Daxing County, Shuntian Prefecture". At that time, it was stipulated that if there were three brothers in a family, two of them should go, and if there were two brothers, one of them should go. At the same time, it was also required that "husband and wife should go together". This was because the purpose of relocation was to enable them to settle down there for a long time, while single people were hard to manage and control. From later observation, it was true that some Jing bannermen did bring their families. In the *Records* of the 10th year of Qianlong's reign (1745), there was a record of "Bannermen who went with servants who could assist in farming"; there was also a record in the existing Manchu archives of "The 750 Manchus who were relocated were divided into six teams, each with nearly 130 people." In addition, they brought their families with them, with a total of 300 to 400 people. However, there were also many people who left their families in Beijing and went alone. Therefore, in the 17th year of Qianlong's reign (1732), the emperor issued an imperial edict: "Many of the people who were sent to Lalin and Alcuka to cultivate land did not bring their families with them. I am afraid they cannot settle down there, or they may come back to the capital or go elsewhere. This is not certain. I will order the officials of the Eight Banners to send their families to Lalin and Alcuka after they arrive. No one is allowed to stay in Beijing." In the 11th lunar month of 1732, specific measures were stipulated. "The Capitals of the Eight Banners and other officers are required to investigate all those who have been sent to the reclamation sites without their wives and children. The court will provide supplies for their families and send them to the reclamation sites, showing the court's sympathy. However, due to the long distance and the fact that most of family members are women, and most of the officials are men, it is inconvenient for the male officials to escort them. If anyone is willing to go, they can be accompanied by their relatives, and they do not need to be escorted by officials." After that, all those who were sent to the reclamation sites by the Eight Banners all brought their families with them. This approach can both increase the labor force and prevent them from returning, forcing them to live in Lalin peacefully. It can be said that this move has a lot of compulsory elements, which can be seen from the neat number of 125 households per banner. It is obviously a result of the distribution according to the Banner and the requirement of every banner should send a full number. For such a large number of reluctant Jing Bannermen, if only the non-commissioned nominal cavalry officer and the leaders of the tuns take charge, it would inevitably be difficult to take care of them and it was hard to guarantee that no incidents would occur. Therefore, the Qing Court decided to "send sufficient officers and soldiers from the capital to escort the troops to Shanhai Pass, and then reassign officers and soldiers from Shanhai Pass to send them to Fengtian, and then replace the officers and soldiers from Fengtian to Jilin Wula, in order to take care of them." Despite this, there were still some incidents. On the 8th of the 9th lunar month, "Manchu Bordered White Banner Hailing died in Fengrun county. His had no descendants and clans, so the coffin and his wife were handed over to the cavalry officers Wen Ying to send to the capital with. On the 26th of the 10th lunar month, Manchu Qiushisan of the Blue Banner died in the Fateha border gate. Because his father was also a soldier who came with him, the coffin was handed over to his father for disposal." After several twists and turns, it took nearly two months to travel from the capital to Lalin, which was originally a journey of more than 40 days. Finally, from the 22nd to 29th of the 10th lunar month, they arrived successively and were placed in various villages of the Banner.

In the 10th year of Qianlong's reign (1745), when the earth thawed, the soldiers of Bodune and Sanxing established the remaining four villages and houses of the Bordered Red Banner and Bordered Blue Banner, and sent two officials and 400 soldiers from Ji Lin Wula to feed the 400 cattle that should be allocated to the Jing Bannermen. The remaining 250 qing of land were cultivated as usual. In the 8th lunar month, the 250 households of Manchuria were also divided into two groups and moved to Lalin as before. In this way, the relocation of the thousand households of the Beijing Banner was finally successfully completed.

(3) Another reclamation of The Jing Bannermen

The second batch of Jing Bannermen's reclamation during the Qianlong era from the 21st year of Qianlong (1756) to the 24th year (1759) can be divided into four parts. Compared with the first batch, there was a 12-year interval, and the scale was even larger, with the number of relocated households doubled to a total of 2,000.

① Terrain assessing and plan preparing before the reclamation

The second relocation of the Jing Bannermen began in the 8th lunar month of 1753 (the 18th year of Qianlong's reign), with an imperial edict: "Up to now, the Manchurians who were sent to cultivate the land in Lalin have been there for many years. What is their current livelihood, and whether they have benefited from the reclamation? You should send letters to Fu Sen and Man Fu to let them evaluate the situation of the Manchurians who are cultivating the land and the people currently residing in Lalin. Also, consider the possibility of adding several thousands of people and carefully plan for it. After finishing this year's work, you should come to the capital and report to me, and I will then decide on the appropriate action." Based on this edict, in the 10th lunar month, general Fu Sen and lieutenant general Man Fu evaluated the surrounding areas of Lalin and Alcuka, and initially selected six fields within the proximity of forests, high terrain, and easy access to water sources as the location for the second relocation of the Jing Bannermen. "One field lies 6 kilometers east of the Deputy Capital's office in Lalin, one field lies eight kilometers southwest of the Alcuka in the Sigeohuolo, one field lies 18 kilometers southeast in the Hojimo, one field lies 8 kilometers southeast of Yooji in Alcuka, one field lies 12.5 kilometers east in Haigou, and one field lies 15.5 kilometers northeast in the Wahun." They planned to establish 48 villages in these six fields, following the structure of the 16 tuns in Lalin, to accommodate 3,000 households. 3,000 qing of cultivated land were selected within 2.5 kilometers of these fields on high-lying fertile ground. Additionally, there were many arable lands within five or ten kilometers of these fields, and firewood was available within 1.5 or 2 kilometers to 3.5 or 4 kilometers. The construction of houses required timber from deep Yaoji. Emperor Qianlong was very satisfied with this survey result and wrote "very good" in his comments.

In the 12th lunar month, Fu Sen and Man Fu once again conducted a detailed survey centered on the Lalin Lieutenant General's Office, covering an area of 140 kilometers east to the Mayan River, 20 kilometers west to the Lalin River, 25 kilometers south to the Molin River, and 70 kilometers north to the Songhua River. They found that, except for 16 tuns and cultivated land inhabited by 1,000 Manchus and the villages and cultivated land inhabited by the officers and soldiers of Alcuka, the rest of the area was vast but dry and low-lying. From the Feiketu River to the Mayan River, there were more than 100 kilometers of mountains and dense forests, making it difficult to divide during reclamation, and it was also far away from

Lalin and Alcuka. Finally, they selected 6 areas including Meimangka, Sigeohuolo, Hojimo, Yooji, Haigou and Wahun which were near the forest with fertile land and could dig wells. They also planned in detail the number of villages and tuns to be established in each area, the number of households to be accommodated, to be reclaimed, and the distance of places where wood and firewood for building houses could be obtained. "One of the areas in Meimangka, a tun located 6 kilometers east of the Deputy Capital's Office, could accommodate 7 villages and tuns with more than 400 households; the mountains in its southeast were covered with trees. Within 2.5 kilometers northwest of the settlement, the area with high land and fertile soil could be reclaimed, with more than 400 qing of land. One of the areas between the field located 8 kilometers southwest of Alcuka, and a field located 18 kilometers in Hojimo, could accommodate 25 villages and tuns with more than 1,550 households; Yooji, located east of Hojimo, is 30 kilometers long and 7.5 to 10 kilometers wide. Within 2.5 kilometers of the west, south, and north sides of the village, fertile land with high elevations can be reclaimed, resulting in more than 1550 qing of land. One of the areas in Yooji, a land located 8ht kilometers southeast of Alcuka, could accommodate 4 villages and tuns with more than 250 households; There are trees on the east mountain, and within 2.5 kilometers of the west, south, and north sides of the villages, the land can be reclaimed from the high and fertile land, with more than 250 qing of land available. One of the fields lies 12.5 kilometers east of Haigou, with a distance of 0.5 or 1 kilometers and 1.5 or two kilometers, can be set up with eight villages to accommodate 500 households. There are trees on the east mountain, and within 2.5 kilometers of the north of the villages, the land can be reclaimed from the high and fertile land, with more than 500 qing of land available. One of the fields is 15.5 kilometers northeast of Wahun, with a distance of 0.5 or 1 kilometer, can be set up with 4 villages to accommodate more than 250 households. There are trees on the southeast mountain, and within 2.5 kilometers of the north of the tun, the land can be reclaimed from the high and fertile land, with more than 250 qing of land available." In this way, there were a total of 48 tuns in six fields, which could accommodate 3,000 households. Within 2.5 kilometers of the tuns, the fertile land was reclaimed, and more than 3,000 qing of land were obtained. The distance from the place where firewood was collected ranged from 1.5 to 3.5 or 4 kilometers. The wood needed for building houses still had to be cut in the forest, which was located more than 5 or 10 kilometers away. At the same time, the surveyed land was drawn into a map for the Emperor Qianlong to view.

Although Fu Sen had pre-surveyed these 6 areas, during the construction of the settlement in the 20th year of Qianlong (1755), it was discovered that it was necessary to fetch wood from Wahun, 7.5 kilometers away, for the construction of houses and land reclamation. Therefore, "the 4 settlements of Yooji were relocated to the Abuqi Valley, 2 kilometers east of Wahun, and 8 tuns were established extending from Wahun."

Due to the inspection tour of Jilin in the 19th year of Qianlong (1754), the matter was temporarily shelved. In the 10th lunar month, Fu Heng, Secretary of the Grand Council and other officials formulated a plan for the Jing Bannermen's second reclamation based on Fu Sen's memorial and the previous relocation regulations.

It was decided that the 3,000 Jing Banner soldiers would be divided into 6 groups, and each group 500 persons. The reclamation of the land, building houses, and other items required by the Jing Banner soldiers would be arranged by the Generals and local soldiers in Jilin in rotation. The payment for the hired workers would be the same as the previous payment. "Starting from this winter, 500 Bannermen will be sent to cut and transport timber for housing, and in the spring of the following year, they will be asked to build houses. Another 500 Bannermen will cultivate arable land, dig wells and springs, and collect thatch for the houses in autumn. In the following winter, in addition to lumbering, another 500 Bannermen will be sent to plant crops before the spring of the year of Bingzi. Starting from the spring, another 500 Bannermen will be sent to build houses, cultivate arable land, dig wells and springs, and collect thatch for the houses in autumn. In this way, 500 persons would be sent each year, according to the plan, until the year of Xinsi, all 3,000 households may be sent to live there."

However, when the 500 soldiers from Jilin set off, 152 of them failed to get there. Among them, 149 were willing to resign because they did not want to separate from their families, while three were dismissed due to illness. One-third of the local soldiers in Jilin preferred to resign and give up their salaries rather than come to reclaim the uncultivated land. This shows how strongly they opposed it. Finally, the Qing Government decided that those who did not want to move would "remain in Sanxing. Only 300 soldiers from Lalin and Alcuka would be relocated, while the rest of the 200 soldiers would not be recruited. Because those Manchu soldiers who were relocated to Lalin and Alcuka needed to learn how to cultivate land, if there were too many empty slots for the soldiers, but still gave them money, then the soldiers would not consider agriculture as their main business." "If there are any vacancies among the 300 relocated soldiers, they should be filled in with the underage soldiers who originally lived in Lalin and Alcuka, and the underage soldiers who have newly migrated to Manchu and from Sanxing." In this way, there were 300 cavalry officers from Sanxing and 200 cavalry officers from Jakunhalai to form a total of 500 cavalry officers to go to Lalin and Alcuka. According to the Manchu archives, the 32 tuns prepared for the second batch of Jing Bannermen's migration, and every four villages were turned into one tun; these groups were equipped with 2,500 houses and four wells were dug for each group. All these facilities were prepared by 500 soldiers.

In addition, it was stipulated that all the migrants should be provided with "30 taels of silver for the preparation of their equipment, and they should be provided with rations, fodder for horses, cart cost along the way. Upon arrival, they should be provided with 50 taels of silver for the establishment of property, one year's rations, cattle, seeds, agricultural tools, and the appointment of an officer, and nominal officer, the people who were sent to teach the land-cultivating soldiers should be provided with ration for one year." The migrants who were sent to reclaim land should be provided with taels of silver equivalent to ration, The craftsmen who build new houses for the Manchu people will be paid 3.3 taels of silver for each room. The seeds, agricultural tools, vehicles, milling and other items used for reclaiming land, as well as the fodder for cattle and the place for building grain warehouses should be handled according to the previous example of placing 1000 Manchurian soldiers. Due to the increase in cattle prices in Jilin over the past few years, the general minister of the region was required to "buy no cattle for unreclaim land but buy them according to their application at the time." The silver required for this migration "should still be disbursed from the reserve silver as before and should be collected by the Ministry of Treasury in Shengjing. The used silver should be reported to the Ministry as usual for expenses."

In addition, in the selection of Jing Banner personnel, it was required that the Eight Banners must "select the sons of the close branch" and "those with wives and children must go". Emperor Qianlong attached great importance to this, in his comments written in red: "When selecting personnel, the Ministry should request the emperor's approval and I will send out princes and ministers to select them separately." According to the saying that is circulated among the villagers of Haigou Village, Liaodian Manchu Township, A'cheng County, before their ancestors moved from Beijing, they lived in a "hutong" called Wulubazi Straw hat in Beijing. According to various investigations, this place is now Xicaoshi East Street, Dongcheng District, Beijing. Most of the Jing Banner personnel selected were indeed from the close branch of the city. According to this plan, it can be seen that "the Eight Banners' ministers should select their clan members and those with dependents". The dependents were not allowed to stay in Beijing, and this is even more compulsory than the first batch. This can also be seen from the fact that some people fled during the subsequent migration.

② Reclamation of Jing Bannermen

According to the plan, the reclamation was to start in the 2nd lunar month every spring, and in the previous year the land, housing, wells, etc. for the entire settlement would be well prepared. The first group arrived at the end of the 2nd lunar month of 1756 (the 21st year of Qianlong's reign), and 8 tuns of villages were established for them in Haigou Alcuka. After that, each year 500 households were relocated and settled in three places: Wahun, Sigeohuolo, and Hojimo, each of which established eight tuns of villages. According to the precedent of the 9th year of Qianlong (1744), each person who left from Beijing was given 30 taels of silver to prepare their facilities, but lessons were learned from the previous experience of running out of silver halfway and being unable to move forward. The silver issued was handed over to the newly appointed Lieutenant General for safekeeping. The specific preparations and relocation conditions were listed as follows:

8 tuns in Haigou. Haigou was the first place where the Jing Bannermen was relocated. The preparatory work began in the 19th year of Emperor Qianlong's reign (1754). In the 12th lunar month, the construction of the Lieutenant General's residence, the idle Manchu housing, and the warehouse timber was collected. By the 1st lunar month of the following year, all timber had been collected. Because of the light snow in winter, large trees were transported in advance to the construction site by sleigh car for carpenters to build. In addition, craftsmen were sent to the mountains to process the small trees such as purlins, beams, and rafters, which had not yet been transported. Afterwards, they were transported by carts to the construction site. By the 10th lunar month of 1755 (the 20th year of Emperor Qianlong's reign), 36 official houses for the Deputy Capitals and 2,500 Manchu houses had been built and accepted. In addition, land reclamation was carried out as scheduled. Since the 12th of the 3rd lunar month of 1755 (the 20th year of Qianlong's reign), "more than 150 qing of land have been cultivated" by the 19th of the 4th lunar month. Because they all chose fertile land with many trees, the land reclamation required a little more time. By the 7th lunar month, 500 qing of land had been cultivated, and the crops were growing well. However, when the rice shoots were about to be harvested, continuous rain fell. Although it was located in a high hill, it was soaked up and the rainwater got nowhere to go. In addition, there was no sun exposure, so on the 9th of the 8th lunar month, it would generally freeze. Therefore, after harvesting and threshing, only "1671 dan and 6 dou (a measure for grain, the same below) of grain, 49 dan and 7 dou of barn grass, and 829 dan and 2 dou of buckwheat, all together 2550 dan and 5 dou were stored in the newly built warehouse." The first 500 Jing Bannermen arrived in Alcuka in the 2nd lunar month of 1756 (the 21st year of Qianlong's reign) and began to cultivate their own land in the 3rd lunar month.

8 tuns in Wahun. On the 8th of the 9th leap lunar month of 1756 (the 21st year of Qianlong's reign), the housing in Wahun were ready for Jing Bannermen, and the acceptance inspection was passed. "Each of the tun has four wells, totaling 32, all of which have been dug." The 500 qing of land had good crop growth this year, and the rainfall was appropriate at the time of head sprouting, resulting in a good harvest. There were 6,668 dan and 5 dou of grain, 1,529 dan of barn grass, and 1,482 dan and 5 dou of buckwheat after harvesting and threshing. Three kinds of crops totally harvested were 9,680 dan, which had been stored in the warehouse. This batch of 500 Manchu households from Beijing, led by Guodohun, lieutenant general, arrived in Wula, Jilin province on the 3rd of the 2nd lunar month of 1757 (the 22nd year of Qianlong's reign). Only one incident happened, "loafer Lao Jile, under the leadership of Neluntai from the Bordered Red Banner, after arriving in Shengjing, escaped alone on the 29th of the 1st lunar month. This matter was immediately reported to the Ministry and the original banner to pursuit him." Other people who moved to Manchuria went without any incidents along the way. From the 4th to the 13th of the 2nd lunar month, they set off for Lalin as usual, from the 10th to the

20th of the 3rd lunar month, they arrived one after another. All the houses, land, cattle, and all kinds of facilities that should be provided were allocated and settled properly.

8 tuns in Sigeohuolo. In the 10th of the 9th leap lunar month of 1756 (the 21st year of Qianlong's reign), the construction of the wooden houses began. In the 4th lunar month of 1757, "700 houses out of the 2,500 houses that should be built in 8 tuns of villages and towns have been completed, and 200 qing land out of the 500 qing of land that should be reclaimed also have been reclaimed, and the cultivation began too." In the 11th lunar month of the same year, the 2,500 houses were well-built in a standard size, sturdy and durable; after the seeding of the 500 qing of land, all the crops were harvested and stored in the warehouse. In the 23rd year of Qianlong (1758), the 500 Manchu families who were transferred from Beijing were led by the Lieutenant General, Badai, and no incidents occurred on the way. "They arrived in Jilin Wula successively from the 7th day of the 2nd lunar month. From the 8th to 14th of that month, they were organized as usual and were escorted by officials from Jilin Wula on their way to Lalin. From the 9th to 25th of that month, they have all arrived in Alcuka." All the houses, land, cattle, and other facilities that should be given had been allocated.

8 tuns in Hojimo. On the 24th of the 11th lunar month of 1757 (the 22nd year of Qianlong's reign), the timber for building houses had been collected and transported to most of the places. Because "the settlement was near the Yooji, and the snow was thick this year, all of them could be transported before the end of the year. The cattle and all necessary facilities for land reclamation were well prepared." On the 25th of the 10th lunar month of 1758 (the 23rd year of Qianlong's reign), the 2,500 houses that should be built had been completed and qualified. There were four wells in each tun, and a total of 32 wells should be dug, all of which were dug. The 500 qing of cultivated land had been harvested, and 6,186 dan of grain, 510 dan and eight dou of barn grass, and 1,370 dan of buckwheat were obtained. The total amount of crop was 7,724 dan and 8 dou, which had been stored in the Lalin warehouse. After moving to Manchuria in the following year, this grain would be allocated as rations according to the actual number of households. The 500 households from Beijing that moved to Manchuria were led by Guo Duohun, and they arrived safely along the way. On the 4th of the 2nd lunar month of 1759 (the 24th year of Qianlong's reign), they "arrived in Jilin Wula one after another. From the 8th to the 11th of that month, they were arranged as usual, and officials from Jilin Wula were sent to take care of them and set off for Lalin. From the 13th to 17th of the 2nd lunar month, they arrived one after another. The houses, cattle, and all necessary facilities that should be provided had been allocated and properly arranged".

In this way, in four years, 2,000 households of Jing Bannermen in total were transferred from Beijing to Lalin and Alcuka. Another 1,000 households should have been sent there, but they were never relocated, so the total number of Jing Banner households relocated to Lalin and Alcuka, both from the beginning to the end, was 3,000. Through the comparisons of the *Records*, *Eight Banners Chronicles*, *The Great Qing Constitution of the Guangxu Dynasty* and the Manchu documents in the Military Council, the records are the same and should be reliable. The relocation of the Jing Bannermen in the Qianlong Dynasty came to an end.

1.3.2 The Jing Bannermen's Reclamation to Shuangchengpu During the Jiaqing and Daoguang Periods

After the Jing Bannermen returned to Lalin and Alcuka in the Qianlong Period, except for temporarily vacating a limited number of soldiers in Beijing, there was no effective solution to the livelihood problem of the Jing Banner. Several years later, no one mentioned this proposal at all. In the 4th year of Jiaqing (1799), Fashishan proposed to send the Eight Banners soldiers to cultivate in the Northwest, "The western region outside the borders is vast and fertile. The idle households of the Eight Banners who are willing to cultivate are allowed to report and go to cultivate on their own." At that critical moment to suppress the uprising of the White Lotus Society in Sichuan and Shaanxi, and the fugitive soldiers were numerous. This practice of relaxing the restrictions on the Banner people was so dangerous that the combat effectiveness of the capital's elite troops could be weakened. Therefore, this proposal was strongly rebuked by Emperor Jiaqing: "The idea of sending Banner people out to cultivate is a big mistake," "If I follow your method, it will make Beijing into an empty city, which is even more absurd." Fashishan was rejected and the proposal was stopped. However, after more than ten years, the Qing Court was eager to send the Jing Bannermen to cultivate in Shuangchengpu in Jilin according to the old practice in Lalin and Alcuka. What were the reasons? By analyzing all aspects of society at that time, Qing Court probably had two things for consideration.

The first one was that the "Eight Banners livelihood" had reached a point where it must be solved, but the Qing Court still refused to relax the restrictions on the Bannermen. Starting from the Jiaqing Dynasty, the decline of the Qing's reigning became increasingly frail: fiscal deficits, corruption in government officials, laxity in military equipment, and intensified class contradiction. The problem of the Eight Banners' livelihood, which was closely related to the rise and fall of the Qing Dynasty, also became increasingly troublesome for the Court. The "livelihood" issue not only affected ordinary Bannermen, but also affected a growing number of descendants of the imperial family. It was not limited to the Bannermen in Beijing, but also extended to the Northeast, Jehol, and the provinces with garrison troops. Land was gradually lost, while the population was increasing year by year. "The old established vacancies have now reached its limit, and the idle people of each Banner are limited by the vacancies and cannot get rations." At the same time, suppressing continuous peasant uprisings and managing river disasters had caused the losses of treasury and social economy had been stalled. The Qing governors could no longer provide generous rewards and pensions to the Jing Bannermen like they did in the

Kangxi, Yongzheng, and Qianlong Periods. The Qing rulers "worked hard to think and finally came out no good strategies." However, at this time, the vast majority of soldiers had a weaker personal attachment to the country compared to the time when they first entered China or even compared to the early Qianlong Period. This forced the Qing rulers to make concessions again and again and relax their control over the Bannermen. However, the more they did this, the more they needed to strengthen their control over the Bannermen. Moving the Bannermen back to cultivate in northeast China was not only beneficial to solving the problem of Eight Banners' livelihood, but it was also a way to keep the Jing Banners under the constraints of the Eight Banners system. Therefore, this action had become the most feasible way for the Qing rulers to choose. This was also one of the reasons why emperor Jiaqing severely rebuked Fashishan in 1817 when he proposed that women and men of the Eight Banners should engage in textile production, but on the other hand was eager to prepare for the Jing Bannermen's relocation in northeast China.

The second one was that the Han refugees violated Qing Government's prohibition on the Northeast. The Han population soared in the Qianlong Period, and the contradiction between land and population became increasingly prominent, while there was still vast fertile land in the Northeast, especially in the north area of the Willow Border. Additionally, "the ginseng fields are moving further away, and there are over a thousand miles of empty land, all of which are rich soil". This piece of land, which was yet to be developed, was great attraction for the Han people. At this time, these migrants, either alone or with their families, came to the Northeast to work and trade in groups. There was a trend that could not be contained. Even some Manchu people in Shenyang also joined the migration. The complete prohibition on state-owned uncultivated land could no longer be implemented. By around 1812 (the 17th year of Jiaqing), due to serious disasters in Shandong and other places, even more refugees went north of Shanhai Pass than before. Although the Qing Court issued strict orders to "drive all the famine victims away", they soon gathered again and would not disperse. The Qing governors were afraid that they would uprise and did not dare to suppress them. Finally, more and more famine victims gathered, and commodity prices soared as the population increased. The Qing Government felt that their efforts to protect this imperial power's rising ground and the livelihoods of the Eight Banner soldiers in northeast China, which were the most important reserve troops in Beijing, were all threatened by these famine victims. Since it was no longer possible to prohibit the famine victims from go north of Shanhai Pass through administrative means as in previous dynasties, they had to send the Jing Bannermen to occupy this fertile land again to strengthen the power of Manchuria in the northeast China.

Under this situation, in the 17th year of Jiaqing (1812), Emperor Jiaqing ordered the Jing Bannermen to reclaim land as before. It can be seen obviously that this time the Jing Bannermen's reclamation to the Northeast was forced by the situation. Compared with the Qianlong Dynasty's long-term plans for the Jing Bannermen, precautions and achievements from the perspective of courage and integrity, Jiaqing's Period prepareness, purposiveness, migration scale and courage were no better than before.

(1) Three tuns in the middle, left and right of Shuangchengpu

Same as in the Qianlong Period, the reclamation of the land still began with sending people to the Northeast to observe the land conditions first. But there was a difference: this time, it was carried out in two separate routes at the same time. One was to send Grand Minister of State Songyun to Shengjing area, and they met with He Ning and Fujun to survey the uncultivated land at Daling River pasture area, Zhangwutai Frontier, Yangshimu River Pasture, and Fenghuang City Area. These places were not to be easily checked, for they were either hundreds of miles away from the provincial capital of Shengjing or they would cost too much in water draining, which was rejected by Emperor Jiaqing. The other was carried out by General Jilin Sai Chong'a and Song Ning. They first found "about 250 kilometers southeast of Ningguta, to Suifen River, Fanjiawopeng and other places surrounded by more than 300 kilometers. Among them, Huarha and other places have convenient water and wood resources, with an estimated cultivated area of about 50,000 shang", but because it was far away from Ningcheng and difficult to control, it was rejected. Then they "surveyed the uncultivated land in the east of Lalin, from Yangyaozi mountain to Tongzi Gully with an estimated cultivated area of about 5,000 shang, and in the southeast of Lalin, there is a place called Jiaxin Gully with an estimated cultivated area of about 20,000 shang", Sai Chong'a and Song Ning said that these two places were about 20-25 kilometers away from Alcuka City, and they worried that the newly settled Bannermen would be difficult to be controlled by the Lieutenant General who lived far away. They also said that recently, the harvest in Jilin was not good. Therefore, they requested to wait for three or five years then they would plan gradually. Unexpectedly, this idea was strongly criticized by Emperor Jiaqing. In the imperial edict, he said, "The purpose of moving the idle Bannermen is to improve their livelihoods. Now it has been surveyed that there are more than 25,000 shang of cultivatable land near Lalin. In Xisandao Kasari, there are still uncultivated land available for reclamation besides the allocated official land. So, there is a lot of uncultivated land in this province. It is better to plan and cultivate it all at once instead of checking it every year. By allowing the Bannermen to cultivate it, we can increase production and make it a stable income. As for the uncultivated land in Lalin, although it was 20-25 kilometers away from the city, but there are many differences between the Bannermen who are there to cultivate land and to be trained with equestrianism skill or archery, as it is not necessarily to appoint officials to check it, the post of lieutenant general for Lalin was removed later. Nowadays, the Bannermen in that area have been living and working for a long time without any problems. There is no need to have a high-ranking official specifically designated for them. If you say that the harvest in recent years has not been good, we cannot relocate the Bannermen there now. All the plans for cultivating the land and calculating the land must be prepared in advance. There is no need to delay for three or five years." In this way, the location for Bannermen's reclamation had been selected.

Although Sai Chonga and Song Ning surveyed the terrain for reclamation, they did not participate in the actual planning. The person who officially planned it was their successor, Fujun. Fujun, whose style name was Songyan, was a man of the Mongolian Yellow Banner. He has a biography in the *History of Qing Dynasty*, *The Biographies of the Qing Dynasty* and *Biographies of Those Seniors Who Made Contributions to the Country and the Court*. He was a famous Prime Minister (in ancient China) who served under Emperors Jiaqing and Daoguang for a long time and was well-known for his achievements in the borderland. He served as General for Jilin 4 times, lasting 13 years, making him the longest-serving and most outstanding one. He was familiar with the situation in northeast China, enthusiastic about practical borderland development, and planned to establish free schools, adjusted courier stations and official land, edit and rearrange books, eliminate bandits, established Shuangchengpu stronghold resettlement, reclaimed uncultivated land in Bodune, prepared to receive Jing Bannermen, opened up a sustainable livelihood for the Banner people, and implemented numerous good policies. He is a person who is worth commending in the history of Jilin Province forever.

Shortly after Fujun held the post of General Jilin for the second time, he discovered that the previously surveyed barren land, although fertile, was generally marshy and unsuitable for settlement. After referring to the old files of the Qianlong Period, he found that "the land between the Bordered Blue Banner village and its western neighboring towns, 12.5 kilometer northwest of Lalin, along the Lalin River towards the northwest to Shuangchengpu's old town, 40 kilometers away, is fertile with easy access to water and firewood. There is no shortage of building materials, and they can be transported down by the Lalin River." After a field investigation, Fujun decided to use this area as a settlement for idle Banner people from Beijing. Shuangchengzi "is located in the center of Lalin, serving as a barrier in the northern part of the province with a broad and open terrain." Fujun selected a land area about 65 kilometers from east to west and 35 kilometers from north to south, which could accommodate 2,000 to 3,000 idle Bannermen families, and decided to establish villages and tuns here, naming it as Shuangchengpu.

When formulating the regulations for the planned resettlement, Fujun clearly considered the lessons learned from the Qianlong Period: "The idle Banner people of Beijing were resettled, and their housing and land cultivation were all carried out by the troops stationed in various cities in Jilin. However, the land was cultivated but not planted, and although a few people were retained to teach farming, they were disbanded after one year. The newly resettled idle Banner people from Beijing had no idea of how to cultivate the land, so they initially hired the Han people, but over time, most of the land was owned by the Han people." Therefore, Fujun decided to first recruit local station troops who open up uncultivated land, which would be beneficial for both sides and would not require too much government funds. After ten years, the idle Banner people from Beijing would be resettled, and they would also be able to cultivate the well tended land. Therefore, in the first ten years, all the participants in the land cultivation were Banner loafers in northeast China.

The people who opened up uncultivated land were sent to Shuangchengpu in two batches. The first batch of 1,000 arrived in 1816 (the 21st year of Jiaqing), including 720 from Jilin, 100 each from the Eight Banner idle people in Alcuka and Bodune, and 80 from the Eight Banner idle people in buthai ulai hoton. These people must be young, energetic, honest, and law-abiding. Four people were grouped together to ensure that there were no unemployed rogues who hoped to obtain government funds for squandering, and it was strictly prohibited to use the elders as replacements. After the station troops arrived at Shuangchengpu, they were divided into five tuns for each of the Eight Banners. Each of the Bordered Yellow Banner and Plain Yellow Banner had 128 households, with three tuns of 24 households and two tuns of 28 households. Each of Plain White Banner, Plain Red Banner, Bordered White Banner, Bordered Red Banner, Plain Blue Banner, and Bordered Blue Banner had four tuns of 24 households and one tun of 28 households. everyone was allocated 30 shang of uncultivated land, 20 shang for cultivating, 10 shang were left uncultivated. all the land was distributed by whether they were on the left or right of the tun. The people were given 25 taels of silver from the reserve funds to purchase farming tools and build huts. They were also given two dan of grain seed from the Alcuka public granary.

Due to the initial establishment, "the Court was not able to fully understand the situation" in dispatching the first batch of a thousand men, there were many careless omissions. Firstly, the men sent from Jilin Banner did not bring their families and had no assistants. Even if they brought their families, because there was only one hut and one stove for four people, so they had nowhere to settle their families. These men who opened up uncultivated land also had no ability to build their own houses. Secondly, these men were all poor people. When they were dispatched to Shuangchengpu, all the cattle and farming tools were provided by the government, so they brought no money with themselves. After arriving at the destination, they were in a difficult situation, so the phenomenon was that these men were escaping constantly. These men didn't have enough assistants, together with those who escaped, caused the shortage of manpower, resulting in insufficient cultivation. Even worse, some land reverted to uncultivated ones.

In response to these careless omissions, Fujun made many modifications on the regulations of land cultivation. For example, "Strictly punishing those who violate orders and escape, in addition to chaining the fugitive for two months and whipping him 100 times, the leader of the Jing Bannermen who sent them will be reproached or removed from their posts, the cavalry officers and nominal officer will be given a major demerit for two years, and the Commander will be given a minor demerit for one year. This is to serve as a warning for those who neglect their duties and are careless." when selecting new ones to replace those who escaped, they would only be allowed to go if they had children or siblings to serve as helpers, after that, no Bannerman escaped. Secondly, they would be given silvers as relocation expenses, with four taels of silver per person, to encourage them to bring their families to the newly cultivated land. The original one utensil for every four men had been replaced by one utensil for every man, so that they could settle down to raise their family. After these measures were implemented, the situation improved, but if compared with the two tuns of 2000 men established later, the middle tun still had the most problems. By the 25th year of Jiaqing (1820), there were still people escaping with farming tools, and the efficiency of cultivating land was still very low, never achieving the expected results.

In the 8th lunar month of 1818 (the 23rd year of Jiaqing's reign), Fujun proposed that "there are still 20% of uncultivated land in Shuangchengpu that have not been cultivated, and it is better to cultivate them now rather than let them be abandoned. Hence, we can also get the grains earlier." He requested that the Bannermen in Shengjing and Jilin, no matter where they were from, Manchu, Mongolian, or Han military, if anyone was willing to go cultivating should be selected and the total number was 2000. In the 24th year of Jiaqing (1819), 1,000 troops arrived at Shuangchengpu. In the 25th year of Jiaqing (1820), another 1,000 troops arrived, and they were divided into two tuns, with the original tun named *the middle tun*. Since then, the three tuns had begun to take shape.

Learned from the first lesson, when sending people for the second time, Fujun made several changes to the regulations. Firstly, no more forced distribution. "There is no need to force them to go there, so there is no need for them to escape. This can avoid the disadvantage of fleeing." Fujun also adopted the method of "those who are willing to go can go freely". Secondly, the arrangements were more thorough and careful compared with the previous time. They selected those who had family members. Each person was given silver as relocation expenses. The station troops from Shenjing received 8 taels of silver per person, while the Jilin local station troops received 4 taels of silver per person. In total, each person received silver that was 22 taels of silvers more than the original 25 taels of silver. Thirdly, among the men who opened up uncultivated land this time, 1,000 were selected from Shengjing. Compared to the men from Jilin, they were more skilled at farming and had a more urgent desire to regain land. It could be said that they needed the land as much as the Han people among the Manchu Bannermen. After hearing the news of reclamation, the men from Shengjing were very enthusiastic. In Shenyang alone, there were "2,000 young and strong Bannermen who were willing to go to the Shuangchengpu in Jilin Province to reclaim uncultivated land." Among the 1,000 selected station troops, "the people sent from Fengtian had their families go with them, and some even went with their entire clans and retired soldiers." "Each household had a total of 15-16 men, women, and children, at least with 7-8 people. They were told that the land here was very fertile, and they were all willing to come as helpers." The distance from Fengtian, Jinzhou, and Fuzhou to Shuangchengpu was more than 1,000 kilometers. The selected men who opened up uncultivated land still had 5 taels of silver as relocation expenses, but the helpers did not receive any silver. However, this did not stop them from traveling long distances. This showed how difficult their living conditions were and how eagerly they were for their own land. The situation of the 1,000 Jilin local men seemed similar to the first batch. 200 of them were "Ningguta idle people who often fled." The reason they fled is that "the Ningguta mountains are high, and the forests are dense, and these idle people make a living by hunting. The land there is also fertile and can be cultivated, so they do not want to leave their hometowns easily." Finally, all the Ningguta idle people were sent back, and more than 200 idle people who were willing to come and cultivate land from Shengjing were selected to replace them. After arriving at Shuangchengpu, these men generally lived and worked in peace. There was no record of their fleeing. This was closely related to the fact that they brought many helpers who could help them cultivate the land, "so they could avoid hiring laborers and save expenses." It can be said that this was the best group of men cultivating land in Shuangchengpu.

According to statistics in the 4th year of Daoguang (1824), there were 3,000 men and 14,770 family members in the 3 tuns of Shuangchengpu. Under the circumstances at that time, this was indeed a considerable number.

(2) Jing Bannermen's Reclamation

On the basis of cultivating 90,000 shang of uncultivated land in the northeast, in the 1st lunar month of 1821 (the 1st year of Daoguang'a reign), the Qing Government officially ordered the relocation of the Jing Bannermen. The specific method was: "After discussion, starting from the 4th year of Daoguang (1824), 200 households will be transferred every year, divided into four times. Preparation will be made in the 2nd year of Daoguang (1822) to build houses, and each household will be given farmland, cattle, and other facilities." According to the initial plan, the 90,000 shang of cultivated land could accommodate 3,000 Jing Bannermen households, but the actual number of people who went there was far less than that. Unlike the allocation method by Banner in the Qianlong Period, this time the transfer was voluntary. The orders were given to "the Generals and Lieutenant Generals of the Eight Banners of Manchu and Mongolian, to inform their subordinate Bannermen the benefits of relocation. Those who wish to relocate should report to their own Banner. At the appointed time, they will be given property and land. The people with bad behavior should not be selected so as not to disturb the good customs. Each Banner will still report the registered households to the Ministry of Treasury. At the end of each year, a report will be submitted." However, what the rulers did not expect was that only 28 households were willing to relocate to Shuangchengpu that year. Therefore, the Qing Court had to once again issue documents to each Banner, "If there are those who wish to relocate later, they may make a register at any time and submit it to the Ministry of Treasury. By the end of the 12th lunar month of 1823 (the 3rd year of Daoguang'a reign), another report will be submitted." It was not until December of the 3rd year of Daoguang (1823) that there was a total of 53 households who wished to go, and they were officially relocated to Shuangchengpu in the 4th year of Daoguang (1824).

In the 5th year of Daoguang (1825), 76 households were relocated, with a total of 243 people. This relocation was divided into 2 stages, with 38 households each stage. The first stage was led by the General of Heilongjiang Lu Cheng, and the second stage was led by the lieutenant general of Ningguta He Fu, who accompanied them. During the journey, the wife of Furgong, a member of the Bordered Yellow Banner, Ms. Zhu, carried their three-year-old son, Lao Shou, ran away secretly. When they arrived at the Hersu station under Jilin, De Chang, a member of the Bordered White Banner, was too ill to walk and was treated at the station. However, the treatment was unsuccessful, and he died. As a single person was not allowed to be counted as a household, these two households were sent back. Therefore, there were 76 households at the start, but only 74 arrived at Shuangchengpu, which matched the record of 74 households in the *Jilin Chorography*. However, in later archives and records, there were 77 households. The reason for this discrepancy is still to be investigated.

In the first 2 years, the number of people who relocated was less than the originally planned 200 households. The reason for this was due to the regulation in the original plan of Fujun that only families were allowed to count as households. Although in the 2nd year of Daoguang (1822), Fujun had proposed that "people who are single between the ages of 20 and 50, if they have parents, brothers, or uncles who are willing to come with them, or if they have widow mothers, or sisters-in-law who are willing to come with them, and have three or more family members, that can be counted as a household without the restriction that people must have married." However, the Qing Court did not immediately approve it, believing that there were still 2 years before the relocation, so there was no need to plan. When it came to the 5th year of Daoguang (1825), it was found that "people were not very enthusiastic about signing up," and some willing to move to could not sign up because they were single. This was contrary to the original intention of regulation. Therefore, Ying He and others proposed that in the future, "all single idle Manchus and Mongolians who are willing to relocate will also be allowed to go. The father and son who are both single will be counted as one household, and siblings will be given full shares. Single idle people will be counted as one household, but the farmland, equipment, and public assistance silver of their own Banner will be halved. When they leave, they will be given wagons with four wheels. After the 2 households arrived at the settlement, how to distribute housing and tools will be arranged by the general." However, due to Fujun's consideration that "single idle people are easy to wander around after arriving at the settlement, and it is difficult to halve the room, cattle, and other facilities for each household." Therefore, it was decided to follow the proposal made in the 2nd year of Daoguang (1822) and treated those who were single but had parents, children, uncles or brothers, and grandparents who were willing to go with them as one household.

After changing the registration method, in the 6th year of Daoguang (1826), a total of 189 households registered. That year, due to difficulties in arranging housing, cattle, and vehicles, it was decided to postpone the relocation of "the 41 households with only two members each who have disposable money and grain to the 7th year of Daoguang (1827) for relocation". In this way, the specific number of people who relocated in the 6th year of Daoguang (1826) was 148. These people were divided into four groups from Beijing. The first group of Jing Bannermen included 40 households, of which soldier Saishabu refused to board the vehicle at the last minute and was deducted from his Banner. The remaining 39 households left Beijing on the 21st of the 1st lunar month and escorted out of the border on 29th of that month. The second group of Jing Bannermen included 30 households, who left Beijing on the 23rd of the 1st lunar month and escorted out of the border on the 2nd of the 2nd lunar month. The third group of Jing Bannermen included 42 households, of which one soldier Ling Bao was deducted in Beijing and replaced with Jilun. In addition, one idle household of Manchus from the Plain Blue Banner named Chenggui, was replaced with one household of Fulong'a, and one household of Mongolian footmen from the Plain Blue Banner, Fuen'e, fled in Beijing. Only 41 households left Beijing on the 25th of the 1st lunar month, and on the way, two people died: Ms. Yan, wife of ordinary soldier Gong'e Bu from the Bordered White Banner of Manchus, and Jilun, son of Hengwen leader of the Bannermen from the Bordered White Banner of Manchus. The remaining households escorted out of the border on the 3rd of the 2nd lunar month. The third group of Jing Bannermen also stated that there were two children under the name of Shi Tai from the Plain Yellow Banner of Mongolians, Shi Tai also mentioned that his second son, Cundebao, died on the 6th of the 1st lunar month of 1826. However, it was found that Cundebao was still alive and in fact his third son died. There was a discrepancy in the book. The fourth batch of sending Jing Bannermen included 32 households who left Beijing on the 27th of the 1st lunar month and arrived at Linyu County on the 4th of the 2nd lunar month. There was one female offspring Rongsheng from the Plain Red Banner of Manchus gave birth to a girl. In this way, the actual number of households in the 6th year of Daoguang (1826) was 142.

Because the registered number was close to 200 people that year, the rulers gained confidence and decided that they did not need to adhere to the number of 200 in the future, but to relocate based on the actual number of registrants. However, in the 7th year of Daoguang (1827), the number of people was less than before, with only 90 households, and in the 7th year of Daoguang (1828), there were only 27 households. As the registration of Jing Bannermen was not very satisfying, on October 19th of this year, Fujun proposed that "each banner of the Eight Banners of Manchus has more than 80 Cavalry Officers, and every year, 20 Cavalry Officers are randomly selected. Each Cavalry Officer will count out those idle people under the age of 50 with wives or father and brothers more than two people in a family and select one household from those people. There are 20 households from 20 Cavalry Officers, 160 households in total from all Eight Banners. For the Eight Banners of Mongolians, five Cavalry Officers are randomly selected from each banner, and one household is selected as those selected in the Manchus, totaling five households. There are 40 households in total from all Eight Banners. The total number of Manchus is 200 households. If there are people who voluntarily want to move, they can be counted as a household without additional registration. If there are a husband and wife, they will be counted as one household. It will take three years for each Cavalry Officer's household to rotate ... This plan is designed to relocate 200 households per year, which will take more than ten years to reach the target of 3,000 households." However, later evidence showed that this proposal was not adopted by the Qing Court. The reason for this, I believe, is mainly because the Qing Court's restrictions on the Manchus' personal freedom became increasingly weaker, and they could no longer adopt the mandatory relocation method on each banner as they did in the Qianlong Period. Moreover, the rulers also anticipated that even if they reluctantly did so, the result would still be the same as before, the Bannermen would flee from the relocation land. It is better not to relocate than to do so. Therefore, in the 9th year of Daoguang (1829), when Boqitu and others proposed that the original plan of relocating 3,000 households of Jing Bannermen to Shuangchengpu should be changed to relocating 1,000 households, the Qing Court immediately approved it. Subsequently, there were fewer and fewer Jing Bannermen came to Shuangchengpu. In the 10th year of Daoguang (1830), only five households were willing to move, but the number was too little, so they had to wait until the next year to gather more than ten households for reclamation. There had been people who moved in every year since then, but the number had not been significant. According to statistics from the Xianfeng period, there were a total of 698 Jing Banner households that were relocated to Shuangchengpu, which was 302 less than the planned 1,000 households of Boqitu's plan and much less than the originally planned 3,000 households.

(3) Bodune reclamation

Bodune (Fuyu city in Jilin province today) is between the Songhua River and the Lalin River, with flat and fertile land, and has long been known as a place of water and land convergence, the most prosperous land in the entire province. As early as the beginning of the reclamation in the Shuangchengpu settlement, Fujun had noticed this old enclosed area with "four plains and approximately more than 50 kilometers long, with no mountains, trees, or livestock," and after investigation, he found that there were "over 200,000 shang of land that can be cultivated" and "can provide food for tens of thousands of people every year." However, at this time, the Qing Government's finances were extremely tight, and they had no spare money to handle this matter, so they decided to postpone this discussion. However, Fujun's focus was not completely consistent with the Qing Court. He believed that "the cultivation of the Fuyu region is not only for the reclamation of Jing Bannermen, but also for the natural benefits of wilderness that are worth preserving," so he strongly advocated the cultivation of this area for future reclamation of Jing Bannermen. He had submitted 6 or 7 memorials to the court, which were rejected by the court, but he still did not waver and ultimately obtained approval.

The reclamation in Bodune was still carried out under the Jing Bannermen's reclamation to their original locations, but in the end, there was not a single Jing Banner that moved there. However, from today's perspective, this reclamation was much more successful than the previous one in Shuangchengpu. The key was adopting the method of recruiting civilians proposed by Fujun to cultivate the uncultivated land. The so-called "Recruiting Civilians to Cultivate the Land" referred to the Qing Court's organized and planned recruitment of Han people to replace the Jing Bannermen in cultivating land. When the Jing Bannermen was relocated, the cultivated land would be handed over to the Jing Bannermen for farming. If we look back at the suggestions of Shu Hede, Sun Jiagan, and other Manchu and Han officials on the relocation of the Jing Bannermen in the early years of Emperor Qianlong's reign, we will find that Fu Jun's proposal was actually in line with Sun Jiagan's suggestion of "Jing Bannermen take 2/3 land and Han people take 1/3". However, Fu jun had practical experience and lessons from the cultivation in Shuangchengpu, and he had a deeper understanding that using Bannermen as the workforce for cultivating land was not feasible. He was quite determined about recruiting Han people to cultivate the uncultivated land. Compared with sending local Bannermen, recruiting Han people had two advantages, which could be summarized as "Increase of Labor Productivity and Decrease of Expense Spending."

"Decrease of Expense Spending." means that large sums of silver could be saved. Although compared with sending the Bannermen from Beijing, sending the Bannermen from Shenyang and Jilin would cost much less, the principle of the state providing everything was the same. The Qing Court would provide them with silver for relocation expenses, sheds for temporary shelter, and all the necessary daily items such as farming tools, pots and pans, etc. The average cost for each Bannerman was 47 taels of silver, and for 3000 men, the total cost was around 178,000 taels of silver. However, when the settlers fled and were replaced with new ones, this cost still needed to be incurred. Additionally, if more land was to be cultivated, more workers would be required, and "subsidies had to be considered," at that time, "one helper was given 3 taels of silver per year." Instead of increasing subsidies and hiring helpers, it was better to recruit Han people for cultivation. Because when recruiting them, all the farming tools were self-provided, and the reclamation expenses were not offered by the state. Each settler only needed to be given 4 taels of silver for building houses. 30 households formed one tun, and the government drilled two wells, with each well they were given 18 taels of silver. In this way, each settler only needed 5.2 taels of silver, and in the "first year of rent collection, the land is 30 shang, and each settler needs to pay nine taels of silver. The annual revenue is still sufficient," "comparing with the expenses in Shuangchengpu, it reduced by 90%." The actual savings were significant. The labor needed for cultivation was huge, and the more labor needed, the more funds saved accordingly. This was only from the perspective of funding at the beginning of cultivation. Compared to the Manchu soldiers, the Han people who cultivated land had to pay a much larger amount of rent to the governor. After 6 years, they were required to pay taxes according to the amount of land they cultivated, which was not a small amount of income for the court. In addition, it could also be used as a special fund for Jing Bannermen's reclamation. Compared to sending Manchu soldiers, this was of course very cost-effective. This was particularly important in the context of the fiscal decline during the Daoguang Period.

"Increase of Labor Productivity" essentially meant that it was easy to improve labor productivity. The effect of the reclamation in Shuangchengpu was not satisfactory, mainly because many of the settlers were not good at or accustomed to farming. "Each settler has 30 shang of land, but after several years, only 20 shang have been cultivated, and there is still one-third of the land that left uncultivated." Additionally, reclaiming new uncultivated lands is much more difficult than reclaiming already-farmed land. "If we reclaim too much new land, we may worry that the already-farmed land will be abandoned. Therefore, the labor of one adult male settler can only cultivate 6-7 shang of land," and the contradiction between having too much land and too few settlers was particularly prominent at that time. Expanding the number of settlers was not easy, as there were a limited number of Bannermen, who also bore heavy military duties. Furthermore, from the performance of the two batches of Jilin Bannermen in Shuangchengpu, it could be seen that many of them were extremely reluctant to cultivate the land. Even if they were reluctantly assigned, the result would still be the same as before that many of them fled. If the labors were assigned from Shengjing and other places, on the one hand, it required correspondingly more spending of large amounts of silver; more importantly, as the Shengjing Bannermen were very enthusiastic and many had withdrawn from the army to join their families, the Qing rulers might fear that this would weaken the combat effectiveness of strong force of Eight Banners in northeast China, and they dared not assign too many of them to land cultivation. Moreover, there were no more idle Bannermen in Jilin and Fengtian provinces to assign. "The three settlements in Shuangchengpu have allocated 3000 households of unemployed Bannermen from Jilin and Fengtian provinces, with men, women, and children totaling over 10,000 people. In addition, all have land to cultivate, and others have family members who serve in the army and receive provisions. With such a prosperous livelihood, who would want to leave their hometown?" This made it necessary to recruit Han people to expand the scale and quantity of cultivation. At the time of the cultivation in Shuangchengpu, due to a severe lack of labor, it was necessary to hire Han people to assist in farming. The restrictions that prevented

Han people from bringing their families into Shuangchengpu and prohibited them from privately pawning Bannermen's land were merely empty words and caused a lot of trouble. It would be better to simply hire Han people for cultivation. In the future, when the Jing Bannermen are relocated, they will be given 20 shang of land by the state for strict verification and management. The remaining 10 shang will be considered as private property for Han people, who can buy and sell them as they wish, as long as they pay taxes on one mu basis. Here, Fujun also specifically proposed that if nearby Bannermen wished to cutivate land, they should be treated in the same way as Han people. The difference was that after cultivation the Bannermen could hand over 20 shang of land to the Jing Bannermen, there was no need for them to pay taxes for the remaining 10 shang like Han people. The ownership remained with the state and could not be sold or pawned at will. However, this was clearly more difficult to implement than in Shuangchengpu's fenced area.

In the 5th year of Daoguang's reign (1825), the tenants were officially recruited to take over the reclamation, and it was planned to reclaim 200,000 shang of land. In the name of the lieutenant general Yamun of Bodune, he presented the edict: "The officials will be sent to survey the land, divide the villages and tuns, draw up the boundaries, and name them Xincheng Tun. From the 5th year of Daoguang (1825), 25 tuns were set up for each banner, and each tun had 30 households." Qing Court selected 8 Chinese characters "治本于农务兹稼穑 (Zhi Ben Yu Nong Wu Zi Jia Qiang)" from the Chinese famous *Thousand Character Classic*, which means "the government must do a good job of sowing and harvesting as the foundation of governance." as names of 8 tuns, and each character represented 25 tuns. There was a total of 200 tuns. The first reported households would be the first character of 'Zhi' if they accumulated to 30 households, they would be classified into the Bordered Yellow Banner first tun, and land would be allocated to them for cultivation. Then, the following reported 30 households would be classified into the Yellow Banner first tun, and the character was assigned as 'Ben', the arrived people would be divided and grouped using the above-mentioned approach, and the Eight Banners' land could be reclaimed and cultivated at the same time." As expected by Fujun, the Han farmers who claimed the uncultivated land were quite enthusiastic. In the first year of arrangements, 1127 households were enrolled and allocated to 43 tuns. The next year, another 917 households were enrolled and allocated to 31 tuns. In the 7th years (1827), 1556 households were enrolled and allocated to 46 tuns. In total, over three years, a total of 3600 households were enrolled and allocated to 120 tuns. If each household was allocated 30 shang, the total area of land would be 108,000 shang, so there would be more than half of the planned reclamation in just three years. It can be seen how the Han people enthusiastically responded to the invitation of reclamation.

By the time of the Guangxu period, the uncultivated land here had all been reclaimed, and the tenant farmers had paid rent to the state according to the regulations. Although no households of the Jing Bannermen had moved there, compared to Shuangchengpu's reclamation, Fujun's painstaking efforts had achieved a more effective result. Of course, the Qing Court's initial concern that it was easy to gather countless Han people together but difficult to scatter them was not without reason, as the 30 shang of uncultivated land that had been recognized for cultivation, including the 20 shang that should be given to the Jing Bannermen, became private property of the Han people eventually. In the 3rd year of Guangxu's reign (1877), General Jilin Ming'an mentioned that when the descendants of the original tenant farmers in Bodune heard that the Jing Bannermen wanted to move there and make them give up two-thirds of their land, they were all surprised and said: "The uncultivated land (Xincheng tun) has been reclaimed by each tenant for many years and has been handed down for several generations. The ordinary people do not understand that the land should be divided as two-thirds for the Banner people and only one-third for themselves. They think that this land is their ancestral property, and some of them have sold it repeatedly. Suddenly hearing that they will be evicted, and their land be returned to the Jing Bannermen, they are all afraid. If we suddenly make them give up their land, their livelihood will be difficult and pitiful. I am afraid that they may become homeless or cause other trouble." By the early years of Guangxu's reign, only 60-70 years later, the descendants of the original tenant farmers did not know that the land they inherited from their ancestors was cultivated by tenant farmers. Some of the tenant farmers had already sold the land they had received. Under this situation, the Qing rulers had to give the 120 tuns in Bodune as the permanent property rights to the Han people, which was originally state-owned land of more than 100,000 shang intended for the Jing Bannermen. Finally, these became private property of the Han farmers. However, the Bodune tenants' reclamation aimed at relocating more than 100,000 shang of uncultivated land the Jing Bannermen had opened up , and these 120 tuns dotted there gradually becoming "a prosperous region on the border."

1.3.3 The Jing Bannermen's Reclamation to Hulan in the Late Qing Dynasty

After the Daoguang Period, the livelihood of the Jing Bannermen became increasingly difficult. Apart from the reasons of the Jing Bannermen, it was also related to the social environment at that time. Firstly, there was internal trouble. The Xianfeng and Tongzhi Periods were full of calamities. Apart from the Taiping Army rising, there were the Nian Army, the White Lotus Society that appeared in the Huanghuai River Basin, and the Heaven and Earth Society that harassed Guangdong, Fujian, and Taiwan. In the northwest, there was the Agubai that occupied Xinjiang, Shaanxi, and Gansu. In the southwest, ethnic people rebelled against the Manchu. These rebellions caused a sharp decline in population, disrupted grain transportation, and caused a continuous rise in grain prices in Beijing. The life of the Jing Bannermen was greatly affected. Secondly, there was external trouble. The huge war reparations of the two Opium Wars caused extreme poverty and exhaustion of funds. The Jing Bannermen's pay and provisions could not be issued on time and in full amount. The poverty of the Jing Bannermen became increasingly severe, and the contradiction between the soldiers and the Qing Court became increasingly intensify. Under these circumstances, some ministers once again proposed Jing Bannermen's Reclamation.

(1) The choice of land for reclamation

In the 4th lunar month of 1876 (the 2nd year of Guangxu's reign), the rulers of the Qing Dynasty instructed the ministers of Grand Council and others: "I have heard that there are still acres of arable land in the cities of the three Northeastern provinces. If it is allocated in different times, we may send a high-ranking officer to supervise the field affairs, and together with the general to inquire whether it is feasible. Chongshi, Mutushan and Fengshen will be sent to find out the land of the Jing Bannermen and the land of the refugees who have cultivated but not reported, and among them, how many lands had been taxed previously. The remaining cultivable land shall be located and measured, and the location and area shall be mapped and presented for review. The situation shall be observed to determine whether there will be obstacles to the reclamation, and the actual situation shall be reported."

Why did the Qing Court put forward this proposal again at this time? It could be that apart from the fact that there was no other way out for the Jing Bannermen in Beijing, what is more important was that the Manchu rulers were unwilling to give up their control over the Bannermen easily, and even more unwilling to revoke the prohibition for free. When forced to allow Han farmers to reclaim large tracts of land in northeast China, they did everything possible to keep as much land as possible for the Bannermen, especially for the Jing Bannermen. This motivation could be clearly seen from the fact that a considerable part of the "Eight Banners livelihood land" was reserved in the Northeast when reclamation was carried out freely. However, at this time in the Northeast, it was difficult to find sections of uncultivated fertile land. As early as the Qianlong Period, in the Shengjing area there were no land left to cultivate, and in Jilin only a few fragments: Ningguta, "from Yangmuding (name of certain area in Ningguta) Qianyang (name of certain area in Yangmuding) to Xiao Renkou (name of certain area in Ningguta), there are about ten places that can be cultivated"; "Hexihe Road, Niao Lang'e Ahada etc., which belong to Hunchun, the mountains ranges are vast and the ground is flat, which is worthy of reclamation"; Except for the establishment of the new city bureau in the 5th year of Daoguang (1845) in Bodune, "the rest of the land have been released successively, and there is no other way to reclaim"; There were "10,570 shang of remaining unallocated land for Jing Bannermen" in the Shuangchengpu. Moreover, after verification, it was found that these areas were not suitable for the reclamation: the land reported by Ningguta "are all separated by mountains, scattered and fragmented", and "located in the frontier, isolated in the east, and bordered by Russia", the men of Bodune and Shuangchengpu had cultivated land for many years, and it was inconvenient to suddenly withdraw them. Therefore, Jing

Bannermen could no longer move to Jilin at this time. In the sparsely populated Heilongjiang area ruled by General Heilongjiang, there were very few places that could be cultivated. "Butha and Hulun Buir are located in the northwest of the provincial capital. The wind is violent, and the soil is thin, and weather there is freezing. There is no public land for planting. The harvest is poor, except for the public fields that are cultivated in the villages, banner camps, and official villages near the cities, as well as the acres of farming land planted by the idle people, there is not much uncultivated land, and the places far away from the city are mostly sandy, rocky and hilly, which make it difficult to cultivate." Hulan had "a section of a deserted land that was kept for Jing Bannermen more than ten years ago, and only 300 households could be accommodated. Due to insufficient funds, it was impossible to carry out the tasks of reclamation, building houses, digging wells, purchasing cattle harness and seedlings, etc. The land remained closed and still needed to be prepared before allocating the Jing Bannermen." As a result, Hulan was chosen as the last reclamation site of Jing Bannermen.

Hulan, means "chimney" in Manchu language. In the 22nd year of Emperor Kangxi's reign (1683), "8 sentry posts of the Hulan River were set up, and one of them set up a chimney at the mouth of Hulan for cooking, so the place was named as Hulan, and the official book also followed it". It has broad and narrow senses. In a narrow sense, it refers to the city; in a broad sense, it refers to the vast area under the jurisdiction of the guard of Hulan City. It refers to the latter meaning here.

From the map, Hulan is not far from Lalin and Shuangchengpu. They are all located in the southern part of Heilongjiang Province and under the jurisdiction of Harbin City. It was said that "the mountains are majestic and splendid, and ginseng is also produced among them." The essence of Heilongjiang is all in the corner of Hulan, the weather is genial, and the soil is fertile, so it is admired by people south of the Shanhai Pass", "the province's tax revenue is 370,000 taels of silver, and the Hulan's tax revenue has reached more than 100,000 taels of silver." As early as Qianlong Period, when Chalaang, Arigon and others surveyed the northeast land and prepared to move Jing Bannermen, they had already been attracted by this area of more than 250 kilometers circumference, and had planned to "cultivate the land, and when it is valid for those who have moved from Beijing to settle in Lalin and other places, and the Hulan area should be kept as a settlement by people from Beijing." Later, reclamation in Lalin was not as successful as expected, and the reclamation in Hulan was naturally not on the agenda. In the first year of Tongzhi (1862), when Tepuqin planned to move the Jing Bannermen to reclaim within 50 kilometers north of Hulan City, north of the Hao River and south of the Hulan River, the tuns where Bannermen lived were connected, and a section of flat and barren land was selected for about 10 tuns. 300 households of idle Bannermen were allocated, and a method of reclamation was planned. "For the resettlement of the first batch Jing Bannermen, it can be modeled on the former General Jilin Fujun's report on the resettlement of the scattered Banner population in Shuangchengpu. It is proposed to pre-recruit local households to cultivate on behalf of the Bannermen, each household is given 70 shang of uncultivated land on preferential terms. When the Bannermen arrive at the settlement, each Bannermen household can receive 15 shang of cultivated land and 20 shang of uncultivated land. These lands can be cultivated by themselves as permanent property. The remaining 35 shang are considered as the personal property of the local household, with each shang initially paying office expenses of 0.06 taels of silver, without advance rent. By the 6th year, taxes are paid, with each shang still levied with major and minor rents of 0.66 taels of silver. At that time, there are no other tenant farmers from other places. If resettlement is done by transferring Bannermen from Shengjing and Jilin, it would be too expensive. It is proposed to try recruiting local households to do so, but there is still concern that the local people may be reluctant to participate. Therefore, it is planned to give each household two cattle in advance to help them cultivate, which will be returned along with the cultivated land. It is requested that the local government should provide a cattle death subsidy 0.000042 taels of silver each year, which would be stopped after the cattle is returned. The local households are required to provide their own farm implements and seeds to save costs. It is also proposed to provide them with bedding and well-digging subsidies, as well as funds for pre-building houses, purchasing cows, farm tools, milling equipment, furniture, and hiring laborers. Each household needs 250 taels of silver, with a total of about 61,500 taels of silver for 300 households. As there is no funding available, it is considered to use the cultivated land leased by local households in the next few years to pay for the construction of houses and other expenses for the Bannermen's resettlement." However, because there was no money to raise, the matter of Jing Bannermen's reclamation to the settlement was put on hold. When the rulers of the Qing Dynasty officially moved the Jing Bannermen here in the 2nd year of Guangxu (1876), this promising land had been waiting for them for more than a hundred years.

(2) The process of reclamation

After the location was selected, starting from the 5th lunar month of 1877 (the 3rd year of Guangxu's reign), a Jing Banner boundary officer was specially assigned to survey the boundary of Jing Bannermen, "to survey the area reserved for the location of the Jing Banner government office and bases, make marks ... If the people, tenants, etc. steal, destroy the marks, go against the rules, they will be convicted and sentenced." Later, due to concerns that local officials would become lax over time and not be able to personally go to the locations under their jurisdiction, in August, they again "assigned local cavalry officer Wuerxiang'e and his troops to carefully check the desolate field and the surrounding for Jing Bannermen. If there are any abuses or behaviors such as illegal occupation, sale, building lodgings, and stacking on the land, the local households will be expelled, their houses will be demolished, and the land will be abandoned. They are not allowed to stay and continue to live there. If there are people who do not comply with the regulations, they should be brought in by cavalry officer Wuerxiang'e and handed over to the court for serious punishment. This is to serve as a warning and to pacify the boundaries." The reason for such strict regulations was mainly because the originally reserved waste land for the Jing Banner was within the boundary of the land for people to reclaim, and naturally there would be some people who wanted to occupy it. After this order was issued, it was successively found that there were 66 legal and illegal households who built houses, occupying land, and opened land, inside and outside the border mark of the Jing Bannermen's reserved land. In the 4th year of Guangxu (1878), the demolition was carried out again, but the households always refused to leave because of the fact that it was winter, and land was covered with ice and snow and there was nowhere to move.

Like the two previous Jing Bannermen's reclamation, it was impossible for the Jing Bannermen to reclaim and cultivate land in person this time, and someone else was needed to come to reclaim the land. However, this time was quite different, especially in the territory reserved for Jing Banners. The number of Han refugees was increasing, and they could not be driven away. Therefore, the Qing Court decided to "prepare the recruiting of Jing Bannermen and wait for the order to reclaim. If it is the land is cultivated well, the officials shall select strong and capable Banner households for resettlement and let them cultivate the land on behalf of the Banner people. If the number is insufficient, then select additional capable residents in the vicinity to make up the 300 households required. All these methods are used to prepare in advance for the Jing Bannermen's reclamation." In the 5th lunar month of 1877 (the 3rd year of Guangxu's reign), the Commander Bodong'a and others followed the memorial and found out 21,000 shang suitable for cultivation that could be cultivated by the 300 households of Manchu and Han people. The houses, fences, wells, roads and pastures were all prepared, and more than 20,000 shang of land that could be reclaimed were obtained after the water was over. In the 4th year of Guangxu (1878), "according to area of the reserved land, there may form 20 tuns, which are divided into four Banners, including the Bordered White Banner, the Bordered Red Banner, the Yellow Blue, and the Bordered Blue Banner. Each Banner is set up with five tuns, and each tun is assigned 15 households to cultivate for another 15 Jing Banner households, and all 600 households including Jing Banners and other people are all under the leadership of the commander of the Beituanlinzi Committee." "The applicants of the Banners and tenants may get 70 shang for each household. Among those lands, 35 shang need to be taxed after five years, 20 shang need to pay the official rent of 0.66 taels of silver for each shang according to the regulation. The remaining 15 shang will be the permanent property for Manchu and other people. The land reclaimed by Manchu and other people for the Jing Bannermen is 35 shang, and the court does not offer cattle. After seven years, it will be handed over to the Jing Bannermen to manage. If it is less than seven years, it will be ordered to pay the official rent each shang, but not the mortgage rent. The court also does not provide the cattle, farm implements, housing and wells, etc." The treatment for these people was much worse than that of the 3,000 local Manchu in Shuangchengpu. Because not only they receive no resettlement silver, but they also had to pay the official rent in advance.

Seven years later, that was the 11th year of Guangxu (1885), there were already 10,000 shang of well cultivated land, so they began to move Jing Bannermen. However, each household needed 250 taels of silver to build houses, dig wells, and purchase cattle equipment. If 300 households were counted, the court still needed more than 61,500 taels of silver. For such a huge sum of money, government in Heilongjiang Province could not raise it. Thus, General Wen Xu of Heilongjiang asked to "send silver first, so as to purchase materials to build houses and other things", so as to avoid delays. However, the number of people who moved in later was relatively small, and the Jing Bannermen only needed more than 2,000 taels of silver, which was distributed by the Heilongjiang General as expense.

(3) The Jing Bannermen's Reclamation

In the 10th year of Guangxu (1884), the year when the Jing Bannermen was transferred, only ten households from four Banners, the Bordered Yellow Banner, the Bordered Red Banner, Red Banner, and the Bordered Blue Banner, and a total number of 28 people wished to go. Later, because of Xingbao, who came from the Mongolia Bordered Yellow Banner led by cavalry officers Yu An died of illness, therefore, only nine households with a total of 26 people actually went to Hulan. The construction of houses, the purchase of cattle harnesses and other items were specifically arranged by Commander of the Beituanlinzi Committee Changde, and Commander Yindeng'e, the committee member who was assigned to the Jing Bannermen for housing refurbishing. In the 10th year of Guangxu (1884), the rooms and furniture were all built and purchased in advance of the Jing Bannermen's arrival. After the arrival of Jing Bannermen, in the 11th year of Guangxu (1885), the courtyard walls were repaired. "Its courtyard wall is five chi (a unit of length in China, the same below) five cun (a unit of length in China, the same below) high, three chi wide at the foot, and each household wall is 16 zhang (a unit of length in China, zhang is larger than chi and cun, while chi is larger than cun, the same below) long and fifteen zhang wide. There are ten households in total, and the walls are 483 Zhang. Construction began on 6th June, completed on 25th July. 9 Jing Bannermen households, signed a joint file to share responsibility ... The money they borrowed was about 293.9 taels of silver. For building houses and digging wells, a total of 832.8 taels of silver was used; for purchasing household furniture and cattle, a total of 773.2 taels of silver was used. The total amount of silver used was 1899.9 taels of silver", which was the cost for the last 9 Jing Bannermen households. In the 9th lunar month of 1884 (the 10th year of Guangxu's reign), 9 households arrived at Beituanlinzi under general Heilongjiang's jurisdiction. ② Because "it was in the midwinter; the newly built rooms were cold. The official would rent a temporary apartment for the households to live. When the weather warms up in the spring, the Jing Bannermen would be moved to the new villages and tuns", "Each household was also provided with 1 dan of millet, 1 dan of sorghum rice, 5 dou of japonica rice, and 1000 bundles of sorghum, these were sufficient for half a year's use. After Jing Bannermen arrived at the settlement in the spring, the households that had been selected to cultivate on behalf of the Banner people will be required to hand over 35 shang of cultivated land, and the Jing Bannermen will cultivate the land as a permanent property themselves without selling it. All the land will be archived and under the jurisdiction of the local Banner." Since then, a vigorous plan to move the Jing Bannermen had only ended hastily with only 9 households relocated.

Although the Jing Bannermen's reclamation in the Qing Dynasty was planned very carefully every time, it was often not satisfactory when it was implemented. The number of migrants was progressively reduced, which was consistent with the rise and fall of Qing's national power. Since then, although ministers had continued to discuss the matter of reclamation, in the 8th lunar month of 1884 (the 10th year of Guangxu's reign), the grand secretary Shang Xian reported that there were many uncultivated lands in Jilin and Heilongjiang, and he planned to transfer the Jing Bannermen from Beijing to the uncultivated lands; In the 9th lunar month of 1898 (the 24th year of Guangxu's reign), Yixuan and others filed a proposal to relocate Jing Bannermen and open new tuns. However, at this time, the Qing Government had no extra funds to spend on this activity, and besides, there was no large section of land in the Northeast and outside the Shanhai Pass that could relocate Jing Bannermen for reclamation. None of these proposals had been put into action.

1.4 Causes Leading to the Failure of the Jing Bannermen's Reclamation Policy and its Objective Effects

1.4.1 Why Did the Jing Bannermen's Reclamation Fail?

Those who first presented their opinions on why the Jing Bannermen's Reclamation failed were some government officials and scholars in the Qing Dynasty. They once published a few analyses about "the Eight Banners' livelihood", the reclamation in Northeast and policies to make the frontier areas rich, from which we can see most of them only focused on the superficial problems. For example, Sun Dingcheng thought that the main reason why the Jing Bannermen's Reclamation in Shuangchengpu wasn't as expected was that no one would take the positions left by Fu Jun and other officials after they died, "The two sirs have passed away, and no one can do it as well as they have done." Even the insightful Wei Yuan couldn't make out why it was so hard to relocate the Jing Bannermen to the Northeast. He said, "In Manchuria and Mongolia, if the troop stations in another place, a thousand households can be relocated. Why is it so hard to relocate even 200 households every year?" and thus he had to believe that if the Bannermen were sent to guard the frontier as warriors, they would go without hesitation; If the Bannermen were sent to cultivate the frontier, they were reluctant to do so because of homesickness. In his opinion, if the government wanted to relocate the Bannermen, it should "in the name of stationing the frontier areas and select the responsible men from the monarch to take charge of one or two commanders as helpers. When they arrive there, the leaders distribute tasks of hunting or farming according to the likes of different people. They should also hire some Han farmers to help them. In this way, they will be satisfied." Of course, that isn't a good idea. In fact, although many people in the same times of Wei Yuan were eager to figure out the essential reason why the Jing Bannermen's reclamation failed, they were not able to do so, nor could they find the way to solve the problem. If we analyze that problem in a scientific and historical way, we can easily see the following three aspects are to blame for the failure:

(1) In terms of the environment, Beijing was incomparable in natural and cultural environment, which is the objective reason for the failure.

Even for now, the natural and cultural environment of Lalin, Alcuka, Shuangcheng, Hulan and other places where the Bannermen stationed are not able to be compared with Beijing. A hundred years ago, what were those places like? In other words, the environmental factor is the direct reason why it failed.

First, in the perspective of nature, the geographical location is important in the forming of climate in an area. The middle part of Northeast is at a relatively higher latitude, about between 45°N and 46°N, which is in the temperate zone of the temperate continental monsoon climate where winter is long and cold while summer is short and warm. *A Chronicle: My Memories as a Magistrate in Binzhou* has a description of the climate, "This is the coldest place in China. From the 11th lunar month to the 1st lunar month, it is always below 0°F. Snow is heavy even in sunny days, and the wind is as strong as a cold knife. The fallen snow on the ground won't melt for a long time, and that snow in the shadow of the mountain is about from 0.66 to 1.33 or 1.66 meters deep, while that the snow under the sun is about 0.33 meters deep. The ice on the surface of the Songhua River is about 2 or 2.33 meters deep. In February or October, even without heavy snow, it is below 20°F. It is a little warmer in the 3rd lunar month, rising to 30°F, and the ice just starts to thaw. The wind from the east blows occasionally, rivers are open to shipping, plants grow, rain falls, and farmers begin to cultivate land. In the 4th lunar month, it is 40°F, rainier. In the 5th and 6th lunar months, the hottest months of the year, it is from 50°F to 80°F. 50% of the days are sunny, 30% cloudy and 20% rainy. It is during that period that sprouts of grains grow fast. In the 7th lunar month, it falls to 50°F with a little less rain. In the 8th lunar month, it is frosty, dropping to 40°F or so, and plants turn yellow and withered, all leaves falling at the end of the month. In the 9th lunar month, it is only 30°F. In the Double Ninth Festival, it snows, and rivers freezes on which passengers can walk. In the 10th lunar month, the source sections of rivers are frozen." According to the conversion formula between Fahrenheit Celsius: 1°C=5/9 (-32°F), we can conclude that in that area at least 6 months are below 0°C around the year, and the highest temperature is just from 10°C to 26.7°C lasting a very short time, about two months, the 5th and 6th lunar months.

In such conditions, the Beijing Bannermen from the warm temperate zone felt very uncomfortable. As they didn't adapt to the climate, lacking medicine they needed, many of them fell ill or died. Let's take the Jing Bannermen's reclamation in the 10th year of Guangxu's reign (1884) as an example. On the 2nd of the 10th lunar month, they just arrived in Beilintuanzi. Many of their family "had caught cold in the journey." Two years later, "Unable to adapt to the environment, among nine households of twenty-six people, two households died out, and the left seven had dead family members too. The total number of people is reduced to seventeen." In the 13th year of Guangxu's reign (1887), another "seven or eight persons were seriously ill, whether they can survive is unknown. The rest who was not ill still didn't fit in. They often had ailments, suffering from agony." Having no choice, Bannerman En Chang and other six households wrote a letter to the emperor, "Your Majesty have mercy on us and let us return to our hometown." Their requirement was not approved. Then "the two households of A Qing and Shuang Fu escaped, and no one knew their whereabouts." Only five households lived there: the En Chang's, the De Chang's, the Ji Run's, the Ji Ling's and the Cheng Chun's. In the 14th year of Guangxu's reign (1887), the En Chang's and the De Chang's escaped as well. There were only three left. From what mentioned above, we can see the main reason is the harsh climate which they couldn't adapt to.

Second, in the perspective of culture, before the Jing Bannermen's Reclamation, that place was wilderness, let alone "culture". However, Beijing is a famous historical and cultural city with a history of over two thousand years, and it has served as the capital of China for nearly a thousand years. In particularly, its unique geographical location connects it with the development of northern minorities such as Jurchen, Mongolian and Manchu, which makes it a melting pot of different peoples.

In the 1st year of Shunzhi's reign (1644), the Manchu troops occupied Beijing. For fear that Manchu would develop "Han people's habits" as well as to relieve the sharp conflicts between Manchu people and Han people, the Manchu emperor took pains to create a social system of two components: the Manchu region and the Han region. In the 8th lunar month of 1648 (the 5th year of Shunzhi's reign), the following imperial order was made, "All the Han officials and ordinary people shall move to the south of Peking." Since then, hundreds of thousands of Bannermen whose job was no other than a soldier lived in the inner part of the city, and what they consumed in daily life all came from the labour of Han people. That explains why the consumption types of Beijing are mainly comprised of commerce, catering and theatre, and Zhengyangmen Street, Di'anmen Street, Dongxi'anmen Street, Dongxisipai Street and the Dongxidan decorated archway area, namely the food market and the flower market in the outer part of the city formed "the shopping district in Beijing". In the reigns of Qianlong, Jiaqing and Daoguang, the Bannermen in Beijing had been accustomed to the extravagant parasitical life, they were the carefree leisure class, and their culture became the so-called leisure culture. Flying a kite, raising pigeons, raising goldfish, going to theatre, playing a role in a Beijing opera or watching crickets wrestling—they lived a life like that. Therefore, the Beijing Bannermen who lived in such an environment for hundreds of years, even though some of them were poor, naturally felt superior to Han people and Bannermen who stationed in frontier areas. If their lifestyle was changed after they moved to the wilderness from the bustling city, they definitely would feel uneasy as they changed from urban consumers to rural producers. Despite the fact that "when they arrived there, land, houses, stables, tools, grains, coal, fowl and pigs were ready", they had lost their social network and communication with relatives and friends as well as the advanced infrastructures in the world—in Northeast, there were "no theatres, acrobatics, tea houses and bars, and they couldn't wander around at will." Consequently, they missed the high citadel of the Beijing, the golden glazed tiles, the straight streets and alleys, the temple fairs and the shopping district where people from all walks of life came, the authentic time-honored brands, the delicious local snacks, the unique customs, the dialect of slang which was not rude, the euphonious voices of hawking goods and the heartfelt friendship between neighbors.

As a result, the huge differences between Beijing and Northeast affected the Beijing Bannermen very much. If they wanted to survive in Northeast, they had to adapt to the surrounding environment, or they would be knocked out. The fact that some of households escaped or died out is an obvious proof.

(2) Since Jing Bannermen preferred being a soldier to being a farmer and thought highly of being a government official, they were unwilling to go to the Northeast to reclaim land mentally.

According to the theories of social psychology, the occurrence, change and development of people's psychological activities are connected with their social life, traditional customs and motivations. Traditionally, Manchu people think a man is born to be a soldier who can ride a horse and shoot arrows. If they have to do productive activities, they only fish, hunt and collect fruits. They never do farming as Han people do. That tradition is another important reason why the Jing Bannermen's Reclamation failed. Before the Ming Dynasty, the ancestors of Manchu people—Jurchen people "didn't do farming but went into hunting and fishing." Fishing, hunting, husbandry and gathering economies were their main livelihoods. In the late years of the Ming Dynasty, although their agriculture developed a little, Jurchen farmers mostly got laborers by looting and buying foreign people, "In Jurchen farmers' fields, most of the laborers were Han people." To us Jurchcen people, if Koreans invade, they would bring geldings and populations of themselves to helps us."

After Nurhachi waged the war against the Ming Dynasty, all the Jurchen people were sorted into the Eight Banners, and fields were distributed to them according to the number of their family members. "They shall be soldiers on the battlefield and civilians in the fields." However, frequent battles left the soldiers no time to produce grains, and thus "slaves cultivated the fields and handed in the grains.

Soldiers all prepared to fight. Nobody did farming." The slaves were "Han people, Liao people or Mongolians" who were plundered in war. At leisure, they liked activities such as fishing and hunting. For example, on the 14th of the 4th lunar month of 1623 the 8th year of Tianming, after the Late Jin Dynasty relocated its capital to Liaoyang, while going on a tour of inspection of the fields along the banks of the Liaohe River, Nurhachi led his sons, daughters-in-law and his grandchildren in hunting and fishing. In the 6th year of the reign of Tiancong (1632), Emperor Huangtaiji described his ideal social life in his letter to the Ming government: "Our two countries are in peace. We are wealthy. Trade between two countries is smooth. We Jurchen people can hunt with our eagles, and we will enjoy peace for ever." From what mentioned above, we can see that representatives of aristocrats such as Nurhachi and Huangtaiji are the same with other Jurchen people who favored fishing and hunting as livelihoods, not farming as Han people did.

In addition, they tended to follow the culture and traditions of Han people, which hindered them from reclaiming land. After the Qing Government took control of China, most of Manchu people moved to the central plains where agricultural civilization had existed for a long time. Influenced by the profound unified culture system of Han people, the Manchu community accelerated the transition from slavery to feudalism and finally adopted the latter. In other words, the establishment of feudalism by Manchu people is the process where they were assimilated into the Han community, though the Manchu emperor created the Eight Banners to organize Manchu people and made them live in special areas which formed a small relatively exclusive society where they were forbidden to communicate with Han people for fear that Han culture would influence them and "the base of the country would be unstable." Nevertheless, since the Qing Government took the initiative in imbibing excellent works of Han culture and released policies to blend Manchu people and Han people together, Manchu people assiduously studied classics and poems of Han culture, and they enjoyed Han culture by creating their own works. In *the Shout Pavilion Diary* by Zhaolian, at that time "On the desks of government officials, there are always *All Men are Brothers* and *The Plum in the Golden Vase or, Chin P'ing Mei* for reading." In the Qing Dynasty, the famous poet Yuan Mei wrote in *Additions to Suiyuan's Thoughts on Poetry*, "Recently, literature is much more popular among Manchu people than among Han people. Even Manchu soldiers and officers can make poems." That was clear in foreigners' eyes, "As time passed by, Tatars have forgotten their traditional focus on merits and their favor for military activities. They become mild under China's entertainment, graceful customs and lasting peace. Han people influence them in every field of life." The mark of the change in their values was the decay of their favor for "the Manchu language and the skills of riding and shooting" as well as their further assimilation into Han culture. In Beijing, where all the excellent pieces of Chinese culture gathered, Manchu people learned Chinese and spoke it, taking the imperial examination to be public servants. No wonder someone commented, "For those who want to be government officials through the imperial examination, cultivating land is toil forced by the government, and how can we complain they don't work?" Under such conditions, the result of the Jing Bannermen's Reclamation was certainly not good.

(3) The system of the Eight Banners, by which the Qing Government used to control the Jing Bannermen, is the essential reason for the failure of the Jing Bannermen's Reclamation.

The environment and the Bannermen should be held accountable for the failure, but beside the superficial phenomena, if we see through the causes and results of the Jing Bannermen's Reclamation and take the system of the Qing Dynasty into consideration, we will recognize that the system of the Eight Bannermen by which the Qing Government used to administrate Bannermen is the main reason for the failure. As what is mentioned above, there were strict divides between Bannermen and Han people. The Bannermen sorted into the Eight Banners who were administrated by military, were a special community. Their household registration was not their geographical location, e.g. in XXX County in XXX Province, but in XXX Zuoling in XXX Banner. They had their own systems of residence, marriage, land, positions in the government and lawsuits. Their social sphere was strictly limited, and all the Eight Banners formed a small community which was completely exclusive. The restraints from the system narrowed the social circle of Bannermen, which resulted in a group lacking enterprise and competitiveness.

Some of the Jing Bannermen returned to the Northeast to reclaim land because of livelihood. The Qing Government, however, managed them according to the original system of the Eight Banners, making no change. In the area where they lived in the Northeast, they were treated as a special group, and the name "the Jing Bannermen" continued until the end of the dynasty. Meanwhile, in order to make the Bannermen willing to live here, the Qing Government tried its best: before relocation, the Jing Bannermen were given settle-down funds; after arrival, they were given career funds; if required, marriage funds, funeral funds, servant funds, cattle harness funds and farm tools funds were given. Even though the treatment was very nice, the Jing Bannermen still faced threats of livelihood. Instead of leaving the problem to society and removing the Jing Bannermen out of the Eight Banners to motivate their enthusiasm for production to save themselves, the Qing Government did as they were in Beijing—it proposed measures to meet the basic needs of the Jing Bannermen by investing more funds and materials to improve their life. The Jing Bannermen were deliberately placed to a superior position compared with Han people or even Bannermen who had lived in the Northeast, and thus they could hardly treat the reclamation area as their homeland mentally. That special psycho made the Jing Bannermen not consider themselves as a member of the reclamation area for a long time, which hindered them from fitting in. What's worse, the policy raised their dependence on the government. They regarded the reclamation as an economic welfare, and most of them planned to inherit the finished results and get supplies from the government for ever. In that area, they became farmers who couldn't farm. When difficulties came, they waited for the supplies from the government. If the supplies were not sufficient, they had no way but to become poor.

That was in contrast with the removal of Han Bannermen. The emperor ordered Han Bannermen to leave the Eight Banners because he wanted to make enough positions for Manchu Bannermen and didn't care Han Bannermen's livelihood. However, to his surprise, most Han Bannermen were extremely enthusiastic about it. In the 7th year of Qianlong (1742), as soon as the order of removing Han Bannermen out of the Eight Banners was given, in just one year 1,396 Han Bannermen would like to do it, including government officials such as cavalries, infantries and Baitanggas (courtiers of no rank) who "got supplies from the government". Besides, most poor Han Bannermen lived better after they left the Eight Banners. As we all know, Han Bannermen are Han people. Their ancestors joined the Banners for different historical reasons. In the system of the Eight Banners, they were strictly restricted in daily life. Furthermore, they were much inferior to Manchu Bannermen and Mongolian Bannermen, and that's why they were willing to move out. After they left the Eight Banners, those useless Bannermen who used to have no livelihoods in the system, made the most of their potential to survive in the farming areas where most of the population were Han people as farmers, and their life definitely became better. In summary, without the restraints of the system, they began their new life. The Qing Government, however, couldn't apply the method to Manchu and Mongolian Bannermen. No matter what the policy was, the removal of the Han Bannermen or the Jing Bannermen's Reclamation, the purpose of the government was nothing but to let Bannermen have livelihoods, especially the Manchu and Mongolian Bannermen, to secure the foundation of the country. Therefore, the "root" of the system of the Eight Banners is not to change. Without the "root", the system will disappear, so does the Qing Empire. As a result, the problems of the livelihood of the Eight Bannermen couldn't be solved within the system or even inside the empire. Finally, the solution of the Jing Bannermen's Reclamation ended up in failure.

1.4.2 The Objective Effects of the Jing Bannermen's Reclamation

Despite the obstacles in the practice and failure to achieve goals, the Jing Bannermen's Reclamation which aimed to solve the livelihood problem of the Beijing Bannermen, had some objective effects of changing the policies of "Supporting the Bannermen with Grace and Provisions" and "Prohibiting Han People from Going North of the Shanhai Pass" which had been applied by the Government for a long time. It led to the fast exploitation of Northeast and brought the advanced culture of Beijing, which promoted the solidarity and amalgamation of different peoples, transforming the frontier areas into inner land as well as the foreign people into Chinese. I will discuss the topic in the following aspects: politics, military affairs, economy and culture.

(1) In politics, the Jing Bannermen's Reclamation provided references for the Qing Government to solve the livelihood problems of the Eight Banners.

From what mentioned above, we know that after passing the Shanhai Pass the Qing Government applied the policy of "Supporting the Bannermen with Grace and Provisions" and prohibited Bannermen from farming or doing business, which was actually against the basic principle of material production because production is the prerequisite for survival, use one's own labour to create social wealth is the first priority of human life. Being away from the labour of production for a long period caused indolence of Bannermen, corrupting their health and national spirits. Despite the difficulties and failure to achieve the goals, the Jing Bannermen's Reclamation made some of the Beijing Bannermen and their descendants stay in the Northeast, and they earned their living by their own labour. The fact changed policy of "Supporting the Bannermen with Grace and Provisions" which had existed for generations, providing referential experience for solving the livelihoods problem of the Eight Banners. To solve the problem, the welfare policies made by the government were useless. The divide between Bannermen and Han people has to be broken. The Manchu Bannermen should do as Han people do—they should make the most of the means of production in the practices of production and different economic activities to make profits, creating economic and social value through their wit and labour. That was obvious in historical recordings of discussions among the officials about the livelihoods of the Eight Banners in the early years of the reign of Daoguang. What the officials discussed and the policies they adopted were apparently different from those before. First, in analyzing the problem, they directly touched the essential problem: Bannermen didn't produce anything. Second, the measures should be adopted by the government were how to use the fund wisely and effectively to sustain their livelihood and loosen the restrictions which were bad for their economic activities, not enlarging the number of Bannerman who could get provisions from the government. Thus, the dilemma of Bannermen would be alleviated.

In the reign of Guangxu, representatives of Manchu and Han officials such as Duanfang, Yuan Shikai and Zhang Zhidong proposed that the system of the Eight Banners should be changed, and the divide between the Manchu region and the Han region should be lifted, so that the Bannermen could have a better life. They thought that "the government don't need to appoint specific positions to them, and as long as they can earn their living, then any trade is OK." "Farmers, craftsmen or businessmen, no matter which career they choose, as long as they can live by their own labour, they can make the choice at will." Under the pressure of the public, the Qing Government was forced to make an order in the 33rd year of the reign of Guangxu (1907). It said that over two hundred years since the foundation of the Qing Dynasty Manchu officials and Han officials or, Manchu people and Han people, were never discriminated. In hard time, now, any member of the officials or the craftsmen of the government should unite to solve the problem, and local governments should give their advice on how to solve the problem between the

Manchu region and the Han region, which the government may adopt as policies. In the 10th lunar month of 1908 (the 34th year of Guangxu's reign), the Qing Government released the List of Tasks of Every Year. According to the list, in the first year since the release of the list, the office in charge of changing the system of the Eight Banners was set, whose task was "to find livelihoods for Bannermen of the Eight Banners and make Manchu people and Han people live on good terms in harmony." In 1915, its task was "to change the system and abolish the divide between the Manchu region and the Han region, which is the purpose of all the measures." Therefore, finding livelihoods for the Bannermen of the Eight Banners is the prerequisite for changing the system, "If by working the Bannermen can live without the supplies from the government, then it is suitable to change the system." From that we can see that the emperor realized the essential way to solve the problem was to erase the divide between the Manchu region and the Han region, provide education to Bannermen and teach them trades to support themselves. In the 12th lunar month of 1908 (the 34th year of Guangxu's reign), the Agency of Changing the Eight Banners was officially established, with prince Pulun, Zaize duke of Zhenguo, grand secretary Natong and ministers Baoxi, Xi'yan and Dashou in charge of it. Well, in the 1st lunar month of 1909 (the 1st year of Xuantong's reign), Shun Pao reported, "the officials of the Agency of Changing the Eight Banners often held meetings in the office. They didn't know what to do. If they didn't stop distributing supplies to Bannermen, they couldn't change the system; if they stopped distributing supplies to Bannermen, they feared that the Bannermen would protest ... After several meetings, they still didn't figure out the solution." A year later, in the 1st lunar month of 1910 (the 2nd year of Xuantong's reign), Shun Pao reported, "duke Zaize, prince Pulun, minister Baoxi, minister Xi'yan and minister Dashou with official En and official Wu all went to the agency to hold a meeting about how to change the system of the Eight Banners, except Grand Secretary Natong. When everyone arrived, no remark was made. In fact, two officials had their opinions, but they remained silent because no one began to speak first. That day, they discussed other things and then broke up the meeting. The participants all said that their positions allowed them to attend the meeting but not to discuss the problem." After several years of discussion, they had no other way than surveying the Bannermen's household registrations and wasteland. So, *Shun Pao* commented, "It has been 3 years since the establishment of the Agency of Changing the Eight Banners. The agency has done nothing for the livelihood of Bannermen. Those officials of the agency should be held accountable for their dereliction of duty." Even so, the Qing Government took the opportunity to establish new economic institutions run by the government around the country—the Bureau of Crafts and crafts factories, of which Mukden got the biggest success: the crafts factory of the Eight Banners, the agricultural school of the Eight Banners, the school of the Eight Banners, school of the Eight Banners for industry and commerce, the school for students from the imperial clan, the elementary school for pupils from the imperial clan in Weicheng, the women's factory of the Eight Banners, the silk enterprise of the Eight Banners and the subsidiary of Jinzhou crafts factory of the Eight Banners along with the Manchu and Mongolian middle school of the Eight Banners and the training school for women workers of the Eight Banners. Bannermen in Mukden were very enthusiastic about learning new skills. According to the report by Xi Liangzou, in 1909 the training school for women workers of the Eight Banners was built in Mukden. The quota of enrollment was 100, while in reality, hundreds of people came to join the course. A large number of Bannermen began to study knowledge and skills on factories and schools of the new type to make their living, which laid a foundation for their survival. Since then, Bannermen started their careers in agriculture, craftsmanship or business, depended on themselves, and they had other ways to support themselves except cultivating land in Northeast, which was the inner reason why few people followed the Jin Bannermen's Reclamation policy applied in the reign of Guangxu with precedents as examples.

(2) In the perspective of military affairs, the Jing Bannermen's Reclamation prepared the army reserves for the Eight Banners, which was a strategic military action.

It was obvious that both ministers and the emperor regarded the Jing Bannermen's Reclamation as a military action. After the Bannermen arrived in the Northeast, Emperor Qianlong gave an order, "Although your task is to reclaim land, you should practise equestrianism and archery in your spare time. If you perfect your skills, you will choose to be a soldier there." Renzong of the Qing Dynasty also said, "If the reclamation is successful and the land becomes fertile, you will become wealthier and wealthier, and you should practise equestrianism and archery. The excellent ones of you can still be selected to be officials in Beijing. So the policy has two advantages." In the 7th year of the reign of Tongzhi (1868), Shen Guifen, the imperial inspector in Shanxi, also suggested that the Jing Bannermen who used to be supported by the Qing Government should "be removed to the Northeast, weather hardships and learn to cultivate land and manage husbandry by themselves." "In that way the active spirit of the early years of the dynasty will be restored, and in decades of years the land in the frontier areas will be cultivated, with Bannermen as the army reserves which can be mobilized to Beijing directly." The above all demonstrates that the Qing Government expected the Jing Bannermen to be transformed for the purpose of reclaiming frontier land and increasing the army reserves. The government did so because when the Eight Banners went south of the Shanhai Pass their efficiency in battles and their martial spirit decayed quickly. After the regime got its hold on the state, the Qing Government kept the Eight Banners without any change, and the Eight Banners became a group of professional soldiers and the army reserves supported by the government. As time passing by, it gradually turned into a social group which lived on the dole and lost its original efficiency in battles. There was a description, "The Bannermen shoot and miss, ride and fall." The phenomenon was quite common. In the 15th year of Daoguang (1835), Huang Jue, the minister of the Honglu Temple (a ministry in charge of foreign affairs and related ceremonies), vividly depicted the increasingly decadent Bannermen in Beijing, "Recently, crowds of Bannermen, holding birdcages and bird racks, idled around the city or gathered to gamble. When they are asked what they do, they answer that they are soldiers who are responsible for patrolling the city, but they don't do their job—they hire other people to register their attendance. That's all." In the 6th year of the reign of Xianfeng, Zeng Guofan reported to the emperor, "Since the 17th year of the reign of Jiaqing, no military parade has been held. Soldiers become strong through practice but weak through idleness. It is natural that the Bannermen become weaker and weaker because they go through no battles in peacetime and hunt no more." In daily life, the Bannermen were indolent; in the battlefield, they were cowardly and unwise. In the battle to suppress the Revolt of the Three Feudatories, Beile Shangshan and Beile Chani commanded soldiers in the front line to attack Yuezhou. On the excuse of lacking ships and oars, they did not dare to fight for a whole year, and on hearing the order of retreating, "all the soldiers roared with joy". The bravery of the old days had vanished in them.

Facing the fast decay of the Eight Banners, the emperor and the officials had to think about how to restore the bravery and strength of the Bannermen. After consideration, they thought the best way was to relocate Bannermen to the Northeast. In fact, as the headquarters, the Northeast was the base of the Eight Banners. To continue its function, the Qing Government tried its best to reserve different peoples' customs, languages and skills of riding, shooting and producing in the Northeast. The Jing Bannermen's Reclamation is killing two birds with one stone—the Bannermen who had lived in Beijing for generations returned to the Northeast, cultivating land and increasing the army reserves, which secured the governance of Manchu aristocrats. It was proved that part of the Qing Government's goal was achieved.

According to the rule at that time, among the jobless Bannermen who returned to the Northeast, "if someone who has lived in the Northeast for three years would like to be a soldier, he may be selected with other jobless men underage in Alcuka." Those Bannermen, "are drilled in every spring and autumn: from the 2nd lunar month to the 5th lunar month in spring, and from the 8th lunar month to the 10th lunar month in autumn. The drill is mainly comprised of equestrianism and archery. In leisure time, they do farming. In the spring after every four years, there will be a military review of the Eight Banners. Every soldier will shoot one arrow while riding and five arrows while standing. Those who excel in skills will be awarded prizes by the Jilin General. Those who fail will be dismissed according to military discipline. In drill, every Banner should prepare dozens of underage strong men to fill the vacancies left by people who are promoted or dismissed, and the excellent ones will be examined and selected by Meilezhangjing (vice general who stations in a province)." In this way, the soldiers of the Eight Banners in Alcuka and Lalin "are good at equestrianism and archery besides cultivating land." And since the reign of Xianfeng, as a base of the army reserves of the Eight Banners, the Northeast gradually came into effect: soldiers and officers were frequently called up in defensive affairs of frontier areas and inner land.

In the 1st year of Xianfeng's reign (1851), "100 healthy and excellent soldiers were called up from Akanmenke and Xuanqiu, accompanying Grand Secretary Saishang'e to enter south of the Shanhai Pass. They were called as 'the First Troop' to attack the Taiping Heavenly Kingdom."

In the 2nd year of Xianfeng's reign (1852), "2, 000 horse carers were called up from Shuangchengpu in Jilin, which were led by Governor Xichang in Shuangchengpu, to attack the revolt forces in Henan."

In the 9th year of Xianfeng's reign (1859), "The Anglo-French Allied Forces occupied Beijing. The army of the Eight Banners in Alcuka were called up again with Prince Seng'gelinqin to combat the invaders. Since there were not enough soldiers, the soldiers underage were also called up, which were called as 'the Second Troop'."

In the 1st year of Tongzhi's reign (1862), "50 soldiers who were underage from Shuangchengpu were called up to Beijing. They were drilled, ready for battle."

In the 6th year of Tongzhi's reign (1867), soldiers in Alcuka "were called up three times a year: the first time 1, 500 to Shandong, the second time 500 to Jilin, and the third time 2, 500 sorted into five battalions of Gang (Fortitude), Yi (Perseverance), Sheng (Victory), Rui (Elite) and Jie (Agility) to Shanxi, and in August 100 cavalries to Shandong."

In the 8th year of Tongzhi's reign (1869), "20 excellent soldiers were selected from Shuangchengpu, who were called up to Gansu."

In the 10th year of Tongzhi's reign (1869), the government selected soldiers from Alcuka, "800 soldiers went to Dihua (Urumqi in China)."

In the 11th year of Tongzhi's reign (1872), "The Hui people in the northwest of China revolted, so the Qing Government called up soldiers and officers of the Eight Banners (from Alcuka) who went with General Jinshun to suppress the revolt. They were called as 'the Third Troop'."

In the 7th year of Guangxu's reign (1881), "The crisis in Beijing made 100 cavalries (from Alcuka) go to Beijing."

It is certain that the soldiers played an important role in suppressing peasant revolts around the country, including the Taiping Heavenly Kingdom, while they paid painful costs for it. Most soldiers "died in the battlefield". Therefore, in the 12th year of Tongzhi's reign (1873), in South Neidongda Street in Shuangchengpu, the Qing Government "asked the soldiers and officers of the Eight Banners to build a memorial hall. There were spirit tablets for the 186 deceased soldiers and officers in the battle."

(3) In the perspective of economy, the Jing Bannermen's Reclamation boosted the economy in Northeast.

On the basis of economics, the development of the economy of an area is determined by three dispensable elements: labour, capital and technology. During the reclamation period of the Northeast, thanks to the national policies and sufficient capital, Han farmers were active in labour, making the most of their productive technologies advanced. Nevertheless, later on, to restrict the migration of population in the Northeast, the Qing Government set barriers to insulate the Northeast from southern areas, causing the geographical isolation of the Northeast from the inner land. Since advanced technologies and methods of management from the inner land were barred outside the area, the underdeveloped Northeast got less and less support. The Jing Bannermen's Reclamation beginning in the early years of the reign of Qianlong was a good opportunity for the Northeast to develop different industries, where the frontier Northeast started to catch up with inland areas.

First, the Jing Bannermen's Reclamation brought the capital that the Northeast needed to develop its economy as well as attracted a quantity of experienced agricultural labour. Before the reclamation, the Qing Government invested a lot of start-up funds and equipment in the Northeast to develop economy, and by the power of the state organized people to reclaim vast wilderness which then became fields. Of course, the Han people who braved the journey to the Northeast couldn't enjoy such government subsides. Given the fact that the Bannermen had lived in Beijing for a long time and been used to extravagance and indolence, the reclaimed fields became barren again, and experienced labour was in demand. Although in that period the government made attempts to solve the problem, such as delivering funds, buying servants and transporting convicts to the Northeast, the measures didn't work, but the nice production environment and the demand for labour attracted quite a lot of bankrupt Han people. The emperor was once afraid that "if so, many people are not checked and not stopped from entering the Northeast, they will harm the livelihood of Bannermen", and he adopted restrict measures to stop it. However, the Bannermen took a different attitude towards the Han people who were important in local agriculture, "Rather than refusing Han labour, they recruited a lot of Han people." As a result, the government had to change the policy to bar Han people, applying the strategy of insulation and development, which drew Han people "like throngs of bees". In the 36th year of Qianlong's reign (1771), in Jilin the population was comprised of just "8, 856 newly registered households and 44, 656 adults," with the total number was not more than 53, 500. By the 17th year of Jiaqing's reign (1812), the number increased to 307, 981, quintupling in two decades. In the 19th year of Guangxu's reign (1893), the number surged to 626, 000. In the past 81 years, the population increased by 318, 200, about 40, 000 per year on average. Despite the climax of the Jing Bannermen Reclamation, from the reign of Qianlong to the reign of Daoguang, however, there were only 6, 000 or so households of Bannermen relocated to Jilin from Beijing, Mukden and Rehe in total. If a household had five persons, there would be only 30, 000 people, and most of the additional population were definitely Han people. From that we can see the Jing Bannermen's Reclamation attracted Han people who came to earn their living, with their population dozens of times more than that of Bannermen, making the population of central Northeast soar, which was beneficial to the cultivation of land in that area.

Second, the Jing Bannermen's Reclamation boosted local agriculture. As the area where the Beijing Bannermen stationed was restricted most. Before the Jing Bannermen's Reclamation the area was isolated and had little agricultural production. With the policy of the government, large quantities of peasants moved into the area, and the barren land was quickly cultivated. In the last year of Yongzheng's reign (1735), "4, 908 shang of land in Alcuka and Lalin was cultivated by the Bannermen." In the 45th year of Qianlong's reign (1780), "The land cultivated by the Bannermen increased to 36, 278 shang", which rose by 31, 370 shang in nearly half a century, with the growth rate of 639%. The growth rate was obviously higher than that of other places in Jilin. According to another record, 64, 912 shang 9 mu 6 fen of land was cultivated in Lalin by Bannermen, 98, 640 shang 3 mu in Alcuka and 151, 145 shang 4 mu 6 fen in Shuangchengpu. The total amount of the three places was over 300, 000 shang, with over 200, 000 shang cultivated by Han people in Bodune, which added up to over 500, 000 shang. At the same time, the land owned by Han people was on the increase. Before Han people came here, the area had little land owned by them. Although according to the law of the Qing Government Han refugees didn't have the right to cultivated local land, in reality they "in the name of peasants of the Bannermen cultivated extra land to survive," and Bannermen also "would like to collect rent from Han peasants and serve as camouflage when the government inspect the situation." The combination of Han refugees and land became possible then. In the 18th year of Qianlong's reign (1743), the Jilin government found 16, 744 mu of land cultivated in the name of Bannermen, and the Qing Government asked Jilin General Fusen to "remove the land from the government category and recruit tenant farmers to cultivate it", collecting rent according to the three levels of wealth: rich, middle and poor. *The Chorography of Mukden* published in the 48th year of Qianlong's reign (1783) recorded that in the 46th year (1781) the land cultivated by Han refugees in Jilin was five times more that that in the early years of Qianlong's reign. In the 17th year of Jiaqing's reign (1812), the cultivated land in Jilin was 1, 492, 251 mu, rising to 1, 559, 848 mu in the 25th year of Jiaqing's reign (1820). In mere 8 years 67, 597 mu of land was cultivated, excluding the land which was secretly cultivated by the refugees. To cultivate such vast land, the massive influx of Han people with their advanced agricultural technologies was necessary. Han people changed the extensive methods of cultivation—local people "chose another field at the end of the year and sow when it rains." In contrast, Han people adopted advanced technologies from the inner land such as "letting their land lie fallow" and "rotating crops", which led to a much higher crop yield. In the last year of the reign of Jiaqing, the crop yield in Alcuka and Shuangchengpu was "eight or nine dan per shang in a good year" and "over five or six dan per shang" in a usual year⑤. Afterwards the crops were not only sufficient to meet local demands but were transported to other places around the country. Even today, Lalin, Wuchang, Shuangcheng, Acheng and Hulan are still important areas of grain production in Heilongjiang.

Third, with the growth of population and the development of agriculture, to adapt to life in the Northeast, various workshops related to daily life appeared. "Shaoguo" was the most prominent one. "Shaoguo, a place where alcohol is distilled. If you travel around Manchuria, within hundreds of steps, you will see high walls around. The place is a Shaoguo. The owners of Shaoguo are local rich farmers who gradually form a clan and have their own name." The Northeast abounded with sorghum—the ingredient of prime spirits, and local people were fond of drinking, so the yield of spirits was extremely high in the Northeast. In the 6th year of Tongzhi's reign (1867), Lalin produced 111, 632 jin of spirits by itself, paying taxes of 44.5 liang. According to the statistics by the Alcuka government in the 2nd of Guangxu's reign (1876), "There used to be 130~140 Shaoguo", and in the 18th year of the reign (1892), "40 Shaoguo tickets (A kind of tickets for owners of Shaoguo. They used the tickets to collect ginseng. If they collected more than the ticket allowed, they had to pay taxes for the excess part) were distributed in Alcuka, Lalin, Binzhou and Shuangcheng, with the total taxes of 20, 000 liang of silver ingots. The newly emerging small Shaoguo each paid taxes of 200 liang of silver ingots, but there were no fixed taxes for them." Those Shaoguo were a kind of cottage industries for the sorghum they used were produced by themselves, and they could begin or stop production at any time, which was a kind of small-scale peasant economy. The bonanza of Shaoguo demonstrated that the grain production in the Northeast could meet the needs of foodstuffs and taxes, and it was in abundance. In addition, the Northeast was rich in soya beans and wheat, and villages of different places had oil and flour mill.

Last but not the least, the Jing Bannermen's Reclamation boosted the development of local cities. Generally, it is impossible to expand a city quickly only through the reproduction of the local population, and the entry of massive quantities of immigrants is quite necessary. ① In the Northeast, the arrival of Bannermen and large numbers of refugees turned the wilderness into fertile land and brought out the flourishing scene where "as I stationed in Manchuria for many days, I saw more and more people come here. There were so many vendors and sellers of livestock that they naturally formed a market." ② Villages and tribes were scattered over the area which used to be isolated. If we open a large-scale map of Heilongjiang province, we still see place names such as the Bordered Blue Banner, the Plain Red Banner, the Plain Yellow Banner as well as "Wopeng (shack in Chinese)" or "Wobao with someone's family name as prefix (the meaning is the same as Wopeng,). The place names with "Banner" are areas where Bannermen from Beijing stationed, while those with "Wopeng" or "Wopu" are areas where Han immigrants lived. As time passed, the places where the yamens administered by Bannermen developed into modern cities such as Acheng (Alcuka), Wuchang (Lalin is under the governance of Wuchang) and Shaungcheng (Shangchengpu). With the influence of the above cities, Harbin, the current capital city of Heilongjiang, gradually takes shape and prospers.

(4) In the perspective of culture, the area where the Jing Bannermen stationed

formed a unique culture of their own.

Although the Jing Bannermen's Reclamation was a wave of migration supported by the Qing Government and aimed at solving the livelihood problem of Bannermen from Beijing, it is not a simple migration from Beijing to the Northeast, which involves all walks of life, and culture is a significant element. Literature, arts, customs, habits and folk religions comprise the important contents of the spiritual life of the society of Jing Bannermen in the Northeast. As we know, Chinese culture features the characteristics of different regions and peoples. Therefore, as a kind of embodiment of their culture, when the Bannermen from Beijing entered the Northeast, they formed a new community and brought their own cultural traditions and lifestyles which unconsciously changed the social culture and social lifestyles of the Northeast. It was recorded, "At the beginning of the reclamation, the Bannermen from Beijing, Mukden and Jilin were relocated here. Besides, more and more Han people from areas south of the Shanhai Pass came here. Since Han people and Bannermen came from different areas, they had different customs and habits, but the longer they lived together, the closer they became, and finally marriage between the two peoples was permitted and their cultures combined gradually. The division between the regions of the two peoples vanished."

By looking up in the genealogies reserved until now, we know that most of the ancestors of the Bannermen from Beijing who stationed in the Northeast originated from Xinbin county in Liaoning, Yitong county and Huichun in Jilin. Their ancestors were soldiers and officers of Nurhachi, going to Beijing with emperor Shunzhi. *The Genealogy of the He* in Shuangqiaozi Village in Wuchang recorded, "The grandfather of my grandfather Sandali was a Bannerman of a family of the Plain Red Banner in Beijing, and his family entered the area south of the Shanhai Pass in the reign of Shunzhi, then moving to Xinhuashi Street, north of the Caomao Alley, Wanping county in Shuntian District of Beijing. In the 9th year of Qianlong's reign (1744), his family moved to the Northeast according to the national policy. My grand grandfather Eleqing'e and his son Balantai moved to the old camp in the south of Lalin in Alcuka (or Acheng) in Jilin on 8th February in the lunar calendar, and then they lived in the Second Village of the Plain Red Banner." Under the potential influence of Han culture of the central plains for over one hundred years, the Bannermen from Beijing had been used to the culture of Beijing, and when they moved to the Northeast, they brought their habits that were formed for over one hundred years. For Manchu people who originated from Jilin, Shengjing and Rehe, the Bannermen from Beijing were newcomers who were different from them, and conflicts and disputes were unavoidable between the two groups. A shared sense of honor, experience, value orientation and certain lifestyle and customs all gave the Jing Bannermen in the Northeast a collective consciousness. As time passed by, the collective consciousness was enhanced. The Bannermen from Beijing, who made a large organic social group, had emotional and psychological identification with each other. Additionally, living and laboring with local Manchu people and

Han people, the Bannermen from Beijing combined Beijing culture and local culture, culturologically turning urban culture into rural culture which was different from local Manchu culture—the Jing Bannermen's culture with the characteristics of Beijing.

So far, the language used by people who live in the region where Jing Bannermen used to live still has a heavy Beijing accent of "ér" which obviously differs from the colloquial Chinese used by Manchu people who originate from the Northeast. For example, they call "yí (aunt)" as "yí er", "huā" as "huā er". Furthermore, some words from the Manchu language remain, e. g. the rag is called as "zhǎn bù", the wall as "pái chà", the shirt as "hàn tǎ", the singlet as "dōu dōu", the marsh as "chí táng", the grassland as "tǎ tóu", and some senior people call their father as "à ma" and mother as "é niáng". Some names of places are still Manchu: in the Shuoduoku Mountain "shuò duō kù" means "flat" in Manchu; Lalin (lā lín) means "refreshing" in Manchu; the Mole'en River (mò lè ēn hé) is today's Muniu River (mǔ niú means the bull in Chinese, and hé means the river).

In terms of customs, the Jing Bannermen paid special attention to what they used in daily life. Women of Bannermen from Beijing were used to wearing veils and washing and starching quilts and cotton-padded mattresses. The traditional Manchu food remained in their diet. Instead of soya bean paste, they preferred pan paste, which is a kind of fermented paste made of soya beans and salt. They also liked boiled pork, Chinese black pudding made of pigs' blood and their small intestines, steamed sticky bean buns, polished glutinous rice cakes, steamed polished glutinous rice rolls with cooked soya bean powder, dumplings, hot pots and fermented soya bean milk (sour tea), and every meal must be served with four dishes of different pickles. Making dumplings in the Spring Festival was one of their customs. Most Manchu people began to make dumplings half a month before the Spring Festival. They would invite several neighbors to sit on the southern side and the northern side of their kang (a heatable brick bed), staying up to make a large jar or a cabinet of dumplings made of over one hundred jin of flour, which they would eat until the 2nd of the 2nd lunar month. As for residential structure, even the newly built house had its chimney erected outside itself. In the Spring Festival, on the New Year's Eve (eve before the festival) all the family worshiped their ancestors by burning incense, laying offerings on the altar and taking turns kowtowing, kneeling and bowing. The memorial tablet of their ancestors hangs on the upper part of the western wall. Beside the tablets was the Bag of Foduo Mama (fó duō in Chinese, Foduo Mama is a goddess in Shamanism who oversees birth and reproduction, similar to Goddess of Descendants or zǐ sūn niáng niáng in Taoism). The wall was also hung with portraits of their ancestors which were called as "Lao Ying (Lao, means old in Chinese, and Ying means image in Chinese)" by local people. Their life was also colourful in culture and sports. In the 1st month in the lunar calendar, some old women liked to play "gachuha (the patella of an animal)", dance the yang'ge, play the song-and-dance duet or listen to the drum ballad. However, as time passed by, those customs are vanishing.

Their literature left abundant heritage. Among the Bannermen from Beijing, many folk works were passed from one person to another. Their literature was sorted into three kinds in form: legends, stories and ballads. The content of their literature was related to Manchu folk religion, worship, customs, fashion, taboos, laboring and seasons. The folk literature was created and handed down by the public. Although most of it was immature in an artistic way, it did have the functions of education and entertainment, especially some ballads which not only vividly depicted the psychology and the history of the Manchu people, but also had fresh and lively wording. The following two examples are typical:

The Ballad of Rocking the Baby in Arms

Rock and rock,
Arms like a wok.
Papa goes there,
Brings back red headgear.
Sleep, sleep, my little dear.
Pat and pat,
Left to right.
Mama sews with care,
A pair of boots to wear.
Sleep, sleep, my little dear.

* *

Gachuha, Four Aspects

Our ancestor Nurhachi no one forgets.
Nurhachi, a hero,
Wins the war by his horse and arrow.
Gachuha, all colours.
Copper coins, strung on threads,
Thrown away above heads,
Let's see who turns Gachuha best.

Most of those ballads were unintentionally created by Manchu women and children while they were laboring, studying or playing. They are the embodiment of the wisdom of the common people in the form of colloquial literature, vividly and profoundly demonstrating Manchu culture and the personalities of Manchu people, which are of the essence to Manchu people's spiritual life.

In addition, the Bannermen still believed in Shamanism, a primitive religion whose content was worshiping nature, the creator of the universe and ancestors, which was popular in northern China. Since the Bannermen living in Beijing for over one hundred years, they frequently communicated with Han people and Mongolian people in economy and culture, the religious cultures where Han people and Mongolian people lived directly or indirectly influenced Manchu religious structure. The service of Shamanism is worshiping gods of nature and dancing to worship totem. It was a complex social and cultural phenomenon as well as a common cultural activity in the community of Bannermen. The purpose of it is to remedy diseases, expel evil spirits and avoid disasters. In fact, the activity of dancing to worship gods was beyond superstition of inviting gods or expelling evil spirits and became a mass cultural activity with skills of artistic performance. From the late years of the Qing Dynasty to the Republic of China, the activity was extremely popular in the area where the Bannermen lived. According to some senior people's memories, "If you walk around the area where the Bannermen lived in the evening, you will hear the sound of drums in every village." The sound of drums accompanied the dance to worship gods, so we can see it was quite common at that time.

The livelihood problem of the Eight Banners was an abnormal aspect of the society in the Qing Dynasty. It upset the Qing Government for a long time. What's worse, it became a burden to the whole society. During the reigns of Kangxi and Yongzheng, despite a lot of methods, the government didn't solve the problem that Bannermen didn't labour to earn their living. The idea of the Jing Bannermen's Reclamation, the proposal of the policy of the Jing Bannermen's Reclamation and the application of the policy showed the purpose of the emperor was to solve the problem through restoring the old system of the combination of farming and soldiering. However, the development of history won't be commanded by any ruler. The environmental differences between Beijing and the Northeast, Bannermen's tradition of worshiping martial merits instead of farming, Bannermen's tendency to follow Han people in taking the imperial examination to become civil servants as well as the lumpish management system and the forcible restrictions on production by the government resulted in the failure of solving the problem through the policy.

After that we can't help wondering why the policy of the Jing Bannermen's Reclamation was applied just three times from the reign of Kangxi to the end of the Qing Government? Or didn't the Jing Bannermen have any livelihood difficulty in other periods? To answer these questions, we need to know the social background of the three waves of the Jing Bannermen's Reclamation. The three waves all during the time when the national financial situation was not good, which proved that the policy seemed pro-Bannerman but in fact in the interest of the emperor. It was the Bannermen from lower social strata who were relocated to the Northeast to reclaim land. Although some scholars researched and thought that "the first wave of the Bannermen coming to Lalin were descendants of senior officials of the Qing Government. Their genealogies recorded the details. For example, the ancestors of the Zhaos in Yingchengzi or other counties and towns had the surname of Aisin Gioro which was the surname of the royal family; the ancestors of the He in Hongqigujiazi Village, Shuangqiaozihanxiang Village and Shiren Village were descendants of the Prime Minister Heseri Sonin and his son the Grand Secretary Heseri Songgotu; the Guans who had a big family in Yingchengzi Manchu Village in Nantu Village were descendants of the hero for the foundation of Hantai, the Qing Dynasty, Nanzheng general and minister of personnel." In addition, there were descendants of Fusheng, Ertai and E'yidu. Those scholars concluded, "It was obvious that Emperor Qianlong was determined to develop the Northeast by the policy, so he ordered the relatives of the royal family and senior officials to take the lead in reclamation in Lalin, and the Bannermen who went there became pioneers of developing the area." However, with some knowledge of the history of the Qing Dynasty, the so-called relatives of the royal family and senior officials had become culprits in the reign of Qianlong. Therefore, their descendants wouldn't live a better life than they did. Furthermore, in that period, the method of choosing people was dividing social classes within the Eight Banners without changing the superior stratum of Manchu people. In other words, the policy applied to the Bannermen by the Qing Government was maintaining the policy of supporting Manchu people but dividing their social classes. It is quite normal for the emperor to sacrifice the interests of some Manchu people to secure his governance. Nevertheless, the change from supporting all the Manchu people to excluding the lower classes foretold that the Qing Dynasty was bound to fail in the application of the policy of supporting Manchu people by imperial grace on the basis of lineage.

Besides, if we analyze the three waves of the Jing Bannermen's Reclamation in a comprehensive way, we will find that the results of the policy went from bad to worse, whether in the number of Bannermen or the level of improving their life, which was in line with the vicissitudes of the Qing Dynasty. Therefore, the three waves of the policy reflect the fall of the dynasty.

If we research the policy in the perspective of history without considering other elements, however, the policy is historically positive because the opportunity to farm was the only practical and feasible method to solve the livelihood problem of the Bannermen. Evidence also proved that quite a few Bannermen from Beijing and their descendants stayed in the Northeast, earning their living through labour. They "did farming by themselves" or "hired hands", and "all of them worked and lived in peace." The change of their life influenced those who lived in Beijing, "The idle Bannermen in Beijing all knew the people in Shuangchengpu lived a happy life, and more and more Bannermen in Beijing were willing to move there." By the reign of Tongzhi, "The Bannermen who moved to Shuangchengpu and Lalin now have their descendants and live happily." From what mentioned above, Lalin and other places where the Bannermen were relocated relieved the dilemma of some Bannermen and brought them a new life of self-support by farming. So far, the villages of the Eight Banners formed hundreds of years ago are still flourishing. Other peoples also moved in during the development, but the main part of the population is still the Manchu people. In a word, the Jing Bannermen's Reclamation led to the fast development of the area, reconnected the Manchu people and the Han people, and promoted the rapport between the two peoples and the exchanges of the two cultures, which accelerated the form of a new type of society.

Chapter 2
The Tradition and Innovation of Inland Immigrants

2.1 | The Jing Bannermen's Reclamation Policy and the Social Issues of Immigrants in Heilongjiang

2.1.1 Review of Academic History

The Jing Banner is a term unique to the Qing army after its entry to Shanhai Pass. After the Qing Dynasty took the central plains of China, the officers and soldiers of the Eight Banners were stationed in the capital and other parts of the country. Those who stationed in the capital were called "Jingshi Banner" or "Zhujing Banner", abbreviated as "Jing Banner" ("Jing" means Qing's capital "Beijing"), and eight banners stationed in other places were called "Eight Banners of Garrison". Centred on the imperial city, the Jing Banner was stationed in the following directions. The Bordered Yellow Banner was placed in the Andingmen, and the Yellow Banner was placed in the Deshengmen. They were both in the north. The White Banner was placed in the Dongzhimen, and the Bordered White Banner was placed in the Chaoyangmen. They were both in the east. The Red Bannner was placed in the Xizhimen, and the Bordered Red Banner was placed in the Fucheng Gate. They were both in the west. The Blue Banner was placed in the Chongwenmen, while the Bordered Blue Banner was placed in the Xuanwumen. They were both in the south. The eight banners in the capital (Jing Banner) had cavalry, vanguard, guard, infantry, Jian-Rui, Shenji and other battalions. And the upper three banners of Manchurian and Mongolian were selected to serve as the bodyguard troops for the forbidden city (like the division of the Praetorian guard). The Qing Government had been practising a policy of grace and support for the soldiers of the eight banners, which were regarded as the foundation of the country, but due to the multiplication of the eight banners, especially the Jing banners, the Qing Court had been overwhelmed since the middle of the Kangxi period and the livelihood of the banners had become a problem. Although measures were taken to alleviate this conflict, such as redeeming the banner lands, offering silver rewards, retiring the Han army from the banners, and increasing the number of troops to be raised, the results were not very satisfactory. In the early years of

Qianlong era, some insightful officers in the government began to discuss how to solve this problem fundamentally by making the Jing Bannermen work for their living. The idea of moving the Jing Banner back to reclaim the land came about at the right time. During the Qianlong era, the Jing Banner began to return to Lalin and Alachuka, then returned to the Shuangchengpu during the Jiaqing and Daoguang eras, and during the Guangxu era, they continued to return to Hulan. It had been lasted for more than 100 years through the ruling of the six emperors.

On the question of the Jing Banner's returning to the northeast for settlement in the Qing Dynasty, some pioneering discussions had been made in the works and articles before the founding of the People's Republic of China. The most representative results are the relevant chapters in *The History of the Development of Manchuria* by the Japanese scholar Inaba Iwakichi. Although there are many mistakes in it, it still provides many valuable historical materials and research clues for later studies. Yoshiyuki Chouto's book *A Study on the Upper Land Policy of Manchuria in the Qing Dynasty* also specifically describes the beginning and end of the settlement of the Jing Banner in Lalin during the Qianlong Period in the relevant chapters about Jilin Banner land. The materials are all taken from *The Records of the Qing Dynasty* and *The Eight Banners General Annals*, which are more systematic and detailed, as well as more accurate. In addition, Gao Yan's *The Jing Banner's Settlement in Manchuria* draws much of its material from *Shilu* and *Holy Hadith of the Qing Dynasty*. Jiro Yonekura's *The Settlement of Northern Manchuria in the Qing Dynasty—Focusing on the Preliminary Report on the Settlement of Shuangchengpu* was distinctively written on the basis of field investigation. However, in the context of the time, its main intention was to create public opinion in conjunction with the Japanese invasion of northeast China, and even to provide information and materials.

In the period of the Republic of China, Liu Xuanmin wrote an article on the very subject, "The Beginning and End of the Settlement of the Jing Banner in the Three Northeastern Provinces", published in *Yugong*, Vol. 6, No.3, 4 (Part 1) in October 1936. However, this article contained few original ideas of its own, and in many places transcribed the views and opinions of Inaba Iwakichi in whole paragraphs without attribution.

After the founding of the People's Republic of China, especially since the 1980s, many scholars in China mainland have published some articles on this issue one after another. The main one is the typescript of Ding Yizhuang's master's thesis, "*The Beginning and End of the Qing Dynasty's Relocation to the Northeast for Settlement*" (1985), which is now stored in the Library of Minzu University of China. It can be said that it has been the most detailed discussion on the question of the Jing Banner's returning for settlement up till now, and it also has a strong influence on the writing of this book. In addition to official documents, this paper also used some archival materials, not only to examine the Jing Banner's return in various eras of the Qing Dynasty, but also to describe the life of the Jing Banner in the returned settlements area and the distribution of land. It opened up the research field of this subject and made people have a more comprehensive understanding of the Jing Banner's return in the Qing Dynasty. However, in the following 20 years, there has been no breakthrough in the research on this issue. Although many articles have been published, the content is almost the same without adding valuable new materials and new content. Ding Yizhuang rewrote "On the Cultivation of Shuangchengpu of the Jing Banner in the Middle Qing Dynasty", published in *Northern Cultural Relics*, No.1, 1987 and *A Brief Report on the Settlement of the Banner People in northeast China in the Middle Period of Qianlong Dynasty*, published in *Chinese National History and Culture* based on his master's thesis. What's more, Cui Yong's master's thesis in Song History Research Center of Hebei University *on the Settlement of Beijing Banner in northeast China in The Qing Dynasty* (1989) can be said to be an article without a word from the author's own views. It's almost a copy of Ding Yizhuang's master's thesis. In addition, Wang Geisheng's "*The Investigation of the Jing Banner Sura's Immigrant*" published in *The Annals of History*, No.4, 1985, Shifang's "*The Jing Banner's Migration in the Middle Qing Dynasty and Han's Migration to northeast China and Its Social Significance*" published in *Population Journal*, No.4, 1987. Zhao Aping's "*Lalin Development History Survey*" published in *Heilongjiang Ethnic Series* No.2, 1988, Chen Bolin's "*Heilongjiang Manchu Immigration Banner Construction Overview*" published in *Heilongjiang Ethnic Series* No.2, 1990, Diao Shuren's "*On the Settlement of Shuangchengpu and Bodune during Jiadao Period—Also on the Development of Jilin by the Refugees*" published in *The Journal Of Qing History Research*, No.3, 1990, and "*On the Migration of the Jing Banner Sula during the Qianlong Period*" in *The Journal of Northern Cultural Relics*, No.2, 1994, Zhao Qichong's "*Argumentation on the Reclamation of the Jing Banner*" published in *Heilongjiang Province Social Science*, 1993 (3), Zhang Lizhen's "The Jing Banner's Reclamation and Its Social Transformation" published in *Journal of Liaoning University* (Zhe Club version) in 1995, No.4. Most of the following articles are an overview of the general outline of the issue, which have few details. The materials used are also relatively simple, and most of them are official documents.

In addition, there were He Rongwei's "*The Administrative System of the Double Castle Area in the Qing Dynasty*" published in *The Research on Manchu* No.1, 1992, Zhao Liyan's "*Brief Introduction of the Qing Dynasty Double Castle Area Compiles Check Baojia*" published in *The Research on Manchu* No.3, 2000, Wei Kewei's "*The Early Development of Fujun and Jilin*" published in *The Journal of Eastern Region* No.1 2000, and He Rongwei and Zhao Liyan's "*The Setting of The Eight Banners in the Double Castles of Qing Dynasty*" published in *Lantai World* in the second issue of 2001. The above articles were written specifically for the reclamation to the Shuangchengpu of The Jing Banner.

The contributions of the above fruits results are mainly reflected in two aspects: first, it's an overview of the process of the Jing Banner's reclamation in the northeast; second, it analyzed the reasons and influence of the Qing Government's reclamation to northeast China. But due to the lack of Chinese literature and the lagging of the archives in Manchu language preserved in the literature translation, sorting, previous research on some basic questions of the Jing Banner's reclamation doesn't really make sense. The research on the setting of the Jing Banner's management organization, the Jing Banner's reclamation regions of rural social organizations and rural infrastructure construction, as well as their life security system was still to be deepened.

In recent years, Li Jianhui published "*Tracing the 'Beijing Youth' 260 Years Ago: A Preliminary Exploration of the Manchu Jing Banner Culture of Wuchang Lalin, Heilongjiang*" in the 10th issue of *China National Newspaper* in 2002. Cui Guangbin and Wang Yulang published *Lalin Town the Jing Banner Cultural Resources in Need of Protection* in *The China Construction News* on December 17th, 2002, and Yu Zidong published "*On the Protection and Development of The Culture of Alchuka the Jing Banner in Lalin Alchuka*" on *Heilongjiang Nationalities Series*, No.2, 2003. Wang Jing's "*Study on the Cultural Tourism Development of Manchu the Jing Banner*" was published in *China Nationalities Daily* on March 4th, 2003, and "*The Tourism Development Value of the Jing Banner Culture*" was published in *China Nationalities Daily* on October 21st, 2003. Yin Hongfeng published "*The Historical Value of the Jing Banner Culture and The Conception of Redevelopment*" in *No.2 Heilongjiang Historical Records*, 2007, etc. In addition, Wang Jing also published a monograph *Lalin Alchuka the Jing Banner Culture* based on field investigation (Harbin Publishing House, 2001).

The contribution of the above research fruits is to discuss the tourism development value of the Jing Banner's culture and Lalin and Acheng reclamation areas, but the discussion of the tourism development value of the Jing Banner's culture in Shuangcheng and Hulan is obviously not detailed enough, and the tourism with the Jing Banner cultural resources as the main content, whether the cultural concept of the main body of tourism culture, or the cultural connotation of the tourism culture object, or the cultural management of the tourism culture intermediary, all have a companion relationship with the history of the Jing Banner's reclamation, all of which is not enough in the Jing Banner cultural research.

To sum up, there are still many gaps in the research on the reclamation of the Jing Banner in the academic circle, and there is room for further study. More importantly, there is no academic monograph of historical value on the reclamation of the Jing Banner.

It is helpful for us to have a thorough understanding of the social nature and structure of Heilongjiang immigrants in different periods and their influence on the overall social development to study the problems of the Jing Banner's reclamation, especially the rural administrative system, rural land management system and rural social security system of the Qing Government in the reclamation area.

The historical enlightenment of "the Jing Banner's Reclamation" is that in a society of peaceful development, when the surplus population is concentrated in the cities without jobs, transferring the surplus labor force to the sparsely populated border areas can be regarded as a way to solve their livelihood. This leads us to observe that contemporary Chinese society, which is also faced with a similar social problem of more than 200 years ago: the population expansion in big cities and the poor livelihood of some people have become an important factor of social instability. Although we cannot copy the Qing Dynasty "return to the village" practice, but its solution to the problem and the direction of efforts are worth learning. In addition, the Jing Banner, who originated from the northeast wilderness and underwent the baptism of Han culture in the Central Plains for hundreds of years, returned to the Northeast and combined with the local indigenous culture to form a unique Jing Banner's culture. At present, Heilongjiang province is taking advantage of the cultural and historical advantages of the Jing Banner's reclamation area to vigorously develop the tourism resources of the Jing Banner culture. Under this circumstance, it is of great theoretical significance and application value to reproduce the historical appearance of the Jing Banner Reclamation area by using the nearly 100,000 characters of Manchu archives excavated for the first time.

All in all, the research on the question of the reclamation of the Jing Banner in the Qing Dynasty is of great value and significance, it is worthy of special and in-depth research.

2.1.2 Difficulties Encountered in Topic Selection

There are three major obstacles in studying the reclamation of the Jing Banner in the Qing Dynasty. The first problem is historical problem. It is not exaggerating to use "numerous" to describe the historical data in the Qing Dynasty. Emperors in the Qing Dynasty all paid great attention to the preservation of historical archives, and they left a lot of original archives. China's first historical Archive keeps many original files, and various official documents, local Chronicles, notes and so on are hard to count. The original records about the Jing Banner's reclamation are buried in a myriad of files and books. To search and verify the relevant historical materials in the files and books in the limited time will be a major problem in our research. What is more difficult is that most of the questions about the return of the Jing Banner in the Qianlong Dynasty are recorded in Manchu. How to accurately and historically translate the files in Manchu which have been preserved and never been used by predecessors is one of the many difficulties in this research. At the same time, this is also the primary cause for the delay in in-depth research on this issue in the past.

Second, there are very limited relevant research results and clues for reference, and many contents cannot be prompted or referred to. Although there are a lot of research results mentioned above, these articles have not carried out a detailed study on this issue due to limited material, which is not very useful for the writing of this book.

Third, the theoretical issues. The scope of the issues to be discussed in this book is relatively narrow, so how to improve its theorical base and expand the study has become another difficulty of this research.

However, these obstacles can be solved with the persistent efforts of the researchers.

2.1.3 Literature and Research Methods

In the use of historical materials, this study first takes the official archives of the Qing Dynasty as the main material. The archives preserve many complete and detailed materials about the previous reclamation of the Jing Banner, many of which can be used as the supplement and evidence of the official history, as one of the main sources of materials cited in this study. Due to the huge volumes of archives and limited time, I could not read them all, and only part of the Manchu files in China's First historical Archives were allowed to be translated, so there must be some omissions in the archives. The archival materials for this research mainly include: The first Historical Archives of China in the Qing Dynasty *Grand Council of Manchu and Chinese Records*, the Chinese part mainly refer to the agricultural archives of Qianlong, Jiaqing and Daoguang dynasties, and the Manchu part mainly composed of some translated archives of the settlement in Lalin Alechuka during Qianlong dynasty. This part of the archive is only quoted in Ding Yizhuang's master's thesis, "*The Whole Story of Jing Banner's Moving to the Northeast and Settlement in the Qing Dynasty*", which is not seen in other articles. It can be regarded as my newly unearthed historical materials and is also one of the most important materials in this paper. *Financial Papers and Manuscripts* collected by The First Historical Archive of China mainly referred to the land tax, disaster relief and reward of silver for weddings and funerals of Jing Banner after it moved to northeast China. The catalog in China's first historical archives' collection of the Qing Dynasty *Eight Banners' Government Fil* is relatively rough, only refer to the register of the Jing Banner in Shuangchengpu during Guangxu. *The Qing Dynasty Yamun Files of Deputy Dutong in Ningguta District, Jilin Province*, collected by the First Historical Archives of China, mainly refers to the livelihood and settlement of the banners in the Shuangchengpu district from the 1st year to the 10th year of Daoguang's reign (1821—1830).

The Qing Dynasty's *Yamun files of Deputy Dutong Yamun files in Alechuka Region, Jilin Province* in Heilongjiang Province Library is also collected in China's first historical archives, but I mainly check the archives of Heilongjiang Province library. However, due to historical reasons, there are only Tongzhi and Guangxu's archives in this file, which is really a pity.

The archives of Liaoning Province collected the *Files of Shuangchengpu Governor Yamun*, which were formed from the 30th year of Daoguang to the 13th year of the Republic of China (1850—1924). Most of the case files ranging from the 20th of Jiaqing's reign (1815) to the end of Xianfeng's reign were destroyed in the 1st lunar month of the 5th year of Tongzhi's reign (1866) when the city was under siege in the "Mashazi" rebellion. Due to the changes of the times, there were not many case files during the time of the Republic of China. The merit of this volume, which is mainly from the Tongzhi and Guangxu's reigns, lies in its detailed account of the historical process from the rise to the decline of the local set-up of the cantonment at Shuangchengpu in the Qing Dynasty and the subsequent living conditions of the banners who moved to the cantonment at Shuangchengpu, Shengjing and Jilin.

And there are some published archives, such as *Imperial Edict Files of Qianlong, Imperial Edict Files of Jiaqing and Daoguang, Imperial Edict Files of Xianfeng and Tongzhi, Imperial Edict Files of Guangxu, Xuantong, Bordered Red Banner Profiles of Yongzheng and Qianlong*, Translation and Compilation of *Manchu Files of Three Deputy Dutong Yamun in Qing Dynasty*, Translation and Compilation of *Manchu and Han's Files of Three Deputy Dutong Yamun in Qing Dynasty, Selected Chinese Archives of Northeast Acheng in Qing Dynasty, Selected Historical Archives of Heilongjiang in the Qing Dynasty* (the first year to the 7th year of the Guangxu's reign), *Selected Historical Archives of Heilongjiang in the Qing Dynasty* (the 8th year to the 15th year of the Guangxu's reign), etc. Through these archives, a great deal of original relevant material can be obtained.

In addition, the "*Lalin Alechuke Jing Banner's Original Case*" in *Lalin Alechuke Jing Banner's Culture* as the form of appendix is also the archives material of considerable value. It is a collection of archives transcribing and collating about the relocation of the Jing Banner to Lalin and the settlement of the Acheng area, including two letters of the 8th year (1743) and 13th year (1748) of the Emperor Qianlong, one letter of the Imperial Court to Jilin General in the 17th year (1812) of the Emperor Jiaqing, and one message of the Ministry of Revenue. And from the 9th year of Qianlong (1744) to the 24th year (1759), Zhang Tingyu, the Head Minister of Grand Council, and others wrote 6 documents, a total of 10 documents from the Imperial Court. According to the Qing Dynasty archives management convention, this file should be stored in Jilin General Yamun or Alechuka Lieutenant General Yamun. But up to now, no such file has been found in the archives of General Yamun in Jilin, and *The Jilin Unofficial Documentary* compiled by Sa Yinge in the 7th year of Daoguang (1827) has not been quoted. *Jilin General Annals*, written during the Guangxu's reign, is incomplete, although it does cite some of the historical material from *The Original Case*. Therefore, this file has the function of verifying and filling history. The archive, which was discovered in 2000 and remains unused, is of great historical value.

The second is official documents. All the previous articles on the settlement of the Jing Banner are based on *The Records of the Qing Dynasty*. The outline of the reclamation of the Jing banner can be drawn from the imperial edict contained in the *Records*, especially in the four dynasties of Gaozong, Renzong, Xuanzong and Dezong.

The third is local Chronicles. *General Annals of the Eight Banners, The First Episode of General Annals of the Eight Banners, General Annals of Shengjing, General Annals of Jilin, Jilin Outer Chronicle, Annals of Hulanfu, Annals of*

Shuangchengxian, Official Documents of Binzhoufu, Local chronicle of Alechuka, Annals of Achengxian, Acheng Topography, Annals of Wuchangxian, etc. These local chronicles of different periods and different natures recorded the relevant historical materials of the Jing Banner' s reclamation.

Finally, notes and other historical materials. For example, *Daily Retinue Record of the East Tour, the Record of Shiquyu, Records of Shengwu* and *A Brief Introduction to Heilongjiang (6th edition)* were used to supplement the missing materials in archives, official documents and local chronicles.

In addition, it is important to note *Shuangchengpu' Tuntian Summary* by Wang Lvtai. The book recorded the specific measures of the Shuangchengpu' s settlement in 10 years from the 19th year of Jiaqing (1814) to the 6th lunar month of the 3rd year of Daoguang's reign (1823). No matter the crucial events or minute particulars, all of them were collected and recorded, reflecting the situation of Shuangchengpu in detail, especially in the early period of settlement, namely the scene of the three thousand banners (from Jilin, Shengjing) developing Shuangchengpu. This is the main source of material for the Shuangchengpu' settlement.

However, in fact, all kinds of historical materials are just like the vast ocean, and it takes a lot of time to collect, sort out and apply. Due to the lack of academic ability, regrets are inevitable. Therefore, this study can only discuss the problems reflected by the collected materials.

To carry out this research, there are three basic methods: the first is the textual research and collection of historical materials. Without historical materials, it is difficult to conduct historical research. Without a full grasp of historical materials, and without textual research and screening of important and key historical materials, it is impossible to make correct analysis and judgment on historical facts. Therefore, the primary and frequently used method to carry out this research is to examine and collect historical data. Second, case studies. In this book, the typical events and special phenomena occurred in the reclamation of the Jing Banner are analyzed by case study to clarify the truth. It also analyzes its particularity, representativeness, and reveals some characteristics of it. The third is the analysis, demonstration and exposition of the combination of history and theory. On the basis of full possession of first-hand materials, a large number of comparative analyses ranging from one to the other, from the outside to the inside, eliminating the false and reserving the true, getting rid of clutter and keeping the beauty, thus analyzing the reasons for the failure and the objective effects of the reclamation of the Jing Banner in Qing Dynasty. In addition, this study will use the immigration social security theory to analyze the Qing Government's social security of the Jing Banner, using the principles and methods of population migration to analyze the psychology of the reclamation of the Jing Banner, the reasons for the failure of reclamation to the northeast and so on.

Through the research of this topic, the author hopes to show the whole system of the reclamation of the Jing Banner, further excavate the existing study of the reclamation of the Jing Banner in Qing Dynasty, correct some mistakes in previous studies, explore areas where no one has stepped in before, add new content, so as to comprehensively and systematically reveals the outline of the return of the Jing Banner in the Qing Dynasty.

2.2 | Re-exploration for the Livelihood of the Eight Banners

After entering the Shanhai Pass, the Qing Government adopted the policy of welfare for the banners. However, with the increase of the population and the corruption of the banners, the livelihood of the Eight Banners became a burden to the court and the society. For this reason, the Qing Government, from the Kangxi Period to the Qianlong Period, spent a lot of money and adopted a number of measures, such as the Han army retired from the banners, anyone whose family name was not on the original list of the Eight Banners Clan became civilian, the establishment of the nine squares system of land ownership, silver rewarding, the redemption of the banners' residence, the establishment of the system of raising soldiers and so on, which were in order to solve and maintain this system. However, they all got little effect. In the early years of Qianlong, some men of insight in the government began to put forward the idea of moving the idle Jing Bannermen to the Northeast, and then put it into practice until the end of the Qing Dynasty. Although this policy failed to fully realize the original purpose of the ruler, quite a few of the children of the Jing Banner did stay in the reclamation settlements.

2.2.1

When the Manchurians, who were backward in culture and relatively small in number, entered the Central Plains, they tried to maintain the rule of the Qing Dynasty with the force of the whole nation, and stipulated that the soldiers of the Eight Banners should all be professional soldiers. At the same time, measures should be taken in politics, economy, law and other aspects to establish and maintain the superior social status of the banner people, so as to strengthen the cohesion of the Manchu and the whole banner people society.

Politically, Manchuria had a dominant position in political power, in the government, Manchu got the principal position and gave the order, and the seal belonged to the Manchus, and they drew a fixed quota as Manchu vacancy. Compared with the size of the Manchu population, it is obvious that Manchu was given special priority over other ethnic groups. On the one hand, it could create more opportunities for the banners to enter the official post. On the other hand, it also ensured that the banners had a legal dominant position in the political power.

Economically, to ensure the stability and high combat efficiency of the Eight Banners' army, the Qing Government prohibited the banners from engaging in agriculture, industry and commerce. Being a soldier became the only legitimate occupation for the banners, and all their household needs were provided by the state.

In addition, distribution system of the land、food and money were successively established.

From the 1st year (1644) to the 4th year of Shunzhi's reign (1647), the Qing Government forcibly occupied civilian land within hundreds of kilometers around Beijing for three times and distributed the enclosed land within the Eight Banners according to grades. In addition, different amounts of rations and silver were distributed according to the ranks of the Eight Banners soldiers, commonly known as "Qian Liang". This includes monthly silver as salary and quarterly rations of rice, which was called "Zuo Liang". In the wartime, there was another "Xing Liang": garrison officers and soldiers in case of business trips, weddings or funerals could borrow silver. In addition, to reduce the economic burden on the soldiers of the Eight Banners, the Qing Government stipulated that in addition to military service, all the banners need not to do corvee, to pay grain and cloth.

In law, banners enjoyed different legal privileges from civilians. "Every banner who commits a crime will be punished with the whipping rod instead of flog and will not be exiled and will wear chains separately." Unlike the Han people, when they commit a crime: those who should be flogged should be flogged, and those who should be confined to the army should be confined to the army.

However, in order to maintain the dignity of the banners and consolidate the Eight Banners system, various restrictions were also imposed on the banner, such as forbidding the exchange of possession, marriage and living together, forbidding the banners from going out for a long distance, engaging in other business such as industry and commerce, acting, and borrowing money from others.

Ought to say, to safeguard such noble status, the Qing Government has formulated a series of regulations system. At a time when the world was unsettled and the regime was unstable, and when strong force was still needed to consolidate the new regime, it did help to establish the self-esteem and self-confidence of the Banner people, which contribute to the enhancement of narrow national consciousness. However, with the war ended and the development of society, the privileges and bondage enjoyed by the banners increasingly constituted a huge obstacle to the further development of the banners, especially the Manchurian banners.

2.2.2

If the financial resources of the state allowed, the Qing Government could still carry out these measures of "supporting" the banners. However, when the state financial resources were limited and the population of banners kept increasing, the livelihood of the Eight Banners became a burden to the court and the society gradually.

As early as in the middle of Kangxi Period, the livelihood of some banners in the capital city was in trouble, the most direct reason was the increase of population and the extravagance and corruption of the banners.

When it comes to the livelihood of the Eight Banners, population is a factor that must be listed in the decrees and official documents of the Qing Dynasty, which is called "breeding and multiplication". After the establishment of the Qing Dynasty, especially after the end of the "Sanfan" war in the 20th year of Kangxi's reign (1681), the population of the Eight Banners grew rapidly after decades of rest and relaxation. According to the official statistics of the Qing Dynasty, the number of men in the Eight Banners increased from 346,931 in the 5th year of Shunzhi (1648) to 696,681 in the 60th year of Kangxi (1721). In more than 70 years, the number of people in the Eight Banners had more than doubled. For the banners, only when they were on military duty could they receive a fixed ration of food and pay. However, there was a quota of soldiers. Although the Qing Government had adopted the way of expanding the number of soldiers to absorb part of the increase population, it still could not solve the problem. With the increase of the banner's population, the number of idle people was increasing too, which was bound to increase the difficulties of family livelihood.

The extravagance and corruption of the banners was another important reason for the livelihood problems of the Eight Banners. Emperor Yongzheng once criticized the Eight Banners: "They are accustomed to living in peace, especially luxury. Furniture, clothes, drink, food were all extravagant and they competed with each other in this lifestyle. They wondered in opera house and casinos, drinking, gambling in place of entertainment." To maintain such a luxurious life, it was necessary to have enough sources of living. However, bannermen's income was fixed, and it was stipulated that their rated grain and rice were distributed by the Eight Banners on a quarterly basis. The purpose of the regular ration system was to support the basic life of banners and their family members and ensure that they do not suffer from hunger. But as a matter of fact, from the middle period of Kangxi, most of the banners sold their grain and rice as soon as they got it. Not only that, but many of the banners were also exploited by usury, the banners borrowed with the unexpired soldiers' salary as collateral, which was called "usury" at that time. This kind of usury asks for interest rate of 50% or 60%. This kind of usury exploitation will inevitably make a part of the banner soldiers bankrupt and suffer from heavy debt.

In order to temporarily relieve the financial pressure, the impoverished banners had to sell their only property—their land. This directly leads to the exhaustion of the income from the land and the loss of a fixed source of living. At the beginning of the Qing Dynasty, the soldiers of the Eight Banners generally set up farms to recruit civilians to cultivate the land they acquired, and they received rent, so that "a plot of land may support banners and civilians together sufficiently and peacefully". The profits from the land were sufficient to support the welfare system. After the middle period of the reign of Emperor Kangxi, the population of the Eight Banners increased rapidly, but the increase of soldiers' salaries was limited. Many banners felt it was difficult to support the increased population with their original income. When it was difficult to make ends meet, they often "sold more farmland and houses under their names to others". The Qing laws stipulated that banner land was generally only allowed to be traded within the original banner and only in exceptional circumstances was it allowed to be sold to other banners, while the trade out of whole banners system was strictly prohibited. However, banners traded land with other people covertly was not rare. As a result, the land owned by the banner people was transferred to the Han people gradually. In the early years of Qianlong, "half of the banner land within 250 kilometers of Beijing belonged to Han people". Quite a number of middle and lower-level banner people have fallen into the situation of "no money and food, no property, and no means of subsistence". This situation shows that the livelihood of banners has deteriorated to an extremely serious level.

2.2.3

The increasingly serious livelihood problem of the Eight Banners not only made the Eight Banners system appear crisis, but also directly affected the rule of the Qing Government. To maintain and rely on the Eight Banners system, we must look for a solution to this problem painstakingly. Therefore, from the Kangxi Period to the Qianlong Period, the Qing Court spent a lot of money, adopting many measures, such as the unorthodox banner of the Eight Banners' becoming civilian, establishment of the Nine Squares System of Land Ownership, Rewarding silver, and so on, in order to solve the problem and maintain this system.

(1) The unorthodox banner of the Eight Banners becomeing civilian

Another practice, similar to that of the Han Army, was to make the unorthodox banner of the Eight Banners becomes civilian. The so-called unorthodox banner was originally the servant of the Eight Banners noble, or obtained the status of the unorthodox banner by means of military merit or redemption, but still belonged to the name of the original owner and only had a semi-independent identity. As the livelihood of the Eight Banners became increasingly difficult, the ruler began to consider letting this part of the people leave the banner system and become civilian. In the 3rd year of Yongzheng (1725), the Qing Court approved the Yi Prince Yunxiang under the premise of the lord's willingness to allow a part of the banner slaves to ransom themselves. It could be the overture of "the unorthodox banner of the Eight Banners becomes civilian". The large-scale action was in the Qianlong Period. It was during the 10th year of the reign of Emperor Qianlong (1745) that the Qing Government first let the servants from the Internal Affairs Department leave the banner system. Then in 21st year (1756), 27th year (1762), 36th year (1771) and so on, the official servant and "Baoyi" of the non-Manchurian descent from the Wanggongfu in the Ministry of Revenue, as well as people registered in other files were required to leave and become civilian. Although the Qing Court stated in the 21st year of Qianlong's reign (1756) "people registered in other files leave the banners system and turn into common people" that it ordered such people to leave the banner because of the "increasing number of the Eight Banners 'population" and the "increasingly difficult livelihood", it seemed that it was for the sake of all Banner people. But what happened soon after showed the ruler's real purpose. In the 27th year of the reign of Emperor Qianlong (1762), some people who had already left from the banner returned to their former owners and re-entered the banner system because they did not fit in. Emperor Qianlong decided that it was a crime to occupy the banner's quota and issued an order forbidding the re-entering to the banner system. It fully revealed the real intention of allowing these people to leave the banner system: To throw off the burden for the Eight Banners of Manchu and Mongolia.

(2) Establishment of the Nine Squares System of Land Ownership

The establishment of Nine Squares System of Land Ownership was an attempt of the Qing Government to recombine the idle Eight Banners with the land. Although it ended in failure, it could be said that it was the harbinger of the return of the Jing Banner to northeast China during the Qianlong Period. In the 2nd year of Yongzheng (1724), the Deputy Capital of the Imperial Investigation Academy, Saide, requested that "the old system of the Nine Squares System of Land Ownership in the Western Zhou Dynasty should be restored". In essence, this was a way of turning the banners into state-owned serfs again. However, this approach to solve the idle livelihood of the Jing Banner by focusing on the permanent property of the Eight Banners soldiers was affirmed by Emperor Yongzheng. In his letter of the 23rd of the 6th lunar month that year, he instructed, "It has been well agreed upon, and shall be carried out accordingly." He ordered the task to be presided over by Yunxiang, the Heshuo Prince. In the 5th year of Yongzheng's reign (1727), officers and soldiers of the Eight Banners who had been demobilized because of crimes were "sent to the field to render service". However, until the 1st year of Qianlong's reign (1736), this method is still not effective. So, the Qing Court had to turn the banners to tun households, stockpiling grain according to the land acres, the rest of the households do not have the ability to cultivate the land were send back to its banner, stop their subsides. The trial operation of Nine Squares System of Land Ownership failed.

(3) Rewarding Silver

The silver reward was the usual means used by the Qing Emperors, Kangxi, Yongzheng and Qianlong, to solve the livelihood problems of the Eight Banners. The Emperor Kangxi gave a great amount of silver to the Eight Banners twice. In the first case, he gave more than 5,415,000 taels of silver, with an average of hundreds of taels of silver for each banner family. In 1703, in the 42nd year of Kangxi's reign, more than 6,554,000 taels of silver were awarded to the soldiers. After Yongzheng ascended the throne, he also awarded the soldiers of the Eight banners several times, each time about 350,000 to 360,000 taels of silver. In 1743, in the 8th year of the reign of Emperor Qianlong, "10,000 silver was awarded to each of the Eight Banners" and the three banners of the Ministry of Revenue received the same. However, the soldiers and others did not use the silver to buy property, "all of silver was spent on food and drink in less than 10 days." Such extravagant consumption made their livelihood even more impoverished than before.

In addition to the reward of silver, during the middle period of emperor Yongzheng's reign, each banner was also issued 100,000 silver to use in loan business, the interests of the silver can be used to cover the cost of marriage and funeral. By the 1st year of Qianlong (1736), soldiers of Manchuria, Mongolia and Han army under the Ministry of Revenue had received 1,100,000 taels of silver. The silver was initially handed over to ministers and other officials to loan and collect interest. Later, due to difficulties in handling the silver, they ordered lieutenant generals to use the silver to purchase the property, or set up pawnshops, or buy the land for rent. According to the *Bordered Red Banner File Records*, from the 1st day of the 11th lunar month in the 10th year of Yongzheng's reign (1732) to the 2nd of the 10th lunar year of the following year, "20,000 taels of silver was invested in five trades, they were market, rice, clothes, money and pawnshop". The interest silver is mainly used for wedding or funeral matters of the Eight Banners soldiers in the capital.

2.3 Social Security of Heilongjiang Immigrants in the Late Qing Dynasty and Early Republic of China

The social security policy of a country or region for immigrants has an important impact on the scale and speed of population migration in the country or region. In the Late Qing Dynasty and Early Republic of China, government authorities at all levels carried out preferential reclamation policies to encourage people in the south of Shan Hai pass to move to Heilongjiang in order to solve the livelihood of refugees, maintain national defense and develop northeast China, and set up immigration security agencies, formulated various rules and regulations, and established various social security mechanisms for immigrants. At the same time, various civil society groups also responded to take measures to ensure the smooth progress of immigration work.

2.3.1 Social Security Institutions for Immigrants

In the Late Qing Dynasty and Early Republic of China, the Qing Government, the Nanjing Provincial Government, the Beiyang Government and the local governments in northeast China adopted policies to encourage and support immigrants, among which the first was to set up various social security institutions for immigrants. These institutions mainly consisted of three parts: One was located in the Northeast around the reclamation bureau, reclamation association, reclamation companies and other institutions; One was the charity relief organizations set up in Hebei, Henan, Shandong and other migrant origin areas; One was the various railway and shipping transportation agencies that carry immigrants. The establishment of these institutions is very effective in attracting and relieving immigrants, helping immigrants to move to Heilongjiang in a planned and purposeful way.

(1) Immigration reclamation institutions

In the Late Qing Dynasty and Early Republic of China, the establishment of various migration and reclamation institutions ranked first among immigrant social security institutions. As early as the 28th year of the reign of Emperor Guangxu

(1902), the General Administration of the Taxes and Drought was set up in eastern Heilongjiang Province. In March 1912, when the Republic of China was just established, Huang Xing and Qiu Liang established the Association of Exploration and Cultivation in Nanjing. The purpose of the association was to "develop the frontier soil, increase production, raise the military expenditure, keep the foreign powers at bay, and alleviate the distress of the mainlanders". In 1914, the Beiyang Government set up the General Bureau of Preparation for Immigration Affairs in the Ministry of Revenue, and the General Bureau of the Land Measurement and Recruitment for Reclamation was set up in Qiqihar in the western part of Heilongjiang Province on the basis of previous land cultivating. Under the general administration there were several districts, almost every county followed the provincial instructions to set up reclamation sub-bureau of reclamation office and set up full-time members to deal with immigration and reclamation affairs. For some counties which were unable to set up branches, offices, the local chamber of commerce was entrusted to the duty. County reclamation agencies surveyed and measured arable land and provided convenient conditions for immigrants to reclaim land according to the local financial situation. The articles of land cultivation recruiting could be determined according to the specific local conditions and could be carried out after being approved. Nenjiang, Luobei, Huma, Baoqing, Ahui and other 12 areas of land reclamation, namely, the focus of land reclamation was on the border areas. In March and November of the same year, the Ministry of Agriculture and Forestry of the Beiyang Government issued the *Regulations on The Reclamation of State-owned Wasteland* and *Regulations on the Reclamation of Frontier Wasteland*, which stipulated that the frontier wasteland was outside the border wall, the northeast border of Fengtian, the border of Jilin, the border of Heilongjiang and Shanxi, the border of Shaanxi, the border of Gansu, and the border of Xinjiang, Guangxi and Sichuan-Yunnan. The private estate of the Qing Dynasty was abolished and reclaimed by local governments, and the government encouraged the rich to invest in this area.

In 1925, Zhang Zuolin set up the General Affairs Office of Reclamation Supervision in the provincial government office and reclamation recruiting office to recruit people for the counties. Heilongjiang Province set up reclamation bureau to take charge of reclamation matters; Reclamation County should have one commissioner of reclamation affairs, who should be elected by the retired governor after consultation with the provincial government. An immigration office was organized in Tianjin to help immigrants who wanted to move north of Shanhai Pass.

In July 1928, after Zhang Xueliang took office as the Commander-in-chief of the Security, he established an organization responsible for the immigration and reclamation work in the northeast region—the Northeast Settlement Committee in order to strengthen the organization and management of the immigration. The committee with Sun Chuanfang as its chairman began to implement "the policy of disarmament and populating the border". In 1928, Zhang Xueliang adopted the settlement proposition of Zou Zuohua, the Commander of the first Army of northeast artillery, announced the grand plan of integrating soldiers in agriculture and developing settlement, and set up the Xing'an Settlement Supervision Office (originally Suolun District Settlement Office), which was "a great feat for the border populating" of the local government in northeast China. Zou Zuohua was appointed as the Superintendent of reclamation, demarcating the reclamation area; Heilongjiang Province borders Hulunbuir in the north, Tai Lai in the east, Feng province in the south, and Mongolia in the west. It is more than 1,500km long from east to west and 2,000km wide from north to south. While stationing troops for reclamation, they also recruited Hebei and Shandong refugees for reclamation, and the reclamation should be carried out by the three provinces at the same time. The financial sources for Xing'an resettlement area were also decided. Half of the money would come from local funds, and the other half would be financed with funds from the disarmament administration. At the beginning of the settlement in Xing'an, the three artillery regiments of the Northeast army and their redundant officers formed the settlement army and the reclamation team of redundant officers. On October 13th of that year, "Zou Zuohua led his troops to Soulun for a trial settlement and set up a preparatory office in Shenyang under the Security Headquarters of the Three Northeastern Provinces". During the trial period, "the areas of settlement were mainly Tao'an county of Fengtian Province and Suolun County of Heilongjiang Province. The soldiers' salaries were paid by the Fengtian Provincial Government, and Zou Zuohua was responsible for the recommendations of the two county magistrates".

In order to strengthen the command of Xing'an settlement area, the office of Xing'an Settlement Office moved to Tao'an County in June 1929 and set up a provincial office in Shenyang named "Xing'an Settlement Office in Liao".

At the same time of military reclamation, Xing'an resettlement area is also implementing civilian reclamation. In 1929, the Xing'an Resettlement Office accepted 4,857 refugees from 944 households in Henan and Shandong Provinces. For land that had been recultivated, measures were taken to promote reclamation. To make the settlement work organized, planned, and to explore and accumulate experience, approved by the council of the northeast China, they promulgated a series of rules and regulations, including the *Regulations for the Supernumerary Officer Cooperative reclamation of the Xing'an area, Regulations of land distribution for Xing'an District Officer of Reclamation*, *Regulations for Xing'an District Reclamation Army* and so on. "While carrying out the military reclamation, Xing'an district also implemented the people's reclamation." Therefore, Xing'an district promulgated the *Xing'an District Settlement Measures for the Immigrants, Xing'an Area Outline of Rural Organization, Xing'an District Two Banners' Land Survey Rules, Xing'an Area Farming Instructor Service Planning, Punishments for Immigrates' Passive Reclamation* and so on. All these intended to have a good management on the immigrates, and if any immigrates fail to cultivate enough land, they would be punished accordingly, including paying fines and withdrawing tenancy.

In order to cooperate with the resettlement work in Xing'an settlement area, Zhang Xueliang established Xing'an Bank in 1929. "The area is doing settlement now; this policy is to populate the frontier with immigration, develop the border, provide aid for the poor and transport goods. All these matters need money." The establishment of Xing'an Bank jointly requested by the government and business should be approved for registration, "As for the issuance of 100,000 yuan of reclamation circulation bonds, which will be limited to one section of Xing'an reclamation area, it will affect the provincial treasury and shall not be approved. If the reclamation in this area needs funding in the future, there will be no difficulty for the government bank or the border bank to set up branches." After the establishment of Xing'an Bank, its business scope was as follows: ① Managing all kinds of deposit and lending; ② Handling bills of exchange; ③ Foreign exchange transaction; ④ Discount or purchase of commercial promissory notes; ⑤ Discount or purchaser of bill of exchange; ⑥ Acting as an agent for Xing'an District Treasury; ⑦ Depositing securities and other valuables on behalf of the customers; ⑧ Receiving payments for various bills on behalf of bank, companies and individuals with whom transactions have been made; ⑨ Taking gold and silver goods or raw gold and silver as collateral for loan; ⑩ Fixed term or current loans secured by bond certificates and various securities. The establishment of specialized banks in immigrant reclamation areas is unheard of in the history of the Republic of China, which shows that the local governments in northeast China attach great importance to settling immigrants and developing the border areas.

In addition, governments at all levels also set up refugee relief centers and shelters and set up immigration offices and reclamation travel agencies and other official organizations in Hebei, Henan, Shandong, Hunan, Anhui, Shanxi, Hubei, Shanghai, Tianjin and other places of immigrants' origin. The establishment of these institutions had the functions of managing and organizing immigration and reclamation in Heilongjiang Province, and undoubtedly promoted the arrival of the climax of immigration in Heilongjiang Province.

In addition to the government agencies mentioned above, there were many non-governmental public organizations dealing with immigration affairs during this period. Among them, the associations of townsmen in each province were the most common organizations. "The community thrives on its financial resources and networks of influence in the city, which facilitate the development of patronage mechanisms that link the poor and the elite among travelers." The traditional Chinese family system makes people accustomed to living in a family culture with blood ties and close relationships. However, due to their departure, immigrants cut off the connection with their familiar atmosphere and enter a completely unfamiliar environment. To solve practical problems in real life, immigrants first think of asking for help from people who speak the same accent. Therefore, in places where immigrants are concentrated, an independent self-protection mechanism will be formed under the banner of provincialism. In this way, the former immigrants of the provinces have established townsmen associations. One of the main functions of the association is the mutual aid function. In their purpose of building the association, generally, there are expressions of the spirit of cooperation and mutual aid, the protection of the welfare of hometown and the handling of public welfare and charity. Another major function of the association is the public welfare function, which is manifested by the relief of disasters such as floods, droughts, winds and wars in the hometown, i.e., fundraising and disaster relief.

Since the founding of the Republic of China, in the eastern part of Heilongjiang Province where uncultivated land was concentrated, local warlords, the rich and bureaucrats had forcibly occupied a lot of land by means of monopolizing, annexing and buying at low prices. They organized large land reclamation companies, such as the Fire Plough company founded by Zheng Yongchang, a plutocrat in Jiangsu and Zhejiang, the Dongjing Company founded by Chen Taoyi, a bureaucrat in Jiangsu, the Zhiyuan company run by Zhou Darong, a landlord in Jiangsu and Zhejiang, the Jinen Company headed by Zhu Qinglan, a landlord in Hebei, and the Guangxin Company headed by Wu Junsheng and Bao Guiqing, warlords and bureaucrats in Heilongjiang. During the thirteen years ranging from 1913 to 1926, there were as many as eighteen such agricultural companies established in the Heilongjiang region, which occupied an unprecedented area of land and had many tenants and abundant funds. These big landlords and bureaucrats, who had a lot of land in their hands, "were able to supply labor with very low wages due to the relocation of refugees. After two or three years, the uncultivated land was turned into fertile land, and the price of land naturally increased. Therefore, the relief of immigrants was the pleasure of the officials." Along the Chinese Eastern Railway, landowners who owned a large amount of land "left things at their discretion, or leave the land untended and uncultivated for lack of tenants." Bureaucratic landlords who owned a large amount of land were also willing to help immigrants out of economic interest. From 1913 to 1926, 18 agricultural and animal husbandry reclamation companies were established in Heilongjiang Province, which strengthened the organization and management of immigration reclamation, and made the immigration enterprise carry on in an organized and planned way. According to the incomplete statistics in the book *A Preliminary Survey of the History of the Landlord Class in Suibin*, only Huoli, Dongjing, Zhiyuan, Jinen and Guangxin had more than 950 tenants and more than 930 employees. Most of these tenants and employees were immigrants during the Republic of China.

(2) Non-governmental charity organizations

Among all the social security institutions for immigrants, many non-governmental charities played an important role in immigrants recruiting and disaster relieving. This was mainly because people from North China moved to the Northeast "to escape the famine, unsure of their future fate. There is no way to survive in the hometown, so they are all forced to leave the hometown. As for how to survive in the north of Shanhai Pass, it is left for the heaven to decide."

Therefore, "The problem of the relief of immigrants is an urgent one, which cannot be delayed." Therefore, the major newspapers, news medias have proposed those relief organizations to help the victims. The famous and influential charity relief organizations at that time were the Red Cross Society of China, which emerged from the International Red Cross Society in Shanghai jointly organized by China, Britain, France, Germany and the United States in 1907. Sheng Xuanhuai, the first president, was mainly responsible for the relief of war. Founded in 1916 in Shanghai by Wang Yiting, Ji Sheng Association of China mainly organized disaster relief in various provinces and sets up shelters for refugees. China Huayang Relief Association, founded in 1921, plans for national disaster relief; Shanghai Federation of Charitable Organizations, founded in 1927 by Wang Yiting, etc., to improve and cooperate with charitable organizations, and better utilize of the functions of charity.

In addition, with the appeal of the whole society, in Heilongjiang, Shandong, Hebei, people in different fields set up Shandong branch of the Universal Red Cross, the international Red Cross, Wushan Club, Tongshan Club, Qiliu Club, Longjiang Charity Chamber of Commerce in Harbin, Shandong Compassion Club, Northeast Charity Society, North China Disaster Relief Society, Northeast Reclamation Committee, Buddhist Phuket, Shanghai Economic Committee, People Immigration Procurator Offices, Charity Federation of Four Provinces (Re, Feng, Ji, Jiang), Taiping Charity, Kailu Officials and Gentry Business Circles, Universal Charity, Central Charity, Universal Moral Society, in addition to Dalian, Changchun, Binjiang, Fengtian refugee counseling centers and relief organizations. Just in Binjiang, there were 7 refugee guidance centers organized by different organizations and a refugee relief association established by the General Chamber of Commerce. These charities provided relief and support to many immigrants. There were also many kind people who denoted a lot of money and things.

(3) Railway, shipping and other transport organizations

At the end of the Qing Dynasty and the beginning of the Republic of China, immigrants who wanted to go to Heilongjiang from Shandong, Henan and Hebei had to go through long distances and hardships. At that time, the land route was mainly through Jinpu, Jiaoji, Jingfeng, Datong, Sitao, Zhengbai, Taoang, Fenghai, Jichang, Jidun, Nanman, Chinese Eastern and Huhai railways. The waterway was mainly through the ship agency—namely Andong, Dalian, Yingkou and Zilu port connected by various cruise company. Immigration routes to Heilongjiang mainly include four routes: Qingdao to Dalian, Yantai to Yingkou, Tianjin to Yingkou, Yantai to Haishenwai. Immigrants in the southeast of Shandong mostly boarded ship from Qingdao to Dalian, and then transferred to the Heilongjiang region by South Manchurian railway. After landing in Yingkou, the immigrants from Yantai area would go on two different routes. One route enters Heilongjiang area via Changchun along the South Manchurian Railway Branch Line (Yingkou Branch line), and the other route enters Taonan via Jingfeng Road and Sitao Road. Immigrants from Yantai to Haishenwai then directly enters the key reclamation areas along

Heilongjiang. Because these groups had a direct interest in the settlers, "The land and sea transportation agencies could increase their income for transportation and hoped that the reclamation of land would contribute indirectly to the development of the railroads." Therefore, they were enthusiastic about promoting immigration and provide convenient and economic conditions for immigrants to migrate.

2.3.2 Social Security Measures for Immigrants

In the Late Qing Dynasty and Early Republic of China, many official and private immigration agencies gave various preferential treatment to immigrants, adopting many policies and measures to take proper care of immigrants, reducing and exempting transportation fees, formulating immigration regulations, protecting, recruiting, transporting and settling immigrants.

(1) Recruitment of immigrants

After the Opium War, the Qing Government gave up the restriction policy to the whole northeast region including Heilongjiang. The immigration to the Heilongjiang region increased sharply after the partial release of the restriction in 1861, especially after the outbreak of the Russo—Japanese War in 1904. Japan and Russia redivided their sphere of influence in the Northeast, and Russia intensified its colonial rule in the Heilongjiang region. "The Qing Court also felt that the Northeast was in urgent need of development, so in addition to setting up more courts and improving traffic, it also set up Courier stations in important towns, so that the people were attracted by the news." Not only so, in the 34th year of Guangxu (1908), from the perspective of immigration, the Governor of Heilongjiang Province, Cheng Dequan, reported to the Emperor and published *Articles of Association for Border Reclamation (5 Chapters and 24 Articles)*, which fully started the Qing Government's process of legalization of immigration policy. *Articles of Association for Border Reclamation* can be roughly divided into 3 parts, the first part of which is the measures to attract immigrates. The government planed to set up Heilongjiang Border Reclamation Reception Offices in "Hankou, Shanghai, Tianjin, Yantai, Yingkou and Changchun, and send personnel to take care of them properly". In the specific implementation process, this policy was carried out. In addition, provinces in the Northeast were invited to recruit in the name of the government, and regulations such as the *Outline of the Colonial Plan of the Northeast Provinces* were formulated, printed, and were sent to Liaoning, Henan, Hebei, Shandong and other provinces by government employees responsible for recruiting.

During the period of the Republic of China, Harbin was the main channel for immigrants to enter Heilongjiang Province. Each immigration agency had its own resident immigration staff. Provincial associations, for example, often sent officers to railway stations, immigrant shelters, and all the places where immigrants might lodge to find out if any settlers had gone up the river from Harbin or to the eastern regions, and if there is any, they would be brought to hotels. And at any time, these officers would find out the schedule of the transportation to guide the immigrants.

The association also issued immigration certificates on behalf of the provincial reclamation bureau, one for each family. It bears the names of the immigrants and the family members. It reads: "Today, ××× took several members of his family to reclaim land in ××× county in Heilongjiang Province. This is to prove it." After arriving at the designated place, the counties also have to recruit reclamation staff manage resettlement for the immigrates with the certificates. Immigration reclamation companies also set up recruitment personnel to attract immigrants in Harbin and other places. Most of the recruitment objects are immigrants who have no relatives to seek refuge in Heilongjiang and their destination is not determined. In addition, the immigration agencies also published reclamation advertisements on the newspaper to attract farmers in the south of the Shanhai Pass. As a result, poor farmers from the other provinces south of the Shanhai Pass flocked to Heilongjiang.

(2) Transfer of the immigrants

To attract more immigrants and maintain the effect of immigration movement, all sectors of society had also given great protection and assistance to immigrants in Heilongjiang Province during the transfer. It mainly involved the means of transportation, the raising of travel expenses, living expenses and so on.

During the 33rd year of Guangxu (1907), Heilongjiang General (Xu Shichang) and Governor (Zhao Erxun) reported to the emperor, "please exempt immigrates' fare for carts and boats". It was requested that "the Postal and Communication Department waive immigrates' road fare and ferry fare, if they are going to Heilongjiang, this would be of great benefit to the colonial administration of the frontier province ... We plan to recruit and transfer people. We will first recruit people and reclaim the land, and it will be easier to do so once people know the benefits of migration and they will think all the pain endured along the road worthwhile." In the 34th year of Guangxu's reign (1908), Cheng Dequan, Governor of Heilongjiang Province, reported to the Emperor and published the *Regulations of Border Reclamation*: "For the reclamation households in Heilongjiang Province, along with reduced ferry fares, train tickets will be halved, and their families will be exempt from charges, all these measures are to attract more people to come." These local officials' documents were all specific to the transfer of immigrants, which put forward specific preferences and protection measures.

In the period of the Republic of China, railway under the jurisdiction of warlord governments at all levels also formulated many immigrations transfer laws and specific implementation methods. For example, on November 5th, 1913 and October 22nd, 1914, Jingfeng and Jinpu Railway Administration twice published "Jinpu and Jingfeng Railway Administration reducing the fare of laborers", which included the following contents: "Every year, poor people of Hebei Province go to the three northeastern provinces to work as laborers, and the fare will be reduced when they travel along the railway. When these people want to return home, as many of them are from Shandong Province, hereby through tickets are sold jointly by Jingfeng and Jinpu road, which can reach all parts of Shandong directly from Fengtian."

In March 1925, the Department of Transport in Beijing announced, "for the sake of promoting immigration reclamation, in particular in Jingfeng, Jingsui two road immigration ticket will be sold on discount." In April of the same year, The Regulations on the Sale of Discounted tickets for Immigrants in Jingfeng and Jingsui Lines were promulgated, stipulating: "The tickets prices for immigrants and their families shall be reduced to ten-fourth or ten-fifths of the original price, and tickets shall be exempted for children under the age of 11, as well as the farm tools brought by immigrants themselves."

On November 12th, 1927, Zhao Lantian, director of Jiaoji Railway Bureau, sent a telegram to the various railway bureaus: "Recently, Shandong Province has suffered from disasters frequently and people's livelihood has been devastated. Due to the drought and locust invasion this summer, the livelihood become worse day by day. Today, at the end of autumn and the beginning of winter, people from all counties take Jiaoji train to make a living in other provinces more frequently. People's hardship and displacement deserve compassion. We should act quickly to help them, we hope the railway company would reinstate the discounted tickets for the laborers as past, to help the disaster victims as soon as possible!" After the order was issued, train No.20 of the Jiaoji Railway was used as a special train to transport immigrants. In late February of the following year, as the trains from Jinan to Qingdao were already full every day in Jinan, so according to the increase in the number of immigrants, 4 more trains were issued, No.23, No.72, No.74, No.38 and 5 to 10 fourth-class passenger trains. The fare for the train from Jinan to Dalian via Qingdao was only 4 yuan.

The Chinese Eastern Railway also actively cooperate with all sectors of the community to transport immigrants at discounted prices. The original price of each ticket from Changchun to Harbin was "3 rubles and 50 kopecks", but after the reduction, it will be "1 ruble and 92 kopecks". Not only were the migrants transported "in the heated cars of the freight train, but each car will also carry five elderly persons over sixty and children under ten years of age, they were transported free of charge." At that time, all the railways in the three northeastern provinces, except the Nanman line, which was administered by the Japanese, were ordered by the authorities to allow immigrants to travel at half price. In June, 1929, the Northeast Transportation Committee developed a more favorable immigration regulations—Provisional Regulations for the Transportation of Refugees on Reclamation, stipulating that: "All reclamation refugees with free vouchers, no matter men or women, old or young, are all free of charge; Reclamation refugees with discount vouchers, thirty percent of the regular third-class fare will be charged, children under 12 free of charge."

The social security measures taken above made part of refugees get social help and successfully got to Heilongjiang. Although it is only a drop in the bucket compared to the huge migration, it will not be easy for the refugees to reach their reclamation destination with limited financial resources, if the transport authority does not help them." The movement has played an important role in promoting the immigration.

Besides the exemption and discount of transport costs offered by transportation departments for the refugees, Heilongjiang Province also sent local officials to the railway stations along to offer reception of immigrants, providing consultancy and help, introducing the location of the immigrant settlements and route to the location. "The local officials sent people in the station or on the vital road to provide immigrates with convenience. The local officials must prepare all the files and documents for the government of the immigrates' destination in advance. Relief Money should be raised for the poor and those without enough travel expenses. If the fundraising was insufficient, they could be subsidized by public funds. Make sure to keep them alive." The refugees should be inquired for "their destination, and be told how to get there, provided with necessary protection. For those who has no one to go and seek refuge with, they should be introduced to the labor market. If they are in the county with implementation of special reclamation policy, they should be introduced to this policy."

The immigrant organizations mentioned above, such as the townsman associations and the immigration reclamation companies, also stationed personnel in Harbin and other immigrants transit cities to give guidance and help to immigrants. It had greatly relieved the hardship of the immigration, ensured the smooth progress of immigration activities, and provided convenience for many immigrants to Heilongjiang.

However, conditions for most poor migrants were difficult. Although the transportation department had reduced the fare, the cost of the trip was still a heavy burden for the nearly destitute migrants, forcing them to sell their land and houses and used all their savings to make the journey. According to statistics, a family of fouror fivepeople's travel by water might cost at least 10 yuan, while the general cost was 30 yuan. This was only the fare to the Northeast port. However, "most of the Shandong peasants who moved to Manchuria would go to North Manchuria. If a family of three plan to travel from Shandong to North Manchuria, the minimum cost would be 100 yuan or more, and the living expenses of the family after arrival would beyond account. We can see that most of the peasants in Shandong who left their hometowns were very poor, and most of them did not have enough travel expenses." According to the investigation of Nankai University school of economics, among the 139 households immigrated from Shandong, 63 households experienced hardships due to insufficient travel expenses, and 17 households even begged for food along the way, accounting for about 12% of the total. Akio Nakajima once wrote in *The Empirical Study of Rural Revolution of China* that the poor people who "brave their journey to northeast" begging along the road, he said: "They only carry a small amount of travelling fee. On the way to the Manchuria from Shandong, they seldom take the train, but mostly on foot, begging from door to door, or just live on a few food), they camp in the open air or lodge in a small inn, extremely frugal on travel expenses." For lack of travel expenses, many immigrants sat on deck of the boats and took lorries. Some travelers take more than 40 or 50 yuan, while others less than 1 to 2 yuan, and the penniless were begging for food along the way. Therefore, there were not a small number of people frozen to death. In Qingdao, poor people had to sell their children, "each daughter costs twenty or thirty yuan, but in Mukden, only ten yuan." This is mainly because Fengtian is a place where too many immigrants were forced to sell their children. From Jining to Harbin, each person needs about 20 yuan, many people who didn't have enough money had to disembark in Dalian, travelling on foot all the way, eating nothing but sorghum, corn and other things. They had endured hunger and cold in their journey to the north of the three Northeastern provinces. For some immigrants without friends or relatives to take refuge in, they did not have a certain destination, but after landing in Dalian, they began to move on foot, looking for places to stay, and settled in random places. When they were not satisfied with the place, they would move again. Therefore, immigrants in the period of the Republic of China had great mobility.

When a large number of refugees rushed north of Shanhai Pass, local authorities, public and private organizations in the area of move-out and move-in did not stand by, they took a series of relief measures to facilitate the immigration and reduce the immigrates' burden. Some social groups and charitable organizations had also set up relief offices to collect donations and organize the transfer of refugees. For example, the refugees from Henan to northeast China were mainly transferred by the Lvping Henan Disaster Relief Association, the Huayang Relief Association and local Henan associations. Lvping Henan Disaster Relief Association supplied refugees with steamed bread 2 jin each day per person. From Henan to Zhengzhou, the supply was distributed everyday according to the distance. Supplies would also be distributed when the refugee was waiting for the train everyday. Wherever these people went, there were hostels to accommodate them. And they would also receive more or less money from philanthropists and charities. Shandong Disaster Relief Office had made detailed and thoughtful arrangements for the subsidies and accommodation for the immigrants who moved to northeast China, and formulated regulations such as *Shandong Disaster Relief Office's Brief Rules for Immigrants and Shandong Disaster Relief Office's Brief Rules for Refugee Hostels*. According to the Provisions: "refugees should be transported in empty food transporting trucks, to the counties in the 3 provinces in the Northeast for a living; The soup kitchen should register the refugees for further inspection, issue travel cards, provide food and be responsible for their settling, issue a migration license; For refugees who lack travel expenses and accommodation, hostels will be set up along the way to receive refugees and provide them with a meal for a night." The North China Disaster Relief Association set up a guesthouse in Tianjin and provided steamed bread for the refugees. Universal Red Cross in Shanhai Pass set up soup kitchen, Zhi Lu Yu Refugee Relief House distributed sorghum rice at Dahu Mountain. Xu Zhongliang, Wang Zhensheng and Zhou Qin handed out steamed bread in Tangshan; Li Fengshan, Ma Qingwu, Dai Guozhang and Officer Ma donated rice, vegetables, sorghum, salt in Tongliao.

In 1927, local officials from Jilin and Heilongjiang were sent to Changchun, the starting point of the North Manchuria immigration, to provide all kinds of help to the immigrants, to make them know the various places suitable for cultivation and the way and method to reach these places. Immigrants who came to Changchun and had nowhere to live were first settled by local rescue teams and then sent to their future settlements.

Along the way, from the aspect of supplement, those organized immigration was much better than those who went to the Northeast by themselves, but there are still some deficiencies. For example, several groups of refugees, escorted by Li Maoxiu, a member of Lvping Henan Disaster Relief Association, were delayed for 5 days from Taonan to Zhendong by military vehicles. There was only one meal of 2dan (1dan=80kg in 1927) millet per day for more than 2300 people. In some transfer stations, people kept coming without going due to the delay of trains. Supply was not enough, some of them died of starvation. *Dagongbao* (Tinjin) also recorded the fact: the immigrants transported by the American Moral Society and the Henan Disaster Relief Association to the Northeast were stuck in Zhujiazhuang for three days, "Because of food shortage, several people die every day, and they now eat grass to survive"; Although some supplies were offered even as usual, there was no firewood, even a bowl of thin soup was not easy to get, because of eating raw bread or drink cold water, people suffer from diarrhea on the way.

Although a variety of public and private organizations offered immigrants who "Brave the journey to the Northeast" a lot of help, in fact, most of Shandong immigrants just "escape randomly and separately", and "towards the places where they had relatives and friends to depend on; There were a lot of refugees went to the Northeast from Yizhou, which is probably due to this reason." "Most of the immigrants were gathered by relatives in the same country, so they stayed in the same place, and most of them moved from the same country. As far as the migrants were concerned, when one of the refugees' fellow villagers lived in the northern part of the three northeastern provinces, his relatives and friends came in a great stream. Therefore, when there were many acquaintances of the refugee, the refugee would be more willing to go to them."

(3) Resettling of immigrants

Most of the people who entered Heilongjiang were peasants who had lost their land in their hometowns and had fled to escape different disasters. In fact, they are all refugees. There was no certain form of organization for the fleeing refugees. The only form of organization was family, bloodline or geographical relationship, which was extremely loose and randomly without any binding force. There was no specific destination, the only thing they know was "Braving the journey to the Northeast", as for where to settle after they go north, where to make a living, there was no plan. Almost none of the refugees had ever been to Heilongjiang and they knew almost nothing about it, except that it was large and sparsely populated and had plenty land to claim. In addition, the refugees who arrived in Heilongjiang always ran out of money, had no farm tools, food and shelter. They had nothing, no basic living material, only bare hands.

The life of immigrants who were organized by the government was relatively better when they just arrived. According to the investigation report of Henan Disaster Relief Association in BeiPing, "Lindian County is divided into eight districts, the first, second, third, fourth and eighth districts are the best for the refugees. Each person is given a bucket of millet every month. The houses are all straw houses, and the victims live in one or two houses. Those who cannot work will get cotton-padded clothes to keep warm. In Suihua County, more than 800 refugees of the disaster came. The local treatment for the refugees was quite excellent. Each family had a room, or two families shared a room. All had heated beds. Although there were not many rooms, they didn't suffer from the cold ... The food and drink of the refugees was provided by the heads of 100 households according to the land distributed to them. Each person was given about 700g rice per day. Regardless of age, clothes were covered by the laborers' wages." According to *Dagongbao* on February 11th, 1930, "The people of Anda County treated the refugees very well ... All the villagers lived in grass-roofed huts with heated beds. They ate millet, corn and buckwheat for most of the time. Since the cotton-padded clothes had been delivered to the victims, they didn't have to worry about cold weather." Such cases did exist, but they were quite rare, and the vast majority of immigrants were still treated poorly. Changchun Toutaogou shelter consisted of three houses, each with 23 meters long and 5 meters wide, with wooden boards and mud walls, roof covered with lead and straw. The total value of the shelter was 500 yuan. Each shelter accommodated 200 refugees, and the total number of refugees in the three shelters was more than 600. It cost less than 1 yuan per person. The refugees in Changchun camps ate millet paste and salted soybeans every day, while the refugees in Yingkou camps ate sorghum, pickles and salted radish every day. The number of camps that could provide a few cotton-padded clothes was absolutely limited.

Due to the large number of immigrants, the Immigration Reclamation Bureau's measures for the immigrants were very simple, "every 5 people a hut, 500 people a well; materials are provided by the official; labor by the immigrants; In addition, preparing the water trough and wheels for public use. If the population number is more than 1,000, a new village will be built, and each man will be lent a set of farm tools, a set of household appliances, and 75kg of ration. The expenses will be reported by the county office to the provincial office and covered by public fund, and the immigrants will cross guarantee each other that after two years all the expenses will be repaid in five years." Although this resettling method was too simple, it was not easy to do so at that time and under that situation. According to the *Journal of the International Association* of 3rd May 1927: "Local administrative authorities have given assistance to collective migration by demanding that residential land be allocated first. In the settlements there shall be a simple house for every five people, a well for every five hundred people, and a simple mill. The building should be made of public materials but paid for by immigrants. In addition, each immigrant will be given money for the purchase of a sickle, a pick, a pickaxe, 75kg of grain, and a special allowance of 10 dollars for household appliances." All the above materials, in the form of loans, could be provided as long as the immigrant had collateral. Therefore, many villages and settlements were formed. All these measures expanded the employment chances of the immigrants and lightened the burden of immigrants, which not only attracted a large number of immigrants to the northeast China, but also enabled them to settle down quickly and promoted the smooth development of immigration.

The most important issue for the immigrants, besides the necessities of life, was how to provide the land they needed.

To settle immigrants, in the 6th year of Guangxu's Reign (1880), the Qing Government stipulated that, "Each household should only use 36 mu of land, regardless of class." The reward method for immigrants was as follows:" ① Every arable and uncultivated land is priced at 2.4 taels of silver per hundred mu, people can buy land at this price, but each person is limited to purchasing 1,000 mu. People who have no money to buy the land but is willing to cultivate the land can pay land tax 0.6 tael of silver per 100 mu. ② People can be paid for cultivating the government owned land and they will enjoy tax exemption for 5 years. When the land is well cultivated, the rent will be 0.66 tael of silver per 100 mu. This 5 years tax exemption is specifically provided for the immigrants who own the fewest land. After several years of taxation (the length of time to pay tax is determined by the amount of cultivated land), the land will be the immigrants' own. ③ Adjacent to the southern Ussuri, the climate is freezing and the land is barren, and there are few people who are enthusiastic about reclamation. Therefore, those who wish to migrate there are not only exempt from taxes, but also receive government subsidies 21 taels of silver to purchase agricultural tools, cattle, horses and build houses."

On the 7th day of the 7th year of Guangxu (July 26th, 1881), Jilin Province issued *Notice on Recruiting for Reclamation in Ningguta, Hunchun and Other Places*, immigrant settlers of Hunchun, Ningguta, enjoyed a preferential policy, "collaterals, 0.66 tael of silver for rent for the land owner and re-rent are exempted, the immigrant should pay rent 5 years later", "Other expenses are all covered by government fund." In addition, as most of the immigrants were refugees of the disaster, they could not afford to buy cattle, so the local government bought them from Korea altogether. The government "charged half the price and ordered the whole price to be paid within three years. The unpaid half price was divided again so that the poor people would not be burdened heavily".

During the 34th year of Guangxu's reign (1908), the Heilongjiang Provincial Governor Cheng Dequan asked the Emperor's permission and published *THE Regulations of Border Reclamation*. The second part of the *Articles* aimed at setting specific provision on land granting rules, "45 hectares of land per household", but no land amount limitation for the land reclamation company, only "reclaimed land can't be sold if the land is not well cultivated." Also stipulated, "Except the first year of reclamation, all the reclaimed land shall be taxed the third year of reclamation ... If the reclaimed land is well cultivated more than two thirds of the reclaimed amount in the inspection year, the remaining reclaimed land but not cultivated yet shall be filed in and be taxed. If the cultivated land is less than two thirds of the reclaimed amount, the land shall be filed according to the actual amount of cultivated land, and the rest of the uncultivated land should be withdrawn and redistributed." The third part containing three chapters and nine entries was about how to aid the reclamation households and other supplementary provisions. In the provisions, if the reclamation households are unable make ends meet, "they can go to the nearest official bank to apply for loan based on the number of people in the reclamation households, and the loan can be repaid in installments". If the owner of the land recruit people to reclaim land, "Seventh-rank official shall be appointed to the man who reclaimed more than 600 hectars of land, the sixth-rank official shall be appointed to the man who reclaimed more than 800 hectars of land, and fifth-rank official shall be appointed to the man who reclaimed more than 1000 hectars of land." *The Regulations of Border Reclamation* was a major measure of land development policy of the Qing Government after it completely opened northeast China.

With the continuous increase of immigrants in the Northeast, "*The Regulations of Border Reclamation*" in 1908 could not meet the needs for reclamation in many aspects, plus it was only aimed at border areas, namely "the regions under the jurisdiction of Xing'an Mountains, Xingdong, Aihui, Hulun Buir and other places." So local governments began to adjust according to their own conditions. During the 2nd year of Xuantong (1910), Heilongjiang Province Halahuoshao Reclamation Bureau regulated: "After granting households to the village, each household will be given 100 mu of well cultivated land, a house, a cattle", at the same time, the land, housing and cattle will be priced and loaned to the farmers, and set a term of payment. "10 mu of prime cultivated land at the price of 5 taels of silver, plus the cost of 1 tael of silver, all together 6 taels of silver; The price of 10 mu of medium cultivated land is 4 taels of silver, plus the cost of 8 qian, a total of 4 taels of silver and 8 qian. A cattle for 38 taels of silver, a house for 36 taels of silver; all the price of housing, cattle must be paid off in 5 years, the farmer doesn't need to repay the price the first year, the farmer only need to pay one tenth in the second and third year, and two tenth in the fourth year, three tenth in the fifth and sixth year. After all the prices are paid in the seventh year, the land will be registered, filed and taxed, the land, house, and cattle will be the farmers for generations." This was undoubtedly a great attraction for those reclamation households who didn't have many assets.

In the period of the Republic of China, the Government also attached great importance to the development of northeast China, and successively issued the *Regulations On Reclamation Of State-Owned Land, Regulations on Reclamation of Frontier Land* and other national laws and regulations on reclamation, as well as *The Regulations On Recruiting For Reclamation In Heilongjiang Province* And

Regulations On Reclamation In Heilongjiang Province.

In 1914, Heilongjiang Province promulgated *The Regulations Of The Land Measurement And Recruiting For Land Reclamation In Heilongjiang Province*, which stipulated that the development policies of the land measurement, people recruiting, and reclamation were adopted simultaneously in Heilongjiang Province. Compared with *The Regulations Of Border Reclamation,* the new regulation had been added new entries, supplemented and revised in many places. First of all, concerning the bandits problem in northeast China, the provisions of sending army and police to protect the reclamation areas along the reclamation route and in the reclamation areas were added. Secondly, restrictions on the reclamation territory had also been relaxed, the provision: "Reclamation households must have a plow, then they will be allowed to reclamation. But the company reclamation is limited by this. The amount of land to be claimed by reclamation immigrants who use fire to burn grass shall be determined at any time." But no matter how to reclaim land, three households vouching for each other was the requirement for reclamation. In addition, the reward to recruit reclamation member and reclamation household also began to pay more attention to practical reward. "Recruiting the reclamation member will not be given government position, if recruit enough to have a plow 50 households to the section of the settlement for cultivation, the allowance of 100 yuan and allowance in the newly released wasteland within the territory of the two halves of the price." "If there are ten reclaiming households, the reclaiming committee will be the head of the household at the end of the section, and the reclaiming committee will be the head of the village for hundreds or tens of households. If there are more than three hundred reclaiming households, the reclaiming land will be reduced by half in the areas."

These policies promoted the implementation of the immigration policy in northeast China, which attracted many immigrants to northeast China. However, the lack of clear restrictions on territories and the lack of supervision of the effectiveness of land reclamation have also caused many large landowner and capitalists to take advantage of the opportunity to seize land and hoard it, resulting in a situation in which large tracts of barren land are left uncultivated.

In order to solve the problem of a large amount of land being released but not cultivated, the northeastern counties have taken various measures, such as promoting, recruiting people to reclamation, and rush-reclamation. In February 1914, Heilongjiang Province General Bureau of Reclamation and Recruitment was established, drawing up *Regulations on Reclamation Recruitment* and *Land measurement Recruitment in Heilongjiang Province*. It stipulated, "Reclamation of newly released barren land ... In the third year, if two-fifth of the land has not been reclaimed, or the reclamation is not finished within time, the unclaimed part shall be revoked without compensation." In the same year, Heilongjiang Provincial Administrative Office issued *The Notice of Reclamation Recruitment*, announcing various preferential policies implemented by the Government for reclamation, such as the establishment of Reclamation Bureau in Longjiang County, the provincial capital, reclamation sub-bureau in each county, and the establishment of guest houses in the provincial capital, responsible for serve reclamation households. When the reclamation farmers arrived, they would "send troops to protect them" and gave seed money and cattle at the discretion of the government. For those who reclaimed land outside the boundaries of the released land, "the land price may be paid in succession." The establishment of the Quanye Bank, reclamation households unable to make ends meet could borrow money from the bank. This prevents reclamation households from receiving without cultivating, while protecting and attracting more reclamation households to settle in the Northeast. According to Nehe County provisions, "If the distributed barren land cannot be reclaimed within three years, the land will be revoked without compensation, and the land will be redistributed. So, the farmers of Tieling County who want to reclaim land prepared cattle, carts, seeds and go to the Northeast immediately."

In 1928, Heilongjiang Province promulgated the *Heilongjiang Province Edgewise the Border of All the Land Reclamation Trial Rules*, regulated that, "All unclaimed land in the reclamation area shall be allowed to be rush-reclaimed regardless of whether it has been laid barren by the people or by the government." At the same time, it also stipulated that "Land rush-reclamation is limited to those with more than 40 shang, and land under 40 shang shall not be rush-reclaimed", which was to protect the interests of small and weak farmers. At the same time, for those occupying large areas of land, their land was not completely deprived of, the provision indicated that "the original households of the land who want to cultivate land should go to the county bureau to be filed within time limit, and then be issued a permit. If the household fails to report or fails to report the actual cultivation of a section by the expiration date, then the cultivated land shall be permitted to be seized by other households." While this attracted settlers to cultivate land, it also forced the large landowners to recruit settlers. This was to prevent the emergence of a new wave of land grabs, this encouraged the recruitment of people to reclaim rather than simply to raise funds. At the same time, these rules and regulations also had a great effect on the Northeast immigrants. According to the statistics of the personnel department of Manchuria, the number of people from North China moving to northeast China soared from more than 500,000 in 1926 to more than 1 million in 1927 and lasted for three years. In the 19th year of the Republic of China (1930), the Government promulgated *The Land Law* on June 30th, and announced that it would be implemented on March 1st (1936) (the 25th year of the Republic of China). Articles 188 to 210 of *The Land Law* had made corresponding provisions on the reclamation of barren land with a total of 23 articles. Article 196 stipulated that from the date of completion of reclamation, the licensee should acquire the land cultivation "right" free of charge, and stipulated (Article 197) that, except as provided in this law, "the provisions of the civil law on permanent tenant rights shall be applied". That was to say, the developer had a partial property right, a perpetual tenant right, but not a full property right. But reclamation was still a big attraction.

According to Article 198, the amount of rent paid to land on which cultivation rights had been acquired "shall not exceed 15 percent of the gross harvest of the main products of the land for five years from the date of acquisition of cultivation rights". This was more than half and a half less than the average mainland rent, and it was free for five years, which was certainly attractive. There were also provisions for reclamation price repayment (Article 205): "The reclamation price shall be paid in installments, with a period of no less than ten years, and shall be paid after harvest." To prevent barren land from being claimed without reclamation, Article 208 stated: Private barren land classified as agricultural land "shall be restricted by the competent land authority to the owner of the barren land to be reclaimed or cultivated within a certain period. If the barren land is not reclaimed or cultivated within a certain period, the land user may apply for expropriation according to law." The promulgation of *The Land Law* clearly stipulated the rules of reclamation of barren land from the legal point of view. It summarized and summed up the previous regulations of reclamation.

Local authorities in the Northeast generally applied preferential policies to land purchases by migrants, especially in Heilongjiang Province in the northern part of the Northeast, which was more than twice as cheap as in Shandong. In the 1920s, 6 mu of medium-quality arable land in Shandong cost "$350-400," while 10 mu of arable land in the fertile and productive Zhuhai County in the Northeast cost "around $250-300. The price of barren land was even cheaper and was categorized into three grades according to quality and location: "the first grade is $10, the second grade is $7, and the third grade is $4."

2.3.3 The Social Security Characteristics of Heilongjiang Immigrants in the Late Qing Dynasty and Early Republic of China

During the social transformation period in the Late Qing Dynasty and Early Republic of China, all aspects of the society were changing. During this period, the immigration process of Heilongjiang Province showed its characteristics in social security ideology, social security legislation, institutional carrier and so on.

Feature 1 The social security thought in the Late Qing Dynasty and Early Republic of China was influenced by the Western social security theory, and people's understanding of social security behavior also changed from the traditional "charity" performance of the ruling class to a part of the Government's responsibility. The particular domestic and international circumstances of the Late Qing Dynasty and Early Republican Period led to the widespread acceptance by the intellectual class and conscientious government officials of modern Western ideas about the relationship between the state and the people, they recognize that: in the modern society, "the people and their country are closely related, sharing weal and woe, as for the relief work, it is signed as the responsibility of the government for the people."

Feature 2 There were special social security legislation to ensure the social security of migrant, providing the legal basis for regular implementing. Both the central government and the local authorities in Heilongjiang had enacted laws to ensure a more effective migration to Heilongjiang for people in short-term distress due to various disasters and for poor people who had difficulty in maintaining a basic living for various social reasons.

Feature 3 Social security for immigrants in Heilongjiang in the Late Qing and Early Republic of China was not just the responsibility of the Government, various civil relief organizations also emerged. And there was an increasing number of social security and social relief acts for immigrants at all levels and in cooperation with various departments.

Table 2–1 General Situation of Heilongjiang Agricultural Reclamation Company (1913—1926)

Name	Time	Place	Total Area (shang)
Heilongjiang Reclamation Company	1913	Baiquan	139
Heilongjiang Reclamation Co. LTD	1914	Baiquan	12,960
Youyi Reclamation Company	1914	Baiquan	3,240
Jianye Company	1914	Baiquan	16,480
Funing Reclamation Company	1910	Dongning	
Funing Reclamation Company	1913	Dongning	2,500
Yuning Reclamation Company	N/A	Dongning	10,000
Yuhua Reclamation Company	N/A	Longmenzhen	16,2000
Shangjichang Agricultural Company	N/A	Suihua	20,000
Huma County three companies	1915	Huma	3,600
Suibin Fire Plough Company	1915	Suibin	57,000
Dongjing Reclamation Company	1915	Suibin	2,400
Zhiyuan Company	1915	Suibin	1,600
Jinen Reclamation Company	1915	Suibin	2,400
Guangxin Company	1925	Suibin	45,000
Taidong Company	1929	Tailai	8,715
Nanyang Reclamation cooperative	1929	Weihe	15,000
Dali Reclamation Co. LTD	1914	Linjiang	36
Total			217,270

Source: *Heilongjiang Immigration Summary*

Chapter 3
The Influence of Immigration and Local Population

3.1 Research on Jewish Immigration to China in Modern and Contemporary History

Since 1978, especially since 1988, professional institutions focusing on the history of the arrival of Jews in China and the study of the Jewish religion have been established in China successively, such as the Shanghai Jewish Research Center of the Shanghai Academy of Social Sciences (1988), the Diane/Gelford Glazer Institute of Jewish Culture at Nanjing University (1992, founded as the Center for Jewish Cultural Studies at Nanjing University, renamed the Institute of Jewish Culture at Nanjing University in 2001. In 2012, it was renamed as the present one, and now it is called the Institute of Jewish and Israeli Studies of Nanjing University). The Institute of Jewish and Israeli Studies of Nanjing University (founded in 1992 as the Center for Jewish Cultural Studies of Nanjing University, renamed in 2001 as the Institute of Jewish Cultural Studies of Nanjing University, and renamed in 2012 as the Institute of Jewish and Israeli Studies of Nanjing University), the Center for Jewish and Interreligious Studies of Shandong University (1994), the Center for Jewish Studies of Heilongjiang Academy of Social Sciences (2000), the Institute of Jewish Studies of Henan University (2002, renamed in 2018 as the Center for Israeli Studies of Henan University), etc. Meanwhile, several well-known experts and scholars at home and abroad have emerged in this research sphere, such as Jianchang Fang, Xin Xu, Guang Pan, Qianhong Zhang, Youde Fu, Shuxiao Li, Shuang Liu. In more than 30 years of research, Chinese scholars have achieved noticeable results in the "regional history" aspect of the history of Jewish immigration to China, especially the study of the Jews in Harbin and Shanghai (this part focuses mainly on the history of the Jewish immigration to China in modern history. Regarding the study of Jews in Kaifeng, our scholars have also made great contributions). However, due to lack of references, as well as the restriction of thinking patterns and other reasons, in recent years, Chinese scholars encounter research bottleneck in this field. Still, the "regional" historical research by Chinese experts and scholars has laid a solid foundation for breaking the "bottleneck" and conducting "holistic" historical study. In the author's view, under the paradigm of "holistic history" of Jews in China, it is worthwhile to explore such paths as the study of Jewish mobility and interaction in China, international relations and Jews in China, and Jewish economic activities in China from a micro-historical perspective.

3.1.1 Historical Periodization and Source Country of Jewish Immigration to China

Regarding the study on the history of Jewish immigration to China, historical staging is the first issue worth exploring. In contrast to the historical phasing of Jews in Shanghai, the chronological phasing of Jews in Harbin was more complex and had attracted scholarly discussion. There were three tides in the arrival of Jews in Shanghai: "The first involved the Sephardic Jews who came from Baghdad, Bombay, Singapore, and Hong Kong China, doing business in Shanghai in the decades after the 1840s; the second included the Russian (Ashkenazi) Jews who came to Shanghai to escape the anti-Semitic wave, revolution, and civil war in the decades after the end of the 19th century; the third consisted of Jewish refugees, the fugitives from Europe under Nazi oppression to Shanghai between 1933 and 1941." The historical phasing of the Jews in Shanghai is basically uncontroversial, since researchers have given relatively clear divisions and explanations.

However, there are five or six different historical staging methods of the Jewish immigration to Harbin. Teddy Kaufman divided the history into four periods: the early Harbin Jewish community (1898—1914), the prosperous period of the Harbin Jewish community (1914—1931), the period under Japanese occupation (1931—1945), and the arrival of Soviet troops. Xu Xin separates the history of the Jewish community in Harbin into five phases: the formative phase (late 19th century to 1902), the development phase (1903—1918), the heyday phase (1919—1929), the decline phase (1930—1949), and the epilogue phase (1950—1985). Based on important historical events and periods, Zhang Tiejiang divides the history of the Jews in Harbin into four periods: the Tsarist period (1897—1917), the period from the October Revolution to the September 18th Incident (1917—1931), the period of Japanese occupation (1931—1945), and the period from the victory of the War of Resistance Against Japanese Aggression to the beginning of New China (1945—1963). According to Liu Shuang, it is more appropriate to separate the historical process of Jews in Harbin into two periods, namely, "the period of development of Jewish historical activities in Harbin (1896—1931) and the period of decline of Jewish historical activities in Harbin (1931—1966)." The reason why Liu Shuang identifies the year 1931 as the dividing line between the development and decline periods is that "the Japanese invasion of northeast China after the September 18th Incident in 1931 was one of the most important events in the modern history of northeast China and an important turning point in the history of northeast China. At the same time, the Japanese occupation of northeast China was a great shock to the Chinese Eastern Railway and even to the businesses and lives of expatriates in Harbin."

But Wang Zhijun points out that "events such as the 'September 18th Incident' in 1931 or the Japanese occupation of Harbin in early 1932 should not be the dividing point that delineates the rise and fall of Harbin's Jewish population." However, he emphasizes later that "for a Chinese living in Harbin, the 28 years' life—from 1918 to the August of 1945—is obviously different from that of other periods (e.g., the period of Zhang Zuolin's rule over northeast China and the period of Japanese occupation), but I am afraid that it is questionable to use this as a criterion to measure the history of Jewish life in Harbin. This is also a question worth discussing in the study of Harbin Jews." According to Wang Zhijun, "No other historical event can surpass the impact of the October Revolution on the Jews of Harbin, as determined by the impact of the 'October Revolution' on the fate of millions of Jews in Russia at that time and the historical process of the Jews of Harbin themselves thereafter." The October Revolution "should become a historical demarcation point in the study of Harbin's Jews." Therefore, Wang Zhijun divides the history of the Jews in Harbin into three periods: "The first period, from the construction of the Middle East Railway at the end of the 19th century to the October Revolution in 1917, which can be regarded as the period of 'incubation and development' of the Jewish community in Harbin; the second period, from 1918 to the Japanese surrender in the August of 1945, a period of 'adjustment and development' for Harbin Jews; the third period ranges from the entry of Soviet troops into Harbin in the August of 1945 to the closing of the Old Synagogue in 1963, a period of 'decline' for Harbin Jews, especially the eight and a half months of Soviet troops in Harbin, which was 'devastating' for the Jewish community in Harbin." In the author's opinion, the historical staging of Jews in Harbin should be considered from the following aspects: first of all, the actual national conditions of China and Russia (Soviet Russia, USSR) at that time; second, the connection between Jews and Sino-Russian, Sino-Japanese and Russian-Japanese relations; third, the relationship between Jews and Russian expatriates, etc. The most important is the first one. In the context of the historical development of China, the history of the Jews in Harbin should be divided by the entry of the Japanese army into Harbin on February 5th, 1932 (Not the establishment of pseudo-Manchukuo in 1932). This is mainly due to the change in the rulers or administrators that the Jews faced in Harbin, previously Russia and then Japan. Wang Zhijun's view is questionable—"whether facing Tsarist Russia, the Soviet Union, local Chinese forces, or Japanese rule, the Jewish community in Harbin basically managed to have good relations with those in power and was basically 'developing' itself" and that "there should be no fundamental difference in the nature of the Jewish community in Harbin during different regimes". The author believes that the history of the Jews in Harbin should not only examine the Jews themselves, but that the connection between the Jews and Sino-Russian, Sino-Japanese, and Russian-Japanese relations is more worthy of consideration. Because the Jews had to deal with different objects of relations, which they could not choose, great attention should be paid to the issue of the relations between the Jews and the Russian diaspora, while studying the history of the Jews in Harbin at the time of the victory of the War of Resistance against Japanese Aggression on August 15th, 1945 and the subsequent entry of Soviet troops into Harbin. The author believes that the Jews in Harbin and the Soviet diaspora in Harbin faced a similar situation. In his article "Historical and Cultural Study of Jews in Harbin", the author points out that "Russian Jews in Russia were first valued for their 'national' identity, that is, for which ethnic group they were first concerned; However, when Russian Jews arrived in Harbin, China, they were first valued for their 'diaspora' identity, that is to say, they were first concerned with which nationality they were from, and later with the 'national' identity of the Jews. Specifically, the Russian Jews in Harbin were first 'expatriates' and then 'Jews'." From the founding of New China on October 1st, 1949, to the closing of the Harbin Taikona Synagogue in 1963, the development of Jews in Harbin was necessarily affected by the course of Chinese history. During this period, issues such as the policy of the Chinese Communist Party toward Jews in China are worthy of study. At the same time, the study of Jews' leaving China is still rare compared to the study of Jews' coming to China.

The history of the Jews in Harbin ranges from 1896 to 1932, and the history of the Jews under Russian administration can be subdivided, and this aspect is mainly concerned with the actual situation in Russia at that time. The factors of "the construction of the Chinese Eastern Railway, (i.e., the Middle East Railway), the expansion of Russian power in China, the Russo-Japanese War, the two Russian revolutions of 1905 and 1917 and the resulting civil war" led to the influx of Russian Jews to Harbin and south to Tianjin, Qingdao and Shanghai. The watershed in this period was 1920, as this was the year when the number of Jews in Harbin peaked at about 20,000. This was mainly caused by the Soviet-Russian Civil War of 1918—1920, while the Jewish community in Harbin was relatively well established and mature after decades of development, such as the construction of synagogues, the establishment of the Harbin Jewish Community Council, and the creation of *Jewish Life*, which had prepared certain conditions for acceptance. The number of Jews who came to Harbin because of the October Revolution was far less than the number of Jews who came to Harbin because of the Civil War. The Far Eastern Gazette on January 17th, 1919, stated that there were 7,500 Jews living in Harbin, of whom 4,500 were over 20 years of age and 3,000 were under 20, and the number of Jews in Harbin in 1913 was 5,032. The author does not deny the relationship between the October Revolution and the Civil War. A condition of this history that cannot be ignored is that Harbin was attached to the Chinese Eastern Railway. The year 1924 saw the establishment of diplomatic relations between the Soviet government and the Chinese Kuomintang. The Kuomintang's policy toward Jews in China and the relationship between Jews in Harbin and the warlords of northeast China and the Kuomintang deserve to be studied.

Linked to the historical chronology is the question of the geographical origin of Russian Jews. At present, there are no in-depth studies on this issue. With the construction of the Chinese Eastern Railway, "In 1898, Jews began to settle in Harbin, and the Jewish community and synagogue were officially established in 1903. The first group of Jews to move to Harbin came from Siberia." In 1904, "a second wave of Jewish immigration came to Harbin from Russia. The rampant pogroms in Kishinev and Odessa in southern Russia forced the Jews to search for a more spacious living in Manchuria." Wang states that "Harbin Jews are an extension of Russian Siberian Jews". He does not develop a specific analysis. The author believes that most of the Russian Jews who came with the construction of the Chinese Eastern Railway were "extensions of Siberian Jews" and belonged to the Asian part of Russia, while most of the Russian Jews who came with the October Revolution and the Civil War were from the European part of Russia, such as Ukraine, Belarus, and Georgia. The main reason for emphasizing the geographical origin of Asian and European Jews is to study and analyze the different Jewish groups, because Jews came to Harbin for different reasons, some to "seek gold" and some to "escape", thus the study of the Jews in Harbin as a whole is realized. The "whole" is not a simple superposition of "regions", but an organically linked "whole" of each "region". Newly published *Harbin Jewish Concise Dictionary* will provide good conditions for such in-depth research. It is known that Guo Qiuping is currently working on the Harbin Municipal Archives and the Heilongjiang Provincial Archives on Jewish household records in Harbin, which will contribute to the study of the geographical origin of the Jews. It is worthwhile to study the relationship between European-Russian and Asian-Russian Jews in Russia and Harbin in this regard. At present, scholars have not yet conducted research on the Russian area of origin of Jews in Shanghai.

In his article *An Analysis of the Rise and Fall of the Jewish Community in Tianjin*, Huang Xiaoyu mentions that "in the late 19th century, anti-Semitic frenzies arose in Russia, and many Russian Jews crossed Siberia to settle in northeastern China and Inner Mongolia to escape the persecution of the Tsar. The 1905 Revolution in Russia and the October Revolution of 1917 triggered another wave of Jewish migration, and some Belorussians who did not recognize the new Soviet regime lost their citizenship, most of them Jews, and left their homeland in search of livelihood opportunities. The Jews who came to the Harbin area built two synagogues, established the leadership of the community, participated in the establishment of the Harbin Chamber of Commerce, and took advantage of the convenient network of the Chinese Eastern Railway to develop commercial trade. It was then that some of the Jews continued to advance south to places like Tianjin and Shanghai." The statement that "some Belorussians who did not recognize the new Soviet regime lost their nationality, most of them were Jews" is questionable. The fact that most of the Russian Jews who came to Harbin in this period were "Belarus" also indicated that the political identity of Russian Jews who came to Harbin in different periods also needs to be studied. Moreover, there were more than two synagogues in the history of Harbin, only two synagogues exist. Huang

Xiaoyu also said, "The Jewish community in Tianjin was founded by Russian Ashkenazi Jews, starting with the establishment of the Tianjin Jewish Congregation in 1906. After decades of development, it has surpassed the Harbin Jewish community in terms of amenities and has become the largest Jewish community in the north and maintains close ties with other Jewish communities in China." Among them, it is questionable that Tianjin "became the first Jewish community in the North China". When and by what criteria did Tianjin become the "first Jewish community in the North China"? The author believes that both Tianjin and Qingdao are a part of the Jewish community in Harbin, merely branches. Tianjin was not the "largest Jewish community in the North China" in terms of the size of the Jewish population in Tianjin or the influence of the Tianjin Jewish community in China and internationally. Moreover, the majority of Jews in Tianjin are Russian Jews, and the demographic changes of Jews in Tianjin need a clear data support.

3.1.2 Mobility and Interactivity Research

After the arrival of Russian Jews in Harbin, due to the influence of Belarus and other factors, they continued to flow to Tianjin, Qingdao, Shanghai and other places inside the Shanhai Pass without settlement. In the course of the movement, economic or political interaction also occurred among Jews in Harbin, Qingdao, Tianjin and Shanghai. The Russian Jews who moved to different parts of the country were more mobile in China. In December 1938, "10 German-Austrian Jewish refugees came to Harbin"; in 1939, "about 150 German Jewish refugees came to Harbin and demanded refuge"; and in 1942, "about 150 German Jewish refugees came to Harbin and demanded refuge". In 1942, "according to the statistics, 31 German Jews came to Harbin for refuge, including 39 men and 29 women, a total of 68 people". During the Nazi massacre of Jews period, "21 German Jewish refugees" came to Qingdao. The "area" of Jewish movement in China and the reasons for it need to be examined in depth. "Of the 250,000 Russians who came to the Far East in 1918—1922, slightly more than half settled in China, in Manchuria and at ports such as Shanghai, Tianjin and Qingdao." One of the reasons was that "Russians generally regarded China as the garden of Eden". Manchuria was "the largest concentration of Belorussians in the Far East: a population of 155,000 in 1922. Shanghai, located in the middle of the Chinese coastline, "was undoubtedly the largest seaport in the Far East in the 1920s. As a trade center for one eighth of the world's population, it connects the vast Yangtze River basin with the ocean. About "30,000 Europeans, including 19,000 Belarus, lived in two enclaves with extraterritorial jurisdiction: the Universal Concession and the French Concession." This was because "the Russians in Shanghai liked their chosen city better than any other Asian city. They were even glad that they did not have to bargain with Parisian landlords or live in the countryside on Balkan farms. In addition, Shanghai gave them the opportunity to earn a living. Lawyers and doctors set up successful businesses. Entrepreneurs opened pharmacies, clothing stores and cafes along the fashionable Nanjing Road." By the mid-1930s, "Russian Jews in Shanghai had reached more than 4,000, far surpassing the Sephardic Jews and becoming the largest Jewish community in Shanghai." In the article Historical and Cultural Research on Jews in Harbin, I analyzed the relevant data and saw a phenomenon that "the migration of Russian Jews from Harbin was 'out of sync' at the same time as the mass immigration of Russians into Harbin. The migration was 'out of sync'." Therefore, "the relationship between Russian Jews and non-Jewish Russians in the process of migration remains to be further analyzed and studied by experts and scholars."

As a "rootless" nation, the Jews have a natural mobility, even a "holistic" mobility in various "regions" of the world. The "interaction" of Jews as a "whole" with each other in various "regions" is worth studying, especially the interaction of Jews themselves, the economic interaction of Jews in China and worldwide, the interaction of Jews with regional regimes and the interaction of Jews with China, Japan, the Soviet Union, the United States, Germany and other countries.

Concerning the self-interaction of Jews themselves, the interaction among Sephardic Jews, Ashkenazi Jews and later German Jews in Shanghai needs to be studied. In 1932, the Shanghai Ashkenazi Jewish Communal Association (SAJCA) was founded to "represent the Russian Jews in Shanghai in their external contacts and internal affairs". Since "most of the Sephardic Jews in Shanghai were naturalized British, they generally joined the British General Council, which had very strict conditions, and did not establish their own General Council. As the number of Russian Jews in Shanghai increased, they urgently needed to establish a place for cultural and social activities, so they set out to establish the Shanghai Jewish Federation." The Shanghai Jewish Club, founded in August 1932, "was also an influential institution founded by the Russian Jewish community," and its founder and life-time director was "Bloch, one of the leaders of the Russian Jewish community."

The relationship between the Shanghai Jewish Religious Congregation and the Shanghai Jewish General Assembly must be sorted out. The "Jews in Qingdao" consisted mainly of German and Russian Jews. "The first Jews came to Qingdao with the arrival of Westerners, especially Germans, at the end of the last century (late 19th century, author's note), so they were mostly German Jews, mainly merchants, bank employees, diplomats, etc. The initial influx of Russian Jews to China came with the construction of the Chinese Eastern Railway, basically from the Russian Far East to Qingdao via Harbin. Most of the Russian Jews lived from hand to mouth at first, and some later ranked among the middle class and only a few became wealthy." "Most of them had lived in Harbin for some time before settling in Qingdao and maintained economic and kinship ties with Harbin." Harbin "was the Jewish religious, political and cultural center of northern China, so the Jews of Qingdao were always under the leadership of the Harbin Jewish community." This interaction between Qingdao and Harbin has not been studied. At the same time, what are the ways and extent and effects of interaction among Jews in Harbin, Shanghai, Tianjin and Qingdao?

Regarding the economic interaction of Jews in China and worldwide, among the early Jewish merchants who came to Tianjin to engage in the fur business, "Solomon Bikhovsky was a pioneer who came to Ulaanbaatar from Belarus via Siberia in 1909. He was one of the first Europeans to buy furs directly from Mongolian hunters. He sold furs directly to Europe and the USA without intermediaries. Later, he established the Bikhovsky Brothers and Shikh Company in Harbin and continued the fur business." The tea trade was an important commercial activity of Russian merchants and Russian Jews in China. For more than 20 years from the end of the 19th century to the October Revolution, "Russian merchants shipped tea from Hankow and Fujian by sea to Vladivostok or the port of Dalian, from where it was shipped to Russia via the Chinese Eastern Railway. According to the *Far Eastern Newspaper*, the tea shipped from Dalian to Harbin in 1910 weighed 54,000 pounds, and the tea exported via the Chinese Eastern Railway between 1912 and 1914 reached 3-4 million pounds per year. The ships of the Heilongjiang Shipping Company, which belonged to the Chinese Eastern Railway Bureau, often traveled to and from Shanghai and Tianjin to transfer tea. Russian scholar Romanova said: 'Every year, 65% of the tea imported into Russia is imported via the Chinese Eastern Railway'." The actual controller of the Jewish Skidelsky family was the eldest son, Jacob. "Jacob's wife Lisa traveled through Paris to invest in securities in the United States, only to be hit by the 1929 blackout of the Wall Street stock market and lost all the capital invested." Her grandson was the later famous Robert Skidelsky, author of the three-volume biography of Keynes and Rediscovering Keynes, who was born in Harbin on April 25, 1939, and was a famous economist and member of the British House of Lords. The author believed that his study of Keynes was closely related to his family's actual economic encounters, and that he is drawing historical lessons from his grandmother's investments. Also in Harbin, the Jewish Gawarski was also "devastated" by the biggest financial storm in history that swept the world, the "earthquake" on Wall Street in the United States, and his plywood factory fell into total loss. This suggests that the "regional" economic activity of the Jews in China was closely linked to the "whole" of the world, but the depth and breadth of this connection needs to be further explored, and the international status of Harbin at the time has not been sufficiently brought to the fore. The just-published *Concise Dictionary of Harbin Jewry* provides abundant study resources for such inquiry.

With regard to the interaction of Jews with the regimes in the region and the interaction of Jews with China, Japan, the Soviet Union, the United States, Germany, etc., "the Jewish community in Harbin was basically able to have good relations with those in power, whether in the face of Tsarist Russia, the Soviet Union, local Chinese forces, or Japanese rule," while the "interaction" of Jews with the Chinese regime in China needs to be studied in depth. The relationship between the Jews in Harbin, where the railroad was attached, and the Chinese regime, the then administrators of Harbin and the Chinese Eastern Railway Administration has yet to be clarified. This problem also exists in the study of Jews in Shanghai. At the same time, John Stephen, professor of history at the University of Hawaii, notes that "Russian exiles caught in the great whirlwind of Chinese nationalism, Japanese imperialism, and Soviet communism had no choice but to move in response to the enormous momentum of political currents. Living in turn under the power of Chinese warlords, Japanese officers, and Soviet commissars, they worked for each in turn in order to survive." The author believes that the Kasper case is not only a question of anti-Semitism and the Russian Fascist Party, but also the intricate relationship among China, Japan, and Russia that needs to be clarified. From February 5th, 1932, when the Japanese army was stationed in Harbin until the Japanese surrender on August 15th, 1945, the relationship between Japan and Russia in Harbin has not been deeply studied in our academic circles. Regarding the Fugu Plan, researchers must excavate the difference between the Japanese methods and the essence. In fact, Japan, like Germany, kept their eyes on the money in the hands of the Jews, and essentially used it for war. At the same time, the researcher must also analyze the mentality of the Jews who were caught in the crossfire; in March 1939 "Lev Zichmann, a Harbin Jew, proposed to Colonel Inuzuka the idea of moving 200 European Jewish leather workers and 600 of their families to pseudo-Manchukuo." In Hongkou, Shanghai, where many Jews lived, "there were also many Japanese living there, so it was also called Little Tokyo." After the September 18th Incident, Japan's policy toward the Jews and the changes in the relationship between Germany and Japan as German allies have yet to be studied in depth, and the American factor needs to be analyzed in depth too.

Interactivity is also manifested in the exchange, influence and penetration of the two cultures. Pan Guang's *Sino-Jewish Cultural Exchange in China since Modern Times*, Fu Youde's *Between Tradition and Modernity: The Reformation of Judaism and its Implications for the Reconstruction of Chinese Culture Today*, Zhang Qianhong's *A Comparison of Judaism in Biblical Times and Confucian Educational Thought in the Pre-Qin Dynasty*, and Zhou Guojian's *A Comparative Study of Traditional Chinese and Jewish Family Concepts* examine relevant cultural issues in the past and at present. Shi Fang's *History of the Russian Diaspora in Harbin* includes a chapter on "The Influence and Role of Russian Culture in Harbin", which involved three aspects: "architectural culture", "customary culture", and "press, publishing, culture and education". Wang Zhicheng's *History of Russian Expatriates in Shanghai* is also covered in this regard. Abraham Olmert (O'Mouran) asked Li Shuxiao in an interview, "What have you learned about the contribution of Jews to this city (Harbin, author's note)?" Li Shuxiao pointed out, "The influence of the Jews on the art of architecture is still evident today. In Harbin, some customs and habits were kept under the influence of the Jews. If you compare Harbin with other cities, you will find that people in Harbin eat more bread and drink more beer than Chinese in other places. You must know that Harbin Beer, the earliest beer in China, was first produced by the Harbin Brewery founded by Jews. Former Israeli Prime Minister Ehud Olmert also said, "We are fortunate to have grown up with two cultures-Chinese and Jewish. The Jewish culture taught us how to choose our path in life, and the Chinese culture taught us how to move forward in life." In his autobiography, Ehud's father wrote about one of his Chinese assistants, Lao Yan. He "learned a lot from Lao Yan's words and character and learned a lot about the strengths of the Chinese." "Lao Yan has all the good qualities of the Chinese people. I think he is a very typical representative of the Chinese people. I talked with him many times and got the strong impression that the Chinese are very hard-working, contented, well-educated, helpful, and always thinking of their families and friends. The Chinese are not conquered by guns but have succeeded in 'engulfing' other nations with their hard work." This is just a blip of the "whole" of the interaction between Chinese and Jewish cultures, and other aspects need to be studied in depth.

3.1.3 Research on the Historical Dependence Between the Past and the Present

Since 1978, scholars in China have been gradually deepening and expanding their research on the history of Jewish arrival in China in modern history. In the historical connection between the past and the present, scholars in China have found a point of academic growth from the "regional" to the "holistic". The Shanghai Center for Jewish Studies at the Shanghai Academy of Social Sciences, the Institute of Jewish Studies at Henan University, and the Institute of Jewish Culture at Nanjing University have all taken their "regional" studies as a basis and expanded them to include the Holocaust, Israel, and American Jewish research as a whole. These studies are at the forefront of research that can be brought into line with the world. The Shanghai Jewish Research Center of the Shanghai Academy of Social Sciences has been awarded the National Social Science Foundation's major project "Research on Jewish Refugees in China" and "Shanghai Jewish Refugee Memorial Hall" serves as a bridge between China and other countries, such as Israel and the United States. The Shanghai Center for Jewish Studies also publishes the *Jewish-Israeli Studies Series*, extending its own academic territory. The Institute of Jewish Culture at Nanjing University held an exhibition on May 20th, 2013, entitled "The Scourge of the Nazis: Postal Evidence of the Holocaust and the European Shoah" to highlight its strengths in Jewish culture and other areas while exploring new areas of research. In 1988, XuXin established the Chinese Society for Judaic Studies and edited and published the *Jewish Encyclopedia* in 1993. He did not confine himself to a specific Jewish community but gave us a comprehensive understanding of Judaism and the Jewish people. Henan University established the Center for Israel Studies in addition to the Institute of Jewish Studies. Based on the study of the Jews of ancient Kaifeng, the Institute has realized the parallel development of Jewish studies and Israeli studies. It is worth mentioning that the Institute's "Qiu Cailian

Dissertation Award" has been successfully held for 11 years and has become a "brand" in the academic community. The Center for Judaism and Interfaith Studies at Shandong University, a key research base in the humanities and social sciences of the Ministry of Education, is well known for its research and translation on Judaism and publishes the *Journal of Jewish Studies* on a regular basis. At the same time, the websites of the above research units have been well established. Based on the original Jewish New Hall, a first-class "Harbin Jewish Memorial Hall" has been built, which comprehensively displays the history of Jews in Harbin and China. The large-scale photo exhibition "Jews in Harbin" put on display in Israel, Russia, the United States, and Australia, and it caused a strong reaction among the Jews living in Harbin. However, the Center for Jewish Studies of the Heilongjiang Academy of Social Sciences has not built its own website or established relevant research publications. The author believes that with the advantage of the historical resources of Jews in Harbin, it can be more unique and attractive in these two aspects, especially in the construction of the website. The Harbin Huangshan Jewish Cemetery is the largest Jewish cemetery in the Far East. The just-published *Harbin Jewish Concise Dictionary* appendixes the "Harbin Huangshan Jewish Cemetery Burial Distribution Table", which introduces the names, locations and dates of death of the graves' owners in more detail and in three languages: Chinese, English and Russian. If published in the form of a website, it would not only facilitate the search for relatives of Jews around the world, but also contribute to the deepening of academic research. Nikolai Zayko (Goliath), a Russian expatriate who lived in Harbin, once organized the "Russian House" association in Harbin and regularly carried out many activities.

Based on the academic research into historical ties between the past and the present, Harbin and Shanghai have developed interstate or interregional cooperation to strengthen the role of historical ties in concrete practice. 2004 and 2006 saw the convening of two "International Symposiums on Harbin Jewish Historical and Cultural Studies" in Harbin; in 2007, the "International Forum on Economic and Trade Cooperation between Harbin and World Jewish" was held in Harbin. Also, 2004 witnessed the opening of Heilongjiang-Israel Economic and Trade Fair in Harbin. Ehud Olmert emphasized that Heilongjiang had made remarkable achievements in electronics, food, science and technology, and Israel has accumulated rich experience in agriculture and industry, etc. He believed that the cooperation between the two sides in the fields of agricultural innovation, irrigation technology, food processing, etc. would achieve more positive results. The 2nd China-Harbin-Israel Cooperation Conference was held in Harbin from January 16th to 20th, 2011, with the theme of "Passing on Friendship, Promoting Cooperation". In the article *Our Family's Root Is in Harbin*, Ehud Olmert pointed out that "most of the Israeli agriculture uses greenhouses to achieve high yield, high quality and high efficiency in agriculture. It is suggested that Heilongjiang Province should open up overseas markets and export livestock and agricultural products to

Russia, Northeast Asia and Europe, acting as the 'winter kitchen' and 'vegetable base' of Europe like Israel." He also mentioned, "I have contacted many delegations from Heilongjiang, and they are interested in science and technology innovation and are willing to develop agricultural science and technology cooperation with Israel." The author believes that in terms of cooperation, both Heilongjiang and Israel have some problems in terms of information not being effectively connected. Israel's advanced agricultural technology with limited land resources and very different climatic conditions may not be suitable for Heilongjiang, which is rich in resources and enjoys good weather conditions. Due to the climate, greenhouses may not be fully functional in Heilongjiang. In the future development, relevant experts and scholars should take advantage of their disciplines in this regard to clear up the misunderstanding and misconceptions between the two sides as early as possible. The second is the effectiveness of implementation and enforcement. In 2007, "Shanghai's volume of trade with Israel was $734 million, an increase of 43%, of which Shanghai's volume of imports reached $504 million, an increase of 44%. Shanghai's main imports from Israel involved electrical machinery, non-metallic mineral products, professional, scientific and control instruments, metal products, etc. Shanghai's main exports to Israel are as follows: land vehicles, clothing, electrical machinery, steel, etc." Compared with Harbin, Shanghai enjoys certain advantages of location and resources. However, the superior conditions of Heilongjiang and Harbin should be thoroughly investigated and introspected, so as to achieve a "whole" win-win situation between Heilongjiang and Israel.

In *China and Israel: A Glorious Past and an Opportunity-Filled Future*, former Israeli Prime Minister Ehud Olmert emphasized that "the development of relations between nations relies on a variety of factors and must be based on common interests and be mutually beneficial." He pointed out that "mutual respect for each other's heritage, history and traditions is a strong bond that cannot be simply seen as a byproduct of business and politics."Abraham Olmert (Omuran), Ehud's brother and Minister of Science, Technology and Agriculture at the Israeli Embassy in China, spoke straightforward, "While holding lectures, seminars and even publishing books are important to strengthen the relationship between China and Israel, and there is a greater need to address practical issues." He also made it clear that "I am promoting the cause of cooperation in China in the hope that what I do will have a positive impact on the reality in China." With the theme of "Understanding and Win-Win", Abraham Olmert analyzed the problems of Israeli side in the economic and trade relations between Israel and China. In his opinion, "for Israelis, when they do business with the Chinese and develop economic and trade relations with China, it is important to pay attention to the issue of cultural differences". Abraham Olmert (Omuran) also discussed "different business concepts", "differences in mentality", "Chinese conditions and suitable strategic considerations", "Bargaining in the Chinese market" and "Patience and sincerity". At present, Chinese scholars are lagging behind in this area of study. Experts and scholars should examine, reflect and summarize the path of Sino-Israeli cooperation in the "region" from the "whole" of Jewish culture and the "whole" of Sino-Israeli relations, instead of emotional reasoning. The academic level of research needs to be deepened. In addition, the Jewish factor in the relationship among China, Russia and Israel is also a subject that needs further research.

In addition, on June 28th, 2013, the Institute of Jewish Culture at Nanjing University, headed by Professor Xu Xin of the Department of Philosophy and Religion of Nanjing University, was established as a research center for international issues in Jiangsu universities. "The Center for the Study of Jewish-Israeli Issues" has defined the main theme of its research as the study of Jewish-Israeli issues in a global perspective. The research focuses are intended to include the following 4 areas: ① the formation and role of global Jewish organizations; ② the study of Holocaust memory; ③ the cultural mechanisms of Jewish economic and technological success; ④ the study of cooperation between Israel and Jiangsu. The study of cooperation between Israel and Jiangsu will be approached from the following aspects: ① a study of cooperation between Israel and Jiangsu. A study of the economic complementarity and cooperation between Israel and Jiangsu; ② the economic miracle of Israel as an example to examine the great role played by the culture of innovation in the economic development of the country and to provide ideas for the establishment of a new way of economic development and cultural support for Jiangsu; ③ in the increasingly close Jiangsu-Israeli economic cooperation, how to provide advisory services to Jiangsu enterprises on Jewish-Israeli issues, including national society, language and culture, customs, religious practices, etc., and to provide information about Jiangsu for the Israeli enterprises concerned, so as to facilitate mutual understanding and promote substantive cooperation and exchanges. On September 30th, 2013, Peretz Lavie, President of the Technion-Israel Institute of Technology (TGIT), and Gu Peihua, Executive President of Shantou University, signed a memorandum of cooperation in Tel Aviv, Israel, to establish the Guangdong Technion-Israel Institute of Technology (TGIT). These regions do not have historical ties with the Jews themselves, but the reality of the "regional" advantage of achieving academic and economic ties with Israel is worth reflecting on and exploring.

3.1.4 Shift from Macro-research to Micro-research

According to the long tradition of historical research, when studying a historical object, the researcher must first examine it at a macro level. Only on the basis of a more adequate argument can the researcher conduct a microscopic study of it, because only in this way can the "region" be systematically studied under the grasp of the "whole". Of course, each "region" can also be studied as a "whole", but this depends on the representativeness and feasibility of the "region". In the process of studying the history of the Jews' arrival in China, Chinese scholars have also taken a research path from the "whole" to the "region," and I do not deny the "regional" research done for the "whole" in the first place. "Region" and "whole" are relative.

The systematic macroscopic study of Jews in Shanghai began with Pan Guang and Wang Jian's *The Jews of Shanghai over a Century and a Half-An Oriental Page in the History of the Jewish People*, which examined origin and development of Shanghai Jews from a holistic perspective. On the basis of macro-studies, micro-studies of Jews in Shanghai are represented by Rao Lihua's *The Spiritual Home of the Exiles: A Study of the Shanghai Jewish Chronicle*, Tang Yating's *The Musical Life of the Jewish Community in Shanghai (1850—1950, 1998—2005)*, and Wang Jian's *A History of Jewish Social Life in Shanghai*. It is noteworthy that these studies were preceded by two monographs published by the Shanghai Jewish Research Center, *The Road to Jewish National Revival* and *Jewish Civilization*. These two books laid a certain academic foundation for subsequent research in terms of the history of the Jewish "whole". In the author's view, this is the first phase of academic research at the Shanghai Jewish Research Center of the Shanghai Academy of Social Sciences. The second stage is the study of Nazis, Jewish refugees and China, which was marked by the award of the National Social Science Foundation's major project "Research on Refugees from China" to the Center for Jewish Studies at the Shanghai Academy of Social Sciences in 2011. Like the first phase, the second phase was preceded by a thorough "holistic" academic preparation: Pan Guang, Wang Shuming, and Sheng Wenqin edited *The Political and Cultural Impact of the Nazi Holocaust* and Pan Guang and Wang Jian's *Jews and China: Interaction and Friendship between Two Ancient Civilizations in the Modern Era*. The academic basis for Jewish studies in Harbin is relatively weak.

The systematic and macroscopic study of Jews in Harbin began with Liu Shuang's *History of the Jewish Diaspora in Harbin*. Liu Shuang's study of Jews as part of the diaspora is of high academic value. This is inseparable from the "holistic" thinking that Liu Shuang has been engaged in the study of the history of Russian diaspora in Harbin. Therefore, Yu Pei, a researcher of the Chinese Academy of Social Sciences, pointed out that "this is a comprehensive academic monograph reflecting the history and culture of the Jewish diaspora in Harbin, which, to a certain extent, makes up for the deficiencies of the previous research on the history of the Jewish diaspora in Harbin and has positive pioneering significance in this research field." In April, 2002, "Song Fatang, then governor of Heilongjiang Province, gave instructions to Zhang Tiejiang, a researcher at the Heilongjiang Academy of Social Sciences, on his proposal to strengthen the study of the Jews in Harbin: 'Please ask Comrade Qu Wei to read it, and hope that the Academy of Social Sciences will make a decision on how to organize and use the remains of these sites for the study and put forward specific proposal.' Heilongjiang Provincial Academy of Social Sciences accordingly established the Harbin Jewish Historical and Cultural Research Center, and President Qu Wei was also the first director of the center." Previously, *Harbin Jews*, edited by Qu Wei and Li Shuxiao, and Zhang Tiejiang's *Unraveling the Mystery of Harbin Jewish History: A Study of the*

Jewish Community in Harbin were published. Li Shuxiao "has made great efforts in collecting, translating, and organizing written and photographic materials of Harbin Jews, and has published and presented a series of significant research results that have promoted the study of the history and culture of Harbin Jews." Zhang Tiejiang "has made initial achievements in research on the Harbin Jewish community, the Harbin Jewish cemetery, and Jewish industrial operations in Harbin." On this basis, the representative works of Jewish micro studies in Harbin are *The Kasper Incident: Cultural and Ethnic Conflict in Harbin 1932—1945* by Dan Ben Kanan of Israel and translated by Tiechao Yin and Han Sun; *History of Jewish Families in Harbin* by Tianyan Han, Hongze Cheng, and Hong Xiao; *A Concise Dictionary of Harbin Jewry* edited by Wei Qu and Shuxiao Li, and *The Religious and Political Life of Harbin Jews in the First Half of the 20th Century* by Zhijun Wang and Wei Li, etc. The author believes that the study of Jews in Harbin is better integrated with the study of local culture in Harbin, such as Li Shuxiao, Shi Fang and Liu Shuang, who were initially experts and scholars in the study of local history of Harbin and the history of Russian expatriates in Harbin.

From the above sorting and reviewing of research achievements, the current Jewish studies in Shanghai and Harbin have basically made the leap from macro-study to micro-study, shifting toward micro themes such as the history of social, religious and political life. In the author's view, economic activities, etc., are an important area of microscopic research. The reasons are as follows: first, Jews are well known for their economic activities or economic power all over the world; second, Jewish economic activities are closely linked to international relations. The Sephardic Jews of Shanghai, such as Hartung, Sassoon, and Kadoorie, and the Ashkenazi Jews of Harbin, such as Skidelsky, Gewalski, Kasper, and Derikin, are important research resources in the history of Jewish arrival in China. Papers such as Pan Guang's *The Development and Rise and Fall of Jewish Merchant Groups in Hong Kong and Shanghai since 1840* and Zhang Zhongli's *The Activities of the Sassoon Group in Shanghai and its Role in the Development of Shanghai at the Beginning of the 20th Century* sort out and justify the activities and roles of Sassoon and other Jewish merchants. According to *A Concise Dictionary of Jews in Harbin,* it can be seen that the Jews in Harbin's banking industry "took the lead"—China and Russia Dawson Bank, Citibank, Faja Bank, HSBC, Concord Bank, Shinji Bank, Jewish National Bank, Far Eastern Bank, Huamei Bank and so on all have the "presence of the Jews". The Jews were either personally present or behind the scenes. "The capital stock of the China and Russia Dawson Bank was 6 million rubles when it was founded. It was founded with the participation of four French banks (Hodinger Bank, Lyon Trust Bank, BNP Paribas, National Discount Bank) and one Russian bank-St. Petersburg International Commercial Bank. The St. Petersburg International Commercial Bank, in turn, was a subsidiary of the German Discount Company, which was run by German Jewish capitalists. A.Iu. Rothstein, the director and the first general director of the Bank, was the representative of the

International Commercial Bank of Petersburg, a close friend of the Russian Minister of Finance, and the central figure in the business of the Bank, the real president and dominator."

In terms of the conditions for micro-research, the state of the sources and the research environment, among others, are crucial. In terms of sources, Teddy Kaufman, President of the Israel-China Friendship Association and President of the Association of Jews Originally from Israel in China, noted in his article "The Revival of Jewish History in Harbin" that it is very unfortunate that "the archives of the Jewish community in Shanghai have not been preserved." "The archives of the Jewish community in Tianjin were taken out of China and were preserved at first by Iglund and later sent to the Jewish Center Archives in Jerusalem for preservation." Of these, "the best preserved and most valuable are the historical archives of the Jews of Harbin. These archives, which are currently kept in the Heilongjiang Provincial Archives, contain the entire 60 years history of Harbin's Jews from 1903 to 1963. We are very familiar with these archives from our social life experience in Harbin, and they will help summarize the history of Chinese Jews, especially the history of Harbin Jews, which used to be the cradle of the Jewish people's political and commercial life in this region." From March 1st to 31st, 2009, "a delegation of young scholars led by Han Tianyan, Associate Researcher of the Center for Jewish Studies, Heilongjiang Academy of Social Sciences, visited Israel at the invitation of the Israel-China Friendship Association and the Association of Israeli Jews of Chinese Origin. The delegation successfully reproduced valuable archival materials of Harbin Jewish history and collected oral materials of Harbin Jews. The delegation made a total of about 60,000 pages of precious Harbin Jewish historical archival materials, about 60 million words. At the same time, a group of Harbin Jews oral history materials were salvaged and nearly 40 Harbin Jews and their descendants who originally lived in Harbin were interviewed." Qu Wei stressed in the Postscript of *A Concise Dictionary of Jews in Harbin* that "the study of Harbin Jewish history and culture is in its infancy, and although the results of our research represent the latest findings and the latest progress in this study, which is fundamental and pioneering, due to the fact that a large amount of information on the study of the history and culture of Harbin Jews has been scattered around the world, and that more collections have not been made due to financial constraints, especially the fact that there are few surviving Jews living in Harbinmw, and that rare oral histories have been rescued, there are still many mysteries to be further uncovered." Liu Shuang also stressed that "objectively speaking, the study of the history and culture of Harbin Jews in the real academic sense is still very weak. Many studies are still at the level of data collection and organization, and the historical data that we can see now is only a part of all the historical data of Harbin Jews."

But Wang Zhijun points out, "It is well known that Harbin and Shanghai are the two most concentrated and influential Jewish communities. In terms of the number and influence of papers and monographs, the study of Shanghai Jews is inferior to that of the Harbin Jewish Institute in many aspects, both for historical and objective reasons and lack of broad vision as well as deep thinking." Firstly, the author believes that from the perspective of macro-study and micro-study, especially micro-study, the Jewish research in Harbin is not inferior to or even superior to the Jewish research in Shanghai, which is mainly caused by the problem of information. At the same time, the author also recognizes that the study of Jews in Harbin "suffers from the problem that the researchers' vision is not broad enough and their thinking is not deep enough", which is weaknesses in the research environment, and mainly involves the research path and paradigm of the history of Jews in China. The study of Jews in Harbin is basically at the stage of "history", while the study of Jews in Shanghai has the advantage of "theory", i.e., academic theory, such as Pan Guang's paper *Nationality and Legal Problems of Jews in China (1840—1945)*. Second, there exists the issue of government support. According to the author, the governments of both places attach great importance to the study of the history of Jews immigration to China. However, the policies in Shanghai were more continuous, targeted and effective than those in Harbin. Among them, Mr. Wang Daohan and Mr. Song Fatang are to be credited. Again, the researchers' own strengths. Pan Guang is not only the director of the Center for Jewish Studies, but also the director of the Shanghai Center for International Studies, the director of the Shanghai Cooperation Organization Research Center, etc., which has better realized the connection, dialogue and cooperation with the international academic community. Finally, language condition should be taken into consideration. The Russian language proficiency of the researcher is an important condition for Jewish research in Harbin. In fact, the current research on the history of Jewish immigration to China in both places takes full advantage of their respective strengths.

With the relevant historical archives under control, the study of the history of the Jewish immigration to China requires multilingual and multidisciplinary participation; Hence, cross-regional research is imperative. Meanwhile, the exploration of research paradigms and research paths is also necessary. The relative concepts of "region" and "whole" provide a path of inquiry for the study of the history of the Jews' immigration to China.

3.2 Historical and Cultural Investigation on "Lithuanians in Harbin"

Settled by water, thriving by the road. Harbin is a city gradually formed with the construction of the Middle East Railway. The flow direction of Songhua River makes the hub of the Chinese Eastern railway finally located in Harbin. With the opening of the Chinese Eastern railway, Harbin gradually developed from a village (fishing village) dominated by natural economy into a modern emerging city. After 20 to 30 years of development, it has grown into the center of Northeast Asia and even one of the world's economic and trade centers. Lithuanians, as expatriates, came with the construction and opening of the Chinese Eastern Railway.

Lithuania (Lietuvos Respublika, литва in Russian, Republic of Lithuania in English, リトアニア in Japanese) was twice occupied by Germany and ruled by Russia. "Lithuanians in Harbin" status is an expatriate at the first place, thus, Lithuanians tended to be included in Russian (Soviet) demographic categories. This created ambiguity and discrepancy in the "Lithuanians in Harbin" demographic data. Lithuania also set up a consulate in Harbin; They carried out economic activities in Harbin and so on. Lithuanians were also an important cultural factor in the characteristic culture of "pluralism, interaction and symbiosis" in Harbin, where "foreign and Chinese cultures blend together".

3.2.1 Demographic Change of "Lithuanians in Harbin"

Litis Sutkauska, the cultural counsellor of Embassy of the Republic of Lithuania in China, once introduced, "In 1923 there were about 1300 Lithuanians in China, of whom 700 were Lithuanian and the rest were Russians, Jews and other nationalities born or residing in Lithuania." "Most of the eastern European nationals entered Harbin with the Russians at the beginning of the construction of the Chinese Eastern Railway, while most of the nationals from other countries entered Harbin with the opening of the international commercial port after the Russo-Japanese War. The expatriates of these countries and regions came to Harbin mostly to do business or run an enterprise. Although the number of expatriates of each country is small, the number of people is stable because they have their own factories or shops. Before 1931, there were about 1,200-1,300 Lithuanians in Harbin".

According to *Foreign Affairs in Harbin Annals*, "In 1928, there were 962 nationals from 18 countries living in Harbin. Among them, 140 were from France, 116 from Britain, 72 from the United States, 164 from Germany, 20 from Sweden, 57 from Italy, 28 from the Netherlands, 30 from Austria, 3 from Portugal, 37 from Denmark and 8 from India. In 1930, there were 1729 nationals from more than 20 countries in Harbin. Among them, 109 were from Czechoslovakia, 333 from Germany, 178 from Britain, 49 from Greece, 84 from France, 10 from Hungary, 81 from the United States, 11 from Sweden, 53 from Denmark, 64 from Italy, 31 from the Netherlands, 24 from India, 3 from Portugal, 1 from Switzerland, 49 from Greece, 36 from Austria, 7 from Romania, 3 from Serbia and 17 from Armenia. Most of them are businessmen, factory owners, bank managers, employees and technicians of foreign enterprises, and a few are lawyers, journalists and doctors." However, the introduction to the population of the nationals in Harbin did not mention the details of "Lithuanians in Harbin".

From 1898 to 1932, the number of "Lithuanians in Harbin" was rarely recorded. If there is any report of "Lithuanians in Harbin" in the *Far East Newspaper* from March 14th, 1906, to March 1st, 1921, it needs to be checked in depth. There were no Lithuanians in the "population" of *Harbin Guide* edited by *Dongchui Business* in 1922; In 1929, the Xinhua Press in Harbin published *The Secular Life of Binjiang* without mentioning the section of "population"; In 1931, the *Municipal Report of Harbin Special City* compiled by Harbin Special City Municipal Bureau, Chapter 7, Volume 3, "Municipal Council", Section 2, "Municipal Registered Residence" and the "population" in the Japanese version of *Harbin Case* published in 1933 did not contain the number of "Lithuanians in Harbin". In the *Introduction to Special City Harbin* published in 1936, the population of "Lithuanians in Harbin" was not introduced. In the book *Population Changes in Harbin* published in 1998, "Changes in the Number of Overseas Chinese population in Harbin from 1916 to 1931" did not mention the number of "Lithuanians in Harbin" and its changes. "Changes of alien population and nationality composition before the founding of the People's Republic of China" in *Population in Harbin Annals* is basically consistent with the data introduction in *Population Changes in Harbin*, mainly concentrated on the period after 1932.

The reports related to population in *Binjiang Times* are as follows: *The Latest Statistics of Harbin Household Registration (Section 6)* on May 22nd, 1923, "The Domestic and Foreign Household Registration in The Special Area of East Province (Section 6)" on September 8th, 1923, "The Population Table of Daoli (Section 7)" on November 22nd, 1925, "Recent Population Survey of the Three Northeast Province (Section 7)" on October 20th,1926, "The Total number of Resident Aliens in Local Port (Section 6)" on December 22nd, 1927, "The Population Survey of Habu" supplemented on January 14th, 1928, the supplement on March 29th, 1928, "The Survey on Resident Aliens in the Special Zone", "The Population Statistics of Harbin (Section 10)" on December 21st, 1930, "The Household Statistics of Harbin (Section 6)" on April 26th, 1932, "The Household Statistics of Harbin (Section 6)" on November 2nd, 1932, "The Household Statistics of Harbin (Section 7)" on November 19th, 1933, and "The Household Survey of Harbin (Section 6)" on June 5, 1934, etc.

The reports on population in *Binjiang Daily* are as follows: Statistics on "The Nationality of Harbin' Population in the third section" on November 27th, 1938, "Population Statistics of Harbin in the fourth section" on July 6th, 1941, "The Number of People Surveyed by City in the fourth section" on April 7th, 1942, "The Check of the City's Population in the third section" on May 10th,1943, etc.

In *Binjiang Times* and *Binjiang Daily*, the author could not find the population data of "Lithuanians in Harbin". One reason for this is "the qualifications of Belarusians". At the same time, the relevant departments in China pay more attention to the "number of households" rather than the specific "number" in demographic statistics. Therefore, we need to clarify Lithuania's historical relationship with Russia (the Soviet Union). Lithuania was twice occupied by Germany and under Russian (Soviet) rule. From a vertical historical point of view, in the 19th century, "Russia occupied the whole Lithuania. During the occupation, Russia adopted the policy of "divide and rule" towards Lithuania. Under this policy, Lithuania was divided into several provinces and actively pursued the policy of 'Russianization'." From the October Revolution of 1917 to 1920, "the

Three Baltic states were in the period of contention between the Soviet regime and the bourgeois regime, and finally ended in the victory of the bourgeois regime". From the early to mid-20th century, i.e., from 1920 to 1940, "Soviet Russia (Soviet Union) was forced to withdraw due to the development of the 'nationalist movement', and the three countries experienced a period of independence for about 20 years". On 3rd August,1940, Lithuania was "accepted into the Soviet Union" and became "a republic of the Soviet Union." In 1990, Lithuania formally declared its independence. September 6th, 1991, "The highest authorities of the Soviet Union recognize the independence of the three countries." This raises the question of whether Lithuanians should be counted as a large group of Russian nationals or as a separate small group.

Lithuanian relations with Russia are related to Polish-Russian relations. "During the partition of Poland in 1772, 1793, and 1795, most of Lithuania was taken by Russia (the rest came under Prussia's control)". "As another result of the partition of Poland in the 18th century, the Russian empire annexed Lithuania. When annexed, Lithuanians could claim the independent status they had long enjoyed, and that they were great as rulers of a vast kingdom in the heart of Europe. No other part of the Baltic under Russian rule has the memory of such an independent nation."

The relationship between Lithuania and Germany proves that "on December 11th, 1917, the Lithuanian commission officially declared Lithuania an independent state with Vilnius as its capital; But the proclamation, which emphasized close ties to the German Empire, also accepted the necessity for military, monetary and customs unions. 9 weeks later, a more intelligently worded announcement emerged. It avoided any mention of German patronage and established 16th February 1918 as Independence Day." "Without the support of the German Empire, they would inevitably fall back into Russia's orbit," Randolph once said. In the Baltic region, the best place to colonize was Lithuania: its people seem malleable. It had large tracts of fertile land, and it had strong pre-war commercial ties with East Prussia."

According to the archives of "The Police General Management Office of Eastern Province Special District (1920—1932)" collected by Harbin Archives, "the management of the alien population became an important task for the police department at that time, and a lot of files in this area were formed. Among them, there were Chinese and foreign account monthly report materials submitted by the first police district, the number of residence years of Chinese and foreign residents and the occupational survey materials of foreign residents; revised rules on residence permits and licenses for overseas Chinese; the documents of unlicensed Russian nationals and temporary resident nationals in the fifth department; the monthly report on the number of various licenses issued by nationals from each foreign country and the materials for the issuance of residence licenses and exit certificates; the materials of Russian nationals' changes of the nationality and Russian nationals' nationality investigation presented by west bridge police station of the third district police station of the east province special region's first district;

There were also materials of prohibiting unauthorized entry of nationals." These files may make up for the demographic situation as well as other situations of "Lithuania in Harbin" from 1920 to 1930.

According to *Harbin Archives Guide*, "The Police General Management Division of the Eastern Province Special Region was established in the 9th year of the Republic of China (1920). In the 11th lunar month of 1927 (the 16th year of the Republic of China), it was renamed the Eastern Province Special Region Police General Management Office (hereinafter referred to as the Special Police Office). "The Special Police Department" is directly affiliated to the Office of the Chief Executive of the Eastern Province Special Region and is responsible for the management of police affairs in the Eastern Province Special Region. The whole region is divided into five districts, each of which has a police general office and sub-offices. Harbin is the first district with five sub-offices. The file consists mainly of documents from the 3rd, 5th and the special police department's offices in District 1. "The archives" were formed between 1920 and 1932, of which the vast majority, 2,459 volumes, were formed after 1927." Upon examination, the author found such files as "Investigation of Household Accounts and Various Affairs to Be Protected during Travel to Different Countries (May 1926)", "Matters concerning the Investigation of the Number of Domestic and Foreign Household Accounts in the Administrative Area and the Request for Household Papers (January 1927)", "Statistical Table of Investigation of Foreigners (October 1929)", and "Matters concerning Domestic and Foreign Household Accounts (June 1931)". However, at present, we could only see the file directory. For some reasons we couldn't refer to the file text.

Compared with the population data of "Lithuanians in Harbin" before 1932, the population statistics after 1932 are more perfect and detailed. For the change in the number of "Lithuanians in Harbin", please refer to *Table of the Population of "Lithuanians in Harbin* from 1933 to 1941 and *The Detailed Table of the Regional Population of Lithuanians in Harbin in 1934*.

In 1934, in the first series of the first volume of *The Census Result Table of Harbin Special City* and *The Second Yearbook of Harbin Special City*, the difference between the "210 men" of the former and the "209 men" of the latter was 1 person, which was due to the statistical error of the former, and the actual total number was "209". Therefore, the total Lithuanian population in Harbin in that year was "387". Second, according to the *Census Result Table of Harbin Special City, volume 1*, *Series 1*, "1 household, 1 male, 1 female, 2 people" of Lithuanians in the Shuixiang District; Lithuanians on The Sun Island "2 women, counting 2 people"; *The Second Municipal Situation Yearbook of Harbin Special City* in Shuixiang District "1 household, 1 male, 3 female". The latter incorporated the Lithuanians of the former Sun Island into Shuixiang District.

In 1933 and 1934, there was a great difference in the number of "Lithuanians in Harbin". In 1933, it was "1 household, 2 men and 1 woman", a total of 3 people. In 1934, it was "143 households, with 209 men and 178 women", a total of 387 people. In the author's opinion, this is mainly because Japan did not carry out a detailed household survey in Harbin. There was also a big difference in the number of "Lithuanians in Harbin" among 1934, 1935, 1936. In the author's viewpoint, on the one hand, Japan redivided the administrative divisions in Harbin; on the other hand, the demographic statistics of 1934 (the first year of Kant in Manchukuo) are closely related to Japan's invasion and colonial rule.

In 1937, there were a total of 242 Lithuanians in Harbin, but there were 229 Lithuanians in *Population Changes of Harbin*, which means that the latter was wrong. This may be due to the omission of Nangang and Xiangfang, both with 13 people. At the end of December 1938, there was no specific population data of "Lithuanians in Harbin" in the "Overview of external hukou" in the sixth edition of The Fake Kant *Harbin City Yearbook* (the sixth edition). At the end of December 1939, there was no specific population data of "Lithuanians in Harbin" in *Harbin Population and Household Statistics by Ethnic Group (Jurisdiction)* in Kant's seventh Annual Book of Harbin City Situation (seventh edition)

As for the population of "Lithuanians in Harbin" after 1945, Heilongjiang Provincial Archives has collected a list of Romanian and Lithuanian Expatriates in 1946, but this file is in a "controlled" state.

3.2.2 Political, Economic, Social and Cultural Activities of "Lithuanians in Harbin"

Regarding the political activities of "Lithuanians in Harbin", our first concern is the establishment of the consulate. At present, the author has not found the detailed information about the Lithuanian consulate in Harbin, only combing some fragmentary historical materials.

In 1922, there was no introduction to Lithuanian consulate in "Attached to Railway Authorities and Foreign Institutions" in the book *Harbin Guide* edited by Dongchui Business Newspaper; it was not mentioned in the location of foreign consulates in Harbin from *The Hubbub of Binjiang* published by Harbin Xinhua Press in 1929. In *Harbin Business Guide*, the introduction to foreign consulates in Harbin did not discuss the consulate of Lithuania in Harbin. According to *A Brief Introduction to Activities of Foreigners in Harbin before the Founding of the People's Republic of China* and other materials, Lithuania "set up an office in December 1921 and changed into a consulate in 1925" in Harbin. Address on Great Straight Street, later moved to Haicheng Street, it withdrew in 1931. "After 1932, due to the strict economic and political rule of the Japanese invaders, the Pacific War broke out in December 1941, and most of the consulates of various countries in Harbin were closed." According to the introduction to *Harbin Annals·Foreign Affairs*, "In 1921, the Republic of Lithuania set up a representative office in Harbin. In December 1925, the consulate was established, first at Great Straight Street, Nangang, and then at Haiguan Street." In 1940, "The museum was closed after Soviet troops entered Lithuania. The consuls successively included Touris,

Katchukilius, and Minkovsky."

On August 16th, 1936, *The Afternoon Newspaper* reported that "Honorary Consul of Lithuania in Harbin Presented His Country's Certificate of Appointment—The Ministry of Foreign Affairs Has Completed the Procedures of Recognition". The specific contents were as follows: "Most of the foreign consuls who work in Manchukuo never take office without any formal procedures, and Manchukuo also acquiesced this temporarily; In the future, however, the formality is to be realized wherever possible, for as a result the honorary consul of Lithuania in Harbin has formally presented the appointment of his government to the Ministry of Foreign Affairs on this day, for which the formal formality of recognition for the performance of his duties has been completed."

On July 12th, 1939, *Binjiang Daily* reported that "Manchukuo and Lithuania Officially Reply to State Relations—To Set up a Consulate in Harbin". Regarding Lithuania's setting up a consulate in Harbin, "The Foreign Affairs Bureau is in the process of applying for permission, and the permission has been decided, and the permission certificate will be issued soon. About 530 Lithuanians in Manchukuo, centered around Harbin, are active in Manchukuo under the qualification of White Russians. For this reason, before the incident, the Lithuanians had been honorary consuls stationed in Harbin. But this time it was abolished, and a new consulate was set up. Mr. Atrius, Consul of Lithuania, visited our Foreign Affairs Office on the 26th of the 5th lunar month this year, and presented the certificate of appointment of consul of Harbin by the government of Lithuania, asking for a certificate of recognition. The Government, on understanding the request, formally recognized Mr. Atrius as consul of Lithuania under mutual conditions and is now applying for a certificate of approval. This time the diplomatic relations between Lithuania's officially dispatched consuls are officially replied." On October 6th, 1939, *Binjiang Daily* reported that "The European Lithuanian State Set up a Consulate in Harbin—The Foreign Affairs Bureau has been Officially Recognized". It was reported that "The Consul of Lithuania in Harbin, Mr. Pyo Tolis, went immediately to visit the Foreign Affairs Bureau in Capital (Note: new Capital, namely, today's Changchun) from Harbin upon his arrival this day, and requested the Foreign Affairs Bureau to establish a consulate of the Lithuanian state in Harbin through formal procedures. After the approval of the Foreign Affairs Bureau, the establishment has been granted. And it published that "photo of Atorius, the first Consul of Lithuania in Harbin". In this period of time, the relationship among Lithuania, Japan and Manchukuo should be further clarified.

According to the archives of *Heilongjiang Province in the Ministry of Foreign Affairs of Jilin and Harbin's Negotiator's Office (1913—1930)*, "there were many foreign consulates in Harbin, and the diplomatic affairs were very complicated, forming many foreign affairs files. In terms of Sino-foreign relationships, there are materials such as the recognition of the official president by various countries, the date of arrival of consuls in Harbin and the establishment of consulates. There is a list of the areas under the jurisdiction of the Russian consulates in China, a list of the migration of the Russian consulates in Harbin, a list of the official records of the Ministry of Foreign Affairs, a list of the names of representatives of the various provinces issued by the Ministry of Foreign Affairs, and a compilation of the decrees issued by the Ministry of Foreign Affairs." These files are the most important material to accurately provide information concerning the establishment of the Lithuanian consulate in Harbin and its activities.

Among Jews in Harbin, there are some whose nationality is Lithuanian. Russian scholar B. Romanova concluded through researching that "Russian Jews account for 90% of the total number of Harbin Jews, and the remaining 10% are of Polish, Lithuanian and Latvian nationalities". According to the statistics of 1936, "of 96 Lithuanian business owners, 70 were Jewish, such as M.M. Coates, who founded a Geneva watch and jewelry shop and the Eskin Brothers, the owner of the Eskin Brothers Chamber of Commerce, accounted for 73 percent of the total." Among them, "Lithuanian Jewish Eskin Brothers Chamber of Commerce, founded in 1915, is located at the corner of China Street and Shangshi Street (now Central Street and Hongxia Street)". The Chamber of Commerce "had a large wholesale warehouse of cloth, daily goods, and did business with Russia, the United States and many European countries and regions."

The 36th Years of the Republic of China (1947) Special Annual Harbin City Industrial and Commercial Roll III in the "Public sector, Public-private Partnerships, Cooperatives, Foreign Department of Industry and Commerce" is related to the foreign industrial metal products, daily chemical, electrical and fiber products, fur, grain processing food, wood, construction, printing, tobacco and other things; metals, daily groceries, fibrous products, furs, groceries, timber and building materials, books, medicines, finance, agency and other articles for the foreign business. There is no Lithuanian manufacturing or operation in Harbin in either case.

The relationship between Harbin and Lithuania since the reform and opening up is as follows: "Harbin Archives keeps *Request for Instructions for Inviting Lithuanian Merchants to Harbin for Business Negotiation* (from August 1992 to 1994)", which has a total of 5 files, and is under "control" at present. Lithuania was invited to Harbin to participate in "The third Border and local Economic and Trade Fair in Harbin, China." This symposium "invited clients coming from 18 countries, including Russia, Ukraine, Belarus, Tajikistan, Turkmenistan, Harbin, Uzbekistan, Azerbaijan, Georgia, Lithuania, Armenia, Moldova, Poland, Bulgaria, the Czech Republic and Slovakia, Romania, Mongolia, up to 1006 trade groups, 4,936 persons in all."

The social and cultural undertakings of "Lithuanians in Harbin" involve religious belief, school education, community pension, etc. Lithuanians, who are mostly Catholic, also established Lithuanian societies in Harbin. In 1902, the Middle East Railway Engineering Bureau "set a Catholic cemetery in the corner of the Eastern Orthodox cemetery (today's Cultural Park)". After 1907, "a number of different denominations' cemeteries were set up, including Catholic, Morogan,

Kalayim, Tartar cemetery, collectively known as the Catholic United Cemetery. Although it is called the United Cemetery, each denomination originally managed its own cemetery. After the 1940s, it remained unsupervised, with merely Catholic cemetery existing. Until 1958, there was still a Soviet old woman in charge, with 487 headstones. In 1958, there were 2,104 graves for foreign nationals in the cemetery, divided by denomination: 1,298 for Catholics, 151 for Morogans, 42 for Lutherans (Bakistes), 92 for Sabbaths, 41 for Kalayim and 480 for Tatars".

As for Lithuanian associations in Harbin, according to Rittis Satkauskas, cultural counsellor at the Lithuanian Embassy in China, "The first Lithuanian association in Harbin was established in 1909 and was named 'Oshla'. Its members are mainly engaged in cultural activities and the preservation of Lithuanian national identity. It ended in 1914. In 1918, a committee was set up to deal with Lithuanian affairs and to provide legal services to Lithuanians who wanted to return. With the help of the community many Lithuanians have been able to return to Lithuania, and those who stayed in Harbin in contact with Lithuania through consuls. In 1923, the consulate was established and took over this part of the work." In 1935, "Harbin Lithuanian Society was founded again with 22 members, more than 100 in 1938 and 184 in 1939. One of the founders of the society, the Reverend Ulladas Marjonas, is the core. The community has clubs, reading rooms, a library, a subscription to Lithuanian newspapers, a chorus, dance rehearsals, and Lithuanian language lessons. Consul Iduadas Arturis came to Harbin in 1939, paid more attention to Lithuanian national culture, published a yearbook of the Far East, organized a Baltic State chorus, raised funds for the New Lithuanian House, and celebrated Lithuanian national holidays every year."

From the development course of Lithuania and the history of "Lithuanians in Harbin", the situation of "Lithuanians in Harbin" should be studied together with the situation of the immigrants from Estonia, Latvia, the other two Baltic countries and Poland in Harbin, so as to Gradually reconstruct the history of "Lithuanians in Harbin".

Table 3–1. Population of "Lithuanians in Harbin" (1933—1941)

Time	District	Partition	Total Households	Number of Males	Number of Females	Total
1933	Bazhan District, Butou District		1	2	1	3
1934	Butou District, Nangang District, Xin'anbu District, Zhengyanghe District, Majiagou District, Old Harbin District, Shuixiang District	99 households in Butou District, men 138, women119; 14 households in Nangang District, 25 men and 20 women; 5 households in Xin'anbu Street, 11 men and 9 women; 4 households in Zhengyanghe District, 5 men and 3 women; Majiagou District 17 households, 25 men, 23 women; 3 households in Old Harbin District, 4 men and 1 woman; Shuixiang District 1 household, 1 man, 3 women.	143	210	178	388

(to be continued)

Time	District	Partition	Total Households	Number of Males	Number of Females	Total
1935	Jingwei Department, Nangang Department, Xiangfang Department, Xinanbu Department	Jingwei Department 2 households, 4 men and 5 women, totaling 9 people; 9 households in Nangang Department, with 11 men and 14 women, totaling 25 people; Xiangfang Department 2 households, 3 men, 2 women, a total of 5 people; Xinanbu Department 2 households, 4 men and 3 women, totaling 7 people.	15	22	24	46
1936	Jingwei Department, Nangang Department, Xiangfang Department, Xinanbu Department	6 households, 9 men and 7 women, total 16 people; 5 households in Nangang Department, including 8 men and 10 women, totaling 18 people; Xiangfang Office 1 household, 2 men, 2 women, a total of 4 people; There were 23 people in 10 households, including 12 men and 11 women	22	31	30	61
1937	Jingwei Department, Nangang Department, Xiangfang Department, Xinanbu Department, Zhengyang Department	118 households in Jingwei Department, there were 97 men and 94 women, a total of 191 people; 6 households in Nangang Department, 6 men, 7 women, a total of 13 people; Xiangfang Department 6 households, 6 men, 7 women, a total of 13 people; 1 household in Xin 'anbu Department, 2 men and 2 women, a total of 4 people; 9 households in Zhengyang Department, 11 men, 10 women, a total of 21 people.	140	122	120	242
1939			about 530			
1941	Butou District, Nangang District, Majia District	There were 116 people in 49 households in Butou District, including 67 men and 49 women; 4 households in Nangang District, 3 men, 2 women, a total of 5 people; There were 18 people in 4households in Majia District, including 7 men and 11 women.	57	77	62	139

Data source: *Harbin Special City Yearbook*, *Harbin Special City Hukou Survey Results Table* volume 1, Number 1 and *Binjiang Daily*

Table 3–2. Detailed Population Distribution of "Lithuanians in Harbin" in 1934

District	Street	Number of households	Male	Female	Total population
Butou District		99	138	119	257
	The Central Street	12	14	7	21
	Paodui Street	8	14	10	24
	Gaoshi Street	5	8	9	17
	Jingwei Street	1	3	4	7
	Maimai Street	1	2	4	6

(to be continued)

District	Street	Number of households	Male	Female	Total population
Butou District	Ertang Street	3	2	2	4
	Santang Street	2	5	3	8
	Sitang Street	4	6	3	9
	Wutang Street		2	1	3
	Qitang Street	1	1	3	4
	Jingcha Street	2	3	2	5
	Shangwu Street	1	1	2	3
	Yaopu Street	2	2	2	4
	Shangshi Street	9	13	7	20
	Mianbao Street	4	9	7	16
	Ma Street	6	6	6	12
	Da'an Street	10	14	12	26
	Xiaman Street	5	7	6	13
	Shangpu Street			2	2
	The First Central Street	2	2	3	5
	The Fourth Central Street	5	7	4	11
	The Fifth Central Street		1		1
	The Ninth Central Street	1	1	2	3
	The Tenth Central Street	3	3	1	4
	The Thirteenth Central Street	3	3	5	8
	Shitoudao Street	1	1	1	2
	Kaiming Street			1	1
Nangang District		14	25	20	45
	Dazhi Street		1		1
	Shenggongshu Street	1	1	1	2
	Songhua River Street	1	1	1	2
	Haiguan Street			2	2
	Majia Street	3	3	3	6
	Hegou Street	1	2	4	6
	Gongsi Street	1	3	1	4
	Yizhou Street	1	1		1
	Ashihe Street	3	7	3	10
	Jilin Street	2	2	2	4
	Longjiang Street			1	1
	Tieling Street	1	1	1	2

(to be continued)

District	Street	Number of households	Male	Female	Total population
Xin'anbu District		5	11	9	20
	Anguo Street	1	2		2
	Anmin Street	2	4	4	8
	Anshun Street	2			3
	Anning Street		1		1
	Anda Street		1	5	6
Zhengyanghe District		4	5	3	8
	Hezhou Street	1	1	1	2
	Xinmin Street		1		1
	Hequ Street	1	1	1	2
	Heqing Street	1	1		1
	Hetu Street	1	1	1	2
Majiagou District		17	25	23	48
	Tongdao Street		3		3
	Shike Street	3	4	3	7
	Guoke Street	1	2	2	4
	Heishan Street			1	1
	Fenbu Street	2	2	1	3
	Lujia Street		1		1
	Yonghe Street	1	1	3	4
	Xiehe Street	1		2	2
	Zhonghe Street		1		1
	Bile Street	2	3	2	5
	Jiaotang Street		1		1
	Baling Street	1	1	2	3
	Xuande Street	1	2	1	3
	Xuanwei Street	1	2	1	3
	Xuanxin Street	1	1		1
	Wanyuanli	1		3	3
	Lianbu Street			2	2
	Cultural Street	1	1		1
Old Harbin District		3	4	1	5
	Lujun Street	1	1		1
	Xinxiangli	1	2	1	3
	Bubing Street	1	2	5	7
Shuixiang District		1	1	1	2
	Taiyangdao			2	2

Source of Data: *Household Survey Results of Harbin Special City* Part 1, Vol.1

Table 3–3. The Establishment of Lithuanian Consulate in Harbin from"Foreign consulates in Manchuria"in Manchuria Yearbook (1924—1932, Japanese version)

Time	Name of the Consul	Provenance
1926	Acting consul	page 73, Book I
1927	Acting consul, A.Polishaits	page 65, Book I
1928	Acting consul Jean Katil-Katilius	page 71, Book I
1929	Acting consul Jean Katil-Katilius	page 69
1931	Acting consul Jean Katil-Katilius	page 77
1932	Acting consul Jean Katil-Katilius	page 50

Table 3–4. The Establishment of Lithuanian Consulate in Harbin from"Foreign consulates in Manchuria" in Manchuria Yearbook (1933—1945, Japanese version)

Time	The consul's name	Provenance
1933	Acting consul Jean Katil-Katilius	page 69
1936	Honorary consul	page 146
1937	Honorary consul	page 130

Table3–5. The Consulate of Lithuania in Harbin from "Consulate in Harbin" in Harbin Business directory (Japanese Version)

Time	Name of the Consul	Consulate Address
1939	ア·メハムス	No.11 Wutang Street, Daoli District Telephone: 4692
1941	ヤ｜トウリス	No.11Xiewenwutang Street, Daoli District Telephone: 4692

3.3 | Reflections on the History and Culture of "Jews in Harbin"

Among the diverse and international migratory features of Harbin and Heilongjiang Province, the trace of Jewish people is particularly prominent. Not only do Jewish people, their descendants and relevant groups who have lived through this history have a strong attachment to it, but other groups here are also fascinated by the traces left by Jewish people in various fields. Scholars and elite social leaders have studied this unique Jewish phenomenon in depth, trying to discover new fruits that will benefit the research on the immigration to Heilongjiang Province.

In the contemporary history of Jewish activities in China, Harbin, one of the largest Jewish communities in the Far East, is renowned both at home and abroad. This valuable history has made Harbin a major international and domestic center of Jewish historical and cultural research. Among the Jewish historical studies in Harbin, Shanghai, Qingdao, and Tianjin, Harbin's Jewish studies have its own uniqueness. Jewish historical and cultural research in Harbin at the Center for Jewish Studies of Heilongjiang Provincial Academy of Social Sciences has become another discipline with special advantages, together with studies concerning Russian.

Since the establishment of the Center for Jewish Studies at the Heilongjiang Academy of Social Sciences in 2000, the first publication in 2003 was the large album, *Jews in Harbin* edited by President Qu Wei, which together with *Jews in China, Jews in Shanghai and Jews in Tianjin* constructed pictures of the life of the Jewish people in different regions of China, and made first impression of the Jews in China. In 2004, a published collection of research articles on *Harbin Jews* presented "the highest level of research on the subject of the Jews in Harbin to some extent". In 2007, the Center for Jewish Studies published another collection of essays by *Harbin and World Jewish* and also saw the publication of Teddy Kaufman's *The Harbin Jews in My Heart*. During this period, the Center for Jewish Studies also held several international symposia, which symbolized that the research on Harbin's Jews took shape.

Books or papers by Li Shuxiao, Qu Wei, Liu Shuang, Zhang Tiejiang are outstanding in Jewish studies in Harbin. Among this, Li Shuxiao has made an impression on a foundation role which his works such as *Harbin Jews Historical Timeline* and *A Brief History of the Harbin Zionist Organization* acted pioneering function. In 2007, Liu Shuang's *History of the Jewish Diaspora in Harbin* deals with the complicated history of Jewish dispersal and migration, making this book not only of high academic value, but also has important practical significance. In 2004, Zhang Tiejiang's book, *Unraveling the Mystery of Harbin Jewish History—A Study of Harbin Jewish Community*, separating Jews in Harbin from the traditional Russian diaspora, focuses more on the study of Jewish ethnicity, and uses historical facts to scientifically corroborate and explain the social legends surrounding Jewish people.

In addition, Pan Guang, Wang Jian, Fang Jianchang and some history experts from other provinces in China emphasis on the study of Jewish history and culture in Harbin. Pan Guang, a researcher from the Shanghai Academy of Social Sciences, published *The Tide of Russian Jews in China and the Formation and Development of the Russian-Jewish Community in Harbin and Shanghai* in *Social Sciences*, No.5, 2005, and *Nationality and Legal Problems of Jews in China (1840—1945)*" in *Social Sciences*, No.2, 2006. *Some Reflections on the Jewish Community in Harbin in the course the Japanese Occupation* by Wang Jian of the Shanghai Academy of Social Sciences and *The Jews in northeast China in Modern Times* by Fang Jianchang of the Chinese Academy of Social Sciences have also discussed and interpreted the history and culture of the Jews in Harbin from different periods and perspectives.

The publication of these monographs, collections and papers have laid a solid foundation for the study of the history and culture of the Jews in Harbin.

In 2007, Teddy Kaufman, former president of Harbin Jewish Community and now president of the Association of Jews of Israel Origin in China, pointed out in his book *The Jews of Harbin in My Heart* that "The Jewish community flourished in Harbin for 65 years since the beginning of construction of Harbin in 1898 to the departure of last group and their return to homeland in 1963. While some were well educated and knowledgeable, others were illiterate and lacked the most basic knowledge of the Jewish religion. Anyhow, these Jews from different backgrounds quickly integrated with the community and adapted to their new environment. This was one of the most striking features of the Jewish community. Unlike the Jews who were dispersed to Germany, Poland and other countries, taking nearly a century to unite and coalesce, the Harbin Jewish community was formed almost overnight."

This quote by Teddy Kaufman provides a more comprehensive remark and evaluation of the Jewish journey in Harbin and its characteristics. In his book *The Jews of Harbin in My Heart*, he also gives an account of the conditions of Jewish life in Harbin. At the same time, there are many experts and scholars at home and abroad who had done a lot of special studies on this subject. But due to the lack of relevant information and knowledge background of researchers, misunderstanding would be inevitable on the recognition, thus the research of Jews in Harbin is only at the "just beginning" stage. Therefore, based on previous studies, this paper presents some views and ideas of myself to discuss and explain the specific history of Jews in Harbin.

3.3.1 Starting Point of the Restudy on Jewish History and Culture in Harbin

After a dozen years of research on Chinese and foreign Jewish history and culture, the author found that some journalists, writers and scholars who are not professional but were keen on Jewish research in Harbin have "misinterpreted" the knowledge, meaning and elaboration of this history, which makes many readers "misunderstand" while reading their relevant materials or discourses. However, their efforts should be awarded.

On August 24th, 2007, *Heilongjiang Daily* published "They Are Writing the 'History of Harbin Jews'" written by journalist Li Shuquan and intern Wang Xiaotang, which described in some detail experiences of Li Shuxiao, Zhang Tiejiang, Zeng Yizhi and others in the field of Jewish studies in Heilongjiang Province and the important role they played in the study of Harbin Jews. One of the paragraphs, "Zeng Yizhi: this is my lifelong career," describes how "in his work of studying and preserving Jewish culture, Zeng Yizhi felt most satisfied with two things. One of them was Liu Yihuan, a researcher at the Institute of Literature of the Heilongjiang Academy of Social Sciences, lent her the book *Fugu Plan*, which describes the history of Harbin's Jews during Japanese occupation of Harbin. What's more, by reviewing the large number of historical materials and analyzing them in detail, Zeng Yizhi wrote two articles, "*Who Accepted the Harbin Jews*" and "*Fugu Plan and Harbin Jews*", in which she concluded: How could the Chinese people accept the persecuted Jews during the humiliating years when they lost their sovereignty and were persecuted by the invaders? The only possibility is that the Tsarist colonizers and the Japanese invaders, who were in control of Harbin's sovereignty at the time, admitted them successively."

In her article "*Fugu Plan and the Harbin Jews*", Ms. Zeng Yizhi states that the *Fugu Plan*, written by the Jews, made her "aware of the Japanese invaders' plot to use Jewish funds to win the war of aggression." In those days, when the Jews of Harbin were fawning over the Japanese invaders again and again for the survival of their own people, the Chinese people in Harbin and in the fallen areas of China, who did not discriminate against the Jews, were living in the misery of the loss of their land and the destruction of their families. Then, "the only possibility is that the Tsarist colonizers and the Japanese invaders, who were in control of the sovereignty of Harbin at that time, successively accepted the Jewish people." This statement was a "misinterpretation" by the reporter or a "misrepresentation" by the interviewee?

In fact, there is no particularly detailed interpretation of the relationship between the Harbin Jews and Japan, Russia and the Soviet Union, and especially Belarus, during the period of Japanese occupation. One of the more persuasive cases was the internationally influential "Kasper kidnapping" case, planned by the Japanese colonial authorities and carried out by Belarus against Simon Kasper as a threat and revenge for the unsuccessful economic plundering of the Kasper family. In 2009, Dan Kanan, a Jew and professor of Spanish at Heilongjiang University, published *The Kasper Incident—Cultural and Ethnic Conflict in Harbin, 1932—1945,* which used many foreign sources from France, Australia, and the United States to provide an in-depth and detailed interpretation of the Kasper Incident, giving a clear understanding of the incident. However, this incident was more than a conflict between culture and ethnicity. Researchers need to dig into more complicated issues underlying, especially the struggles among the Kasper family, the Japanese, Russian, French, and other regimes and forces in this case.

Dan Ben Kanan pointed out that the "Fugu Plan", a project aiming at consuming "Jewish money from all over the world" to strengthen Japan's war-torn economy and to find a solution to the "Jewish problem", which did not succeed in Manchuria.

In 2008, Chongqing Publishing House published the book *Wandering with God-The Jewish Refuge in Harbin* by the famous writer from Heilongjiang Province, Ah Cheng. In this book, Ah Cheng excerpted from the Harbin Specialized Advisory Committee's article *Harbin and the Jewish Economic and Trade Cooperation Research Group*, mentioning that "in the first half of the 20th century, millions of Jews immigrated from Europe to Asia, Australia and North America to avoid the Nazi fascist persecution, while Harbin was an important stop in this century-long migration." He also quoted former U.S. Secretary of State Dr. Henry Kissinger's comments on the situation of the Jewish in Harbin in his article *I know That the Chinese Treat Jews Well*, "The information you presented and the picture book *Jews in Harbin* and related materials you brought me indicate that before and after World War II there were once more than 20,000 Jews who fled from persecution and discrimination then settled in Harbin."

Mr. Li Shuxiao, an expert in Jewish studies in Heilongjiang Province and former deputy director of Jewish Research Center of the Provincial Academy of

Social Sciences, listed in the *Harbin Jews Historical Timeline* that in 1920 "a large number of Jews moved from Vladivostok and other places to Harbin making the population of Harbin Jews up to 20,000"; in 1938, "10 German and Austrian Jewish refugees came to Harbin who were settled in by Harbin Jewish religious guild and other community organizations"; In 1942, "according to statistics, a total of 31 German Jews families came to Harbin for refuge, including 39 men and 29 women, adding up to 68 people". Ah Cheng also used all of Mr. Li Shuxiao's *Harbin Jews Historical Timeline* in the Appendix of his book, however it seemed that he did not find the contradiction in it.

In the afterword of *Wandering with God-The Jewish Refuge in Harbin*, "By the Blessing of Harbin, by the Blessing of Jews", Ah Cheng points out that "those foreigners living in Harbin who claimed to be Russians, Germans, poles, etc., were in fact Jews, or had Jewish origin. Among them, only a few were brave enough to face up to their Jewish identity. This creates the illusion for outsiders that there are not many Jews in Harbin (just over 20,000) in this way. In fact, at least 70% of all foreign exiles in Harbin were Jews or had Jewish ancestry. Since foreign exiles accounted for 51% of Harbin's population, I call it 'Harbin-The Jewish Life's Harbor'." However, Ah Cheng did not give any supporting evidence for the "seventy percent" claim.

Mr. Xue Lianju, an expert on Harbin population research, points out in his book *Population Changes in Harbin* that "according to *The Railway Industry and Commerce Guide (Russian version)*, there were 43,091 Russians in Harbin in 1912, accounting for 63.7% of the total population of Harbin at that time." He also introduces that "before 1922, Jews accounted for more than 10% of Harbin's expatriate population. Since this nationality was mainly business-oriented and characterized by frequent mobility, the number decreased, and the proportion declined with the change of objective circumstances."

In 2009, in the book *Footsteps of the Exiles*, edited by Li Xingsheng and published by Heilongjiang Education Publishing House, He Hong, an official of the Heilongjiang Provincial Museum of Literature and History, mentioned in the article "Foreign Exiles Should Be Taken Seriously" that "the refugees of Russian expatriated into northeast China in 1917, Harbin, also included many Jews. From 1899 to 1985, the first Russian Jew set foot on Harbin to the last Jew Agore passed away in Harbin, they had resided in Harbin for nearly a century. Their population in Harbin once peaked at 20,000, which should not be ignored as a major flow of people. They created numerous economic miracles depending on their own wisdom on business in Harbin." Mr. He added, "It is a pity that all of Li Xingsheng's writings happen not to cover this aspect of the study. I would like to make some supplements." Obviously, Mr. He has not read or understood Mr. Li's argument on the "flow of people".

Dan Ben Kanan also inquired that "Most publications on Harbin try to portray the city as a heaven for the Jewish people and other ethnic communities. Is that real?" "Is that narrative objective?" He emphasized that "in the study of historical reality, nostalgia may overtake science, and thus the conclusions will not be based on fact. History is for all. So, a lack of truth can lead to historical error, controversy, and intentional or unintentional misinformation." He also directly states that "nostalgia is often idealistic and impractical, and it often confuses feelings with the past when it generalizes and omits certain parts of historical existence. Therefore, the researcher should not be an editor. By whatever means or method, the researchers should promote, utilize, and rely on authentic history."

3.3.2 Conceptual Interpretation: The Definition of Immigrants, Refugees, and Exiles

In the study of the history and culture of Harbin Jews, researchers need to sort out and define the concepts of immigrants, refugees, and displaced persons.

(1) Immigrants

The specific meaning of immigrant is in varies among the academic circle and still inconclusive. *The Modern Chinese Dictionary* (5th edition) defines "immigrant" as a resident moving from one place or country to settle in another place or another country, a person who migrates to a foreign country or a foreign country to settle down. However, *CiHai*, on the other hand, has two explanations: ① a person who moves to a foreign area to settle permanently; ② a larger, organized migration of population. Professor Ge Jianxiong, a famous expert in the history of population and migration in China, pointed out that migration is "the flow of people from their original place of residence to other places", which is in the sense of a verb; as a noun, immigrants refer to "people who carry out such migration behavior".

"From the definitions of immigrants given in various dictionaries and works, the focus of disagreement lies mainly in the question of how long a person stays in place B after moving from place A to place B." Some researchers believe that immigrants who permanently residents are "immigrants", while others believe that only the acting of migrating is "immigration".

(2) Refugees

Lexically speaking, a refugee is "a person who has stayed outside his country because of events that took place before January 1st, 1951, and because of a well-founded fear of persecution on account of race, religion, nationality, membership of a particular social group or political opinion, and who is unable or unwilling to be protected by that country because of such fear; or a person who does not have a nationality and who has stayed outside his country former residence because of the above-mentioned events, and who is unable or unwilling to be protected by that country because of the above-mentioned fear.

Geographically speaking, refugees are a special form of population migration. Many people are forced to leave their homes and live in other countries because of natural disasters, war, class and ethnic oppression, religious and racial discrimination, and changes in national borders, resulting in compulsory migration. After the Second World War, the world refugee problem has become increasingly prominent. Refugees are a special group in the international community, a group unable or unwilling to return to their country of origin due to war, racial persecution, tribal conflicts, national territorial changes, political asylum, natural disasters, economic deterioration, etc. They are characterized by their nature, helplessness, mobility, spontaneity, and passivity.

Convention relating to the Status of Refugees of the United Nations provides that States Parties shall accord certain treatment to refugees in their territories, including national treatment in primary education, public assistance, labor and social security; treatment at least not less favorable than that accorded to foreigners in general and as favorable as possible in movable and immovable property, free occupation, housing, etc. States shall respect the right of refugees to acquire personal status, grant them identity documents and protection from deportation, and facilitate naturalization and assimilation of refugees as much as possible.

In the book *Russian Expatriates in China (1917—1945)*, which was published in 1997, the term "expatriates" is explained as "those who are forced or voluntarily moved from their home country to other countries for some political, economic, religious, or other reasons. There have three common situations: ① Some still retain their original nationality; ② Some renounce or lose their original nationality but do not acquire a new one, thus becoming "stateless"; ③ Some acquire the nationality of the country of their residence." Professor Zhao Xinsan introduced in his book *Shanghai Baie Lalisha* that "The so-called Russian expatriates include old Russians, Russian Jews, Ukrainians and Russians who have been naturalized in China."

(3) Exiles

What is an exile? Li Xingsheng, a famous expert in the study of the exiles, the history of the exiles and the culture of the exiles, pointed out in his book *Chinese Exiles History and the Culture of the Exiles* that "the exiles are a kind of guest inhabitants who were forcibly moved (exiled or deported) to remote places with certain control measures because they were considered guilty by the rulers whose purpose is guided by punishment, reinforce border garrison or plundering of wealth. In class societies, it is the product of class dictatorship. In short, the exile is the type of person who is considered guilty by ruling class and forced to move (exile or deportation). It refers to both the exile as a whole, and an individual (a person) or part of it". At the same time, Li Xing sheng also outlined five characteristics of the exiles: First, the exile was the object of punishment, and in class societies, the object of class dictatorship; Second, the exile was the product of the ruling class's policy of plundering wealth or reinforce border garrisoni; Third, the exile was considered guilty by the ruler; Fourth, forced migration was the fundamental mark of the exile that distinguished it from the spontaneous exile and organized and planned migration; Fifth, the places of migration were mostly remote.

After understanding the concepts associated with the Jews, the "origin" of the Jews in Harbin is the key issue that needs to be clarified first.

3.3.3 The Origins of Russian Jews

Historically, Jews can be divided into Ashkenazi and Sephardic (also called

"Sephardim") peoples. According to the *Encyclopedia Judaica*, edited by Xu Xin and Ling Jiyao, renowned experts in Jewish studies at Nanjing University, Ashkenazi was the term used in medieval writings to describe the Jews who lived on the banks of the Rhine and later throughout the Germanic region. Over time, it came to refer not only to German Jews, but to all Jews who were descended from German Jews in the Middle Age by origin. According to modern interpretation, the term refers to that part of the Jewish population of the above-mentioned social and cultural complex. The term Ashkenazi is used to denote a certain contrast with Sephardic, which refers to the Jewish cultural complex formed in Spain and Portugal. The term "Ashkenazi" denotes cultural commonality of the Jewish community that includes northern France, Germany and the Slavic countries. Pan Guang and Wang Jian, renowned Jewish experts from the Shanghai Academy of Social Sciences, summarized in *Shanghai Jews over a century and a Half-An Eastern Story in the History of the Jewish People* that Ashkenazi Jews originally referred to European Jews, then later mainly referred to Jews from Central and Eastern Europe and Russia. Sephardic Jews, originally referring to the Jews expelled from Spain, later came to refer generally to the Jews who emigrated from the Mediterranean coast, especially from the West Asia and North Africa to all parts of the world. The Jews of Russia belong to the Ashkenazi Jews.

Around the 1st century AD, a number of Jews migrated one after another to the Crimea, Ukraine, Belarus, Poland and Lithuania in Eastern Europe. A devastating plague of glanders (later known as the Black Death) in European history occurred in 1348—1361. After the Black Death, the criminals, the nobles, the disabled and Jews were suspected, especially Jews, who were suspected of intentionally spreading the plague by contaminating the water of wells with a so-called poison or by smearing houses and people". "In Freiburg, all identified Jews were driven into a large wooden house and burned to death. In Strasbourg, it is said that more than two thousand people were hanged on gallows erected in a Jewish cemetery. The persecution was so cruel that the enlightened Pope Claremont Ⅵ issued two papal bulls declaring the Jews were innocence. Many Jews in Western Europe fled to Germany and Poland." "There, they were tolerated, and they established communities that grew rapidly in number, a phenomenon that partly explains the large Jewish populations in western Russia, eastern Germany, Poland and northeastern Austria in the 19th and early 20th centuries."

It was not until in the second half of the 18th century that Jews entered Russia as foreign people in large numbers. This was achieved primarily through the three annexations of Poland by Tsar Ekaterina Ⅱ (1762—1796). Poland, located between the Baltic Sea and the Black Sea, was always the territory coveted by Russian tsars due to its important geographical position, and the policy of annexing Poland was pursued from Peter Ⅰ (1682—1725) to Ekaterina Ⅱ . On August 5th, 1772, Russia, Prussia and Austria signed the first treaty of partitioning Poland in Petersburg. According to the treaty, Russia received Belarus and partial territory of Latvian between the Druch, the Western Dvina and the Dnieper rivers with 92,000 square kilometers and 1.3 million people. In 1793, Russia and Prussia signed the second agreement on the partition of Poland in Petersburg. Accordingly, Germany received a total of more than 250,000 square kilometers of Belarus and part of Lithuania and most of Ukraine west of the Dnieper River. On October 24th, 1795, Russia, Prussia and Austria signed the third agreement on the partition of Poland. Based on the agreement, Russia annexed 120,000 square kilometers of Lithuania, Courland, Western Belarus, and the western part of Volyn, extending the border to the line of the Neman and Bug River. Through three annexations, many Polish Jews were incorporated into Russia. In 1815, there were about 1.2 million Jews in Russia (including Russian Poland). By the middle of the 19th century, there were about 2.4 million Jews in Russia, and the population reached nearly 5 million by the end of the 19th century, thus making Russia a country with most Jewish people in the world, which accounted for two-thirds of the world's Jews at that time.

From the beginning of the 19th century Russian Jews were excluded from Russia's mainland and were confined to the "Pale of Settlement", which stretched from the Baltic Sea to the Black Sea. In the "Pale of Settlement", most of the Jews lived in dark basement or small, crude houses with wet walls and roofs, 10 people sharing one room, in a cramped and oppressive atmosphere. They worked mainly in wood, lock, hosiery, tanning, cigarette and match industries and generally worked for 16-18 hours in crowded and air stagnating working conditions. A Russian government commission on the condition of Jews in the 1880s reported that 90 percent of Jews was "proletarians with barely enough to live on". By the end of the 19th century, nearly half of them was living on charity payments from those who had jobs among them. Besides, not only did they lack citizenship rights, but special laws severely restricted their residence, economic development, and even marriage in Russia.

The Tzarist government adopted a policy of assimilation, exclusion, anti-semitism, and massacre of Jews to "prevent the Jews from corrupting Russian society" as it was called. After the reign of Ivan Ⅳ in the 16th century, he banned Jews' residence in Russia. In the 17th and 18th centuries, the Tsarist government repeatedly refused to allow Polish Jews to live in Russia, and Peter I said: "I would rather accept Islamists and pagans than Jews."In 1762, Ekaterina Ⅱ allowed foreigners to travel and live in Russia except Jews. The exception, however, was the former Tatar territory in southern Ukraine, which Russia took over from Ottoman Turkey in the 1870s. This new Russian region was opened to Jews and other minorities to increase the local population and develop the local economy. Odessa, the main city of this region, soon became a major center of Jewish life. In 1791 Jewish merchants were forbidden to live in central Russia because of the demands of orthodox merchants in Moscow for protection in competition with Jewish merchants. During the reign of Paul I (1796—1801), a "Jewish ghetto" decree was issued, stipulating that Jews could only live in Belarus and Ukraine and were not allowed to live in the capital. During the reign of Alexander I (1801—1825), Jews were expelled from the Belarusian countryside by decree; at time of the Nicholas I

(1825—1855), an antisemitic decree was enacted, and these two tsars carried out a policy of massacre of Jews; in the early years of Alexander Ⅱ's reign (1855—1881), Jewish literacy increased rapidly, and the number of Jewish high school students rose significantly, accounting for 13.2% of the whole middle-school boys by 1873. In the later part of his reign, however, anti-Semitic newspapers accused Jewish university and high school students of being overrepresented in Russian national schools, leading the Russian government to repose harsh restrictions on Jewish enrollment. At the same time, the growing number of Jews receiving a university education fueled widespread suspicion and hostility toward Jews as they believed it would give rise to socialist and revolutionary idea.

In 1871 there was an anti-Semitic riot in Odessa in which nearly 100 Jews were killed or injured.

On March 1st, 1881, Tsar Alexander Ⅱ was assassinated in Petersburg. The Tzarist government claimed that a Jewish woman was a member of the Party of the People's Will, which aimed to turn over the Tzarist government as the result of the murder. The Russian authorities tried to describe the persecution to provoke public wrath against Russian Jews. The nation went on a massacre spree of Jews. Tsar Alexander Ⅲ, the successor of Alexander Ⅱ, suppressed revolutionary activities, and all free resistance and revolutionary activities were put down. Over the next few months, riots broke out in more than 160 cities and villages, concentrated initially in southern Russia and the Ukraine, and later at times in Warsaw and Novgorod. John Foster, the U.S. ambassador in Petersburg, reported to the U.S. government that "these recent events are more worthy of the name 'Dark Ages' (the years of civilization declined in Europe between about 500 A. D. and about 1000 A.D) than the present century." And indeed, as Lenin put it, this was "directing the hatred of the workers and peasants of poor countries against the Jews." This persecution "led to growing and uncontrollable unrest and increasingly virulent anti-semitism in Russia, which also provoked the spread of anti-Semitism throughout Western and Central Europe."

These two persecutions caused a sudden change in the mind of hundred of thousand of Jews who had previously advocated assimilation into Russian society as a solution to the problem of Jewish persecution. The massacres made Russian Jews clearly wake up to the fact that there was no hope at all for Jews to achieve emancipation and equal rights as citizens in Russia. For these massacres showed that such riots were not only the misdeeds of odious peasants but were actively encouraged by students and populist revolutionaries in the press. Even the most admired Russian writers of the time (with the exception of Kropotkin and Lavrov) tacitly approved of it. This made "the already assimilated Jews feel insecure" as well. Russian Jews began to reflect on the series of attempts to renounce their own faith, which led directly to the development of Jewish homecoming in the direction of a national liberation movement and inspired more and more Jews to become active in the emerging Zionist movement. Pinsker, one of them, wrote *Auto-Emancipation* due to the stimulus of this persecution.

For related discourses on Russian Jews, we can also read the article *Exploring the Origin of Harbin Jews* by Liu Shuang of the Heilongjiang Academy of Social Sciences, *The Trend of Russian Jews Coming to China and the Formation and Development of Russian-Jewish Societies* in *Social Sciences* by Pan Guang of the Shanghai Academy of Social Sciences, published in Social Sciences, 2005, No.5, and *The History of Jewish Migration to Harbin and Its Role* by Shi Yan and Dai Wei. The thesis completed in 2005 by Bao Zhong, a 2001 undergraduate student at East China Normal University, entitled *A Preliminary Study of the Causes of the Anti-Semitic Wave in Russia in the Nineteenth Century*, is also worthy of reference. In exploring the history and culture of Jews in Harbin, the "earliest" or "first" Jew to come to Harbin and his identity are often the first concerns of researchers or readers.

In 1896, Russia signed the *Sino-Russian Secret Treaty* with the Qing Government, acquiring the right to build the Chinese Eastern Railway. After the survey and design by Russian engineers and technicians, Harbin was designated as the hub of the Chinese Eastern Railway, and in 1898, construction of the railroad began in three directions: west, east and south. Many Russian engineers, managers and road construction workers began to pour into Harbin.

3.3.4 "Identity" of the First Comers of Jews to Harbin

At present, there are divergent views and inconclusive opinions about who was the first Jew came to Harbin. At the same time, few scholars have emphasized the significance of their "identity" and the international "background" of their arrival in Harbin.

Theodore (Dieter) Kaufman, in his book *The Jews of Harbin in My Heart*, mentions that "Jews began settling in Harbin in 1898, and the Jewish community and synagogue were formally established in 1903. The first Jews coming from Siberia immigrated to Harbin." He adds, "Jews came to Manchuria at the end of the 19th century with the laying of the Middle East Railway tracks." "The first arrivals were railroad workers of varying ranks, followed by investors, contractors, suppliers and freelancers (including doctors, engineers, lawyers and architects)."

Li Shuxiao in his *Harbin Jews Historical Timeline* tells that "With the construction of the Middle East Railway, S.L. Berserzeli became the first Jew to arrive in Harbin." In his article G. B. Derikin's Person, he testifies that "according to the article on the 35th anniversary of the founding of the Harbin Jewish Religious Congregation in January 1939, 3-4 issue of the magazine *Jewish Life*, the first Jew was Yakov Ilyich Bertseri who got to Harbin in 1899." He emphasizes that this statement is "reliable and that the magazine *Jewish Life* is more authoritative."

In his article *The First Jew to Harbin-The Discovery of Gregory Derikin's Tombstone*, Zhang Tiejiang talks about how "the author found the Hebrew tombstone of the first Jew to come to Harbin in the Jewish cemetery in the eastern suburbs of Harbin, uncovering the century-old mystery of who was the first Jew to arrive in Harbin." "The discovery of the Hebrew tombstone confirms that Grigori

Borisovich Grigori Derikin was the first Russian Jew to come to Harbin (in 1894) and made here permanently residence, which was also the first "Ashkenazi" Jewish immigrants (meaning Jews from the East, Central Europe and Russia) arrived in Harbin.

Xue Lianju points out that "after 1898, Harbin became a base for imperialist and capitalist countries to exploit the blood and sweat of the Chinese people and a paradise for merchant capitalists from various countries to get rich. Jewish merchants came to Harbin in this historical background." He also emphasized that "the Jews who entered Harbin were first construction engineers who came with the Russians when the Middle East Railway was established, and then came the Jewish merchants from Russia, Poland, Lithuania, Estonia, Latvia, and Western European countries."

Li Xiqi writes in the article *The Introduction of Judaism into Harbin* during the construction period of the Middle East Rail ranging from 1898 to 1903 that "Judaism was introduced into Harbin by Imperial Russia in 1898. At that time, as the construction of the Middle East Railway, engineering technicians came to Harbin one after another, mostly of them believed in Judaism."

Dan Ben Kanan in *The Kasper Incident—Cultural and Ethnic Conflict in Harbin, 1932—1945* emphasizes that "Jews came to Harbin for a variety of reasons, which included business opportunities and what they believed would be a free environment." Gregory Grossman, a professor at the University of California, Berkeley, in his article *Building the Northeast: Jewish Enterprise in Manchuria between 1900 and 1940*, states that "Jews were drawn to Manchuria for reasons other than purely economic, but more importantly for the relatively tolerant and liberal atmosphere in Manchuria: official, economic and social. Private enterprises and private capital were in great demand and generally welcomed here."

After introducing and summarizing various points of view in his book *History of the Jewish Diaspora in Harbin*, Liu Shuang points out that "We date the initial arrival of Russian Jews in Harbin to around 1896, and, also, do not want to confirm who was the first Jew to arrive in Harbin." He explains, "To be honest, for historical facts that cannot be determined at all, this slightly vague determination may be closer to the historical truth in a sense."

The author agrees with Liu Shuang's view, but it is necessary to emphasize the issue of the "identity" of these first Jews in Harbin and the international "background" of their arrival in Harbin. First, the Jews who first came to Harbin were "gold seekers", not "refugees", even though they were living in the Russian "Pale of Settlement". This was to show why they came to Harbin. Second, in 1896, the signing of the *Sino-Russian Secret Treaty* provided an "opportunity" for Russian Jews to come to Harbin. On June 3rd, 1896, Russia and China signed the *Sino-Russian Secret Treaty*, paragraph 4, which states, "Now Russia, for the future transfer of Russian soldiers to defend the enemy and to receive arms and food, with a view to the proper speed. The Chinese state allows the construction of a railroad in Heilongjiang and Jilin to reach Vladivostok."

Thus, Theodore (Dieter) Kaufmann says, "In 1896, China and Russia signed the *Sino-Russian Secret Treaty* in St. Petersburg, a treaty that was pivotal in increasing Russian influence on the Russia-China border. In Russia, the Jews were severely restricted in general, while the situation was greatly improved when they came to the railroad dependencies in China that Russia had acquired. This change was closely related to the Russian policy of the time. At that time, Russia spared no effort to increase its influence in China, and they abolished religious and ethnic discrimination. As a result, not only Russians, but also Georgians and even Jews, who had been suppressed by them earlier, lived on that land with full citizenship rights. From then on, Jews began to move into the area." These statements of Kaufmann clearly claim that the Jews who first came to Harbin were not for "refuge." In a sense, the Jews, like other non-Jewish Russian expatriates, considered Harbin as "theirs" and they were its "owners". Undoubtedly, it has a certain tint of "colonial" or "invasion".

The author believes that the Russian Jews is first valued of their "national" identity in Russia, that is to say, the first concern was which ethnic group they were, while the Russian Jews were first valued for their "expatriate" identity when they came to Harbin, China, that is to say, the first concern was which ethnic group they belonged to. To be exact, a Russian Jew in Harbin was first considered as an "expatriate" and then a "Jew". The Jews themselves were very clear about the "national" identity of the Jews in Harbin. They had their own cemeteries, hospitals, churches, religious congregations, schools, and a complete set of institutions and facilities. There was a clear "line" between Russian Jews and non-Jewish Russians.

3.3.5 "Wind and Cloud": A Probe into the Changing Population of Jews in Harbin

At present, the academic cycle shows great interest in the number of Jews in Harbin, especially the peak of the population of Jews, which is the focus of the discussion. Representative works or articles include Li Shuxiao and Fu Mingjing's *Exploring the Demographic, International and Occupational Composition of Harbin Jews*, Wang Zhijun and Li Wei's *On the Number of Jews in Harbin in the Early 20th Century*, and Xue Lianju's introduction to the population in the section "Jewish Diaspora" in the book *Population Changes in Harbin*.

Firstly, the author would like to list reliable numbers of the population of Harbin Jews. In 1924, according to the Russian version of the book *Harbin-Fujiadian Commercial and Railway Guide*, there were "5,848 Jews in Harbin, of whom 2,885 were men and 2,963 were women". The May 5th, 1926, edition of the *Binjiang Daily* described that "1,367 people, of whom 807 were men and 560 were women in the district." *Far Eastern Newspaper* of January 17th, 1919, recorded, "7,500 people. Among them, 4,500 were over 20 years old and 3,000 were under 20 years old." In the table "Changes in the number of Jewish expatriates in Harbin from 1916 to 1930", Xue Lianju misspelled the year as "1918". According to Japanese newspaper *Luya Times*, in 1920, Harbin had 20,000 Jews.

The fourth section of the second chapter of *The Secular Life of Binjiang* records that the population of Jews in Harbin during the construction period of the Middle East Railway was "1,400" from 1898 to 1903 in October 1925; In 1929, the number of Jews in Harbin was 1,324. Xue Lianju notes that Jews "often held double identities: they held the nationality of their residential countries and were Jews at the same time." "A number of statistics from 1920 onwards often indicate under the item of Jews that they are 'included in the stateless population' or 'unknown'." Thus, "the actual number of Jews after the 1920s was greater than the number on the statistical tables." During the period of Japanese Puppet Regime, the number of Jews in Harbin and northeast China had detailed records. The Japanese Manchurian Survey Mission also had a detailed survey of Jews in the Northeast.

In March 2010, at the former Danish Consulate in Harbin (now the Harbin International Friendship City Exhibition Hall), 91 Tiandi Street, Daoli District, the translator of this book came across a copy of the "Questionnaire on the Number of Aliens in Harbin City by Race March 1946 "at the Harbin Hall. This questionnaire shows in detail that "There were 1,680 Jewish people in total, of whom 804 were men and 876 were women: 78 men and 79 women under 14 years of age; 539 men and 626 women from 14 to 60 years of age; 187 men and 171 women over 60 years of age" This is the first demographic file of Jews in Harbin in 1946, which should have certain reference value and meaning.

To demonstrate the demographic changes of Jews in Harbin, the translator quotes the number of Jews in representative years from Mr. Li Shuxiao's *Harbin Jews Historical Timeline* again. By the end of the 1902, there were 300 Jews in Harbin and more than 10 Jewish stores. While in 1906, there were 3,000 Jews in Harbin, and in 1908, the number of Jews reached 6,000 in Harbin. In 1913, 5,032 Jews lived in Harbin, accounting for 11.5% of the total number of expatriates at that time. On 17th January 1919, the *Far Eastern Newspaper* reported that 7,500 Jews lived in Harbin, of whom 4,500 were over 20 years old and 3,000 were under 20 years old. In 1920, many Jews moved to Harbin from Vladivostok and other places, and the Jewish population in Harbin increased to 20,000. In 1922, there were 11,000 Jews living in Harbin, and in 1924, there were 5,848 Jews living here, 2,885 men and 2,963 women, of whom 2,580 were working, accounting for 44.12% of the total population. In 1926, there were 1,367 Jews in Harbin, of whom 807 were men, 560 were women (including merely Daoli, Nangang and Xiangfang districts). In 1927, there were 1,352 Jews in Harbin (including only urban area). In 1931, there were 2,600 Jews in Harbin, compared with 1,100 Jews in 1937. By the mid-1930s, 70% of the Jews had left Harbin.

By analyzing the trend of population change of Jews in Harbin, it is obvious that the population change of Jews in Harbin was particularly dramatic, especially between 1920 and 1922, which was surprisingly reduced by 9,000 people, and according to the current data it was greatly reduced year by year after 1922. Experts and scholars should analyze in depth the root causes of the change in the Jewish population in Harbin. The reasons for such large fluctuations can indicate that the

Russian Jews only regard Harbin as a transfer station to Tianjin, Shanghai and other mainland cities. Zhao Xigang points out that "in 1920 there was a large migration of Jews to other countries, with more than 10,000 leaving Harbin for Shanghai and Tianjin by July, and more going to the United States, Britain, France, etc." At the same time, "large waves of emigration often occurred during periods of great historical change." The fluctuation of the Jewish population in Harbin was also closely linked to the domestic and international situation in Russia at the time. However, there exists rare deep analysis on this issue.

According to the *History of Oversea Russian in Harbin*, "after the Russian October Revolution in 1917, a large number of Russian expatriates moved to Harbin, but the peak of Russian expatriates moving to Harbin was after 1922." According to the statistics, the number of Russian expatriates in Harbin was 60,200 in 1918, up to 131,073 in 1920, and 155,402 in 1922. And by 1923, the end of the Soviet-Russian civil war, "the number of Russians settled in Harbin was once as many as 200,000, even more than the local Chinese residents. Harbin became the largest center of Russian Jews localities in China."

The author finds that the mass migration of Russians to Harbin coincided with the gradual decline of Jews in Harbin, and that the two migrations were "out of sync". Was the migration of Russian Jews out of sync with the migration of non-Jewish Russians? The relationship between Russian Jews and non-Jewish Russians during the migration process needs to be further analyzed by experts and scholars.

Regarding the discussion of the maximum number of Jews in Harbin, the author believes that it is very meaningful to discuss the situation when the information and other aspects are relatively not sufficient. This is because the current generally accepted figure of 20,000 already makes Harbin as the largest Jewish community in the Far East, although Xue Lianju mentioned in the table "Changes in the Number of Jewish Expatriates in Harbin from 1916 to 1930": according to the Times of the Harbin Japanese Commercial Conference House that there were more than 55,000 Jews from 1921 to 1922. This is the real historical significance of the Jewish community in Harbin. Just as the discussion of Wang Tifu's insurance of transit visas for 12,000 Jews to enter Manchuria, we should also pay close attention to the significance of this move. It is important to focus on the significance of the event itself, rather than the amount of population. Wang Tifu recalls, "At that time, I held the title of consul in the embassy (Note: the pseudo-Manchukuo embassy in Berlin), and I personally handled the above matters, so I knew the Jewish issue better. The German government permitted the Jews who left the country to wear mere one set of clothes, hats and shoes, and $10 in cash, in addition to the clothes they carried. From the spring of 1939 to the end of May 1940, more than 12,000 Jews obtained entry permits (Note: visas) from the pseudo-Manchurian embassy in Berlin." Specifically, first, "the American Jewish Masons proposed a rescue package for the persecuted Jews in Germany, and those who wished to go to the U.S. were given 400 U.S. dollars to cover their travel expenses.

Romanova, a professor of the Department of Political History at Khabarovsk

State Pedagogical University in Russia, points out in the article "Charity Activities of the Jewish Religious Congregation in Harbin" that "in March 1938, the first group of about 20,000 European Jewish refugees came to 'Manchukuo' via the Soviet Union." Her figures come from *Jewish Life*, No.1, 1943 (p. 17). At the same time, she goes on to describe that "Here the refugees received sympathy and support, as always. The Sanhedrin often helped the refugees without any interference from the Japanese authorities." However, the translator questions this statement.

In the late 19th and early 20th centuries, as Jews gradually migrated to Harbin, The Jews formed a complete system of community in Harbin with Central Street as the center: ① The old synagogue on Tongjiang Street and the new synagogue on Jingwei Street were used as places of religious activities in the Daoli District of Harbin; ② The Jewish Women's Charity Society on Tongjiang Street, the Jewish Poor People's Canteen, and the Harbin Jewish Nursing Home were used as places of charitable protection; ③ The Jewish Private Hospital on Red Brick Street and the Jewish Hospital on West Fifth Street were used as places of medical and health care; ④ The first Jewish elementary school on Dongfeng Street, the second Jewish elementary school on Hongxia Street, and the Judean high school on Tongjiang Street were used as places of education and teaching; ⑤ The Judean People's (Adult Association, later called the Judean Religious Congregation) of the Harbin Science Officer on Upstream Street was used as a place of public administration; ⑥ The banks and shopping malls opened by the Judeans concentrated on both sides of Central Street were used as places of financial and commercial business.

3.3.6 "All For Profit": Jewish Business and Economic Activities in Harbin

The author believes that the business acumen of the Jews was "forced" to mold during their thousands of years of dislocation, and as a "rootless" people without land and country, they had no choice but to engage in business activities in other countries, from which they developed a set of the way of doing business.

In Harbin, there is a jingle that has been said for many years: "Daowai is hell, Daoli is earth, while Nangang is heaven." This jingle illustrates the different living conditions of people in the three districts of Harbin during certain time, but it cannot be used to fully depict the actual economic conditions at that time. the translator believes that before 1945, especially in the 1920s and 1930s, 8 districts were formed as the core of Harbin's production and processing center in Daowai, Central Street in Daoli was regarded as the core of Harbin's financial and commercial center, meanwhile, the East and West Dazhi Street in Nangang was considered as the core of Harbin's administrative center. Historically, the three districts functioned differently in Harbin and were formed as an orderly operating system. Jewish activity in Harbin was concentrated in the Jewish community in the Daoli district, centered on Central Street, but they had a "presence" in Nangang and Daowai districts. It should be noted that although Daoli, Nangang, and Daowai were administratively part of different countries or governments at the time, showing a municipal administration pattern of "two countries, three provinces, and four quarters", they were economically interconnected. Duan Guangda, an author from the College of History and Culture of Heilongjiang University pointed out in the article "Rumination on the Characteristics of the Early City of Harbin", "In 1926, Harbin's municipal administration was still not unified, and the city was divided into four, still in the special pattern of multiple administrative jurisdictions. Their respective jurisdictions were as follows: "Fujiadian belonged to Binjiang County, Jilin Province; Daoli District and Nangang District belonged to Harbin Special City; the remaining districts in the south of the river, such as Majiagou, Guxiang, Xiangfang, Yifanzi and Zhengyanghe, belonged to the Special Municipal Administration of Eastern Province and Harbin City; Songpu District on the north bank of the Harbin section of the Songhua River was under the jurisdiction of the Songbei Municipal Council, a subsidiary of the Heilongjiang Provincial Governor's Office (When the bureau was established in early 1920, it was called the Majiafangkou Municipal Council)."

"In the main streets of Harbin, 80% of the businesses were in the hands of Jews." Jews such as Skidelsky, Gewarski, Kabarkin, Soskin, Derikin, Kagan, Zicherman, Kaisp, etc., established banks, shopping malls, insurance companies, breweries, cigarette factories, high-class hotels, etc., in Harbin, and with their business wisdom, they created numerous economic miracles in Harbin, "becoming the early financial industry, industrial and commercial founders and Harbin's earliest pioneers to the world." "In the first half of the 20th century, Jews occupied a pivotal position in Harbin' housing estate as well as industry and commerce." In this article, the author does not plan to describe in detail the specific economic activities of the Jews in Harbin. For more information on the economic activities of Jews in Harbin, readers can further research Zhang Tiejiang's *Unraveling the Mystery of Harbin's Jewish History—An Investigation into Harbin's Jewish Community*. The large picture book *Jews in Harbin* edited by Qu Wei and Li Shuxiao also provides an illustrated look at the "economic miracle" created by the *Jews in Harbin*.

Regarding the study of the economic activities of Jews in Harbin, the author believes that the case studies of Kasper and Zickerman are only in their "initial stage" and have not been studied in great depth. For example, in the case studies, the houses of Skidelsky and Gwilski were in Nangang, while most of the Jews lived around Daoli Central Street. Why did they build their houses in Nangang? The relationship between Skidelsky, Gwaryski and the Middle East Railway, and the relationship between them, has yet to be sorted out. Also, there is no overall study of the economic activities of Jews in Harbin. In 2017, Zhang Tiejiang published *Study on Jews in Northeastern China* by Heilongjiang People's Publishing House. The study examines and argues by different historical periods to make an objective and fair historical assessment of the integration of Jews into the society of northeast China and their organizational activities in forming Jewish communities and societies, religious, political parties, economic, cultural and educational undertakings in various cities, their performance in joining the cause of modernization in the three northeastern provinces, and even the development of Jews in northeast China as a whole.

In the use of Jewish resources to promote the economic development of Heilongjiang and Harbin, researchers in Heilongjiang province have also made "Study on the Introduction to Israeli High Technology to Promote the Economic Revitalization of Heilongjiang Province", "Study on Economic and Trade Cooperation between Harbin and the Jews", "Research Report on Giving Full Play to the Province's Historical and Humanistic Advantages over Israel (Jews) to Promote Foreign Economic and Trade Cooperation", "Study on the Establishment of Research", "Report on the Establishment of 'Harbin an Israeli Ecological Agricultural Science and Technology Demonstration Park'", "Research on the Investment Status of Israeli and World Jewish Enterprises in China" and other research reports have also achieved some results. But do we really know the Jews and what are the concrete effects? The phrase "culture sets the stage, economy sings" has become an empty phrase. At the International Forum on Jewish History and Culture in Harbin in 2006, Australian Professor Eric pointed out in his "Proposals for Friendship and Commercial, Cultural and Talent Exchange between the Chinese and Jewish Peoples" that "contrary to typical Chinese beliefs, the essence of Jewish identity does not imply a form of unity and collective action. Therefore, some misconceptions about the existence of Jews need to be corrected before a message can be effectively conveyed to them." He proposes, "What might appeal to the former Jewish residents of China and engage them in actions that would benefit not only China but both sides?" "In addition to giving investors, tourists and other interest groups a financial incentive, the ideal way to unite and stimulate the interest of the former Jewish population is to bring them together and encourage them to work together." The author believes that "passion" alone is not enough for economic activity with Jews. However, it seems that we are not yet out of this "misunderstanding".

3.3.7 "Spiritual Ties": The Religious Life of Jews in Harbin

Synagogues, religious congregations, cemeteries, etc. were integral parts of a well-established Jewish community. The synagogue was "a place of public prayer, charity, recreational activities, and scripture study, and was the center of Jewish religious, educational, and public affairs." The synagogue is the "iconic" condition for the formation of a Jewish community and the spiritual anchor of the Jewish people. Because of the large number of Jewish expatriates, there were four synagogues (prayer houses) in Harbin. The earliest synagogue was called "Sinagoga Synagogue", built in 1903 in Paodui Street (now Tongjiang Street), the second in 1908 in Daoli Shangwu Street (now Shangyou Street), "Gallai Mother Religious Congregation", and the second in 1916 in the next is the "Majiagou Chapel" built in 1916 in Majiagou Xiaorong Street (now Guangmang Street), and again in 1920 in Xiewen Street (now Jingwei Street), also known as the "Sinagoga Synagogue". When the Harbin Synagogue was about to be closed, the Soviet diaspora Gishelyov oversaw two of the synagogues. The emergence, popularity, and development of synagogues "played an extremely important role in maintaining the common faith, common culture, common feelings, and common identity of the Jewish people. It was not only a center of spiritual life during the Jewish diaspora, but also a link of communication between Jews." Teddy Kaufman notes, "Of all the communities, the Jewish community of Harbin is considered the only religious community. The other communities, although religious ritual activities are still performed, the community members live secular lives."

The Sanhedrin "refers to the highest house of Judaism and the judiciary in the *Bible*." The members of the Sanhedrin "consisted of three types of people: the high priests, who were in office or retired, the scribes, and the social dignitaries. The priests represented the clergy, the scribes represented the intelligentsia, and the scribes represented the ordinary people." The Jewish Religious Congregation was the highest governing body of Harbin Judaism and the civil administration. "In 1903 the Sanhedrin was registered in Harbin, the center of construction of the Middle East Railway. Its official name was the Harbin Jewish Religious Guild, which had nearly 500 members at that time." The Harbin Jewish Religious Congregation managed the city's synagogues, libraries, baths, cemeteries, and relief canteens for the poor, all under the direction of the Religious Congregation Council. The Council of the Harbin Jewish Religious Congregation consisted of 10 people, with 3 supervisors, which was the last board of directors, at the time of social group registration in 1951. *The Constitution of the Harbin Jewish religious Association*, printed in 1927, defines the main functions of the association: "to subsidize the needs of the Jewish religion in the Harbin community, to manage the church and its teachers (priests), to manage the prayers for the slaughter of animals, and to manage and register the births, deaths, marriages, divorces, etc. of Jewish residents in the city. It also manages and registers the births, deaths, marriages, divorces, etc. of the Jewish community in the city; requests permission from the Chinese government to build schools for the Jewish community and to manage their funds or to organize other cultural and educational activities for the Jewish community in accordance with Chinese laws; and requests permission from the Chinese government to carry out various charitable projects to help the poor and needy."

The Jewish cemetery is an important part of Harbin's Jewish history and culture. The present Jewish cemetery in Harbin's Huangshan Cemetery is the largest surviving Jewish cemetery in the Far East. Zhang Tiejiang and Zhao Liantai introduced issues such as the changes in the Jewish cemetery in Harbin in the article "Study on the Examination of the Cemeteries Jews in Harbin". In the article, it is pointed out that the original address of the Harbin Jewish cemetery was at the back of the cemetery of the Harbin Orthodox Church (Note: there are several Orthodox churches in Harbin, this should be the Orthodox Church of Our Lady of Guardianship on Dongdaizhang Street), and the burial of the dead Jews began in 1903. It was later moved to Taian Street Cemetery in Taipingqiao, Daowai District, Harbin, covering an area of about 37,500 square meters. According to a proclamation of the Harbin Municipal People's Government on May 6th, 1958, the old Jewish cemetery was moved to the new Jewish cemetery on the newly formed Arakan Hill (Note: now called Huangshan) of the Harbin Jewish Congregation on August 6th of the same year. "According to the death register of the Harbin Jewish Congregation and combined with the comprehensive statistics of the cemetery rolls, there were 3,173 Jewish burials in the 55 years since the first burial (in the old style) in the old Jewish cemetery on May 28th, 1903, until the last burial on March 5th, 1958. Of these, 1,923 were men and 1,250 were women." The Harbin Jewish Cemetery is a resting place for Jews who were active in the political, economic, religious and cultural circles of Harbin, such as Rabbi Aaron Moses Giseleff, the spiritual leader of Harbin Jews, A. Kaufman, the president of the Jewish Congregation and his relatives, Olmert, Derikin, etc.

Li Fangbin, director of the Harbin Huangshan Cemetery Administration, in his article "The Opening and Management of the Jewish Cemetery in Harbin", describes "the 605 graves of the Jewish cemetery that are currently well preserved inside Huangshan Cemetery, the largest Jewish cemetery in Northeast Asia." "There are 583 documented graves."

As Teddy Kaufman recalls, Jewish funeral mutual societies were also formed in Harbin, which was established on an entirely voluntary basis. If the deceased was poor, the burial place and the headstone would be donated by the community, free of charge, and all died Jews, whether poor or rich, had headstones in front of their graves. However, when a rich man dies, his family must pay many expenses, 20% of the expenses for the burial and the remaining 80% for the expenses of the Jewish communal welfare institutions."

The author believes that development and utilization of the Jewish architectural remains in Harbin need to be further developed and enhanced. For example, the transportation problem of the Jewish cemetery in Huang Shan has become a "bottleneck" for people to visit and study. It is a problem that needs to be solved. At the same time, a key issue is how to play the "economic card" when playing the Jewish "cultural card", and properly handle the relationship between "culture" and "economy". "Culture on the stage, the economy sings", it is important to do the job properly, to make it possible.

The Zionist movement, with "return to the homeland" as its core, is a product of the combination of religion and reality. The author will not discuss in detail the Zionist movement of the Jews in Harbin. For related articles, you may consult Teddy Kaufman's "Zionist Activities in Harbin" and Li Shuxiao's "An Overview of Zionist Organizations in Harbin" for reference.

3.3.8 "Pull together in times of trouble": Jewish Charitable Security Activities in Harbin

The Jewish Women's Benevolent Society, the Jewish Poor People's Canteen, the Jewish Nursing Home, the Jewish Hospital, the Jewish Burial Society, and other Jewish charitable organizations in Harbin were not only an integral part of the Jewish community in Harbin, but also played a pivotal role in the life of the Jews in Harbin.

The Harbin Jewish Women's Benevolent Society was founded in 1907 and was located on Daoli Gun Team Street (now Tongjiang Street). The president of the society was Zitlin. The society was dedicated to the relief of poor Russian Jewish women, and the number of its relief recipients reached a maximum of more than 190 people. The relief was financed by members' dues and donations, and the annual income and expenditure was about 3,000 yuan. The Jewish Women's Benevolent Society's "primary responsibility is to provide community welfare and vocational training for the poor, so that these people can become self-reliant and ease the burden on the community." To this end, the Jewish Women's Benevolent Society "financed the purchase of work tools for artisans and helped them to set up handicraft workshops; purchased cows for dairies; and helped families who wanted to leave Harbin. The Jewish Women's Benevolent Society also provided wood and coal to poor families, as the cold winter in Harbin lasted for more than seven months, from October to April."

The Jewish People's canteen (free canteen) was founded by the Jewish Religious Congregation of Harbin in September 1917 on Daoli Gun Team Street, with Muburger as its president. Two meals per day were provided to the common Russian immigrants for free or half price. It was financed by members' dues, charity performances and social donations, with an annual income and expenditure of about 10,000 yuan. Because of its financial security, this poor people's canteen continued to operate until the 1950s. The "Jewish Free Canteen" provided meals to many Jewish immigrants who came to Harbin before World War I. For a full year, the Free Canteen provided hot lunches for a nominal fee. During the Jewish holidays, it also provided meals to Jewish prisoners, who have been imprisoned for theft and illegal possession of foreign currency. During the week of Passover, the free cafeteria prepares three meals each day in strict observance of the kosher food—clean food based on Jewish religion. On Yom Kippur, it serves meals before and after the fast, and 70% of those who come to the free cafeteria are Jews, but Russians and Chinese can also come here for help. The free cafeteria provided 170 meals a day, but not all were used where they were served, as some people tended to take the food home with them." In the author's opinion, the specifics of the "large number of Jewish immigrants who came to Harbin before World War I" needed to be further studied.

The Harbin Jewish Home for the Aged was founded in Daoli Gun Team Street in January 1921. The director was Rabinovich. The purpose of the home was to provide Jewish and Russian Jewish invalids, and in 1934 there were 34 elderly people in the home. The annual funding was about 6,000 yuan, which was financed by the Jewish religious guild and social donations. In the Jewish nursing home, "the elderly receive medical care and attention from the community, including medicine. At home, an internist came regularly to make rounds of the elderly and infirm, while Arkadi Futran, an assistant doctor at the time, came every day."

In July 1932, heavy rains fell 27 days in a row. On August 5th, the Songhua River was flooded, with the water level reaching 133.16 meters above the sea level, and Harbin Sun Island and Cross Island were completely submerged. The people in Majia port fled as their houses collapsed. On August 7th, the river rose sharply, and the riverbank of Jiudao Street, Daowai District broke a hundred meters long, and Daowai was flooded. Banks closed, stores closed, and the phone was cut off. On that day, the water level of the Songhua River reached 133.51 meters above the sea level. August 8th, Daoli, ranging from Gu Xiangtun area, diffused into the flood. By the 10th, all Daoli had been flooded, and water was everywhere. In Harbin, more than 100,000 refugees of flood escaped from Daoli and Daowai districts, rushed to Nangang, Majiagou, Xiangfang, the districts with high sea level. About 50,000 people were sleeping in the fields in Jile Temple, Wenmiao, Dazhi Street and Shan Street. How miserable they were! There is no place to shelter from the wind and rain, people crying for hunger and cold. *Harbin Flood Document in 1932* said, "It is a heart-breaking scene, making the angles weep." It is recorded that "about 240,000 people were victims, 20,000 people were killed, 120,000 people displaced among the city's 380,000 residents, and the whole economic losses amount to more than 100 million dollars." According to the Japanese authorities, during the entire flood period, 621 people suffered from Cholera (first emerges in the hardest-hit areas, rapid spread and high mortality rates) in Harbin, 248 died and 149 killed on the road; 168 people suffered from other infectious diseases and 62 died.

Facing with the floods, the Jewish community in Harbin organized rescue teams to provide emergency assistance to the affected refugees. According to Teddy Kaufman, "Many Chinese lives were swallowed up, but not a single Jew died. Jewish community leaders worked tirelessly to organize people and provide bread and water to families in distress. Doctors went around in small boats to check on patients and were active in the infectious disease wards. Because the first floor had also been flooded, "Beta Israel" youth—the black-skinned Jewish transported Jews from the affected areas to the second floor of the kosher cafeteria. Volunteers reached out to the elderly and the sick, bringing food from the free cafeteria. It was not until five weeks later that the flood waters receded."

3.3.9 "Capital of Music": Jewish Cultural and Artistic Activities in Harbin

Jews in Harbin also published newspapers, ran schools, publicized the state of Jewish life in the Far East, cultivated music, art and other talents, and carried out a rich and colorful cultural and artistic life, leaving a rich memory in Harbin. A report "United Nations awarded Harbin the title of 'Music City'" issued by *Modern Evening Times* on June 24th, 2010. The article said "June 22nd, Harbin, China, was awarded by the United Nations 'Music City—Harbin, China!'" However, the author believes that the title of "Music City" is a result of the rich musical heritage of Harbin in the first half of the 20th century, especially in the 1920s and 1930s, which witnessed the contribution of Jewish musical talents in Harbin.

According to the book *Russian Press Publications from 1917 to the Early 1930s*, the following Jewish publications came out: *Bulletin of the Council of the Harbin Jewish Association*, *Jewish Diaspora and Palestine* (magazine for the agency of the Jewish National Socialist Ideology), *Jewish Speaks* (magazine for the agency of the Far Eastern Zionist Local Committee), *Towards a New Shore* (published by the Harbin Women's Zionist Organization), *Our Life* (founded by Russian Jews in Shanghai), *Zionism* (founded by the Young Zionists Group), *Our Speech, Siberia-Palestine*, etc. According to the Table of the"Publication Status of Harbin Newspaper in the First and Second Decades", the Jewish newspapers were as follows: *Jewish Language* was published in 1918, *Our Language-Jewish* was published in 1919, *Rustan Exile* and *Bulletin of the Jewish Society of Harbin* was published in 1920. *Jewish Life Newspaper* was published in 1925, which was devoted to the interests of Jews, especially the life of Jews in the Far East, and this newspaper continued to be published after 1935. According to *A Brief List of Newspapers in Heilongjiang Province (1901—1985)*, *Jewish Life Newspaper* was a weekly newspaper, with the year of its founding on January 4th, 1925, and its organizer or director was Kaufmann. The newspaper continued to be published after 1935, but the year in which it ceased publication is still unknown. This summary table also mentioned a Jewish-language newspaper with Russian and English descriptions, *Del Weiter Mizrahi,* founded on December 2nd, 1921, and ceased publication on October 6th, 1922, under the sponsorship or direction of Biermann. Another account mentioned that "In 1920, *Jewish Life* was founded at 59 Bieler Street, edited by A. Y. Khauvermahn. This newspaper was rich in content, covering society, politics, and literature, and was an authority on Jewish issues in the Far East. It was a daily newspaper whose circulation was not limited to Harbin. The newspaper office was later moved to Gun Team Street in the Butou district."

Among the Russian Jews who founded and published various newspapers in Harbin, "the most famous was Lembich, who had published the *Tsarah Newspaper* in Harbin, Shanghai, and Tianjin, *Tsarah Evening Newspaper* and *Tsarah Pictorial Newspaper*. According to Mr. Fang Hanqi, a famous expert in the history of journalism in China, and also a professor of Renmin University of China, *Xiaguang Newspaper* was founded in 1920 in Harbin; *Shanghai Tsarah Newspaper* was founded in 1925 in Shanghai; and Russian *Xiaguang Newspaper* was founded in 1928 in Tianjin. *Xiaguang Newspaper* was first published in Harbin on April 15th, 1920. The address was in China Street (now Central Street), Daoli District, and the founder was Lembich. It was published twice a day, in the morning as Morning Sunshine and in the evening as Evening Sunshine. In the past in Harbin, it is the most dominant force, and also set up branches in Shanghai", and that it is famous for "its well-informed, incisive discussion." During the period of Japanese occupation, *Xiaguang Newspaper* became the only Russian language newspaper in addition to Harbin Times. It was still published and distributed after 1942, but the date of discontinuation is unknown. The newspaper was managed by "Kaufman, and the responsible editor-in-chief was Satovsky." Zhang Xueliang also wrote inscription to celebrite the 10th anniversary of the founding of the *Xiaguang Newspaper*.

According to the relevant material, before he came to China, Lien Bich had worked as a reporter for the largest Russian commercial newspaper *Russkaya*

Pravda and was already famous. After fleeing to Harbin, he made a correct assessment of the local cultural and political situation and bravely decided to start a "city" newspaper, or a "popular" newspaper. Thus, on April 5th, 1920, he and the journalist Shipkov co-founded *Xiaguang Newspaper* in Harbin, located at No.5, China Street, Butou (present-day Daoli District), with Lien Bich as its editor-in-chief.

In 1909, Jewish Diaspora Association Primary School was opened, and in 1918, Harbin Jewish High School was opened. In 1919, the Harbin Jewish Church School was opened. According to the List of Private Russian High Schools and Elementary Schools in 1928, the Jewish Primary School No.1, established in 1920 on Ma Street (now Dongfeng Street), had 5 teachers and 111 students that year; the Jewish Primary School No.2, established in 1925 on Shangshi Street (now Hongxia Street), had 4 teachers and 40 students that year.

After 1909, the following schools were also established by Jews in Harbin: The Music School (Central Street), headed by Gershgorinoi F. Commercial accounting school, with Haday A. I. as the principal. Violin school in Bread Street (today's Hongzhuan Street), the principal of which was Tritjenberge F. G. Piano and vocal school in Commercial Street (today's Shangyou Street), whose principal was Shjetn Zilizer Titmar. In 1912, the Jews founded a library in Paodui Street with a collection of 13,000 books.

Regarding the Jewish school education in Harbin, the author believes that music education is an educational activity which was exceptionally outstanding and left a valuable legacy. The author briefly describes these Jewish musicians. Burstyn, a male Jewish violinist who was born in 1922, lived in Harbin in 1928, and attended the First Higher Music School in Harbin in 1935. He left Harbin for the United States in 1941. Dillon was a female Jewish pianist and musician educator. She graduated from the Leipzig Conservatory of Music in Germany with a degree in piano, lived in Harbin in 1925, and left for Europe in 1936. Giscint, a male Jewish cello player who studied at the Russian Royal Conservatory of Music, lived in Harbin in 1922, and left Harbin in 1935. Kirov, a male Jewish flutist, was born in Harbin in 1915 and graduated from Harbin Medical College. He engaged in musical activities in Yantai, Qingdao and Shanghai. He was a musician of the Harbin Railway Club, and left Harbin in 1961 to settle in Chile, etc. In the List of *Some Expatriate Musicians* compiled by Liu Xinxin and Liu Xueqing, famous music history experts in Heilongjiang province, there are 14 famous Jewish musicians, music educators or performers, and all of these Jews are "famous" in the history of music in Harbin, China and even the world. These Jews have trained many excellent musical talents for Harbin and even for China.

In his article "Contemporary Chinese Music Masters and the Historical Achievements of Jewish Musicians in Harbin", Miao Di of the Institute of Art Research of Heilongjiang Province emphasized that "Harbin was an important window for the introduction to Western music into the East, and the Russian music schools trained the first Western music artists for China. They made an outstanding contribution to the spread of Western music in China, and among these musicians, a group of Jewish musicians played a major role." For example, Wang Lobin, the "King of Western Song", was taught by Jewish music educators or conductors Ai Meijer, Trachkinberg, and Gerscholina when he studied at the Harbin Music School. Jin Tielin, Li Shuangjiang, Guo Song and other outstanding musicians who went out from Harbin are all the fruits of music education by Jewish musicians or Russian musicians in Harbin.

In the author's opinion, at present, Harbin's musical status in the country has not been fully studied and demonstrated, and it is necessary to further explore the excellent musical wealth of Harbin, especially the influence of the Jewish musicians or Russian musicians in Harbin on China's music in the first half of the 20th century.

3.3.10 "What Course to Follow?" The "Interaction" of Jews in Harbin

The author believes that the study of Jews in Harbin, Shanghai, Tianjin, Qingdao and other cities in China, especially Harbin and Shanghai, has already achieved certain results, but now there is a "bottleneck" in the study of this area, and no more new research findings. It is not only due to the shortage of data or archives, but also the fact that researchers in different regions have focused on the Jews in respective areas, neglecting to study the "interaction" of these Jews in the economic, cultural and musical aspects and so on in China. This "interaction" appears not only among different parts of China, but also among China and other countries. The "interaction" within China is not limited to Jews, but also exists among Jews, Chinese or other nationalities. Likewise, there exists problems with the study of the Russian diaspora in China too.

In terms of music, on July 24th, 2010, Mr. Liu Xueqing, a member of the Chinese Musicians Association, who has devoted himself to the study of Western music in Harbin for many years, gave a 3 hours' lecture on the "Impact of Western Music in Harbin on China" at the 150th Heilongjiang Provincial Library's "Heilongjiang Forum", he talked about the "interaction" of Jewish musicians in different places of China, this lecture was an important "attempt" and "beginning". He told the story of the female Jewish piano pedagogue, Czaplik—she graduated from Odessa Music College; lived in Harbin in 1924 and taught piano in Harbin from 1924 to 1933; went to Shanghai to study and teach piano from 1933 to 1938; returned to Harbin in 1938 to teach piano, and taught at the Soviet Higher School of Music in Harbin from 1946 to 1955; returned to the Soviet Union in 1955. The Jewish violin pedagogue Tonov, who graduated from the violin class of the St. Petersburg Conservatory of Music, lived in Harbin since 1918: he went to Beijing and Tianjin in 1925 to teach violin; went to Hong Kong in the late 1940s. Jewish flutist Kirov, born in 1915 in Harbin, graduated from Harbin Medical College; engaged in musical activities in Yantai, Qingdao and Shanghai. Tang Yating, a professor at the Shanghai Conservatory of Music, also mentions in his book *The Musical Life of the Jewish Community in Shanghai 1850—1950, 1998—2005* that "In 1934, Longstrem, a Jewish student at the Harbin Institute of Technology, established a jazz band with his brother, playing tango, waltz, foxtrot, and blues, which became an instant hit. In 1935, with the sale of the Middle East Railway to the Japanese regime, and the Soviet employees' return to their home countries, the Rostelem Jazz Band went to Shanghai and took its place in the "Paramount" dance hall. In 1937, when the Japanese occupied Shanghai, they went to Qingdao and returned to Shanghai in 1941, where they played at the Paramount until 1947. They returned to Shanghai in 1941 and remained there until 1947."

In the economic sphere, the Jewish businessmen Kasper, Skidelsky, Gevarsky, Soskin etc. left behind a "legendary" economic activity in Harbin. Kabarkin, with whom we are more familiar, run a soybean business that spread to Europe; Zicherman, who bought the Ash River Sugar Factory, specialized in importing sugar from Java and selling it wholesale. As a secondary activity, he also began importing jute sacks ("burlap bags") from India, which were used primarily for the already thriving Manchurian soybean exports of the time. His business went very well. He also set up an office in Yokohama, Japan. The Harbin office was opened in the North Market on Shitoudao Street. In 1902, the Lurie brothers, Jews born in Nikolaevsk, were engaged in salmon fishing and fur business, and in 1902, the business of the Lurie brothers expanded dramatically, both in terms of business and geographical scope. Within a few years, in addition to Nikolaevsk, the Lurie family established its own offices in Vladivostok, Yokohama, Tokyo, Shanghai, Harbin, Shenyang and Dalian." Later, "the business gradually grew into an 'industrial empire.'" Jewish-American Plessey, in partnership with Qi Zhushan and Hao Rujiu (born in Shandong), ran a large pastry store in Harbin called "Yishunhe". Yishunhe's business was so prosperous that in addition to the main store in Harbin, it also set up branches in Changchun, Dalian and Shenyang, and was famous for its pastries and candies, which were sold in the Northeast. Orlun Brothers specialized in dog skin business and had a chain of companies in Tianjin and Harbin. They purchased from the Northeast long-haired dog skins, from Tianjin through Dalian to New York, where the skins were processed into a variety of fine leather products; Jinshan Foreign Company founder Luo Guwen came to Harbin from Russia in 1918. He was originally a Lithuanian Jew and used to run Western medicine. He came to Harbin, first as a Western medicine broker, after having a certain amount of savings, went to Shanghai in 1927. In 1930, He established Jinshan Foreign Company with others, bought a few rooms in Zhabei as a stack house, and focused mainly on business of Western medicine ...

In terms of music and economics, the "interaction" of Jews in China and abroad is still very frequent, and the questions of why and how they moved are worth exploring in depth, which still remain "blank" in domestic research. Although limited by some materials or archives, the study of "interaction" can be studied in depth based on the existing Chinese materials or archives in China, especially those in Russian, English, Japanese, German and other foreign languages, such as the issue of the routes of movement, and it is also "very useful" and valuable for the research of international relations, ethnic exchange, economic history, cultural history, anthropology, etc. This chapter of the book is only the author's insights or experiences in five-or six-years research of Jewish issues, and it provides a framework for the history of the Jews in Harbin based on previous research, and further research on the Jews in China is still needed.

3.4 | Harbin YMCA in Immigrant Society

The development and activities of Harbin YMCA are one of the important contents of immigrant cultural life in Heilongjiang Province today. It shows the abundance of the cultural activities in Heilongjiang, especially in Harbin, where immigrants are the main human resources, and reflects the regional characteristics of the international, diversified, and inclusive immigrant society.

The Young Men's Christian Association (YMCA) is an international Christian social service organization. That is, in Christ's spirit of "serving the world", according to the needs of social groups (especially vulnerable groups), engaged in a variety of social service work. These services are guided by the concept of "promoting the moral, intellectual, physical and social growth of the whole person" and serve people regardless of gender, age, nationality, race, or religious belief. Services include civilian education, sports and recreation, camp services, community services, youth work, refugee work, employment services, etc. Some YMCAs also run low-cost hostels and hotels. "The YMCA" is not a missionary organization, nor is it a charity. Its mission is to spread love, encourage the undertaking of social responsibility and promote social harmony.

In 1844, George William (1821—1905), a young Englishman, founded the YMCA Ecumenical Movement in London. At first, it was a Gospel gathering to enrich the souls of professional youth who were lost in the wave of Industrial Revolution. Later, it gradually added moral, intellectual, physical and group elements to promote the development of the whole person. The YMCA is a Christian organization that aims to understand and practice the Christian spirit of caring for the world through personal experience of serving the society and serving others. It has been recognized by the society, the church and the young people, and has developed rapidly. It has expanded to the whole Europe and North America in more than ten years. YMCA was first established in China in 1885 as youth clubs by missionary George Blood Smyth in Fuzhou Yinghua Academy and missionary Harlan Page Beach in Beijing Tongzhou Luhe Academy. Since then, youth clubs had been set up in Tianjin, Shanghai, Harbin, Hangzhou, Hankou, Qingdao, Jinan and other places.

3.4.1 The Development of Harbin YMCA

In the General Database of CNKI (China National Knowledge Infrastructure), there are 53 theses under the entry of "YMCA" from 1979 to 2008, including two excellent master's theses. In these 53 papers, the YMCA in Beijing, Shanghai, Tianjin, Hankou, Hangzhou and other places is introduced, but there is no special article to systematically discuss the development of Harbin YMCA. The problems about the establishment and ending time of Harbin YMCA, social activities and the establishment of the school need to be further discussed. The YMCA established in Harbin, where the Russian diaspora is gathered, has its own characteristics compared with the YMCA in Beijing, Shanghai and Tianjin.

There are different opinions about the time, place and initiator of Harbin YMCA. In "During the Preliminary Stage of Harbin Underground Party Organizations and YMCA" Gao Zhichao said that "Harbin YMCA was founded in 1914 (the address is now located at 62 Nansi Street, Daowai District)". In the context of "Harbin YMCA and Revolutionary Propaganda", Fu Shang said that "Harbin YMCA was established at 62 Nansi Street in 1915 after the birth of the Christian faith organization. At the beginning of establishment, Fengtian YMCA sent people to Harbin for guidance and preparation. Pastor Hua Maoshan from Denmark, director Shi Duer from America and director Yan Baohang from China of Fengtian Youth Association worked in Harbin Youth Association successively." However, it is recorded in *Religious Dialect in Harbin Annals* that "in 1925, the Lutheran Church was changed to 'Xin Yi Church' by the resolution of northeast congress." Shi Xu, an international student from Ukraine in Harbin Institute of Technology, points out in "A Review of the Cultural Activities of Russian Expatriates in northeast China" that "The YMCA in Harbin was formally established in 1919". Zhao Xiaoyang, associate researcher of the Institute of Modern History of the Chinese Academy of Social Sciences, summarized the statement of the book *Religious Dialect in Harbin Annals* in the book *The YMCA in China: Local and Modern Exploration*, "In 1926, The Youth Association of Harbin was founded by the Christian priest Shang Kuiying and the national capitalists Wu Baixiang and Zhao Chantang. The venue is next to the Sanyu Elementary School run by the Xin Yi Church in Sanyu Street, Daowai District. To facilitate the staffs of Tongji Shopping mall to participate in religious activities, another activity room was set up on the third floor near Nansi Street shopping mall in Daowai District." It is recorded in the section of "Young Christian Association" in *Religious Dialect in Harbin Annals* that "In 1926, Harbin Young Christian Association was founded. Its founders were Shang Kuiying, pastor of Shuangcheng Christian Church, and national capitalists Wu Baixiang and Zhao Zentang." The author has not found the exact founding time of Harbin YMCA at present, but the author believes that Harbin YMCA was founded in 1917—1918. This is because "The Cause of Organizing the Youth Association" from the 22ed, February 1917, *Far East Newspaper* once reported, "the local Christian pastor Ma (namely Ma Deliang) has long been interested in organizing the youth association, but due to the lack of funds, he failed to set it up for the time being. We also regret that most of the young people are incapable of self-government and throw away their precious time at will. Therefore, he discussed the method of organization with comrades yesterday." This indicates that Harbin YMCA was not established before. On June 27th, 1918, *Far East Newspaper* reported, "It was reported yesterday that the number of Members of the Chinese Youth Association is now about 28,000, according to a recent survey." "YMCA member" should be a member of Harbin YMCA, indicating that Harbin YMCA has been established at this time. Later, on September 14th, 1918, *Far East Newspaper* reported, "The Local Christian Church received a letter from the Beijing Youth Association yesterday and sent two youth association officers to the Chinese Eastern Railway to investigate the situation of the Chinese army, and then set up the Youth Association of Chinese soldiers." This also indicates that the Harbin YMCA has been established. On January 31st, 1919, *Far East Newspaper* reported, "The Youth Association of the Jesuits received a letter from the general Assembly of The Jesuits yesterday saying that the membership of the society is still too small and that it is planning to expand its ranks. It posted a notice urging all who wish to join the society to register early."

The address of the Harbin YMCA was also not explained clearly. Gao Zhichao and Fu Shang mentioned that it was in "62 Nansi Street in Daowai District"; It is stated in *Religious Dialect in Harbin Annals* that "the activity place is next to The Sanyu Primary School run by the Xin Yi Church in Sanyu Street, Daowai District. To facilitate the religious activities of the staff of Tongji Shopping mall, another activity room is set up on the third floor near the Nansi Street of Daowai District." On June 28th, 1925, Harbin Women's Association, the earliest women's group established in Harbin, held its founding meeting on the 3rd floor of the YMCA in Nansi Street, Daowai District. Therefore, the author believes that Harbin YMCA was founded in the road outside the Nansi Street. March 27th, 1925, *Binjiang Times* published that the Harbin YMCA held a memorial service for Sun Yat-sen in the enlightenment, also mentioned that it is the fourth street of Daowai District.

The YMCA consists of three departments: intellectual education, moral education and sports. The Intellectual Education Department has daily classes, Bible study classes, principle learning classes, singing classes, health classes; The Moral Education Department offers a variety of ethical lectures; Sports Department set up various chess, ball games, literature and sports activities. Later, the YMCA also established schools, added clubs, and published its own publication, *The Citizen's Weekly*. Gao Mang later recalled, "I remember I was just 10 years old and studying in Harbin YMCA School. Xialiyabin was talked about in the streets and alleys. I had heard about him from my school music teacher and textbooks."

In 1921, Zhu Jiqing paid a visit to the Soviet Union. In the following year, he returned to China and hosted *The Citizen's Weekly* in Harbin. Zhu's original name was Guo Sheng and styled Ji Qing, later renamed Zixin and styled Zaizaozi. He was born in a wealthy family in Beizhen (Binzhou, Shandong Province) in 1882. He studied in the private school when he was young. In 1899 (the 25th year of The Reign of Emperor Guangxu of the Qing Dynasty), he studied in Shenyang Wenhui Academy. In 1901, he went to Japan to study abroad at his own expense and entered Dongbin School in Tokyo to learn military affairs. During his stay in Japan, he accepted Sun Yat-sen's democratic revolutionary ideas and joined the Chinese Tongmeng Hui. In 1912, Zhu was responsible for propaganda and presided over the founding of the *People's Daily of the Three Northeastern Provinces*. In 1924,

Sun Yat-sen appointed Zhu and others as temporary members of the Kuomintang propaganda committee to promote party affairs in Harbin. He died in Taiwan in 1955.

After 1929, E. Arndt, a Russian mining engineer and geologist, was "elected the head of the new natural science and geography club of the Young Christian Church." Arndt was born in Novogorkievsk, Russia, on July 25th, 1865. He was the son of a Russian military engineer and a Russian mother. In 1875 Arndt entered a military sports school in Orenburg. He graduated from the Alexander Rovsk Military Academy in St. Petersburg in 1883 when he was 18 and then spent six years at the Catherine Ⅱ School of Mines in St. Petersburg, graduating in 1889. From January 2nd, 1923, to June 1st, 1924, he served as chairman of the Far Eastern Branch of the Russian Geological Committee. During the same period, from 1920, he continued his exploration work in the northeast. And from this year, he worked as the long-term Muling coal mine general engineering consultant. This position continued until 1939. In 1923, Arndt joined the Manchurian Research Association (also known as the Eastern Province Cultural Relics Research Association) in Harbin and was one of the 17 founders of the organization. In 1924, he was elected the head of the society's geological society. He was also appointed as the director of the Museum of Manchurian Studies (now Heilongjiang Provincial Museum) and was awarded honorary membership for life. He collected a large number of rock and mineral specimens for the museum and organized quite wonderful geological exhibitions (some of the complete sets of rock and mineral specimens are still properly preserved in the Heilongjiang Provincial Museum). "In 1929 Arndt was elected an honorary member of the Chinese Society of Geological Exploration in Beijing. In the same year, Arndt was appointed by the relevant Chinese authorities as the head of the Cultural Relics Research Institute of Eastern Province."

Founded in 1925, Harbin YMCA Middle School is located in No.59 Huayuan Street, Nangang District. At that time, the school principal was Hagrid. There were Russian and American teachers at the school, and the wife of the principal, Hagrid, was teaching for the first time, she was teaching the history of the ancient world. Miss Hopkins of the United States taught English, and other members of the church staff taught Russian history and geography. Vorobyova, a Russian, taught Russian linguistics, Tomilov mathematics, and Nosov botany. All three taught in commercial schools and were experienced teachers. "The Christian Church was run on the basis of the Russian school syllabus, which was seven years at the beginning and had 263 students in 1928. After the school system was changed to 10 years, 329 students were enrolled in 1938." According to Gao Mang, who entered the YMCA mission school in Harbin in 1933, "most of the students in Harbin YMCA middle school came from different nationalities, including Poles, Ukrainians, Estonians, Lithuanians, Jews, Koreans, Chinese and so on. Most of them are Russians. The common language is Russian. The teachers were mainly Russian nationals and gave lectures in Russian. They teach English with a strong Russian accent that a real Englishman would shake his head on hearing it." Such a situation is rare even in

Shanghai, where there is a large expatriate population. Talking about his classmate, the Jewish painter Ji Na Gilevich, Gao Mang added, "In the 1930s, when I was studying at the YMCA in Harbin, there were people of many nationalities among my classmates, including Russians, Poles, Latvians ... There were Jews, too. There was no concept of nationality at that time. We were friendly classmates." According to the "Teacher and Student Scale of Harbin Russian Expatriates Private Middle School" in the *Monthly Statistics of Harbin Special City*, No.1-10 in 1936, the principal of YMCA Private Middle school was Jole Jinxin. There were 37 faculty members, including 24 males and 13 females; there were 38 students in the primary department, 19 male and 19 female; there were 217 students in the middle school division, 116 males and 101 females. "Harbin Russian Expatriates Literature, Art, Culture and Education and Press and Publication Activities" shows that the YMCA private business Foreign Language School, located at No.59 Huayuan Street, Nangang District, the principal is Milandov. There were 20 teachers, including 7 men and 13 women; there were 192 students, 62 males and 130 females. The YMCA private Standard Chinese Institute with Milandoff as principal had 15 teachers, including 7 males and 8 females; there were 72 students, 25 males and 47 females. Scholars have come to regard Harbin YMCA school as a Russian(Soviet) school.

When the YMCA ended is as controversial as when it was founded. According to *Religious Dialect in Harbin Annals,* "In 1936, YMCA was banned by the Japanese occupational force." Fu Shang mentioned it in "The Harbin YMCA and the Revolutionary Propaganda" at the same time, "Because the Harbin YMCA often hold lectures, seminar, and spread anti-Japan ideology which attract the attention of the Japanese. They sent spy surveillance and persecuted the staff and finally closed the Harbin Youth Association in 1936." Shi Xu, a Ukrainian student in Harbin Institute of Technology, pointed out in *A Review of The Cultural Activities of Russian Expatriates in northeast China* that "Until the late 1940s, the YMCA played a certain role in youth activities and youth education in Harbin." The author agrees with the statement "late 1940s", because Gao Mang, a famous translator and painter, was born in Harbin in 1926. "He entered the church school of the Harbin YMCA in 1933 and studied for ten years." This indicates that Gao Mang "graduated from the Harbin YMCA in 1943." It proves that the Harbin YMCA did not end at this time. The end of the Harbin YMCA should have come with the mass migration of the Russian diaspora.

The Harbin YMCA emblem is also different from the emblem of the YMCA National Association. Harbin YMCA certificate of 1923, 1936 and 1941 collected by Mr. Cao Zengshen, a famous collector in Harbin and member of Harbin Village Culture Salon, with Harbin YMCA emblem and steel seal on the certificate. The 1923 certificate was written in White Russian; the emblem on the 1941 certificate is in old Russian for intellectual education, moral education and physical education. Although the YMCA was introduced into China from the United States, it is often called the YMCA of America. However, Harbin YMCA was founded by Danish priest Madelian and other people, and Harbin YMCA school is mainly based on Russian teachers, communicating in Russian. This is an important feature of Harbin YMCA.

3.4.2 Main Deeds of Harbin YMCA

After the establishment of Harbin YMCA, Wu Lishi, Chen Weiren and other leaders of Harbin's early party organizations took advantage of the favorable conditions of the YMCA to strengthen and expand the party's influence and consolidate the party's mass base in Harbin. On March 12th, 1925, after Sun Yat-sen passed away, Harbin YMCA responded to the call of YMCA national Association and actively carried out memorial activities in Harbin to commemorate Sun Yat-sen. After the Wusa Movement broke out in Shanghai, Harbin YMCA immediately organized "the Rescue Club" to strongly support it. At the same time, it worked together with "Harbin Women's Association" and other organizations for Shanghai donations, supported compatriots' patriotic action. In the school founded by Harbin YMCA, the "Chulaiyevka" Literature Association was founded by the famous Russian poet Grezov (pseudonym Achyil), which united a group of literature lovers and organized various activities, which had a great influence in Harbin at that time, especially among the Russian expatriates.

In October 1923, the Beijing District Committee of the Communist Party of China sent Chen Zuolin (Chen Huisheng) to work in Harbin. Chen Weiren, Li Zhenying and Chen Zuolin formed the Harbin Group of CPC. From then on, the first party organization in northeast China was formally born. To combine revolutionary propaganda and organizational development, Chen Weiren and Li decided to set up a place to train and educate young people. In October 1923, "Harbin Youth College of the Three Northeastern Provinces" was founded in Waiguoerdao Street (now Zhongyi Street), Daoli District. Meanwhile, to responded to the requirements of the party's central organization to create and use the civilian schools to carry out revolutionary activities, the Harbin Party and League decided that Li Tiejun, a member of the Socialist Youth League, should be in charge of civilian education. Later, "Li Tiejun joined the Harbin YMCA as a secretary, and founded 15 civilian primary schools in the name of the YMCA and set up two civilian evening classes in a commercial school. Most of the students were workers, and the courses taught were civil knowledge, Chinese language, abacus calculation and so on." The party and league organizations achieved good results by carrying out civilian education and making use of night schools for the civilian population. On the one hand, they organized students to learn cultural knowledge and on the other hand, they propagated revolutionary ideas to them. "The party's principal leaders Wu Lishi and Gao Hongguang went to youth associations and night schools to make friends with young people, identify and inspect activists among them, and recruit advanced young people who were willing to devote themselves to the revolution into the party and league organizations. Gao Chengru, a student of Sino-Russian University of Technology at that time, Ji Jinzhang, a young shop assistant, and others received Marxist theory and revolutionary thought education here and embarked on the path of revolution. At the same time, the Party built a bridge between students and the public through them." Ji Jinzhang said in"Memories", "I attended the night school organized by the YMCA of Daowai District. During the night school study, I got to know Su Ziyuan, the secretary of the YMCA, and Yang Shouyu. They both lived on the third floor of the YMCA, where they had a lot of progressive books and periodicals, such as *Chinese Youth, Guide* and *Political Life*. They lent them to me, which broadened my horizon and made me embrace revolutionary ideas." In the autumn of 1925, under the leadership of the party and league organization, Ji Jinzhang, Liu Xinghan, Liu Bingzhe, initiated and established the Harbin Shop assistants' Association. The purpose of the association is to unite young shop assistants, oppose exploitation and oppression, demand better treatment, and participate in the patriotic struggle against imperialism. At that time, Su Ziyuan was a member of the Communist Party of China and Yang Shouyu was a veteran of the Kuomintang. They were both introduced to Harbin YMCA by Yan Baohang, who was the secretary of Mukden YMCA in 1918.

On October 5th, 1923, Sun Yat-sen appointed Zhang Jin as the head of the Harbin branch of the Kuomintang and set up the Harbin organization of the Kuomintang. In January 1924, Zhang Jin attended the first National Congress of the Kuomintang in Guangzhou. On March 12th, 1925, the news of the death of Sun Yat-sen, the founding father of the People's Republic of China, spread to Harbin. The two parties organized people from all walks of life held memorial activities. Zhang Jin actively contacted the person in charge of the associations to prepare for the memorial meeting of Dr. Sun Yat-sen. "On March 29th, a memorial meeting for Sun Yat-sen was held at Harbin YMCA. After the meeting, *the Citizens' Weekly* published a special issue on Sun Yat-sen's memorial service to publicize Sun's will and revolutionary spirit." Qin Fang and Tian Weiping introduced in "A Preliminary Study on the Relationship between Sun Yat-sen and the YMCA—A Speech Centered Discussion" that Sun Yat-sen attached great importance to the YMCA because its members were mostly young people. He believed that young people were flexible and would be revolutionary forces. Sun Yat-sen once made a lot of remarks, giving full recognition to this youth organization. He not only pointed out that the YMCA of China is a progressive organization, but also said, "Is there any group that has a stronger union, a wider spread, a faster development, and a larger number of volunteers than the YMCA of China? If not the Chinese YMCA, who else would take the duty of Josiah and lead the Chinese people to Cannan, the land of Milk and honey?" ("Josiah" was a king at the end of Judah, and "Canaan" is a place name, both of which can be found in the *Bible*.)

At this time, YMCA Director General Yu Rizhang, also issued a letter to the national YMCA, launched a memorial service. On March 26th, 1925, *Shen Newspaper* published "Mourning for the Death of Dr. Sun Yat-sen (13)" by Yu Rizhang, "Dr. Sun Yat-sen died in Beijing on the 12th of this month. Those who know, both at home and abroad, sigh deeply. After 40 years of striving for the doctrine, he narrowly escaped death and created the Republic of China. In recent years, especially, our nation has fought for freedom and equality, and its positive spirit of implementation and perseverance are due to Christ. State affairs are now at an important stage. No one should express special condolences but should express a feeling of remembrance. The plan is to let the youth of the whole country hold memorial services to express their respect when the body is buried in Nanjing. As for the order and etiquette of the memorial service, it is now left to the members of the association to prepare, as soon as they are ready, they will serve." March 27th, 1925, *Binjiang Times* published a memorial service for Dr. Sun Yat-sen held by Harbin YMCA, "Dr. Sun Yat-sen, who created and built the Republic of China, died in Beijing on the 12th. The nation is in deep sorrow like a child losing his parents. It is a misfortune to lose this popular leader at a time of political instability and people's livelihood. All the members of our association will hold a memorial meeting this Sunday (29) at 2:00 PM in the auditorium of our association (Nansi Street, Daowai District). We would appreciate it if you could send us your representatives or couplets on Saturday."

April 1st, 1925, *Binjiang Times* published "Detailed Records of YMCA Mourning Sun Yat-sen". "Yesterday, the Youth Association held a memorial meeting for Dr. Sun Yat-sen. It was snowing heavily, and the roads were muddy. The men and women who braved the snow were extremely enthusiastic; there were more than 200 people. All groups were represented. The gate of the youth association is a high archway, above the archway were the inscribed board with four Chinese characters meaning 'Super Star Falls Down'. The venue layout was extremely perfect, couplets (about 50) were hanging around the wall. In the rostrum, there was Mr. Sun Yat-sen's portrait photo with a white wreath, covered with green gauze. People were in deep sorrow by the sight of it. At 3 o'clock, the bell rang for a meeting. Its order was as follows: ① Music performance of the Children Welfare Home; ② Mr. Yu Fangzhou announced the purpose of the meeting; ③ Singing hymns; ④ Mr. Shang Junchen prayed; ⑤ The whole congregation bowed three times to Mr. Zhongshan's portrait photo; ⑥ Zhang Zicai told the life story of Sun Yat-sen; ⑦ Guests offered funeral orations; ⑧ The guest delivered speeches, including Zhang Shuping, Yang Shouyu, Liu Tianyou and others; words were sorrowful and touching; ⑨ Singing hymns; ⑩ music performance of the Children Welfare Home, signifying the end of the meeting."

Here are some of the best written elegiac couplets: "We advocate freedom, solve problems through democratic means, change the old system of Chinese tradition, overthrow dictatorship, establish a republic, and add a glorious page to history." from YMCA. Binjiang Governor Zhang Shuhan pointed out, "Through our joint efforts, we will create a republic that truly respects equal rights, proclaims the zeal and virtue of the masses, and leaves a glorious legacy. Seeing the suffering of our people, we have come together with the desire to save our country and shoulder to shoulder to share the responsibility. Who is willing to come forward and take up this wonderful mission and live up to the expectations of Dr Sun." East China

News Agency reported, "The debate between standpoints will be concluded in the long course of history, with deep meanings contained in every word and sincere sentiments conveyed in every voice. The angry nationals are not unpatriotic, they just see some unfairness and hope to improve people's lives. May we be able to weave together bits and pieces of public opinion so that the people's voices will be taken seriously." *Harbin Chenguang Newspaper* also inscribed the elegiac couplet. This report proved that Gao Zhichao mentioned in the article "Early Stage of Harbin Underground Party Organization and YMCA" that "on March 29th, more than 500 people from 14 mass organizations in Harbin held a memorial meeting for Dr. Sun Yat-sen in the YMCA", which needs to be discussed.

The Yu Fangzhou mentioned above at the memorial service for Dr. Sun at the Harbin YMCA, where "Mr. Yu Fangzhou announced the purpose of the meeting", is Yu Huanfei, born in 1894 in Binzhou, Jilin (now Bin County, Heilongjiang Province). After graduation from middle school, he was admitted to Harbin Medical College. After graduation, he returned to his hometown and founded Bin County Hospital with his friends. After the May 4th Movement in 1919, Yu Huanfei, influenced by the trend of democry and science, began to be keen on social activities, travelling around Binjiang, Harbin and Shenyang, communicating with comrades, spreading Dr. Sun Yat-sen's national revolutionary thought and engaging in the anti-imperialist and anti-feudal new cultural movement. In February 1923, Yu Huanfei, together with Han Tiesheng and Zhang Shuping, founded the newspaper *Harbin Morning Light* in Harbin. Yu Huanfei was the main planner and writer of the newspaper. This is a progressive newspaper which propagates the ideas of the national revolution. Li Zhenying and Chen Weiren, who were sent by the Beijing District Committee of the Communist Party of China to build the Party in Harbin, were engaged in revolutionary activities under the cover of the identity of the newspaper reporters. The newspaper also churned out new literature. Together with a group of progressive young people, Yu Huanfei founded the first new literary group in Heilongjiang—"Spring Lake Society". The two weekly magazine *Literature* and *Art*, published by *Harbin Morning Light*, made a great contribution to the rise and development of Heilongjiang new literature. In 1924, after the first KMT National Congress, KMT native Zhu Jiqing was assigned to the Harbin Development Organization to set up the KMT Party headquarters in Harbin. With the consent of Zhu Jiqing, Yu Huanfei actively developed the Kuomintang organization in Bin County and prepared for the establishment of the Party headquarters of The Kuomintang Bin County. After the September 18th Incident in 1931, Yu Huanfei actively engaged in counter-Japanes propaganda activities. He launched the industrial and commercial circles to boycott Japanese goods, donated money and materials to support Ma Zhanshan, Su Bingwen, Li Du, etc., to fight against the Japanese invaders and defend Heilongjiang and Harbin. In 1932, Yu Huanfei left Harbin and served as the manager of *Daguang Newspaper* founded by Zhang Xueliang. In 1947, he was elected as a representative of the "National Congress" and went to Taiwan Province on the eve of the liberation of Nanjing. Yu

Huanfei died of illness in Taizhong in 1978.

After the "Wusa Massacre" in Shanghai in 1925, the anti-imperialist patriotic movement against British and Japanese atrocities in Harbin began rapidly. On June 7th, the Harbin YMCA held an emergency meeting attended by the Party and league members and established the "Harbin National Salvation Support Association", telegraphed Shanghai workers and students, and telegraphed the whole country, in the telegraph "... Hearing this tragic event, we feel deeply saddened and will uphold justice to support the Shanghai case. We will not be satisfied until the unequal treaty is abolished." On the same day, *Harbin Morning Light* published a commentary titled "Voice", calling for "the overthrow of the inhuman imperialism" and "400 million beloved compatriots united to create a new world and transform greater China." On June 17th, 1925, *Binjiang Times* pointed out that "The momentum of national progress is fast, as fast as you can walk a thousand miles in a day." "The popular spirit of Harbin is not weaker than other places". Wu Lishi, then secretary of Harbin Special Branch of the Communist Party of China, gave a speech to the YMCA in person. He said passionately, "Why do foreigners randomly shoot Chinese workers in China? This is because our country is a semi-colonial country, and foreigners can establish concessions in China and set up a state within a state. We must overthrow this social system and drive out all imperialism in China!" Harbin's support for the "Wusa" anti-imperialist patriotic struggle continued till September 1925. On September 6th, YMCA also held the "Wusa Movement Report Meeting". Tong Xingmen, who returned from Shanghai to participate in the National Youth Association Cadres' Committee, made a long report at the meeting, accusing the imperialists of killing Chinese workers and students. The participants were "all extreme indignant, and some even sobbed in secret."

On June 28th, 1925, Harbin established the earliest women's group—Harbin Women's Association and held its founding meeting on the 3rd floor of the YMCA in Nansi Street, Daowai District. More than 60 people attended the meeting, and Chai Jingshi reported on the preparatory process of the Women's Association, adopted the constitution of the association and the first newly recruited 30 members. Guests from all walks of life warmly congratulated the establishment of the Women's Association. Chai Jingshi was elected president, Wang Shuyun vice president, and Kong Fanzhen, Zhang Tielan and Zhang Weizhi were elected officers. In the "Wusa" movement under the influence, Chai Jingshi, Wang Shuyun and Kong Fanzhen and others who had the advanced thinking (Chai Jingshi was a teacher of First Woman Primary School in Binjiang county; Wang Shuyun is a student at Harbin Industrial University; Kong Fanzhen graduated from Shanghai Southeast Higher Normal School), initially often get together and discuss issues of women's rights and women's liberation. Later, they decided to take practical actions to guide women to get rid of the shackles, participate in society and move towards independence. Under Chai Jingshi's advocacy, in 1924 they began to build their own organization—Harbin Women's Association. After more than a year of efforts, they overcame various resistance, and finally obtained the approval of

Binjiang Provincial Office. After the women's association was established, they led women to take an active part in social activities. In Harbin people support "Wusa" movement of anti-imperialist tide, women's association in the First Stage of Tianxian in Daowai District held a fund-raising performance. With the support of all aspects of society, they earned a total of 2,800 flat silver, except part of which was reserved for the funds of the association, most of which was donated to the workers and students in Shanghai, contributing to the anti-imperialist struggle of the people in Shanghai.

The educational director of Harbin YMCA School, Grezoff (pen name Achyer), initiated the organization of "Chulaiyevka" literary association. This literary club, located in the Harbin YMCA school, united a group of literary lovers, and became very influential among the Russian diasporas. The name "Chulaiyevka" cames from the name of the main character in the novel *Bratja Chulaewy* by the famous Siberian writer Georgiy Grebenschikov at that time. The organizer was Alexey Gryzov, a poet and educator who writes with the pen name Acharya. He was fond of writing poems since he was a child. After he came to Harbin in 1922, he often published his works in different magazines and published 5 volumes of poetry successively. His poems are full of Chinese feeling, because he often describes landscapes, statues of gods, typhoons and so on. His poems are musical, easy, delicate, and sweet to read, and the rhymes of the peoms "Little Birds" and "Sorrow" have great appeal. Some poems, such as "A Blazing Sunset Bathed in Mist" and "The Mountain Breeze is My Cheerful Guide" vividly depict the scenes of nature that the author was enchanted with. "Chulaiyevka" holds two meetings a week, "every Tuesday is a special day for lecture or music and literature program evening". The main purpose is to invite some famous scholars and writers of the old generation to give lectures. Every Friday is for the youth group members activities, "group discussion of literary theory, exchange of creative methods, recitation of members of the poetry, selection of outstanding works." On July 3rd, 1932, "Chulaiyevka" began to publish its own literary weekly, *Young Chulaiyevka*. But it only lasted a month, publishing only 6 issues. "Chulaiyevka" also organizes poetry competitions. In the first competition, 14 people and 45 poems entered, and the judges specified 2 types of poems for the competition: Oriental theme or free topic. "Poetry readings and concerts also attract large audiences, sometimes up to a thousand people, and such events are usually free of charge." Members of "Chulaiyevka" often published poems in Harbin newspapers. Many writers and poets got their start here. They are Andersen, Volin, Cranin, Rabikin, Obhov, Perelesin, Rasinskaya, Reznokova, Shatovski, Svetlov, Slobochkov, Geritovt, Schegolev and others. As the Japanese occupied northeast China, members of the "Chulaiyevka" began to flee to Shanghai in 1933. In addition, Harbin YMCA school was also a "heaven" of arts. Gao Mang had learned painting from Ye Stepanov. "He is an oil painter and has a certain reputation." Through studying painting with Stepanov, Gao Mang realized that "color can speak, and color is a kind of beauty that is pleasing to the eye."

On September 29th, 1926, the members of Harbin Three Churches Association and the Youth Association welcomed Dr. Yu Rizhang, general director of the National Association. On September 29th, *Binjiang Times* published the news "Welcome Yu Rizhang", "Harbin Youth Association yesterday issued a general news, this year's national association director Dr. Yu Rizhong scheduled on the 28th evening of this month at 11 o'clock to arrive in Harbin. At Xi Men Lian Church, Daowai District, we will hold a tea reception with photography as a memento at 3 p.m. on 29th (next Wednesday), which will charge 2 Jiao of Da Yang (money unite in the period of the Republic of China) per person. If you are interested in participating, please inform Shen by letter of 29th so that you can reserve your seat. Please don't miss the once-in-a-life opportunity." Mr. Cao Zengshen, a famous collector in Harbin and a member of Harbin Village Culture Salon, collected a group photo of "Harbin Three Churches Association and Youth Association members welcoming Dr. Yu Rizhang", which were signed on September 29th, 1926. The Xi Men Lian Church is in the background. Yu Rizhang(David Z.T.Yui) was born in Wuchang in 1882. In 1895, he entered Wuchang Wenhua Middle School. Later, he entered St. John's University in Shanghai. After graduation in 1905, he returned to Wenhua Middle School as a physical education teacher and founded *Wenhua Academic Circle*. In 1908, he went to the United States, majoring in education at the Graduate School of Harvard University, and got a master's degree. Two years later, he became vice president of the North American Christian Student Congress. In 1911, he returned to China and became the principal of the high School attached to Wenhua University. He initiated the first summer camp in Hankou, and actively participated in political activities. During the 1911 Wuchang activity, he founded the Red Cross, engaged in the work of healing the wounded and saving the dying; He also served as Li Yuanhong's English secretary and participated in foreign affairs activities. When Sa Zhenbing led the Qing navy arrived in Han and wanted to bombard Wuchang, Yu Rizhang advised Li Yuanhong to write a letter to dissuade him and deliver it on his behalf. After the founding of the Republic of China, he was invited by the minister of education Cai Yuanpei to attend the first national education conference and served as the assistant editor of Beijing *English Daily*. In 1913, he became the chairman of the Speech Department of the Chinese YMCA National Association. In May of the same year, he attended the 8th meeting of the World Youth Student Association. After the meeting, he traveled around Europe. In 1915, he joined the Chinese Industrial League and held the post of secretary. In 1916, he became the director general of the National Youth Association and participated in the compilation of Sun Yat-sen's *Outline for Founding the Nation*. He attended the executive meeting of the New York Youth Association in 1919. In 1921, he went to Washington to attend the Disarmament and Far East Issues International Conference. He also served as consultant of Shanghai Ministry of Industry and Bureau and secretary of Association for Shandong Railway redemption. In the same year, he received his doctor degree in liberal arts from St. John's University, Shanghai. In 1923, he became president of the All-China Christian Council. In 1924, he went to the United States to attend the International

Conference of the YMCA, unaware and still had illusions of the aggressive nature of imperialism. In 1927, when he attended the Pacific National Conference in Tanxiangshan, he "persuaded" Japan, Britain and the United States, which had invaded China, to show "benevolence". In August 1932, when he went to the United States for medical treatment, he met with Secretary of State Stimson and "persuaded" the United States to curb its invasion of China. In 1933, he heard Shanhai Pass's lost, and suddenly suffered from cerebral hemorrhage, and then died of illness in the January of 1936.

In May 1931, the "Wanbao Mountain Incident" (the bloody incident in Changchun's Wanbao Mountain created by Japanese imperialists to find an excuse for invading northeast China) aroused public indignation. After the September 18th Incident, the Japanese imperialist aggression became more arrogant. Harbin people's counter-Japanese thought became more intense, and the Harbin YMCA organized the "Anti-Japanese National Salvation League". In the battle of Harbin in February 1932, the underground Communist Party of China organized a broad mobilization of the masses, organized all sectors of society to support the frontline. The YMCA also organized medical teams to bandage the wounds of injured officers and soldiers.

In October 1916, before the Harbin YMCA was founded, at the invitation of the president of Jilin YMCA, Zhang Boling, the principal of Nankai Middle School and the president of Tianjin YMCA, went to northeast China and gave a lecture tour entitled "China will not perish as long as I am here". Zhang Boling "introduced modern European and American sports into Tianjin's universities and middle schools through the YMCA". He believed that "the Christian spirit could encourage him to overcome various difficulties and persevere in the cause of education and national salvation." On October 28th, after the successful speech at Shenyang YMCA, Harbin Christian Church and the business community invited Zhang Boling to give an education speech in Harbin. As soon as Zhang Boling got off the train, he was warmly welcomed by all walks of life in Harbin. Wu Baixiang, a famous entrepreneur in Harbin, specially invited Mr. Zhang to Tongji factory and warmly welcomed him. On the afternoon of October 31st, Zhang Boling gave his first speech in Harbin at Harbin Christian Gospel Church. At that time, Harbin people from all walks of life came to see Zhang Boling's elegant appearance. As many as 400 people, including students from Jilin Tier-1 Commercial School, Daoli Middle School, teachers and staff from various schools under Binjiang Persuasion Institute and representatives of Harbin business community, surrounded the Gospel Hall. At 3p.m., the speech began. First of all, Diao Zimin, the leader of Harbin education circle and the director of Binjiang Persuasion Institute at that time, introduced Mr. Zhang Boling's life to the guests, and expressed sincere gratitude to Mr. Zhang Boling for coming to Harbin on behalf of all circles in Harbin. In the crowd's applause, Zhang Boling stepped onto the stage. Zhang Boling was a burly man who speaks the authentic Tianjin dialect with a loud voice and simple speech. He told the audience about his own experience in founding Nankai Middle School and the concept of the Chinese YMCA to serve the community. Zhang Boling's humorous and profound thoughts made the Gospel Hall filled with warm applause.

Speaking of the responsibility of young Chinese to their country, Mr. Zhang surprised the audience by saying: "If we are here, China will never fall!" "Everyone must be self-reliant. If everyone has a sense of self, China can't fall. We must have the courage to think so." At that time, the country was in a state of civil strife and warlords were on the verge of war. After the signing of "Twenty-one Demands", Japan's ambition to invade China had been clearly revealed, and the worse international and domestic situation had put the majority of young people in a pessimistic mood. Zhang Bolin's speech gave a profound enlightenment to the young people in the midst of uncertainty and wandering, so that every Chinese person in the audience were invigorated by it. After Zhang Boling finished his speech which lasted for more than an hour, Mr. Fan Junfu, the principal of Jilin a Commercial School, introduced to Mr. Zhang Boling the situation of Harbin High School focusing on cultivating students' ability and carrying out industrial education in combination with the needs of Harbin's commercial development. Zhang Boling has always insisted on the concept of "education to save the country" and "industrial education", and the speech of Principal Fan resonated greatly with Mr. Zhang. He had a wide range of discussions with the majority of secondary school teachers and students attending the lecture, which lasted until 5:00 p.m. before the end. In the days following his speech, Zhang visited business leaders and friends in press in Harbin. He planned to return to Tianjin on November 4th. At the invitation of Huang Fumei of Binjiang County Girls' Primary and Secondary School, Zhang Boling especially visited this distinctive girls' school before his departure. The school was located in the east of Badao Road in Daowai District. The school aims at "promoting women's family education" and follows the model of the Russian Business School girls' school in Harbin, with one senior class and four junior classes. Before Zhang Boling's arrival, the school had just held a grand "The First Anniversary of New School" commemoration activity.

3.4.3 Elites of All Walks from the Harbin YMCA.

The high school founded by the Harbin YMCA has produced many Chinese and foreign social talents, leaving a rich legacy in the history of China and the world. Many people who graduated from Harbin YMCA High School went on to become scientists and literary figures. Professor Volkov, a world-renowned nuclear physicist and one of the builders of Canada's first nuclear reactor. Professor Volkov and famous poet and translator of Chinese literature Valery Perereshin studied at Harbin YMCA Middle School. Another alumnus, Mikhail Volin, was a poet, writer and journalist who later lived in Australia and England. The outstanding Chinese translator, writer and painter Gao Mang, the famous film actor Wang Shu and the famous film translator Meng Guangjun are also "outstanding students" cultivated by Harbin YMCA School.

The Oscar winner for the best actor, "The Bald Movie Star", Yubreiner, was born in Vladivostok, Soviet Union on July 1st, 1920. His father was a Swiss-Mongolian engineer and inventor, and his mother was the daughter of a Russian doctor. When he was young, his father abandoned the family, and his mother took him and his sister to Harbin, China, where they enrolled in a school run by the YMCA, the Harbin YMCA. In 1934, his mother brought them to Paris, where she sent him to elite school, but Yubrynner often skipped school and became an accomplished traveling entertainer who began singing in nightclubs and found a home among a group of Russian gypsies. In 1951, Mary Martin, who had performed with him in *The Song for a Pipa*, recommended him to be cast in the musical that would immortalize him: *The King and I*, which ran for 1,246 performances and was an unprecedented success. In 1956, he was cast as the lead in a film adaptation of the play and won the Academy Award for Best Actor. In the same year, he also starred in two classic films, *True and False Princess* and *The Ten Commandments*, which catapults him into the ranks of Hollywood stars and makes him known as the "The Bald Movie Star" in movie history.

Jewish female painter Jina Gilevich (Jina) was a classmate of Gao Mang at the Harbin YMCA. Gao Mang found the entry about Jina from the *Russian Jewish Encyclopedia* published in 1997, "Shmshkevich (formerly named Gilevich) Leonina Solomonovna, born in Harbin in 1933, an oil painter. She studied in the private studio of the painter Ya Ni Kemdiyev (a student of Liebin). She graduated from the Piano Department of Harbin Conservatory of Music in 1949. Since settling in Israel in 1951, she studied oil painting in Professor Fermanti's studio in Rome. In 1972, she taught in the piano class of the Conservatory of Music, and also engaged in oil painting, painting portraits, landscapes and still lives. Shmshkevich was characterized by an organic combination of Russian realistic painting with traditional Chinese painting. Shmshkevich's works are in the collections of museums and individuals in many countries, and her portraits of Israeli Presidents Naon and Gerzog are preserved in the Israeli Presidential Palace in Jerusalem." Jina later told Gao Mang, the birth date in the *Russian Jewish Encyclopedia was wrong*, she was born in 1928 rather than 1933.

Gao Mang, under the pen name Ulan Khan, was born in Harbin in 1926. He entered the Harbin YMCA Church School in 1933 and graduated from the Harbin YMCA Middle School in 1943. He worked in Sino-Soviet Friendship Association and foreign literature research institute at all levels for a long time, engaged in translation, editing, Russian and Soviet literature research and cultural exchange and foreign friendship activities, and also engaged in literature and art creation. After 1945, he served successively as translator and editor of Harbin Sino-Soviet Friendship Association, translation chief and editor of Northeast Sino-Soviet Friendship Association, Director of the Liaison Department of Sino-Soviet Friendship Association, editor, director, chief editor and editor of *World Literature* magazine, Director of Sino-Russia Friendship Association, Director of China Translation Workers Association, Honorary Member of Russian Writers Association. His publication began in 1943. He joined the Chinese Writers Association in

1954. As translators, the works are Pushkin (Lyrics), Lemontov (letter collection), Akhmattova (long poem Requiem), Ye Senin (group poem), Pasternaq (prose autobiography *People and Things*), Mayakowski (Script *Bug*, *Bath*) and others. Before his retirement in 1989, he was the chief editor of *World Literature* magazine. In 1997, the Russian Writers Association absorbed him as an honorary member. In the same year, the Russian president awarded the Medal of "Friendship" for his contribution to the literary and art exchanges between China and Russia. In 1999, he was awarded the "China-Russia Friendship Memorial Medal" by the Sino-Russia Friendship Association and the "Russia-China Friendship Memorial Medal" by the Russia-China Friendship Association. In the same year, the Far East Institute of the Russian Academy of Sciences awarded him the honorary title of doctor.

Wang Shu, born in Harbin in 1928, attended the YMCA School in Harbin in 1943. From 1945 to 1948, he served as the translator of Changchun Office of Soviet Film Export and Import Company, member of Northeast Film Production and leader of the projection team. From 1949 to 1962, he served as the translator and deputy leader of the Northeast Film Studio and the translator of the Soviet teacher in the acting class of Beijing Film Academy. In 1963, he was transferred to Beijing Film Studio Actors Troupe as an actor. He played the Great Lama in *Spring in Inner Mongolia*, Zhu Botao in *After the Armistice*, translator Wang in *Little Soldier Zhang Ga*, Commander Niu in *Enemy at the Gate*, white porcelain in the fairy tale *Journey to the "Next Time depaart" Ship Port* and Huang Mo in *The Horse to the Screen*. And he had translated the Soviet film *Great Setbacks* (Joint translation), *Xia Boyang*, *Red Scarf*, *Little Captain*, *Small Navy*, *Zhuo Ya* (Joint translation), *Tiger Taming Girl*, Czechoslovak film *Sister*, Hungarian feature film *Fire*, Bulgarian film *Dan Ka*, democratic German film *Cold Heart* and more than 30 others. Other translations have been published in relevant domestic journals. "Wang Shu and Gao Mang once studied at the Harbin YMCA School together. Wang Shu was two years later than Gao Mang in school and participated in the revolution without graduation. After Wang Shu's father died, he and his mother moved to a building near the Railway Garden (now Children's Park), next to Gao Mang. Wang Shu's father was in charge of Tongxing Company, a brick kiln, and Gao Mang's grandfather also has a stake in the company."

Meng Guangjun, a native of Laizhou, Shandong Province, once studied in Harbin YMCA School when he was young. In 1946, he entered the Harbin Soviet film export agency and translated Chinese subtitles for Soviet films. In 1948, he went to Xingshan, as the Northeast Film Studio (now Changchun Film Studio) translator, and with Fuming, Liu Chi, Yuan Naichen and others together to complete China's first Chinese dialogue Soviet translation production *Ordinary Soldier*. Since then, he served as the leader of the factory translation film office. Between 1949 and 1952, he had translated nearly 30 Soviet film scripts, including *The Baltic Representative*, *The Scoutor's Great Service* and *The Angry Fire*. In 1954, he visited the Soviet Union and several countries with the Chinese film delegation in Eastern Europe. After returning to China, he served as the deputy director of the Expert

Office of the Film Bureau of the Ministry of Culture. In 1957, he was transferred to China Film Press as the deputy director of the Editorial Office of Foreign Film Books, in charge as the chief editor of *International Film*. In 1958, he served as the director of the Editorial Office of Foreign Film Books. In 1959, at the beginning of establishment of the Film Institute, he was transferred to take charge of foreign film research, organized and compiled the compilation of a number of foreign film materials, which expanded the vision of people in the film and cultural circles. In 1960, when the China Film Workers Association was founded, he was elected as a member of the Board of Directors and served as a member of the Foreign Liaison Department and as an editor of the China Film Publishing House. He was elected as the standing director, secretary general and executive secretary of the secretariat of the 4th China Film Association; a member and director of the presidency of the 5th China Film Association; and once served as the vice president of China Film Publishing House.

The Harbin YMCA was founded and developed in Harbin, where Russian expatriates gathered in the first half of the 20th century and later under Japanese rule. In such an environment, Harbin YMCA created a distinctive YMCA different from other places. Harbin YMCA not only had inextricable links with the early construction of Harbin Communist Party, but also actively organized anti-imperialist patriotic movement. At the same time, under the influence of famous teachers of Russian literature and painting in Harbin YMCA, a number of outstanding scientists, painters, actors and translators have been cultivated. These achievements are commendable, and Harbin YMCA is a "wonderful flower" in the YMCA National Association.

It is impossible for a person to master all the information he needs under certain conditions, despite the great effort to "find something". Using their own ideas to collect the data to form a kind of "own views" will often form some "prejudice". As the data gradually "appears", we will also "revise", or even "subvert" the same issue. These problems should be a normal phenomenon in academic research and become a "normal" thing. Go beyond oneself is "valuable", and the correct treatment of the discussion is more "precious".

3.5 | On the Business Philosophy of Jews in Harbin

Harbin is a representative of the rise of modern cities in Heilongjiang, whose prosperity may attribute to the establishment of the Chinese Eastern Railway. The so-called "internationalization" procession of Harbin also started there. It is the golden period of urban development in Harbin ranging from having trade relations with foreign countries after the Russo-Japanese War to the establishment of the Puppet Manchukuo. The economic and political elements of various countries entered Harbin which gave the Jews there a once-in-a-lifetime opportunity. The Jews in Harbin came mainly from Russia and a few from Poland, Germany and France. The Jews soon made forays in industry and commerce in Harbin, and the outstanding contribution they made to transform Harbin from a small fishing village to a modern metropolis was a significant part of development miracles created by the Jews around the world. The way in which Harbin Jews made their fortune expressed their shrewd and wisdom in every aspect.

Harbin began to take shape as a modern city with the construction of the Chinese Eastern Railway in 1898, and it became a famous industrial, commercial cosmopolitan city in the Far East in less than a quarter of a century, creating a miracle in the process of Chinese modern urbanization and leaving an intriguing page in the history of modern Chinese urban development. The business philosophy of Harbin Jews is worthy of further research.

3.5.1 The Rise of Harbin as a Modern City

Harbin, as a typical city of modern times, was neither transformed on top of a traditional city, nor did it have a long natural preparation or accumulation phase.

Until the end of the 19th century, the Harbin area had already reverted to the agricultural area in which the traditional natural economy played a dominate role. When the Chinese Eastern Railway Engineering Bureau moved to Harbin on June 9th, 1898, a huge and profound change took place here—the process of urbanization started. First, many Chinese and foreigners rapidly converged here by various means. Secondly, the scattered natural territory condition began to evolve into a concentrated urban territorial pattern and an orderly spatial structure. Thirdly, various industrial enterprises, represented by "Eastern Railway", various financial institutions represented by China-Russia Dosheng Bank and new cultural and educational facilities such as weather stations, schools, hospitals, clubs, etc., which is the unique structural organization of modern cities, appeared in succession. Harbin broke through the fence of the original natural economy and quickly completed the orderly combination of the constituent elements of the modern city, appearing in a new urban posture on the banks of the ancient Songhua River. Since then, Harbin's overall urban growth has remained phenomenal.

The whole line of Chinese Eastern Railway opened to traffic in July 1903. Since then, Harbin gradually became the biggest water and land translation hub in the northeast area. It was the easternmost end of of Eurasia Land Bridge and the transportation pivot of Chinese Eastern Railway, which extended 2489.34 kilometers long. Meanwhile, Harbin was also the biggest hub of inland navigation in the northeast area, which may trace back along the Songhua River to Jilin Province, Qiqiha'er, Nenjiang in Heilongjiang Province, and down to Jiamusi, Tongjiang, and even Khabarovsk. Due to the convenience of transportation, Harbin soon became the largest center for goods in the northeast. After the Russo-Japanese War, while Harbin was forced to open a port for business, capitalist countries across the world rapidly surged into it. By the middle of the twentieth century, Harbin has developed into one of the largest international trade cities in the Far East. From 1924 to1928, Harbin was the first favourable balance of trade among the 45 national customs and has always maintained the advantage of trade surplus, trading with the Soviet Union accounted for an average of 85% of the total trade between China and the Soviet Union. Harbin was not only the "general sink of goods distribution", but also the "financial transfer center" in the northeast area. During this period, Harbin's total amount of trade and capital circulation accounted for 40% of the Northeast region. As an important industrial center in the northeast, Harbin in the 1920s had already had forty industrial sectors, including about 200 large and medium-sized enterprises and more than 1,150 small factories. The industries consisted of Chinese Eastern Railway General Factory, the once biggest one across China, and flour milling, oil making and brewing industries, which mainly controlled by Chinese National Capitalism, all ranking tops. In the 1920s, 20 countries had chronologically set up consulates here, and Harbin became the"main source"of political, military and diplomatic information in the Far East. When the Chinese Eastern Railway went into operation in 1898, Harbin had a telephone line stretched from the easternmost end of Suifenhe to the westernmost end of Baikal. In 1907, the Qing Government opened an international circuit in this bureau directly reaching to the major radio stations across the world. In addition, Harbin's major trade and financial institutions and consulates had their own telecommunications facilities. As an information center of the city, the function of Harbin was very prominent and important while much famous news agencies at home and abroad had sent staff stationed in Harbin in a long period time. In 1922, Harbin, one of the most advanced cities which had achieved the automation of the telephone prior to the Shanghai and other cities, was then one of the most advanced cities of China's municipal telephone communications.

3.5.2 The Historical Background of Jews' Immigration to Harbin

In the 1920s Harbin became a city with the most population of Jews in the Far East, which was about 12,000-13,000 Jews, and even up to 25,000 at the most. The Jews in Harbin came mainly from Russia, with a few from Poland, Germany and France. At that time the Jews still had no homeland of their own. "As early as the 16th century, Tsarist Russia stipulated in a special law that Jewish merchants or citizens had to pay double tax. In the Tsar' s pardon of 1827, Jewish youths aged 12 to 18 were obliged to serve in compulsory military camps as reservists, and then to serve 2.5 years of active service. When Tsar Alexander Ⅱ was assassinated in May 1881, the new governments' anti-Semitic policy became even more radical. From this time onwards, Russian Jews began a mass emigration. The largest migration took place between 1881 and 1882. Until the end of the 19th century, Jews living in Russia, who made up about two-thirds of the world's Jews, still did not acquire citizenship". For Jews suffered from years of religious conflicts, political persecution, racial discrimination, occupational restrictions, human rights violations, and exclusion of foreigners forced, they had to wander for long periods of time to find a secure home. At this time, the construction of the Chinese .Eastern Railway, Russia's defeat in the Russo-Japanese War, the October Revolution and the outbreak of civil war brought objective conditions for Jews to move to Harbin. The Tsarist

Russia's "Yellow Russia" plan led the Jews rush to Harbin, following the Russians in the construction of the Chinese Eastern Railway. Russian Finance Minister Witte, a "pro-Jewish" official, "established a series of 'preferential' policies, including the freedom of religion and the right of unrestricted commercial and access to schools without quotas." That made Jews put aside all their ideological burdens and worked hard to make a fortune in the virgin land of Far East.

3.5.3 The Business Philosophy of Harbin Jews

Jews have acquired extraordinary commercial talents after experiencing the dispossession of land, the loss of farming opportunities, the exclusion from running handicrafts and the formation of transnational trade networks, and the rich experience of the great wanderings. They are never averse to making money, which bring them a sense of security and elevate their status too. With a wealth of knowledge and wisdom, spirit of innovation and adventure, risk and reward being directly proportional to each other, the Jews soon rose to prominence in industry and commerce. The Jews made an outstanding contribution to the transformation of Harbin from a small fishing village of the past to a modern metropolis, which is an important part of the miracle of development created by Jews in the world, rewarding Harbin for treating its Jews well. The Harbin Jews displayed their shrewd and wisdom everywhere in the path to make their fortune.

(1) Business operates beyond domain and broad vision makes great business

Initiating the export of the Northeast soybeans to Europe was the Harbin' s earliest trade. Harbin was the first city to export soybeans to the European market. At the beginning of the 20th century, northeast China' s soybeans were well known overseas, and they were mainly utilized for cooking, feeding and oil-making raw materials. "A large number of northeastern agricultural products, mainly soybeans, soybean cake and soybean oil are exported to Japan, Europe and the United States which expanded the avenues for trade in soybean specialties and contributed to the dramatic development of the trade in specialties." The specific timing and operators of Harbin's soybean exports have various statements in the academic world. The Russians, Japanese, British, and Danes all have different statements about that issue. Zhang Tiejiang argues that "Harbin soybeans were first sold to Europe in 1907 by the Harbin Jews Bitkernovsky, who pioneered the export of Harbin soybeans to Europe. After Bitkernovsky' s first successful sale of Harbin soybeans to Europe, the Harbin Jews entrepreneur P. M. Kabalkin sold soybeans to London in 1908, which was the beginning of the 'massive' export of soybeans to Europe, thus making Harbin soybeans famous in the world."This testimony confirms that Harbin was the first city to export the Northeast soybeans to the European market, and also confirms that Harbin's land transportation preceded Dalian port's sea transportation in the Northeast soybean export route. The first to advocate the export trade of the Northeast soybeans shows the unique vision and drive of Harbin's businessmen, as well as their boldness to be the first in the world. Indeed, the history of soybean exports from the Northeast to Europe can be traced back to 1907. Starting from that year, about 4,000 tons of soybeans were shipped to the port of Vladivostok via the Ussuriysk Railway. Since then, the export volume increased year by year, and at its peak in 1929 it exceeded 2,010,200 tons, accounting for 81% of the 2,480,000 tons of soybeans shipped on the entire Northern Railway line. The export of soybeans contributed to the rapid development of the economy in the northeast of China which made the Northeast economy inseparably with the world economy and be an important part of the world economy. The export of northeast soybeans to Europe is representative of international trade in the northeast region. Northeast soybeans have this opportunity to become famous in the world, mainly by three reasons: First, the superiority of the northeast soybean itself. Compared with Japan's mainland soybeans, Hokkaido soybeans and other origins of soybeans, Northeast Chinese soybeans are superior in a number of indicators, including protein content, fat content, and carbohydrate content, and are rich in nutritional value and high in oil yield.

Second, Harbin has the unique geographical location and solid economic foundation. From the economic geographic conditions, Harbin is in the middle of the Songhua River Plain, whose hinterland is known for its fertile land, virgin forests, rich mineral deposits and other natural resources by the North Manchurian region of Heilongjiang, Jilin and Hulun Buir provinces. After the Late Qing Dynasty and Early Republic of China immigration and settlement, the Songhua River Plain had been initially developed into a crop production area known as the granary of North Manchuria. Soybeans were produced in Harbin and nearby areas, and the local production can save the freight cost of transportation. The opening of the Chinese Eastern Railway in 1903 made Harbin a transportation hub in northeast China and a link to the Russian Far East. The Chinese Eastern Railway was built and operated by Russia in northeast China after the signing of the Sino-Russian Treaty between the Qing Government and Tsarist Russia in 1896. A line from Manchuria to Suifenhe via Harbin with a total length of more than 2,480 kilometers was the main line and a line from Harbin to Dalian via Changchun was branch line, called South Manchurian Railway with a total length of more than 980 kilometers. They are collectively combined to the Chinese Eastern Railway. In July 1903, the whole line of Chinese Eastern Railway was opened to traffic and started its official business. It was the first big railroad in China that connected with the world. "Harbin is the management center of the Chinese Eastern Railway and the intersection of railroad trunk lines."Taking a train from China to Western Europe via Harbin into the Great Siberian Railway could take 15-18 days less than by sea, and the cost was reduced by 2 thirds. After the Russo-Japanese War (1904), the Changchun-Dalian section of the South Manchurian Railway was occupied by Japan. Harbin's water transportation was increasingly active, and its port became busy as well. In 1905, Harbin set up the "Binjiang Customs Office" and opened the port to commerce, which stimulated the export of goods. At that time, the freight of the Chinese Eastern Railway was controlled by the Russian. Besides, the cost by sea was cheaper than land transportation, so that Kabalkin chose the water transportation. In February 1908, Kabalkin chartered the British freighter "Golenesque" in the name of the St.

Petersburg exporters Natanzon Company, operated by Captain Rafelt, and shipped 300,000 to 400,000 pounds of agricultural products mainly with the soybean from Harbin to London via Vladivostok and received by James and Sons Company. Since then, soybeans have become a popular commodity on the international market and are known as a "worldwide commodity".

Third, the ability of Harbin businessmen to capture business opportunities. At the end of the 19th century, with the construction of the Chinese Eastern Railway, Harbin quickly became a city of immigrants. The Russians were the first, followed by Europeans and Americans, and also Jews, Japanese and Koreans came in succession. The reasons for the arrival of multinational expatriates in Harbin varied from the government dispatch, making lives and escaping from a crackdown on exile and so on. Objectively, expatriates from various countries brought in their business ideas and injected exotic genes into Harbin's economic and cultural form. Roman Kabalkin is a typical example. Kabalkin was a bold innovator in business methods and thinking. He combined the grain business with building grain barns on the railroad, and first of all sent grain in bulk in wagons, without sacks, using only train gates, which greatly saved the cost of freight from the warehouse to the railroad and the purchase of sacks. During the Russo-Japanese War, it was believed that the most promising commodity was wheat from Manchuria. But Kabarkin had the ability to capture business opportunities and found a unique way to achieve great success in the soybean trade.

(2) Seizing new trends, combining with old projects

Harbin is the first to establish high-class hotel which pioneered the construction of the luxury hotel. In 1913 Joseph Casper founded the Modern Hotel, the most luxurious high-class hotel in the Far East at that time. Kasper started by running a watch repair store, and later developed into a big jewelry store. At the beginning of the 20th century, soon after the invention of films, Joseph Kasper immediately realized the importance of cinema and combined it with hotels and restaurants. The Modern Hotel was a comprehensive enterprise hotel integrating with hotel, restaurants and theaters. "Almost every night, the Modern Cinema Park staged the latest films, performed Chinese and foreign new plays, and held grand fashionable balls. This immediately caused a sensation in the whole industry, which led to a greater development of the hotel industry." The advertisement at that time was as follows, "100 clean and gorgeous rooms, 50 rooms with bathrooms, comfortable and safe; Restaurant, café, large living room, reception room, dancing hall, movie garden, flower hall, pergola, American food, playing room, beauty saloon, car room all in it. And also sold cosmetics, tobacco, cigarettes, sugar, stationery, books, and so on." It illustrates the luxury of Modern Hotel.

(3) Choosing the right place is more important

The first stores established in Harbin were the Samsonovich Brothers Chamber of Commerce, before the Churin Company. The Samsonovich brothers came to Harbin from Russia via Hailar in 1901—1902 and were the first Jewish merchants to open clothing and textile stores in Daoli District. The flag-ship store of the

Samsonovich Brothers' Chamber of Commerce was located at the corner of Central Street and Xishidao Street in Daoli District, a three-storey building with a very advantageous location and a large flow of customers. According to Mr Li Shuxiao's testimony, this building was built prior to 1909. Moreover, the Samsonovich Brothers' Chamber of Commerce also had branches in Moscow, Berlin, Khabarovsk, Chita and other places.

(4) Following the laws of science, achieving machine-based production

The first machine-made flour enterprise was founded in 1908 by Aron Josefovich Kagan, a Russian flour company. Kagan was a Russian Jew. The Russian Flour Company was based on the Russian capital, with a running capital of 1.5 million yuan and an annual turnover of about 15 million yuan. The company had branches in Dalian and Kobe, and its Kobe branch had a working capital and inventory of about 1.5 million yuan. After Kagan established the Russian Export Company, which was engaged in exporting soybeans, soybean meal and hemp seeds, and imported sugar from Java for sale in Harbin. At the same time, wheat warehouses were established, and grain was sent to Khabarovsk, Chita and Blagveschensk to supply for flour mills, civilian use and seeding. In 1921, Kagan reorganized the Russian Flour Company, after purchasing the Songhuajiang Flour Company, its name was changed to Songhua River Flour Company Ltd, also known as Yongsheng Company. With a maximum annual production capacity of 6 million pounds (about 100,000 tons), the Yongsheng company produced all grades of wheat flour, as well as millet, corn, buckwheat and other milling and flour making operations. Songhua River Flour Company Ltd. is the earliest machine-made flour enterprise in Harbin, and the company owned first-class building and equipment in North Manchuria. There were three wheat flour plants, one rice milling plant, one corn milling plant, one refined rice plant, one steam drying plant, one machinery plant and one power generation plant, all of which were the latest machines imported from Britain and the United States. "By 1924, Citibank of America had invested 2 million yuan in the company to set up more than 100 sales offices in various places. By 1925, the company had become the strongest and largest flour processing enterprise in North Manchuria."

(5) Capturing business opportunities, making innovations

Beet-sugar enterprise was pioneered. In 1908 the Polish Jew Tzadov invested 1.8 million rubles to establish the Ash River Sugar Factory, which was transferred to the Songhua River Flour Company in 1923 due to poor operating and production conditions, but it still remained under his own management. In 1926, the sugar factory was transferred to Aron Josefovich Kagan for operation. The crude sugar factory was built in 1908 and put into operation in 1909. The refined sugar factory was built in 1915, and all its equipment was imported from England. The brewery was originally small in size but was expanded in 1927 with the installation of the latest equipment, and its production increased significantly. The beet-sugar residue drying plant offered poultry feed by pressing sugar beet residue into cakes. In addition, there were soybean meal crushing plants and soybean meal refining plants.

The total valuation of the Ash River Sugar Mill amounted to 1,541,279 Yuan.

(6) Taking risks bravely, making bold attempts

Multinational corporations were first established. In 1916, Shemin Soskin founded the "Soskin Shipping Company". At that time, the problem of exporting Manchurian grain to the American and European markets was still being explored, and Soskin was bold enough to take risks and entered the shipping business. Due to the defeat of the Russo-Japanese War, Russia's economy suffered from depression, which created space for its involvement in the shipping industry. The ports of the Heilongjiang, Songhua and Ussuri rivers were connected only by water, and in the face of the huge demand for transportation of grain, timber, coal and other materials, the risk was always proportional to the profit, and Soskin made a big profit. Later, he joined hands with Amur Merchant Shipping Company and formed Amur Shipping General Company. With its strong strength, fighting in a big price war and enhancing its services, Amur Shipping General Company turned into a giant scale in the shipping industry.

(7) More fields, more fortune

The Soskin family was a Jewish family with international influence in Harbin's history. It was involved in grain import and export trade, flour and soybean processing, finance, shipping and municipal construction, and was one of the wealthiest families in Harbin. The Soskin family founded or co-owned the Soskin Shipping Company, the Amur Shipping Corporation, the She-Soskin Joint Stock Company, the Soskin Flour Mill, the Soskin Oil Mill, the Far Eastern Jewish Commercial Bank, and the Harbin Jewish National Bank, making the family's fortune grow larger and larger.

(8) Wide horizon, down to earth

In 1904 the Russian Polish Lithuanian Ilya Aronovich Barzai Sr of Jewish origin founded the Barzai Sr Tobacco Company in Harbin. His tobacco store was in Moscow and had been operating for six years at that time. He came to Harbin alone to investigate the tobacco market here and prepared to set up a factory. For the moment, with the operation of the China Eastern Railway, Harbin became the center of the railroad in the eastern province and the economic center of northeast Asia, having convenient water and land transportation. Harbin's economic environment was very ideal. In 1904 Ilya founded Gwanna tobacco shop and founded the Old Barzai Father and Son Tobacco Company in 1909 and renamed the British Old Barzai Father and Son Tobacco Company in 1914 as a result of joint venture and reorganization, then joined the Qidong Tobacco Company in 1930. He had an absolute advantage in the competition with the Japanese East Asia Tobacco Company. Every step of the company's development showed the vision of its entrepreneurs. They adjusted their countermeasures from the practical point of view to make themselves always in the leading position of the North Manchurian tobacco industry.

(9) Valuing contract spirit, entering the financial and insurance industry

The Jewish people are a contract-oriented people who place great importance on making and keeping covenants. This is especially true in business activities. The financial and insurance industry needs the spirit of contract to support.

In modern times, Harbin was the financial center of Northeast Asia, and the financial institutions established by Jews occupied an important position. The Sino-Russian Dawson Bank was founded in 1895, and its first director general was the Jewish Rothstein. In 1898, its branch was set up in Harbin. In 1910, it was renamed as Russian Asian Bank, and its manager was a Jewish man named Schedelman. The Sino-Russian Dawson Bank was the first foreign bank in Harbin and even in the Northeast area. It marked the entry of international Jewish capital into Harbin and the beginning of the formation of Harbin's financial system, which laid the foundation of financial capital for the construction of the Chinese Eastern Railway. After that, HSBC and Citibank set up branches in Harbin in 1911 and 1919 in sequence. The Universal Savings Association, the Far Eastern Jewish Commercial Bank, the Jewish National Bank, the Far Eastern Bank, the Harbin Union Bank, the Anglo-Manchu Savings and Trade Chamber of Commerce, and the Shinji Bank was founded, all of which were large financial institutions with considerable economic strength. Among them, the Jewish National Bank, founded in 1923, was the earliest and longest-running foreign bank in Harbin. It was nationalized and changed to an expatriate bank in 1957.

After the opening of the Chinese Eastern Railway, the Jews founded several insurance agencies to act as agents for foreign insurance business. The Ginzburg Insurance Company and the Norwegian Foreign Bank acted as agents for Russian and Norwegian insurance companies respectively. Ogrelensky Insurance Company was an insurance agency founded by Ogrelensky, a Lithuanian Jew, to operate insurance agency business.

(10) Knowledge economy, education first

Jews attach great importance to education. Only those full of knowledge can be invincible in the business world. Jewish tradition imposes an obligation on the father to teach his son the Jewish classics. The book is smeared with honey for the child to lick as soon as they are born. When the child starts to learn words at five-year-old, they are supposed to read and recite the Torah. In 1907, the Harbin Jewish Primary School was founded, also known as the Harbin Private Jewish School of Excellence, and in 1909, the Jewish Diaspora Primary School was opened, also known as the Harbin Private Jewish National School. In 1912, the Harbin Jewish National Library was founded, and later was renamed the Zionist Organization Library. In 1933, it was merged with the Imardaq Library and renamed the Harbin Jewish Public Library. The collection of the library covered 15000 volumes. In 1918, the Harbin Jewish High School was founded, also known as the First Social High School of Harbin, which was the only synagogue high school in Harbin. In 1921, the Talmudic College was opened, offering courses mainly related to Judaism such as Hebrew, Torah reading, selected Bible readings, Rabbinic Judaism, etc., as well as some secular courses. In addition, the Jews established a number of vocational schools in Harbin, such as a commercial accounting school, a piano and vocal music school, a music and art school, and a violin school and so on.

Chapter 4
The Role of Celebrities in the Development Process of Immigrant Society

4.1 | New City of Immigrants—"Chicago of the East"

The diversity of immigration structure and the multiculturalism it brought with contributed directly or indirectly to the economic prosperity of Harbin. This prosperity was so dazzling in the early years of the Republic of China that it was internationally acclaimed as the "Chicago of the East" in the midst of chaos of China. This is a reflection of the economic and commercial success of the area in its time and space. When we reflect on the migration in Harbin during this era and within the boundaries of today's Heilongjiang province, the special relationship between the two must be highlighted, and we have to marvel at the fact that the characteristics and influence of immigration in this era must have some inevitable relationship with the outstanding economic and social achievements here!

The following paragraph examines the impact, development and achievements of the diverse immigrant culture on the urban landscape of Harbin from a "city card" of Harbin.

In 1930, the *Chinese Eastern Railway Economic Monthly* carried an article summarizing the state of trade in Harbin in 1929—"An Introduction of Trade and the Trade of Harbin". "The state of trade in Harbin is of great interest to the European and American. In terms of commerce, Harbin is worthy of being called the 'Chicago of the East'".

The recognition of any appellation must not depend on the words of one or two foreigners, but on whether it is worthy of the name. This is true of the "Paris of the East" and the "Moscow of the East", and it is also true of the "Chicago of the East". Harbin is surrounded by an immensely rich, vast rural hinterland; the constant influx of immigrants from Shandong, Hebei and other places has accelerated the development of agriculture here. In just a few years, Harbin has formed a huge grain production area. This is the natural condition of Harbin as a commodity food base. Harbin is located at the intersection of the Chinese Eastern Railway, the economic artery of the north-east, and the Rabin and Binbei Railways and the Songhua River, making it extremely convenient for transportation.

As a result, the Northeast Plain, China's "breadbasket", allows two different developed economic spheres, Europe and Japan, to be connected here, with Harbin becoming one of the hubs for their interaction. Even before it made a decisive contribution to China's economic take-off, Harbin played a role in the international economic cycle. In addition to being a cosmopolitan city in terms of architecture, ideology and culture, Harbin is also a truly 'cosmopolitan' city in terms of economic trade.

In 1907, the Japanese were the first to act. Mitsui & Co. exported about 4000 tons of soybeans to Europe via the Ussuri Railway which pass through the port of Vladivostok. This was the first large-scale export of soybeans from the Northeast to Europe. The Sino-German relation was back to normal from tension shortly after the World War I. Massive soybeans were poured from Northeastern China to Germany through export. Meanwhile, grain trade in Harbin city soared to its full accordingly, followed by the Grain Future in the end. In April 1924, to restrain the "exporters" from continuing to drive down the purchase price of soybeans, the Chinese government set up the Binjiang Currency Exchange in Harbin, rebuilt the Binjiang Grain Exchange, and established the Harbin Stock Exchange. These created a more sophisticated system of grain futures trading in Harbin. From there we can see that Harbin played an important role in the modernization of China.

By 1929, soybeans from the Northeast of China were exported to Germany, the Soviet Union, the United Kingdom, and the British colonies via Vladivostok through the Grain Export Department of Danish, French, and British chambers of commerce and the Soviet in Harbin, and to Japan and Korea (under the Japanese occupation at that time) via Dalian (a city in northeast China). Soybean exports were no longer only dependent on the German market but showed a trend of blossoming everywhere. Under the guidance of the government, the Harbin Grain Exchange restricted grain exports several times, which directly led to the fluctuation of grain prices in Europe and Japan and established its reputation in the world grain futures trading market. They saw similarities between Harbin at this time and Chicago in the United States, which was also a transportation hub and a center for grain futures trading. So, they took the lead in calling Harbin the "Chicago of the East".

There are always amazing coincidences in history, just like the Republic of Belarus "The sign transformation party" calling Harbin 1919 "Paris of the East" and "Moscow of the East", which were both the accident of history. But in view of Harbin's important position in the world grain futures trading market in the 1920s, didn't this coincidence contain a kind of historical necessity? The "Paris of the East" showed that Harbin in 1919 accepted the Western civilization in terms of architecture and lifestyle, while the "Chicago of the East" showed that Harbin 1929 integrated into the world market in terms of economy.

At present, Wuhan (a city in south China) and Zhengzhou (a city in north China), relying on the characteristics of the city, have launched the slogan of building the "Chicago of the East". As a kind of city symbol," Chicago of the East" plays an important role in publicity. Therefore, nowadays there is heated discussion in Harbin on the importance of the establishment of oil futures trading market and grain futures delivery market. How to put "Chicago of the East", the name card of Harbin, into good use should be a test.

4.2 Study on Administrative Power of Chinese Eastern Railway Affiliated Area

The "Railway Negotiation Bureau" was developed from the negotiation organization under the control of the General Magistracy (government office in feudal China) of Heilongjiang and Jilin provinces at the end of the Qing Dynasty and spawned by the Russian Chinese Eastern Railway Administration to intervene between the Chinese and the Russians in the territories of the Chinese Eastern Railway. It became, under certain conditions, the "quasi-administrative body" of the Chinese in the Chinese Eastern Railway territories and the areas under its influence. The name of the agency and the evolution of its intelligence, as well as the story behind these changes, was almost tainted with the times. The history of changes in this organization fully reflects the unique history of the development of Harbin and the affiliated areas of the Chinese Eastern Railway from a unique perspective, and also reflects the basic features of the formation process of the city of Harbin. From the initial establishment of this agency, it was branded as the expansion of Tsarist Russia, to its later emergency as an important counterweight to the aggression of Tsarist Russia, the transmutation of the agency "Railway Negotiation Bureau" clearly outlines for us a controversial history of development process of Harbin, which is a special history product of the encounter between the two political civilizations of the East and the West since modern times.

In modern times, China took a turn in its position in foreign relations and began to engage passively with the powers. The Manchu Government of the time in China adapted passively to the different rules and circumstances of diplomacy and began to set up special diplomatic agencies at various important points of contact. As a result, the word "diplomacy" was tainted with humiliation and the agency was branded with shame, so that the nation regarded it as a "scarlet on the face" and was ashamed to mention it. Even its functions and the work of its staff were kept secret. Because of the weak state and cowardly government behind it, it seems that its work was always linked to "Betrayal of national interests". In fact, it was not (Such is not the case). In the course of our modernization and in the midst of a difficult and troubled evolution, the diplomatic agency and their interlocutors have made an indelible contribution. A proper and accurate understanding of history is a prerequisite for a nation and a people to be able to move forward.

These institutions were called by slightly different names at different times and in different regions. In the administrative offices of important open commercial ports and cities, there were departments such as the "Customs Office", "Bureau of

Negotiation" and "Department of Negotiation". The Jilin and Heilongjiang Railway Negotiation Bureau was an important agency in its "territory" after the construction of the Chinese Eastern Road. As it was historically controlled by the Tsarist Chinese Eastern Railway Administration, and in terms of institutional settings, functions and staffing, it overlapped with the Jilin General Bureau of Negotiation, the Heilongjiang Negotiation Office and the Harbin Customs Office. The inherent complexity of its nature and functions caused great problems for the practice at that time as well as for later generations' perception of the institution. Moreover, as most scholars considered the establishment of Harbin Customs Office as an important event within the Chinese government's possessions in the China Eastern Railway and proposed that the date of its establishment is regarded as the birth of Harbin, more scholarly attention has been paid to Harbin Customs Office, while research on the Railway Negotiation Bureau has been relatively rare. This part of the book compares the changing nature of the functions of the Railway Negotiation Bureau from Late Qing Dynasty to Early Republic of China and restores the historical relationship between the Railway Negotiation Bureau, the General Bureau of Negotiation of Jilin, the Heilongjiang Negotiation Office and the Harbin Customs Office.

4.2.1 Railway Negotiating between Jilin and Heilongjiang Provinces before the Establishment of the Provincial Railway Negotiation Bureau

When the China Eastern Railway was first built, the Heilongjiang and Jilin regions along the railway were economically backward and sparsely populated compared to the mainland. The Qing Government exercised loose administrative jurisdiction over this vast territory and did not have a top-down and complete system of foreign diplomacy in the region, which was chaotic and disorganized.

After the Sino-Japanese War of 1894—1895, because of the gradual devolution of the Qing Government's foreign diplomatic power, local governors and generals involved in many foreign diplomatic activities, with a succeeding situation that "the power to handle negotiation cases between provinces and foreign countries was exercised by frontier officials". The Jilin and Heilongjiang regions were no exception to this rule, with the General magistracy mainly responsible for foreign diplomacy. But there were many drawbacks in this system. First, there was no fixed diplomatic staff, and when it came to foreign affairs, they often transferred people from the "staff of the five departments" as temporary personal to "handle foreign affairs concurrently". Most of these foreign affairs officers were local officials who were diligent and cautious in handling affairs and understood the general situation. Although they had practical experience in dealing with Russia at the border for many years, they were not specialized in foreign affairs, and most of them even did not speak Russian and did not undergo systematic diplomatic training. Secondly, the Qing Government had a tradition of setting up "customs offices" at coastal ports, which were specifically responsible for local taxation and certain foreign diplomatic matters.

From the beginning of the construction of the Chinese Eastern Railway there was a steep increase in the number of Negotiations with Russia and related matters of civil, economic, political and even international relations in the provinces of Jilin and Heilongjiang. However, the Qing Government did not set up a permanent diplomatic office in this area. Without an organizational structure, naturally there was no permanent office. Local diplomacy was mainly handled by the relevant magistracy (outside Harbin, such as Hulan Office, Shuangcheng Office, Binzhou Office, etc.). Small matters such as theft, could be dealt with by the magistrate, but concerning major matters of national sovereignty, the local magistracy would "blame each other" for reasons of authority and jurisdiction. The role of diplomatic agencies was not accomplished. Thirdly, shortage of diplomatic funding result in lack of fixed office funding; meanwhile, vehicle requirements and staff salaries were not guaranteed.

In 1897, many Russian railroad engineers flocked to the Chinese territory in the Heilongjiang and Jilin regions. The pressure on the local Chinese authorities to deal with foreign affairs increased dramatically. In practice, the disadvantages of having local officials running diplomacy were soon revealed. Due to the lack of awareness of the importance of diplomatic institutions and inadequate preparation time, the Qing Government did not have a specific reform program; besides, Jilin and Heilongjiang provinces are located in the border area, with money shortage, and diplomatic talents in short supply, thus the establishment of the negotiation agency with Russia was hasty and the work was in disorder. On October 10th, 1897, the General's magistracy of Heilongjiang Province approved the establishment of "Heilongjiang Negotiation Office" in Qiqihar, which was specifically in charge of the diplomacy with Russia. Ten people were selected from the officials who dealt with foreign affairs in peaceful time, among which included a "General Officer", an "assistant", a "Russian language meeting officer", two "council members on affairs", and five "principal manuscript translators" and "scribes". In the same year, the General of Jilin also established Jilin Negotiation Administration in Changchun. It was stipulated that, "Negotiation Administration of Jilin Province shall be responsible for local negotiation affairs of Jilin province exclusively. In case of serious incidents, literary affairs shall be verified and handled by this Administration jointly with the Russian Foreign Minister in Jilin, military affairs shall be verified and handled by the Foreign Minister of Russia in Jilin Province, and trivial affairs on the street shall be verified and handled by this Administration jointly with the Russian Chief of City Guard in Jilin Province." The relevant negotiation events "are always endorsed by the General of Jilin Province to handle." It was stipulated that specific local negotiation affairs with foreign countries shall be dealt with under the command of General Jilin. In terms of staffing, the General Bureau of Negotiation of Jilin was staffed with more than 60 people, the institutional set-up is much the same as that of the Negotiation Office of Heilongjiang, but with more clerical staff—10 guards, 10 civil servants, 14 temporary scribes, and 15 dispatching members.

Although the agency was established, its members were almost exclusively a patchwork of non-professional diplomats, far from being able to cope with the increasingly complex diplomatic incidents along the Chinese Eastern Railway. And the real headache for the "diplomatic office" was not the frequent diplomatic incidents per se, but its opponent, the Chinese Eastern Railway Bureau. The Russian-controlled Chinese Eastern Railway Board was an administrative structure from the outset. Almost everything it did for the Chinese Eastern Railway was related to the sovereignty of the state and railway negotiations. It was responsible for land occupations, logging claims, and judicial incidents between railway employees, Russian soldiers and personnel along the line. Although the above were called "railway intercession", it was in fact related to state sovereignty and its jurisdiction. However, the Heilongjiang and Jilin Negotiation Offices were just "service agencies" for the generals of Heilongjiang and Jilin, which did not have the decision-making power for foreign affairs. They were only information transfer agencies, and did not have the ability or power to handle such events. They were only information transfer agencies for transmission, without the ability and power to deal with such matters. Therefore, in the face of diplomatic affairs, they either shirked their responsibilities, or delayed the prime opportunity, trapped in a more disadvantageous situation. Responsible officials handled matters in violation of regulations, no matter what the result was, they would face the system of picketing, impeachment, so that officials worked as if walking on thin ice. How many heroes wandered around, lamenting that there was no way to serve their country or suffered heavily, leaving the right and wrong to be judged by the future generations.

4.2.2 Heilongjiang Railway Negotiation Bureau within the Chinese Eastern Railway Administration System

On 9th June 1898, the ship Blagoveshchensk arrived in Harbin (now called Xiangfang District) with a shipload of engineers and technicians for the Chinese Eastern Railway and road-building materials. Based on the negotiations with the Chinese authorities, the Russians designated 21,000 acres of land in Harbin, including the old Harbin (Xiangfang), the new Harbin (Nangang), the port area (Daoli) and the Jiangbei Dockyard, as subsidiary land for the railway, making Harbin the terminus of the Chinese Eastern Railway. This led to large-scale railway negotiations between China and Russia.

At that time, in the administrative division of the Qing Government, the south of Harbin was under the jurisdiction of Shuangchen Office and Binzhou Office, whose commander was the subordinate of General Jilin, the Vice General of Alacuka; while the north of the Harbin was under the jurisdiction of the Hulan Office, whose commander was the General of Heilongjiang. Although the Qing Government already had the administrative system of "diplomatic office" and "general bureau of diplomacy", the Tsarist Russia was very dissatisfied with this kind of diplomatic organization. They believed that the two institutions still retained a strong feudal magistracy in terms of personnel allocation and institutional nature, and that many practices were different from modern diplomatic practices. Consequently, the two sides were unable to integrate with each other in system and channel of diplomatic and document processing. In 1899, the chief engineer of the Chinese Eastern Railway, Ruggievich, urged General Enze of Heilongjiang and General Yanmao of Jilin to sign "The Statute of the General Bureau of Railway Negotiation of Heilongjiang" and "The Charter of the General Bureau of Railway Negotiation of Jilin", because "after the railroad has been built and opened to traffic, China and Russia were involved in it, therefore, entanglements were indispensable". Besides, he also pressed the Qing Government to set up a "Railway Negotiation Bureau" in Harbin in accordance with the modern diplomatic system that "specialized in railroad negotiations". Both charters stipulated that the Bureau "shall be exclusively in charge of negotiation matters within the railway boundaries, and in case of incidents, the Bureau shall handle them in conjunction with the chief engineer". "All matters of great importance, no matter where there is disagreement among the officials of the Harbin General Bureau and the chief engineer, shall be handled by the general according to the request of the members of the bureau and by the chief engineer. Other matters may be handled by the General Bureau and the chief engineer or his agents at any time through consultation. The General Council Office first drew up a plan to deal with the case, and then informed the General while transferring the case to the negotiation office (Heilongjiang Negotiation Office, Jilin Negotiation General Bureau) for record. From the above provisions, it is easy to see that Heilongjiang and Jilin Railway Negotiation General Bureau, in the early days, was only a group responsible for specific matters, and did not have the decision-making power on important matters but the general. In nature, it was not much different from the Heilongjiang Negotiation Office and the Jilin Negotiation General Bureau. It was not very different in nature from the Heilongjiang and Jilin General Bureau of Negotiations. The power to deal with matters was still vested in the local government of the Qing dynasty, up to the general. Its important feature is that the Railway Negotiation Bureau was established under the influence of the Chinese Eastern Railway Administration and was able to negotiate directly with the Russian side on behalf of the Chinese side's interests.

It is important to highlight that the above-mentioned "Statute of the Railway Negotiation General Bureau" states that the Railway Negotiation Bureau "shall send all the cases it draws up to the Negotiation General Bureau for the record", which shows that there was no subordinate relationship between the Railway Negotiation General Bureau and the original Heilongjiang Negotiation General Bureau and the Jilin Negotiation General Bureau, but a parallel relationship of division of labor. The Railway Negotiation General Bureau oversaw the negotiation affairs within the railway, and matters outside the railway were all dealt with by the Negotiation General Bureau. Due to the increase of relevant negotiation affairs and the active endeavor of the Chinese staff, the functions of the Railway Negotiation General

Bureau changed greatly and gradually played an important role in the administration and diplomacy of the Chinese Eastern Railway. However, at the same time, the institutions of the Heilongjiang Negotiation Office and the General Bureau of Jilin Negotiation continued to be retained and, during the New Deal period in the Late Qing Dynasty, were renamed the Department of Negotiation, which developed into an independent Chinese diplomatic institution at the local government level, different from the model of the Railway Negotiation Bureau.

In 1900, the Boxer Movement spread to the Chinese Eastern Railway. In a few months, the Boxers in northeast China destroyed almost all of China's railways, including the Railway Negotiations Bureau. When China and Russia became hostile, Enze and Yanmao abolished the railway charter, and the Railway Negotiations Bureau was abolished before it was officially opened. The Russian government took this incident as an excuse to send troops into and occupy the "railway zone." In just a few months, Tsar Nicholas Ⅱ mobilized 116,000 troops to northeast China and quickly took control of the area along the Chinese Eastern Railway, taking full control of the construction and management of the railway zone. The Chinese Eastern Railway Engineering Bureau (which became the Chinese Eastern Railway Administration after the opening of the railway in 1903) took advantage of its power to exclude Chinese personnel from important posts on the Chinese Eastern Railway, and completely took off the disguise of "commercial railway". It established a railway administration system in the Chinese Eastern Railway subordinate territory that functioned similarly to the Russian "Central Asian Railway Bureau" and "Ussuri Railway Bureau" and answered directly to the Russian Ministry of National Defense, becoming the highest administrative body of Tsarist Russia in the region. Since then, Russia had ignored the previous Sino-Russian treaty on the Chinese Eastern Railway, wantonly trampled on, tampered with and eroded China's rights and interests at will. Besides, the Chinese side lost the only weak legal guarantee on the Chinese Eastern Railway issue and had to negotiate with Russia again on a new basis.

By 1902, heavily armed Russia forced the Qing Government to resign The Statutes of the Jilin Railway Negotiations Bureau and The Heilongjiang Railway Negotiations Bureau, which were under even harsher conditions. Compared to the 1898 regulations, this time the following changes were made: Article 3, which stated that "in all cases ... the whole case shall be referred to the General Administration for consultation with the Director General of Railways in the Eastern Province", together with Article 8, which stated that "the appointment of the Director General, the General Administration and those who are to take on important duties shall be discussed with the Company first"; Article 9 said, "the General and Branch Bureaus shall be set up within the railway boundaries, be assigned to deal with each other, and be subsidized by the Chinese Eastern Railway Company, and their buildings shall be built with funds from the Company." These two changes significantly altered the nature of the 'Railway Negotiations Bureau". The Bureau of Railway Negotiations was no longer responsible for the Heilongjiang and Jilin Generals but became a subordinate body of the Eastern Provincial Railway Company.

In addition, the two statutes further expanded the functions of the Railway Negotiation Bureau. Article 2 stipulated, "all miscellaneous cases involving the railroad and railroad theft, no matter how far from Harbin, must be delt by the General Administration of Railway Negotiation; all contracts for the purchase of public or private lots shall be verified and sealed by the General Administration of Railway Negotiation", which further strengthened the administrative power of the Railway Negotiation Bureau in land leasing and administration of justice. Although the power of the Jilin and Heilongjiang General magistrate was emphasized in the appointment and dismissal of personnel, the funds and offices were allocated and prepared by the Chinese Eastern Railway Administration; therefore the Chinese Eastern Railway Administration also had the right of veto in the appointment and dismissal of personnel; and the establishment of institutions followed the "establishment idea" of the Tsarist Chinese Eastern Railway Administration, that was, a centralized institutions integrating negotiation, justice and economy were set up around the Chinese Eastern Railway subordinate territory. At this time, the Heilongjiang and Jilin Railway Negotiation Bureau was no longer a simple "foreign negotiation organ". In fact, it had broken away from the control of the General magistrate and had some local administrative decision-making power and became a quasi-local administrative organ focusing on foreign negotiation in the Chinese Eastern Railway subordinate territory. The reason why it was called a "quasi" administrative organ was that it was an organ in the Chinese Eastern Railway subordinate territory, which was free from the local administrative system of the Qing Government. Although it represented the interests of China, the statute stipulated that it was subject to the jurisdiction of the Tsarist Chinese Eastern Railway Administration and was not entirely an administrative organ of the Qing Government (and the local governments of the Republic of China). On the other hand, its officials had the status of administrative officials of the Chinese government and represented the Chinese government externally. Therefore, the "Railway Negotiation Bureau" had its special dual identity and status in this special period of hostility between China and Russia. However, the ambiguity of its status inevitably led to the breeding of conflicts.

After the reform, because of the internal functional conflict, the "Railway Negotiation Bureau" soon led to adverse events. From 1902 to 1904, the Jilin General Administration of Railway Negotiation had few contacts with Russia. Zhou Mian, the general office of the Heilongjiang Railway Negotiation Bureau, was mainly responsible for negotiating with Russia, who had overseen negotiations with Russia for many years. At the beginning of his term of office, he enjoyed a good reputation as "He is a fair and impartial person, with excellent talent and ability, and his reputation is well known and admired by both Chinese and foreigners". However, after a period in office, Zhou Mian was obviously not mentally prepared enough for realize the function of the Heilongjiang Railway Negotiation Bureau.

He did his duty in strict accordance with Statutes of the General Bureau of Railway Negotiation in Heilongjiang—he maintained good communication with the Chinese Eastern Railway Administration, and handled sensitive events such as land leases and banditry suppressing properly, which did not lead to conflicts between Russia and China and ensured the normal construction of the Chinese Eastern Railway and to a certain extent eased the tension between Russia and China after the Boxer Movement. However, for institutional reasons, he did not "keep the General of the Heilongjiang informed" when dealing with major events. So, he received the opposite of what he was getting at the beginning of his tenure. The Heilongjiang General magistrate thought that Zhou Mian "ignored all the official affairs of the province", but "catered to everything that was beneficial to the foreigners", and blindly made concessions to the Russian Chinese Eastern Railway Administration. Besides, his attitude toward leading the people to sell the land outside the boundary of the Chinese Eastern Railway was rude and arrogant, which aroused public discontent and greatly damaged the image of the Heilongjiang Railway Negotiation Bureau.

After ascertaining the "baneful" influence caused by Zhou Huang, Heilongjiang General Da Gui and Vice-general Cheng Dequan thought that he was no longer suitable to continue to serve as the chief office of the Heilongjiang Railway Bureau, so they jointly submitted a letter to the court, requesting that he held responsible for his crimes and be removed from office. However, due to the provision of Article 8 of the Statute of the Heilongjiang Railway Negotiation Bureau mentioned above, "the appointment and removal of the General Office shall be subject to the consent of the company", the sixth-ranking Daotai Zhou Mian, under the patronage of the Russian Chinese Eastern Railway Administration, refused to leave his post for two months after receiving the removal order. After being dismissed from public office, Zhou Mian was not severely punished and was soon handed over to the Beiyang Minister for commission. In 1909, Empress Dowager Cixi awarded him two Red Cross medallion and two merit medals, which indicated that Zhou's "crime" was not unforgivable, just "privately signing a treaty with the Russians that humiliated the country" as described, during his impeachment. After the "Zhou Mian Incident", there was a power vacuum for the Qing Government in Heilongjiang and Jilin provinces near the Chinese Eastern Railway. There was a lack of sound administrative setup that could take care of the interests of all parties, and an independent and effective mechanism and staff that could respond to unexpected and major diplomat matters, and many contradictory issues within the system had also emerged as never before.

4.2.3 The "Railway Negotiation Bureau", Which Was Attempted to be Incorporated into the "Harbin Customs Office" System

Northeast China, after the Russo-Japanese War, lost its sovereignty and became the sphere of influence of Japan and Russia, but it became more open to the outside world. The exploration of land and sea routes opened up land links between Russia and the northeast of China, Britain and other European countries. The wharves along the river nearby Chinese Eastern Railway had established a shipping network with ports at home and abroad, such as Dalian, Yantai, Vladivostok, Osaka and Busan. In a short time, the closed geographical unit of northeast China was broken up rapidly. Moreover, as a result of the defeat in the war, the Russian monopoly once established in northeastern China was destroyed, which aroused great interest in the Chinese Eastern Railway and its dependencies among the political and economic forces in China and the rest of the world. Hundreds of thousands of immigrants flocked to the Chinese Eastern Railway and its dependencies, so, traditionally, the relatively closed northeast was brought into the world economic circle. Besides Tsarist Russia, other powers also became stakeholders in the northeast China, and the importance of the Chinese Eastern Railway suddenly increased.

To adapt to the real condition of the Chinese Eastern Railway after the Russo-Japanese War and strengthen the management of the Chinese Eastern Railway and its dependencies, Tsarist Russia supplemented the existing railway administration system and set up a “city council” for the first time (such bodies had not yet been established in Tsarist Russia and the frontier provinces). Tsarist Russia ’s intention was to diversify the forms of management of the Chinese Eastern Railway in response to the democratic reform at home and the growing protests from China and other powers against its monopoly on the management of the Chinese Eastern Railway and its subordinate territories, and to relieve the pressure on the Chinese Eastern Railway Administration. More insidiously, Tsarist Russia took the opportunity of legal construction to perfect the management mechanism of the Chinese Eastern Railway to blur the sovereignty of the area.

The United States strongly opposed this, and Britain and France also took a negative attitude. What they would like to see was the situation of “national condominium” rather than parliamentary forces, which represented other interests except their own, controlling thc Chinese Eastern Railway and its subordinate territories. Of course, the powers knew that the Chinese Eastern Railway was a commercial enterprise. Under the scope of international law, the Qing Government was the undoubted master of the Chinese Eastern Railway’s subordinate territories and had the legal power to govern the area politically and carry out public management. But to expand their power base in northeast China and weaken the influence of Russia and China, the powers all tried to meddle in all the affairs of the Chinese Eastern Railway’s subordinate territories by “condominium”. Japan, with the same ambition of monopolizing northeast China as Russia in the past, was indifferent in either the “parliamentary” reform of Russia or the so-called “condominium” of the powers, while Japan had no absolute power to monopolize the management of the Chinese Eastern Railway, it was happy to see the powers hooked up with each other to achieve nothing, .

The Qing Government of China firmly opposed to the implementation of the “parliamentary system” in the Chinese Eastern Railway, whether out of the idea—

The opposition between imperial power and democracy, or the pragmatic interest-conflict of juridical belongings in the Chinese Eastern Railway territory. At the same time, the growing economic and social activity in the then-formed urban area of Harbin, especially the increasing number of matters involving the Chinese, made both central and local officials of the Qing Government aware of the urgency of establishing their own administrative system.

However, strictly speaking, although China had never legally lost its "territorial ownership"—its territorial sovereignty—in this area, the actual control and administrative power had always been in the Russia side, and it had always been the "Jilin and Heilongjiang Railway Negotiation Bureau" that represented the Chinese right to leverage against Russia and asserted its sovereignty. Whether in jurisprudence, in the material basis of its existence, or in the process of its practice, this institution, which was subject to the constraints of others, could play its role in safeguarding state power less by the explicit and effective directives of the central government or the administrative system of the country, and more by the conscience and efforts of the officials themselves. After the Russo-Japanese War, Chinese sovereignty in Harbin was represented by such an institution, it's just like walking on wire, it had to be carefully and vaguely maintained until now. Now there are more Chinese interests to safeguard, and more urgent territorial sovereignty and jurisdiction to be clarified and asserted. But what was the effective way to realize these aspirations? How could a new modern government be established in the Chinese Eastern Railway's subordinate territories, which was in line with the international model, could adjust the interests of the great powers and carry out public management of people from all over the world? One of the most pressing and thorny issues was how to make an effective cut between the Railway Negotiation Bureau and China East Railway Administration, and how to set up a body to fill the power vacuum created by Zhou Mian's departure.

In legal terms, China enjoyed sovereignty in the Chinese Eastern Railway Territory, but the uncompromising attitude of Russia's Chinese Eastern Railway Administration and the profound institutional differences between China and the West prevented the Qing Government from setting up a government office in the Chinese Eastern Railway Territory. In 1905, the Qing Government tried to introduce the "Customs Office", a foreign affairs agency usually set up at a treaty port and on leased land around it, to the Chinese Eastern Railway Territory, and set it up in Harbin. Compared with other ports of commerce and leased areas "where sovereignty was clearly defined in law and foreigners played an absolutely dominant role", the newly established Harbin Customs Office (also known as Binjiang Customs Office) was not primarily tasked with collecting taxes. Harbin Customs Office "handled the negotiations between the two provinces and supervised the collection of customs duties". In principle, the original diplomatic agencies of Jilin and Heilongjiang provinces, such as the Heilongjiang and Jilin Railway Negotiation Bureau, the Jilin Negotiation Bureau and the Heilongjiang

Negotiation Office, were combined into one agency under the authority of Harbin Customs Office. Its establishment marked the formal separation of the diplomatic agencies of Jilin and Heilongjiang provinces from the General magistrate, and the establishment of an independent diplomatic system at the provincial level with Harbin Customs Office as the center and the Heilongjiang and Jilin Railway Negotiation Bureau, the Jilin Negotiation Administration and the Heilongjiang Negotiation Office as the assistants. The primary purpose of Harbin Customs Office at that time was to resist the disguised colonization of Russia and safeguard national sovereignty by establishing a highly centralized diplomatic agency in the Chinese Eastern Railway Road Territory.

In 1905, the Jilin and Heilongjiang generals proposed to the court, "remove the Jilin, Heilongjiang and Harbin Negotiation Bureau and set up a customs officer", to weaken the Railway Negotiation Bureau through Harbin Customs office. However, because it was indicated in many Sino-Russian treaties that "the Railway Negotiation Bureau was responsible for all the negotiations along the Chinese Eastern Railway", until 1906, Tsarist Russia still only recognized the status of the Railway Negotiation Bureau, and resisted Harbin Customs Office in leasing land and judicature. As a result, the status of Harbin Customs Office in the Chinese Eastern Railway Subordinate Territories could not be established, and the rights of railway negotiation could not be recovered.

The Qing Government had no choice but to compromise. On the 22nd of the first lunar month of 1906, the Qing Government officially appointed Du Xueying the general officer of the Jilin General Administration of Railway Negotiations, "who should go to his post immediately to be dedicated to his duties", and issued a wooden seal with the following text: "The official seal of Harbin Customs Office Concurrently Jilin and Heilongjiang Negotiation" (It is said in the archives as "Border Defense of Harbin Customs Office Concurrently Jilin and Heilongjiang Negotiation", but the seal was stamped on the official documents as "Border Defense of Harbin Customs Office Concurrently Jilin and Heilongjiang Negotiation", so the function of the seal should be based on the real object). It is stipulated that this Customs Office shall be under the jurisdiction of Jilin and Heilongjiang Provinces, with Hulan and Yilan under its jurisdiction. All railway negotiations should be handled by this Customs Office. In terms of personnel, Harbin Customs Office also used the former personnel of the Railway Negotiation Bureau of Jilin and Heilongjiang Provinces. In terms of staffing, Harbin Customs Office also used the old staff of the Jilin and Heilongjiang Railway Negotiation Bureau. The chief office of the Jilin Railway Negotiation Bureau was appointed as the officer of the Binjiang Customs Office, while the other personnel were five, each from the Jilin and Heilongjiang Railway Negotiation Bureau. This move was intended to blur the distinction between Harbin Customs Office and the Railway Negotiation Bureau, so as not to leave a pretext for Tsarist Russia to refuse to negotiate.

This compromise showed that the Qing Government did not have a correct understanding of two issues. First, the Qing Government did not realize the reason why the Jilin and Heilongjiang Railway Negotiation Bureau, which it wanted to deprive, could play a role in the territory of the Chinese Eastern Railway and be recognized by the Chinese Eastern Railway Administration—first, a series of treaties were signed between China and Russia, which endowed the Railway Negotiation Bureau with the power to negotiate with Russia; second, its centralization of diplomacy and administration was objectively in line with the complex reality of the Chinese Eastern Railway territory. Therefore, the Qing Government tried to replace the power of the Railway Negotiation Bureau with Harbin Customs Office which was only in name but not in reality. Hence, in the negotiation practice, most of the former officials of the Railway Negotiation Bureau had to be retained in the personnel arrangement, and the operational mode of the Railway Negotiation Bureau was still followed in the organizational functions. Second, the Qing Government did not understand the status and function of the Railway Negotiation Bureau. It was a diplomatic agency to deal with the issues related to the Chinese Eastern Railway between China and Russia, and to represent the interests of China in the field of non-full sovereignty, so it was not quite equal to the equivalent diplomatic agency of equal countries. Therefore, the status of the Railway Negotiation Bureau was delicate and special, and "unprecedented" in the history of China's diplomacy.

The facts showed that this compromise of the Qing Government could not change the situation that the Chinese Eastern Railway Administration of Russia had the diplomatic dominance over Jilin and Heilongjiang provinces. It also did nothing to protect the national power it sought to maintain. Taking advantage of the treaty signed between China and Russia, Russia had already grasped the diplomatic initiative in the subordinate territories of the Chinese Eastern Railway. Relying on its powerful military and economic strength, and with the help of its control over Jilin and Heilongjiang Railway Negotiation Bureau, the Chinese Eastern Railway Administration ignored the naive approach of the Qing Government to weaken the negotiation power of the Railway Negotiation Bureau by "building a customs office" and resisted the "Harbin Customs Office" under construction in every possible way. The Chinese Eastern Railway Administration branded the Qing Government's setting up of Harbin Customs Office as "a blatant violation of the existing treaties and a challenge to the international law and the international order", and constantly put pressure on the highest authorities of the Qing Government.

In desperation, the Qing Government reformulated regulations, stipulating that "Lawsuits between China and Russia within the railway domain which are not related to railways shall be tried jointly by the customs authorities and the Russian consuls, while those involving railways shall be handled jointly by the Railway Traffic Bureau and the Russian Railway Traffic Bureau." The position of the Railway Traffic Bureau as the subject of railway negotiations was re-emphasized in terms of jurisprudence. Since then, Harbin Customs Road continued to be retained, but it no longer had the practical significance of weakening the Railway Negotiation

Bureau. Instead, it began to seek to use the legal basis that "the dependencies of the Chinese Eastern Railway were Chinese territory" to collect taxes from Chinese and foreign merchants in the dependencies of the Chinese Eastern Railway. It also began to take charge of the management of the Chinese people outside the subordinate territories of the Chinese Eastern Railway, towards the goal of establishing an independent and sound administrative organization. It also began to take charge of the management of the Chinese people outside the subordinate territories of the Chinese Eastern Railway, towards the goal of establishing an independent and sound administrative organization. But the realization of this target was also very bumpy. When it was founded in 1906, Harbin Customs Office set up a tax bureau in Angangxi and set up checkpoints to extract taxes from Chinese and Russian merchants on the ground that "there was no stipulation in the railway contract that Chinese officials were not allowed to collect taxes within the railway boundary". Faced with repeated obstructions from the Russian Empire, the Russian Bali Department (the Russian tax authority) often led troops to raid the tax collection offices, arrest Chinese officials and confiscate tax revenues. They even took extreme measures to obstruct the Chinese officials from exercising their tax collection power, such as smashing up shops, "damaging plaques", "sealing the doors with nails", and "driving people and goods out of the territory". To completely deprive Harbin Customs Office of its power to collect taxes in the subordinate territories of the Chinese Eastern Railway, from 1906 to 1907, Russia forced the Chinese merchants in the subordinate territories of the Chinese Eastern Railway to join the Russian Autonomous Association and compelled them to "subscribe". The state rights were infringed upon by Russia. Du Xueying, a Harbin Customs official, as the chief of the Jilin Railway Negotiation Bureau, negotiated with the Chinese Eastern Railway Administration many times about the berthing of ships on both sides of the Songhua River and the taxes, but in vain. After successive setbacks in taxation and diplomacy, Harbin Customs Office had in fact collapsed.

In order to ease the deadlock, the Qing Government also delegated Song Xiaolian, a Heilongjiang dignitary and second-grade Advisory Officer to take over the head office of Heilongjiang Railway Negotiation Administration, hoping to take advantage of the subject status of Railway Negotiation Bureau within the territory of the Chinese Eastern Railway to try to "retrieve the lost rights" and change the disadvantageous situation of Qing Government in negotiations with Russia. Song Xiaolian implemented official system reform of Heilongjiang Railway Negotiation Administration. After carefully studying the Articles of Association of the State Administration of Railway Negotiation of Heilongjiang Province, Song continuously sent notes to the Negotiation Bureau of Railway of Heilongjiang Province 4 times in respect of the dispatch of negotiation personnel and official seals during half a year from the 3rd of the 3rd lunar month to the 18th of the 7th lunar month of 1907. On the one hand, Song required the Chinese Eastern Railway Administration to reformulate relevant "measures of issuing documents" and strengthen self-management. Issuance of documents, required to be affixed (stamped); Chargé d'affaires shall not issue archives "in the name of general office" under the circumstances that the general office is "not on a business trip or sick", otherwise it will not be recognized by Railway Negotiation Bureau. On the other hand, Song Xiaolian began to strengthen the internal management of Railway Negotiation Bureau by setting up posts as conference director, examination director and section member under the management of general office. The functions were refined, and each performed its own duties. Song Xiaolian repeatedly requested the Chinese Eastern Railway Administration to respect the subject status of Heilongjiang Railway Negotiation Bureau and to negotiate with Horvath on major issues to improve the status of Heilongjiang Railway Negotiation Bureau in terms of "formality".

At that time, the Chinese Eastern Railway was in an eventful period. On June 7th, 1906, the Japanese Mikado approved the preparation for the establishment of "South Manchurian Railway Co." under the overall control of the Japan government. The Japanese northward chariot advanced from Korean Peninsula to the southern part of northeast China. After the Russo-Japanese War, Russia's strategy in northeast Asia was also adjusted, changing from the original policy of preventing Japan from entering Manchuria and vying with Japan for hegemony in northeast Asia to the policy of "Japan-Russia coordination", a new route to jointly seek interests of Manchuria with Japan. On July 30th, 1907, both sides first signed *The Japan-Russia Agreement* and *The Japan-Russia Secret Agreement. The Russia-Japan Secret Agreement* stipulated, "northeast China is divided into northern and southern part, which are the spheres of influence of Japan and Russia respectively and they guarantee mutually that each party would not be hindered from seeking more interests within its sphere of influence and not to expand its own power within the sphere of influence of the other party." The Supplementary Clause stipulated the boundary line of "South Manchuria" and "North Manchuria". In the process of Japan and Russia approaching Manchuria, from 1906, the Qing Government had opened the gateway of the Northeast. The Yingkou port was opened to the outside world in succession at Andong, Dadonggou, Fengtian, etc., and consular officials were accredited one after another from Japan, the United States, Germany to Great Britain. In order to strengthen its control over Manchuria, the Qing Government unified the military and political affairs of the Northeast (provinces of Liaoning, Heilongjiang, Jilin) in 1907, and the pro-American Qing Government appointed Xu Shichang to be the Governor, and Tang Shaoyi, Zhu Jiabao, and Duan Zhigui (later modified to Cheng Dequan) to be the Governor of Fengtian (Liaoning), Jilin, and Heilongjiang provinces. It was planned that, through the establishment of the "Bank of Northeast" with the help of American capital, a Chinese railway network in the northeast region that could contend with the Russian-Japanese Railway with the support of American capital was to be built, and the American capital might also be used to stabilize the local currency and launch other industries. In the face of competition, Tsarist Russia strengthened its control over the Chinese

Eastern Railway, sent troops and stationed police, and sought for the establishment of autonomy. The Chinese Eastern Railway Administration, which was on the offensive, was indifferent to Song's approach, and Holwart, who sneered at him for "not benefiting the facts at all but hurting your feelings and becoming a hindrance to your future work" closed his door to Song. Song "can't meet with Horvath for 3 months", and his "reform" also provided an excuse for the Tsar. Consequently, the Heilongjiang Railway Bureau almost paralyzed.

Knowing the importance of the matter and that he was powerless to change the overall situation, Song Xiaolian, together with Du Xueying and Sa Yintu of Harbin Customs Office (who did not hold office), presented a memorial to the General Magistrate of Heilongjiang and Jilin Provinces and submitted a "Method for the Merger of the Railway Negotiation Bureau", again trying to deprive the Railway Negotiation Bureau of its power and transfer it to Harbin Customs Office which was set up independently by China. It proposed that the organizational system of the Railway Negotiation Bureau of Jilin and Heilongjiang provinces should be abolished, and a special "Railway Negotiation Unit" should be set up in Harbin Customs Office to take charge of railway negotiation. The size of the Chinese Eastern Railway Magistrate should follow the original local official setup of the Qing Government, and a "Railway Negotiation Department" should be set up in the original magistrate. It advocated that the previous method of unified negotiation with Russia by the Railway Negotiation Bureau should be changed, and that each place should handle railway negotiation with Russia separately, to decentralize the negotiation power. Soon after the abolition plan was put forward, Song Xiaolian was reinstated, and no longer directly involved in the reorganization of the Railway Negotiation Bureau. But the call for abolishing the Railway Negotiation Bureau continued to grow. On September 8th, 1907, with the support of the Generals of Jilin and Heilongjiang Provinces, Du Xueying, the General Officer of the Chinese Eastern Railway and Jilin Railway Negotiation Bureaus, sent a note to the Chinese Eastern Railway Administration on "the abolition of the Railway Negotiation Bureau of Jilin and Jilin Provinces and the establishment of a separate bureau under the jurisdiction of Binjiang Customs Office". But the Chinese request was immediately rejected by the Chinese Eastern Railway Administration. Moreover, Horvath, the Director of the Chinese Eastern Railway Administration, especially ordered that the funds of the Jilin Railway Negotiation Bureau should be given to Du Xueying in the spring of the previous year (1907), to emphasize the subordinate relationship between the Chinese Eastern Railway Administration and the Railway Negotiation Bureau as an insult to Du. After that, the abolition of the Railway Negotiation Bureau was left unsettled.

4.2.4 The Loss and Recovery of Power on the Chinese Side—Li Hongmo's Revival of the Railway Negotiation Bureau

On January 8th, 1908, Tsarist Russia implemented the *Harbin Local Charter of*

Public Governance in Harbin and set up a council in the Chinese Eastern Railway. By governing the "people of all countries in the Chinese Eastern Railway", the increasingly prosperous Chinese Eastern Railway was about to fall into the hands of the Russians. In this situation, Harbin Customs and Border Office took all measures to curb Russian's aggression, actively organized the Sino-Russian joint railway police, set up checkpoints in the Chinese Eastern Railway to collect taxes, and tried to mobilize people in the industry and commerce to set up a local autonomy council. But these measures did not stop Tsarist Russia's aggression.

At the level of national diplomacy, the Tsarist government came forward directly to put pressure on the highest authorities of the Qing Government, trying to force the Chinese side to yield to Russian demands and set up a "council" in the Chinese Eastern Railway. In the Chinese Eastern Railway subordinate territories, the Chinese Eastern Railway Administration sent the so-called Chinese Eastern Railway Guard to wreak havoc, arresting Chinese officials, destroying the Agricultural Bureau, sealing up Chinese shops, and deliberately framing the Chinese by falsely claiming that they had caused the chaos in the Chinese Eastern Railway, so as to build momentum for Russian diplomacy with China. On May 10th, 1909, the representatives of China and Russia, after more than two months of negotiation in Beijing, finally reached an agreement that the Chinese and Russian governments would jointly establish a council within the boundaries of the Shandong Province railway to manage local autonomy, on the premise that "China enjoys sovereignty within the territory of the Chinese Eastern Railway", and signed the 18 articles of The Outline of the Council Measures. It was signed by Shi Zhaoji, a member of the Binjiang Customs Road Administration (Du Xueying, the former Binjiang Customs Road Administrator, was dismissed in April 1909 for "decadence, selfishness and ignorance of the regime"), Yu Sixing, the alternate Heilongjiang Road Administrator, and Horvath, the general officer of the Chinese Eastern Railway Administration. At this point, the Chinese government completely lost the administrative power over the Chinese Eastern Railway. Later, Tsarist Russia set up a "special committee" under the Chinese Eastern Railway Administration to further coordinate the relations between the various Russian departments in Harbin. To some extent, the committee gained the authority of the Governor-General's Office, and the status of the director of the Chinese Eastern Railway Administration was similar to that of a colonial governor. The Chinese Eastern Railway was another colony of Tsarist Russia and a "state within a state" in the territory of China. Although the formal signing of The Outline of Methods for the Council in Beijing legally recognized that China still enjoyed sovereignty over the Chinese Eastern Railway, the specific administrative power had been completely seized by Tsarist Russia. This marked the complete exclusion of the Qing Government's power in The Chinese Eastern Railway Company. However, it also provided an opportunity for the Qing Government to establish systematic and standardized diplomatic and administrative agencies around the Chinese Eastern Railway.

Since then, the Jilin and Heilongjiang Railway Negotiation Bureau became the main force to safeguard national sovereignty. After several twists and turns, the Railway Negotiation Bureau, which had a delicate and fragile power, was completely deprived of its power, but, presided over by Li Hongmo, Li Jiaao and other professional diplomats. After many institutional reforms, the Railway Negotiation Bureau underwent great changes in its functions.

The opportunity for change came from the skillful handling of civil affairs by Chinese officials, such as non-diplomatic and non-political issues of Sino-Russian commercial interests. By this time, the Railway Negotiation Bureau had been kettled and rendered null and void. Because China's own documents had revoked it, Russia, although still nominally recognizing it, had also taken the opportunity to transfer its power to an agency under its control. However, the active efforts and achievements of the Chinese officials in the Railway Negotiation Bureau became a new starting point for the return of Chinese power. After the railway opened to traffic, the Chinese Eastern Railway's subordinate territories became increasingly prosperous, and Chinese businessmen poured into the railway subordinate territories in search of business opportunities. But because of the lack of relevant laws, local officials could not sign and file the land leased by Chinese businessmen, leading to difficulties in the lease of land by Chinese businessmen in the territory. In 1910, Li Hongmo, the then General Officer of Heilongjiang Railway Negotiation, believed that "if there is no involvement of Chinese officials and private individuals are left to sign the lease contract on their own, it is difficult to convince outsiders of the validity of this contract", and if let Chinese businessmen and railway companies "vaguely admit the contract on their own, then it is bound to be very disturbing in case of disputes", and advocated that the Railway Negotiation Bureau should be responsible for the lease of land in the territory of Chinese Eastern Railway subordinate territories. Based on The Charter of the Heilongjiang Railway Negotiation Bureau, which stated that "whenever thc railway purchases public or private lots, the various contracts shall be verified and sealed by the Railway Negotiation Bureau", he sent a note to the Chinese Eastern Railway Bureau, stating "the purpose and authority of Chinese officials to collect taxes in the territory". On September 29th, 1910, the Chinese Eastern Railway Bureau announced that "If a Russian merchant enters into a lease contract with our company, the contract will be witnessed by a Russian official on his behalf, and if it is a Chinese merchant, it shall be witnessed by the Bureau of Foreign Relations." Heilongjiang Railway Negotiation Bureau's right to lease land in the Chinese Eastern Railway subordinate territories was formally recognized. The power of representation of Chinese institutions was reconfirmed by the Russian side. This was the starting point for the return of lost Chinese power. Substantive progress was made not only in name, but also in safeguarding China's practical interests. On this basis, Li Hongmo established an effective land lease system in light of the actual situation of the Chinese Eastern Railway's subordinate territories at that time. Specialized personnel should be set up in the Railway Negotiation

Bureau's sub-bureau. "If a Chinese businessman or a railway company sent requests to the Negotiation Bureau, the sub-bureau commissioner should check the situation. If there is no problem, the sub-bureau commissioner should sign the lease contract, stating that it should be kept. At the same time, the lease should be sent from the Negotiation Bureau to the Russian diplomat for signature and filing. After the lease is signed and returned to the other stations, the Russian personnel in charge will handle it." If the Chinese businessmen in this territory needed to lease land again, the Railway Negotiation Bureau was responsible for the filing of the contracts, and if they encountered disputes with the Russians, the Railway Negotiation Bureau was responsible for negotiating. The land leasing power all belonged to the Railway Negotiation Bureau.

On 5th November, 1910, Li Hongmo introduced to Zhou Shumo, the Governor of Heilongjiang, the successful experience of using the Qing Shan Station Taxation Bureau to set up a blockade outside the railway boundary of the Chinese Eastern Railway territory, and requested Zhou Shumo to allow "the taxation within the railway boundary to be handled by the Bureau of Negotiation", with the Railway Bureau of Negotiation sending personnel to "take turns to station at the blockade". The taxation was to be handled by the Bureau of Railways. With the support of Zhou Shumo, from November to December 1910, Li Hongmo sent three notes to Horvath, the general manager of the Chinese Eastern Railway Administration, and Daniele, the chargé d'affaires of the Chinese Eastern Railway Administration Bureau, in accordance with the previous Sino-Russian peace treaties and the international practice, and finally forced the Chinese Eastern Railway Administration Bureau to "accommodate", and finally reached a consensus. Firstly, changed the original tax regulations of Heilongjiang Province, imitated the tax system of Russia within the Chinese Eastern Railway subordinate territories in the areas around the Chinese Eastern Railway subordinate territories, and uniformly named all kinds of governmental levies as tax, abolished the poll tax, combined donation with tax, and only collected tax from businesses; specified the name of tax collection and formulate more standard tax collection regulations. A new tax system in line with international practice was to be established in the Chinese Eastern Railway subordinate territories, which was in line with international practice. Second, according to international practice, combined with the relevant provisions of The Treaty of Land Trade in The Sino-Russian Treaty of Renewal, argued with the Russian officials along the Yangtze River. Officials of the Railway Negotiation Bureau were stationed at the ports and checkpoints on the Chinese side of the Chinese Eastern Railway subordinate territories and tax authorities were set up. Import taxes were levied on grain, cattle, horses, sheep, grass, hides and other "local goods" entering and leaving the Chinese Eastern Railway subordinate territories. Third, a sound tax collection system was established. When merchants bought and sold goods in the Chinese Eastern Railway subordinate territories and passed through the checkpoints outside the boundary, they should first go to the Railway

Negotiation Bureau to "file tax returns and collect invoices before they are allowed to sell". Fourth, the Russian officials in the Chinese Eastern Railway subordinate territories were required to assume the corresponding responsibility and fulfill their obligations to assist the Railway Negotiation Bureau officials in arresting tax evaders. Russian officials were required to bring the tax evaders to the nearest Railway Negotiation Bureau once they found that the goods sold by merchants had not been declared and collected in the Railway Negotiation Bureau. The Railway Negotiation Bureau officials "punished according to the regulations" and Russian officials were not allowed to interfere.

In February 1911, Governor Zhou Shumo informed Li Hongmo that Heilongjiang Railway Negotiation Bureau would set up an outpost of the tax office on the Chinese side of the Chinese Eastern Railway subordinate territories. Jilin Railway Negotiation Bureau also implemented a new land lease on the Jilin side of the Chinese Eastern Railway subordinate territories and set up checkpoints outside the boundary to collect taxes. So far, the long-pending case of collecting taxes in the Chinese Eastern Railway subordinate territories was finally solved.

The handling of these two long-pending cases made the Heilongjiang Railway Negotiation Bureau get the important rights of leasing land and collecting taxes around the Chinese Eastern Railway subordinate territories under the objective framework of "railway as the center". Since then, the Railway Negotiation Bureau in the Chinese Eastern Railway subordinate territories continued to take measures to secure China's legal rights, using Chinese parliamentarians, chambers of commerce, fellow townsmen association and other social organizations to infiltrate the politics and power of the Chinese Eastern Railway subordinate territories, and gradually enjoyed jurisdiction over the taxation, land leasing, justice, and police establishment in the Chinese Eastern Railway subordinate territories, and became an independent administrative agency of the Chinese Government in the Chinese Eastern Railway subordinate territories, playing the role of a "shadow government". At the same time, given that the "Customs Office" had no room for negotiation and tax payment, and the benefits of opening of the Chinese Eastern Railway subordinate territories on the economy was increasingly significant, and the periphery of the Railway subordinate territories also attracted a large number of Chinese businessmen, the Qing Government urgently needed to improve its administrative and judicial jurisdiction. On the 4th of the 5th lunar month of 1910, the Qing Government approved the establishment of the 3 northeastern provinces. At the request of Governor Xiliang and Governor Chen Zhaochang of Jilin, "Binjiang Customs Office (i.e., Harbin Customs Office) was changed to Northwest Administration, still stationed in Harbin, patrolling Northwest Jilin and other places, and in charge of Harbin customs duties and commercial port negotiations." At this point, "Harbin Customs Office" was renamed "Jilin Northwest Office Sub-Patrol Preparatory Office" as the supreme authority set up by the Chinese Government in the periphery of the Chinese Eastern Railway subordinate territories (the office was located in today's Daowai District, Harbin) (later changed to Jilin Northwest Office and Binjiang Customs Office). Its chief secretary was Dao Yin, who was concurrently appointed by the Jilin Railway Negotiation Bureau. So, since then, Dao Yin of Jilin Northwest Office held two posts, both as the local Governor of the Chinese Eastern Railway Subordinate Territories and as the Head of the Chinese "Shadow Government" in the Chinese Eastern Railway Subordinate Territories. By implementing the "dual system" of administrative jurisdiction inside and outside the Chinese Eastern Railway subordinate territories, the Chinese Government formed a joint check and balance over the Russian Chinese Eastern Railway Subordinate Territories. China's control of real interests in the region has been boosted for the first time since the Tsar Russia invasion.

4.2.5 The Railway Negotiation Bureau as a Quasi-administrative Body during the Republican Period

With the outbreak of the First World War in 1914, Harbin, as an important economic and information center in the Far East, played an unprecedented role. At the same time, because of the provocation of the Russians, there existed conflicts between Jilin and Heilongjiang Railway Negotiation Bureaus. Although they were both institutions of the Chinese Government and were in the same place, they were respectively responsible for the governors of Heilongjiang and Jilin Provinces. They share similar functions, but they all had independent powers and responsibilities. Taking advantage of the characteristics of decentralized power and vague responsibilities of the railway negotiation bureaus of the two provinces, the Chinese Eastern Railway Administration Bureau often sent separate notes to the general offices of the two parties on the same matter, and once a contract was concluded, it requested that "the whole Chinese Eastern Railway subordinate territories be handled according to the regulations". In 1914, "Russian troops trespassing Lanxi incident" brought the contradiction of the two bureaus into the public.

On 24th April, 1914, Horvath, the General Officer of the Chinese Eastern Railway Administration Bureau, sent a note to Li Jia'ao, the Director of Binjiang Customs Office and the General Officer of the Jilin Railway Negotiation Bureau, requesting the Chinese Eastern Railway Negotiation Bureau to protect the road and to "cross the border to suppress the bandits". Li Jia'ao agreed to Horvath's request without knowing the intention of the Russian troops and without informing Li Hongmo, the General Director of the Heilongjiang Railway Negotiation Bureau. He also telephoned Li Hongmo in the tone of a superior, asking him "not to argue over opinions to avoid unnecessary misunderstandings and conflicts" about the Chinese Eastern Railway escort. At the same time, he irresponsibly informed Li Hongmo that "in the event of an accident, he should only take up the matter with the Company (the Chinese Eastern Railway Administration Bureau)". As a result, on 24th April, two hundreds Russian cavalry were sent from Harbin "without translators and without army unit number" to Hulan County and then straight to Lanxi County (now Lanxi

County, Suihua City, Heilongjiang). In the name of the "criminal police", they stayed in Lanxi County and "temporarily stationed". In 1911, when the Russian army "crossed the border to suppress the bandits", it requested that if any Chinese troops near the route passed through the railway or entered the railway boundary for a temporary stay, "they must inform the nearest Russian railway guard so as not to complicate matters". It even stipulated that "The same notice must be given even if the Chinese troops cross a railway switch". However, as the two provinces of Heilongjiang and Jilin were independent administrative bodies of the same level and governed different territories, the two provinces disagreed on the regulations governing the Russian army's "interception of bandits", so the regulations were delayed. The two provinces disagreed on the regulations governing the Russian army's "manning of the border" and "manning of the border", so the regulations were delayed. so the regulations were delayed. Before the Russian army crossed the border this time, there were no cases of banditry in Heilongjiang, which had just been cleared of banditry. Therefore, at this time there was no "banditry" in the area as claimed by the Russians. If Li Jia'ao, the head officer of the Jilin Railway Negotiation Bureau, had actively liaised with Li Hongmo, the head office of the Heilongjiang Railway Negotiation Bureau, they could have argued with the Russians. However, Li Jia'ao's unauthorized promises led to the Russian army using this as a pretext to "move freely" in China. In the following months, the Russian army, under the pretext of "suppressing bandits", was active in the river ports of Fujin and Lahasusu (now Tongjiang, Heilongjiang), setting up garrisons at the river ports of Fujin and Lahasusu (now Tongjiang, Heilongjiang) in the following months.

At the same time, materials came to light that Yilan Director of Fujin County and other local officials submitted a petition to the Railway Negotiation Bureau of Jilin Province, exposing the fact that Li Jia'ao had "not sent any reply" to the documents submitted by the local authorities, that his response was slow, and that in his dealings with Russia, his statements were erratic and unreal; as a "simple and honest" person, he "always follows the traditional tracks firmly". In a word, Li Jia'ao was not suitable to serve as the Intendant of Circuit of Binjiang and General Office of Jilin Railway Negotiation Bureau any longer. They requested that another official be sent to "argue with Russia on strong grounds". So far, the Jilin and Heilongjiang Railway Negotiation Bureau had been divided into two independent agencies, resulting in unclear authority and responsibility, so the disadvantages of administrative inefficiency has been fully revealed.

In addition, since the outbreak of World War I, in view of the important strategic location of the China Eastern Railway, Japan, Russia and other countries intensified the aggression around the Chinese Eastern Railway Road belongings. The integration of the authority of the Heilongjiang Railway Negotiation Bureau and the Jilin Railway Negotiation Bureau could not be delayed.

In view of the outbreak of World War I, the major changes in the international situation and the importance of Harbin's role in Northeast Asia, the Beiyang Government decided to upgrade Harbin's diplomatic status. The Railway Negotiation Bureau was incorporated into the diplomatic system at the central level. In Harbin, the core city around railway subordinate territories, a system of "diplomats" was set up, similar to that in Tianjin, Yantai and Changchun, where the Central Government directly dispatched professional diplomats to serve as "Harbin diplomats". The "diplomats" reported directly to the Central Ministry of Foreign Affairs and the Ministry of Communications. The jurisdiction of the Jilin and Heilongjiang Provinces over the Railway Negotiation Bureau was transferred to the Central Government. As one of the first students to study in Petersburg, Li Hongmo, the Head of the Heilongjiang Railway Negotiation Bureau, had spent many years in Russia and knew the Russian system well. In order to cope with the complex reality of the Japanese and Russian powers gathering in the Northeast and Harbin, the Beiyang Government decided on October 1st, 1914 to retain the Jilin and Heilongjiang Railway Negotiation Bureau, with Li Hongmo, former head of the Heilongjiang Railway Negotiation Bureau, as the Head of the Jilin Railway Negotiation Bureau, and also as the Harbin Negotiation Officer. At the same time, it was expressly stipulated that the newly appointed General Office of the Heilongjiang Railway Negotiation Bureau, Ma Zhongjun, would be under his control. Previously, the General Office of the Jilin Railway Negotiation Bureau had also been appointed as the Yin of Binjiang Customs Office, so Li Hongmo held 3 positions-that of Harbin Intercessionaire, General Office of the Jilin Railway Negotiation Bureau and Yin of Binjiang Customs Office and had great diplomatic and administrative autonomous power.

During World War I, China's state power increased, while Tsarist Russia, in a more complex international situation, relaxed its control over the China Eastern Railway subordinate territories. This Chinese mode of power centralization in Ha was then of great relevance to the governance of both the China Eastern Railway subordinate territories and the adjacent Chinese jurisdictions. Although the Jilin Railway Negotiation Bureau is still under the jurisdiction of the Governor of Jilin Province, it can bypass the governor and report directly to the "Ministry of Foreign Affairs and Ministry of Transportation". The status of the Jilin Railway Negotiation Bureau had been unprecedentedly elevated. After the integration of power, the Jilin Railway Negotiation Bureau changed its previous image as a "shadow government" that focused on managing Chinese people who were "lodging" under the management of the Chinese Eastern Railway Administration in Russia. It used the changes in the international situation to challenge the Chinese Eastern Railway Administration Bureau in many fields such as diplomacy, military, and administration and achieved many results.

In 1915, "the Russian soldiers, who were illegally providing escort for Russian ships, occupied Demerit Street, the Ur River and Xindian in Fangzheng County and refused to retreat, setting up Permanent fortifications in Xindian. Li Hongmo sent note to Horvath, stating that Binjiang Administration had ordered the military to be stationed along the river, and reiterating the Chinese government's full responsibility to protect the safety of Russian ships. On the 2nd of the 7th lunar month of 1916, Li Hongmo, as Harbin interlocutor and chief interlocutor of the Jilin Railway Negotiation Bureau, took note of the International Law and the relevant treaties of the Russian and Chinese Governments after 1898, and seriously confronted Horvath. He (Horvath) "sat in silence for a long time, out of reason," and was forced to make concessions. He was forced to make concessions and eventually made a promise to withdraw Russian troops by a certain date. 2 years later, in 1918, the Chinese army expelled the Russian troops on this basis and took back Lakhasusu. In the summer of 1918, in accordance with the agreement between Li Hongmo and Horvath, the Chinese government recovered the land, established a regimental headquarters and took control of the river navigation.

In 1916, during the formulation and implementation of the *Sino-Russian Treaty on the Prohibition of Tobacco and Alcohol*, Li Hongmo, as Interlocutor and the Intendant of the Circuit of Binjiang Customs Office in Harbin, negotiated painstakingly with the Russian Consul Trauscholit on the prohibition of alcohol in the whole of the Chinese Eastern Railway Territories, under the premise that the Beijing Government and Tsarist Russia had already signed a treaty. This forced the Russian side to make certain concessions. On May 21st, 1916, Li Hongmo signed the *Sino-Russian Agreement on Prohibition of Alcohol Sales in Several Areas of North Manchuria* with Russian Consul Trautvetter as the highest representative of the Chinese side in the China Eastern Railway, ultimately minimizing the losses of Chinese merchants.

In 1917, when the February Revolution broke out in Russia, Li Hongmo explained to the Governor of Jilin twice in succession the chaotic situation in Harbin and advocated that the Chinese Government should take advantage of the Russian mutiny and the lack of Russian military power in Harbin to make use of the provision in Article 8 of The Statute of the General Bureau of Railway Negotiation in Heilongjiang that "the branch offices of the General Bureau of Railway Negotiation may have soldiers". Under the leadership of the Railway Negotiation Bureau, utilizing the power of Chinese merchants, the Chinese were actively elected to the Harbin Public Council, and the Harbin Chamber of Commerce was used to exert pressure on Horvath by acting as an "expatriate group". He asked the Russians to protect the rights and interests of Chinese businessmen in the railway subordinate territories; he asked for the stationing of a police force in Harbin, converted from the army, to protect the "expatriates" and to station troops in Harbin. On 1st April, the Governor of Jilin, Meng Enyuan, and the Governor of the province, Guo Zongxi, called the President and the Ministries of Foreign Affairs, Internal Affairs and the Army, proposing 3 measures to station army converted police officers in Harbin and to station troops in Harbin on the pretext of protecting the expatriates.

At this point there was a difference of opinion between Li Hongmo and

Guo Zongxi on the specific measures to be taken to recover the China Eastern Railway. Li Hongmo did not agree that Horvath's power should be weakened, or that Horvath should be left alone to deal with the matter. He believed that once the left-wing Socialist Revolutionaries took control of the "provisional administrative preparatory office", the order of negotiation that the Chinese Government had previously established with Horvath would no longer exist. The agreements that had been signed over the years to facilitate the gradual recovery of the Chinese Eastern Railway would also lose their validity. Li Hongmo therefore resisted the pressure of the Governor of Jilin and refused to carry out Guo Zongxi's order to support the Provisional Administrative Preparatory Office, and using his position as Harbin's Interlocutor to consult the Central Government directly and avioding to discuss important matters with the Provisional Administrative Preparatory Office, such as the joint operation of the police.

During this period, Li Hongmo set aside the Provisional Administrative Preparatory Office and insisted on negotiating with Horvath on important matters, working as General Director of the General Bureau of Railway Negotiations. In August 1917, with the acquiescence of the Russian Chinese Eastern Railway Administration Bureau under Horvat's chairmanship, the Chinese troops stationed in Fuyu changed into "police uniforms" and formed a Chinese "commercial police" under the guise of protecting "expatriates in Harbin". The Chinese "commercial police" were formed in the name of protecting "expatriates in Harbin". The Chinese merchant police entered the center of Harbin (a Russian-controlled area) from Daowai, replacing the Russian patrols and taking back the right to police the city. This was a major event in the history of the Chinese administration in Harbin.

Looking at the transmutation of the Jilin and Heilongjiang Railway Negotiation Bureau, we learned about this complex process in the history of the growth of the city of Harbin. What's more, it is thought-provoking to consider how the work of the Railway Negotiation Bureau should be evaluated. In addition to the assessment of administrative capacity and performance, shouldn't the tasks that this body is meant to fulfil also be considered? Although the Railway Negotiations Bureau was coerced by the Chinese Eastern Railway Administration to manage the territories of the Chinese Eastern Railway, it would neither be a study of historical materialism nor a study of "patriotism", if the mission of the Railway Negotiation Bureau as a local Negotiations agency in a colonial and semi-colonial country was given too high an expectation. For such a study would not give us the correct historical perception, nor would it naturally lead to the correct inspiration.

4.3 Li Hongmo (Intendant of Binjiang) and Jilin Railway Negotiation Bureau

The Railway Negotiation Bureaus of Jilin and Heilongjiang Provinces and Binjiang Customs Office were government agencies of Chinese side (Qing Dynasty) that played an important role in the history of the city of Harbin, which negotiated with foreign countries, mainly with Russia. Li Hongmo served as the Head of these offices and as the general officer of Heilongjiang General Administration of Railway Negotiation in Heilongjiang (and later as the general office of Jilin General Administration of Railway Negotiation in Jilin) and concurrently served as the Governor of Binjiang in Jilin and Negotiator of Harbin. Li Hongmo lived and worked in Harbin for more than 40 years and made important contributions to the development of Harbin. His legacy leaves many questions worthy of in-depth study.

For many years, there has been a lack of research on Li Hongmo in the academic community. The existing research is also debatable. In *Harbin History Chronicles*, *The Chinese Eastern Railway Chronicles* and other chronicles have sporadic records of Li Hongmo's career. And there are also some problems with the existing research results. For example, in the above-mentioned materials, it was stated that on March 10th, 1915, Li Hongmo was removed from the post of Intendant of Binjiang and was replaced by Wang Shuhan. On March 4th, 1916, Li Hongmo was reappointed as Binjiang Intendant. This means that Li Hongmo served as Binjiang Intendant twice. However, the *Far East* Newspaper and historical archives of the same period indicate that Li Hongmo was still the Binjiang Intendant and was not removed from office during this period. This part of the book is only a cursory discussion of Li Hongmo's life, official position, and other relevant circumstances, with a view to promoting the development of Li Hongmo's research.

Li Hongmo (1863—1944), styled yuchen, a native of Ninghai (now Muping Xiejiazhuang) in Yantai, Shandong, was admitted to the Russian School of Imperial Tung Wen College (founded during the Kangxi Period, the foreign affairs faction created the school on the basis of the Russian Language Institute) in Beijing in 1886 and studied Russian and diplomacy. During his time at the school, Li Hongmo excelled in his studies and was praised by Emperor Guangxu's teacher, Wen Tonghe, as "a man with a solid foundation in reading and a high moral character". In May 1896, with the approval of Guangxu, Li Hongmo, Bi Guifang, Shao Hengjun, and Chen Jiaju were invited to study in St. Petersburg, Russia, as the first batch of students at Imperial Tung Wen College to study aboard, funded by the General Taxation Department. During their stay in Russia, the four of them lived in the Russian Embassy, where they assisted the Russian ambassador in dealing with diplomatic affairs, and at the same time studied language and negotiation skills to gain diplomatic experience. 1898 saw the end of their 3-year study period and the return to Beijing. Li Hongmo was awarded the honorary title of "5th-ranking official of the 7th rank of the magistrate" in the Imperial Tung Wen College. During the Russo-Japanese War, Li Hongmo was ordered to come to Fengtian to act as a diplomat. He was awarded the official title of "Honourrable Candidate Official of Fengtian".

In July 1905, the Russo-Japanese war was in a stalemate, and despite the mediation of the United States, Russia, which was militarily inferior, unexpectedly resisted Japan's peace terms. Li Hongmo, with his knowledge and relationships accumulated in the past, contacted the Japanese and Russian sides and was ordered to persuade the stubbornly resisting Russian troops, Li Hongmo made Strenuous efforts to make peace between the two sides. For this reason, Li Hongmo was not only commended by his superiors, but also won the goodwill of Russia, which increased the leverage for subsequent negotiations with Russia. The Japanese side was so grateful that the emperor of Japan gave him a second-class medal as a token of appreciation. Later, he followed Song Xiaolian, who was appointed as the head of the Heilongjiang Railway Negotiation Bureau at that time, to work for the Heilongjiang Railway Negotiation Bureau, dealing with the Chinese side's negotiations with Russia in Harbin and the territories of the Chinese Eastern Railway.

On January 8th, 1908, the Russian Authorities introduced the *Harbin Local Charter on Public Governance* in Harbin, a subordinate territory of the Chinese Eastern Railway, and tried to establish a public council to govern "the peoples from different nations in the subordinate territories of the Chinese Eastern Railway". The Russian side kept sending "road guards" to arrest Chinese officials in the territories, destroy Bureau of Agricultural Reclamation, and seize Chinese shops, causing the "Min Chen Arrest Incident". The increasingly prosperous territories of the Chinese Eastern Railway were about to fall into the hands of the Russians. Yu Yixing, who was then the General Office of Heilongjiang Railway Negotiation Bureau, negotiated with Horvath on this matter for many times without success. The Chinese side again assigned the former General Officer Song Xiaolian together with Li Hongmo (then a member of the Heilongjiang Railway Negotiation Bureau) to consult with Russian diplomats again. After arduous negotiation, 6 measures were finally drafted: ① Manchurian Border Reclamation Bureau shall still be established within the railway boundary; ② The Russian side shall send Min Chen back to Manchurian Border Reclamation Bureau from Hailaer in a first-class carriage; ③ After Min Chen's arrival in Manchuria Russian taxation officials shall meet him at the station and send him to Manchuria Border Reclamation Bureau, and the company shall hoist the Chinese dragon flag; ④ The Bureau guarding soldiers' guns which confiscated by Russian taxation office shall be returned; ⑤ The Border Reclamation Bureau shall still have 10 guarding soldiers with guns; ⑥ Before a decision is made by China and Russia, the Border Reclamation Bureau shall not collect taxes within 100 kilometers of the border temporarily, and the Russian livestock tax it collected before shall be returned in full. Because of the proper handling of the "Min Chen Arrest Incident", Li Hongmo, who was a civil servant, was appreciated by Heilongjiang Governor Zhou Shumo and others. But on May 10th, 1909, after more than 2 months of negotiations in Beijing, *the Outline of Measures for the Council* was finally signed. Although the treaty legally recognized that China still enjoyed sovereignty over its possessions in the Chinese Eastern Railway subordinate territories, the specific administrative power had been completely seized by Tsarist Russia. With this as the beginning, the Qing Government completely sidelined in the Chinese Eastern Railway Company.

On August 1st, 1910, The General Office of the Heilongjiang Railway Negotiation Bureau, Yu Yaixing, stepped down, and Li Hongmu took over as the General Office of the Heilongjiang Railway Negotiation Bureau, and he was awarded the title of "General Office of the Heilongjiang Railway General Bureau of Negotiation in Harbin, Honourrable Candidate Official of Fengtian". Due to the growing economic and cultural prosperity of the Chinese Eastern Railway subordinate territories, Chinese merchants from the mainland continued to flock to the railroad subordinate territories and their surrounding areas in search of business opportunities. However, due to the lack of relevant laws, Chinese officials are unable to facilitate and protect Chinese businessmen in terms of business such as drawing and filing of land leases, and the Chinese in Harbin reacted strongly to this. In view of this, Li Hongmo took the initiative to negotiate with the General Office of the Chinese Eastern Railway Administration, based on the second clause of the Charter of the General Bureau of Negotiation of the Heilongjiang Railway, and made a "practical declaration" with the Chinese Eastern Railway Administration on the Chinese officials' purpose and authority of tax collection within the boundary. Since all negotiations were in accordance with the "international practice" accepted by the Powers and based on the signed treaties, Tsarist Russia had to make concessions. On September 29th, 1910, the Russian side officially announced that "if a Russian merchant establishes a lease contract with the Company, his signature shall be testified by a Russian official on his behalf, and if it is a Chinese merchant, it shall be testified by the Bureau of Negotiation". The right of the Chinese Heilongjiang Railway Negotiation Bureau to lease land in the territory of the Chinese Eastern Railway was officially and legally confirmed, and the authority of the representatives of the Railway Negotiation Bureau was once again confirmed by the Russian side. Thus, the Chinese side not only declared the rights of the Chinese side in name, but also made substantial progress in safeguarding the practical interests of the Chinese side. Li Hongmo also took into account the actual situation of the Chinese Eastern Railway territories at that time and set up a detailed charter of charges in the Chinese Eastern Railway territories near Heilongjiang Province, following the Russian method of reporting the monthly payments received and keeping them for proper expenses. It was stipulated that special personnel were allocated in each branch of the railroad to deal with Chinese business affairs involving Russian rights. So far, the Chinese merchants in the Chinese Eastern Railway territory who needed to lease land again were put in charge of the Railway Negotiation Bureau for the record, and the Railway Negotiation Bureau was responsible for negotiating with the Russians in case of disputes. The right to lease land was unified under the responsibility of the Railway Negotiation Bureau.

In order to further fight for the national power, Li Hongmo introduced the successful experience of the "Qing Shan Station Tax Bureau" in setting up the tax checkpoints outside the railroad boundary of the Chinese Eastern Railway to Zhou Shumo, the Governor of Heilongjiang, on November 5th, 1910, and suggested that "the taxation within the railroad boundary should be handled by the Bureau of Negotiation". The railroad bureau would send its staff to "take turns to station at the checkpoint" to handle all of them. Li Hongmo, with the support of Zhou Shumo, sent three successive notes to the Russian General Office of the Chinese Eastern Railway Administration, Horvat and Chargé d'affaires in November and December 1910, requesting that the specific details of the "taxation outside the boundary" be exchanged in accordance with the successive Sino-Russian peace treaties and international practice, finally forcing the Chinese Eastern Railway Administration "The two sides reached a consensus under the arguments of the Chinese side: ① To amend the original taxation regulations of Heilongjiang Province, and to model the taxation system around the territories of the Chinese Eastern Railway on the Russian taxation system in the territories of the Chinese Eastern Railway, deleting the name of taxation and calling it "tax". The "tax" was abolished, and the "tax" was merged with the "donation", and the "tax" was collected from the southern families; the name of the tax was refined, and the regulations of the tax were standardized. A new taxation system was established in the territories of the Chinese Eastern Railway, which was in line with the international practice of "eliminating the excuse of foreigners and facilitating the implementation". ② In accordance with the international practice and in accordance with the relevant provisions of the "Regulations on Land Trade" in the *Sino-Russian Renewal Treaty*, the Chinese officials were stationed at the ports and checkpoints along the Chinese Eastern Railway outside the Chinese side, and taxation organs were established. The "import tax" was levied on "local goods" such as grain, cattle, horses, sheep, grass, hides, etc. that entered and left the territories of the Chinese Eastern Railway. ③ Establishment of a perfect tax collection system. ④ The Russian officials in the Chinese Eastern Railway territories had to assume the responsibility of assisting the Chinese officials of the Railway Bureau in detecting the tax evaders. In February 1911, Li Hongmo was finally informed of the instructions from his superiors and his proposal was approved. The approval. The Heilongjiang Railway Intercession Bureau set up a tax card on the Chinese side outside the Chinese Eastern Railway territory. The Jilin Railway Bargaining Bureau also followed the method of the Heilongjiang Railway Bargaining Bureau to implement the new lease on the Jilin side of the Chinese Eastern Railway and set up a tax card outside the boundary to collect taxes.

In the same year, "Harbin Customs Office" was renamed "Jilin Northwest Office Sub-patrol Military Preparation Office", responsible for the management of the Chinese Eastern Railway subsidiary to the periphery of the vast area (the headquarters in the present-day Harbin Daowai District), and then successively changed to Jilin Northwest Office, Binjiang Customs Office. After the establishment of the Republic of China, its official house chief from the road member to be called the Intendent, by the Jilin Railway Intercourse Bureau chief office. Thus, there was a phenomenon that the Provincial Governor of Jilin Northwest Office was holding two important posts, he was the local governor of the Russian Chinese Eastern Railway in the periphery of Binjiang Customs Office, and he was also the General officer of the Jilin Railway Interchange Bureau, which was located in Harbin Chinese Eastern Railway Territory. Li Hongmo made use of social organizations such as the Chinese Chamber of Commerce in the public councils and hometown associations to infiltrate politics and power in the railroad subordinate territories: with the acquiescence of Tsarist Russia, he exercised partial administrative jurisdiction over the Chinese in the Chinese Eastern Railway Subordinate Territories in such matters as taxation, land leasing, and justice.

In 1914, the First World War broke out, the international situation changed greatly, and Harbin played an important role in northeast Asia. The Beiyang Government set up a "negotiator" system in Harbin, like that in Tianjin, Yantai, Changchun and other important foreign-related cities, that is, the Central Government sent professional diplomats as "Harbin interlocutor", who reported directly to the Ministry of Foreign Affairs and Communications of the Central Government of China when major negotiation events occurred. Li Hongmo, who had been appointed General Officer of Heilongjiang Railway Negotiation General Administration, had rich experiences because of his status as one of the first batch of students in Imperial Tung Wen College to study in Petersburg, and thanked to his many years in Russia, he was familiar with the Russian system of negotiation, and he had many years of experience in dealing with Russian government. More importantly, Li Hongmo had contributed to the end of the war between Japan and Russia and had always communicated smoothly with both sides. To deal with the complex reality that Japan and Russia and other powers caused in northeast China and Harbin, on October 1st, 1914, the Beiyang Government of China officially decided to "retain the organizational system of Jilin and Heilongjiang Railway Negotiation Bureaus, Li Hongmo, former General Officer of Heilongjiang Railway Negotiation Bureaus, shall be appointed General Officer of Jilin Railway Negotiation Bureaus and Harbin negotiator." It was also expressly stipulated that the newly appointed General Officer of Heilongjiang Railway Negotiation Bureaus, Ma Zhongjun, was under its control. So far, Li Hongmo had held three posts—Harbin Negotiator, chief director of Jilin Railway Negotiation Bureaus, intendant of Binjiang.

Taking advantage of the changing international situation, Li Hongmo challenged the rights of the Russian "Chinese Eastern Railway Administration" in many fields, such as diplomatic, military and administrative aspects, and achieved many successes. In 1915 Russian soldiers illegally entered our country along the Songhua River under the pretext of protecting the ships, forcibly occupied Founder County Demerit Street, Ur River, Xindian and other places and refused to retreat their troops, and built permanent fortifications in Xindian. Li Hongmo noted to

Horvath, stating: Binjiang Customs Office had been stationed to maintain law and order, reaffirming that the Chinese Government fully assumed responsibility for the protection of Russian ships. On July 2nd, 1916, Li Hongmo, in his capacity as a diplomat of Harbin and the Chief Negotiator of Jilin Railway, made a serious dialogue with Horvath with reference to the international practice and the relevant treaties of the Russian and Chinese Governments after 1898. Horvath was forced to make concessions and finally made a promise to withdraw his troops within a certain period of time. Two years later, in 1918, the Chinese army expelled the Russian soldiers on this basis and took back Lakhasusu. In the summer of 1918, in accordance with the agreement between Li Hongmo and Horvath, the Chinese government took back the Russian territory, established a Chinese military and police command, and took control of the river navigation. In 1916, during the process of the *Russian-Chinese Treaty on the Prohibition of Tobacco and Liquor*, Li Hongmo, in his capacity as the consul of Harbin and intendant of Binjiang, and the Russian consul, Trautius Sholit, agreed with the Russian consul on the implementation of the Treaty on the Prohibition of Tobacco and Liquor. Li Hongmo, as the highest representative of the Chinese side in the Chinese Eastern Railway Territories, signed the *Agreement on the Prohibition of the Sale of Alcohol in Certain Areas of North Manchuria with the Russian Consul in Harbin on May 21st, 1916,* which finally minimized the losses of Chinese merchants.

When the February Revolution broke out in Russia in 1917, Li Hongmo explained the chaotic situation in Harbin to the Governor of Jilin twice in a row and advocated that the Chinese Government should take advantage of the mutiny of Russian soldiers and the emptying of the Russian military force in Harbin to fight more for national power. He pointed out that Article 8 of the Statute of the General Bureau of Railway Negotiation in Heilongjiang, which was recognized by the Russian side, contained the clause that "the branch of the General Bureau of Railway Negotiation may set up soldiers", and that the Chinese side could, under the leadership of the Bureau of Railway Negotiation, make use of the power of Chinese merchants to actively elect Chinese people to the Harbin Public Council and make use of the organization of the Harbin Chamber of Commerce. The Chinese side could take advantage of the Chinese businessmen's power to elect them to the Harbin Public Council, and use the Harbin Chamber of Commerce to organize the function of "overseas Chinese groups" to ask the Russian side to protect the rights and interests of the Chinese businessmen in the railroad annexes, and to request the stationing of the police in Harbin, which was converted from the Chinese army, to protect the "overseas Chinese" on the occasion of the Chinese garrison in Harbin. His proposal was adopted by the Jilin Authorities, and on April 1st, Jilin Governor Meng Enyuan and Governor Guo Zongxi called the President and the Foreign, Internal Affairs, and Army Ministries and agreed to Li Hongmo's proposal. At this time, Li Hongmo and Guo Zongxi disagreed on the specific measures to take back the Central East Road. Li Hongmo thought that it would be disadvantageous for

China to weaken Horvath's power at this time or to leave Horvath behind to deal with the matter. Because once the "provisional administrative preparatory office" controlled by the left-wing social revolutionaries (the provisional government after the February Revolution) gained power, it was bound to be "proud of its wisdom and exceeded the autumn norms", so that the order of negotiation previously established by the Chinese Government with Horvath would no longer exist. All the agreements signed over the years to help the gradual recovery of the Chinese Eastern Railway will also lose their effectiveness. There were so many uncertainties in starting from scratch that it would be better to continue to extend the benefits already gained. Therefore, Li Hongmo resisted the pressure of the Governor of Jilin and refused to carry out Guo Zongxi's order to support the "provisional administrative preparatory office", and instead used his position as a member of Harbin Jiaosha to directly consult the central government, not to discuss with the "provisional administrative preparatory office" to run the police patrol and other important matters. During this period, Li Hongmo left the "Provisional Administrative Preparatory Office" and used his position as the General Officer of the General Bureau of Railway Intercession to insist on negotiating important matters with Horvath, who was still in power even though he was in dire straits. In August 1917, the Chinese side was recognized by the Allied Powers, represented by the British ambassador Jules, and the Russian the Chinese Eastern Railway change into "police costumes" and form the Chinese side. The "commercial police" "protected Chinese nationals in Harbin". The Chinese commercial police entered the center of Harbin (Russian-controlled area) from Daowai and replaced the Russian patrols, thus the Chinese side recovered the right to set up police in Harbin. This was a major event in the history of the Chinese government's administrative jurisdiction in Harbin.

Although the "right to set up police" was recovered and order was stabilized in Harbin, Li Hongmo's actions still aroused the discontent of the Governor of Jilin, Guo Zongxi. Guo Zongxi demanded that Li Hongmo be removed from his post on the grounds of "failure to report in time and failure to ask for instructions on the larger case". As a result, on November 27th, 1917, the Ministry of Foreign Affairs removed Li Hongmo from the post of Intendant of Jilin Binjiang Customs Office and the Chief Officer of Jilin Railway Negotiation Bureau and replaced it with Shi Doyin. Li Hongmo resigned from all his posts in anger. After leaving office, Li Hongmo was once discouraged and told the *Far East Daily News* that "After the task is completed, I will return to the hermitage, after which I will not consider taking up any position in the Court".

During this period, Li Hongmo returned to Muping in Shandong to purchase land. In December 1917, as a member of the Allied Powers, the Chinese Beiyang Government, with the support of the Allied Powers, forcefully expelled more than 4,000 Russian troops stationed on the Chinese Eastern Railway, and thus took full control of the Chinese Eastern Railway. However, the British, Japanese, American and other members of the Allied Powers supported the Chinese move for their own anti-Soviet purposes and their own interests in the Chinese Eastern Railway, rather than to protect Chinese sovereignty, so the Powers expressed their discontent with the complete control of the Chinese Eastern Railway by Chinese troops, and a Siberian Conference was held in March 1919 in Haishenzhan, discussing how to share the control of the Chinese Eastern Railway with other countries. As a Chinese official who was familiar with the negotiation of the Chinese Eastern Railway, drafted the rules for the joint management of the railroad between China and Russia, and was good at negotiating with the Russian side and striving for state power, Li Hongmo, as a special agent of the Ministry of Foreign Affairs of the Republic of China in Beijing, went to Vladivostok to attend the Siberian Conference with Zhan Tianyou, the chief engineer of the Chinese Eastern Railway, and Liu Jingren, the Ambassador to Russia.

In the mid-1920s, Li returned to Harbin and bought house and property. In the retirement, Li Hongmo continued to have close contact with socialites in Harbin, exerting his personal influence and participating in social affairs, becoming influential in the field of culture and education in Harbin. Li Hongmo loved calligraphy, and he also joined the Harbin Confucian Church with He Shouren and supported the Harbin Government and people in running schools. In 1937, he was suspected by the Japanese occupation authorities of being a member of the Communist Party for participating in a patriotic theater group with Chen Yuanting, Guo Zhongheng, En Yuzhi, Qiao Artaudou, Bao Danting, Bo Xinting, and Shi Zhe Sheng. "They were wanted and hunted down by the Japanese occupation authorities and went south to join the Counter-Japanese forces of the Nationalist government. Li Hongmo and his family members were saved from being persecuted by Japanese authorities because of his participation in mediating the peace negotiations of the Russo-Japanese War in 1905. He died in 1944 in Harbin, and his body was buried in his hometown of Dongxiejiazhuang, Shandong Province, by sea from Dalian to Yantai. Throughout his life, he was upright in nature, intelligent and wise, with both the traditional sentiment of national power and public interest, which is honored by Chinese civil officials, and modern consciousness. By virtue of his own learning and courage, he bowed in a position of urgency and devoted himself to his work. Although for various reasons, his performance is seldom found in systematic research topics and official histories, we can sketch a relatively complete image of a patriotic official who was able to uphold justice at the expense of fame and gain in the turning period of history.

4.4 The Interactive Relationship Between Aboriginal People and Heilongjiang Immigrant Society—A Study on the Time and Space Issues in the Transformation of Oroqen's National Life and Production Mode

Through a case study of the Oroqen people living in northeast China, this paper takes the changing view of time and space in people's minds as the research content to reveal a series of problems that emerged in this transitional period for this people who originally lived by hunting. Although it is believed that our country has provided Oroqen people with a good way of life, Oroqen people living in the northeast of China still feel lost in the face of the new way of living. Despite the long transition period of nearly half a century, most Oroqen people still cannot fully adapt to the settlement lifestyle. This part of the book mainly focuses on the villages of Inner Mongolia, except for a small part of Heilongjiang, so the further research perspective should be expanded to more areas. Today, there are still many ethnic groups similar to the ethnic Oroqen group. A report or research on the Oroqen ethnic group may provide a reference to find out the commonness among various ethnic groups. Based on the author's research in this field, this part of the book tries to reveal the commonality of adaptation difficulties that different ethnic groups have in this transitional period, such as the Maasai in Kenya today and the Ewenki and Hezhen in northeastern China, which all reveal the same problems to a greater or lesser extent. This part of the book focuses on the adaptation of human psychology and lifestyle to help document the evolution of those declining forms of civilization, as well as the patterns of evolution, which may provide us with parameters and templates for the future development of non-mainstream ethnic groups and multi-ethnic families in this specific region.

The Oroqen people live in the mountainous areas of northeast China, and until the 1980s they used to live mainly by hunting and gathering. Before the Oroqen people settled down and started farming, they often formed hunting groups, either in groups of several families or in groups of several men and rode into the forest on horseback. The only chance for them to get out of the forest was to trade daily necessities, such as salt, flour, millet and gunpowder or lead for making bullets. At the end of winter, competitions and various recreational activities are held to prepare for the approach of spring.

The hunting area of Oroqen people is extremely wide, which is thousands of square kilometers, so it seems that Oroqen people will never know where the ultimate of their march is. However, because there are more hunting groups, they will naturally divide the hunting area, for example, they will naturally divide some tribes into lesser Khinganling group (today in Heilongjiang province) and Great Khinganling group (today in Inner Mongolia Autonomous Region) according to the area. Even within the same group, each hunting group had its own small area of activity.

Since the establishment of New China in 1949, the government has allocated land to the Oroqen people according to the way of life of most farming people, and built brick houses for the former hunters to settle and live in. After nearly fifty years of transition from hunter to farmer, most of the other ethnic groups think that they are able to finish this transition and are fully capable of adapting to the new agricultural production methods. However, this is not the case for all Oroqen people, especially for the older generation of Oroqen people, where the change in lifestyle is one thing and the change in time and space is another.

Something about human nature determines that people do not always like change in lifestyle, economic mode, or political system. There are two main reasons. First, getting rid of the old, and adapting to the new is not easy for everyone. Second, people who have adapted to a certain way of life often do not see the beauty of change that others think will present for their future life. However, for anyone, change is a fact that must be accepted, while adaptation is often in the form of gradual change, and people are gradually paralyzed by it. History has shown the fact that sudden changes often trigger physical and psychological difficulties for most people to adapt. For example, the North American Indians often adopted different strategies for adaptation after the European invasion. They first cooperated out of ignorance, then rebelled because of attack and persecution, and finally submitted passively because of differences in political, economic, and military capabilities. The transformation of the Oroqen way of life is very different from that of the Indians, but they accept the change passively.

4.4.1 Changed Politics and Ethnic Intermingling

The reasons for the changes that Oroqen people have to accept are multiple, mainly in the following aspects: ① government policies; ② the continuous influx of foreigners; ③ the breaking of the natural food chain; ④ the sharp decline of natural resources.

(1) Policy factors

Out of the understanding of the farming people, the Government introduced the policy of hunting settlement which was considered appropriate soon after the national liberation. But until the end of 20th century, Oroqen people have not fully adapted to this settlement life. "Oroqen ... is one of the 11 ethnic minorities in China who entered the socialist society directly from the end of primitive society. The people have been living without cloth and silk, without grain and corn, without medicine for illness and without a fixed location". Therefore, under the guidance of such view, the government partly adopted the practice of previous governments and allocated land and built brick houses for Oroqen people, so that they could gradually "leave the history of ... hunting and living in wooden pole house for generations and live ... a happy life with a fixed location to live."

The settlement policy started almost simultaneously in the Greater and Lesser Khingan Mountains, where the Oroqen people live. However, how did the settlement affect the Oroqen people psychologically and physiologically? Many reviews and studies have tried to show the good results of the policy implemented, for example, "In the process of Oroqen's transformation from hunting to farming, the government plays a pivotal role, without the participation, intervention and support of the government, this transformation cannot be achieved. History of the two settlement of farming practice proves that the nature and function of the government plays a direct role in the success or failure of settlement of farming. According to the objective law, take the route of the masses and fully play the function of the government, so that the Oroqen people have completed the historical social change from hunting to farming." "The role of the government can be said to be the only driving force."

However, this is not the case. A set of data can explain this from one aspect: "After Oroqen Banner implemented the 'hunting ban' in 1996, Oroqen hunters realized the complete transformation from hunting production to agricultural production, but due to the lack of agricultural technology and management, coupled with the poor soil of arable land and the inability to cope with natural disasters, the production income is small, resulting in most of the land was abandoned and sublet, the hunters had almost no productive income and had to live on the national minimum subsistence allowance every year." "Oroqen people only started to have some improvement after 50 years of settlement, after careful planning in Inner Mongolia Oroqen Banner, a number of projects to support the development and production of Oroqen hunters have been carried out. The hunter's enthusiasm to participate in the production of wealth is high, and the per capita productive income is rising. This year, for the first time in 50 years of settlement, Oroqen hunters achieved a per capita productive income of more than 1,000 yuan."

A similar situation can be seen in the author's fieldwork on ethnic groups in the Greater and Lesser Hinggan Mountains. In the Xiaoxinganling area, the Oroqen people are better adapted to settlement than the Oroqen people living in the Greater Xing'anling area, as the farming peoples around them far outnumber the Oroqen people. Almost all Oroqen people in Heilongjiang have learnt the basic skills of farming and understand the economic environment, so their change of mind is a direct result of the increase in income. However, the above data does not really reflect the actual income of Oroqen people in the Xiaoxing'anling region. The reality is that the income of Oroqen people in this region is not yet one half of the "thousand dollars". In contrast, the Oroqen people in Inner Mongolia are even further away from the "thousand dollars" benchmark.

Northeast China has always been known for its fertile land. Other farming peoples living in this region, especially the Han Chinese, are able to make good use of the land resources to obtain higher economic income, and the land allocated to Oroqen people by the government is often better than that of other farming peoples. In addition, the government has given considerable tax and subsidy policies to Oroqen people. Therefore, the reason that Oroqen people do not have the same or similar economic income as other ethnic groups after the transition to farming is not the land, but other issues.

(2) Ethnic integration and dominant cultural influences

In the period of nomadic hunting, the Oroqen people had little contact with other ethnic groups. Although they did not live in a pure closed ethnic environment, they had to contact with other ethnic groups because of economic exchange. But, traditionally, the Oroqen people maintained a basically self-sufficient way of life. They only had commercial contact with other ethnic groups when they had to.

After settling down, Oroqen people inevitably have cultural contact with the ethnic groups around their own residence. In this way, the combined influence of foreign people on the lifestyle and culture of the Oroqen people becomes more and more obvious. In the field work, the author found that there is hardly any Oroqen village where there is no population of other ethnic groups. The farming people living in this area are not exclusively farmers, but they have adopted many ways to sustain their lives. For example, farmers also increase their intake of animal and plant nutrients by gathering and hunting, and they often increase their economic income by hunting, fishing, clearing land and cutting, leading to an increasing number of new competitors in production methods. Secondly, the change of hunting tools of the farming people and the habit of acquiring resources without any concern for the natural ecology have led to the short-term non-renewal of a large amount of natural resources. Traditionally, the Oroqen people often had a deep understanding of the regenerative habits of animals and their dependence on nature, and therefore set the time and rules for hunting. Whereas the agricultural output of the farming people was almost completely sufficient for survival, hunting and gathering were additional food supplements. Since they does not depend entirely on the flora and fauna of the forest for their livelihood, they naturally does not have similar dependencies and regulations. Thirdly, as the Oroqen people are forced to live in a smaller area part of the time due to the decreasing resources after settlement, the lifestyle, diet habits, clothing, rhythm of life of the farming people have a great assimilating effect on them. The result of this assimilation is naturally a change in people's life, a change in their lifestyle, a change in their clothing, an adaptation of their diet and a weakening of their traditional production skills. Fourthly, the cultural power of the farming people in the narrow sense, such as education, and the state policy also greatly break the traditional education of the Oroqen people. Traditional festivals are disappearing with the strong culture, and the ethnic language skills are weakening due to the increased interaction with other ethnic groups. The state established schools at different levels, mainly in Chinese, where appropriate, and required school-age children to attend them. The traditional language heritage of the Oroqen people has been devastated in the form of formal education. Once children leave the village to receive an education and see the outside world and the possibility of economic gain, they rarely return, breaking the chain of ethnic language transmission. The consequence of the loss of language is the disappearance of ethnic culture, ethnic ways of thinking and ethnic wisdom.

When the Oroqen people encountered these great changes, it took them nearly half a century to adapt, both naturally and unnaturally.

4.4.2 Spatial Transformation: Social, Personal and Psychological Shift

Spatial changes are the most direct and obvious changes that people feel.

Hunter-gatherers generally need more living space than farmers. Therefore, the first thing that makes the Oroqen feel uncomfortable is the phenomenon of "space congestion" when they share the same living space with their peasant neighbors. Like hunter-gatherers in other parts of the world, the Oroqen used to be a people shuttling through the dense forests. But, since settling down, farming has confined them to a "limited" area, which is extremely large for central and southern China. Although the Oroqen do not know how much land they should be able to use for farming, they seem unable to disconnect from their traditional hunter-gatherer way of life, so they are still very uncomfortable with this "space congestion." In fact, the farmlands in northeast China are generally known for their vastness. Compared with the farmers in the south, the Oroqen peasant neighbors never feel crowded. An Oroqen elder once said: "Agricultural production makes us feel particularly uncomfortable, but as village leaders we have to teach people to adapt slowly. Except for some modern young people, most of us still prefer to live the way we used to live. Back then, in the deep forests, we had clean rivers and fresh air, which is now polluted by crowded people."

These words are a true reflection of the psychological state of the older generation at this stage: they are less talkative, less smiley, and less generous. Because they know little about farming, to a large extent, they are more resistant to learning how to farm. It is difficult for the Oroqen to adapt to agricultural production.

The Oroqen people in Inner Mongolia often lease their land to their peasant neighbors and wait for the rent when autumn comes. In the long run, the profit they get from this kind of land lease is minimal, but they don't seem to be worried about it, because their natural history and folklore never lecture them on this issue. It is in the nature of the Oroqen people to aspire to life in the forest, as some of them do: to spend a whole day without expecting much in return. After stalking the prey on foot, going deep into the forest, returning home to show your friends the results of the day's hunting and share them with everyone.

Nowadays, Oroqen people live in brick houses arranged in an orderly manner, and there are streets between the houses. To the peasants who still live in mud houses, such houses are indeed fascinating. However, this still does not make Oroqen people interested in this kind of mixed living. Because they find the heat unbearable in this environment, they build small huts (ɕilan-ʤu) next to the main house. A female Oroqen singer, Guan Changyun, once told the reporter that when she saw the brick courtyard given by the government, her first thought was to build a ɕilan-ʤu in the courtyard, which at first surprised the reporter, but only later did she realize that only the previous kind of house could realize the peace in their spiritual world.

Their rejection of such houses was perhaps due to their construction, but more than anything else it was due to a lack of private space. They felt that everything they did seemed to be "public", whereas the hunting life in the woods gave them more space to be alone. They saw farming in the fields as a form of "publicity". As the land was divided up, each family had to work on its own land and watch others work on another, as previous generations had done, so they called their generation the "loose generation".

Although Oroqen people also like to sit together and talk in their free time, they do not like the way in which the peasants around them get together. In winter, the northern farmers often get together to drink, talk about their families and play cards. The number of people is about four or five. Oroqen people tend to have a large group of at least ten people together. They never gamble when they get together because they have never learnt the secret of it. One of the most common gambling games played by peasants in northern China is called mahjong or pai gow. The Oroqen men prefer to drink, and sometimes the women do too, but the women prefer to talk about family matters and smoke (of course smoking is also a preference of the men).

Like the North American Indians, who often indulge in cigarettes and liquor, the Oroqen people are also alcoholic. Whenever they drink, they never stop drinking until they reach the limit. In the past, Oroqen people started to learn how to make liquor even before it became widely consumed. Xiao Mei, in her book *Echoes of the Field-Notes on Musical Anthropology*, talked about a phenomenon that there are few male singers among Oroqen people because they are so obsessed with drinking that they do not have time to practice. She says that although there are many songs to persuade men not to be too obsessed with drinking, such as "My dear brother, put down the glass of wine, the visitors will laugh at you" (*My Dear Brother*), there are also many songs to try to persuade women to stop drinking, such as "mother of the baby, put down the glass of wine, if you are drunk, you should starve the baby" (*Mother of Man*), but these songs cannot stop the desire of Oroqen people to drink. Xiao Mei asked a female singer why the Oroqen people did not stop drinking, and the female singer was "furious": "Can't you see that we don't have any distillery? All this wine is given by you Han people." She sobbed, "We drink because we are sad. We are a people who live in the forest, why should we be allowed to work in agriculture? We don't know how to farm at all, and we haven't had any good harvests ..."

In fact, for almost all peoples that were formerly hunting peoples, the problem of booze drinking was a problem when other peoples or cultures invaded. The drinking problem of the North American Indians has been documented in many books. Drinking helped them to escape from facts that they could not understand but had to face. Nowadays, the Oroqen people do not drink as much as they used to, because the Oroqen people in Inner Mongolia no longer have hunting guns and farming has tied them firmly to the farm, so they have less opportunity to drink. In addition, the Government has been persuading people to stop drinking, widely using radio, television, newspapers and other news media to report on "exemplary sobriety" and to publicize that "a certain person" has been able to get out of poverty and become rich because he stopped drinking and worked hard at farming. The children of Oroqen, the ambassadors of public opinion, have seen drinking as a vice from the very beginning. Nowadays, people see electricity as a symbol of an advanced way of life, but older Oroqen people think that it has disrupted their old way of life. They used to be able to go around and talk about family life from time to time, but now they can only stay at home and watch TV with their families, and their drinking patterns have also changed.

Traditionally, Oroqen people have to share all the hunting and wild vegetables they get. Nowadays, the situation is different, what a family gets is the family's belongings, no longer sharing collectively, and the change of understanding on the issue of distribution is also a change of consciousness on the ownership system, this change is due to economic factors, the increasing shortage of natural resources, so small families become the model. At that time the Government required the peasants around them to carry out family planning, but not the Oroqen people, yet these policies also influenced them in an invisible way. Nowadays it is rare to see a family with more than four children. Modern Oroqen society has shown a rule that the smaller the family, the less goods are shared with other relatives, let alone with other families. The mode of production determines the size of the family and the system of ownership. A similar phenomenon can be found elsewhere in the world: When human beings gradually got rid of the primitive state, in addition to their own family members, people inevitably tended to be stingy with other members of the family and people outside the family. This law was clearly reflected in the transitional period of the Oroqen people.

4.4.3 Time Shifts: Natural And Spiritual Transformations

The Oroqen people did not keep track of the months as the agricultural peoples did. Han farmers counted time differently from the Oroqen, who used to be hunters and gatherers. For example, instead of dividing the year into twelve months, the Oroqen people divided the year into three broad periods: spring (from mid-March to mid-April, when beautiful deer were caught), summer (from mid-May to June, when fresh antlers were obtained), and autumn (from October to February, when leather was removed). The Oroqen people also traditionally had no concept of "hours", but only two periods of daylight, such as noon (when roe deer were caught) and morning (when moose were caught).

Although there are words like "moon" and "month" in the Oroqen language, they do not mark the months by the movement of the moon or the sun, and there is no clear delineation of dates. For the peasants, especially in China, their lunar calendar is clear. They keep track of the days by the waxing and waning of the moon and work out which days are suitable for farming.

After the Oroqen people settled down, they began to use the local farmers' way of counting the months: aɳi-January, ʤur-February, ilan-March, dojon-April, unʤa-May, ɳuɳun-June, nadan-July, apkun-August, ujun-September, o:n-October, ujɐun-

November, and oron-December. But even with the names given to each month, most people are still not quite sure which month should be used for which farming activities. There is a generally accepted theory in anthropology that there is no difference between human populations in terms of intelligence and stupidity. So, we cannot conclude that Oroqen people are slow in thinking, but their attitude to agricultural production has prevented them from learning how to sow and harvest. Although their previous nomadic life taught them to read the sky, they did not connect the weather with the seasons, but paid more attention to the direction of the procession, the running of the prey, the cycle of life and the influence of the sky on the physical and mental health of people. Some researchers believe that the power of the shaman's drum is equivalent to that of the sun, while the Oroqen people see the shaman's drum as the moon, just as the North American Indians associate the moon with the dream catcher. Oroqen people believe that when the night comes, ghosts can easily enter their bodies and souls, so the shaman's spell can prevent and cure diseases. Observation of the moon and stars is only used by Oroqen people to guide the above aspects, but not related to agricultural production. Nowadays, the older generation of Oroqen people still like to go outdoors at night and sit around with their friends to talk about their feelings about folklore and discomfort in their minds, but the shaman is no longer a topic of conversation. In contrast, when Chinese Han peasants get together to talk about the moon, they are more or less involved in agricultural production. For example, the names of the main characters in stories about the moon (Niulang and Weaving Maiden) are closely related to agriculture. In addition, the traditional Chinese New Year Festival is also dedicated to farmers. In the past, Oroqen people used to meet several times during the year, but not because of the harvest, but only for exchanging their needs or for weddings. Watches and clocks are essential tools for urban dwellers to tell the time, and with the increasing number of peasant gatherings, clocks have become more important to peasants as well. However, for the Oroqen people who still live in the villages, these are only useful for the village leaders. Although the common people are also very "organized and disciplined", they still feel that clocks are just a decoration. The Han peasants often complained about the lack of discipline of the Oroqen people, who were always habitually late for meetings and gatherings, so the Chinese made up many jokes to show that punctuality was not the rule of the Oroqen people.

Recreation is an indispensable part of life, but the Oroqen people have their own definition. Winter in the Northeast creates a world of ice and snow, farmers have no farm work to do, so they often choose winter as a good time for leisure. The traditional Oroqen people have no clear boundary between rest and work. Winter is the best time to go hunting in the forest because it is easy to catch prey in that season. Not only during the hunting period, but also in any season, people can enjoy it so much that they often say that hunting is also one of their pastimes. Although the new way of life has started, Oroqen people still cannot separate their pastime from their work, because they often try to have some fun while farming and it seems to be their ethnic tradition to wander around, but in fact, the "idleness" shown by Oroqen people is caused by the inability to adapt to the change of time. In addition, this idleness of Oroqen people is also related to the change of the nature of work or the intensity of work. Farming requires the repetition of certain actions and uninterrupted work. When hunting in the forest, the prey appears at different times and in different places, so the hunters can work with a combination of relaxation and relaxation. Once these hunters are engaged in physically intensive farming, they can not escape their old habits and inevitably preferred to wander and work at the same time, seemingly "at leisure".

It is difficult for outsiders to understand how the Oroqen people will feel in this changed environment. Like many other ethnic groups with small populations (the Oroqen are one of the least populated ethnic groups in China, with less than 7,000 people). The Oroqen are a relatively submissive people and do not have many objections to policy making and implementation. Most people, even some who are Oroqen chiefs themselves, think that it is not a bad thing to settle down, according to their own judgment. However, the chiefs of these Oroqen settlements had been educated when they were still very young, even when they didn't really understand the way of life of their own people, and thus the root causes of the social and psychological problems of the Oroqen people have never really been studied.

4.4.4 Conclusion

Similar problems can be found among other Chinese peoples who have moved from non-agricultural to settled farming production methods. For example, some of the Ewenke people have returned to the forest after three major settlement policies. Therefore, the cases studied in this part of the book are in fact somewhat general.

The author has seen many of the maladjustments discussed above in another linguistic and cultural survey in July 2019, e.g. some Oroqen people over 60 years old in Shizhang Township, Tahe County, Heilongjiang Province, still rely on renting out land rather than farming it themselves; Oroqen people of this age group still do not know how to cook; they still prefer to live in their own boarded houses in summer; some of the better-off Oroqen people still prefer to buy and entrust others to raise now-defunct hunting horses. In Oroqen Autonomous Banner of Inner Mongolia Autonomous Region, some Oroqen people prefer to rely on government subsidies rather than follow the example of the local Han Chinese who go out to work or grow crops on their own land for extra income.

Accordingly, the lifestyle of the current Oroqen people, especially the elderly, can also be seen to be incomprehensible and confusing in terms of the settled way of life. Although they are not immigrants, they are living in a world that is alien to them in terms of both their spiritual and physical environment.

第五章 清末民初黑龙江移民文献英译研究

5.1 | 犹太移民文献译介相关研究

5.1.1 国内外相关研究的学术史梳理及研究动态

改革开放以来，尤其是1992年中以建交使犹太学在中国勃兴，以色列研究进入学术界视野。随着“一带一路”倡议的提出和中以创新全面伙伴关系的建立，犹太—以色列研究成为我国区域与国别研究的典型案例，其成长模式与发展态势引起广泛关注。

5.1.1.1 犹太—以色列研究梳理

中国首批犹太研究机构出现于20世纪90年代，以上海社会科学院犹太研究中心等为代表，潘光、徐新、傅有德、肖宪等都是我国犹太学研究的先行者。21世纪以来，黑龙江省社会科学研究院犹太研究中心、北京大学希伯来和犹太文化研究所等陆续建立。

我国犹太—以色列研究的特点为科研成果快速增长、研究内容不断深化，并呈现出热点纷呈的局面。犹太历史文化研究一直是研究的热点，潘光、徐新、傅有德、肖宪、张倩红、徐向群等均对此进行过深入研究。国家社科基金、教育部人文社科项目中有关犹太—以色列研究的立项超过40项，其中，潘光主持的“来华犹太难民研究”、张倩红主持的“犹太通史”被列入国家社科基金重大课题。越来越多的学者开始尝试多视角、多维度地研究以色列：以色列的地缘环境、国家政治与安全问题，以色列的经济发展模式及创新体系研究，以色列外交关系及中以合作研究。

中国的犹太—以色列研究既有国际视野，又不乏中国特色，其特点如下。

① 注重现状研究。21世纪以来，由研究传统的犹太历史文化向研究以色列国家转型明显。从研究导向来看，现实意识与当下情怀明显上升；从成果内容来看，描述以色列国家特性与发展历程、挖掘以色列因素在世界舞台上影响力的研究日益增多。

② 注重从区域研究的视野观察以色列个案。中国学者从中东大格局观察以色列个案，总结其经验教训，并分析对其他发展中国家的启示。

③ 关注非主流及少数族裔的学术表达。一方面，中国学术界聚焦以色列的主流意识形态及官方历史叙事，尤其是以色列民族国家建构的历史篇章、移民社会的发展及国际影响力等；另一方面，对非主流的学术表达（如多元文化主义、以色列国家的异质表达等）也予以关切。从研究对象上来看，既聚焦主体民族在以色列的发展历程，也关注少数族裔的生存状况及其社会诉求与现实困惑。

5.1.1.2 黑龙江犹太移民文化译介研究梳理

清末民初的黑龙江移民是中国历史上最大的人口迁徙浪潮之一。随着中东铁路的修建，哈尔滨成为近代国内最早接纳犹太人的城市。在哈犹太人从事各种经济文化活动，哈尔滨也成为犹太文化遗存最多的城市，这些历史遗存成为研究近现代世界历史和哈尔滨城市历史的重要资源。国内学者对哈尔滨犹太文化的研究聚焦于政治、经济、文化、宗教、建筑等多个方面。目前，学术界对哈尔滨犹太文化遗存的研究分为学术、经济开发、情感交流 3 个方面。

在学术方面，郭宇春、程红泽、张铁江等的研究整合并挖掘了哈尔滨犹太历史文化资源，主要聚焦于哈尔滨犹太历史文化及犹太宗教两个方面。

在经济开发方面，张宇浩、杨光、杨彦君、詹宇婷、张崴、谷万佳、卫大可、黄晶、魏秀秀、鞠超、王启龙等阐述了近代犹太人在哈尔滨的一系列经济活动及他们给哈尔滨经济发展和城市近代化带来的影响，并针对哈尔滨犹太文化遗迹的开发和利用提出了合理化建议，著述颇丰。

在情感交流方面，国内围绕哈尔滨犹太家族及哈尔滨犹太人历史方面的著作较多，肖洪、韩天艳、曲伟等分析了犹太人移居哈尔滨的内外因素，《哈尔滨犹太简明辞书》等著作为研究哈尔滨犹太文化提供了史料依据。国外的研究多为在哈犹太人及其后裔的回忆录和传记。Y. 利伯曼、特迪 · 考夫曼、赫尔穆特 · 斯特恩等对当时哈尔滨的音乐文化成就及发展状况进行了详细的记述，是研究近代哈尔滨音乐文化发展历史的重要史料。

近年来，随着世界各国对犹太人关注度的持续升温，有关犹太人的各种译著不断增加，在“二战”时期作为犹太人避难所的哈尔滨与上海这两座城市，国内外关于它们的译作更是不胜枚举，其中，具有代表性的包括：刘全顺翻译的特迪 · 考夫曼先生的英文版著作《我心中的哈尔滨犹太人》；张以群翻译的法国犹太小说家米雪尔 · 卡娜的《上海犹太城》；美国著名翻译家葛浩文翻译的加拿大华裔女作家贝拉“犹太人在上海”三部曲中的第一部《魔咒钢琴》，这也是葛浩文翻译的众多中国题材小说中第一部涉及犹太难民主题的作品。

除此之外，国内外关于犹太史的译著也颇多，其中包括阎瑞松翻译的阿巴·埃班的《犹太史》一书，郭小凌、王皖强等翻译的英国历史学家阿诺德·汤因比的《历史研究》一书。

总的来说，虽然目前国内外对有关犹太人经济、社会、宗教与文化研究的译作颇多，但是有关哈尔滨犹太人的来源、犹太人迁居哈尔滨的历史背景、哈尔滨犹太人的社区活动，以及维系他们生存的物质、文化、宗教和精神因素等方面的学术专著译作极为罕见。

5.1.1.3 国内外研究简评

中国的犹太—以色列研究兴起较晚，仍存在很多不尽如人意之处，如习惯某些套路式的观点，深入的个案分析不够，富有学术深度与创新性的成果不足，等等。因此，真正形成具有中国特色、中国风格、中国气派且与国际学术界深度接轨的犹太—以色列研究体系仍任重道远。

由于研究起步较晚，加之仍有大量的原始文献史料未能发掘，目前，在开发和利用哈尔滨犹太文化当代价值这座极其丰富的“资源宝库”方面的研究成果尚存不足，亟待进一步挖掘。在现有学术研究价值方面，很多研究侧重探讨犹太人的历史活动、文化价值等。研究的新视角、新领域如犹太妇女、在哈犹太民众结构层次和阶级构成、在哈犹太人经营理念和精神文化研究等虽有所涉及，但成果较少，对各种新角度如哈尔滨犹太人饮食文化、服饰文化等有关哈尔滨与犹太文化交流融合方面的新学术资源，挖掘、利用不充分。另外，在宏观视角上，近代哈尔滨接纳犹太难民的开放包容心态和兼收并蓄的文化心理，也是研究文化开放与包容特性的独特切入点。微观领域的研究角度、宏观领域的研究深度均缺乏创新性探索，成为制约学术价值开发的主要障碍。在经济开发方面，研究多侧重学术价值的探讨，对哈尔滨犹太文化的宣传力度和规模都有局限，进而导致哈尔滨犹太文化知名度低、竞争力较弱等问题，这些都有待各界提出进一步的解决方案。研究中对哈尔滨犹太文化遗址遗存的开发利用措施和建议都局限于被动保护，开发利用模式和途径较为传统与固化，未能结合现代化信息技术提出创新性开发措施。因此，无法进一步打响“边疆文化大省”的文化招牌，这也在一定程度上制约了哈尔滨犹太文化的国内外影响力。在情感交流价值方面，目前只局限于学术界交流和学术价值探讨，未能深入两国人民的民间友好往来。虽然有关哈尔滨犹太人的教育、音乐文化等学术研究较多，但并未在两国优秀文化成果具体交流的过程中发挥实质性作用，仅停留在理论研究层面。目前，立足哈尔滨城市本身，现有的研究没有凸显地域性优势，资料性、学术性研究成果多，但指导性作用未充分在实践中发挥，应用性研究成果还有进一步发展的空间。应以此为契机或突破口进一步发掘哈尔滨犹太文化的当代价值，从而加大推进哈尔滨城市文化发展的力度。

5.1.2 该研究角度的独到学术价值和应用价值

国际竞争日趋激烈，归根结底是综合国力的较量，而文化发展是综合国力发展的一个重要推动因素。"全球化背景下，国家间的交流越来越密切，文化在外交领域也日益发挥着重要作用，想要在国际上展现大国形象，离不开文化软实力的支撑。"对我国来说，如何开发和利用好本国特色文化资源推动文化软实力发展至关重要。哈尔滨犹太文化作为黑龙江特色文化资源，是建设"边疆文化大省"、以文化促发展战略的重要基础和坚实保证，其在黑龙江省多元文化中独树一帜。进一步发掘哈尔滨犹太文化的当代价值对于填补学术研究空白，推动文化资源开发与哈尔滨国际化建设，搭建中犹沟通桥梁，促进中以两国文化交流合作与发展具有重要意义。

5.1.2.1 学术价值

聚焦新视角、新领域，利用好哈尔滨犹太文化的丰富资源，不仅对于犹太学、历史学、宗教学、翻译学等学术领域具有重要的研究意义，而且能为当代经济文化活动提供借鉴和启示。

①从国际视角出发，对黑龙江在犹太移民浪潮中的开放包容、和平共处心态及当时两国人民友好交往的研究，不仅可以作为研究城市文化多样性和兼收并蓄的包容开放理念的重要史实，还可以为当代反对种族歧视和促进人类和平研究提供参考价值。

②在微观视角上，可以进行多角度、多领域的交叉研究，诸如哈尔滨犹太人经营理念文化的研究，可以为当代黑龙江工商业的发展提供启示；民俗史中有关犹太人饮食文化、服饰文化的记载，可以为民俗史研究提供新的学术资源补充。

③为文献类翻译提供了一套行之有效的翻译批评和鉴赏批判方法。

5.1.2.2 应用价值

① 发挥哈尔滨犹太历史文化旅游资源的作用，促进旅游业发展，带动对外开放和招商引资，产生良好的社会效益和经济效益。

在修缮保护方面，目前，哈尔滨犹太建筑如位于中央大街57号的犹太国民银行旧址存在楼体破损及墙皮脱落、"一楼三色"、窗户被广告牌盖住等修缮不到位的问题。文物保护部门一方面可以借助档案馆保存的犹太建筑原有图片、影像史料及研究成果，进一步修复中央大街上的犹太建筑，破除失修违建现象，彰显犹太文化风貌，提升中央大街旅游竞争力；另一方面，可以在现存哈尔滨犹太遗址如哈尔滨卷烟厂等地建立犹太人纪念馆或纪念室，实现修缮保护与文化重塑一体化。

在开发利用方面，主要考虑结合当今新型网络媒体、信息技术对犹太文化资源进行创新性开发。

首先，网络自媒体方兴未艾，可以合理利用各自媒体平台投放哈尔滨犹太文化旅游宣传片，扩大宣传途径。其次，“5G背景下的新型数字化文化旅游，是传统旅游的升级换代，走高质量发展的必由之路”。为打破文化与公众交流的障碍，提升哈尔滨犹太文化的知名度，哈尔滨犹太文化经济价值开发利用应紧跟“互联网+”和5G时代的浪潮。可将旅游服务与学术研究成果，如旅游景点文物建筑的保护性开发、博物馆文创商品的犹太文化元素设计等相结合。社交平台可以通过数字化博物馆，让哈尔滨犹太文化“走出去”“活起来”。

② 景区可以利用5G技术开发出“手机游哈尔滨”等线上旅游服务软件，将哈尔滨犹太文化景点纳入哈尔滨城市游一体化旅游路线，这不仅可以给人们带来具有互动性的创新旅游方式，还是一个可以让人们足不出户体验“云旅游”的新举措。再者，文创纪念品的开发可以融合当代文创理念，以哈尔滨各种犹太教堂为图样，制作各类相关的文创产品，作为学术交流会、联谊会等活动的纪念品，将其作为旅游资源的创新开发形式以发挥其经济价值。

③ 发挥情感交流的纽带作用，通过人文交流深化中以两国人民友谊。作为犹太人的“第二故乡”，犹太文化元素成为当今哈尔滨犹太人后裔维系其对“第二故乡”情感的重要精神纽带，具有重要的情感沟通价值。这不仅仅有利于中以两国的国际文化交流，更能增进两国人民之间的友谊。

首先，历史名人效应有助于黑龙江旅游业形成自身鲜明的特点，历史名人具有独特的民族性、传承性和巨大影响力，能使本地旅游业更具独有气质，增强竞争力。我们要利用好这一珍贵的纽带，在广泛搜集资料的基础上，进行走访与口述史整理，利用访谈、拍摄纪录片等形式进行记录，发挥历史名人效应。

其次，犹太人艺术教育理念对哈尔滨城市艺术文化传统产生了深远影响，目前，学界研究也对哈尔滨犹太人的教育文化、音乐文化进行了多角度分析，在这一方面可供利用的资源丰富。在哈尔滨高校中，可以开展哈尔滨犹太文化展览会、邀请在哈犹太留学生参加学生联谊会、举办研学夏令营、开展重走哈尔滨犹太人生活历程的遗址遗存等一系列文化沟通交流活动。另外还可以采用线上、线下相结合的方式，邀请中犹教师进行线上教学理念交流研讨会。用哈尔滨“音乐之都”旅游招牌及中央大街现有“音乐阳台”特色资源，举办两国音乐家演奏交流会，实现中犹艺术家合奏，达到音乐文化交流的目的。普通民众交流则以旅游为主要形式，这可以通过上文提到的5G技术，打造线上“海外游”，以及互赠旅游纪念品等民间特色产品等方式实现两国人民“云游玩”，从而通过此类活动促进人文交流，深化中以两国人民友谊。

哈尔滨犹太文化的当代情感沟通价值，不应只局限于学术研究研讨及国际官方领域的交流合作，更应深入两国人民的日常生活，促进两国人民友谊。这既能使哈尔滨犹太人后裔在“寻根之旅”中寄托他们对先辈的无限追思，又能通过中以两国人民的沟通交流丰富两国文化，从而促进两国文化进一步发展。

5.1.2.3 国家社科基金已立同类项目综述

2011 年至 2021 年，国家级社科立项结题项目中，79 项聚焦译介研究，涉及中国典籍英译 8 项、戏剧英译 1 项、中国文学作品英译 3 项、中国哲学思想英译 2 项、英译研究 14 项。移民研究项目庞杂，大致可分为 9 类：涉外移民 24 项；国内区域移民 63 项；移民社会生产模式 43 项；古代移民类 3 项；移民与文化体育类 23 项；战争与移民 7 项；扶贫与移民经济 24 项；移民细化研究 14 项；移民史 4 项，分别为以色列移民史 1 项（以河南省开封市为主）、巴西的日本移民史 1 项、德国移民政策史 1 项、中朝移民史 1 项。龙江文化研究共计 5 项，涉及中俄黑龙江流域旧、新石器文化过渡遗存研究，中俄边境侨民研究，侨民教育和红色档案研究，以及与本项目最接近的国家级社科项目研究（主题为“犹太人在近现代中国东北的历史考察”）。

综上所述，目前国家级社科项目中涉及地区类犹太移民文献的译介项目凤毛麟角，有很大的拓展空间。

5.1.3 研究新方向

5.1.3.1 研究对象

从本土译论角度解析清末民初黑龙江犹太移民文献中体现的犹太历史文化资源的显态形式（有形遗产）和隐态形式（无形遗产），总结适用于本土国情的犹太移民文化译介范式。

5.1.3.2 框架思路

为探清上述对象，拟由五大板块建构框架，充以 11 部分的具体内容。

① 清末民初黑龙江移民文化图景。

在犹太人在华“整体史”的范式下，了解犹太人来华史的历史分期和来源地域，犹太移民的流动性和自身互动性，厘清犹太人来华的过去与当下历史性联系，从宏观研究逐步定位到微观研究，勾勒黑龙江移民文化的整体轮廓。

② 哈尔滨犹太文化研究综述。

国内学者对哈尔滨犹太文化的研究聚焦于政治、经济、文化、宗教、建筑等多个方面。综合学术界现有研究，根据研究侧重点的不同，可以归纳为以下 3 个方面。

在学术研究方面，整理学者对有形的犹太文化资源和无形的犹太文化精神两个方面的研究，总结哈尔滨犹太文化的内涵构成，包括对异质文化和自身传统文化的吸收与保存及对两者的调和。

在经济开发方面，梳理现有研究，归纳犹太人在哈尔滨的经济社会活动及其对近代哈尔滨城市发展的积极作用，以及对当前哈尔滨犹太建筑的保护与利用。

在情感交流方面，厘清现有研究考察在哈犹太人生活历史的成果，分析犹太人移居哈尔滨的内外因素，提出开放、兼容的城市风格和语言的相似性是移居的人文环境因素，中国人和犹太人重视教育与家庭伦理的文化融通性是移居的民族文化因素的观点。

③ 哈尔滨犹太历史文化资源的显态形式译介：变译理论视角。

作为 21 世纪中国本土主要翻译理论之一的变译理论中的 12 种变译方法，均可运用于有形犹太历史文化遗产的翻译中。

遗址遗迹资源。哈尔滨犹太遗址遗迹数量众多，保存最完整的、最具代表性的是建筑文化和艺术。运用变译理论有利于更好地体现黑龙江移民文化的多元性。

文献档案资源，大量的犹太人档案资料现主要散存于黑龙江省档案馆、哈尔滨市档案馆和黑龙江省博物馆等地，其中，保存犹太人档案资料最多、最完整的是黑龙江省档案馆。黑龙江省档案馆现存大约 5000 份犹太人档案，用俄文、英文和希伯来文等书写，这些珍贵的档案资料和生活遗物对于深化犹太历史文化研究具有不可估量的意义。因此，尽快进行抢救性整理翻译具有极其重要的意义，运用变译理论有利于更好体现文献的历史原貌。

家族历史材料，对犹太家族史的译介不仅能加深对犹太民族的了解，而且能为延续原居哈尔滨犹太人及其后裔与中国人民的感情搭建桥梁，从而促进中华民族和犹太民族这两个伟大民族历史友谊的传承。

④ 哈尔滨犹太历史文化资源的隐态形式译介：生态翻译理论视角。

生态翻译理论是由清华大学著名教授胡庚申提出的全新翻译理论，一经提出便受到许多学者的认可。“翻译生态环境”是原文、源语和译语呈现的世界，采用生态翻译理论有利于构建语言、交际、文化、社会，以及作者、读者、委托者互联互动的整体。

社区文化。哈尔滨犹太社区是哈尔滨犹太人的共同家园，各种福利、救济和慈善机构的设立是犹太社区的显著特点，社会功能齐全是犹太社区长久存在的基石，是犹太民族的情感和血脉。译介犹太社区文化文献对今天的社区建设仍起着极大的启示作用。

商业贸易。20 世纪初期，哈尔滨已发展成为具有国际影响力的著名都市，而哈尔滨犹太人的经贸活动几乎涉及哈尔滨各领域。哈尔滨犹太人贸易、金融方面的文献译介有利于总结犹太移民在哈尔滨城市化进程中起到的作用。

文化教育。民国初期，犹太人在哈尔滨开办了一批幼儿园、学校，创建了电影院、剧院、图书馆等文化设施。对文化教育领域文献的译介有利于分析在龙江大地异质文化与文明“并存”且“共生”的现象，追索其存在的根源，为今天提供借鉴。

⑤ 犹太移民文献译介模式探索。

以本土译论为理论基石，从变译理论及生态翻译理论视角出发，以黑龙江犹太移民文化文献译介为案例，总结出适用于犹太历史文化资源显态形式及隐态形式译介的多元本土路径。

5.1.4 创新之处

①展示民族形象名片。犹太移民文化对外宣传与翻译具有时代特殊性，是弘扬我国民族精神内涵的重要手段。

②夯实文化传播基础。通过本土译论，在外宣翻译过程中强化“三立足”（意识形态协调发展、国民教育基础建设、科技手段载体传播）传承基石的构筑。

③拓宽本土译论范围。以根植于本土的变译理论和生态翻译理论为依托，结合翻译实践，拓展本土译论诠释移民文化的高度和宽度。

④构建多维传承网络。面对文明互鉴的时代新要求，以语境为切入点，构建体现犹太历史文化资源显态形式与隐态形式的多视角移民文献译介模式。

参考文献

[1] BASSNETT S. Translation Studies [M]. London: Methuen, 1980.

[2] NEW MARK P A Textbook of Translation [M]. Shanghai: Shanghai Foreign Language Education Press, 2001.

[3] Nida, E A. Translating, Language and Culture [M]. Shanghai: Shanghai Foreign Language Education Press, 1993.

[4] NORD C. Text Analysis in Translation [M]. Amsterdam: Rodopi, 1991.

[5] 程红泽 . 哈尔滨犹太文化与中华文化交融述略 [J]. 重庆科技学院学报（社会科学版），2012（11）.

[6] 崔巧凤 . 犹太移民在哈尔滨城市化进程中的作用 [J]. 黑龙江史志，2007（11）.

[7] 韩天艳，程红泽，肖洪 . 哈尔滨犹太家族史 [M]. 哈尔滨：黑龙江人民出版社，2010.
[8] 黑龙江省社会科学研究院犹太研究中心 . 犹太人在哈尔滨 [M]. 北京：社会科学文献出版社，2006.
[9] 胡庚申 . 生态翻译学：建构与诠释 [M]. 北京：商务印书馆，2013.
[10] 黄忠廉 . 翻译方法论 [M]. 上海：华东师范大学出版社，2019.
[11] 李长栓 . 非文学翻译理论与实践：第 2 版 [M]. 北京：中译出版社，2012.
[12] 李明，等 . 清末民初黑龙江移民史研究 [M]. 哈尔滨：黑龙江人民出版社，2019.
[13] 李述笑 . 哈尔滨历史编年 [M]. 哈尔滨：哈尔滨出版社，2000.
[14] 刘爽 . 哈尔滨犹太侨民史 [M]. 北京：方志出版社，2007.
[15] 穆雷 . 翻译学研究的方法与途径 [M]. 上海：上海外语教育出版社，2021.
[16] 曲伟 . 哈尔滨犹太人 [M]. 北京：社会科学文献出版社，2004.
[17] 王琦，杜禹萱 . 对哈尔滨犹太历史文化遗存价值的思考 [J]. 黑龙江史志，2021（6）：15–20，29.
[18] 王志军 . 新成果 · 新观点 · 新阶段：评《哈尔滨犹太侨民史》[J]. 中国边疆史地研究，2009（3）：137–139.
[19] 许钧 . 翻译论（修订版）[M]. 南京：译林出版社，2014.
[20] 张倩红 . 我国犹太—以色列研究的新进展 [N]. 光明日报，2020-01-06（14）
[21] 张倩红 . 犹太史研究新维度 [M]. 北京：人民出版社，2015.
[22] 张莹 . 当代中国译学发展史（1979—2019）[M]. 天津：南开大学出版社，2020.

5.2 《近现代史上犹太人来华史研究路径探究》英译研究

5.2.1 引言

犹太移民历史文献记录了犹太人来华的历史。该段历史阐述了清末民初犹太人来华的原因，以及在当时特定历史时期产生的影响。犹太移民历史文献英译可以有效地传播历史，促进历史文化的交流，吸引犹太人来华投资，推动经济发展，并为历史研究学者及历史爱好者提供参考与借鉴。

历史文献是一种特殊的文体，在翻译时要注意源语与译语之间的关系，尽可能在译语文本中体现历史文献的严谨性、历史性及科学性。译者在翻译时将宏观的理论细化到微观层面，并在生态翻译理论的指导下，从词汇角度、句子结构等方面入手，细化翻译工作。首先，译者从中文文献入手，分析该文献的语体，以历史文献的语体为基准，明确历史文献的特征。其次，分析文献中通用词汇和特殊词汇的区别，根据不同词汇的差异性应用，确定不同的翻译策略和方法。在重点句子翻译上，译者结合历史文献的背景知识，合理运用语言知识精准地对源语文本进行表达，考虑句子的逻辑性和句子间的连贯性，对比中英文语言表达的差异，尽可能保证源语与译语风格的一致性。

生态翻译理论首先阐释了译者对翻译生态环境的适应和译者在翻译过程中的选择，为更系统地构建翻译适应和选择翻译方法铺平道路。生态翻译理论借助达尔文自然选择理论中的“自然选择”和“适者生存”原则，并将这些原则引入翻译研究领域。译者在翻译文本时注重提高读者的生态意识，在生态翻译理论的指导下对犹太人移民文献进行翻译探究，在翻译时不仅要考虑其语言环境，还要考虑社会、文化、交际、原文与译文等众多因素，讲究翻译中的动态平衡，体现生态之美。译者运用三维转换方法，即在“多维度适应与适应性选择”原则之下，相对地集中于语言维、文化维和交际维的适应性选择转换，顺利完成该历史文献的翻译任务。

古人云：“纸上得来终觉浅，绝知此事要躬行。”译者在完成此次翻译实践任务的过程中，通过解决翻译过程中遇到的种种困难，深刻体会到翻译工作的不易与艰苦。回顾整个翻译过程，译者深深感受到，做一名合格译者任重道远，不但要具有充足的专业知识储备，还要具有熟练运用翻译技巧及处理问题的本领。这些困难和挑战，让译者更加坚定了翻译之路，确立了进步的目标。

5.2.2 翻译任务描述

本次翻译任务与犹太人来华史有关，原文内容复杂、结构严谨。因此在翻译任务开始之前，译者需要对翻译任务进行分析，以便在翻译过程中更好地把控翻译的各项步骤。本节对任务背景和内容、英译目的及意义，以及委托方要求 3 部分进行详细阐述。

5.2.2.1 任务背景和内容

黑龙江省地处中国东北，北部和东部与俄罗斯隔江相望，拥有特殊的地理位置。改革开放以来，随着经济的快速发展，我国历史文化也受到了广泛关注。黑龙江历史文化从众多地域中脱颖而出，受到了国内外历史研究者的喜爱。因此，高质量的历史文献翻译对促进历史文化传播具有重要意义。

《清末民初黑龙江移民史研究》一书是一本高质量的历史文献资料，对黑龙江的移民历史进行了详尽的阐述，自 2019 年 12 月出版以来，深受历史研究者好评。该著作内容丰富，条理清晰，以历史研究方法探讨区域文明的发展、转型、特征等问题与移民的关系，旨在丰富黑龙江移民史，促进历史文化的发展与交流。译者在导师的带领下翻译《清末民初黑龙江移民史研究》历史文献，目的在于为外国历史研究者和相关历史学者提供历史资料，促进业内外人士对黑龙江移民文化的了解。

译者受黑龙江大学李朋教授委托，选取《清末民初黑龙江移民史研究》之八——《近现代史上犹太人来华史研究路径探究》作为翻译实践源语文本。犹太人来华史是中国近代研究史中的一个薄弱点，而《近现代史上犹太人来华史研究路径探究》是围绕犹太人来华史的历史分期和来源地域研究、流动性和互动性探究、过去和当下的历史性联系研究等内容进行描述的，并且作者提供了细致的阐述以帮助读者了解近现代史上犹太人来华的历史。该文本合计 15065 个汉字，满足此次翻译实践的字数要求。

5.2.2.2　英译目的及意义

当今，黑龙江省的发展史日益成为历史研究学者关注的热点。译者通过此次翻译实践，了解犹太人来华史的相关知识，掌握相关领域词汇，将日常学习的生态翻译理论应用于实践中，同时，练习文本分析，就实践过程中使用的翻译策略和翻译技巧进行总结，进一步学习相关知识，为日后的翻译工作积累经验。

然而，了解黑龙江省的历史，对每个人来说都不是简单的工作。对每个想要了解未知区域历史文化的学者来说，都会碰到各种问题——如何详尽了解该地域的发展史、如何入手研究、如何查找资料等，译者将针对翻译过程中可能遇到的问题进行分析，从而让更多历史研究学者了解犹太人来华史，促进文化传播交流，并希望为从事历史研究的学者提供帮助。此次翻译实践研究目的如下：

①分析文本类型并概括历史文献翻译的特点；

②总结此次翻译实践中涉及的专业术语；

③运用生态翻译理论并结合案例分析，归纳针对历史文献翻译运用的翻译技巧。

本次实践是对《近现代史上犹太人来华史研究路径探究》进行汉译英的过程。在翻译过程中，译者不仅要对犹太人来华史进行翻译研究，还要对黑龙江移民史的相关信息进行介绍。因此，本次翻译实践具有一定的理论意义、实践意义及现实意义。

① 理论意义。此次翻译任务采用胡庚申教授提出的生态翻译理论来指导历史文献翻译，促进历史文献翻译的发展。在翻译过程中，译者基于生态翻译理论在“多维度适应与适应性选择”的原则之下，从语言维、文化维和交际维 3 个维度对源语文本进行分析和翻译，并总结相应的翻译技巧。理论与

实践相结合，拓宽生态翻译理论在历史文献翻译中的研究视野。

② 实践意义。历史文献的翻译可以促进国内历史传播，促进文化交流，推动跨文化交际发展。此次翻译实践系统地介绍了近现代史上犹太人来华史的研究路径，译者将生态翻译理论与实践相结合，总结术语翻译并对每个案例进行分析，找到合适的翻译技巧，从而为历史研究领域人士提供更多的参考资料。

③ 现实意义。随着中国改革开放，有大批“中国犹太人”纷纷重返故里参观并参与故乡的发展。中国各地也出现了犹太居民群体。而犹太移民史英译可以使海外犹太人更加了解犹太人来华的历史，更有效地促进历史文化传播与交流，并吸引犹太人再次来华了解该地区的发展，加强合作交流，推动经济发展。

5.2.2.3 委托方要求

译者在翻译过程中严格遵守国家相关标准规范、法律法规和行业标准规范，准确翻译，使译文符合历史文献文本准确性、严谨性、科学性的特点，以期为国外犹太移民史研究学者提供可靠资料。基于上述翻译出发点，译者对本次翻译项目进行汉译英的同时，按照行业标准对本次翻译实践制定了如下具体要求：

① 委托方对终稿译文的预期质量是达到 98% 及以上的精确度；

② 译文要做到语言流畅，用词准确，客观严谨，专业细致；

③ 译文要最大限度上贴近源语文本，表达地道，忠实原意，文本信息不可错译漏译；

④ 译文要逻辑清晰，行文连贯，便于译语读者阅读；

⑤ 委托方要求此次翻译实践始于 2022 年 5 月 4 日，终稿的预期完成时间不晚于 2022 年 12 月 31 日。

5.2.3 翻译过程描述

翻译实践任务的成功与否在很大程度上取决于翻译过程是否完整、全面。译者在翻译过程的前、中、后各阶段都做了充分准备。为保证翻译工作顺利进行，译者在译前阶段积极分析文本内容、查找平行文本、制作并校对术语表、采用合适的翻译工具，并根据需要选择合适的翻译理论；译中阶段制订翻译过程计划及记录翻译计划的执行情况，以此把控翻译任务的进度；译后阶段通过自我校对、同行审校、导师审核、专家审查及委托方反馈保证翻译质量。

5.2.3.1 译前准备

① 源语文本分析。

恰当而详尽的源语文本分析是翻译实践圆满成功的前提条件。德国翻译功能派领军人物克里斯蒂安·诺德（Christiane Nord）从功能概念视角出发，提出了更详尽的翻译导向文本分析模式。她认为，译者只有了解影响文本分析的文内因素和文外因素，才能较好地解读源语文本的特有功能，选择合适的翻译策略。

译者据此针对文内因素和文外因素对源语文本进行分析。文内因素包括文本主题、文本内容、前提、词汇、句子结构等，文外因素则包括文本发送者、文本接受者、发送者意图、媒介、文本接受场所、文本接受时间等。

《近现代史上犹太人来华史研究路径探究》文内因素主要包括以下几项。

文本主题。《近现代史上犹太人来华史研究路径探究》的主题是通过不同学者对犹太人来华历史的研究来展开，以此促进犹太人来华历史的传播与发展，增强人们对历史文化的学习意识，并为相关研究的学者提供宝贵资料。以史为鉴，温故知新，促进交流合作，推动经济发展。

文本内容。《近现代史上犹太人来华史研究路径探究》通过介绍犹太人来华的历史分期和来源地域、犹太人的流动性和互动性、过去和当下的历史性联系等内容，从历史、文化方面阐述犹太人来华的历史并剖析犹太人来华的背景原因及影响。

前提。《近现代史上犹太人来华史研究路径探究》为历史文献文本，首先，在将其翻译成英语时译者需要考虑历史文本准确性、严谨性、科学性的特点，在翻译时应摒弃口语化表达，多使用正式的书面语。其次，译者需要充分了解犹太人来华历史的背景信息，同时，分析源语文本要传递的信息，对内容的关联及文本结构有清晰的把握。最后，译者需要分析英汉两种语言之间的表达差异及文化差异。选取适当的翻译理论与翻译技巧对源语文本进行翻译，让更多外国学者了解犹太人来华史，促进历史文化的传播。

词汇。《近现代史上犹太人来华史研究路径探究》源语文本在阐述犹太人来华史的同时涉及大量的历史文化负载词及专有名词。在翻译历史文化负载词时，译者需要考虑词汇的本身含义及引申含义。译者将以生态翻译理论为指导，考虑文化差异并分析词汇的生态环境，从语言、文化、交际等维度进行适应性选择，从而找到两种语言转换的平衡点，表达准确，忠实原文。

句子结构。《近现代史上犹太人来华史研究路径探究》多为不同学者及作者对犹太人来华史的分析，以陈述句为主，句子较长且逻辑关系紧密。为保证句子通顺，以便译语读者能快速提取文本信息，提高阅读效率，在翻译时，译者需要从语言维、文化维、交际维 3 个维度对句子进行拆句重组、语态转换、语序调整等处理，并适当补充关联词及标点符号来完善句子间的逻辑关系。

《近现代史上犹太人来华史研究路径探究》文外因素分析如下。

译语文本将由中国经济出版社出版发行。

该译文的接受者主要为英语语言受众、犹太移民历史兴趣爱好者、来华移民史研究学者、出版社发行的相关技术人员、英语翻译的专业译员、学生及教师等。

发送者意图如下：作为历史文献的资料，为研究犹太人移民史、犹太人来华史、黑龙江移民史等方面的历史研究学者提供帮助。将犹太人来华史进行英译，可以为外国对该部分历史感兴趣的学者提供资料，以此促进犹太人来华史在世界范围的传播。

② 平行文本准备。

翻译过程也是再创造的过程。鉴于译者翻译的文本需要充分了解犹太人来华的原因、过程等一系列历史情况，为准确、客观、流畅地传递原文信息，译者借助万方数据知识服务平台、中国知网等网上资源，以及图书馆等线下形式查阅了大量翻译平行文本。

历史类文献——了解背景知识。

译者在中国知网找到《中国省别全志（贵州卷）》汉译初探、《对哈尔滨犹太历史文化遗存价值的思考》，以及 Seidelman Rhona、Kuhne Jan、Blum Nava 和 Fee Elizabeth、Dal Bo Federico、Presner Todd Samue、Blum Nava 和 Fee Elizabeth 等发表的关于犹太人移民的文献。通过阅读外文犹太移民史文献，译者可以了解到更多关于犹太移民的历史信息，以及与移民相关的词汇和句子表达，这些为译者提供了翻译历史文献的思路。

翻译理论文献及著作——确定理论内涵。

译者查阅胡庚申教授著作《翻译适应选择论》《生态翻译学》；查阅论文期刊《生态翻译学的研究焦点与理论视角》《中国翻译理论话语：内涵与意义》《翻译研究“生态范式”的理论建构》及 *Eco-Translation: Translation and Ecology in the Age of the Anthropocene* 等文本，这些文本帮助译者了解生态翻译理论的内涵，并使译者更好地运用生态翻译理论指导历史文献的翻译。

翻译技巧论文——掌握翻译技巧。

译者查阅《跨文化差异与词汇翻译》《翻译过程中的转换现象浅析》《名词性从句的拆句译法》《标点符号的语篇衔接功能与英汉翻译中的信息处理》《标点符号辅助翻译研究》《破折号辅助英汉翻译》等文本，使译者更好地将中文词语翻译成英文词语，并加深对语句结构的了解。从语言维度，对译文进行换词改译、拆句重组等适应性转换。在翻译历史文化负载词时，译者查阅《论翻译中文化意象的保留》《成语的直译和意译》《也谈如何翻译汉语的四字格词语——基于 MTI 课堂教学的观察所得》及 *About the Definition Classification, and Translation Strategies of Idioms* 等文献。这些文献使译者受到启发，能更好地从文化维度翻译历史文化负载词，避免文化差异。译者查阅《基于语料库汉语四字格英译直译与意译研究》《英译汉中的补译法》等文本后获得启发，在翻译时要考虑译文交际性，在忠实原文作者的同时，方便译语读者阅读，从交际维度对四字格词语进行意译，并运用增词补译、语序调整等方式促进译文的传播与交流。

译者认真研读平行文本，以便更好地理解原文内容，帮助提升译文的质量和水准，推动翻译任务顺利完成。

③ 翻译术语整理。

“中华思想文化术语的整理、诠释和翻译，是向世界传播中华文明和中华思想文化的关键。”（陈海燕，2015：13）而《近现代史上犹太人来华史研究路径探究》文本涉及很多复杂的专业术语，为了确保译文质量，在翻译过程中，译者整理编辑出 20 多个专业术语，并第一时间运用搜索引擎查询、查找纸质及电子词典、比对平行文本及向专业人员请教，反复确认与检查，避免术语出现偏差与错误。并利用 SDL Trados 对专业术语进行翻译整理，经过多次仔细斟酌校对输出术语表。部分术语如表 5–1 所示。

表 5–1　部分术语

Table 5–1　List of terms (Excerpts)

中文	英文
满洲国	Manchukuo
侨民	Expatriates
十月革命	October Revolution
远东	Far East
巴尔干半岛	Balkan Peninsula
纳粹大屠杀	Nazi Holocaust
内战	Civil War
苏联侨民	Soviet Expatriate
苏联政府	Soviet Government
苏维埃政权	Soviet Regime

在对专业术语的翻译过程中，译者本着严谨、负责的态度，将能在目标语中找到对应词义的术语进行总结归纳，针对部分难以对应的术语，译者根据生态翻译理论，从语言、文化、交际等维度进行词义引申，来保证译文的准确性及可接受性。

④ 翻译工具准备。

译者在面对客观严谨的翻译工作时，尤其是对历史文献的翻译，无论是词语还是句段，都不能掉以轻心。为此，译者利用翻译软件来提高翻译质量和翻译效率。

表 5–2 为部分翻译辅助工具，译者灵活运用翻译辅助工具，在提高翻译效率的同时，还可以保证译文的质量。

表 5–2　翻译辅助工具
Table 5–2　Translation Aids

工具类型	工具名称
纸质词典	《牛津高阶英汉双解词典》（第 9 版）
	《英汉大词典（陆谷孙主编）》（第 2 版）
	《新世纪汉英大词典》（第二版）
	《韦氏高阶英汉双解词典》（第 1 版）
	《柯林斯高阶英汉双解学习词典》（第 8 版）
	《现代汉语词典》（第 7 版）
电子词典和网络在线翻译工具	欧路电子词典
	金山词霸
	谷歌在线翻译
	百度翻译
	网易有道翻译
	DeepL 翻译
计算机辅助翻译软件	AntConc
	Trados
网络搜索引擎	百度
	谷歌
语法审校工具	Grammarly
	火龙果写作
	批改网
文献浏览工具	学校图书馆电子浏览室
	中国知网
	万方数据知识服务平台

⑤ 翻译理论准备。

历史文献翻译是促进文化交流的翻译，为确保其准确性，在翻译时译者应遵循特定原则和特殊要求，充分考虑译语读者的文化背景、语言表达等。此外，历史文献翻译还要想尽一切办法去吸引读者阅读，激发读者的阅读兴趣，并向其传播历史文化知识。因此，历史文献翻译一般都需要对译文做出适当调整以满足译语读者需求，从而增强译文的可读性，提升译文可接受性，着重弘扬历史文化。

在研读各种翻译理论时，译者发现，尤金·奈达从语言学角度出发，提出“功能对等”理论。所谓“功能对等”，就是翻译时不求文字表面的死板对应，而是要在两种语言间达成功能上的对等。而皮得·纽马克的“交际翻译”和“语意翻译”中提出，“翻译关联法”即源语文本或译语文本语言越重要，就越要紧贴原文翻译。两种理论均适用于旅游类文本或文学类文本，而犹太移民文献为历史文献类文本，含有大量历史文化负载词，因此译者应着重文化因素对翻译的影响。在众多翻译理论之中，生态翻译理论中“多维度适应与适应性选择”的原则能较为合适地满足上述历史文献翻译的种种要求。

2001 年，胡庚申教授提出生态翻译理论，该翻译理论对中国翻译学者产生了非常深远的影响。生态翻译理论主要是从生态学的角度出发研究翻译，把翻译活动放到整个生态环境中去。参照生态翻译理论，在翻译历史文献文本时，译者需要结合西方人的语言表达及文化背景，融合西方的生态环境，原著作者、译者及生态翻译环境等多个因素，在“多维度适应与适应性选择”的原则之下，将历史文献从语言、文化和交际 3 个维度进行分析与翻译。

语言维度，把握英语的形合特点和汉语的意合特点，通过换词改译、语态调整和拆句重组等方法使译文在语言维度更加符合译语读者的表达，使词语更加准确，语句更加通顺。

文化维度，在翻译历史文化负载词时，译者通常考虑文化意象的显化与隐化、文化缺省及文化借用等方式灵活传递文化信息，避免文化差异给译语读者造成困扰。

交际维度，通过词语意译、增词补译、语序转换使原文更易于读者理解，促进译文的交流与传播。

随着生态语言学的快速发展，生态翻译学研究在国内呈现出蓬勃发展的态势。在中国当代译学研究领域，作为开发本土学术资源的一面旗帜，生态翻译学自 2001 年创建以来一直备受关注。胡庚申教授的专著《翻译适应选择论》（2004 年）被看作生态翻译学的奠基之作。

随着研究的不断深入，生态翻译学理论已经引起了翻译界学者的广泛关注，被应用于翻译实践各领域，如文学翻译、公示语翻译、外宣翻译、广告翻译、旅游翻译等。国内译界对生态翻译学这门新兴学科的研究逐渐升温，相关会议增多，全国多所高校运用生态翻译学作为理论框架来指导研究生完成硕士和博士学位论文。

国外翻译界对生态翻译学研究的学者也日益增多，2003 年，米歇尔·克罗尼恩在《翻译与全球化》一书中提出，要关注语种“翻译的生态”问题，呼吁在不同语种的翻译之间要保持健康平衡。安德烈·勒非弗尔与苏珊·巴斯奈特于 1990 年提出“文化转向问题”，多次将翻译的语境描述为“文化环境”，并使用“发现树木生存之地”“描述植物生长之状”等生态类比翻译研究中语言学家的“天堂”。

2011 年至 2022 年，应用生态翻译理论指导翻译的文本逐渐增加。译者在中国知网上搜索“生态翻译理论应用”这一词条得到多篇生态翻译理论在翻译中的应用，而其中，历史信息翻译中的应用仅有 15 篇。因此，译者选用生态翻译理论对犹太人来华史文献进行翻译，旨在拓宽翻译视野，使译文既忠实原文，又全面准确。

综上所述，译者经过深入分析，发现生态翻译理论是指导历史文献翻译的重要理论，可以根据不同的翻译生态环境对翻译策略和方法进行相应选择。

5.2.3.2　译中工作

翻译任务的完成需经历 3 个阶段，即开展充分的译前准备工作、进行翻译及译后审校事项，缺一不可。其中，翻译的中间过程尤为重要。译者在导师的指导下，分析该项目的文本类型、文本特点；在试译、修改及讨论的过程中，总结翻译过程中需运用的翻译策略和技巧；探究历史文献翻译领域的翻译特点及中英文表达的差异性；系统地翻译文本内容；找出翻译文本中的重难点并提出解决办法，高质量完成翻译任务；扩充翻译所需的历史知识，并按时、按量完成本次翻译实践。

① 翻译过程设计。

为保证翻译进程顺利推进，译者将翻译过程分为 3 个阶段，即译前、译中、译后，并制图 5–1。

图 5–1　翻译过程设计

（Figure 5–1　Translation Process Schedule）

译者严格执行翻译过程计划表，根据相关的时间安排，合理分配翻译工作，保证翻译工作顺利进行。在此期间，译者与导师密切联系，不断完善译文。与此同时，译者结合翻译理论，记录一些典型案例，为之后翻译案例的编制做好准备，进一步提高撰写翻译实践报告的效率。

② 翻译计划执行。

本次翻译任务文本属于历史文献文本，要求译文忠实原文、客观准确、逻辑清晰、严谨专业。在翻译时，译者遇到了前所未有的困难与挑战。这时，就需要译者有大量的知识储备作为基底，还要具备高度的翻译素养。为此，译者严格按照预先制作的流程图进行。译前准备阶段较为顺利，这一阶段主要是输入的过程，难点主要是确认查找到的资料是否全面、准确。然而，译者在译中遇到了一些问题，如发现个别专业术语的表达存在差异，或者个别术语解释较少，难以验证译文的准确性等。译后审校阶段也按照计划如期进行，经过多轮自我及同专业同学的校对，将译文移交给导师进行审核，按照导师提出的修改意见进行修改润色，最终请从事学术论文写作教学的教授进行专业审核。

③ 难点汇总。

译者将本次翻译实践中遇到的最棘手的 3 个难点收集汇总出来，辅以译者的突破思路和解决办法，具体如下。

第一，语言表达对等的困难。由于汉英两种语言之间存在的文化差异较大，实现译文与原文在语意方面完全对等的难度也相应提升，译者需要克服文化差异带来的翻译障碍。译者在网络上查询相关文化常识，也经常向导师请教一些翻译过程中遇到的由文化差异引发的问题，最终顺利突破该项阻碍。

第二，文本中的大量历史文化负载词及四字格结构词汇增大了翻译难度。受现实条件影响，译者对历史文献文本的翻译经验较少。为此，译者需要查找大量的历史文献和资料，翻阅各类中英文词典，及时请教导师和委托方专家，弥补该项不足。

第三，译文案例分析过程复杂，操作难度大。译者要从语言、文化、交际 3 个维度对翻译案例进行分析，译者曾多次与导师和同学探讨生态翻译理论在本次翻译实践中的应用。经过多方面考虑，在不断努力下，经过合理的分析，得出在各方面都非常贴近原文的译文。

5.2.3.3 译后事项

译后事项属于翻译的收尾工作，也是译文最后总结与改进的重要阶段。为了保证译文的专业性，译后阶段需要进行自我校对、同行审校、导师审核、专家审查、委托方反馈 5 部分。总结翻译过程中的优点和不足，积累自身翻译经验，为未来的翻译工作打下基础。

① 自我校对。

自我校对是译文完成后的第一项任务，也是最基本的自查环节。译者对译文共进行了 7 次自我校对。第一次，侧重译文格式、词汇拼写、语法错误、语句不通等问题。译者通过 Microsoft Word 智能审阅拼写和语法错误功能，共找出拼写错误 6 处，标点格式错误 8 处；通过 Grammarly 软件的语法勘误功能和批改网的自我检测功能，找出语法错误 7 处。这些错误是译者在翻译过程中不注意细节造成的，译者通过审校及时改正了错误。

第二次，译者侧重检查历史文献中的一些历史文化负载词、四字格词汇的英译是否正确。译者通过火龙果写作软件的校对功能，找出历史文化负载词汇和术语表不对应的错误 4 处，这主要是未能及时根据译文修改术语表，造成了不对应的情况，译者及时更新术语表，避免类似的错误发生。

最后一次，译者侧重检查案例分析是否合理，句子是否通顺且贴近原文，语篇结构是否恰当，语意是否通顺，未发现明显错误。最后，同导师就自查出来的问题和改进办法进行沟通与交流，听取导师所给意见，商讨并进行润色。

② 同行审校。

在自我校对后，译者邀请 5 名就读于北京外国语大学翻译系的英语笔译专业硕士研究生，进行同行之间的审校。经过 3 次审校，主要侧重检查译文是否准确流畅，逻辑是否合理等方面的问题，共发现了译文衔接错误 5 处，译文翻译与原文表达偏差等情况 3 处，经过共同讨论，译者修改掉其中 6 处错误。询问各位同行对译文翻译的修改建议，综合他们对译文给出的建议对译文进行再次修改。

③ 导师审核。

导师审核是译后阶段不可或缺的一个部分。译者在翻译过程中，与导师密切联系，积极沟通，及时汇报翻译任务的进展情况。向导师请教词汇、句法、语篇逻辑中难以理解的问题，就选词准确性、信息完整性、译文专业性及流畅性等方面进行讨论。导师指出译文中存在 3 处词语译文翻译不当及两处翻译方法使用不当的问题。导师在出现问题的地方，进行标红处理，并给出详细的修改建议。在译文中，有 2 处翻译出现偏差，在与导师分析沟通后发现这两处是译者选择的翻译方法出现偏差，在导师的帮助下，译者加深了对翻译方法的理解。经过反复的修改，译者将译文再次提交给导师，进行二次审校。在二次审校时，导师认为译者在词汇、句子、语篇上做到了对应，但导师也对相同汉语词汇的不同表达给出了替换建议，建议在同一个句子或段落尽量使用不同的词汇去表达相同的含义，进而使译文更加丰富流畅。将译文修改完成并得到导师认可后，提交给委托方。

导师对译文中出现的用词不当之处提出修改建议，并帮助译者区分部分词汇差异，以及总结译语语言习惯，并帮助译者解决了一些操作 AntConc 和 Trados 等翻译软件时遇到的障碍，提高了翻译效率。在导师的帮助下，译者顺利地完成了此次翻译实践。

④ 专家审查。

译者在完成上述审校后，第一时间与学校翻译硕士教育中心的专家教授及中国经济出版社编辑张博取得联系，申请对译文进行专家审查。专家针对原文与译文对应的精准性、译文的专业性及篇章全文安排的合理性等方面对译文进行审校。专家给出的结论是，译文和原文对应处理较好，整体篇章结构没有过多需要修改的地方，但在一些词汇的专业表述上仍有一定欠缺，需要继续完善。在专家审核后，译者针对专家提出的建议对译文再次进行了调整，最终顺利完成翻译任务。

⑤ 委托方反馈。

在提交方终稿后，译者再次询问了委托方对译文的建议。委托方肯定了译者的努力和大部分译文的质量，但也对译文的部分文本提出了建议。

在词汇层面，对于历史文化负载词及四字格成语的翻译，委托方给出的建议是译者在翻译时要体现词语的引申含义，以及源语作者在文本中使用该词的意图，力求忠实原文，表达准确，便于读者理解。

在句子及语篇层面，委托方建议译者尽量将译文翻译成符合译语读者阅读的被动句或从句，且在一句话中尽量使用不同的英文词语翻译同一个中文词语，提高译文的可读性，使读者便于阅读，提高阅读效率。

首次提交给委托方的译文在翻译精准度上没有完全达到客户要求，其中仍然存在专业性欠缺的情况。但在规定期限内，根据委托方意见修改后又提交了两次译文，最终达到了委托方的要求。委托方对译文最终稿审核完毕后，认为提交的译文内容准确、格式严谨、通俗易懂，对译文质量表示满意。译文终稿与委托方的预期标准相符，此次实践取得了良好的反馈。

5.2.4 英译案例分析

译者在此处结合生态翻译理论共选择了 28 个案例来对整个翻译实践进行总结。译者从语言、文化、交际 3 个维度研究词语、句子的选择与适应，并针对翻译过程中遇到的问题或典型案例进行总结，对总结出的案例进行分析。

5.2.4.1 语言维的适应性选择转换

“语言维的适应性转换，即译者在翻译过程中对语言形式的适应性选择转换。”（胡庚申，2011：8）汉语起源于亚洲，属于汉藏语系；而英语起源于欧洲，属于印欧语系。两种隶属不同语系的语言，其表达方式在用词和造句上也截然不同。因此，在翻译时，译者需要充分考虑语言维的转换，使译文更加贴近译语的表达习惯。

源语文本中存在的大多数词汇、句子通俗易懂，简明扼要，可以按照词语和句子的本身含义直接进行翻译。但该文本中包含了少量的历史文化负载词和长难句。因此，在翻译时，要求译者考虑中英两种语言在表达上的差异。另外，译者需要从语言维出发，考虑词汇的词性、词义及句子的语序、语态。为了更好地实现语言维的适应性转换，在翻译时，译者可以进行换词改译、语态转换、拆句重组，使译文更加专业自然。

① 换词改译。

在某些语境下，中文词汇表达的含义在英语表达中没有直接的对应词。“由于两种语言在表达上的差异，在保证原文意思不变的情况下，译文的词类时常需要进行相应的改变。”（丁伟祥，2003：110）因此，译者需要分析中文词汇要表达的含义，以此来确定词汇的译文。同时，在语言表达习惯上，两种语言也存在差异，中文常常使用相同词语，而英文为了避免重复则会使用不同的词语。在面对这些情况时，译者需要从语言维对中文词汇与英文词汇进行对比分析。在没有直接对应词时，译者需要对词语进行换词转译，以此在忠实原文的基础上，使译文更贴近译语读者的表达习惯。

例 1

原文：经过对以上研究成果的梳理后，目前犹太人在上海和哈尔滨的研究基本实现从宏观到微观研究的跨越，向微观的社会生活史及宗教和政治生活等主题迈进。

译文：From the above sorting and reviewing of research achievements, the current Jewish studies in Shanghai and Harbin have basically made the leap from macro-study to micro-study, shifting toward micro themes such as the history of social life, religious and political life.

分析：在翻译前半句“经过对以上研究成果的梳理后”时，译者查找《英汉大词典（陆谷孙主编）》（第 2 版）、《牛津高阶英汉双解词典》（第 9 版）、《柯林斯高阶英汉双解学习词典》（第 8 版）、《韦氏高阶英汉双解词典》（第 1 版）、《朗文当代高级英语辞典》第 6 版、《新世纪汉英大词典》（第二版）搜索“梳理”一词，得到的结果均为“comb”，但在词典中该词的含义有：（1）梳理头发；（2）梳理羊毛、棉花等；（3）仔细搜索，搜寻。“comb”的确有梳理的意思，但是主要指寻找证据和线索，字典里的例句基本没有和科研相关的，因此不适合此句的语境。“为达到预期的翻译目的，在翻译时对原文的形式或/和内容做一定程度的修改和变化。”（方梦之，2019：184）因此，译者根据生态翻译理论，从语言维将“梳理”一词进行换词改译。译者根据语境对“梳理”一词进行分析，发现在原文中“研究成果的梳理”一词的引申含义为“将研究整理分类、复查审核”。译者查阅《牛津高阶英汉双解词典》（第9版）、《柯林斯高阶英汉双解学习词典》（第8版），发现词典中“sorting”的含义为“资料研究的整理分类”，而“reviewing”在《牛津高阶英汉双解词典》（第9版）、《柯林斯高阶英汉双解学习词典》（第8版）中的含义为“资料的复查审核”。因此，译者从语言维将“comb”转换成“sorting and reviewing”，避免出现“comb”一词与“research”搭配不当而使译文中式化的情况，增加译文的可读性。

例2

原文： 刚刚出版的《哈尔滨犹太简明辞书》为这样的探究提供了许多门径。

译文： The just-published *Concise Dictionary of Harbin Jewry* provides abundant study resources for such inquiry.

分析： 在翻译该句时，译者对“门径”一词的翻译颇为困惑。为此，译者首先在《现代汉语词典》（第7版）中查找“门径”一词的中文解释为“门路”，也有“做事的途径、方法、窍门”之意。随后，译者在金山词霸、百度、有道等在线翻译平台逐一对该词及该句进行翻译，结果均为“many avenues”。而译者在中国知网学术在线翻译查询平行文本中得到的结果为“stage-gate”，“stage-gate”多出现在经济类的文本中，在历史文献文本中不常出现。译者根据上下文的理解，发现“门径”在句中指“研究方法”。因此，译者从语言维将“门径”一词进行换词改译，翻译为“study methods”。然而，中国经济出版社编辑张博在对译文进行审校后，认为将该词翻译为“study methods”过于局限，“门径”一词的引申含义可以包含研究方法、途径等各方面。因此，译者在与研究学者商讨后将“study methods”换成“study resources”，而译者在《牛津高阶英汉双解词典》（第9版）中查到“resources”，“resources”常与“资料研究”等词语连用，与文本中作者表达的含义相符。译者从语言维将作者的意图表达完整，使译语读者更容易理解文章内容。

例3

原文：建议黑龙江省开辟境外市场，把畜产品、农产品出口到俄罗斯、东北亚和欧洲，像以色列一样成为欧洲的“冬季厨房”和“菜篮子”。

译文：It is suggested that Heilongjiang Province should open up overseas markets and export livestock and agricultural products to Russia, Northeast Asia and Europe, acting as the “winter kitchen” and “vegetable base” of Europe like Israel.

分析：在翻译该句时，译者发现，句中“菜篮子”一词带引号。在大多数情况下，带引号的词语一般多有引申含义。“根据上下文的语境及逻辑关系，从该词语的基本意思出发，将词义进行引申，从而选择出恰当的汉语词汇来表达。”（徐昌和，2009：10）因此，译者对“菜篮子”一词在句中的含义进行了深入分析。文中“菜篮子”使用比喻修辞，把以色列比喻成菜篮子。而随着网络信息的发展，“篮子”一词联想意义不佳。如果译者采用直译的方式，就会使译语读者对原文含义的理解出现偏差。而译者在平行文本《跨文化差异与词汇翻译》中获得了启发——该文本中采用“代换法”对词语进行转化。为此，译者从语言维出发，规避比喻修辞，并对该词进行换词改译。鉴于黑龙江省内有大面积的农田可以种植蔬菜，译者选择将“菜篮子”一词转化为“蔬菜基地”，翻译为“vegetable base”，“基地”一词表达恰当，能凸显黑龙江的种植规模，且该词积极正面，使词汇更加正式合理，向读者传递隐含信息，避免译语读者对原文含义的理解出现偏差。

经过上述案例分析，原文本作者在表达时会使用源语中通俗易懂的词语对文章进行撰写。但由于中文和英文属于不同的语系，一些中文词汇在句中的含义会发生转变。因而，在翻译时，译者不能直接将词语翻译成英文的对应词，而是需要从语言维的角度结合上下文对该词进行换词改译，从而使译文更加贴近原文含义，避免因词汇使用不当而出现理解偏差。

②语态转换。

原文作者秉承汉语的表达习惯，在写作时常常使用主语、谓语清晰的主动语态语句。而在英文的表达中，常常会使用被动语态。在翻译某些中文语句主语表达不清或缺少主语的句子时，为了保证句子结构完整、译文准确，以及丰富译文表达的多样性，译者也会从语言维角度将汉语中的主动句转换成被动句。“对被动语态语言的理解和翻译，关键在于抓住它表达的事件实体和功能实体。这样才能主干突出，枝叶分明。”（杨红，2010：57）因此，译者通过分析源语文本中的句子结构，对部分句子进行语态转换，以此来顺应译语读者的语言习惯。

例 4

原文：在哈尔滨，存在着许多受犹太人影响而遗留下来的风俗习惯，将哈尔滨与其他城市做比较，你会发现，哈尔滨人比其他地方的中国人吃面包、喝啤酒来得多。

译文：In Harbin, some customs and habits have been left over under the influence of the Jews. If you compare Harbin with other cities, you will find that people in Harbin eat more bread and drink more beer than Chinese in other places.

分析：该句“存在着许多受犹太人影响而遗留下来的风俗习惯”符合汉语的表达习惯。在翻译该句时，译者首先对该句进行分析——该句为主动语态，主语省略，谓语为“存在”，宾语为“受犹太人影响遗留下来的风俗习惯”。英语中则常常使用被动语态，强调“风俗习惯是被遗留下来的”。原句中“受”字也给译者带来启发，“受”为被动语态的标志词。因此，译者想要将其翻译成被动句。为确定该句译文的翻译，译者在欧路、百度、有道及DeepL 翻译软件中查询，结果该句均被翻译成被动语态。因此，译者从语言维，对该句的语态进行转换，将“some customs and habits”作为主语，“have been left”作为谓语动词。在语态转换后，译文更加标准规范，并且凸显该句所强调“风俗习惯被留下”这一主要信息，使译文表达更加通顺地道。

例 5

原文：哈尔滨以原犹太新会堂为依托建立了一流的“哈尔滨犹太人纪念馆”，较为全面地展示了犹太人在哈尔滨及中国的历史。

译文：Based on the original Jewish New Hall, a first-class “Harbin Jewish Memorial Hall” has been built, which comprehensively displays the history of Jews in Harbin and China.

分析：在翻译该句时，译者首先对原文进行梳理，按照原文的顺序将译文翻译成主动语态。但在后期审校时，译者发现该句虽然没有语法错误，但表达不够地道。面对该问题，译者在查找平行文本《翻译过程中的转换现象浅析》时得到启发，“即两种语言中都存在表达同一概念的表达方式，但是这两种表达方式却是截然不同的。要解决这些因语言表达方式不同所产生的差异，翻译过程常用的方法是转换，即采用译文语言中习惯的常规表达方式来取代原文中独特的语言表达方式。”（王宁霞，2006：55）译者也发现，在汉语中有些句子是以主动语言形式表现出来的，而在英语中则是以被动语言形式表现出来的。对此，译者重新将句子进行梳理，找到该句的主语为“哈尔滨”，谓语为“建立”，宾语为“哈尔滨犹太人纪念馆”。译者考虑到汉语和英语之间表达的差异，在生态翻译理论的指导下，从语言维对该句进行语态转换，把原语句的主动语态转换成被动语态进行翻译。其次在不改变句意的情况下，为使语言简洁，译者从语言维对句子进行化繁为简处理，将“以原犹太新会堂为依托”翻译为“基于原犹太会堂”。把“一流的‘哈尔滨犹太人纪念馆’”与后半句话进行整合，做非限定性定语从句处理，实现语言维的适应性选择。采用译语中习惯的常规表达方式来取代原文中独特的语言表达方式，是为了让译语读者能看懂和欣赏译文，有效地获得原文传达的信息。

例 6

原文：同时，抢救性地收集一批哈尔滨犹太人口述历史资料，采访原居哈尔滨犹太人及其后裔近 40 人。

译文：At the same time, a group of Harbin Jews oral history materials were salvaged and nearly 40 Harbin Jews and their descendants who originally lived in Harbin were interviewed.

分析：在翻译该句时，译者发现该句缺少主语，面对这一情况，译者需要补充主语，或对原句进行转换。对此，译者首先分析了该句的结构——原句由 3 个短句构成，第一个短句为时间状语，第二个和第三个短句为无主语句。这种并列的无主语短句在汉语中极为常见，而在英语中则不常使用。针对两种语言的表达差异，“即译者在翻译过程中对语言形式的适应性选择转换。这种语言维的适应性选择转换是在不同方面、不同层次上进行的”（胡庚申，2008：2）。因此，译者从三维转换翻译方法中的语言维对该句进行分析，在不给读者造成理解困难的前提下，摒弃按照汉语结构直接译成英文的翻译。通过分析，译者发现该句主要强调“一批哈尔滨犹太人口述历史资料被及时地抢救收集”，而并非强调“抢救收集”这一动作。而后面的短句也是强调“近 40 人的原居哈尔滨犹太人及其后裔被采访”，而并非强调“采访”这一动作。译者在《牛津高阶英汉双解词典》（第 9 版）、《柯林斯高阶英汉双解学习词典》（第 8 版）中查找“salvaged”“interviewed”发现，在词典的例句中这两个词多用于被动。因此，在尊重语言表达差异的同时，译者从语言维角度将该主动句转换成被动句，使译文既符合译语读者的语言习惯，又能更好地促进译语读者对译文的理解，增强文本的语言传播效果，避免造成句子成分残缺，影响译语读者理解译文。

译者总结发现，源语语言经常使用主动句进行表达，且句子成分复杂、语句较长；而译语语言在表达时多为被动句，且使用从句作为正式的书面语进行表达。“在英译汉过程中，这也是一种对立统一现象，即两种语言中都存在表达同一概念的表达方式，但是这两种表达方式是截然不同的。”（王宁霞，2006：55）因此，译者从语言维出发，将语态进行转换，帮助译语读者更好地理解作者要传达的信息。

③ 拆句重组。

就历史文献而言，语句前后的逻辑关系十分重要，清楚紧密的逻辑关系有助于读者阅读。“研究适当的翻译方法就是既从表层又从深层去比较翻译所涉及的两种语言，然后以语言为基础采取最恰当的译法。”（张梅岗，1999：27）因此，为更好地传递原文信息，使译文符合译语的表述方式和习惯，译者在生态翻译理论的指导下，从语言维对原句进行拆分重组找到适合每个句子的翻译方法。以此做到语言维的适应性选择，使译文更便于理解，进而促进历史文化的传播与发展。

例 7

原文： 哈尔滨啤酒最先是由犹太人创办的哈尔滨啤酒厂生产的，而且这是中国最早的啤酒。

译文： You must know that Harbin Beer, the earliest beer in China, was first produced by the Harbin Brewery founded by Jews.

分析： 在翻译该句时，译者发现句中“最先是由”“最早的”等表述较为相近。因此，译者希望除按照原句顺序翻译外，能找到更好的翻译方法。对此，译者对句子进行分析，该句前半句的主语为“哈尔滨啤酒”，系动词为“是”，表语为“犹太人创办的哈尔滨啤酒厂生产的”。而后半句也是主系表结构，主语为“哈尔滨啤酒”，系动词为“是”，表语为“最早的啤酒”。随后，译者在阅读平行文本《名词性从句的拆句译法》一文时，看到同位语的翻译受到启发，该句后一分句正是对前一分句主语“哈尔滨啤酒”的补充说明。

因此，译者从语言维将句子进行拆分重组，把后一句“这是中国最早的啤酒”翻译为“哈尔滨啤酒”的同位语，省略简化句子中冗杂的信息，使句子更加简洁通顺，易于读者阅读，促进信息传递。

例 8

原文：因为犹太人要处理的关系对象不同，这是犹太人不能选择的。1945 年 8 月 15 日中国抗日战争胜利及后来苏军进入哈尔滨时，犹太人在哈尔滨的历史研究应注意犹太人与俄国侨民的关系问题。

译文：Because the Jews had to deal with different objects of relations, which they could not choose, great attention should be paid to the issue of the relations between the Jews and the Russian diaspora, while studying the history of the Jews in Harbin at the time of the victory of the Chinese War of Resistance against Japan on August 15, 1945 and the subsequent entry of Soviet troops into Harbin.

分析：该处句子结构复杂，因此译者首先对句子结构进行深入分析。第一句前半句和后半句的主语均为“犹太人”。由此，译者想要将这两句整合成一句。考虑到译语读者习惯使用从句的表达方式，于是选取定语从句的形式进行翻译。而第二句句子较长，在中国经济出版社编辑张博的建议下，译者对第二句进行了拆分，拆分成“1945 年 8 月 15 日中国抗日战争胜利及后来苏军进入哈尔滨时”“犹太人在哈尔滨的历史研究”“应注意犹太人与俄国侨民的关系问题”。在拆分后，译者根据上下文对两句话含义进行理解，并将其从语言维进行重组。第一句表示原因，根据句子间的逻辑关系，接下来应该突出翻译重点信息。因此，译者将“应注意犹太人与俄国侨民的关系问题”放在前面进行翻译，把“犹太人在哈尔滨的历史研究”翻译成状语，并与“1945年8月15日中国抗日战争胜利及后来苏军进入哈尔滨时”进行衔接，使句子简洁明了、逻辑清晰，便于译语读者阅读。

例 9

原文：然而，他又强调，对于一个生活在哈尔滨的中国人来说，从 1918 年至 1945 年 8 月的 28 年，它的差异性是明显的。

译文：However, he emphasizes later that for a Chinese living in Harbin, the 28 years' life—from 1918 to the August of 1945—is obviously different from that of other periods.

分析：在该句中出现了叠加的时间表达，而大多数译者将时间放在句首作为时间状语翻译。译者为了使该表达更加清晰易懂，对该句进行思考，并查阅了相关翻译资料。译者查找平行文本，在《从社会符号学角度研究翻译的必要性》一文中找到了利用标点符号将句子拆分重组，辅助翻译的方法。“标点符号作为文字语言不可缺少的辅助，在语篇中的衔接作用是很明显的。”

（梁丽、王舟，2001：26）译者发现，在案例中常常出现通过运用符号简化复杂句子。在与导师商讨后，译者从语言维选择用“—”对时间进行翻译：“—from 1918 to the August of 1945—”，既保持与源语文本形式的一致，又使译文清晰易懂。借助符号，将句子进行拆句重组，使译文结构更加清晰，增强译文的可读性。

由以上案例可知，在翻译该文本时，译者充分发挥主观能动性，总结源语和译语的语言特点。译者发现，源语文本语言特点为：句子成分复杂且语句较长。而译语语言特点为：从句较多，句子成分完整清晰。因此，译者从语言维出发，将句子进行拆句重组及省略简化等，帮助译语读者更好地理解作者要传达的信息。

综上所述，就历史文献而言，语句前后之间的逻辑关系十分重要，清楚紧密的逻辑关系有助于读者阅读。为更好地传递原文信息，使译文符合译语的表述方式和习惯，译者根据生态翻译理论的指导，从语言维对原文中的词汇、句子采用换词改译、语态转换、拆句重组等翻译方法，以此做到语言维度的适应性选择，使译文忠实原文，便于理解，且从语言表达层面消除阅读障碍。

5.2.4.2　文化维的适应性选择转换

“一种语言代表一种文化。文化包括民族的思维方式、心理意识、语言习惯、历史传统、习俗信仰、地域风貌等一系列因素。从某种意义上说，翻译就是翻译文化。”（方梦之，2013：3）语言是文化的符号，文化通过语言传递，不同的语言传递出不同的文化。面对不同的文化差异，文化维的适应性选择转换，要求译者更多地关注双语文化内涵的传递和阐释。译者要准确把握两种语言背后的文化现象及文化差异，在源语与译语中找到翻译的平衡点。在面对文化负载词的翻译时，译者应适当地采取文化意象保留或省略处理、增加注释或文化借用等方式，避免文化差异造成阅读影响。

① 文化意象去留。

历史文献著作中常常富含历史文化因素，作者在写作时常常会使用成语、俗语，以及一些特殊的历史文化负载词。在翻译这些词汇时，译者首先应考虑词汇中的文化意象以及文化特征。“文化意象并不是孤立的语言符号，而是由表示文化意象的语言符号与文化意义化合而成的。”（王青，2015：230）面对词语中的文化意象，译者需要分析源语与译语的文化差异，从文化维对词汇中的意象进行保留或去除处理，将源语与译语中相同的文化意象进行保留，不同的文化意象进行省略处理。例 10、例 11 保留了文化意象，例 12 省略了文化意象，以此做到文化维的适应性选择，促进文化交流与传播。

例 10

原文：第二次是 19 世纪末叶以后数十年里为逃避<u>反犹恶浪</u>、革命和内战来沪谋生的俄国（阿什肯那兹）犹太人。

译文：The second wave referred to the Russian (Ashkenazi) Jews who came to Shanghai in the decades after the end of the 19th century to escape the <u>anti-Semitic wave</u>, revolution, and civil war.

分析：在该句中，"反犹恶浪"一词的翻译较为复杂。在翻译"反犹恶浪"一词时，译者首先在百度翻译和有道翻译进行查询，分别得到了"The Anti-Semitic Wave of Evil"和"Anti-semitism sea"的英文翻译。百度翻译将"恶浪"翻译成"Wave of Evil"，带有情感色彩；而有道翻译则进行了省略翻译。另外，"Anti-Semitic"翻译为反对犹太人的，而"Anti-semitism"翻译成反犹主义，为了突出两个词的区别，译者在"Bing"搜索引擎中查找，询问历史系教授及查阅文本后，得到了关于"反犹恶浪"的文化背景信息。在一般情况下，"反犹"是一种把整个犹太人群体作为迫害和排挤对象的社会现象、社会思潮与社会行为，而"恶浪"则是指凶猛的势头。面对带有历史性质的词语，译者首先要考虑文化背景的适应性选择。"反犹恶浪"一词充分地体现了反对犹太人这一历史现象。因此，译者根据生态翻译理论的指导，从文化维进行剖析，保留文化意象，将"反犹"翻译成更便于理解的"Anti-Semitic"一词，旨在表明反对犹太人的一切现象、思潮和行为。而"反犹恶浪"中的"恶"字则被省略处理，翻译成中性词语"waves"，规避文化差异及译语读者可能为犹太人的尴尬现象，保留文化痕迹。

例 11

原文：之所以强调亚俄和欧俄的来源地域，主要是可以对不同的犹太群体进行研究和分析，因为犹太人是由于不同原因来到哈尔滨的，有的是来哈尔滨"<u>淘金</u>"，有的是来哈尔滨"逃难"，从而实现犹太人在哈尔滨的"整体"研究。

译文：The main reason for emphasizing the geographical origin of Asian and European Jews is to study and analyze different Jewish groups, because Jews came to Harbin for various reasons, some to "<u>seek gold</u>" and some to "escape", thus the study of the Jews in Harbin as a whole is realized. The "whole" is not a simple superposition of "regions", but an organically linked "whole" of each "region".

分析：在翻译"淘金"一词时，因为原文作者将"淘金"一词添加了引号，所以译者并不知道是应该保留文化意象进行翻译，还是应该对词语进行意译处理。面对这一困境，译者首先在百度网页搜索“淘金”一词，得到的解释为“用水选法去沙取金，也比喻在繁复的事物中寻找出有益的、适宜自己的事物”。译者查找有道、DeepL 等翻译工具，得到的结果为“gold washing”“panning”等词。面对不同的翻译，译者查询了“淘金”一词的出处与起源。在《魏书·食货志》中记载：“又汉中旧有金户千余家，常于汉水沙淘金，年终总输。”而在 19 世纪，美国加利福尼亚曾出现淘金热。该词在两种语言中表示相同的含义，有着相同的文化背景。而译者在查询平行文本《论翻译中文化意象的保留》中得知，具有相同文化背景的词语，可以保留文化意象。对此，译者从文化维角度出发保留文化意象，将“金”译为“gold”，将“淘”译为“seek”。面对相同的文化背景，译者保留文化意象，使译语读者能更好地理解词汇要表达的含义，从而加深读者对源语文本的理解。

例 12

原文：俄国国内的 1905 年革命和 1917 年十月革命再次引发了犹太人的迁移浪潮，一些不承认新生苏维埃政权的白俄便失去了国籍，其中，大部分是犹太人，背井离乡去寻求谋生机会成为他们唯一的选择。

译文：The 1905 Revolution in Russia and the October Revolution of 1917 triggered another wave of Jewish migration, and some Belorussians who did not recognize the new Soviet regime lost their citizenship, most of them Jews, and left their homeland in search of livelihood opportunities.

分析：在翻译“背井离乡”时，这一词语为汉语成语，面对特殊词汇的翻译，译者需要仔细斟酌其译文。为此，译者首先在《现代汉语词典》(第 7 版）中进行查询，得到的结果为“离开了故土，在外地生活（多指不得已的）”。而该成语中“井”为文化意象。译者查阅《孟子·滕文公上》得到的结果为：“方里而井，井九百亩，其中为公田。”因此，“井”的引申含义为“家乡、故乡”。而在译语文化中，“井”常常翻译成“wells”，“wells”在英文中多指“油井”。面对两种文化中的差异，译者在有道、CNKI 学术在线翻译、百度等在线翻译得到结果均为“Uprooted from home”“leave one’s hometown”“be forced to leave one’s hometown”。翻译软件均省略了“井”这一意象。译者参考了《中国古典诗词意象翻译策略——兼谈中国文化对外传播》一文根据上下文含义进行分析，该句重点强调犹太人离开家乡去寻找新的发展机会。因此，译者从文化维对该词中“井”的文化意象进行省略处理，将该词译成“left their homeland”。从文化维省略文化意象，使译文更容易理解，避免文化差异。

综上所述，在翻译源语文本时，译者常常会遇到文化负载词。面对文化负载词的翻译，首先，译者需要了解两种语言间的文化背景知识、考虑源语与译语的文化差异，以及充分了解源语文化负载词中意象的含义与该词的整体含义。其次，译者需要根据译语文化，从文化维出发，对意象的翻译进行保留或省略处理，以此达到两者文化之间的平衡，实现文化维的适应性选择。

② 文化缺省。

“文化缺省是指作者在与其意向读者交流时双方共有的相关文化背景知识的省略。”（王大来，2004：68）在源语文本中，常常会出现源语文化中特有的词汇，而这些词汇在译语文本中没有与之对应的词汇，或者这些词汇在译语文化中代表截然不同的含义。面对这一情况，译者在翻译时应考虑文化缺省问题，从文化维出发，对词语加以解释或规避文化差异带来的困扰。

例 13

原文：俄国犹太人到哈尔滨后，由于受到白俄等因素的影响，没有站住脚就继续向关内的天津、青岛和上海等地流动。

译文：After the arrival of Russian Jews in Harbin, due to the influence of Belarus and other factors, they continued to flow to Tianjin, Qingdao, Shanghai and other places inside the Shanhai Pass without settlement.

分析：在该句中，“关内”是一个中国特有的历史文化负载词，而译语中并不存在与之对应的词语。因此，首先，译者在百度搜索“关内”一词，得到的结果为“山海关以西或嘉峪关以东一带地区”。面对历史文化负载词，译者需要考虑文化维的适应性选择。在翻译时，译者应将该词指代的地理文化进行翻译，尽可能找到约定俗成的翻译。其次，译者查找相关的平行文本翻译、相关论文的历史文化负载词翻译，以及在CNKI学术在线翻译中得到山海关的翻译为“Shanhai Pass”。最终，译者将“关内”一词翻译成“inside the Shanhai Pass”，使译语读者便于理解译文。

例 14

原文：犹太人在上海的系统宏观研究开始于潘光、王健的《一个半世纪以来的上海犹太人——犹太民族史上的东方一页》，此书从“整体”考察了上海犹太人的来龙去脉。

译文：The systematic macroscopic study of Jews in Shanghai began with Pan Guang and Wang Jian's *The Jews of Shanghai over a Century and a Half-An Oriental Page in the History of the Jewish People*, which examined origin and development of Shanghai Jews from a holistic perspective.

分析：“来龙去脉”一词为汉语成语，有着极其浓厚的语言文化气息。成语中含有“龙”这一动物，而这种动物在英汉两种语言中有着天差地别的含义。在中国，“龙”为褒义，代表吉祥高贵；而在西方，“龙”代表恶魔。面对文化差异，译者应对文化缺省问题进行规避处理。

因此，译者根据生态翻译理论的三维转换翻译方法，从文化维对该词进行分析。首先，译者查询《现代汉语词典》(第7版)，“来龙去脉”是指“山形地势像龙一样连贯着。本是迷信的人讲风水的话，后来比喻人、物的来历或事情发展的前因后果”。面对两种语言的文化差异，译者充分考虑文化维的适应性选择。其次，译者在查询百度、谷歌等翻译辅助工具后得到“cause and effect”和“origin and development”两种翻译，大多数平行文本也将该词翻译为“origin and development”。在与导师商讨后将该词义译成“origin and development”，既能表达出源语的含义，又能规避文化差异，不影响译语读者阅读。

例 15

原文：1904年，第二波犹太人移民浪潮从俄国涌向哈尔滨。俄国南部基什尼奥夫、敖德萨等地肆虐的集体大屠杀迫使犹太人到满洲寻找飞翔的广阔天空。

译文：In 1904, a second wave of Jewish immigration came to Harbin from Russia. The rampant pogroms in Kishinev and Simodessa in southern Russia forced the Jews to search for a more spacious living in Manchuria (The Manchu nationality)

分析：在翻译“满洲”一词时，译者首先在语料库中搜索，得到该词语的翻译结果为“Manchuria”。而该词的英文是根据汉语的发音进行音译而成的。译者充分考虑到部分译语读者存在不太了解中国历史名称的可能性。面对文化的缺省，可以添加注释。为此，译者根据生态翻译理论，从文化维对该词进行加注翻译。

译者在搜索引擎中查找到对“满洲”的解释为：“满洲”一词原指满族的族称，皇太极改旧族名“诸申”(女真)为“满洲”，清末帝国主义入侵东北以后，把“满洲”一词移用作地名，实则是妄图对中国东北地区进行分裂活动。因此，译者在“Manchuria”后添加了（The Manchu nationality），旨在对该词做进一步解释，从文化维进行转换，帮助译语读者加深对该词的理解，减少阅读障碍。

根据上述案例的分析，面对文化缺省问题，译者应从文化维分析源语与译语的翻译环境，充分考虑两种语言间的文化差异，并思考词语的背景文化，以及词语要表达的含义，进而找到适合源语文本的翻译方法，避免文化差异带来的阅读障碍。

③ 文化借用。

文化借用是通过模仿和应用，有选择地接受外部文化的行为。其中，文化借用是对文化进行适应性选择的过程。译者根据源语文化的特点和含义选取与之相符的外部文化。在翻译时，可借用其他文化来翻译相似的文化，做到文化间的转换，从而避免文化差异。

例 16

原文：第三次是1933—1941年从纳粹统治下的欧洲亡命来沪的犹太难民。

译文：The third consisted of Jewish refugees, the fugitives from Europe under Nazi oppression to Shanghai between 1933 and 1941.

分析：在翻译“亡命来沪”一词时，译者首先结合上下文及译者自身的文化基础对该词进行理解。译者认为，“亡命来沪”一词中“亡命”是指难民，即逃难者，而“来沪”是指来到上海。因此，译者首次将“亡命来沪”翻译成“Refugees coming to Shanghai”。然后，译者在有道翻译对该词进行查询得到的结果为“Escape to Shanghai”，译者在CNKI学术在线翻译查询得到的结果为“Death to Shanghai”。译者将得到的翻译进一步分析，有道翻译将该词翻译成动词——逃跑到上海，而CNKI学术在线翻译将“亡命”翻译成“Death”，名词，指代死亡。因为该词是历史文化负载词，在翻译时应翻译成通俗易懂或约定俗成的词语，使译语读者能快速理解该词的含义。所以，在翻译时，译者在生态翻译理论的指导下，从文化维对该词进一步进行思考并查找相关资料。最终在导师的帮助下，译者找到一部电影，电影的名字为《亡命天涯》，英文名为 *The Fugitive*，该北美电影为奥斯卡获奖作品，1994年在中国大陆地区上映。因此，译者将“亡命来沪”一词结合语境翻译成“the fugitives from Europe under Nazi oppression to Shanghai”，从电影文化角度出发，结合百度翻译将该词翻译成名词形式。既避免与前面一词“refugees”重复，又能引起外国读者共鸣。

例 17

原文：部分原因是"俄国人一般觉得中国更像安乐窝"。

译文：One of the reasons was that "Russians generally regarded China as the garden of Eden".

分析：在翻译"安乐窝"一词时，译者首先在百度上搜索，得到的结果为"安乐窝"是汉语成语，形容安逸的生活环境。译者在有道词典查找到的翻译为"nest of comfort"。"nest of comfort"是对"安乐窝"一词的直译，"nest of comfort"是指舒适的巢穴，但"安乐窝"的含义更广泛，它不仅包括巢穴，还指"安逸的生活环境"。因此，简单地翻译成"nest of comfort"并不能完全契合成语的含义。针对这一情况，译者想到文化的借用。"伊甸园"在《圣经》的原文中含有乐园的意思，指《圣经》中上帝为亚当、夏娃创造的乐园，后世用以比喻幸福美好的生活环境。"安乐窝"和"伊甸园"都指安逸、美好的生活环境。因此，译者从语言维对"安乐窝"一词进行适应性转换，借用"伊甸园"一词进行翻译，翻译成"the garden of Eden"。经过上述调整，译文更加贴近源语文本，加深译语读者对源语文"安乐窝"一词的理解。

由上面两个案例可知，文化借用是指借用读者知道的词汇对源语文本中有相同含义的词语进行翻译，可以使译语读者更好地理解源语文本中特殊词汇的含义，加深对源语文本的理解。在翻译历史文化负载词时，译者需要充分考虑源语国家和译语国家的文化背景，以及两种文化的交集与差异，借助译语读者了解的文化去解释源语中的词汇，并结合作者表达的含义，做到文化维的适应性选择，增强文本的可读性，避免文化差异。

历史文化负载词往往与其悠久的历史文化密不可分，常常引用成语或俗语，给翻译带来一定难度。在生态翻译理论的指导下，译者从文化维对历史文化负载词进行翻译，充分考虑文化意象去留、文化缺省及文化借用来翻译源语文本，使译文更加准确无差异。

5.2.4.3 交际维的适应性选择转换

"交际维转换指的是译者翻译过程中关注双语交际意图的适应选择转换，其要求译者除了考虑语言维和文化维之外，还应当将翻译选择转换的侧重点放在译文的交际层面上，考虑原文中的交际意图是否在译文中得以体现。"（胡庚申，2006：51）换言之，面对译语读者，首先，译者在关注语言表达和背景文化的同时，应充分考虑译语读者的阅读感受。该文本为历史文献文本，面对文本中出现的词语和句子，译者应进行增词补译，以使句子表达得更加充分完整。其次，译者应补充衔接词或句，使句与句之间的逻辑关系更加紧密，以及调整句序，使译文结构更加合理。让读者领悟到原文作者想要表达的深层含义，在情感、思想上与作者产生共鸣。

① 四字格意译。

该文本中出现了少量四字格汉语成语，“语言学家陆志韦于 1965 年提出‘四字格’这个术语”。在翻译这些成语时，译者首先需要分析特定语境中成语的含义。在翻译成语时，应从交际维出发，考虑作者要表达的整体含义，必要时可以省略解释成语的背景知识，将成语进行意译处理。“意译是深悟原意而尽情达意的一种途径。”（周领顺，2019：173）在忠实原文作者的同时，使译文通俗易懂，便于阅读，促进读者的沟通交流。

例 18

原文：俄籍犹太人来时大多一贫如洗，后来有些跻身中产阶级，大富者不多。

译文：Most of the Russian Jews lived from hand to mouth at first, and some later ranked among the middle class and few became wealthy.

分析：“一贫如洗”为汉语成语。在翻译该词时，译者需要考虑作者要传达的含义从而进行翻译。面对成语的翻译，译者秉承严谨认真的态度，首先在谷歌和 DeepL 翻译软件中搜索，得到“poor as church mouse”“as poor as dirt”等翻译，而在中国知网的论文中有 395 篇将该词翻译成“abject poverty”。这些翻译软件均从该词的含义出发，摒弃直译。译者又参考了《成语的直译和意译》一文，文中列举了多个成语的直译与意译翻译。在对比后，译者发现，成语四字格的意译从词语的含义出发，使译语读者便于理解。因此，译者从交际维对该词的翻译逐一进行剖析，并尽最大可能实现交际维的适应性选择。首先，“poor as church mouse”对成语中的比喻进行了翻译，但该词的表达过于陈旧，不利于年轻译语读者阅读。“abject”一词有贬义，而源语文本并未带贬义。最终，译者从交际维考虑，省略修辞，将该词译为“lived from hand to mouth”，而“lived from hand to mouth”的汉译为勉强糊口度日，与“一贫如洗”意义相近，并且该短语更加地道，符合译语读者语言表达习惯，常在交际时使用。在与导师讨论后，译者将该词翻译成“lived from hand to mouth”，从交际维度出发，最大限度地减少文化交流障碍，使译文既忠实原文，又通俗易懂。

例19

原文：结果遭遇到华尔街股市1929年的黑色风暴，血本无归。

译文：only to be hit by the 1929 blackout of the Wall Street stock market and lost all the capital invested.

分析：在翻译“血本无归”时，译者首先在《现代汉语词典》(第7版）中查找了“血本”的中文解释，词典给出的解释为“辛苦积攒起来的本钱；老本儿”，译者还咨询了经济管理学院的教授关于“血本无归”在经济学中的含义，得到的答案为投资失败。而词语中“血本”这一意象翻译较为复杂。在《也谈如何翻译汉语的四字格词语——基于MTI课堂教学的观察所得》这一平行文本中，译者发现可对四字格成语进行意译。由此，译者从交际维出发对该词进行意译，分析这句话中作者要表达的含义是在投资失败后损失了拥有的全部钱财。而译者在有道词典中找到的对应翻译为“lost everything”，结合上文中提到的“华尔街股市”，译者以交际为最终目的，结合该句的上下文，保留“lost”、将“everything”转换成“all the capital invested”，更大限度上强调投资的失败，与“血本无归”的程度相同，忠实原文。

例20

原文：这仅是中国和犹太文化互动“整体”的冰山一角，其他方面还有待深入研究。

译文：This is just a blip of the “whole” of the interaction between Chinese and Jewish cultures, and other aspects need to be studied in depth.

分析：在翻译“冰山一角”时，译者首先在《现代汉语词典》(第7版）中查找到该词语的中文解释为“比喻事物已经显露出来的一小部分”。该词既含有褒义，又含有贬义。译者在百度上查到该词的出处发现，它是由英语“tip of an iceberg”衍化而来的，因为“tip of an iceberg”的字面意思就是“冰山一角”。随后，译者在谷歌和有道等翻译软件上发现该词的翻译“tip of an iceberg”多用于含有贬义的句子中。而该句作者想要表达的含义是已研究探讨了小部分，还需要深入研究，并不含有贬义。对此，译者从交际维出发，根据上下文，将该词义译成中性词语“just a blip”进行翻译。既保留了原文作者表达的含义，又避免了在交际中褒贬理解的偏差，从交际维强化历史文献译文的准确性与严谨性。

例 21

原文：从《哈尔滨犹太简明辞书》可以看出，犹太人在哈尔滨的银行业“叱咤风云”，华俄道胜银行、花旗银行、法亚银行、汇丰银行、协和银行、信济银行、犹太国民银行、远东银行、华美银行等都有犹太人的“影子”，犹太人或亲自出马，或潜居台后。

译文：According to *The Harbin Jewish Concise Dictionary*, it can be seen that the Jews in Harbin's banking industry "took the lead"—China and Russia Dawson Bank, Citibank, Faja Bank, HSBC, Concord Bank, Shinji Bank, Jewish National Bank, Far Eastern Bank, Huamei Bank and so on all have the "presence of the Jews". The Jews were either personally present or behind the scenes.

分析：该句中出现带引号的成语“叱咤风云”，它在《现代汉语词典》(第7版)中的含义为“形容声势威力很大”。而该词在有道翻译和百度翻译均为“all-powerful”，在 CNKI 在线翻译中为“Riding the Whirlwind”。译者对翻译结果逐一分析：“all-powerful”一词主要指全能的，无所不能的，而“Riding the Whirlwind”主要指气吞山河，两词代指“叱咤风云”一词的不同角度。在翻译四字格的历史文化负载词时，应尽可能避免文化差异。因此，译者根据生态翻译理论，对该词所在的语境进行源语情况分析，原文作者想要表达的含义为“犹太人在哈尔滨的银行业占据主导地位”。因此，译者从交际维出发，仿照 CNKI 在线翻译的“Riding the Whirlwind”形式，将该词义译成“took the lead”。译者从交际维出发，将四字格成语意译化繁为简，增强译文的可读性，便于译文的传播与交流。

由以上情况可知，源语文本的翻译目的在于历史的传播与发展。因此，面对文本中四字格成语的翻译，译者应从交际维出发，采用意译的翻译方式对文本进行翻译。以传达作者的意图为根本目的，化繁为简，实现交际维度的适应性选择。

② 增词补译。

历史文献是对特定地区发生的重大事件进行记载，往往是面向国内大众的，因此文本中对共识的知识背景或部分语句的引申含义进行了简化处理，没有进行详细解释。而且，文本中常常会出现汉语中特有的省略成分的表达习惯。然而，译文受众多是外国读者，缺少原文生态语境，在表达方式上也存在差异。“源语中总有某些表达方式在目标语中无法找到对应的词句，这就需要译者在翻译中始终要有跨文化意识，灵活运用增译和补译。”(赵远珍，2006：191)因此，在翻译时，译者多从交际维出发，根据上下文含义，考虑译文的可接受性，进行适应性转换，力求最大限度地保留源语风格，明确交际意图，对信息进行转化或补译，便于读者阅读。

例 22

原文：从宏观到微观研究

译文：Shift from macro-research to micro-research

分析：在翻译这个小标题时，译者根据其含义，首先将该标题翻译为“from macro to micro research”。但根据文章内容译者发现，下文提到的研究是从宏观研究到微观研究的一个转变，直译会导致标题不能充分体现下文内容的变化，且无法保证信息的完整性。译者得到启发，将缺少的信息词汇进行补译，使句意完整。基于以上，译者结合生态翻译理论，从交际维出发，增加词语“转变”这一信息，确保标题含义准确严谨，促使原文与译文的信息等值传递。因此，译者在《牛津高阶英汉双解词典》(第 9 版)、《柯林斯高阶英汉双解学习词典》(第 8 版）中分别查询，“shift”和“transform”“convert”3 个词语，“shift”是指情况、意见、政策、态度等的改变，“transform”强调外观或性质的改观，“convert”则为宗教信仰、观点、习惯的转变。经过分析，译者选择“shift”一词进行翻译。译者在“宏观”后面也添加了“research”一词，突出研究的转变，让行文流畅。增词补译的方法使标题与正文内容保持联系，从交际维加深了读者对下文内容的精准理解。

例 23

原文：笔者认为，经济活动等是微观研究的一个重要领域。一是因为犹太人是以经济活动或经济实力而为人所瞩目的，犹太人是以此而著称于世界的；二是犹太人的经济活动与国际关系紧密相连。

译文：In the author’s view, economic activities, etc., are an important area of microscopic research. The reasons are as follows: first, Jews are well known for their economic activities or economic power all over the world; second, Jewish economic activities are closely linked to international relations.

分析：译者在翻译这一段话时发现，第一句话为作者观点，第二句话则为原因。起初，译者直接按照原文的顺序进行翻译。但译者根据上下文理解，发现作者主要强调观点的原因，即“经济活动等是微观研究的一个重要领域”的原因。在与导师商讨后，译者在作者观点与原因之间添加过渡句，来凸显句子间的逻辑关系。许家金和徐秀玲（2016）说：译文中增添了有助于译文读者理解的显化表达，或者说将原文隐含的信息显化于译文中，使意思更明确，逻辑更清楚。因此，译者从交际维出发，在观点与原因中添加"The reasons are as follows"来显化句子和句子之间的内在逻辑，体现作者要表达的意图，让读者感受到犹太人的经济活动值得深入研究与探讨。

例 24

原文：但黑龙江和哈尔滨也具有自身的优越条件，应进行深入细致的"区域"考察和反思，实现黑龙江和以色列的"整体"共赢。

译文：However, the superior conditions of Heilongjiang and Harbin should be thoroughly investigated and introspected, so as to achieve a "whole" win-win situation between Heilongjiang and Israel.

分析：在翻译这个句子时，译者发现，前半句"但黑龙江和哈尔滨也具有自身的优越条件"是完整的"主谓宾"结构，而后半句"应进行"前面缺少主语。对此，译者将该句分别在百度、有道等在线翻译器中进行翻译，百度翻译与有道翻译分别用"they"和"it"进行代替。但根据上下文译者发现，"they"或"it"并不能清晰地表明主语。译者从交际的意图出发，将该句"但黑龙江和哈尔滨也具有自身的优越条件"进行转换，转换成所属关系即"黑龙江和哈尔滨的优越条件"为主语，把"应进行深入细致的'区域'考察和反思"的动宾结构转换成谓语动词，即"深入地考察和反思"。在确定主干的关系后，译者考虑到译语读者习惯用被动的表达方式，将两句话整合成一个句子，翻译为"the superior conditions of Heilongjiang and Harbin should be thoroughly investigated and introspected"，并在句中添加"so as"进行增词补译，加强句子间的逻辑关系。译者对影响译文阅读的"区域"一词进行省略处理，充分考虑交际维的适应性选择。

汉语文化博大精深，汉语的表达形式多样。在汉语的语言习惯中，会出现省略主语，或出现词语的引申含义等情况。面对这些情况，译者要从交际维对源语文本进行增词补译。在翻译时，补充句子结构，使之更符合译语读者的语言习惯。此外，补充作者的引申含义，也能使译文更加清晰明了。

③ 语序调整。

"翻译，既有其人文艺术学科的特质，也有其作为语言交流手段的属性。"（施屹立，2011：194）在汉语中，定语修饰语和状语修饰语往往位于被修饰语之前；在英语中，许多修饰语常常位于被修饰语之后。不同的表达，在译文中就会有不同的体现。因此，根据生态翻译理论，译者从交际维进行适应性选择的转换。在翻译时，往往要对原文的语序进行调整，将汉语长句按照英语的交际习惯，进行前后调换，或按意群进行倒置，其原则是使英语语句安排符合英语的逻辑顺序，从而便于交际。

例 25

原文：然而，由于相关资料的限制和研究思路的制约等原因，近几年我国学者对犹太人来华史的研究出现“瓶颈”。

译文：However, due to lack of references, as well as the restriction of thinking patterns and other reasons, recently, Chinese scholars encounter research bottleneck in this field.

分析：在翻译“研究出现‘瓶颈’”时，“瓶颈”一词带引号，而在汉语中，带引号的词语大多有其引申含义。因此，译者首先在《现代汉语词典》(第7版)中查找“瓶颈”一词的全部解释后得知，“瓶颈”的本身含义是指瓶子最细、最窄的一部分。但是，随着词语的更新换代，“瓶颈”的深层含义是指易生阻碍的部分。译者最开始按照其引申含义将“瓶颈”翻译成“barrier”，而《牛津高阶英汉双解词典》(第9版)将其翻译成“bottleneck”，“bottleneck”本身就含有阻碍的意思。因此，译者确定“瓶颈”一词翻译为“bottleneck”。

而“瓶颈”一词带有引号，从交际维来看，译者将“bottleneck”一词置于句中，并分析句子结构。该句的主语为“研究”，谓语为“出现”，宾语为“瓶颈”。但经过译者反复阅读原文，研究主语为物，“物”不能主动“出现”。在加以分析后，译者发现，作者想要表达“我国学者在对犹太人来华史的研究中遇到困难”。因此，译者从交际维出发将“研究出现‘瓶颈’”颠倒词语顺序，翻译成“遇到研究‘瓶颈’”即“encounter research bottleneck”。在调整语序后，原句中“研究学者”为主语，“遇到研究‘瓶颈’”为动宾结构。在语序调整后，使译文逻辑更加清晰，句意通俗易懂，提高译文翻译质量，促进信息交流。

例 26

原文：对于犹太人在上海的历史分期，研究者给出比较明晰的划分和解释，基本没有争论。

译文：The historical phasing of the Jews in Shanghai is basically uncontroversial, since researchers have given relatively clear divisions and explanations.

分析：在翻译该句时，最后半句“基本没有争论”如果直接按照字面顺序进行翻译，就可能会给译语读者带来困惑——是“犹太人在上海的历史分期，基本没有争论”还是“研究者给出比较明晰的划分和解释，基本没有争论”？对此，译者首先对该句的结构进行梳理，试图通过分析句子结构，找到翻译突破口。

在原文中，“对于犹太人在上海的历史分期”为状语，“研究者”为主语，“给出”为谓语动词，“划分和解释”为宾语，“基本没有争论”是补语，表用以解释说明。在分析完句子结构后，译者又在百度、有道、谷歌等翻译软件进行翻译，得到的结果均将该句拆分成两个分句“As for the historical stages of Jews in Shanghai, researchers have given relatively clear division and interpretation, and there is no debate”。译者发现，翻译软件都是按照正常语序对译文进行翻译的。但根据生态翻译理论，译者应充分考虑译语读者的阅读习惯——重点优先地表达。因此，在与导师商讨后，译者从交际维对该句的语序进行调整。将“犹太人在上海的历史分期”作为句子的主语，将句子翻译成主系表结构，以此强调“犹太人在上海的历史分期是没有争议的”，把“研究者给出比较明晰的划分和解释”作为从句进行翻译。忠实原文作者表达的含义，规避表述不清造成的交际偏差。

例 27

原文：然而，犹太人来哈尔滨的历史分期却有五六种不同的说法。特迪·考夫曼的分期是早期哈尔滨犹太社区（1898—1914）、鼎盛时期的哈尔滨犹太社区（1914—1931）、日本占领下的哈尔滨（1931—1945）和苏联军队的到来四个时期。

译文：Teddy Kaufman divided the history into four periods: the early Harbin Jewish community (1898-1914), the prosperous period of the Harbin Jewish community (1914-1931), the period under Japanese occupation (1931-1945), and the arrival of Soviet troops.

分析：在翻译该句时，译者发现，该句出现了“四个时期”，“四个时期”的名称和时间在前，总结语在后，直接按照原文顺序翻译，不能显化句子与句子之间的逻辑关系。在中国经济出版社编辑张博的建议下，译者对句子进行语序调整，以此显化句子间的逻辑关系。译者在分析后发现，该句强调的重点即为“四个时期”，应在译文中加以提示，突出强调。

从交际维出发，应该使译文更加简洁，逻辑性更强。译者受到《标点符号辅助翻译研究》平行文本的启发，发现在翻译时可以添加特殊符号来提示重要信息。因此，译者将“四个时期”放在句首，对句子进行语序调整，并添加冒号引起读者对下文中重点信息的注意。以此帮助译语读者进行阅读，使译文条理清晰，逻辑关系明确。

例 28

原文：王志军的“无论面对沙俄、苏联、中国地方势力，还是日本人的统治，哈尔滨犹太人社区基本上能与当政者搞好关系，自身基本在‘发展’中”“哈尔滨犹太人社区在不同的政权时期，性质上不应该存在根本的区别”的观点是值得商榷的。

译文：Wang Zhijun's view is questionable—“whether facing Tsarist Russia, the Soviet Union, local Chinese forces, or Japanese rule, the Jewish community in Harbin basically managed to have good relations with those in power and was basically ‘developing’ itself” and that “there should be no fundamental difference in the nature of the Jewish community in Harbin during different regimes”.

分析：在翻译该句时，译者发现句子较长，逻辑关系不明确。对此，译者对该句进行语法分析，该句主要强调“王志军的观点是值得商榷的”。译者从交际维对句子的语序进行调整，将句中“观点是值得商榷的”放在句首，将句中语序进行调换。为凸显“王志军的观点”这一关键信息，译者受到《破折号辅助英汉翻译》这一平行文本的启发，在翻译时添加破折号对句中“王志军的观点”进行解释说明。经过上述调整，避免了译文头重脚轻的情况，增强文章的可读性，实现语言环境的适应性选择，增强信息交际。

由以上案例分析可知，语序调整在历史文献文本中常常发挥着重要的作用，适当的语序调整可以使译文逻辑性紧密，便于译语读者阅读，对文化的交际起着至关重要的作用。

综上所述，译者充分考虑到源语文本内容，从语言、文化、交际三个维度对译文进行分析。语言维主要采用换词转译、语态转换、拆句重组；文化维主要分析文化意象去留、文化缺省、文化借用等问题；交际维主要进行四字格意译、增词补译、语序调整等翻译，争取做到译文逻辑严谨、忠实通顺。基于生态翻译理论得到的译文在内容上达到了规范、准确的预期效果，体现了生态翻译理论对历史文献文本的指导性作用。

5.2.5 总结

本次翻译实践是译者初次接到的笔译任务，在导师的帮助下，译者根据翻译任务查找资料、规划时间、制订计划、选取理论等来完成此次翻译实践，在此次翻译过程中，译者收获颇多。本节着重从翻译心得与收获、翻译过程中遇到的问题与对策等角度，对本次翻译实践进行阐述总结。

5.2.5.1 心得与收获

经过此次翻译，译者不但积累了大量的翻译经验，而且阅读了 *Jewish migration and the development of the Swedish and Finnish garment industry*, *Israeli-Jewish immigrants in Germany: An assessment of the destination-language acquisition model and the role of Holocaust memory* 等外文平行文本，提高了阅读速度及信息提取能力。本次翻译实践经过了长期的翻译、修改、润色，译者甚至会为一个单词的翻译查询大量的平行文本，这一过程大大提高了译者的搜索能力，锻炼了译者的心性。

① 深入了解历史文献文本语言风格与特点。

此次翻译实践的译本具有语言简练规范、严谨实用的特点。在译前准备阶段，译者通过对文本类型及内容的分析，对该文本的行文特点有了初步了解。

在词汇层面，《近现代史上犹太人来华史研究路径探究》文本中有较多历史文化负载词及四字格词汇，有强烈的文化色彩和时代特征。

在句法层面，《近现代史上犹太人来华史研究路径探究》文本中大量使用严谨、正式的句子结构，主要为作者的观点及阐述，部分句子充满历史文献类文本浓重的历史色彩。

经过深入的实践操作和与平行文本的对比，译者在术语翻译的准确性及语言表达的规范性等方面均有所提升。由于翻译文本具有历史性，前期需摄入大量背景知识，进而扩充了译者在该领域的知识储备。

② 灵活掌握生态翻译理论在历史文献翻译中的运用。

在翻译过程中，译者积极检索纸质书籍及电子书籍，深入学习生态翻译理论的相关知识，阅读大量与生态翻译理论相关的资料文献，探求该理论对本次翻译实践的指导作用。译者细致研究翻译技巧与翻译方法及策略间的差异，运用恰当技巧进行英译实践，把翻译活动放到整个生态环境中去。在翻译历史文献实践材料时，译者结合西方人社会思想的翻译方法和思维方式，融合西方的生态环境因素、原著作者、译者及生态翻译环境，在“多维度适应与适应性选择”的原则之下，将历史文献从语言维、文化维和交际维进行分析与翻译。

5.2.5.2 问题与对策

在本次翻译实践过程中，译者虽然收获颇多，但也发现了在翻译过程中存在的不足。译者对术语翻译与理论选用两个问题进行分析总结，并寻找解决问题的策略，以期为下次的翻译实践做充足的准备并奠定良好的基础。

① 术语翻译之难——多方研讨、验证表达。

译者通过分析历史文献术语的特征，明确了术语应当如何确定与统一。

其一，历史文献文本重点在于历史传承和文化的交流传播，其历史性、严谨性与逻辑性较强，因此译者运用了多种翻译辅助工具进行查阅，通过纸质词典、电子词典、术语查询网站等多方横向比较，根据新闻背景类型选择数据库，确定和统一词义。

其二，文章中含有较多历史事件等名称类术语，这种词汇具有一定的历史背景，为了避免翻译错误造成不便，译者查询大量的平行文本及在线翻译软件，确定约定俗成的表达形式。

其三，一些术语具有一词多义的现象，在不同领域、不同语境下有不同的含义，这种术语没有统一规范的译文，给译者带来了巨大挑战。因此，译者灵活运用各种翻译辅助工具，结合生态翻译理论中的三维转换以及目的语读者的表达习惯等来确定词义，灵活变通地传递等值信息，消除交流障碍。

② 理论选用之难——缜密分析、确定理论。

翻译任务能否顺利完成，在一定程度上也取决于翻译理论的选择。首先，译者借助文本类型理论，深入分析《近现代史上犹太人来华史研究路径探究》的历史文本类型，并对照平行文本掌握该书的行文特点。其次，译者通过多方搜集资料，探究多种翻译理论的内容及特点，结合数篇高质量论文及书籍，筛选出符合该文本翻译的理论。最后，译者选择生态翻译理论来指导本次翻译实践。译者在数月的翻译历程中发现，根据生态翻译理论中的三维转换完成的译文既能完整准确地传达源语信息，又能实现译文的可交际意义。经过不断地修改润色，最后达到内容忠实原文、形式连贯通顺的效果。与此同时，也反向印证了该理论在本次实践中发挥的指导作用。

5.2.5.3 努力方向和展望

在此次翻译实践后，译者感触颇多，对翻译有了进一步的认识，找到了自身的不足与努力方向，对未来的翻译事业有了全新的期待。

译者深刻地认识到翻译这门学科的博大精深。翻译之深奥要求译者不断通过实践提升自己的翻译能力。译者会继续努力学习翻译知识，夯实基础。只有努力地进行一次又一次的实践，才能时刻更新自己的翻译思维，提高翻译水平，以便未来可以从容不迫地应对各种翻译。以后再遇到类似文本或其他类文本时，译者会良好地运用这次实践收获的经验，继续使用生态翻译理论对文本进行分析和阐释，合理利用本次实践掌握的大量专业词汇和翻译方法，争取产出质量更高的译文。

作为一名翻译硕士研究生，不仅要坚持不懈地刻苦钻研，坚持向身边的同行与导师请教，还要对自己的专业保持热情。翻译过程的每个步骤都有需要学习的地方，翻译过程中的每次成功都需要集结身边人来共同取得，一山更比一山高。译者希望未来能继续进行更多的翻译研究，学习各种不同的翻译理论，请教身边的诸多良师益友，以此来取得翻译生涯的长足进步。经过这次实践，译者下定决心提高自己的专业水平，继续保持谦逊，勤学好问，与人为善，成为一名触类旁通的译者，立志在翻译的路途上走得更远。

参考文献

[1] BLUM N AND FEE E. The Sungari River Flood and the Jewish Community in Harbin, China[J]. American Journal of Public Health, 2008, 98(5): 823.

[2] DAL B F. “book–review” A Universal Art: Hebrew Grammar across Disciplines and Faiths (Studies in Jewish History and Culture 46)[J]. Speculum, 2018, 93(1): 281–283.

[3] EKHOLM L. Jewish Migration and the Development of the Swedish and Finnish Garment Industry[J]. Jewish Culture and History, 2023, 24(1): 76–95.

[4] GABRIELLA K. About the Definition, Classification, and Translation Strategies of Idioms[J]. Acta Universitatis Sapientiae, Philologica, 2016, 8(3): 85–101.

[5] KATO D. Eco–Translation: Translation and Ecology in the Age of the Anthropocene[J]. Interdisciplinary Studies in Literature and Environment, 2017, 24(4): 827–829.

[6] KUHNE J. Canon in Exile. Readings by German–Jewish Emigrants in Palestine/Israel[J]. German Studies Review, 2021, 44(2): 416–419.

[7] PRESNER T S. The Translated Jew: German Jewish Culture outside the Margins by Leslie Morris (review)[J]. AJS Review: The Journal of the Association for Jewish Studies, 2022, 44(1): 218–220.

[8] REBHUN U. Israeli–Jewish Immigrants in Germany: An Assessment of the Destination–language Acquisition Model and the Role of Holocaust Memory[J]. Population, Space and Place, 2022, 29(1).

[9] SEIDELMAN R. Between Exile and Exodus: Argentinian Jewish Immigration to Israel, 1948–1967 by Sebastian Klor (review)[J]. AJS Review: The Journal of the Association for Jewish Studies, 2022, 44(1): 222–224.

[10] 陈海燕 . 浅析中华思想文化术语翻译中的难点 [J]. 中国翻译，2015，36

（5）：13–17.
[11] 丁伟祥 . 德汉翻译中的词类转换和翻译技巧 [J]. 同济大学学报（社会科学版），2003（4）：109–115.
[12] 方梦之 . 论翻译生态环境 [J]. 上海翻译，2011（1）：1–5.
[13] 方梦之 . 再论翻译生态环境 [J]. 中国翻译，2020，41（5）：20–27，190.
[14] 耿强 . 中国翻译理论话语：内涵与意义 [J]. 上海翻译，2020（3）：7–11，95.
[15] 过家鼎 . 成语的直译和意译 [J]. 上海翻译，2008，94（1）：66–68.
[16] 胡庚申 . 从术语看译论：翻译适应选择论概观 [J]. 上海翻译，2008，95（2）：1–5.
[17] 胡庚申 . 翻译适应选择论 [M]. 武汉：湖北教育出版社，2004.
[18] 胡庚申 . 翻译研究“生态范式”的理论建构 [J]. 中国翻译，2019，40（4）：24–33，188.
[19] 胡庚申 . 例示“适应选择论”的翻译原则和翻译方法 [J]. 外语与外语教学，2006（3）：49–52，65.
[20] 胡庚申 . 生态翻译学 [M]. 北京：商务印书馆，2013.
[21] 胡庚申 . 生态翻译学的研究焦点与理论视角 [J]. 中国翻译，2011，32（2）：5–9，95.
[22] 李海军 .《中国评论》汉英翻译和中国文化西传研究 [J]. 中国翻译，2022，43（5）：30–37，191.
[23] 梁丽，王舟 . 标点符号的语篇衔接功能与英汉翻译中的信息处理 [J]. 中国翻译，2001（4）：26–29.
[24] 刘川，段跃萍 . 跨文化差异与词汇翻译 [J]. 中国翻译，1996（1）：31–32.
[25] 刘岩，陈胜能 . 历史文献翻译与《中国省别全志（贵州卷）》汉译初探 [J]. 东方翻译，2021，69（1）：20–26，58.
[26] 吕守贵 . 英译汉中的补译法 [J]. 外语与外语教学，1987（1）：40–44.
[27] 彭桂芝 . 论翻译中文化意象的保留 [J]. 华中师范大学学报（人文社会科学版），2002（4）：133–137.
[28] 唐根金 . 也谈如何翻译汉语的四字格词语：基于 MTI 课堂教学的观察所得 [J]. 上海翻译，2020，150（1）：71–75，95.
[29] 佟颖 . 从社会符号学角度研究翻译的必要性 [J]. 天津外国语大学学报，2013，20（5）：21–25.
[30] 王大来 . 从翻译的文化功能看翻译中文化缺省补偿的原则 [J]. 外语研究，2004（6）：68–70，77.
[31] 王宁霞 . 翻译过程中的转换现象浅析 [J]. 语言与翻译，2006（4）：55–57.

[32] 王琦，杜禹萱 . 对哈尔滨犹太历史文化遗存价值的思考 [J]. 黑龙江史志，2021，425（6）：15–20，29.
[33] 王青 . 文化意象的互文性与翻译补偿 [J]. 沈阳大学学报（社会科学版），2015，17（2）：230–233.
[34] 徐昌和 . 英汉翻译中的词义引申 [J]. 中国科技翻译，2009，22（2）：10–13.
[35] 许家金，徐秀玲 . 基于可比语料库的翻译英语衔接显化研究 [J]. 外语与外语教学，2016（6）：94–102，122，150.
[36] 杨红 . 被动语态的翻译研究 [J]. 中国科技翻译，2010，23（3）：23，57–59.
[37] 施屹立 . 英汉翻译中语序调整的就近原则 [J]. 上海理工大学学报（社会科学版），2011，33（3）：194–200.
[38] 张梅岗 . 名词性从句的拆句译法 [J]. 中国翻译，1999（5）：26–28.
[39] 周领顺 . 意译：文学性增强的有效途径 [J]. 中国翻译，2019，40（4）：173–177.

5.3 《关于“犹太人在哈尔滨”的历史文化研究的几点思考》英译研究

犹太人移民哈尔滨这一事件在中国近代历史上具有不可忽视的重要性，众多犹太人在该地组建家庭，发展事业，并在当地社会中扮演着不可或缺的角色。除此之外，犹太人移民哈尔滨还对犹太人移民史有着至关重要的影响和意义，它不仅是犹太人在中国移民历史中的重要部分，而且是世界犹太人历史中一个不可或缺的、值得深入探究的篇章。

据此，译者选取了历史文本《清末民初黑龙江移民史研究》中的研究之十作为翻译实践源语文本。因其文本的专业性，在翻译时，译者需要保持严谨的学术态度，运用科学的翻译方法，以确保译文准确和可信。译者遵循了变译理论的指导，即在翻译过程中要注意保留原文的文化背景，并利用科学的翻译方法，使翻译能更好地传达原文的意义和情感。通过这种方式，译者希望能更好地传达历史文献的精髓，同时也使读者能更好地理解原文传达的信息。

目前，中国关于哈尔滨犹太人的英译历史文献相对较少。尽管国内许多学者对哈尔滨犹太人的历史进行了深入研究，但是大部分研究成果还没有被翻译成英文，并且国外对这方面的研究也相对较少。因此，目前仅有少量关于哈尔滨犹太人历史的英译文献，主要包括一些学术论文和专著的部分章节。

通过这次翻译实践，译者也深刻地领悟到“变通”这一变译理论核心在翻译过程中的应用。

5.3.1 翻译任务描述

《清末民初黑龙江移民史研究》一书是由黑龙江大学李朋教授委托给导师的翻译项目，译者完成了该项目研究之十——《关于“犹太人在哈尔滨”的历史文化研究的几点思考》的翻译任务。在此次翻译实践中，译者遵循黄忠廉教授提出的变译理论，针对翻译过程中的难点进行分析，选择适当的变通手段及翻译方法顺利完成翻译任务，随后总结并撰写了本篇翻译实践报告。这里将介绍翻译实践的任务背景和源语文本的主要内容，阐述英译目的与意义及委托方要求。

5.3.1.1 任务背景和源语文本的主要内容

当今，有关哈尔滨犹太人的历史文献英译作品相对较为缺乏。尽管国内许多学者深入研究了哈尔滨犹太人的历史，但是国内的相关研究成果并未被翻译成英文，同时，国外对这一领域的研究也相对较少。因此，翻译这些历史文献对于增进国际学术交流、促进跨文化了解具有重要意义。随着中国国力的日益增强，“走出去”的步伐刻不容缓，为促进国内学者犹太人移民史研究成果与国外学者的交流分享，英译犹太移民史历史文献势在必行。

译者参与《清末民初黑龙江移民史研究》之十——《关于“犹太人在哈尔滨”的历史文化研究的几点思考》的英译，该部分从哈尔滨犹太人的历史、人口情况、社会组织、文化传承等方面入手，试图探讨犹太人在哈尔滨的历史和文化价值。犹太人在哈尔滨的历史可以追溯到20世纪初，他们主要从事商业、银行、医疗等行业，在哈尔滨市中心建立了犹太人社区及相应的宗教场所。此外，文章还介绍了犹太人在哈尔滨的文化传承，包括他们的语言、信仰、文学、音乐、艺术等方面。译者以其作为翻译实践文本素材，素材总字数为23044个汉字，可以满足本次翻译实践要求。

5.3.1.2 英译目的与意义

英译中国历史文献对于增进中外文化交流，提高中国在国际上的知名度和影响力具有重要的现实意义，随着中国在世界舞台上的地位日益提升，通过英译中国历史文献，可以为中国赢得更多的国际认同和支持，推动中国文化的全球传播和提升影响力。但目前，中国历史文献英译本很少，与犹太移民相关的历史文献英译作品更是少之又少，因此译者希望通过本次翻译实践，实现以下三个目标：

第一，分析历史文献翻译的特点并概括文本类型；

第二，编辑、整理、总结此次翻译实践涉及的专业术语，建立专业术语表；

第三，运用变译理论并结合案例分析，归纳针对历史文献翻译运用的技巧。

在确定文本选择目的的基础上，译者对历史文献在变译理论指导下的翻译方法做进一步归纳，为翻译打开新视野和总结翻译经验。

历史类文献具有专业性、严谨性等特点，在翻译时不能出现遗漏、篡改等情况，要准确地将原著内容翻译出来，这样译文才能高质量传达出原著要表达的意思。在上述基础上，译者归纳出英译具有的理论意义与实践意义。

①理论意义方面。

第一，对变译理论进行实践检验和验证：此次翻译实践可以作为对变译理论的实际应用，进一步验证其在实践中的可行性和有效性。

第二，丰富变译理论的应用领域：此次翻译实践涉及的领域和文本类型，可以为变译理论的应用领域提供新的拓展。

第三，对变译理论进行深入探讨和研究：此次翻译实践可以为变译理论的深入研究提供更多具体案例和实践经验，推动理论的不断完善和发展。

②现实意义方面。

第一，通过翻译犹太人在哈尔滨的历史文献，可以加深中外文化的交流与理解，杨仕章（2015）曾说语言与文化关系密切，语言转换过程中必须解决相关的文化问题，因此可以推动文化多样性和互惠发展。

第二，加深业界对犹太人移民史的认识和理解，为后续国内学者乃至海外学者研究哈尔滨犹太人移民史提供一些可供参考的语料。

第三，激发更多人的翻译兴趣，提升翻译技能，促进全球范围内的文化交流。

5.3.1.3　委托方要求

委托方为黑龙江大学李朋教授，他及他的团队对译者的要求主要有以下几点。

①时间方面。

李朋教授计划于 2023 年 6 月底在中国经济出版社出版该书，因此要求译者在 2022 年 12 月前完成审校并提交最终稿件。

②文本内容方面。

第一，准确性：必须真实准确地传达原文意思，尤其是在涉及专业术语和概念的翻译中，必须准确无误。

第二，流畅性：文稿语言应流畅且自然优美，符合英语语言习惯和读者的审美需求。

第三，语言风格：翻译文本的语言风格要符合读者的习惯和要求，且尽量避免使用过多的俚语或不当的文化隐喻。

第四，格式规范：翻译文本要按照一定的排版格式规范出版，包括字体、行距、段落、图表等。

第五，审校把关：英译书稿须经过专业审校程序，确保翻译质量和准确性。

5.3.2 翻译过程描述

只有做好充分准备，才能事半功倍，为了保证翻译质量，对全文特点进行分析的步骤非常重要。本章将介绍本次翻译实践的步骤，包括译前准备、译中工作和译后事项 3 个主要部分。

5.3.2.1 译前准备

译前准备工作对于加快翻译速度和提高翻译质量至关重要。David Katan（2004）曾将翻译者的角色定义为“文化传递者”（cultural mediator）。这一角色不同于传统翻译者，因为文化传递者具备理解和建立不同文化框架的能力，并且通过文化传递过程将源语文化中的信息转化成目标语言文化中的信息，同时，确保该信息在译文读者脑中产生的解读与源语文化读者的解读相同。一个合格的译者需要做好充分的准备工作。本次翻译实践的译前准备主要包括源语文本分析、翻译理论选择、平行文本准备、术语表整理和辅助工具使用。

① 源语文本分析。

为了保证翻译质量，译者对源语文本的特点进行了分析，主要集中在词汇、句子和语篇 3 个方面。这些特点和难点对翻译的影响很大。

从词汇层面来看，本次翻译实践是典型的移民历史文献文本，其中涉及历史、文化、经济和宗教等领域的专业术语与概念。因此，在翻译过程中，译者必须特别注意专有名词的准确性和习惯用法。为了确保翻译的准确性，译者需要参考文献和英汉词典，并与平行文本进行比较以确定词语的含义。有些词语在平行文本中没有对应的英文译词，这时译者需要根据上下文和语境进行灵活改译，或引申其原始含义并添加相应的信息。

在句子层面，原作客观地陈述事实，讲述有关犹太移民的经济、政治、文化和宗教，形成了大量的复杂长难句。连淑能（2010）曾说，英语是刚性的，而汉语是柔性的；汉语没有严格的形态变化，具有多样性、复杂性和灵活性等特点，是重语感和重变通的语言。英语强调句法结构，重形合，句式复杂，多复合句及并列结构；而汉语重意合，句式简练。英语和汉语在表达习惯、叙事风格方面均存在差异。因此，在句子翻译过程中，要注重语序的调整，把握主语、谓语的逻辑关系，确保译文符合英文表达习惯，力求将译文再现出原文的叙事风格。

在语篇层面，该书句子及段落长度不一。在处理由这些句子组成的语篇时，需要正确传递出原文含义，厘清语篇主旨，突出句子之间、段落之间的逻辑关系，同时，灵活处理英语的表达特点，考虑前后文的衔接关系，进行灵活变译，以展现原文的意义和风格，使得译文更加流畅易懂。

在翻译工作中，源语文本的分析是至关重要的环节。通过文本分析，译者既能深入了解原文的含义、结构、语言风格及文化背景上的特征，也能更加精准地翻译出目标语言要表达的内容。

② 翻译理论选择。

在研究生期间，译者阅读了大量有关翻译理论的文献、书籍。在接到这个翻译项目委托时，译者通过分析源语文本的特点，参考一些平行文本后，决定采用黄忠廉教授的变译理论。

变译理论是一种新型的翻译理论，与以全译为研究对象的传统译论有所不同。黄忠廉（2011）曾说，在信息时代，变译越来越显示出强大的生命力。许钧（2002）曾说，变译理论研究的是一种创新，一种思想革新，它跳出了我国传统全译观的研究平台。

中国变译现象的出现最早可以追溯至古代时期对佛经的翻译。厉平（2014）曾提到，在全球翻译事业飞速发展、信息交流频繁的背景下，变译理论是基于对国内外变译现象进行分析和总结而创立的科学理论体系。黄忠廉（2002）曾说，变译理论主要探究变译过程的特点，反映变译的本质，探索变译在翻译过程中的合理运用。黄忠廉（2011）曾指出，译者通过采用增、减、编、述、缩、并、改、仿等变通手段，以满足特定读者在特定情境下对原作有关内容的特殊需求，来进行翻译活动。由此可见，变译力求摆脱内容逐字对应及形式固定的桎梏，以读者的阅读体验及阅读需求为重，强调以变通的手法处理译文，以达到更好的阅读效果。黄忠廉（2011）曾强调，变译理论诞生于变译实践，是一种反映变译本质和规律的科学原理与思想体系。在发展过程中，黄忠廉教授通过分析比对原著变译及全译两者信息量之间的异同，划分了变译系统，致力于研究读者、译者、变译和原作4部分之间的关系，最终总结出7种变通手段，即增、减、编、述、缩、并、改。随着研究的不断深入，黄忠廉教授后续出版了《翻译理论》（2001）和《翻译方法论》（2019）等论著，让变译理论不断完善发展。“目前，变译理论逐渐形成主体论、行为论、客体论和渊源论等四大研究方向，全面覆盖译者论、读者论、摄取论、范畴论、原作论、译作论、关系论和史论等八大领域，在学界逐渐产生较大影响，成为中国翻译理论学派构建的代表，后来，变译理论研究走向学科和方法论研究。”（黄忠廉、杨荣广，2018：6）2020年，黄忠廉教授的新作 *Variational Translation Theory*（2020）一书由新加坡斯普林格出版社（Springer）出版，这是中国翻译理论走向国际道路的一大进步，也是中国翻译理论“走出去”的一大成功实践。

译者在中国知网检索“变译理论”，从1991年到2023年与“变译理论”主题相关的文章共785篇，主要集中于文学文本、新闻与传媒和旅游等学科翻译，如2016年，唐羽婷在《从变译理论视角分析〈三体Ⅰ〉刘宇昆译本》中讨论了变译理论对科幻小说的指导作用；2022年，甘霖在《〈酒国〉文化负载词变译策略探究》中讨论了变译理论对莫言小说翻译的指导作用等，皆体现了变译理论在指导实践方面的重要意义。

“变译方法以西方读者的阅读兴趣和阅读习惯为导向，在战略上能多快好省、有的放矢地传播中国文化，在战术上能以摘译、编译、译述、缩译等变通手段来化解各种文化传播障碍、提升传播效果、讲好中国故事，能灵活地实现以西方之术传中国之道。”（张永中，2018）综合来看，使用变译理论翻译移民历史文献能更好地传达文化差异，保持原有文化特点，使翻译更具有目的性，同时，还能提高翻译质量。

③ 平行文本准备。

根据百度词条，平行文本是指任何接近原文内容或目标语言内容的语言材料。对译者来说，平行文本可以帮助译者找到合适的表达方式来呈现原文，最大限度地保证翻译的准确性。更重要的是，平行文本既可以帮助译者加深对原文的理解，也有助于积累更多对应的目的语表达，从一开始就养成良好的翻译习惯。在本次翻译实践中，译者借鉴了以下平行文本：《变译理论指导下的中国文化翻译研究》（姜盼盼，2022）中用“增”的翻译策略翻译北京在不同朝代的称呼，译者以此为启发，运用到词汇翻译例1“哈埠”的翻译之中。《变译理论在文学翻译中的应用：以〈你快乐吗？〉为例》（时锦瑞，张孟琳，2017）例2中增加连接词以更好地表现事件准备顺序，译者以此为启发，运用到例18的翻译中。《翻译方法论》（黄忠廉，2009）中对“中山大学概况”使用了编译手段，译者受此启发，在语篇翻译例22中对例句采用“编”的翻译手段，使例句重点集中突出、句子条理清晰。

除上述及其他论文外，译者还查阅了有关网站，如哈尔滨史志网、非物质文化网等。

使用平行文本进行翻译，不仅能使译者更好地理解原文的意思，对于一些专业术语和语言表达上的迥异，平行文本也能提供帮助。在参考平行文本时，译者可以学习和借鉴翻译方法与技巧，掌握一些常用的表达方式和惯用语，同时，了解不同语言在表达上的特点，以便更好地进行语言转换和文化转换。此外，平行文本可以帮助译者缩短调整和修改的时间，提高翻译效率和准确性。

④术语表整理。

本次犹太移民史历史文献文本涉及很多跨学科专业术语，其中包括文化、历史、宗教、经济等领域。在翻译过程中，为保持术语表述上的一致性，确保翻译速度和译文质量，译者使用搜索引擎和翻译工具全面查询其释义，确认统一表述，同时，按术语英文首字母排序方式进行排列组合，制定了相应的术语表。表 5–3 只展示部分术语，完整术语表收录在附录 2 中。

表 5–3　部分术语

Table 5–3　List of Terms (Excerpts)

原文	译文
阿什肯纳兹犹太人	Ashkenazi Jews
塞法迪犹太人	Sephardi Jews
纳粹法西斯	Nazi–fascist
政治避难	political asylum
《关于难民地位的公约》	*Convention relating to the Status of Refugees*
上海社会科学院	The Shanghai Academy of Social Sciences

犹太人移民文献翻译中涉及特定文化或历史事件等专业术语。通过术语表可以确保翻译的一致性和准确性，避免在翻译过程中出现术语使用不一致、错误或误解等问题，从而提高翻译效率，提升译文翻译质量。

⑤ 辅助工具使用。

工欲善其事，必先利其器。翻译辅助工具的正确使用会给翻译过程提供便利，减少麻烦。在本次实践中，译者主要使用纸质词典、电子词典和网络在线翻译工具、计算机辅助翻译软件、网络搜索引擎、语法审校工具与诸多文献浏览工具等一系列辅助手段以解决翻译过程中遇到的问题，现将其以表格的形式分类整理出来，如表 5–4 所示。

表 5-4 翻译辅助工具
Table 5-4 Translation Aids

工具类型	工具名称
纸质词典	《牛津高阶英汉双解词典》(第 9 版)
	《英汉大词典(陆谷孙主编)》(第 2 版)
	《新世纪汉英大词典》(第二版)
	《新华字典》
	《世界人名翻译大辞典》
	《世界地名翻译大辞典》
电子词典和网络在线翻译工具	欧路电子词典
	金山词霸
	谷歌在线翻译
	百度翻译
	网易有道翻译
	DeepL 翻译
计算机辅助翻译软件	AntConc
	Trados
网络搜索引擎	百度
	谷歌
	夸克
	必应
语法审校工具	Grammarly
	批改网
文献浏览工具	学校图书馆电子浏览室
	中国知网
	万方数据知识服务平台

在翻译过程中，译者使用了列表中的辅助工具，有一些是经常使用的，如 AntConc、Trados，利用此类辅助工具建立术语库，避免了重复查询相同

术语，提高了翻译效率；用中国知网、万方数据知识服务平台查询平行文本；用 Grammarly、批改网对译文的拼写、语法等进行校对，提高译文质量。简言之，翻译辅助工具在翻译过程中的作用必不可少，可以有效减少翻译错误和不一致性，提高翻译效率和质量。

5.3.2.2　译中工作

译中工作也是翻译的实施过程，其重要性不言而喻。为了确保翻译过程的顺利进行，译者制订了翻译计划，并且向相关人员交代了计划执行情况，以保证翻译工作顺利进行。

① 翻译过程设计。

为确保翻译工作顺利进行，译者将翻译过程分为译前、译中、译后 3 个不同的阶段，并根据每个阶段的时间需求，制定了详细的翻译项目计划表，如图 5–2 所示。

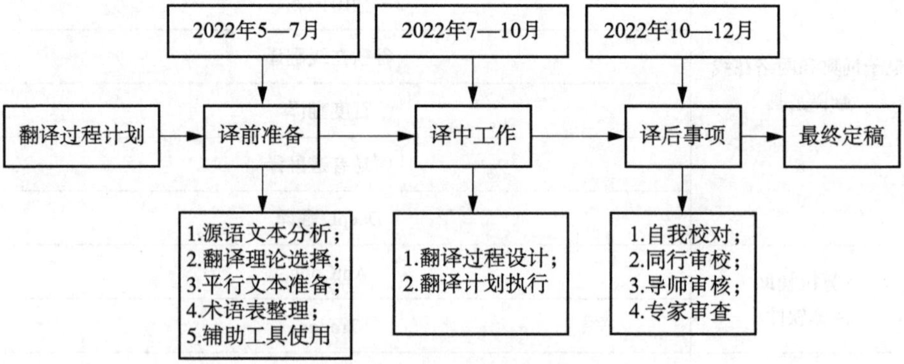

图 5–2　翻译项目计划表

（Figure 5–2　Translation Project Process Schedule）

译者一丝不苟地执行翻译计划表，按照表中规定的时间完成各阶段的任务，保持高品质的译文，并按时推进翻译工作的进度。在完成任务的同时，译者保持与导师的密切联系，不断完善译文。译者还在翻译理论的基础上记录了一些典型案例，为之后翻译案例的编制奠定了坚实的基础，同时，也进一步提升了撰写翻译实践报告的效率。

对委托方来说，翻译项目计划表作为项目实施过程中的一项重要监控指标，能帮助委托方及时了解项目的翻译进度并进行调整。译者认真对待委托方的观点和要求，并在项目执行过程中及时向委托方汇报项目进展情况。在与委托方进行紧密合作、有效交流的基础上，能对翻译过程进行更好的管理，保证翻译任务按期优质完成。

② 翻译计划执行。

译者将本次翻译实践的执行分为 5 个步骤，具体如下。

第一，仔细阅读理解源语文本和变译理论，参考平行文本中使用的变译手段，学习其翻译方法。归纳翻译过程中出现的历史事件、历史人名及地名等。

第二，调试各类翻译辅助工具，运用 AntConc 和 Trados 软件建立语料库与术语库，设计翻译流程，正式开始翻译。在翻译过程中，通过查询纸质词典、网络词典和运用翻译软件等一系列翻译手段得出译文，对比其不同表达方式，记录使用的各种翻译方法，及时与导师沟通遇到的重点和难点问题，定期向委托方报告翻译进度，按进度完成译文初稿。

第三，使用 Grammarly 等软件对初稿进行多次自我校对，检查是否有低级错误，在修改后联系同行进行审校，检查前后是否承接连贯，检验译文能否适应国外读者的文化背景和语言环境。

第四，联系导师和客户方的专业人士对译文进行导师审核与专家审查，之后再进行修改，提交译文终稿。再次整理和总结翻译过程中遇到的重点、难点问题，与导师和同学交流探讨。

第五，分析文中典型案例，总结变译理论在实践中的具体应用，撰写实践报告，结束本次翻译任务。

5.3.2.3 译后事项

翻译的译后事项既是收尾工作，也是译文总结与改进的重要阶段。为确保译文的专业性和准确性，本次翻译实践的校对分为自我校对、同行审校、导师审核和专家审查 4 个方面。

① 自我校对。

第一轮翻译中难免会出现许多问题，因此自我校对尤为重要。译者在翻译前后共进行了 3 次自我校对。第一次校对主要检查汉字书写和标点符号的使用是否准确，例如，“作”与“做”、“的”与“地”等；第二次校对主要关注词汇使用、语序和语法等内容方面；第三次校对，译者则着重检查格式是否规范。

经过自我校对，译者进行了深刻反思，总结出现错误的主要原因：对原文理解不够深入、翻译不够细致。随后，译者不断修改与完善译文，进一步提升了质量。同时，译者及时总结经验，改进了不足，以减少和避免类似错误在日后的翻译实践中再次出现。

② 同行审校。

在进行完自我核对后，译者联系了同翻译项目下的两名英语笔译研究生进行译文审校。校对重点在于是否准确表述原文内容，译文是否通顺流畅、是否符合目的语读者阅读习惯，等等。在同行审校后，笔者收到20多个专业性建议，如词语搭配、句式结构、连接词等方面。译者询问各位同行对译文修改方面的其他建议，之后再对译文进行修改和完善。

③ 导师审核。

导师审核是至关重要的一个环节，必不可少。在经过李靖教授3次细心审校后，经过反复修改和完善，译文达到了较高水平。在第一轮审校中，共发现了27处错误，李靖教授将其标红并为译者提供修改思路。在李靖教授的帮助下，译者进行第一轮修改；在第二轮审校后，李靖教授发现了7处词语、句式运用不恰当的地方，标注为紫色，译者进行了第二轮修改；在第三轮审校后，李靖教授发现了3处符号使用和排版上的错误，标注为红色，译者进行最终修改。在多次审校和修改的过程中，李靖教授和译者持之以恒，坚持反复修改和审校，直至最终译文质量达到要求。经验收，导师认可译文质量，同意译者联系委托方专家进行下一步审校工作。

本次翻译实践始终处在导师的指导和定期检查督管之下。译者经常向导师请教一些翻译难题，也定期向导师汇报自己阶段性任务的完成情况。尤其是译者自身对于一些文化负载词、文言文等英译不甚了解，曾多次请教导师某些词汇和语句的翻译方法。

④ 专家审查。

在进行完上述审校后，译者第一时间与原作者黑龙江大学的李朋教授及其团队取得联系，申请对译文进行专家审查。专家在原文与译文对应的精准性、译文的专业性及篇章全文安排的合理性等方面进行审校。专家给出的结论是译文和原文对应处理较好，整体篇章结构没有过多需要修改的地方，但在一些词汇的专业表述上仍有一定欠缺，需要继续完善。在向专家多次请教之后，译者对译文的篇章安排进行了适当的修改，对专家特别指出的几处欠缺专业性的翻译进行了补充和修改。

中国经济出版社编辑张博对译者提交的最终稿件进行语法、拼写、标点、格式等方面的校验，以确保译文的准确性、规范性和易读性；还确认译著是否满足出版方和读者的要求与需求，如排版、字体、封面设计等方面，确认达到译著出版要求。

5.3.3 汉译案例分析

在变译理论指导下，译者通过黄忠廉教授提出的4种变通手段——“增、减、改、编”并结合下文26个案例分析，来具体展示如何运用变译理论解决在词汇、句子和语篇3个方面遇到的问题。

5.3.3.1 变译理论指导下的词汇翻译

词汇在翻译中扮演着至关重要的角色，它既是句子结构和语言功能的基本单元，也是表达意思最基本的手段。因此，在翻译过程中，正确处理词汇对于保证翻译的准确性和流畅性非常关键。如果词汇翻译不当，就很容易造成译文信息传达的偏颇，从而导致译语读者无法获得与原文读者相同的信息。

词汇翻译的难点主要有文化负载词、宗教词汇和历史词汇等，译者在变译理论指导下，采取“增、减、改”3种手段指导本次实践中的词汇翻译工作。

① 历史宗教术语——增译。

“增”是指在原作基础上增加信息，增加的方式可分为3种，分别是释、评、写（黄忠廉，2002：94）。其中，“释”即阐释，也是最常见的方式，阐释的目的是通过解释原文部分内容，使译语读者更易于理解，释一般不会另外加注，而是融入译文中，不会破坏原文的结构。本次翻译实践中有许多文化负载词、宗教词汇、历史词汇等，这些都是译语读者的阅读障碍点，而“增”的变通手段可以增加译文的“透明度”，使译文更好地被目的语读者理解。

例1

原文：哈埠

译文： Habu—the name for Harbin during the construction period of the Middle East Rail ranging from 1898 to 1903

分析：“埠”是商埠的简称，现在被称为“口岸”。商埠是与外国通商之地，也称“通商口岸”。哈尔滨为什么能称“埠”呢？通过查阅《哈尔滨史志网》译者得知，哈尔滨在1898年被确定为中东铁路的总埠，因此在这段时间，哈尔滨被称作“哈埠”。“哈埠”是一个特定历史时期里哈尔滨的称呼，具有历史韵味，现代中国的城市名称中并不包括这个词。

姜盼盼（2022）在《变译理论指导下的中国文化翻译研究》一文中对北京在不同朝代称呼采用“增”的变译手段，增添了北京作为“大都”这个名字出现的朝代及具体年限。受她的启发，译者在翻译此处时，也采用“增”的变译手段，对“哈埠”的历史背景进行增补说明，避免给目的语读者造成误解。

例2

原文：“卡斯普绑架案”这个具有国际影响的事件，就是一个比较有说服

力的案例。

译文：One of the more persuasive cases was the internationally influential **"Asperger kidnapping" case, planned by the Japanese colonial authorities and carried out by Belarus against Simon Asperger as a threat and revenge for the unsuccessful economic plundering of the Asperger family.**

分析：在搜索"卡斯普绑架案"事件的来龙去脉时，译者发现这一事件发生在哈尔滨日伪统治时期，白俄罗斯人和日本人对犹太人卡斯普开办的具有丰厚利润的马迭尔酒店觊觎已久，他们想以低价强制收购马迭尔酒店，但是卡斯普不同意，于是白俄罗斯人和日本人策划联手绑架他，想以此逼迫他拿出高额的赎金。然而，卡斯普出行非常谨慎，白俄罗斯人和日本人未找到下手机会，于是转而绑架了卡斯普的儿子，以要挟卡斯普支付高额赎金。卡斯普拒绝支付赎金，并向哈尔滨伪警察厅和法国驻哈领事馆寻求帮助，但哈尔滨伪警察厅督察也是计划此绑架案的幕后黑手之一，卡斯普寻求帮助无果，也错过了支付赎金的时间，最终未能救回自己的儿子。这起绑架案是针对犹太人的众多绑架案之一，因其赎金数目巨大，在国际上也产生了重大影响。

在翻译此句时，译者使用"增"的变译手段，增加"卡斯普绑架案"发生的背景原因，如此一来，既可以让译语读者了解这起绑架案发生的根本原因，以及隐藏在背后的国际势力斗争，也可以从侧面展现当时犹太人在哈尔滨的生存状况。

例 3

原文：据日伪当局统计，整个洪水期间，哈尔滨全市患**虎列拉**的共 621 人，死亡 248 人，路毙者 149 人；患其他传染病的 168 人，死亡 62 人。

译文：According to the Japanese authorities, during the entire flood period, 621 people suffered from **Cholera (first emerges in the hardest-hit areas, rapid spread and high mortality rates)** in Harbin, 248 died and 149 homelessness died; 168 people suffered from other infectious diseases and 62 died.

分析：该例句描述的是在洪灾期间，由于感染疾病而死亡的人数。结合上下文，可以推断虎列拉是一种疾病的名称。百度百科上对其介绍为："虎列拉（Cholera）病名，急性传染病霍乱的旧称，亦简称'虎疫'"，是重灾区最容易出现的疫情，其特点为传播速度快，致死率高。虎列拉是霍乱的旧称，早先根据其发音译为虎列拉，属于历史医学术语。文中整段话在讲述 1932 年水灾的惨烈情况，如果只是采用直译术语的手段，就不能传达出与原文中相同的感情色彩。因为译者采用"增"的变通手段，增译其出现时间及特点，所以把其翻译为“Cholera (first emerges in the hardest-hit areas, rapid spread and high mortality rates)”，这样可以使目的语读者对这种传染病的特征一目了然，同时，也可以体会当年洪灾后百姓生活的惨状。

例 4

原文：在逾越节的一周里，免费食堂每天均严格遵循犹太教规**“科谢尔”（洁净食物）**准备三餐。

译文：During the week of Passover, the free cafeteria prepares three meals each day in strict observance of **the kosher food—clean food based on Jewish religion**.

分析：首先，译者在北京大学中国语言学研究中心在线语料库查询“科谢尔”，得到的查询结果为 0；其次，译者查询犹太教规，得到 9 条查询结果，其中，9.1 中查到“Kosher”一词。根据对英文名用相似发音的翻译方法，译者开始考虑例句中“科谢尔”是“Kosher”的音译。同时，译者在使用网络搜索引擎查询“Kosher”后，分别得到其意为符合犹太教规的、清洁的、可食的，泛指与犹太饮食相关的产品，犹太洁食。

译者在百度上查询到，洁净食物的基本定义为选择纯天然、富含营养的食品，避免对其进行任何形式的加工或精制。译者从知识网（http://www.tested.com/lii/4039.html）查询到，犹太洁食是根据《圣经》中的条例制定的，如不能吃宰杀方式不符合犹太教规定的食物，禁止吃动物的血或血制品，避免同时摄入肉类制品和乳制品。因此，译者从网上搜索后确认“科谢尔”洁净食物和常规洁净食物的定义并不同。译者采用变译理论中“增”的翻译手段，解释此处出现的洁净食物是依托犹太教教规处理的食物，而并不是常规认识中的洁净食物，从而可以避免给目的语读者造成误读，使源语信息传达准确明了。

例 5

原文：**“贝塔”青年**

译文：**“Beta Israel” youth—the black-skinned Jewish**

分析：在翻译此句时，译者看到文章出现的“贝塔”青年，心中瞬间产生很多疑问：“贝塔”青年是指什么样的青年？他们为什么叫“贝塔”？相信如果只采取直译的方式，那么也会给译语读者带来阅读困扰。译者使用谷歌浏览器进行搜索，了解到贝塔以色列（Beta Israel）意为“以色列家园”，即信奉犹太教的埃塞俄比亚人，是世界上唯一的黑皮肤犹太人。从而可以分析出，句中所说的“贝塔”青年是指来自贝塔以色列的青年。

但是，对犹太民族不了解的普通读者，一想到犹太人，在脑海里浮现的可能就是白皮肤的犹太人，并不知道“贝塔”青年是特殊的黑皮肤的犹太人。因此，在变译理论的指导下，译者采用变译手段中的“增”，添加和补充“贝塔”青年背后隐藏的民族特征，从而减少宗教背景给目的语读者带来的阅读障碍。

在历史文本中，我们不可避免地会遇到与宗教、历史事件和特定历史时期相关的词汇，其中，有些词汇晦涩难懂，会降低读者的阅读兴趣。为了解决这些问题，译者需要对这些词汇的含义进行解释。在翻译过程中，我们可以通过增加一些信息，将解释融入译文中，而不是简单地单独注释。在符合译文语言条件的情况下，尽可能地增加细节，使译文内容更加清晰明了，这是一种有效的变通方法。当然，最理想的情况是让译文在表达清晰的同时也尽可能地保持原文的神韵，这种要求与翻译历史类文本时的要求一致。

② 成语——减译。

黄忠廉（2002）曾强调，“减”是指去掉原作中译者认为读者不需要的信息，有时是去掉原作中的残枝败叶，有时是挤掉多余的水分，在变译中表现为对原作的取舍。由此可见，在应用“减”这一变通手段时，就是在捕捉原文信息的同时做出取舍，从读者的角度出发，充分地展现有用、有价值的信息。在本次翻译实践中，译者适当运用“减”这一变通手段，对信息进行了筛选，力求原文的简洁性和通畅性。“在成语翻译实践中，要做到‘以貌传神’‘存色入味’和‘情真意切’，关键是要在目的语中恰当地激活并重建决定源语篇概念结构的认知模式。”（王红利，2009：73）

例 6

原文：李述笑、曲伟、刘爽、张铁江等的著作或论文在哈尔滨犹太人的研究中“各领风骚”。

译文：Books or papers by **Li Shaanxi, Bu Wei, Li Huang, Bhang Zhejiang** are **outstanding** in Jewish studies in Harbin.

分析：“各领风骚”出自清代赵翼的《论诗五首·其二》：“江山代有才人出，各领风骚数百年。”其意为在自己所在的领域有作为。海词词典对“各领风骚”的英文翻译为“each side shows its own prowess; each side tries for all its worth”。但是，译者认为采用直译法会使例句拖沓烦琐，因此译者对其他平行文本进行搜索，得到如下译文。

原文：一大批国内外知名企业纷至沓来，群星璀璨，**各领风骚**。

译文：Therefore, many domestic and foreign well-known enterprises come in a continuous stream, like bright stars, and they are all **excellent**.

原文：行走在路上的人，就像《水浒传》中的英雄，虽然**各领风骚**，但脑里始终有一个杀人的念头。

译文：Walking on the road, just like the heroes in the book "Water Margin", although each **leading the trend**, but in their mind, there is always an idea to kill.

这两个平行文本都没有采用直译法，而是根据句意翻译成"excellent""leading the trend"。"各领风骚"在例句中的含义是，这几位专家在哈尔滨犹太人的研究上是重要突出的人物。因此，译者受其启发，采用"减"的变译手段，剪掉"各领风骚"中的枝杈，只保留其核心"重要突出"。译者用 DeepL 搜索具有杰出含义的词语，得到"outstanding"和"prominent"。译者对两个词语进行分析，prominent 突出的是 immediately noticeable 和 widely known，引起了广泛的关注，成为众所周知的事实；而 outstanding 则是 standing out among others of its kind，这个是和其他同类相比的结果，因此这种突出是杰出、优秀，或许仅限于某一特定范围内为人所熟知。

根据上下文分析译者认为，作者想要表达这些专家在此领域研究上比其他专家做得杰出优秀。因此，译者最终选用"outstanding"一词。把核心内容充分展示给目的语读者，使文本轻松易读。

例 7

原文：关于这方面的深入分析还是"**凤毛麟角**"。

译文：However, there exists **rare** deep analysis on this issue.

分析：结合上下文，以及根据例句的句意判断，"凤毛麟角"在句中的意思是数量稀少。《新华字典》中关于"凤毛麟角"的定义为：指凤凰的羽毛和麒麟的角，比喻珍贵稀有的人或事物。形容罕见、稀有、珍贵、出类拔萃的人或物。此词 DeepL 翻译为 phoenix feather and rare horn，这是直译的方法。随后，译者用有道词典翻译，找到了几个例句：第一，中文为"能写出如此诗句的人，现在已经是凤毛麟角了"，英译为"Persons who can write such poems now are already very rare"；第二，中文为"总的来说，理解一枝完美玫瑰的价值的男人真是凤毛麟角啊"，英译为"After all, it's the rare man who understands the value of a single, perfect rose"。在这两个平行例句中，都把"凤毛麟角"翻译为"rare"，取其意义。谷青松

（2010）曾说，在减译中，译者通常从逻辑需要、译语习惯等方面考虑，适当对原语中的冗余信息进行删减，使译文更准确、更地道。译者由此得到启发，在此例句中，本意强调数量上的稀少，因此译者在不改变原文的基础上翻译为“rare”，适当删除冗杂信息，达到既言简意赅而又形象生动的效果。

例 8

原文：在哈尔滨、上海、青岛、天津的犹太历史研究中，哈尔滨的犹太研究独树一帜。

译文：Among the Jewish historical studies in Harbin, Shanghai, Qingdao, and Tianjin, Harbin's Jewish studies are **unique classes of their own.**

分析：独树一帜是四字汉字成语，可以追溯于（清）袁枚《随园诗话》：“所以能独树一帜者；正为其不袭盛唐窠臼也。”比喻与众不同，自成一家。在文中，是为表达哈尔滨犹太历史研究与其他地方的研究不同，且有自己独特的风格。译者查询到英语中有类似的表达方式，如“one of a kind”或“stand out from the crowd”，都表示独一无二、脱颖而出。此外，译者使用在线翻译 DeepL、有道词典翻译独树一帜，得到的分别是 one of a kind、develop a school of one's own。DeepL 翻译强调的是独一无二，有道词典翻译的重点是自成一家。再次分析源语后，译者认为这一词具有“与众不同，有自己独特风格”的双重意义。因此，译者认为使用两种翻译方式都不太适合。在变译理论的指导下，译者决定采用变译手段里的“减”，在不改变原意传达的基础上，脱去其“外壳”，保留其核心“与众不同又有独特风格”的含义。

用变通手段中的“减”翻译历史文本可以减少翻译中的重复、烦琐和晦涩的地方，让读者更轻松地理解文本内容。此外，还可以使译文更加简洁易懂，符合现代人的阅读习惯，提高阅读体验。“英语读者和汉语读者生活在不同的文化环境，在知识结构上自然存在不少差别，对语篇中信息的理解和接受也会很不相同，译者在译语读者难以理解的地方应适当进行减译，令译文信息性维持在合理水平。”（李立业，2005：419）总之，通过减少不必要的翻译，可以更好地传达原文的含义，提高译文的可读性和可理解性。

③ 纪年计量术语——改译

“改”即为“改变”的含义，通过改换内容或形式，让原作发生明显的变化，这种手段包括改换、改编和改造（黄忠廉，2002）。其目的是使译文更加本土化，使译者更加容易理解和接受。在翻译过程中，不能拘泥于对原词的机械对应，否则会让译文显得生硬难懂，同时，还应考虑文本特点，保证用词的准确性。黄忠廉教授提出的“改”对解决这类问题具有极大的指导意义。

纪年计量术语是人类社会对时间的一种记录和感知方式，反映着人类社会的历史变迁。在不同的历史时期和地区，人们根据当时的文化、宗教、政治和经济等方面的特点，选择不同的起点和时间单位来进行纪年计量。纪年计量术语是一个涉及历史、文化和宗教等多个方面的话题，不同的纪年计量术语有着不同的含义和用法，因此在翻译前，译者需要先了解该术语涉及的历史背景和文化差异，确定该术语的具体含义和用法；在翻译时，应该根据实际情况和目标读者的需求，选择最合适的翻译方式，使翻译结果更易于理解和接受。

例 9

原文：《壬申哈尔滨水灾纪实》讲道，水灾时“几似人间地狱，殊甚酸鼻”。

译文： Harbin Flood Document in 1932 said, “It is a heart breaking scene, making the angles weep.”

分析： 译者在查询非物质文化网站（http://www.feiwuzhiwenhua.net/）后，查到壬申属于古代纪年历法，大概对应的公历年份如 1812 年、1872 年、1932 年、1992 年等（60 年一周期）。古代纪年历法是中国古人记录时间的传统纪年方式。而目前，全球约定俗成使用的是国际通用公历年份。国内学者廖七一将文化负载词定义为“经过中国漫长历史沉淀、具备独特文化内涵的词组”，因此“壬申”可以被归纳为文化负载词。然而，由于文化的多样性，在翻译文化负载词时会面临无法在英文中找到对应词语的问题，即所谓的“词汇空缺”。

因此，在翻译此处时，译者采用变译理论中“改”的变译手段，把“壬申”改为公历年份的具体年号。根据上文第一句“1932 年 7 月，大雨滂沱，连降 27 天”，可分析出这份水灾纪实是 1932 年的壬申年。因此，译文中的古代纪年历法壬申改成公历年份 1932 年。

例 10

原文： 而《滨江尘嚣录》第二章第四节记载，迨民国十四年度十月调查，哈埠人口，“犹太一千四百人”。

译文： The fourth section of the second chapter of *The Dust and Hustle of Binjiang* records that the population of Habu—the name for Harbin during the construction period of the Middle East Rail ranging from 1898 to 1903 was “1,400 Jews” **in October 1925**。

分析：译者通过浏览器查询到民国起止时间为 1912—1949 年，从而可以推算出民国十四年度是 1925 年。随后，译者使用 DeepL 翻译网站、百度在线翻译、有道在线翻译得到了同一个翻译结果“the 14th year of the Republic of China”，这些翻译软件都是用直译的翻译方法。

金隄（1985）曾说，在翻译的过程中，需要做到灵活变通，而关键是需要译者打破自身意识中一些机械对等的公式。然而，从直译的翻译法中，目的语读者并不能清晰抓取这份人口调查发生的时间。此外，本例句的上下文都使用公历年份。在思考之后，译者决定使用变译理论中“改”的变译手段，改变词汇形式，保留词汇内容，把“民国十四年度”改为“1925 年”，这样不仅可以使前后的时间表达一致顺畅，还可以使目的语读者对原文信息理解更加透彻，减少阅读障碍。

例 11

原文：据记载，“全市 38 万居民中，约 24 万人受灾，2 万人丧生，12 万人颠沛流离，经济损失至少 **2 亿银圆**”。

译文：It is recorded that “about 240,000 people were victims, 20,000 people were killed, 120,000 people displaced among the city’s 380,000 residents, and the whole economic losses amount to more than **100 million dollars**”.

分析：银圆俗称“大洋”“洋钱”或“花边钱”。银圆起源于 15 世纪的欧洲，是银本位制国家的主要流通货币。大约在明万历时期（1573—1620 年），银圆流入中国，民国时期建立银本位货币制度以后，也以银圆作为主要流通货币。根据当时报纸上的记载，民国时期普通工人的工资每月 4 ~ 6 块银圆。当时，每块银圆的重量大约为 27 克，每块银圆的含银量都在 90% 以上，含银量相当高，而金银的价格在 20 ~ 30 元，按照这样计算的话，1 块银圆的价格相当于 1 克黄金的价格，现在市场上黄金的价格在每克 350 元左右。得出结论：1 块银圆换算成人民币的话，大约是 350 元。

按黄金含量推算：1 银圆 =0.103 英镑 =2.607 法郎 =0.503 美元 =0.211 德国金马克 =0.9767 卢布 =1.01 日元。因此，2 亿银圆换算成美元约为 1 亿美元。因为目的语受众是英语国家，译者认为，把货币单位从银圆转换成美元，会使读者有直观清晰的概念。所以，译者使用“改”的变通手段，改变句中的货币单位。

用“改”的变通手段改变句式结构、使用更加通俗易懂的词汇，不仅能使翻译更贴近读者的阅读习惯和实际需求，还能提高译者的创造性和灵活性，让翻译工作更具艺术性和个性。这样可以使译文更加生动有趣，更容易引起读者的阅读兴趣。通过“改”的变通手段，可以让译文更加符合读者的需求，提高译文的质量和可读性。

5.3.3.2 变译理论指导下的语句翻译

“句子是表达思想和进行语言交际的基本单位，也是进行翻译的基本单位。”（陈柳悦，2010：78）中英思维逻辑的不同和语言结构表达形式的不同，使汉英两种语言句法结构差异尤其明显。为达到忠实的翻译原则，需要对核心进行摄取，抽汲内容，改造形式。在变译理论指导下，译者通过“编、改”变通手段使句子更有序化和逻辑化。

① 长难句式——编译。

黄忠廉（2002）曾阐述，“编”即编辑，指将原作内容条理化、有序化，使之更完美、更精致的行为。“编”这一手段中包括编选、编排和编写，其中，编排是指对原文的顺序加以整理。因此，在本文的翻译过程中，“编”对处理复杂长难句和调整逻辑顺序有很大的帮助。

英语长难句通常结构复杂、含义深奥、长度较长。翻译英语长难句需要注意句子结构、句意和连接词等多个方面，需要理解和把握句子整体结构与意义，选择恰当的连接词进行翻译，保持句子的连贯性和整体性。

例 12

原文：针对“河豚计划”，丹·本—卡南指出，“河豚计划”，一个吸纳“全世界犹太人的金钱”，来加强日本在战争中遭到破坏的经济并为“犹太问题”找出解决办法的秘密计划，并没有在满洲成功。

译文：Dan Ben Canaan points out that the **“Fugu Project”**, a project aiming at consuming “Jewish money from all over the world” to strengthen Japan’s war-torn economy and to find a solution to the “Jewish problem”, failed in Manchuria.

分析：译者发现，这个例句中出现了“河豚计划”在通读全句、充分理解后，译者得知此例句是在描述“河豚计划”是一个怎样的事件。随后，译者分析例句结构，发现这段文字中包含了 6 个小句子。因为中英句子结构差异，中文喜短句，英文喜长句。此后，译者思考怎样才能把短句之间的逻辑顺序厘清，再用英文句子结构表达出来。译者通过分析句意得知，这段的主题是“河豚计划”，因此可以把它选作主语，其余则是句子的谓语和宾语部分，而余下的小短句都是“河豚计划”的定义，译者采用主语从句结构，短语变状语的方式来进行翻译。依据以上分析，译者采用“编”的变译手段，在保持原作内容完整的情况下，删减句中重复内容，重组顺序，使例句脉络分明。

例 13

原文： 这份调查表详细显示，犹太人“十四岁以下，男 78 人，女 79 人；自十四岁至六十岁，男 539 人，女 626 人；六十岁以上，男 187 人，女 171 人。**总计 1680 人，其中，男 804 人，女 876 人**”。

译文： This questionnaire shows in detail that “**There were 1,680 Jewish people in total, of whom 804 were men and 876 were women**: 78 men and 79 women under 14 years of age; 539 men and 626 women from 14 to 60 years of age; 187 men and 171 women over 60 years of age”.

分析： “翻译工作要求尽可能做到忠实、通顺、尔雅，因此在英汉互译时应按照英语和汉语各自的习惯灵活处理翻译语句。”（陈柳悦，2010：69）在中文思维表达中，注重逐步深入，将核心观点置于末尾；英文则不然，它的表达方式常常以直截了当的方式呈现，通常将重点放在前面。Nord (2001) 曾指出，在翻译时，应从目的语读者的需求出发，照顾目的语读者的阅读习惯，在让译文更加通畅流利的同时，避免翻译腔。例句是典型的中文思维模式，细节在前，结论在后。考虑到中英表达习惯差异，译者采用“编”的翻译手段，调整句子语序，把“总计 1680 人，其中，男 804 人，女 876 人”放在译文的首句，使译文更符合目的语读者的阅读思维模式。

例 14

原文： 1898 年，哈尔滨城市开始兴建。此前，这里仅是一个小村庄。第一批犹太人随着哈尔滨城市的建设而来，最后一批于 1963 年归国离去，犹太社区在哈尔滨生息繁衍了 65 年。

译文： The Jewish community flourished in Harbin for 65 years since the beginning of construction of Harbin in 1898 to the departure of last group and their return to homeland in 1963.

分析： 例句中出现了 3 个时间，分别是 1898 年、1963 年、65 年，并且有时间顺序。从叙事方式来看，英语一般按照时间顺序从现在向过去推进，而汉语恰好相反；从逻辑推理方式来看，英语一般是先结论 / 结果，后分析 /

论据 / 原因，而汉语也是正好相反。陈定安（2000）提到，解决长句的问题通常需要采取两步，第一步是分析句子的结构和形式，第二步是确定句子的功能和意义。因此，根据以上中英句子特点，译者对此句进行编译，首先把结论“繁衍了 65 年”放在句首；其次因为“哈尔滨城市开始兴建”和“哈尔滨城市的建设”内容，从而把两个分句整合；最后按照时空顺序，把“1898 年”“1963 年”处理成时间状语。为避免译文文化表达方式与原文不同而导致的思维逻辑矛盾，需要在翻译过程中尽可能地与原文思想保持一致。

用变译理论中“编”的翻译手段可以编排译文中的词语、句子结构和表达方式等，使得译文更加贴近目标语言的语言表达习惯。这种翻译方法不仅可以让读者更加容易理解和接受译文中表达的内容，还可以让翻译更加自然、流畅和易读。

② 文言句式——改译。

“改”即“改变”，是一种对源语内容、形式和风格进行某种改变的变译方法，以适应译语读者的文化背景。

文言句式是古代汉语的书面表达方式，文言文的句子通常比现代汉语的句子更紧凑，较少使用烦琐的描绘和修饰语。使用改译的方式翻译文言文句，一是为了增加可读性，使句子更易懂；二是为了减少歧义，使翻译更加准确；三是适应现代社会需要，使经典文献更好地适应现代社会的需求；四是为了传承经典文化，准确传递古代文献蕴含的思想精髓。

例 15

原文：有无一席以避风雨者，人们啼饥呼寒，其状惨不忍睹。

译文：How miserable they were! There is no place to shelter from the wind and rain, people crying for hunger and cold.

分析：这个例句出自《壬申哈尔滨水灾纪实》，是文言文体。文言文作为中国的特殊文化遗产，其词语和句子都有其特定的用法，因此在翻译过程中要先对文言文有全面的认识。在翻译文言文之前，译者首先对文言文的内容进行全面理解，保证准确无误；其次寻求学校文史老师的帮助，经老师的校对后，这句话翻译为现代汉语是：没有任何地方可以给老百姓挡风遮雨，大家因为饥饿寒冷不断地哀号，此景惨不忍睹。初译时，译者不知采用哪种翻译手段，直到发现卓别林的无声电影《摩登时代》用武汉方言改译为话剧，其形式和内容都发生了改变，但深受观众的欢迎。译者由此得到启发，可以采用“改”的变译手段，不受原文文体和结构的局限，坚持忠实原文本意，遵循现代英语的思维模式和规范的语言表达。同时，根据英语句子结构特点，评价性语句在前，把最后“其状惨不忍睹”分句放在句首，以满足特定文化背景下读者的需要。

因文本特点，文内含有文言文的句式，“把体裁改换掉，或者把原文的篇章结构重新整理排序，是改译手段的应用”（魏望东，2023：120）。通过变译理论中“改”的手段改变语言表达方式和句式结构，能使目的语文本更贴近目标语言的语言习惯和文化背景，可以更好地传达原文的意义和情感，使读者更容易理解和接受译文的内容。

5.3.3.3　变译理论指导下的语篇翻译

Cook（1989）指出，语篇是一串有意义的语言单位。常用语篇翻译手段：调整词序，即根据汉语的表达习惯，对原文的词序进行适当调整，以使翻译更符合中文表达的习惯和规范；补充逻辑连接词，适当添加逻辑连接词，以使原文的语言和意思更加清晰、易懂；等等。

语篇翻译往往体现了文本整体的逻辑性。在翻译过程中，英语通常暗含了一定的逻辑关系，译者需要进行补充。在语篇的处理上，译者运用了变译理论中“增”和“编”两种变通手段，具体分析如下。

① 连接词添加——增译。

“语篇的结构是有条理、上下连贯、前后一致的有机的语言整体。”（黄国文，1988：）在译文中，往往通过表示因果、转折、递进含义的连接词来传达行文间的逻辑关系，有时，原文中通过连接词表现出句子间的逻辑，但是有时，逻辑关系需要通过语境判断，因此译者需要将暗含在原文中的逻辑关系通过连接词体现出来。

例 16

原文：俄罗斯哈巴罗夫斯克国立师范大学政治历史系教授罗曼诺娃在《哈尔滨犹太宗教公会的慈善活动》一文中指出，“1938 年 3 月，约 20000 名第一批欧洲犹太人难民经过苏联来到‘满洲国’”。她的数据来自 1943 年第 1 期的《犹太生活》（第 17 页）。同时，她接下来还介绍，“在这里难民们一如既往地得到了同情和支持。犹太公会经常帮助难民，日本当局没有进行任何干涉”。译者质疑这种说法。

译文：Romanova, a professor of the Department of Political History at Khabarovsk State Pedagogical University in Russia, points out in the article *Charity Activities of the Jewish Religious Congregation in Harbin* that “In March 1938, the first group of about 20,000 European Jewish refugees came to 'Manchukuo' via the Soviet Union." Her figures come from *Jewish Life*, No.1, 1943 (p. 17). At the same time, she goes on to describe that "Here the refugees received sympathy and support, as always. The Sanhedrin often helped the refugees without any interference from the Japanese authorities". **However**, the author questions this statement.

分析：作者首先引用了罗曼诺娃教授在《哈尔滨犹太宗教公会的慈善活动》一文中犹太工会对待难民的态度。然而，在后一句，作者表达了自己对同一事件的不同观点。"However" 表示对比、转折、相反的关系，经分析后，译者认为最后一句与前面表相反的意思，前后句之间存在转折关系，因此译者使用了"增"的翻译手段，增加了转折关系连接词"However"，连接词可以帮助读者理解句子之间的关系和逻辑，使译文更加清晰明了。在英语翻译中，连接词的使用比中文更加频繁，因为英语在语法上要求较高的连贯性和一致性。增加连接词"however"使得前后句之间的逻辑关系更加明显。同时，这种翻译手段还符合"译文可读性"原则，即翻译应该更贴近目标语言的语言习惯和文化背景，使得读者更容易理解和接受译文的内容。

例 17

原文：难民是指"由于 1951 年 1 月 1 日以前发生的事情，并因有正当理由畏惧，由于种族、宗教、国籍、属于某一社会团体或具有某种政治见解的原因遭受迫害留在其本国之外，并由于此项畏惧而不能或不愿受该国保护的人；或者不具有国籍并由于上述事情留在以前经常居住国以外，而现在不能或由于上述畏惧不愿返回该国的人"。

从地理学角度讲，难民是人口迁移的特殊形式。因天灾、战争、阶级压迫和民族压迫、宗教和种族歧视、国界变更等，导致大批人口被迫离开家园，流落他乡，形成强制性的迁移。第二次世界大战后，世界难民问题日益突出。难民是国际社会的一个特殊群体，是战争、种族迫害、部族矛盾、国家领土变动、政治避难、自然灾害、经济恶化等原因造成的一个不能或不愿回原籍国的群体，具有群体性、无助性、流动性、自发性和被动性的特征。

译文：Lexically speaking, a refugee is "a person who has stayed outside his country because of events that took place before January 1, 1951, and because of a well-founded fear of persecution on account of race, religion, nationality, membership of a particular social group or political opinion, and who is unable or unwilling to be protected by that country because of such fear; or a person who does not have a nationality and who has stayed outside his former residence because of the above-mentioned events, and who is unable or unwilling to be protected by that country because of the above-mentioned fear".

Geographically speaking, refugees are a special form of population migration. A large number of people are forced to leave their homes and live in other countries as a result of natural disasters, war, class and ethnic oppression, religious and racial discrimination, and changes in national borders, resulting in compulsory migration. After the Second World War, the world refugee problem has become increasingly prominent. Refugees are a special group in the international community, a group unable or unwilling to return to their country of origin due to war, racial persecution, tribal conflicts, national territorial changes, political asylum, natural disasters, economic deterioration, etc. They are characterized by their collectiveness, helplessness, mobility, spontaneity and passivity.

分析：在这段话中，译者使用了"增"的变译手段来提高译文的质量和可读性。这种变译手段可以通过在翻译中增加适当的语言或者词汇，来更好地表达原文的意思和情感。"微观层面的增译表现为语言单位的增加，目的是实现语句结构完整，语意明确，符合译语表述规范。"（朱英丽，2021）在这个例子中，译者在第一段的首句前，增加了"Lexically speaking"这个短语，从语言学角度更好地说明了原文的意思，与第二段的"Geographically speaking"形成上下呼应，使得译文的结构更加整齐明了，有利于读者理解和接受译文的内容。

同时，这种变译手段符合翻译理论中的"变通翻译"原则，即在翻译过程中，根据原文的特点和目标读者的需求，适当增加、删除、调整或者替换翻译内容，以达到最优的翻译效果。

例 18

原文：此外，国内省外的潘光、王健、房建昌等人也关注犹太人在哈尔滨的历史文化研究。上海社科院潘光发表于《社会科学》2005 年第 5 期的《俄国犹太人来华之潮流和哈津沪俄犹社团的形成与发展》和发表于《社会科学》2006 年第 2 期的《来华犹太人的国籍和法律问题（1840—1945）》，上海社科院王健的《关于日占时期哈尔滨犹太社区的几点思考》及中国社科院房建昌的《上海和哈尔滨犹太圣衣社述略》《近代中国东北的犹太人》等论文，也从不同时期、不同角度对犹太人在哈尔滨的历史文化进行了论述和阐释。

译文： In addition, Pan Guang, Wang Jian, Fang Jianchang and **some other history experts** from other provinces in China emphasis on the study of Jewish history and culture in Harbin. Pan Guang, a researcher from the Shanghai Academy of Social Sciences, published *The Tide of Russian Jews in China and the Formation and Development of the Russian-Jewish Community in Harbin and Shanghai* in *Social Sciences*, No.5, 2005, and *Nationality and Legal Problems of Jews in China (1840-1945)* in *Social Sciences*, No.2, 2006. *The Jews in Northeast China in Modern Times* by Wang Jian of the Shanghai Academy of Social Sciences and *Some Reflections on the Jewish Community in Harbin in the course the Japanese Occupation* by Fang Jianchang of the Chinese Academy of Social Sciences have also discussed and interpreted the history and culture of the Jews in Harbin from different periods and perspectives.

分析： 这段话介绍了几位中国历史专家对犹太移民史的研究，但原文中只是用“等人”来代替这些专家的名字，可能会让读者感到困惑。刘颖（2019）曾说，根据上下文语境，进行了增益补充，以使其语意更加明确。这样做可以填补潜在的语意空缺，使读者更容易理解该句的含义。同时，这也有助于衔接该句与前后文的语意关系，使整篇文章行文流畅。在翻译过程中，我们可以通过化隐为显的方式，使用一些必要的语言单位来加强文章的表达效果，使得译文与原文的修辞效果和审美体验更加相似。

译者以此为启发，对句中提到的潘光、王健等采用增译的变译手段，点明身份性质，翻译过程中的增译，是在尊重源语言和目标语言规律与文化因素的前提下，用简洁明了的语言增补原文中表达不清或存在歧义的部分，以便读者对原文有更准确的理解。

例 19

原文： 特迪·考夫曼的这段话比较全面地记述和评价了犹太人在哈尔滨的历程及其特点。在《我心中的哈尔滨犹太人》一书中，他也就犹太人在哈尔滨的生活状况做过叙述。同时，国内外也有许多专家、学者对此做过大量的专门研究。但是，由于相关资料的缺乏、研究者知识背景的“欠缺”等原因造成了认识上的“误读”，犹太人在哈尔滨的研究仅仅处于“刚刚开始”阶段。所以本文在前人研究的基础上，提出一些自己的观点和想法，就具体的关于犹太人在哈尔滨的历史再做进一步论述和阐释。

译文：This quote by Teddy Kaufman provides a more comprehensive remark and evaluation of the Jewish journey in Harbin and its characteristics. In his book *The Jews of Harbin in My Mind*, he also gives an account of the conditions of Jewish life in Harbin. At the same time, there are many experts and scholars at home and abroad who had done a lot of special studies on this subject. **But** due to the lack of relevant information and knowledge background of researchers, misunderstanding would be inevitable on the recognition, thus the research of Jews in Harbin is only at the "just beginning" stage. **Therefore**, based on previous studies, this paper presents some views and ideas of myself and continues to discuss and explain the specific history of Jews in Harbin.

分析：要想翻译好这段话，译者就要理顺这段语篇里的逻辑顺序。作者在前两句阐释了研究目的，随后提出了出现"误读"的原因，这句与前句的逻辑关系是转折。在翻译中，认识文本中的逻辑关系非常重要，文本中的逻辑关系直接影响译文的流畅性与准确性。因为对于历史事件并不是十分了解，往往会使不熟悉这一领域的读者对译文产生误读。最后一句描述作者想要再做进一步论述和阐释的原因，属于因果关系。译者受到时锦瑞和张孟琳（2017）《变译理论在文学翻译中的应用——以〈你快乐吗？〉为例》例2中增加连接词以更好地表现事件准备顺序的启发，将"但是"和"所以"两个逻辑关联词加入翻译中，符合英语表达习惯。在翻译过程中，译者需要了解并适应不同语言语篇结构和表达方式之间的差异，以便能准确地传达原始信息和逻辑关系。

例 20

原文：而曾一智老师在《"河豚鱼计划"与哈尔滨犹太人》一文中写道，犹太人所写的《河豚鱼计划》让她"知道日本侵略者想利用犹太人的资金打赢侵略战争的阴谋"。"在当年，哈尔滨犹太人为了本民族的生存一次次极尽谄媚地向日本侵略者表示赞美时，哈尔滨和全中国的沦陷区的那些不歧视犹太人的中国人，正生活在国土沦丧家破人亡的苦难之中。"那么，"唯一的可能性是当时掌控哈尔滨主权的沙俄殖民者和日本侵略者先后接纳了他们"。**（这个陈述）**是记者的"误读"，还是被采访者的"误述"？

译文：In her article *The Puffer Fish Plan and the Harbin Jews,* Ms. Zeng Yizhi states that the *Puffer Fish Plan*, written by the Jews, made her "aware of the

Japanese invaders' plot to use Jewish funds to win the war of aggression". "In those days, when the Jews of Harbin were fawning over the Japanese invaders again and again for the survival of their own people, the Chinese people in Harbin and in the fallen areas of China, who did not discriminate against the Jews, were living in the misery of the loss of their land and the destruction of their families." Then, "the only possibility is that the Tsarist colonizers and the Japanese invaders, who were in control of the sovereignty of Harbin at that time, successively accepted them". **This statement** was a "misinterpretation" by the reporter or a "misrepresentation" by the interviewee?

分析：通读上下文，这段话最后一句"是记者的'误读'，还是被采访者的'误述'"，译者读后发现，这句话缺少主语，那么这句话的主语是什么呢？这两段都是写曾一智老师对当时谁接纳了哈尔滨犹太人的看法，在《黑龙江日报》(2007)中，记者写的是当时的沙俄殖民者和日本侵略者先后接纳了他们。但是，在曾一智老师《"河豚鱼计划"与哈尔滨犹太人》一书中写道，日本侵略者想要利用犹太人资金的阴谋。她书中的表达和报纸文章的表达不同，因此原作对此提出疑问，到底是记者的误读还是采访者的误述。本句中虽然提到了报纸采访的观点，但是并没有体现出和后句之间的逻辑关系。黄忠廉(2022)曾说，句子之间要有语意和语气上的联系，可用承前省略、代词呼应、关联词语、重复词语等来确保上下文呼应。因此，为了使语篇表达更清晰明了，译者采用"增"的变通手段，给最后无主语的句子增加了"这个陈述"作主语，从而既使句子结构更完整，也使句间衔接更连贯。

② 语篇重组——编译。

胥瑾(2004)曾强调，在语篇翻译过程中，准确翻译单词和句子是非常重要的，但仅凭单词和句子层面的翻译是不够的。必须全面理解上下文，突出主题，使前后文意连贯，上下文自然过渡。因此，译者认为，不管语篇的长短，在翻译时都需要根据原文语境进行加工，更好地表现原文的逻辑关系和传递的信息。这要求译者具备灵活处理原文的能力，能站在读者的角度根据汉语的特点再现原文。在这个翻译过程中，黄忠廉教授提出的"编"这一变通手段发挥了重要作用。

例 21

原文：19 世纪末 20 世纪初，随着犹太人逐渐地迁移到哈尔滨，在哈尔滨道里区以通江街的老会堂、经纬街的新会堂作为宗教活动场所，以通江街的犹太妇女慈善会、犹太贫民食堂、哈尔滨犹太养老院作为慈善保障场所，以红砖街的犹太私人医院、西五道街的犹太医院作为医疗卫生场所，以东风街的犹太第一小学、红霞街的犹太第二小学、通江街的犹大中学作为教育教学场所，以上游街哈尔滨科学馆的犹太人侨民会（犹太人协会，后称"犹太宗教公会"）作为公共管理场所，以及以集中于中央大街两侧的犹太人开设的银行、商场作为金融商业场所，犹太人在哈尔滨以中央大街为中心形成了一个体系完备的社区。

译文：In the late 19th and early 20th centuries, as Jews gradually migrated to Harbin, The Jews formed a complete system of community in Harbin with Central Street as the center: (1) the old synagogue on Tongjiang Street and the new synagogue on Jingwei Street were used as places of religious activities in the Daoli District of Harbin; (2) The Jewish Women's Charity Society on Tongjiang Street, the Jewish Poor People's Canteen, and the Harbin Jewish Nursing Home were used as places of charitable protection; (3) The Jewish Private Hospital on Red Brick Street and the Jewish Hospital on West Fifth Street were used as places of medical and health care; (4) The first Jewish elementary school on Dongfeng Street, the second Jewish elementary school on Hongxia Street, and the Judean high school on Tongjiang Street were used as places of education and teaching; (5) The Judean People's (Adult Association, later called the Judean Religious Congregation) of the Harbin Science Officer on Upstream Street was used as a place of public administration; (6)The banks and shopping malls opened by the Judeans concentrated on both sides of Central Street were used as places of financial and commercial business.

分析："英汉语篇在信息分布模式和语篇结构上有诸多区别，因此英汉翻译中需对原文语篇进行结构重组，以使译文符合目的语的语篇信息分布模式或语篇结构规范。"（熊兵，2014：87）在翻译过程中，重构语篇结构是一项必要的任务，以确保信息的传递、读者的理解和作者原意的一致性。"在某些情况下，如果汉语原文自然段结构安排不够合理，完全按照原文翻译就会使英语读者感到译文逻辑混乱，这时就应该根据原文的中心思想、发展线索及语篇内部照应的原则，加强逻辑联系，重新安排译文，使之'前后呼应'。"（夏乙琥，1992：129）此段是描述 19 世纪末 20 世纪初，犹太移民在哈尔滨中央大街形成的社区，其中包含宗教活动场所、慈善保障场所、医疗卫生场所、教育教学场所、公共管理场所和金融商业场所，共 6 个场所。原文是中文逻辑推理方式，把结论放在句尾，但因为目的语读者是英文思维模式，所以译者用“编译”中调序方法，把结论句移到句首，把译文结构调整成总分。同时，在句间添加序号，使译文条理清晰，可以帮助读者迅速抓住有效信息。

例22

原文：1997年出版的《风雨浮萍——俄国侨民在中国（1917—1945）》一书中对“侨民”的解释是，“通常把那些由于某种政治的、经济的、宗教的或其他的原因，被迫或自愿地从自己的祖国迁居到其他国家的居民称作‘侨民’。**这些人中，有的仍保留原先的国籍；有的则放弃或失去了原先的国籍，但并未加入新的国籍，从而成为无国籍者；还有的加入了侨居国的国籍**”。

译文：In the book *Russian Expatriates in China (1917—1945)*, which published in 1997, the term “expatriates” is explained as “those who are forced or voluntarily moved from their home country to other countries for some political, economic, religious or other reasons. **There have three common situations: (1)Some still retain their original nationality; (2) Some renounce or lose their original nationality but do not acquire a new one, thus becoming stateless; (3) Some acquire the nationality of the country of their residence**”.

分析：对照原文不难发现，译者增加了3个序号，目的是使原文中提到的3种不同侨民类型一目了然。除此之外，译文中还有一处明显的增译——There have three common situations。此处，增译的句子在修复了原文缺失的连接词的同时，也更加精准地总结了前文所述的3种情况，使得译文更加清晰易懂。在翻译过程中，有时需要对原文进行必要的增、删、改，以便让译文更好地传达原意，并且让读者更好地理解。译者对例18的翻译得益于《翻译方法论》（黄忠廉，2009）中对“中山大学概况”的编译手段。从而，在这个例子中，译者选择了“编”的翻译手法，使得例子的集中展示更能突出原作的信息，同时，让句子的排列更有条理、逻辑更清晰。

例23

原文：2007年，犹太研究中心又出版了《哈尔滨与世界犹太人》论文集。**2007年，**还出版了特迪·考夫曼的《我心中的哈尔滨犹太人》一书。这期间，犹太研究中心还多次举办国际学术研讨会，哈尔滨犹太人问题研究初具规模。

译文：In 2007, the Center for Jewish Studies published another collection of essays by *Harbin and World Jewish* and also saw the publication of Teddy

Kaufman's *The Harbin Jews in My Heart*. During this period, the Center for Jewish Studies also held several international symposia, which symbolized that the research on Harbin's Jews took shape.

分析：英国翻译家和评论家彼得·纽马克（Peter Newmark）的著作《翻译教程》中包含处理重复信息的技巧，它被归类为“语言变体”一章中语言简化和修辞等处理技巧中的一部分。其主要技巧有删除重复信息、换用同义词、改变语序、使用代词、合并句子等。句中出现两次2007年，在分析语篇后，译者认为这两处是信息重复，语意啰嗦，删掉一个并不会对原文的语意造成影响，因此译者使用“编”的变通手段及纽马克的翻译技巧，删掉其中一个“2007年”，然后把两句合为一句，使结构更紧凑、流畅。

例 24

原文：其中，“曾一智：这是我终身不变的事业”一段介绍，在研究和保护犹太文化的工作中，让曾一智觉得最满意的是两件事。其一，黑龙江省社会科学院文学研究所研究员刘以焕借给她《河豚鱼计划》一书，该书描述了哈尔滨犹太人在日军占领哈尔滨期间的历史。

译文：One of the paragraphs, “Zeng Yizhi: this is my lifelong career”, describes how “in his work of studying and preserving Jewish culture, Zeng Yizhi felt most satisfied with two things. **One of them** was Liu Yihuan, a researcher at the Institute of Literature of the Heilongjiang Academy of Social Sciences, lent her the book *The Puffer Fish Project*, which describes the history of Harbin's Jews during Japanese occupation of Harbin.”

分析：这段话主要针对原文中表述不清的问题，在翻译中，译者用“编”的变通手段使翻译更加准确和流畅。曾一智在采访中提到了她对于哈尔滨犹太人研究中两件最满意的事情，但是在新闻稿件中只写了其中的一件，而“其一”这个词会让读者不知道还有第二件事情，导致信息表述不清。因此，译者需要通过合理的变通方法来解决这个问题，避免读者误解。

在这个过程中，译者采用了“编”的方法来理顺逻辑关系，强调语言的连贯性。“翻译就是要在目的语文本中重新构筑源语文本中连贯的叙事模式，让目的语读者获得完整而有效的叙事解读。”（杨志廷，2021：106）在译文中，译者将初稿中“firstly”这个表述方式改成了“one of them”，以减少读者的疑惑。这样做可以使整段文本的逻辑关系更加流畅和连贯，保证读者对信息的理解更加准确。

例 25

原文：李述笑、曲伟、刘爽、张铁江等人的著作或论文在哈尔滨犹太人的相关研究中“各领风骚”。其中，李述笑老师的奠基作用，功不可没，他的《哈尔滨犹太人历史年表》《哈尔滨犹太复国主义组织述略》等具有开创作用。2007 年，刘爽老师的《哈尔滨犹太侨民史》，**“涉及犹太人流散迁移史、犹太复国主义史、俄国侨民史、东北亚国际关系史、东北近现代史、东北经济史、哈尔滨地方史等诸多领域，对这些错综复杂的因素进行综合研究，使本书不仅具有较高的学术价值，而且也有着重要的现实意义”。**2004 年，张铁江老师的《揭开哈尔滨犹太人历史之谜——哈尔滨犹太人社区考察研究》一书，“把哈尔滨犹太人从传统的俄侨中分离出来，更加注重研究犹太人的民族性，把社会上关注哈尔滨犹太人的传说，用历史事实科学地加以印证和阐释”等。

译文：Books or papers by Li Shuxiao, Qu Wei, Liu Shuang, Zhang Tiejiang are prominent in Jewish studies in Harbin. Among this, Li Shuxiao has made an impression on a foundation role which his works such as *Harbin Jews Historical Timeline* and *A Brief History of the Harbin Zionist Organization* acted pioneering function. In 2007, **Liu Shuang's *History of the Jewish Diaspora in Harbin* "deals with the complicated history of Jewish dispersal and migration, making this book not only of high academic value, but also has important practical significance".** In 2004, Zhang Tiejiang's book, *Unraveling the Mystery of Harbin Jewish History—A Study of Harbin Jewish Community, separating Jews in Harbin* from the traditional Russian diaspora, focuses more on the study of Jewish ethnicity, and uses historical facts to scientifically corroborate and explain the social legends.

分析：本次翻译实践的目的语读者可能是历史相关从业人员，也有可能是历史爱好者。作者在介绍刘爽老师的《哈尔滨犹太侨民史》时，提到了很多历史经济术语。译者在初译时对每个术语都进行了检索并询问了原作者，以防出现术语错译。但是，在第二次审校后，编辑根据实践文本的特点，提出是否要把此处所有术语都翻译出来，因为本书的译文受众不仅仅是专业人士，还有历史爱好者。文中出现太多历史术语会消磨读者的阅读热情。译者根据编辑的意见，再次对语篇进行分析，重点突出李述笑、曲伟、刘爽、张铁江等对犹太人在哈尔滨这个领域做出的显著贡献。李述笑老师的作品有开创作用；刘爽老师的作品学术价值高，有重要的现实意义；张铁江老师的作品是历史科学的验证。

因此，最后译者采用“编译”手段，对例句中加粗句子进行编辑，摘取出此句核心重点：“刘爽老师的《哈尔滨犹太侨民史》中对犹太人复杂的流放和移民史的研究有很高的学术价值与重要的现实意义"，然后全部进行翻译。

例 26

原文：①在欧洲历史上具有毁灭性的瘟疫出现在 1348—1361 年。②这是一场腺鼠疫天灾。③后来一般称为"黑死病"。黑死病发生后，"罪犯，贵族，残疾人和犹太人相继遭到怀疑，尤其是犹太人，其被怀疑有意用一种所谓毒药通过污染井水或是涂抹房屋和人来传播瘟疫"。

译文：A devastating plague of glanders (later known as the Black Death) in European history occurred in 1348-1361. After the Black Death, "the criminals, the nobles, the disabled and Jews were suspected, especially Jews, who were suspected of intentionally spreading the plague by contaminating the water of wells with a so-called poison or by smearing houses and people."

分析：这段话主要是针对原文中重复语意问题进行的处理。在本段中，前后三句话都提到了 1348—1361 年欧洲历史上发生的一场毁灭性瘟疫，这个瘟疫是腺鼠疫天灾，后来被称为"黑死病"。然而，在这三句话中，瘟疫的描述出现了重复，需要进行调整以使文本更加流畅和准确。

因此，译者采用了"编"的变通方法来解决这个问题。首先，将②这一分句改成①中瘟疫的前置定语，将③改成①中瘟疫的后置定语，以减少语意的重复。其次，将整个句子重新编写为"在欧洲历史上一场具有毁灭性的腺鼠瘟疫（后来被称为'黑死病'）出现在 1348—1361 年"通过这种方式，译者成功地删减了重复语意，调整了句序，使得整个句子更加清晰、流畅和准确。

在语篇翻译中，译者经常会遇到语言表达中重复或者不必要的信息，这样会导致译文过长和难以理解。采用"编"的变通手段可以通过删减多余信息，调整句子结构或使用不同的表达方式，以减少译文中的信息冗余，使得译文更加简洁有力，易于理解。同时，通过调整句子结构、变换词序等手段，"编"可以帮助译者保持语言的逻辑关系和连贯性，从而使得译文更加易于理解和吸收。

5.3.4 翻译实践总结

译者在变译理论的指导下，以《清末民初黑龙江移民史研究》之十作为案例研究对象，完成了本次翻译实践。在翻译实践任务中，译者获得了许多宝贵经验，但也遇到了不少问题。在本部分中，译者将总结本次翻译实践的收获与启示，同时，反思自身不足，并指出本报告的局限性。

5.3.4.1 心得与收获

此次翻译实践历时较长，从最初阅读原文和收集资料到翻译时把握原文并选择翻译理论和方法，再到最后对译文不断地进行校对和修正。整个过程充满了困难和艰辛、挑战和收获，让译者深刻地感受到翻译工作的真实状态。翻译并不是简单的文字转换，好的译文也不是一蹴而就的。

本次翻译实践让译者受益匪浅，首先，译者了解到在翻译开始之前，应当充分了解任务的性质及写作背景，以便更好地解读文本。其次，译者需要确定翻译文本的目标读者和预期效果，预测翻译阶段可能遇到的问题，及时找到解决办法。“翻译从来就不是一项纯语言的活动，翻译实质上是对原作意义、信息、思想和文化的传递。而译者则是这种传递信息、思想、文化的使者。”（吴志芳、邱棠，2007：15）因此，译者并不是单一的角色，还要扮演编辑的角色，具备一定的分析能力，具备责任心、耐心和恒心，成为一名积极的学习者，不断学习掌握不同领域的知识。

方梦之和王志娟（2022）曾阐明，翻译学科是一门经验学科，其基本特征是实践性。在本篇翻译实践报告中，黄忠廉教授的变译理论及其中的变译策略起到了至关重要的作用。使用该理论有助于译者做到目标文本简洁通顺，并有序地组织句子及语篇之间的逻辑关系。就任何类型的翻译而言，读者是影响译文可读性和可接受性的重要因素之一，因此译者应考虑读者的需求。根据变译理论，译者的主体性得到充分发挥，以目的语读者为出发点，从而决定翻译的策略和方法，提高目标读者的阅读体验。

此外，变译理论当中的变译手段及策略为译者提供了具体的翻译方法，进一步体现了变译理论对移民文本翻译的适用性。在词汇方面，译者可以根据读者的阅读习惯及原文的语境，运用“增”的变通手段适当增加扩展信息，运用“减”的变通手段删去文中多余的水分，运用“改”的变通手段将相关词汇翻译得更简洁。在句子方面，译者用“编”恰当调整语序，让译文层次更加分明；根据句子的意思，用“改”灵活地转述为符合目的语文化语境的表达。在语篇方面，译者用“增”和“编”的变通手段，让语篇的衔接更加连贯，增强了上下文之间的逻辑关系及联系。

5.3.4.2 问题与对策

翻译的过程也是不断进行改进和积累经验的过程，在这次翻译实践中，译者遇到了下列困难，并作出了改进。

第一，文本处理方面。由于译者对移民历史文献文本接触甚少，对专业术语的意义及历史背景的知识了解不足，难免会与专业要求产生一定差距。因此，在初稿中出现了几处词句的表述不够专业，这也对项目的顺利进行产生了一定影响。译者通过查阅资料和参考相关平行文本等方式自行解决了一部分问题；在与导师和客户方专业人士的共同努力下，剩余的疑难问题也得到了较为妥善的处理。

第二，翻译辅助工具使用方面。由于对 Trados 软件的使用不够熟练，译者在本次实践中遇到了一些困难。尽管在计算机辅助翻译课上学习过相关知识，但本次实践是第一次独立操作，导致在建立术语库和导出文件格式的处理上出现了一些失误。幸运的是，译者在向导师和计算机辅助课老师求教后，最终顺利地解决了 Trados 软件的使用难题。

第三，译后审校方面。由于注意力不够集中，译者在翻译过程中出现了一些低级失误。这给译者敲响了警钟，提醒译者要认真仔细地处理每处译文，不能有丝毫马虎。即使是微小的误译，也可能对译文质量造成严重影响。在译后审校阶段，译者必须认真负责地检查译文，在自我校对后，要及时请同行、导师和专家来对译文进行审校。

5.3.4.3　努力方向与展望

这次翻译实践让译者深刻认识到翻译的复杂性和挑战性，同时，也找到了自己努力的方向。在实践结束后，译者获得了丰富的经验和感悟，对未来的翻译生涯有了更加充实和明确的规划。

通过这次翻译实践，译者深刻认识到翻译这门学科的广博和深奥。翻译是一门十分复杂的学问，需要译者具备丰富的知识储备、扎实的语言功底、敏锐的观察力和理性的思考能力，要求译者不断通过实践提升自己的翻译能力。只有在不断的实践中，译者才能逐渐掌握翻译思维模式，拓宽翻译视野，提高翻译水平。“业精于勤荒于嬉”，通过反复实践，不断积累经验，发现问题，解决问题，从而逐步提高自己的翻译能力。译者会继续努力学习翻译知识，夯实基础。在学习中，译者会注重理论知识和实践能力的结合，将所学知识应用到实践中，不断积累经验和提高技能。正如何刚强（2018）所说：“在努力探索建立中国特色翻译基础理论的过程中，我们不仅要继续汲取国外译学的精华，为我所用，更要努力从博大精深的中华传统文化中（包括中国古典哲学、广义文论、文章学、文字学、艺术论等）寻找有益的养分。”

谚语有云：读书百遍，其义自见；行万里路，其事自知。只有通过不断的学习和实践，才能真正理解事物的本质，获得更深刻的认识和经验。作为一名翻译硕士研究生，译者需要坚持不懈地刻苦钻研，不断向身边的同行与导师请教，同时还要对自己的专业保持热情，不断提高自己的翻译水平。在翻译过程中，每个步骤都有着需要学习的地方，每次成功都需要集结身边人来共同取得，因为一山更比一山高。

译者希望未来能继续进行更深入的翻译研究，学习各种不同的翻译理论，读更多的翻译书籍。向身边的诸多良师益友请教，以此来取得更长足的进步。通过这次实践，译者深刻认识到提高专业水平的必要性，下定决心要不断学习，保持谦逊，勤学好问，与人为善，成为一名触类旁通的译者。译者坚信，在未来的翻译路上，只要不断努力，就能走得更远，追求更卓越的翻译成果。

参考文献

[1] COOK G. Discourse and Literature[M]. London: OUP, 1989.
[2] FAWCETT, PETER. Translation and Language[M]. London: Taylor &Francis e–Library, 2014.
[3] HUANG ZHONGLIAN, ZHANG YONGZHONG. Variational Translation Theory[M]. Singapore: Springer, 2020.
[4] KATAN D. Translating Cultures: An Introduction for Translators, Interpreters and Mediators[M]. Shanghai: Shanghai Foreign Language Education Press, 2004
[5] NEWMARK P. Approaches to Translation[M]. Shanghai: Shanghai Foreign Language Education Press, 2011.
[6] NORD, CHRISTIANE. Translating as a Purposeful Activity: Functionalist Approaches Explained[M]. Shanghai: Shanghai Foreign Language Education Press, 2001.
[7] VENUTI, LAWRENCE. The Translator's Invisibility A History of Translation[M]. London: Taylor &Francis e–Library, 2004.
[8] LAWRENCE VENUTI. Rethinking Translation: Discourse, Subjectivity, Ideology[M]. London: Taylor &Francis e–Library, 2018.
[9] 陈柳悦 . 论英汉句子的异同与翻译 [J]. 山西财经大学学报（高等教育版），2010（S1）：69，78.
[10] 陈定安 . 英汉比较与翻译 [M]. 北京：中国对外翻译出版公司，2000.
[11] 方梦之，王志娟 . 变译论的理论贡献和实践意义 [J]. 外语教学，2020（1）：82–86.
[12] 谷青松，焦春 .《豫园》英译中的“减译”[J]. 山西师范大学学报（社会科学版），2010（S3）：84–85.
[13] 何刚强 . 变译的多重意涵与理论地位 [J]. 外语与翻译，2018（2）：7–10.
[14] 黄国文 . 语篇分析概要 [M]. 长沙：湖南教育出版社，1988.
[15] 黄忠廉 . 汉译组构流畅性优化原则 [J]. 天津外国语大学学报，2022（1）：

9–19，111.
[16] 黄忠廉 . 变译的七种变通手段 [J]. 外语学刊，2002（1）：93–96.
[17] 黄忠廉 . 变译理论：一种全新的翻译理论 [J]. 国外外语教学，2002（1）：19–22.
[18] 黄忠廉 . 变译理论 [M]. 北京：中国对外翻译出版公司，2001.
[19] 黄忠廉 . 变译理论研究类型考 [J]. 外语学刊，2011（6）：101–104.
[20] 黄忠廉 . 翻译方法论 [M]. 上海：华东师范大学出版社，2019.
[21] 黄忠廉，杨荣广 . 变译理论：深究与拓展 [J]. 民族翻译，2018（2）：5–6.
[22] 金隄 . 灵活用词，准确达意：翻译中的词汇对应关系 [J]. 中国翻译，1985（2）：2–5.
[23] 姜盼盼 . 变译理论指导下的中国文化翻译研究：以《中国文化读本》英译为例 [J]. 空中美语，2022（2）：257–259.
[24] 李立业 . 从英汉规律性差异谈减译策略 [J]. 辽宁工程技术大学学报（社会科学版），2005（4）：419–420.
[25] 厉平 . 变译理论研究：回顾与反思 [J]. 外语学刊，2014（1）：94–98.
[26] 连淑能 . 英汉对比与研究 [M]. 北京：高等教育出版社，2010.
[27] 刘颖 . 论翻译中的“变译”[J]. 清华大学学报（哲学社会科学版），2019（4）：92–98，201.
[28] 时锦瑞，张孟琳 . 变译理论在文学翻译中的应用：以《你快乐吗？》为例 [J]. 华北水利水电大学学报（社会科学版），2017（6）：118–121.
[29] 吴志芳，邱棠 . 译者主体性的发挥：制约中的能动 [J]. 上海翻译，2007（2）：15–17.
[30] 魏望东 . 正体全译中的变译手段：以《论语》英译为例 [J]. 语言与文化研究，2023（1）：117–122.
[31] 王红利 . 成语翻译新论：互文性视角 [J]. 西安外国语大学学报，2009（4）：71–74.
[32] 夏乙琥 . 漫谈汉译英的段落组织 [M]//《中国翻译》编辑部 . 中译英技巧文集 . 北京：中国对外翻译出版公司，1992.
[33] 熊兵 . 翻译研究中的概念混淆：以“翻译策略”、“翻译方法”和“翻译技巧”为例 [J]. 中国翻译，2014（3）：82–88.
[34] 胥瑾 . 翻译与语篇分析 [J]. 中国科技翻译，2004（3）：9–12.
[35] 杨仕章 . 翻译界说新探 [J]. 外语教学，2015（6）：99–103.
[36] 杨志亭 . 认知叙事学视域中语篇连贯的翻译重构 [J]. 外国语文，2021（1）：105–112.

[37] 朱英丽 . 增译研究述评：名实之辨 [J]. 社会科学战线，2021（9）：266–270.
[38] 张永中 . 变译和全译在文化对外传播中的不同效度 [J]. 上海翻译，2018（4）：78–82，95.

5.4 《中东铁路附属地行政管理权研究》英译研究

中国的日益发展激起了全球范围内中国历史爱好者的研究热情，而翻译特定时期历史文献，有助于海外专家或相关研究者更全面客观地了解中国相关史实，以促进相关领域研究的发展。此次翻译实践选取李朋教授等的著作《清末民初黑龙江移民史研究》之十四——《中东铁路附属地行政管理权研究》作为源语文本，属于历史文献类文本范畴，具有一定的客观性。该部分主要介绍了清末民初哈尔滨中东铁路“铁路交涉局”的演变及发展，包括该机构的名称及职能的演变，以及这些变迁背后的故事。本次实践报告旨在促进国内外学者和历史爱好者对中东铁路附属地行政管理权的相关研究，并深入探索目的论对历史研究文献的指导作用。

本次翻译实践以翻译目的论为指导，在词汇、句子和语篇 3 个层面对翻译实践进行分析与总结。在词汇层面，基于“忠实原则”及“目的原则”，译者采用意译和释义来翻译古代官职与文书词汇等较难理解的特色词汇；在句子层面，译者选择增译来处理文言句式，对于其他句子，译者则选择用主被动语态转化和定语后置的方法进行翻译，并深入探析三大原则对本次翻译实践的适用性；在语篇层面，译者基于“目的原则”及“连贯原则”重点分析增加逻辑衔接词和语序调整对增强语篇衔接、语意连贯的影响，以增强译文逻辑的合理性和结构的一致性。最终，译文实现了语句通顺、结构连贯、逻辑紧密的预期效果，验证了翻译目的论对于本次翻译实践的指导性作用，为相关翻译研究提供了更多具体案例。

通过本次英译实践，译者对翻译目的论在历史文献文本翻译实践问题中的指导作用有了更深刻的认识和把握。本次翻译实践不仅能为撰写清末民初中东铁路研究的学者提供有价值的规范与标准，还能为研究中东铁路的翻译工作者提供翻译技巧方面的参考与借鉴。

5.4.1 引言

随着全球化进程的持续推进，中国的综合国力不断提升，前有改革开放经济腾飞，一跃成为世界第二大经济体；后有中华文化扬帆出海，向世界展现中国自信。实力之下，更具底蕴，作为四大文明古国唯一延续至今的国度，中国拥有上下五千年璀璨的历史文明。因此，有关中国历史文献类的翻译颇受重视，已然成为我国翻译研究的重要领域之一。

在翻译历史文献一类的文本时，要保持严谨客观的态度。“作为译者，我们肩负的责任是传播历史文献中蕴含的文明和内涵”（李靖、侯玉、缪丽伟，2021：133–135），不能添加过多的主观色彩，以保证译文的质量及历史本身的客观性。译者在翻译目的论的指导下，选取《清末民初黑龙江移民史研究》之十四——《中东铁路附属地行政管理权研究》进行实践，希望通过此次翻译实践，在契合目的语读者阅读习惯的前提下，将历史文献研究者的研究本意全面且客观地呈现出来。

目前，学术界与之相关的文献研究外译本非常少。通过查阅中国知网文献译者发现，“素来历史文献的翻译注重于技术实践，同文学类翻译相比，在理论研究方面一直处于滞后的状态”（刘岩、陈胜能，2021：20–26）。分析该类文本英译研究现状的原因得出以下结论：首先，相较于历史文献文本的英译，其对应的文献研究译本则不足为数，因为历史文本多为客观描绘史实，而历史研究各有不同，对内容的解读也是因人而异的，所以与历史研究有关的英译则寥寥无几。译者选取的文本偏向历史研究方向，文白兼杂，对于这类翻译，学术界相关的资料更是少之又少，历史文献偏于客观展现相关史实，而不同专家学者的研究过程和研究结果则可能有所区别。在这种情况下，翻译工作者的任务就不是纯粹地只做翻译，而是要经过一定的筛选，选择主流的、符合史实且容易为大众所理解和接受的研究结果进行翻译。

历史研究翻译要求译者有较高的知识水平及翻译素养，通过本次翻译实践，译者深刻地认识到翻译目的论的“目的原则“忠实原则”连贯原则”在翻译过程中的应用。在翻译过程中，译者明确了“翻译目的论”在历史文献类文本的适用性，灵活建立起译者自身对文本类型的理解，再结合具体案例对译文进行解读分析。对于其中夹杂的文言文或者特色术语，译者也进行了多方询问，例如，利用各大搜索引擎，寻求导师及原作者的帮助，等等，结合相关史实融入自己的理解，最终得出客观结论进行翻译。除此之外，译者还掌握了很多有关历史词汇的术语，并制定了术语表，为今后翻译此类文本提供参考资料。译者热切希望通过本翻译实践报告，为研究相关历史文献英译的学者提供一些借鉴，献出自己的绵薄之力。

5.4.2 翻译任务描述

为做好本次翻译实践，在翻译任务开始前，译者需综合把控翻译工作的各项步骤，以下就《中东铁路附属地行政管理权研究》的翻译实践任务进行具体描述。本部分主要介绍此次实践的任务背景和源语文本的基本内容，阐述翻译目的和意义，传达委托方要求。

5.4.2.1　任务背景和源语文本的基本内容

本次翻译任务选自李朋教授等编著的《清末民初黑龙江移民史研究》之十四——《中东铁路附属地行政管理权研究》，该项目由李靖教授和张春烨教授共同执行，译者被分配的任务为《清末民初黑龙江移民史研究》之十三、十四、十五及十六。其中，选取十四作为翻译实践报告部分。

《清末民初黑龙江移民史研究》一书由黑龙江人民出版社于 2019 年 12 月出版。作为一本较为系统、详尽的黑龙江移民史专著，该书详细论述了清朝末年至民国初期黑龙江移民的历史、过程、背景及其重要意义。该书从黑龙江移民的类型、地区、组织、目的、规模等方面着手，深入分析了黑龙江移民对当地经济、政治、文化、民族关系等方面的影响，并探讨了黑龙江移民与中俄关系的演变等问题。它不仅丰富了我们对黑龙江移民历史的认识，还为研究近现代东北地区历史和民族关系提供了重要的参考。

本项目的源语文本选自《清末民初黑龙江移民史研究》之十四——《中东铁路附属地行政管理权研究》，其中包括吉黑两省铁路交涉局设立之前的铁路交涉，中东铁路管理局体系内的黑龙江铁路交涉局，被试图纳入“哈尔滨关道”体制内的“铁路交涉局”，中方权力的失而复得。本项目计划由中国经济出版社出版，本人翻译字数为 16261 个字，可以满足本次翻译实践要求。

5.4.2.2　翻译目的与意义

本文选取的实践板块含有大量清末民初的特色词汇与表达，涉及当时文化背景下设立的一些外交机构名称，本次翻译项目以准确传递出原文信息和内容为前提，以一名专业翻译人员的要求为导向，向目的语读者讲述一段清末民初哈尔滨城市发展进程中颇具争议的历史，供国外相关领域学者对此进行下一步的研究。因此，译者希望实现如下目的：

① 掌握清末民初有关中东铁路变迁史的专业术语并积累翻译经验；

② 为研究同类型文本内容的历史学者、历史爱好者以及历史文献英译者提供帮助；

③ 深入探索翻译目的论对历史研究文献类文本的指导作用。

译者通过明确文本选择的目的，进一步总结了翻译目的论指导下历史研究文本翻译的方法，通过实践加强了对各类翻译方法的理论理解，并总结翻译经验。

历史类文本专业性与严谨性较强，在翻译时不能出现遗漏与篡改，要准确无误地翻译原文内容，才能译出传达原始信息的优质译文。基于以上，译者总结了英译的 3 层意义：理论意义、实践意义与现实意义。

① 理论意义。

本次历史文献英译翻译实践，作为信息类文本形式的一种，具有一定的翻译理论意义。根据莱斯的观点，“信息型文本主要是表现事实、信息、知识、观点等，其语言特点是逻辑性较强，文本的焦点是内容而不是形式；翻译时应以简单明了的白话文传递与原文相同的概念与信息文本”（Reiss，2000：30–48），如本次选取的实践材料内容写实化，但部分内容（如下设机构的规章及派遣用语）引用的是原稿流传的文本，因此需要将此部分原稿先转化为符合现代汉语习惯的用语，再将其转化为译语。从学术视角来看，本次翻译实践为译者提供了更广泛的历史研究类翻译领域的知识，同时，也拓宽了自身的视野。在翻译过程中，可以对此过程应用到的目的论做进一步分析与研究，借用目的论中的“目的原则“忠实原则”连贯原则”，即“翻译过程最主要的因素是整体翻译行为的目的”（Nord，2000），对文本进行翻译研究，进而总结出相关的翻译策略与技巧。此次实践可为日后相关文本的汉译英提供帮助和借鉴。

② 实践意义。

通过本次翻译实践，就专业的角度而言，译者能够提升自身的翻译技能，更深入地理解和应用各种翻译理论，从而达到更高的翻译水平；就社会方面而言，可以丰富中国历史文献研究的外译本，为国内外学者提供更多英文文献作为参考和选择。

③ 现实意义。

中东铁路交涉局的变迁史，从一个独特的角度充分体现了哈尔滨及中东铁路附属地的独特发展史，也反映了哈尔滨城市形成过程的基本特征。然而，学术界与之相关的文献研究外译本非常少。因此，通过此次翻译实践，既可为我国研究中东铁路附属地变迁史类翻译提供参考，也可为国外研究者提供专业参考资料，同时，促进不同国家和民族之间的交流，加快文化的传播。

5.4.2.3 委托方要求

译者受黑龙江大学李朋教授的委托进行英译工作。在翻译时，委托方希望充分调动目的语读者的阅读积极性，保证相关领域读者的参与性，最大限度地保留原文含义，符合原文编写的目的与要求。终稿的预期完成时间为2022年12月底。委托方对译者提出如下要求：

①本文选取内容中含有清末民初相关铁路机构等专业词汇、中国历史专业术语，因此对这些词汇的处理，要广泛查找资料，以求对其进行准确的翻译；

② 基于真实准确的文本类型特点，在翻译过程中，译者需要不断地修改

和反思，寻找符合目的语阅读和表达方式的翻译，并在译后阶段做好充分的检验以确保译文的词汇准确、句子流畅、语篇连贯。

5.4.3　翻译过程描述

想要顺利完成一项翻译任务，译者需要在翻译任务进行之前，熟悉整个翻译流程，并制订翻译流程的基本计划。本章翻译过程描述主要包括翻译实践开始之前的一系列准备工作、翻译过程的详细内容和翻译实践结束后的一些注意事项，一共 3 部分内容。

5.4.3.1　译前准备

译前准备是保证翻译质量的必要条件。在翻译之前，译者没有足够的经验来完成这项任务，因此做好充足的译前准备必不可少。那么，在译前阶段，译者需要了解相关背景知识、平行文本、专业术语、翻译辅助工具，最重要的是对翻译理论的准备，即便译前准备工作繁重且复杂，但译者的心态仍要热情饱满，保持高度的责任感，这样才能给委托方一份完美的答卷。

① 源语文本分析。

“翻译是一种带目的性的跨语交际活动，翻译活动本身必然涉及对文本的处理。”（张美芳，2013：5–10）确立翻译任务的文本特征是展开翻译研究的核心步骤，这不仅有助于推进翻译方法的选择，还为翻译理论的应用和实例分析奠定了基础。译者从源语文本的内容与结构出发，从词汇、句子和语篇 3 个层面来分析。

该文本为历史文献类，时间段在清末民初，文本内容主要为清末民初中东铁路的变迁史，因此词汇专业性较强，例如，涉及古代官职，清末民初时期的文书词汇及古代公文词汇等。针对此类翻译，译者应充分理解原文表达的含义，在目的论的指导下选取意译、释义等方法进行翻译。

在句子层面，译者翻译部分多涉及一些地域之间的官职调动及行政处理，在这些表述方面，原作者要么引用旧时函件原文，即文言句式，要么用简单的白话告知，其特点为文白夹杂，因此译者结合目的论，对文言句式采用增译的方法，对其他句子则采用主被动语态转换及定语从句后置的方法。在语篇层面，则存在一些语篇结构的调整重组与逻辑衔接。

以上都是译者在本实践报告中提到的典型案例。从整体分析来看，这些文本内容是相互关联、上下联系的，因此在翻译该文本的过程中还需要保证传达信息的准确性，以及翻译为目的语后的可读性。

② 翻译理论选择。

翻译实践的成果受到翻译理论选择的直接影响，因为翻译理论不仅为实践提供基础支撑，还会对译文的最终质量产生深远影响。因此，通过阅读大量的文献及理论书籍，译者最终选取翻译目的论作为本次《中东铁路附属地行政管理权研究》英译实践的理论指导，为翻译过程提供启示，使译文更贴近目的语读者的阅读习惯，更规范、得体。

20 世纪六七十年代，功能主义翻译理论（functionalist translation theory）中的核心理论——翻译目的论（skopos theory）诞生了，skopos 源自希腊语，蕴含着“目的、动机、意图、企图”等多重含义。其最初主要研究翻译行为的目的性问题，后来扩展到对翻译过程进行解释。17 世纪，德国的翻译理论家弗米尔（Hans J Vermeer）率先提出了功能主义翻译目的论，该理论基于赖斯（Katharina Reiss）的功能派思想。它强调翻译过程是一个动态、复杂而又充满创造性的心理活动，翻译的最终结果就是译文与原文达到完全对应，即意义上的对等关系。功能主义翻译目的论的代表著作是 1984 年由弗米尔和赖斯合著的《一般翻译的理论基础》(*Grundlegung einer allgemine Translations-theorie*)，该著作从哲学、美学及社会学角度探讨翻译问题，并结合具体实例阐述了如何运用这一理论来指导翻译实践。翻译目的论的提出，打破了以往将翻译视为静态语言学理论中的一部分这一观点，重新定义和解释了翻译，强调了译者的主观能动性，摆脱了等值翻译的限制，将翻译视为有目的性的人类行为，是一种跨越文化的语言交际行为。在这本书里，翻译目的论得到了极大重视，成为众多学者研究的重点之一。随后，贾斯塔·霍茨·曼塔（Justa Holz Manttan，1984：17）提出了翻译行为理论（translation action theory），将翻译视为一种由目的驱动的复杂行为活动，将其视为涉及各种参与者的交际过程，从而进一步发展和传承了翻译目的论。他认为，任何翻译都要以目的为中心，而在翻译过程中，目的语读者的接受能力也成为一个重要因素。最终，诺德对翻译目的论进行了全面系统的归纳和总结，并提出了一种文本分析模式，旨在限制译者在翻译过程中的自由度，同时强调了“功能 + 忠诚”的理念。本部分从这 3 个方面探讨翻译策略研究在翻译领域的重要性，以及存在的问题与不足。总体而言，“翻译理论需要系统地研究双语转换规律，通过描述翻译过程，总结一定的原则、理论与模式，以解释和预测一切在翻译范畴之内的现象，从而构建一套宏观结构框架和微观操作原则的翻译理论体系”（刘军平，2009）。

赖斯根据文本的不同体裁和功能，将其归为 4 类：第一类是传递原文信息的信息型（informative text），第二类是传递原文审美和情感的表达型（expressive text），第三类是为目的语接受者传递译文预期反应的呼吁型（operative text），第四类是辅助增加文字表达效果的视音型（audio medial text）。赖斯主张根据文本的不同功能，采用相应的翻译策略和手段，以达到最佳的翻译效果。具体到本文中东铁路附属地行政管理权的翻译，根据赖斯的文本分类，本文本属于信息型、表达型和呼吁型文本。传递清末民初清政府下设交涉机构等相关史实属于信息型文本；文中对李鸿谟复兴交涉局的描写属于表达型文本；呼吁型文本表现为作者在末尾提出，在殖民地半殖民地色彩下，我们应当正确地从历史唯物主义角度来看待评价交涉局的工作。因此，在进行翻译时，译者应当根据文本的不同功能，采用相应的策略，以目标为导向的翻译原则应得到贯彻。

根据翻译目的论，主要遵守3项原则。第一，位于首要地位的是“目的原则”（skopos rule），“目的原则主要是指译文应能在目标语言的文化和情境发展中，按照目的语接受者期待的方式发生作用”（卞建华，2008：89），在通常情况下，翻译目的是指译文在交际层面上的目的，即“译文在译入语的社会背景文化以及语境当中对译入语的读者所生成的交际的功能”（韦努蒂，2001）。第二，“连贯原则”（coherence rule），又称“语内连贯”（intra-textual coherence），芒迪（Munday）在《翻译学导论——理论与实践》一书中强调译本的可读性和可接受性，关注译文能否让读者理解，并在译语文化中有一定的实际意义。因此，在翻译时，译者应以目标文化中的目标读者为导向（Nord，2000）。第三，“忠实原则”（fidelity rule），亦即“语际连贯”。“翻译的忠诚性指的是翻译者是否能够将读者所擅长理解的语言环境通过翻译把原文内容完整地翻译呈现出来，并且在保证原文构架内容系统不变的情况下，完整且全面地呈现给读者。”（黄婕，2019：14）在本部分，这3项原则将得到详细的阐述和说明。一是关于“目的原则”与方法原则的关系。首先探讨3项原则之间的相互关系。在这3项原则中，“目的原则”被赋予了至高无上的地位，“主要为译者使用某种特殊的翻译手段，来实现其所要达到的翻译目的（如译者使用特别的翻译技巧来实现其所想呈现的翻译结果）”（张锦兰，2004：43），这两个原则皆为其所属，彼此相辅相成。二是在进行译文和原文的比较之前，必须先考虑原文接受者的文化背景及其受教育程度，以确保“忠实原则”与“连贯原则”的一致性。如果译者认为译文违背了“连贯原则”，就会导致翻译中对原作体现内容或形式的误读。需要注意的是，如果翻译目的不要求译文遵循“连贯原则”，那么译文可放弃“连贯原则”，而是以翻译目的为指导原则。如果我们希望在翻译过程中忠实地呈现原文特点，那么无论是在语言、风格还是写作技巧上，就都必须遵循“忠实原则”。因此，我们认为“忠实原则”是翻译目的的指导原则，它可以最大限度地展现原文的原汁原味。“但是，要想忠实地展现往往过于理想化，所以目的论越发地体现出其优点，并摆脱了以源语文本为核心的枷锁，译者也摆脱了传统翻译中等值理论的桎梏。”（潘平亮，2006）

通过在中国知网进行搜索，译者发现以目的论为指导的翻译研究一共有 11339 条结果，以目的论为指导的历史文献翻译实践一共有 394 条结果，由此可知，目的论在历史文献的翻译领域作出了卓越的贡献，其价值不可估量。

在翻译目的论的指导下，欧飞兵（2011）对景德镇陶瓷文化的翻译策略进行了探讨，从工艺流程、陶瓷历史文化及陶瓷器物名称的翻译 3 个层面，介绍了目的论在陶瓷历史文化翻译中的应用价值，在翻译目的论的指导下，他提出了文化翻译的两种观点和一个目的，即翻译目的决定翻译行为，介绍了音译法和省译法等，同时，提出了历史文化翻译应考虑目标受众的文化心理和语言习惯等因素，做到既准确又规范，为历史类文本翻译提供新的翻译思路。

以上诸多学者在翻译目的论的指导下，研究历史文本相关翻译，这些具体案例为该理论适用于历史文献文本的研究增加了说服力。历史文献文本属于信息型文本，而翻译目的论“目的原则”在指导译者选择翻译方法时，同样以文本交际目的为第一准则，两者在翻译目的上一致，且历史文献类文本的翻译是一种跨人文的文化交际行为，而翻译目的论突破了语言对等的限制，将翻译的边界扩展到交际层面，两者在交际方面一致，由此可见，翻译目的论适用于历史文献类文本的翻译，具有指导意义。

③ 平行文本准备。

“如今，平行文本指的是并排放在一起，可以逐字逐句对照阅读的原文及其译文。”（李长栓，2009）查阅平行文本是译前必不可少的一项准备工作。由于历史研究类文本的专业性比较强，其中会涉及很多无法在词典、术语库等资源中找到的词汇，为了保证译文的专业性与严谨性，需要译者查阅平行文本，找出与词汇所在源语文本相似的语境，进一步确定词义。通过中国知网和万方数据知识服务平台，译者查找到由 Charles Hucker 整理的《中国古代官职英译大辞典》（*A Dictionary of Official Titles in Imperial China*）。在该辞典中，Charles 整理了从西周到清代晚期的中国官职，收录词条 8291 个，涵盖绝大部分中国古代不同官职的英文对照译名，并关注同一官职名称在不同历史时期意义上的变化，内容全面、条目清楚，对中国古代官职的英译有很大帮助。除此之外，《文化翻译理论视域下的历史文献翻译研究》和《文化输出视角下汉语专有名词的英译研究》也为译者在翻译历史文化词汇方面提供了思路，《文言文典籍英译模式与策略研究——基于〈中国十大古典悲剧故事〉的翻译实践》及《以林语堂译〈兰亭集序〉观文言文英译之难》为译者研究文本中文言句式的英译提供了借鉴和参考。

归纳而言，“平行文本的作用主要体现在两个方面：一方面是能够快速地帮助译者了解原文，另一方面是为译者找到合适的表达方法，翻译出地道、专业的译文”（汪晶晶，2014）。

④ 术语表整理。

本次翻译文本属于历史文献文本，涉及很多复杂的专业术语，为了确保译文质量，在翻译过程中，译者整理编辑出专业词汇，并第一时间通过查阅平行文本、运用搜索引擎和翻译工具，以及咨询导师和原作者等方式全方位查阅其释义，并反复确认与检查，避免术语出现偏差与错误。在该过程中，一共确认了22条本次实践中出现的专业术语，按术语首字母拼音排序方式进行排列组合，制定了相应术语表，全部收录在本文附录章节的附录2中，表5–5只做部分术语的特点展示。

表 5–5　部分术语

Table 5–5　List of Terms (Excerpts)

原文	译文
帮办	assistant
笔贴式	letter clerk
局勇	guard
疆吏	frontier official
书识	temporary scribe
局夫	civil servant
总办	general official
关道	custom officer
商埠	commercial port
道尹	intendant of circuit

历史文献类文本大量涉及有关特定时期的历史专业词汇，例如，本实践报告涉及古代官职、文书词汇及清末民初年间下设的机构名称，且这类历史专业性很强的词汇在文本中出现频繁。通过确定并统一这些术语，不仅可以加快译者的翻译速度，保持译文的一致性并提高译文的质量，还可以使目的语读者更容易理解，提高阅读体验。

⑤ 辅助工具使用。

为了确保高质量、高效率完成翻译工作，译者必须在翻译前确定适当的翻译辅助工具，这对于后续的翻译工作具有至关重要的辅助作用。以下列举的是译者在翻译过程中使用的翻译辅助工具，如表5–6所示。

表 5–6　翻译辅助工具
Table 5–6　Translation Aids

工具类型	工具名称
纸质词典	《牛津高阶英汉双解词典》（第 9 版）
	《英汉大词典（陆谷孙主编）》（第 2 版）
	《柯林斯高阶英汉双解学习词典》（第 8 版）
	《古代汉语词典》（第 2 版）
电子词典和网络在线翻译工具	欧路电子词典
	有道词典
	金山词霸
	谷歌在线翻译
	百度翻译
	网易有道翻译
	DeepL 翻译
计算机辅助翻译软件	AntConc
	Trados
网络搜索引擎	百度
	谷歌
	夸克
	必应
语法审校工具	Grammarly
	批改网
文献浏览工具	学校图书馆电子浏览室
	中国知网
	万方数据知识服务平台

翻译过程往往枯燥乏味，但在这些翻译工具的辅助下，通常能节约翻译时间，我们在挑选翻译工具时也要选择一些便于操作的翻译工具。例如，以上列出的翻译工具，都是译者在翻译过程中整理出来的，这些工具不仅提高了翻译效率，还大大节省了翻译时间，为后续的审校工作预留了充足的时间。

5.4.3.2　翻译过程

在翻译过程中，译者设计了一套完善的翻译流程，汇总了需要突破的翻译难点，结合案例分析需要详细阐释的典型例句。

① 翻译流程设计

译者将本次翻译实践流程分为 5 个步骤，具体内容如下。

第一，通读全文本后总结源语文本的风格特点，熟悉选用的翻译目的论，参考平行文本中相关的词汇译文，适当总结应用。在充分了解所要翻译文本的内容主要为历史文献类的信息文本后，开始整理其中较难理解的专业词汇并广泛查询有关平行文本；归纳总结出在梳理过程中遇到的难点，比如，一些无法通过现有资料及仅凭译者无法解决的疑难杂点，将其及时反馈给原作者或寻求导师帮助，做好笔记；规划整体任务时间安排。

第二，调试各类翻译辅助工具，设计翻译流程，正式着手翻译。在翻译过程中，通过查询纸质词典、电子词典和运用网络在线翻译工具等一系列翻译手段得出译文，对比其中不同的表达，结合文本具体语境，选用最适合的版本。遇到疑难杂点，及时与导师沟通或寻求原作者的帮助，定期与委托方交流对译文的要求和需求，按进度完成译文初稿。

第三，使用批改网等软件对初稿进行多次自我校对，检查是否存在语法不当等低级错误，在修改后联系同行进行审校，检查前后是否连贯，译文是否符合目的语读者的阅读习惯。

第四，联系导师与委托方的专业人士对译文进行导师审核和专家审查，在审校后再进行修改，在时间充裕的前提下对译文不断进行打磨和润色。再次整理和总结翻译过程中遇到的疑难杂点，与导师和同学进行交流探讨。

第五，分析文本中经典案例，总结翻译目的论在实践中的具体应用，撰写实践报告，根据导师和答辩组委会的意见，对实践报告进行修改，结束本次翻译实践任务。

为保证翻译进程顺利推进，译者根据译前、译中、译后所需时间，将翻译过程分成了 3 个时间段，制定了翻译计划表，如图 5-3 所示。

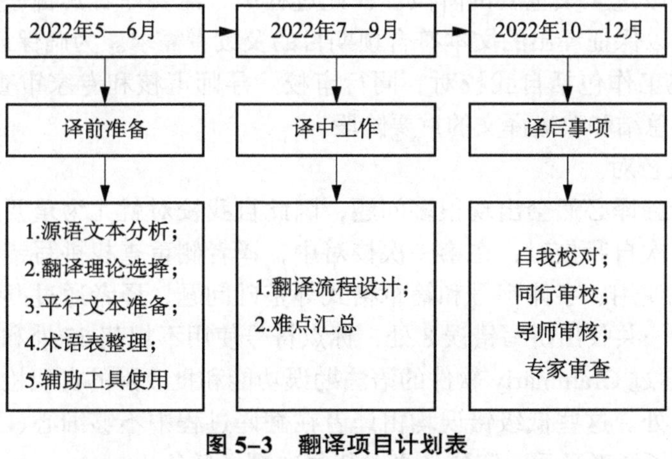

图 5-3　翻译项目计划表

Figure 5-3　Translation Project Process Schedule

② 难点汇总。

译者对本次翻译实践中遇到的 3 个难点进行了分析，附以突破思路和解决办法，具体如下。

第一，英汉表达对等的困难。由于英汉双语之间存在的文化差异较大，现代汉语的翻译有时都需要反复推敲、磨炼，更别说本翻译实践报告中的古文词汇及句式，实现译文与原文在语意方面完全对等的难度显著提高。因此，译者需要克服文化差异带来的翻译障碍。除广泛查找阅读平行文本，搜索相关文化背景外，译者也经常向导师和原作者请教一些难以理解的问题，最终顺利突破该项阻碍。

第二，古文理解的准确性较难把握。由于古文本身的特殊性，在古文英译过程中，译者不仅要能透彻理解古文，还要能恰当地将其表述出来，才有可能使译作规范。而很多词汇古今异义，加之现代汉语存在一词多义的情况，就涉及词义选择的问题，因此在正确理解古文这一难点上，译者通过结合上下文语境，利用百度百科和维基百科等在线工具大量查找相关文献与资料，翻阅各类词典，及时请教导师和原作者，正确理解古文含义，满足英汉转化对等。

第三，语篇层面合适案例的选取。在结合翻译目的论分析语篇的过程中，译者一开始选取的案例都不是很典型的结合三原则的案例，分析得较为浅显，不具有代表性，因此，译者在多次与导师共同商量，不断筛选案例后，最终选择了符合本翻译实践的案例。

5.4.3.3 译后事项

在翻译的收尾工作中，译后事项是不可或缺的一环，同时，也是对译文进行总结和改进至关重要的阶段。在此过程中，需要译者具备一定的综合素养和能力，以保证译出的文本符合预期目的及读者需求。为确保译文专业性，翻译的收尾工作包括自我校对、同行审校、导师审核和专家审查 4 个方面，这也是最终总结和改进译文的重要阶段。

① 自我校对。

第一轮翻译必然会出现很多问题，因此自我校对就尤为重要。译者前后共进行了 3 次自我校对，在第一次校对中，译者侧重查找拼写错误、标点符号的不规范使用、字体字号和篇章格式等基础问题，译者通过办公软件的智能审阅功能一共找出拼写错误 8 处，标点符号使用不规范 65 处和格式上的错误 12 处，通过 Grammarly 软件的语法勘误功能和批改网的自我检测功能找出语法错误 7 处。这些低级错误均由译者在翻译过程中不够细心、态度散漫造成，这提醒了译者日后一定要认真对待每次翻译任务。

第二次校对，译者主要集中在内容上，其中包括用词、语序，以及对前后术语做统一规范，比如，对“交涉局”做了统一规范，摒弃了原来的 Bargaining Bureau，而统一规范为 Negotiation Bureau。

第三次校对，译者侧重检查选取的案例是否具有代表性，译文结构是否清晰，语句是否通顺且符合目的语读者的阅读习惯，最后同导师对自查出来的问题和改进办法进行沟通与交流，咨询导师的意见，商讨并进行润色。

译者在进行自我校对后，进行了深刻反思，总结归纳出现错误的主要原因：对原文理解不够透彻、翻译时不够仔细。在此之后，经过译者的不断修改与完善，译文质量得到进一步提升，与此同时，译者及时总结经验，改进了不足，力求在日后的翻译实践中减少和避免出现类似的错误。

② 同行审校。

在自我校对后，译者联系曾经的本科同窗刘丽红、周小青和学姐万雨晴，她们分别就读于广东外语外贸大学高级翻译学院、上海海事大学外语系英语笔译专业和江西师范大学外语系英语笔译专业，与他们进行同行之间的译文审校。前后进行了 3 次同行审校，主要审校译文是否通顺流畅。在同行校对后，译员们给予译者专业性建议 30 余处，如词语搭配、句式结构、连接词等方面。同行审校可促进译员们深入探讨，给予译者建议，更好地发现译文的不足之处，推动译者及时查漏补缺。

③ 导师审核。

导师审核是译后阶段不可或缺的一个部分。在进行同行审校后，译者及时联系导师，申请导师对译文进行质量审校。导师指出了案例分析板块中古代官职翻译不够契合原文含义的问题，以及 11 处翻译方法选择不当的错误，指导修改不恰当的地方，不论是在定题之前还是在翻译过程中，李靖导师都经常关照译者的翻译过程，耐心解答译者提出的问题，认真负责地帮助译者修改译稿。经过多次与导师的商量和修改，最终敲定了译文，并同意译者联系委托方专家进行下一步的审校工作。

④ 专家审查。

在进行完上述审校后，译者第一时间联系委托方，申请对译文进行专家审查。本部分对翻译工作的过程进行了详细的描述。专家在原文与译文对应的精确性、译文的专业性，以及篇章全文结构的贯通性等方面进行了审查。专家给出的结论是译文在原文对应处理上较好，整体篇章连贯性较好，但一些文言句式的英译其可读性仍然有待加强。在向专家多次请教之后，译者对文言句式的英译进行了适当修改，对专家特别指出的几处欠缺专业性的翻译进行了补充和修改，最终顺利完成翻译任务。

5.4.4 英译案例分析

在汉斯·弗米尔翻译目的论的指导下，译者顺利完成了本次翻译实践，并从中挑选了 24 个案例来对整个翻译任务进行回溯总结，论证了目的论在此次翻译实践中起到的指导性作用。译者选择从目的语所要达到的功能角度来确定翻译的策略。例如，在古代官职和公文词汇的确定上，译者选取目的论指导下的“目的原则”及“忠实原则”，采用意译及释译的方法；在句子层面（包括原文中引用的大量文言官话）译法确定上，译者选取目的论指导下的“目的原则”及“连贯原则”，采用增译的方法对句子进行分析；在语篇翻译的确定上，译者选取目的论指导下的“目的原则”对语篇进行分析、逻辑梳理及语序调整达到形式衔接和语意连贯。

5.4.4.1 基于目的论的词汇翻译

“任何翻译活动必定有其目的，在文化输出的时代背景下，翻译的目的是把中国传统文化和特色事物传播到世界各地。”（丁应强，2015）历史文献文本类的词汇翻译在目的论指导下，能最大限度地发挥其独特的作用。首先，在翻译特定类型的词汇时，可以将不同时期的历史事件进行合理分类，从而使译文更加符合目标读者的阅读习惯和接受能力。在进行特殊历史词汇的翻译时，译者不仅需要关注词汇本身的含义，还需要考虑译语对目的语读者的可读性，以确保翻译的准确性和有效性。其次，通过目的论可以更好地把握翻译策略及语言风格之间的关系，从而提高译文质量。再次，历史词汇的翻译方法因目的论而呈现出多元化的特征。最后，目的论指导下的翻译方法的应用，能更好地实现译文与原文之间的信息交流。考虑到本实践报告涉及历史词汇类型的多样性，包括但不限于古代官职和文书词汇等，译者必须在遵循目的论三原则的前提下，采用恰当的翻译方法，以有效地传递历史词汇的内涵，从而使国外读者更深入地了解中国相关的历史文化。

①“目的原则”下古代官职的意译。

中国封建传统延绵时间长，朝代更迭频繁，给古代官职的翻译带来了一定困难。根据汉斯·弗米尔的指导，在英汉双语转化过程中，“目的原则”是三原则中的首要原则，即翻译应能在译语情境和文化中，按译语接受者期待的方式发生作用。因此，为使译语读者对中国古代官职名称有一定的概念，译者采用意译的翻译技巧，即根据原文的大意来翻译，不做逐词逐句的翻译，以较好地阐述官职的作用及意义。

例1

原文： 从平时处理外交事务的官员中间筛选出10人，其中“总办”一名，“帮办”一名，“俄文会办委员”一名，“办事委员”两名，“主稿翻译”“笔贴式”五名。

译文： Ten people were selected from the officials who deal with foreign affairs in peaceful time, among which included one “general officer”, one “assistant”, one “Russian language meeting officer”, two “council members on affairs”, and five “principal manuscript translators” and “letter-clerks”.

分析： 该文本中出现的“总办”“帮办”及“笔贴式”均为清末设置的政府职位，经百度百科检索，“总办”为旧时官府的总负责人；“帮办”相当于秘书助手等职位；“笔贴式”则指清代官府中低级文书官员、执掌部院衙门文书档案的官员，主要职责是抄写、翻译满汉文。目的论认为，原文的功能只是提供信息，因此此处译者在完全理解原文意思的基础上，在“目的原则”的引领下，采用意译的方法，将“总办”译为“general manager”，“帮办”译为“assistant”，“笔贴式”译为“letter-clerk”，翻译过程主要是凸显原文的内涵，原文“笔贴式”虽有翻译职责，但由于前文提到“主稿翻译”，此处则省略其做翻译的特点，直接概括为“文书官员”。整体简洁，通俗易懂，方便目的语读者理解，译文满足在目的语情境中的发展，符合“目的原则”要求。

例2

原文： 在人员配备上，虽然吉林交涉总局配有60余人，但机构设置与黑龙江交涉处大同小异，不过是多配备了办事人员——“局勇”10人，“局夫”10人，“书识”14人，“差遣委员”15名。

译文： In terms of staffing, the General Bureau of Negotiation of Jilin is staffed with more than 60 people, the institutional set-up is much the same as that of the Negotiation Office of Heilongjiang, but with more clerical staff, which included 10 “guards”, 10 “civil servants”, 14 “temporary scribes”, and 15 “dispatching members”.

分析： “目的原则”不仅要求译者在翻译时按照目的语读者接受的方式进行翻译，还要求译者注意协调目的语和原文作者意图间的关系。“在翻译实践中，背景知识缺失的影响首先会出现在对原文的理解上，紧接着会体现在译文的表达上，最终的结果是造成不合格译文的出产。”（贾璞，2019）该文本中出现的“局勇”经《古代汉语字典》和维基百科查证，是指旧时公署的卫兵，“局夫”是指旧时公署的公务员，“书识”是指清代正额书吏之外的一种临时性书吏。这类词具有明显的文化特色，故译者在翻译此类词汇时应避免复杂晦涩，切忌直译，而应充分理解原文内涵及原作者意图，通过意译将“局勇”译为“guard”，“局夫”译为“civil servant”，“书识”译为“temporary scribe”。此处就内容而言，不仅正确表达了原文意思，还使译文简洁易懂，满足“目的原则”要求。

例3

原文：认为为人“憨直”，“欲行古道”，李家鳌不适合继续担任滨江道尹兼吉林交涉局总办的职务，请求另派官员与俄国“据理力争”。

译文：In a word, Li Jia'ao was not suitable to serve as intendant of circuit of Binjiang and General Officer of Jilin Railway Negotiation Bureau any longer.

分析：“道尹”经谷歌检索得知，其为中华民国时期的官名，“道尹”隶属省长，由清末“观察使”一职演变而来。其主要职责为管理各县所辖行政事务，为流动职位。译者使用有道词典对其初译，得到“Daoyin”，中国历史悠久，朝代更迭不断，使得古代官职种类名称也庞杂繁复，中英双语缺乏相对应的职务，有道词典选择将其直接音译，结果导致目的语读者不知所云，难以理解，故根据“目的原则”的要求，为满足目的语读者对译文的期待，更好地理解原文意思，译者采取了意译的翻译策略，将其意译为“intendant of circuit”，意思为“巡查的监督员”，既很好地传达了原作者的意图，也满足目的语的情境，符合目的论中的“目的原则”。

在翻译一些词句的过程中，现代汉语经常找不到对应的英文词汇，更别说有着中国特色的古代官职词汇了。而目的论中“目的原则”认为，翻译应能在译语情境和文化中，按译语接受者期待的方式发生作用，因此在翻译古代官职这类特色词汇时，译者根据原文内涵，选用意译的方法来翻译具有中国特色的旧时官职。

②“忠实原则”下文书词汇的释译。

“忠实原则”要求译文忠实原文，即原文与译文之间应该语际连贯一致，但与原文忠实的程度和形式取决于译文的目的与译者对原文的理解。本部分研究的文书词汇均选自原文中的公文、书信、契约或从事公文工作的岗位，因而在翻译此类词汇时，译者选用释译的翻译技巧，即“去形存意”，剥离源语外壳，抓住意义实质，使译文表达更自然。

例4

原文：规定：在铁路交涉各分局内设立专门人员……如无关碍，该分局专员即在该租帖为之签字，声明存案。

译文：stipulating that: a special officer was set up in each branch of the railway negotiation... if there is no obstacle, the commissioner of the branch shall sign the leasing contract and declare it for the record.

分析："忠实原则"要求译者在不违背"目的原则"的前提下，忠实原文。译者认为，此处的文书词汇可采用释译的翻译技巧。首先，译者借助百度百科查询到"租帖"是指中国旧时佃农租种地主土地时订立的契约。内容包括田地面积及坐落地点，租佃期限，地租种类、数额及交租期限，中人责任等项。一开始，译者根据有道词典、欧陆词典等工具词典得到其英译结果均为"lease post"，直译过来也是"租帖"，而此处的"post"虽有"帖"之意，但比"contract"少了契约与签订合同之意。因此，根据原文的理解，译者认为可运用文言释译的翻译技巧将该文书词汇释译为"lease contract"，证实了文言释译对古代文书词汇翻译的准确性，达到了贴近原文含义的翻译目的，提升了译文的准确性，于内容上合乎"忠实原则"。

例5

原文："不得已，清政府想到了折中的办法，……并札发木质印章一颗，文曰："哈尔滨关道兼吉黑交涉事宜关防……规定……"

译文：The Qing government had no choice but to think of a compromise ... and issued a wooden seal with the following text: "The official seal of Harbin Custom Office and Jihe Negotiation Matters ..."

分析：要准确传达源语言的意义，译者必须在翻译过程中对原文词汇及术语进行深刻理解，从而达到对原文的忠实。译者查询百度百科，得知"关防"有以下解释：①防备，防守；②关隘有军队驻守的地方；③印信的一种，长方形，始于明初，又称"大印"。结合上文"木质印章"可知，此处的关防为印信的一种。实质可理解为一种"官印"，故在翻译时，为区别于上文的wooden seal，此处则将其译为"The official seal"，既可将原文意思保留，也能使目的语读者清楚地了解并体会到原作者的意图，即当时清政府在确立哈尔滨关道交涉权的过程中，明明可以正常行使权力却仍然要刻意下发官印来行使的无奈。准确地传达了原文意思，满足了"忠实原则"。

例 6

原文：“均归将军按局员掌请情，与总监工照会核办。”

译文：“the general will be allowed to report the situation according to the information already available to members of the Bureau, and will verify the matter with the chief engineer ...”

分析：译者与导师及原作者沟通后得知，此处的“掌”为“掌握”的意思，“请”是指“提出”，“情”在此处则是指前文提到所掌握的情况。而在不同文体的前提下，“忠实原则”的用法也略有不同，若完全直译为“掌握提出所掌握的情况”，别说给目的语读者带来阅读障碍，就连源语读者都会感到困惑，因此，通过联系上下文理解得知，“掌请情”可释译为“报告已掌握的信息”，因而目的语翻译为“report the situation according to the information already available to”，这样既满足了“忠实原则”，也满足了目的语读者的期待。

在“忠实原则”的前提下，古代文书词汇的英译应尽可能保留其原汁原味的文化内涵和意义，同时，也要使译文具有现代英语的表达方式，因此，在翻译古代文书词汇时，译者选用释译的翻译技巧，在以“目的原则”为指导的前提下，满足“忠实原则”的要求，既使源语信息得到了最大限度的传递，又满足了目的语读者的期待。

③“连贯原则”下动名词相互转换。

“连贯原则”强调，译文必须符合语内连贯，即译文具有可读性和可接受性。“词性本身往往是障碍，翻译时不能死盯着原文词性。”（叶子南，2007）众所周知，由于思维方式的不同，中文多为动态，英文多为静态，在英汉双语转换的过程中，为满足这一特点，经常会采用动名词相互转换这一翻译技巧，这样能使译文表达更地道，贴近译语读者的阅读习惯，大大增加了译文的可读性和可接受性。

例 7

原文：正视和准确认识历史是一个国家、民族得以勇往直前的前提。

译文：A proper and accurate understanding of history is a prerequisite for a nation and a people to be able to move forward.

分析：由于英汉不同的语言结构，汉语中多用动词，英语中多用名词。在较为正式的英文文体中，使用名词的倾向尤为明显。因此，英汉互译时往往需要根据语境，在英语名词和汉语动词间灵活转换。此句位于一章结尾，具有呼吁的特点，若将其直译为“Facing up to and accurately understanding history is a prerequisite for a country and a nation to march forward”，则不仅具有严重的翻译腔，而且过于生硬，达不到源语作者想要传达的情感，故在“连贯原则”的指导下，将动词短语“准确认识”名词化为名词短语“accurate understanding”，顺带处理“正视”一词，共同构成名词短语“A proper and accurate understanding of history”，如此一来，不仅符合学术论文的写作特点，更正式，而且能将原作者想要呼吁的情感很好地表达出来。

例 8

原文： 虽然有了机构建制，但是其成员几乎都是由非专业的外交官拼凑起来的，远远不能应对中东铁路沿线日益繁杂的交涉事件。

译文： Although the agency was established, its members were almost exclusively a patchwork of non-professional diplomats, far from being able to cope with the increasingly complex diplomatic incidents along the Middle East Railway.

分析： 为防止漏译，译者使用有道词典对该句进行初译，得到“its membership is almost entirely cobbled together by non-professional diplomats”，其中，将“拼凑”翻译为“be cobbled together by”，考虑到英语偏静态、汉语偏动态的语言差异，译者采用动名转换的技巧，将动词“拼凑”名词化为“拼凑物，混杂物”，译为“a patchwork of”，准确传达了源语信息，增加了译文的严谨性，贴合学术论文写作的行文特点，符合“连贯原则”即翻译需要考虑译语情境与文化的要求，从而提升译文的可读性，再一次印证了“连贯原则”对本实践文本的指导作用。

例 9

原文： 中国清政府无论出于理念——皇权与民主的对立，还是出于现实利益——中东铁路属地法理上归属权的冲突，都坚决反对在此地实行“议会制度”。

译文： The Qing government of China firmly opposed to the implementation of the “parliamentary system”in Middle East Railway, whether out of the idea-the opposition between imperial power and democracy, or the pragmatic interest-conflict of juridical belongings in the China Eastern Railway territory.

分析： 乍一看，该句子复杂烦冗，但其实主谓明显，成分清晰，主干为

“中国清政府……坚决反对在此地实行‘议会制度’”，译者用有道翻译对该句进行初译，得到“The Qing government of China firmly opposed to carry out the ‘parliamentary system’ in Middle East Railway”，此处将“实行”直接翻译为“carry out”，从语法角度来看，并无不妥，但结合文本特点及作用来看，缺少书面语的正式，因此在“连贯原则”的指导下，译者将此处的“实行”名词化为“implementation”，这样不仅简化了语言结构，表达简练，而且更具有英文表达的书面正式感。浓缩的名词化结构在表达过程中常常失去与动词相关的语气，也不具有任何感情色彩，提高了英语表达的客观程度，满足了“连贯原则”。

在翻译过程中，顺句驱动一般虽无错误语法，但呈现的译文会显得刻板生硬。因此，为使译文更加地道自然，译者在遵循“连贯原则”的前提下，将动态的中文词汇转化为静态的英文词汇，使译文表达更加自然、通顺。

5.4.4.2　基于目的论的句子翻译

考虑到英汉语言的不同，以及本次翻译实践的严谨性，译者选取《牛津高阶英汉双解词典》(第8版)、欧陆词典等作为辅助工具，借鉴平行文本相似语句的表达方式与翻译技巧，遵照“目的原则”、“忠实原则”及“连贯原则”，运用“增译”、“主被动语态转换”及定语从句后置的翻译技巧对原文中的文言句式等进行翻译，以使译文符合目的语读者的期待并且更加符合目的语读者的阅读习惯。

①“目的原则”下文言文句式的增译。

“目的原则”强调，译者在进行翻译活动时，应着重考虑翻译语境和目的语读者的阅读感受，并以此为依据采取恰当的翻译技巧。文言文句式讲究押韵，行文简洁。中文翻译时，讲究“信达雅”，但在文言文句式英译的过程中，由于英汉双语的行文特点不同，在英译时为了保证译文的语法结构完整及意思明确，通常会采用增译的技巧，以贴近目的语的表达习惯。

例 10

原文：有关交涉事件，经由“吉林将军等随时饬由该局相机”。

译文：The relevant negotiation events are “all rectified by General Jilin and others depending on the situation at any time”.

分析：“饬”为“整治，整改”之意，“相机”则为“看情况而决定”的意思，文言文句式的英译要在完全理解其内涵的基础上翻译。将该句翻译为现代话为“由吉林将军等看情况随时进行整治”，故在“目的原则”的指导下，译者采用增译的翻译技巧，增添动词“整治”的主语“有关交涉事件”，又因汉语多使用重复词，而英语则习惯用代词代替前文所指，故此处增添的主语可用代词“all”代替，如此一来，整体译文看起来更流畅，意思表达完整，满足目的语读者的阅读感受，符合“目的原则”要求。

例 11

原文：要求：路线附近所驻华兵队今后如需经过铁路，或入铁路界内暂驻，“务须知照就近铁路护路军营俄员，以免滋生枝节”。

译文：it requested that if any Chinese troops near the route passed through the railway or entered the railway boundary for a temporary stay, “they must inform the nearest Russian railway guard, in order to avoid any unnecessary conflicts”.

分析：基于英汉双语在语言表达形式结构上的差异，即汉语多为“意合”，而英语多为“形合”，汉语表达中随处可见的无主语或无逻辑关联词的省略句在文言文句式中更是比比皆是。“目的原则”要求，翻译的过程应该以译文在译语文化中要达到的交际目的为原则。因此，在英译过程中，对动作“务须知照”增添施动者“他们”，即增补了主语“they”，以及后文中“以免滋生枝节”中增添形容词“不必要的”——“unnecessary”，如此一来，不仅句式结构完整，在句意上也更贴近原作者意图，在感官上使得译语读者与源语读者相同，符合译语读者的期待，满足“目的原则”要求。

例 12

原文：1910 年，时任黑龙江铁路交涉总办的李鸿谟认为“华商界内租地，若华官概不与同，任其私于授受，自立租帖，亦难见信于外人”……

译文：In 1910, Li Hongmo, the then General Officer of Heilongjiang Railway Negotiation, believed that “it’s hard for Chinese officials to be convinced if they don’t allow Chinese businessmen to lease land in this region while the land is allowed to be traded privately”...

分析：该句为明显的流散型汉语结构，因此在汉译英时应调整其语序，使其符合英文的聚集型结构。文言文英译的过程一共分为两步即由文言文到现代汉语，再由现代汉语到英文。最关键的一步则是第一步，由于文言文句式具有高度精简凝练的特点，在转化为现代汉语的过程中我们要通过调整语序，适当增减逻辑关联词等，将其内在逻辑舒展开来，在“目的原则”下为实现翻译效果可采用恰当的翻译技巧，将该句翻译为“如果中国官员不同意中国商人在该地区租赁土地，而这些土地却允许被彼此私下交易，那么中国官员则很难为外人所信服……”可见在此过程中不仅调整了语序，还增补了主句的主语——（华官）亦难见信于外人及逻辑关联词“而”“那么”，又为了避免英文结构中的“头重脚轻”，最终译者主句选用it做逻辑主语，得到“it's hard for Chinese officials to be convinced”，逻辑连词选用“while”来表示转折。最后，翻译结果呈现为“it's hard for Chinese officials to be convinced if they don't allow Chinese businessmen to lease land in this region while the land is allowed to be traded privately”，在结构和句意上都满足并符合英语表达习惯的预期目的，且目标受众能清晰掌握原文信息，最终体现了“目的原则”的指导作用。

在翻译文言文句式时，译者需要经过两步转换，从文言文到白话文，再到英文，其中，最重要的便是第一步，只有理解原文真实含义才能正确英译出译文。故译者在“目的原则”指导下，即翻译行为所要达到的目的决定整个翻译行为的过程，译者选用增译的方法先对原文做出理解后的正确阐释，再进行下一步的汉英双语转化。

②“忠实原则”下主被动语态转换。

“忠实原则”要求译文忠实原文，除在内容上要忠实外，还强调在文体风格上也要忠实目的语读者的阅读习惯。在现代观点看来，语言文字的表达大体上是按照先主位后述位、先已知后未知的规律进行的。英语句法囿于如不及物动词须使用被动以顺应主述位理论；而中文则由于语法限制宽松，可以自由使用主动形式的表达，也能很好地契合主述位理论，因而有了中文多用主动而英文多用被动的现象。故在某些句子的英译过程中，采用主被动语态的转换技巧能使译文更加准确、流畅，满足目的语读者的阅读习惯。

例 13

原文：诸如偷盗之类的小事情上，各衙门尚可应付，但一旦涉及国家主权的重大事件，各地方衙门就会因权限、辖区等原因“互相推诿”。

译文：Small matters such as theft can be dealt with by the magistrate, but concerning major matters of national sovereignty, the local magistracy will “blame each other” for reasons of authority and jurisdiction.

分析：由于中英双语差异除呈现出汉语重意合、英语重形合，汉语重心在前、英语重心在后等特点外，还体现在中文多用主动，而英文多用被动等方面，因此在“忠实原则”的指导下，将“衙门尚可应付”调整为被动“can be dealt with by the magistrate"。再者，中英文相互间的关系多为中文"先分后总"，而英文总是"先总后分"。在"偷盗之类的小事情"中，"偷盗"属于"小事情"，即分总关系，故译者在翻译过程中调整语序，形成"small matters such as theft"的总分关系，更符合英文的行文特点，使得译文结构更地道、规范及流畅，继而提升译文的准确性。满足"忠实原则"——译文忠实目的语的文体风格要求。

例 14

原文：俄方再次确认了中方机构的代表权力。

译文：The power of representation of Chinese institutions was reconfirmed by the Russian side.

分析：该句结构清晰明朗，译者开始用百度翻译进行初译得到"Russia reconfirmed the representative rights of Chinese institutions"，源于中西方思维的差异，"中国人崇尚'以人为本'，注重个人感受，认为人起主导作用，因此多采用主动语态；而西方人讲究主客体对立，重视逻辑，因而在英语中强调时则多采用被动语态"。"语言运用要求体现客观性和普遍性，多避免使用人称作主语，因而使用大量被动句。"（翟宗德，2007：73）虽然百度翻译的结果于语法、语意上都没有问题，但是译者联系上下文语境可知，此处原作者意图为在经历了中方交涉机构的几次维权后，俄方终于肯做出一丝妥协后的又一次让步，中方机构的权力再次得到了俄方的确认，强调的是中方机构的权力，故在英译时，选择将其语态转变为被动语态，翻译为"The power of representation of Chinese institutions was reconfirmed by the Russian side"，突出强调主体，符合"忠实原则"下的忠实原文内容、意义、情感诉求等特点。

例 15

原文：至此，吉林、黑龙江两省铁路交涉局分头交涉，导致权责不明，行政效率低下的弊端已经完全显露。

译文：So far, the Jilin and Heilongjiang Railway Negotiation Bureau has been divided into two dependent agencies, resulting in unclear authority and responsibility, so the disadvantages of administrative inefficiency have been fully revealed.

分析：译者使用有道翻译进行初译得到的译文为"At this point, Jilin and Heilongjiang railway negotiation bureau negotiated separately, leading to unclear powers and responsibilities, the drawbacks of low administrative efficiency have been fully revealed”。此处，有道翻译将句中的“分头交涉”直译为“negotiated separately”，乍一看没问题，可细究却发现，“negotiate”做谓语的话，主语一般是人，人作为施动者，而此处实际为两处不同的铁路交涉局，因此在“忠实原则”的指导下，译者采用主被动语态转换的翻译技巧，使汉语主动语态转换成英语被动语态，但意义仍为主动，两处机构“分头交涉”其实也可转化为“划分为两处独立的交涉机构”，故翻译为“has been divided into two dependent agency”，更符合常见的英语表达方式，使译文流畅自然。

为使译文结构更加地道且符合目的语的表达习惯，译者遵循“忠实原则”的指导，即译语除要忠实原文内容、风格等问题外，还要忠实目的语读者的文化背景、阅读习惯，因此在一些主动句的表达上，译者选用主被动语态转换的翻译技巧进行翻译，使译文符合目的语读者的期待，满足“忠实原则”的要求。

③“连贯原则”下定语从句的后置法。

“英、汉两种语言具有不同的语言表达习惯：英文重形合，而汉语重意合，两者在句法上往往很难兼容。”（何刚强，2009：50）因此，译者在翻译过程中进行了必要的局部调整，在英译过程中将汉语中的定语从句后置，以提高句子结构的完整性、内容的忠实性及文本的可读性，进而符合“连贯原则”的特点。

例 16

原文：“铁路交涉局”是由清末黑吉两省将军衙门控制下的交涉机构发展而来的（1），由俄国中东铁路管理局催生的（2），在中东路属地内中方与俄方交涉的（3）机构。

译文：The Railway Negotiation Bureau was developed from the negotiation organization under the control of the Yamen of Heilongjiang and Jilin provinces at the end of the Qing Dynasty, (1) and spawned by the Russian Middle East Railway Administration to intervene between the Chinese and the Russians in the territories of the Middle East Railway (2)(3).

分析：“汉语长句英译时，断句的原则一般是先分析汉语语意，然后以逻辑事理为基础，区分主从，加以拆分。”（伍小军，2006：75）首先，译者对本句进行结构逻辑分析，将句子划分为主语 + 定语（1）+ 定语（2）+ 定语（3），原文强调机构的由来及属性，一个句子中连用 3 个定语，这在汉语中不少见，汉语重意合，然而英语重形合，如此叠加定语的句子虽在英语当中也有，但在英译中时也多译为多个意合的短句，因此，在中译英时，如果也选择将其译为定语套定语，那么译文就会显得烦冗复杂，不符合英语平行结构表达的特点。因此，译者将其重组为两个长句，定语（2）与定语（3）合并，由 and 连接定语（1），由此使句子结构清晰完整。将机构的由来及发挥的作用清晰明了地展现给目的语读者，满足“连贯原则”中译文与目标接受者情境相连贯的要求，最大限度做到语意连贯，有助于目的语读者理解原文信息。

例 17

原文：这些外事人员大都由“办事勤慎，明白大体”的地方官员出任。虽常年在边境对俄交涉，有实际经验，但“实无专责”，又大都不通俄语，也没有经过系统的外交训练。

译文：Most of these foreign affairs officers were local officials who were diligent and cautious in handling affairs and understood the general situation. Although they had practical experience in dealing with Russia at the border for many years, they were not specialized in foreign affairs, and most of them even did not speak Russian and did not undergo systematic diplomatic training.

分析：首先，译者利用百度翻译及欧陆词典对句子进行初步翻译，基于对行文特点的把握，译者认为有必要对结构进行拆分重组。两句话的主语均为“这些外事人员”，而“办事勤慎，明白大体”在原文中做前置定语，然而翻译成英语则显得过于冗长，在英文中，长的定语句子一般放在先行词之后做后置定语，形成“... local officials who were diligent and cautious in handling affairs and understood the general situation”的结构，符合英文遣词造句的方式，保证译文的流畅性。基于此，译语读者可以清晰明白地汲取原文作者传递的信息，高度提升了译文的可接受性和可读性，满足“连贯原则”的要求，即在译语文化中和使用译语的交际语境中产生意义。

例 18

原文：而黑龙江交涉处、吉林交涉总局不过是黑龙江、吉林将军（1）不具备涉外事件决策权的（2）“办事机构”，只是事件上传下达的信息中转机构，根本没有处理此类事件的能力和权力。

译文：However, the Heilongjiang and Jilin negotiation offices are just “service agencies” for the generals of Heilongjiang and Jilin(1), which do not have the decision-making power for foreign affairs events(2). They are only information transfer agencies for events, and do not have the ability or power to handle such events.

分析：在初译时，译者困惑于此句的结构难以下手，经过 DeepL 进行初译，译者厘清了全句的结构，全句主语为“黑龙江交涉处、吉林交涉总局”，“办事机构”为表语，而“不具备涉外事件决策权的”则是“办事机构”的前置定语。除此之外，句子中的“黑龙江将军、吉林将军”也属于“办事机构”的前置定语，属于多个定语叠加的现象，因此，在“连贯原则”的指导下，即以译文要符合译语语内连贯的原则，译者选择将前置定语（1）及定语从句（2）均后置，定语（1）使用介词做后置定语，定语从句（2）则后置为非限制性定语从句，最终得到符合目的语读者期待且贴合目的语读者阅读习惯的流畅译文，满足目的论下“连贯原则”的要求。

在翻译过程中，如果一味地顺句驱动而不调整结构顺序，则很难做到译文结构清晰明朗，而且有严重的翻译腔会使目的语读者感到味同嚼蜡。“因此，译者在翻译汉语流水句及长难句时，要在理解句子表层意思的基础上厘清内在逻辑结构和隐含含义。之后，将汉语流畅、随意、极具弹性的语言转化成有明确主谓结构的‘树式框架结构’，然后将其余成分合理恰当地安插其中”（高迎慧，2012），译者遵循“连贯原则”，对部分句子的定语从句采用定语从句后置的翻译技巧，使句子结构清晰，语意完整，以此提高译文的流畅性及严谨性。

5.4.4.3 基于目的论的语篇翻译

“目的论认为，我们最关注的不是原文，而是译文的使用者，这样就把译者的上帝换成了和源语文本没有任何关系的使用者（译文的用户）。”（叶子南，2013：142）因此，语篇翻译的重点和难点在于如何保证段落在目标语语境下做到通俗易懂。译者通过增加逻辑衔接词增强语句间的紧密性，通过语序调整提高篇章逻辑的连贯性，进而达到准确传递原文信息的目的。

①“目的原则”下的逻辑衔接。

逻辑衔接可以通过添加衔接词使语篇中各部分相互连接，从而实现篇章段落的自然过渡。在这一部分，译者将分析增加逻辑衔接词对增强语句之间逻辑关系的作用。

例 19

原文：认为这两个机构在人员配置、机构性质等方面还保留着浓重的封建衙门做法。许多做法不同于近代外交惯例，双方在交涉体制、交涉渠道、文件处理等方面无法接轨。

译文： They believed that the two institutions still retained a strong feudal magistracy in terms of personnel allocation and institutional nature, and that many practices were different from modern diplomatic practices. Consequently, the two sides were unable to integrate with each other in system and channel of diplomatic and document processing.

分析： 由于汉语属于意合语言，往往会省略其主语，但在英语中不行。经过仔细分析，不难发现原文省略了主语“他们”，因此在翻译这类无主语的句子时，鉴于目的论的“目的原则”，译者根据句子本身或上下文含义选用了代词“they”来补充主语，以构成完整的句子，使目的语读者充分理解其中的隐含意义。且经上下文理解，原文两句间具有因果关系，因此在翻译过程中，译者选择增加逻辑连词“consequently”来提升句子衔接效果，从而使语篇衔接更加紧密、句型结构更加饱满，实现“目的原则”下译文具有交际意义的效果。

例 20

原文： 此后俄国无视先前中俄合办中东铁路的约章，肆意蹂躏、篡改，任意侵蚀中国权益。在中东铁路问题上，中国方面也失去了仅有的法律上的微弱保障，只得在新的基础上与俄国重新交涉。

译文： Since then, Russia had ignored the previous Sino-Russian treaty on the Middle East Railway, wantonly trampled on, tampered with and eroded China's rights and interests at will. Besides, the Chinese side lost the only weak legal guarantee on the China Eastern Railway issue and had to negotiate with Russia again on a new basis.

分析： 该段落由两个独立的句子组成，第一句主要表达中国在与俄国交涉过程中遭受的不公对待及损失，第二句则再一次强调了中国在与俄国合作期间遭受的不公与歧视，在对原文进行深刻理解后发现二者之间存在层层递进的关系。译者使用百度翻译、DeepL 所得译文均未体现两句间的逻辑关系。根据“目的原则”的定义，即目的决定方法，译者在第二句前添加逻辑连接词“besides”即“除此之外”，使得段落内语句层层递进。由此提高了译文的连贯性，使得语篇衔接更加紧密，符合“目的原则”中译文满足目的语读者期待的要求。

例 21

原文：吉林铁路交涉局虽然还受吉林省省长管辖，但可以越过省长，直接“向外交部、交通部”汇报，吉林铁路交涉局的地位得到空前提高。权力整合后的吉林铁路交涉局一改此前侧重管理属地内中国人作为“寄居”在沙俄中东铁路管理局之下的“影子政府”的形象，利用国际形势的变化，在外交、军事、行政等诸多领域向中东铁路管理局发起了挑战，并取得了诸多成效。

译文：Although the Jilin Railway Negotiation Bureau is still under the jurisdiction of the Governor of Jilin Province, it can bypass the governor and report directly to the “Ministry of Foreign Affairs and Ministry of Transportation”. The status of the Jilin Railway Negotiation Bureau has been unprecedentedly elevated. Ever since the integration of power, the Jilin Railway Negotiation Bureau changed its previous image as a “shadow government” that focused on managing Chinese people who were “lodging” under the management of the Chinese Eastern Railway Administration in Russia. It used the changes in the international situation to challenge the Chinese Eastern Railway Administration in many fields such as diplomacy, military, and administration and achieved many results.

分析：该段落由两个独立的句子组成，第一句的主要内容为“吉林铁路交涉局的地位得到空前提高”。第二句为“由于吉林铁路交涉局地位的提高，权力进行整合后，交涉局趁热打铁实行一系列操作获得许多成就”。经过对译文的深入理解，译者发现两句暗含因果关系。译者使用有道翻译、DeepL 所得译文均体现了两句间的逻辑关系。根据“目的原则”的定义，即目的决定方法，译者在第二句前添加连接词“ever since”，使段落内语句间的因果关系一目了然。由此，提高了译文的连贯性，使语篇衔接更加紧密，符合“目的原则”中译文满足目的语读者期待的要求。

在翻译过程中，译者一贯注重文本整体的连贯性，在“目的原则”的指导下，通过增加连接词并根据实际情况结合其他翻译技巧，最终大大提升了译文的贯通性及衔接性。

②“连贯原则”下的语序调整。

“连贯是词语、小句、句群在概念、逻辑上合理、恰当地连为一体的语篇特征。”（李运兴，2001：132）在翻译过程中，译者不仅需要保证篇章逻辑紧密衔接，还需要考虑段落语意是否连贯通顺。因此，译者遵循“连贯原则”，为了最大限度地满足译文语意连贯，通过语序调整及适当技巧对译文进行修改，以达到结构清晰、篇章逻辑完整的效果。

例 22

原文：近代以来，中国在对外交往的地位上发生了转折，开始被动地与列强接触。在不同以往的交涉规则、环境中，中国当时的满清政府被动地适应着，开始在各个重要的接触点上设置专门的交涉机构。于是在迎接和融入世界潮流之际，“交涉”一词便染上了屈辱的色彩，交涉机构也就被烙上了耻辱的痕迹，以至于国人视之如“脸上的红字”，耻于正视它。

译文：In modern times, China took a turn in its position in foreign relations and began to engage passively with the powers. The Manchu government of the time in China adapted passively to the different rules and circumstances of diplomacy and began to set up special diplomatic agencies at various important points of contact. As a result, the word “diplomacy” was tainted with humiliation and the agency was branded with shame, so that the nation regarded it as a “scarlet on the face” and was ashamed to mention it.

分析：原文“在……环境中”在句子中做地点状语，运用 DeepL 初译为“In the different negotiation rules and environment, the Manchu Government passively adapted to them ...”，虽然语法表达上没有问题，但缺乏整体的连贯性，且模糊了“passively”对“adapted”和“began”的修饰，可能造成语意理解有误。因此，译者进一步理解原文，发现“满清政府被动地适应着”的其实正是“不同以往的交涉规则、环境”，进而运用“连贯原则”，对句式语序进行调整，将原句中的地点状语融入英文中做定语，全句结构由地点状语+复合句转变为一句复合句。如此一来，不仅正确传递了原文信息，更使译文简洁流畅，也证明了“连贯原则”在翻译实践中的指导性作用。

例 23

原文：1899 年，中东铁路总工程师茹格维志以“铁路开筑，汽车通行以后，中俄杂处其中，纠葛必不可少”为名，……催促黑龙江将军恩泽、吉林将军延茂签订了《黑龙江铁路交涉总局章程》《吉林铁路交涉总局章程》……

译文：In 1899, the chief engineer of the Middle East Railway, Ruggievich, urged General Enze of Heilongjiang and General Yanmao of Jilin to sign The Statute of the General Bureau of Railway Negotiation of Heilongjiang and The Charter of the General Bureau of Railway Negotiation of Jilin ... in the name of “after the railroad has been built and opened to traffic, China and Russia were involved in it, therefore, entanglements were indispensable".

分析：本句具有汉语表达习惯的典型特点，即中文喜欢先说原因（状语），后说结果（主句）；而英文则是先出结果（主句），后出原因（状语）。分析句子意思可知，本句的结果是"工程师茹格维志催促……签订……"，原因则是"以……为名"，因此根据英文的习文特点，译者决定先翻译主句内容，后翻译原因状语，形成"Ruggievich，urged ... in the name of ..."句式，使得译文更加符合英文表达方式。如此一来，译文在流畅通顺的基础上，也符合目的语的语法习惯，不仅准确呈现了原文传递的信息，还验证了"连贯原则"的指导作用。

例 24

原文：1916 年，在《中俄互禁烟酒条约》的制定实行过程中，在北京政府与沙俄已经订立条约的前提下，李鸿谟以哈尔滨交涉员兼滨江道尹的身份与俄国领事特拉乌绍利特就整个中东路属地内的禁酒事宜进行了艰苦的协商，迫使沙俄方面做出了一定让步。1916 年 5 月 21 日，李鸿谟以中东路属地中方最高代表的身份与驻哈尔滨俄国领事特拉乌绍利特签署了《中俄北满若干地区禁卖酒精协议》，最终使华商的损失降到了最低。

译文：In 1916, in the course of the formulation and implementation of the *Sino-Russian Treaty on the Prohibition of Tobacco and Alcohol*, Li Hongmo, as interlocutor and the intendant of the circuit of Binjiang Road in Harbin, negotiated painstakingly with the Russian Consul Trauscholit on the prohibition of alcohol in the whole of the East China Eastern Territories, under the premise that the Beijing government and Tsarist Russia had already signed a treaty. This forced the Russian side to make certain concessions. On May 21, 1916, Li Hongmo signed the *Sino-Russian Agreement on Prohibition of Alcohol Sales in Several Areas of North Manchuria* with Russian Consul Trautvetter as the highest representative of the Chinese side in the Middle East Road, ultimately minimizing the losses of Chinese merchants.

分析：通过分析该句子结构，译者发现该句为典型的中文流散句，即短句较多，分析句子并且结合上文可知将该段落"在北京政府与沙俄已经订立条约的前提下"，即整个事件的背景情况放在句子末尾，可以突出当时情况紧急，整个过程非常艰辛，作为结果的句子"迫使沙俄方面做出了一定让步"，单独成句，算是一个比较好的结果，更凸显出李鸿谟交谈过程的不易。

在翻译过程中，保持语意上的连贯通顺也同样重要，译者以翻译目的论为“指向标”，根据实际情况进行语序上的调整，并结合其他技巧，经过多次润色，最终提升了译文的流畅度及规范性。

5.4.5 翻译实践总结

在本次翻译实践中，译者既收获了许多经验，也遇到了不少问题，清楚地认识到了自己的不足。本章将从翻译实践中遇到的问题及思考、对今后学习工作的启示与展望两个方面对整个翻译任务进行简要总结。

5.4.5.1 心得与收获

经过此次实践，译者详细地了解到历史研究类文本的风格特点，也对翻译目的论的理论精髓和应用价值有了一些心得，可谓收获颇丰。

通过本次翻译实践，译者了解到历史文献通常采用描述性语言，语言规范、严谨，以便更准确地还原历史，表达方式更精练，简洁明了、言简意赅。以往译者在翻译历史文本时往往习惯性选择直译的方式以求保留原文的原汁原味，但经过此次英译实践，译者学会了首先结合文本语言特点和风格特色进行整体分析，其次归纳文本特点类型，最后运用适合的理论，如本次实践中译者选取的是弗米尔的翻译目的论，结合案例具体分析。

5.4.5.2 问题与对策

首先，译者的知识储备远远不足。专业知识不全面影响了译者的理解与表达。在翻译的早期阶段，因为缺乏与译文相关的专业背景知识，译者的进度缓慢，在查阅和思考中耗费了大量精力。其次，译者自身的综合素质不高。作为一名翻译员，单凭语言能力是不足以胜任的，必须具备深厚的专业领域知识，方能在翻译实践中以更广阔的视野理解原文要传达的信息，从而减少翻译错误的可能性。最后，还要从多个方面着手完善自己的知识结构。因此，译者主张在接到翻译任务后，首先进行充分的译前准备，通过深入阅读原文并收集平行文本，以建立对翻译任务和内容的全面认知。此外，在日常工作中需不断学习新的专业术语，掌握不同行业的相关词汇，这样可以帮助译员更好地理解原文。“磨刀不误砍柴工”，建立知识储备是提升整体翻译质量不可或缺的关键步骤。除针对某项任务建立知识储备外，译者还需要在日常生活中不断积累各领域专业知识，以便在紧急情况下能从容应对。

译者在翻译初期花费了大量时间和精力，从网络上五花八门的术语查阅结果中甄别正确规范的译法，很大原因在于译者缺乏理论知识的指导。理论与实践相辅相成，脱离了理论指导的实践将缺乏严谨性。译者随即制订了解决方案，大量阅读并探究翻译领域专家、学者的相关研究成果，找到适用于本次实践的翻译理论指导。在翻译实践中，译者意识到，只有具备了适用的理论知识，为实践建立起评判准则，才能使实践更具方向性。

译者的搜索和总结能力较弱。通过此次翻译实践，译者意识到，在实践中面对术语翻译，除了掌握翻译策略，查阅能力也很重要。同时，如果仅仅满足于词典和百度的简单搜索，而不去学习互联网的深度交叉检索方式，并总结筛选评判规律，那么翻译质量和翻译速度都将受到影响，译者也很难从翻译实践中获得能力上的提升。

5.4.5.3　努力方向和展望

翻译实践事毕，译者明白“翻书破万卷，译笔如有神”，实践才能出真知——一名优秀的译者，必然也必将是从一次次的翻译实践中磨砺而出的。因此，译者要努力的方向就是在全面学习翻译理论和积极储备知识之余，不论是现在的学业，还是将来的职业生涯，在每次翻译实践中，都保持全身心的投入，汲取师友的指教，让每次的翻译实践都成为迈向一名优秀译者的坚实脚印。

相较于本科阶段潜藏在注重学分与证书之下的迷惘，在成为翻译研究生的这段时间里，译者觉得这是一个消除迷惘的过程，不单单是因为研究方向的细分，更是由于师长营造的氛围，“无论身处哪个方向或哪个领域，‘深耕细作’都是一名翻译硕士研究生应当具备的情怀”。而这种情怀抑或心态，对我们的学习状态也是耳濡目染的，更深深浸润着我们的生活态度。在这次翻译实践之前，译者只想未来从事与翻译相关的工作，而经历了这次翻译实践，翻译将成为译者为之努力一生的事业。

“译者对自己忠诚的表现为总是提交自己最好的译文。”［田璐、赵军峰，2018（4）：86-90］。这次翻译实践历时漫长，从最初的深入研读原文和搜集资料到翻译时对原文的准确理解和翻译理论方法的精选，再到最终的反复校对和修正，这个过程充满了挑战和艰辛，但也带来了丰硕的成果，让译者深刻感受到了翻译工作的真实状态。翻译不是一项简单的文字转换工作，好的译文也不可能一蹴而就。

在本次翻译实践中，译者深刻感受到自己的英语实际应用能力得到了显著提升。在进行具体翻译的过程中，译者发现很多时候都需要根据原文的内容和文体特征来选择合适的表达方法。在进行英汉、汉英翻译时，通常倾向于采用顺句驱动的方式，而忽略了汉语词汇与英语词汇之间的一一对应，从而导致译文的结构不够流畅，与目的语的表达习惯不符，常常带有翻译腔。因此，要想提高自己的语言表达水平，就需要掌握一定的翻译学知识和技巧。在本次翻译实践中，译者遵循汉斯·弗米尔的翻译目的论，重点关注英汉双语表达的差异及中西方文化的差异，以确保译文符合英语的表达习惯。

以本次实践报告为例，在着手翻译前，译者先熟悉了现阶段被广泛应用的各类翻译理论，在整体分析源语文本内容和风格之后，译者认为翻译目的论与本文本的适配性较高，因此在确定了要运用的翻译理论后，结合文本风格及特点，译者在遵循目的论三原则的前提下，分别对文本中具有代表性的词汇、句子及语篇进行分析，例如，对具有中国特色的古代官职及公文词汇采用意译和释译的翻译方法。在句子层面，译者选用增译的翻译方法以及主被动语态相互转化的方法来处理主动句，从而使译语更加贴近译语读者的文化与表达方式。在语篇层面，译者则主要分析了两个方面，即通过增加文中隐含未表达的逻辑衔接词实现篇章的自然过渡。比如，增加因果连接词consequently、ever since来显化前后文的联系，充分考虑目的语读者的阅读感受，并通过调整语序达到篇章的紧密衔接，根据英汉语言的差异，使译文更加符合目的语的行文方式。翻译绝不是单纯的一种语言向另一种语言的转换，其中包含的知识与选择值得译者在日后的每次实践前细细回想、认真揣摩。

译者衷心希望这篇《中东铁路附属地行政管理权研究》英译实践报告能为其他从事相关学术研究的翻译人员提供一些新的思路，帮助国外研究学者正确认识这段历史，正确树立哈尔滨在历史中的形象。

参考文献

[1] HUCKER C. A Dictionary of Official Titles in Imperial China[M]. California: Stanford University Press,1985.

[2] HOLZ-MANTTARI J. Translatorisches Handeln: Theorie and Methode[M]. Helsinki: Tiedeakatemia, 1984.

[3] MUNDAY J. Introducing Translation Studies: Theories and Applications[M]. London and New York: Routledge, 2016.

[4] NIDA E A. The Theory and Practice of Translation[M]. Shanghai: Shanghai Foreign Language Education Press, 2004.

[5] NORD C. Text Analysis in Translation[M]. Beijing: Foreign Language Teaching and Research Press, 2000.

[6] REISS K. Translation Criticism: The Potentials and Limitations[M]. Shanghai: Shanghai Foreign Language Education Press, 2004.

[7] REISS K. Towards a General Theory of Translation Action[M]. London and New York: Routledge, 2014.

[8] VENUTI L. The Translation Studies Reader[M]. London and New York: Routledge, 2000.

[9] VERMEER H J. Andrew Chesterman. Skopos and Commission in Translation

[M]. London: Routledge, 2021.

[10] VERMEER H J. Skopos and Commission in Translational Action[C]// Venuti L. The Translation Studies Reader. London: Routledge, 2000.

[11] 卞建华 . 传承与超越：功能主义翻译目的论研究 [M]. 北京：中国社会科学出版社，2008.

[12] 丁应强 . 文化输出视角下汉语专有名词的英译研究 [J]. 林区教学，2015（11）：20.

[13] 付琼 . 目的论视角下《朝花夕拾》文化负载词翻译 [J]. 现代交际，2011（10）：49–50.

[14] 高迎慧 . 思维转向："意合" 到 "形合"：从汉英结构差异谈汉语长句、复杂句的翻译方法 [J]. 教育理论与实践，2012（12）：52–53.

[15] 何刚强 . 笔译理论与技巧 [M]. 北京：外语教学与研究出版社，2009.

[16] 胡壮麟 . 语篇的衔接与连贯 [M]. 上海：上海外语教育出版社，1994.

[17] 黄婕 . 目的论视角下的翻译策略研究与思考 [J]. 当代教研论丛，2019（3）：14.

[18] 贾璞 . 英汉翻译中背景知识的重要性：以历史文献翻译为例 [D]. 太原：山西大学，2019.

[19] 姜文倩 . 目的论指导下的历史文本翻译研究：以 *Belgium: From the Roman Invasion to the Present Day* 的汉译为例 [D]. 太原：山西大学，2020.

[20] 李靖，侯玉，缪丽伟 . 文化翻译理论视域下的历史文献翻译研究 [J]. 散文百家，2021（1）：133–135.

[21] 李运兴 . 语篇翻译引论 [M]. 北京：中国对外翻译出版公司，2001.

[22] 李长栓 . 非文学翻译理论 [M]. 北京：外语教学与研究出版社，2009.

[23] 刘军平 . 西方翻译理论通史 [M]. 武汉：武汉大学出版社，2009.

[24] 刘宓庆 . 翻译教学：实务与理论 [M]. 北京：中国对外翻译出版公司，2003.

[25] 刘岩，陈胜能 . 历史文献翻译与《中国省别全志（贵州卷）》汉译初探 [J]. 东方翻译，2021（1）：20–26.

[26] 罗选民 . 典籍翻译的历史维度：评《翻译研究的多维视角：1691 年以来的〈中庸〉英译研究 [J]. 上海翻译，2019（6）：93–96.

[27] 欧飞兵 . 翻译目的论视域下的陶瓷文化翻译 [J]. 中国科技翻译，2011（2）：53–56.

[28] 潘平亮 . 翻译目的论及其文本意识的弱化倾向 [J]. 上海翻译，2006（1）：13–17.

[29] 田璐，赵军峰 . 新世纪的功能翻译理论：克里斯蒂安 · 诺德教授访谈录

[J]. 中国翻译，2018（4）：86–90.
[30] 田申 . 以林语堂译《兰亭集序》观文言文英译之难 [J]. 学教育（上），2019（4）：140–141.
[31] 朱湘军 . 翻译硕士（MTI）学位论文之“规”与“范”[J]. 上海翻译，2019（2）：20.
[32] 王洪涛 . 中国古典文论在西方的英译：历史进程与基本特征 [J]. 国际汉学，2018（1）：43–48.
[33] 王军，陈诗月 . 翻译目的论研究综述 [J]. 现代交际，2017（18）：102–103.
[34] 伍小军 . 论汉语长句断句译法 [J]. 外语教学，2006（2）：75–76.
[35] 叶子南 . 高级英汉翻译理论与实践 [M]. 北京：清华大学出版社，2013：142.
[36] 叶子南 . 对翻译中“词性转换”的新认识 [J]. 中国翻译，2007（3）：11.
[37] 翟宗德 . 翻译中的语言学 [M]. 上海：上海译文出版社，2007.
[38] 张锦兰 . 目的论与翻译方法 [J]. 中国科技翻译，2004，17（1）：13，35–37.
[39] 张美芳 . 文本类型、翻译目的及翻译策略 [J]. 上海翻译，2013（5）：5–10.
[40] 张茜 . 目的论指导下史料文献的翻译探究：以约翰 · 德贞的 *The Land Question*（节选）为例 [D]. 南京：南京农业大学，2020.

Epilogue

This book is revised on the basis of the 2008 Heilongjiang Philosophy and Social Sciences Planning Project—"*Research on the History of Heilongjiang Immigration in the Late Qing Dynasty and Early Republic of China*". Members of the project team are responsible for the preparation of various sections: Wei Ying in charge of Section 2, Section 3, Section 4, Section 5, and Section 6; Gao Longbin in charge of Section 8, Section 9, Section 10, and Section 11; Yin Tiechao in charge of Section 16; Gao Zhenling in charge of Section 1 and Section 13; Huang Yanzhen in charge of Section 12; and Li Peng, the Project Leader, in charge of the draft unification and the remaining section.

Thanks to the members of the project team for their hard work! The publication of the book is not the end of this work, but the beginning. We will continue the work that we have started and launch a further study of the "Heilongjiang Immigration History" based on the existing research. Thanks to the leadership of the Provincial Social Science Planning Office for their firm support, and to the Heilongjiang People's Publishing House for their extremely professional guidance! Thank you all for the sincere support to the publication of this work.

Appendices

Appendix Ⅰ Works Cited

Chapter 1 Government-organized Immigration

1.1 History of "Shunzhi and Shandong Guildhall" and "Shandong People Association in Harbin"

1. 石方 . 黑龙江区域社会文明转型研究 [M]. 哈尔滨：黑龙江人民出版社，2006.

2. 哈尔滨市地方志编纂委员会 . 哈尔滨市志 · 人口 [M]. 哈尔滨：黑龙江人民出版社，1998.

3. 李鸿文，张本政 . 东北大事记 [M]. 长春：吉林文史出版社，1987.

4.《帝俄霸占哈尔滨市政的几个问题》,《哈尔滨史志》,1986 年（3）：74–90.

5. 郑长椿 . 中东铁路历史编年 [M]. 哈尔滨：黑龙江人民出版社，1987.

6. 朱寰，王恒伟 . 中国对外条约辞典（1689—1949）[M]. 长春：吉林教育出版社，1994.

7. 钱单士厘 . 癸卯旅行记 [M]. 长沙：湖南人民出版社，1981.

8. 李述笑 . 哈尔滨历史编年 [M]. 哈尔滨：哈尔滨出版社，2000.

9. 黑龙江省档案馆 . 黑龙江历史大事记 1900—1911[A]. 哈尔滨：黑龙江人民出版社，1984.

10. 尼鲁斯 . 中东铁路沿革史 [M] // 吴文衔，张秀兰 . 霍尔瓦特与中东铁路 . 长春：吉林文史出版社，1993.

11. 朱显平 . 帝俄霸占哈尔滨市政的几个问题 [J]. 哈尔滨史志，1986（3）.

12. 梅尼希科夫，等 . 北满 吉林省 [M] // 辛培林，王敬荣 . 黑龙江疆域历史与现状问题研究 . 哈尔滨：黑龙江人民出版社，2006.

13. 黑龙江省档案馆 . 黑龙江历史大事记 1912—1932[A]. 哈尔滨：黑龙江人民出版社，1984.

14. 道里区志 [M]. 哈尔滨：黑龙江人民出版社，1998.

15. 哈尔滨史略 [M]. 哈尔滨：黑龙江人民出版社，1994：155.

1.2 Origin of the Jing Bannermen's Reclamation Policy of the Northeast

1. 杨宾 . 宁古塔杂诗 [M]// 龙吟诗社 . 黑龙江历代诗词选 . 哈尔滨：黑龙江人民出版社，1990.

2. 赵毅，王景泽 . 对清前期（1644—1840）开发东北经济的检讨 [J]. 中国社会经济史研究，1999（1）：12.

3. 李兴盛 . 东北流人史 [M]. 哈尔滨：黑龙江人民出版社，1990.

4.《何陋居集》，转引自衣保中、吴北战《论清前期东北垦荒政策的演变》一文，《长白学刊》，1999 年第 6 期。

5. 曲淑岷 . 清代东北封禁政策述评 [J]. 中国边疆史地研究，1989（2）：1–7.

6. 赵中浮 . 东三省的移民问题 [M]// 王戎笙 . 台港清史研究文摘 . 沈阳：辽宁人民出版社，1988.

7. 辽宁《清史简编》编写组 . 清史简编 [M]. 沈阳：辽宁人民出版社，1980.

8. 张杰 . 试论清前期的东北封禁 [J]. 社会科学辑刊，1994（5）：113–121.

9. 李自然 . 试论乾隆朝东北禁边与八旗生计之关系 [J]. 中央民族大学学报（哲学社会科学版），2000（6）：52–55.

10. 马建石，杨育棠 . 大清律例通考校注 [M]. 北京：中国政法大学出版社，1992.

11. 佚名 . 清初编审八旗男丁满文档案选译 [J]. 历史档案，1988（4）：10–13.

12. 张玉兴 . 包衣汉姓与汉军简论：八旗制度兴衰的一个历史见证 [J]. 辽宁大学学报（哲学社会科学版），2003（4）：37–45.

13. 乾隆十年六月内务府会计司呈稿 []// 载中国科学院民族研究所，等 . 满族历史档案资料选集 .1963 年铅印本。

14. 刘厚生，译 . 清雍正朝镶红旗档 [M]. 长春：东北师范大学出版社，1985.

15. 中国第一历史档案馆 . 雍正朝满文朱批奏折全译：上、下册 [A]. 合肥：黄山书社，1998：1879.

16. 李澍恩 . 宾州府政书 [M]. 北京：商务印书馆，1984.

1.3 The Whole Story of the Jing Bannermen's Reclamation Policy

1. 中国历史第一档案馆 . 乾隆朝上谕档：第一册 [A]. 桂林：广西师范大学出版社，2008.

2. 嘉庆道光两朝上谕档：第十七册 [A]. 桂林：广西师范大学出版社，2000.

3. 李澍田 . 双城堡屯田纪略 [M]. 长春：吉林文史出版社，1990.

4. 中国历史档案馆 . 清代黑龙江历史档案选编：光绪元年—七年 [A]. 哈尔滨：黑龙江人民出版社，1986.

5. 中国社会科学院边疆史地研究中心 . 光绪朝黑龙江将军奏稿 [M]. 北京：全国图书文献缩微复制中心，1993.

1.4 Causes Leading to the Failure of the Jing Bannermen's Reclamation Policy and its Objective Effects

1. 李澍恩 . 宾州府政书 [M]. 北京：商务印书馆，1984.

2. 中国历史档案馆 . 清代黑龙江历史档案选编：光绪八年—十五年 [A]. 哈尔滨：黑龙江人民出版社，1986.

3. 卫匡国 . 鞑靼战纪 [M]//. 杜文凯 . 清代西人见闻录 . 北京：中国人民大学出版社，1985：3.

4. 刘坤一，张之洞 . 江楚会奏变法三折 [M]. 台北：台北文海出版社，1977：94.

5. 故宫博物院明清档案部 . 清末筹备立宪档案史料：上册 [M]. 北京：中华书局，1979：61+66.

6. 故宫博物院明清档案部 . 清末筹备立宪档案史料：下册 [M]. 北京：中华书局，1979：918.

7. 锡良 . 锡良遗稿 [M]. 北京：中华书局，1959：917-922+925-926+1044-1045.

8. 黄爵滋 . 敬陈六事疏 [M]// 黄爵滋奏疏许乃济奏议合刊北京：中华书局，1959：47.

9. 罗尔纲 . 绿营兵志 [M]. 北京：商务印书馆，2012：8.

10. 萧一山 . 清代通史：第 2 册 [M]. 上海：华东师范大学出版社，2006：227.

11. 萨英额 . 吉林外记 [M]. 长春：吉林文史出版社，1986：118.

12.《阿城县志》编纂委员会 . 阿城县志 [M]. 哈尔滨：黑龙江人民出版社，1988.

13.《双城县志》编纂委员会 . 双城县志 [M]. 北京：中国农业出版社，1990.

14.《大清会典事例》卷七〇九。

15. 钱公来，《东北五十年来社会之变迁》，《逸斋随笔》，转引自田志和《关于清代东北流民》社会科学集刊，1983 年第 5 期。

16. 曹明国 . 中国人口：吉林分册 [M]. 北京：中国财政经济出版社，1988.

17. 梁方仲 . 中国历代户口、田地、田赋统计 [M]. 上海：上海人民出版社，1980.

18.《阿城市土地志》编纂委员会 . 阿城市土地志 [M].[出版地不详]：[出版者不详]，1998；又见 [清] 鄂尔泰等修《八旗通志》(初集) 卷二十一,《盛京通志》卷三十八。

19. 李澍田 . 吉林志书造送会典馆清册 [M]. 长春：吉林文史出版社，1988.

Chapter 2 The Tradition and Innovation of Inland Immigrants

2.1 The Jing Bannermen's Reclamation Policy and the Social Issues of Immigrants in Heilongjiang

1. 和龚，张山 . 中华民族历史与文化 [M]. 北京：中央民族学院出版社，1988.

2.2 Re-exploration for the Livelihood of the Eight Banners

1. 马建石，杨育棠 . 大清律例通考校注 [M]. 北京：中国政法大学出版社，1992.

2. 安双成 . 清初编审八旗男丁满文档案选译 [J]. 历史档案，1988（4）：01.

3. 张玉兴：《包衣汉姓与汉军简论——八旗制度兴衰的一个历史见证》。

4.《辽宁大学学报》(哲学社会科学版)，2003 年第 4 期。

5.《乾隆十年六月内务府会计司呈稿》，中国科学院民族研究所等编《满族历史档案资料集》，1963 年铅印本。

6. 刘庆，魏鸿 . 八旗军由盛转衰的历史教训 [J]. 军事历史研究，2004（1）：10.

2.3 Social Security of Heilongjiang Immigrants in the Late Qing Dynasty and Early Republic of China

1. 田方，陈一筠 . 中国移民史略 [M]. 北京：知识出版社，1986.

2. 董惠石，张秀春 . 张学良与东北新建设资料选 [M].[出版地址不详]：香港同泽出版社，1998.

3. 顾德曼 . 家乡、城市和国家：上海的地缘网络与认同 1853—1937[M]. 宋钻友，译 . 上海：世纪出版集团，2004.

4. 王日根 . 乡土之链 [M]. 天津：天津人民出版社，1996.

5. 朱偰 . 满洲移民的历史和现状 [J]. 东方杂志，1928，25（12）：17，20.

6. 东省铁路经济调查局 . 北满农业 [M]. 哈尔滨：哈尔滨中国印刷局，1928.

7.《黑龙江省国营农场经济发展史》编写组 . 黑龙江省国营农场经济发展史 [M]. 哈尔滨：黑龙江人民出版社，1984.

8. 陈翰笙 . 难民的东北流亡 [J]. “中央研究院”社会科学研究所集刊，1930（2）：15，19，23.

9. 农保中 . 试论民国时期朝鲜移民大量迁入东北地区的原因 [J]. 东北亚论坛，2002（2）：77–80.

10. 龚维航 . 清代汉人拓殖东北述略 [J]. 禹贡，6（3–4）106.

11. 王慕宁 . 东三省之实况 [M]. 北京：中华书局，1929.

12. 津浦京木铁路局减收小工车价广告 [N]. 大公报，1913–11–05.

13. 张振之 . 人祸大灾下之山东人民与其东北移民 [J]. 新亚细业，2（3）：39–40.

14. 满铁庶务部调查课 . 民国十七年满洲出稼者：日文版 [Z]. 大连：南满洲铁道株式会社，1929.

15. 胡天 . 六十年来中国农村人口之增减与山东移民 [J]. 政治月刊，1934，2（1）：60–69.

16. 陈翰笙 . 难民的东北流亡 [J]. “中央研究院”社会科学研究所集刊，1934（1）：23–24，29.

17. 剑虹 . 汉族开拓满洲史 [J]. 东方杂志，1919，16（1）：188.

18. 夏如冰 . 清末及北洋政府时期的农业法规 [J]. 古今农业，2004（3）：20–21.

19. 惠民 . 由天灾人祸说到移民：第 6 卷 [J]. 中东经济月刊，1931（4–6）.

Chapter 3 The Influence of Immigration and Local Population

3.1 Research on Jewish Immigration to China in Modern and Contemporary History

1. 潘光，王健 . 一个半世纪以来的上海犹太人：犹太民族史上的东方一页 [M]. 北京：社会科学文献出版社，2002.

2. 徐新 . 哈尔滨历史上的犹太人 [J]. 辽宁师范大学学报（社会科学版），1995（1）：80–84.

3. 张铁江 . 哈尔滨：近代东亚犹太人最大的活动中心 [J]. 学习与探索，2000（6）：125–132.

4. 刘爽 . 哈尔滨犹太侨民史 [M]. 北京：方志出版社，2007.

5. 王志军，李薇 .20 世纪上半期哈尔滨犹太人的宗教生活与政治生活 [M]. 北京：人民出版社，2013.

6. 高龙彬 . 关于“犹太人在哈尔滨”的历史文化研究 [J]. 俄罗斯学刊，2012（2）：84–92.

7. 薛连举 . 哈尔滨人口变迁 [M]. 哈尔滨：黑龙江人民出版社，1998.

8. 考夫曼 . 我心中的哈尔滨犹太人 [M]. 刘全顺，译 . 哈尔滨：黑龙江人民出版社，2007.

9. 石方，高凌，刘爽 . 哈尔滨俄侨史 [M]. 哈尔滨：黑龙江人民出版社，1998.

黑龙江人民出版社，2003 年版，第 448–449 页；黑龙江人民出版社，2011 年版，第 314 页。

10. 曲伟、李述笑 . 哈尔滨犹太简明辞书 [M]. 北京：社会科学文献出版社，2013.

11. 房建昌 . 本世纪三四十年代中国各地犹太人概貌 [J]. 近代史研究，1997（6）：34–38.

12. 斯蒂芬 . 满洲黑手党：俄国纳粹黑幕纪实 [M]. 刘万钧，等译 . 哈尔滨：黑龙江人民出版社，1989.

13. 宋安娜 . 神圣的渡口：犹太人在天津 [M]. 天津：天津人民出版社，2007.

14. 郭蕴深 . 中俄茶叶贸易史 [M]. 哈尔滨：黑龙江教育出版社，1995.

15. 阿唐 . 斯基德尔斯基家族：哈尔滨的洛克菲勒 [M]// 老哈尔滨 · 历史档案 . 哈尔滨：北方文艺出版社，2012.

16. 潘光 . 犹太人在亚洲：比较研究 [M]. 上海：上海三联书店，2007.

17. 欧慕然，唐建文 . 从耶路撒冷到北京：一个杰出犹太家庭的中国情缘 [M]. 北京：世界知识出版社，2012.

18.《本研究所被确定为江苏高校国际问题研究中心》，http://a200980278.oinsite.cn

19. 潘光，余建华，王健 . 犹太民族复兴之路 [M]. 上海：上海社会科学院出版社，1998.

20. 李述笑 . 哈尔滨历史编年（1763—1949）[M]. 哈尔滨：哈尔滨市人民政府地方志办公室，1986.

21. 李述笑 . 哈尔滨历史编年（1763—1949）[M]. 哈尔滨：黑龙江人民出版社，2013.

22. 石方 . 黑龙江区域社会文明转型研究（1861—1911）[M]. 哈尔滨：黑

龙江人民出版社，2006.

23. 石方 . 黑龙江区域社会史研究（1912—1931）[M]. 哈尔滨：黑龙江人民出版社，2009.

24. 石方 . 20 世纪一二十年代哈尔滨多元文化研究 [M]. 哈尔滨：黑龙江人民出版社，2012.

25. 石方，高凌，刘爽 . 哈尔滨俄侨史 [M]. 哈尔滨：黑龙江人民出版社，1998.

石方，刘爽 . 哈尔滨俄侨史 [M]. 哈尔滨：黑龙江人民出版社，2003.

石方，刘爽 . 高凌 . 哈尔滨俄侨史 [M]. 哈尔滨：黑龙江人民出版社，2011.

26. 曲伟，李述笑 . 哈尔滨犹太人 [M]. 北京：社会科学文献出版社，2004.

27. 刘爽 . 哈尔滨犹太侨民史 [M]. 北京：方志出版社，2007.

28. 潘光 . 来华犹太人的国籍与法律问题（1840—1945）[J]. 社会科学，2006（2）：121-130.

3.2 Historical and Cultural Investigation on "Lithuanians in Harbin"

1. 哈尔滨市地方志编纂委员会 . 哈尔滨市志 · 大事记　人口 [M]. 哈尔滨：黑龙江人民出版社，1999.

2. 哈尔滨市地方志编纂委员会 . 哈尔滨市志 · 外事　对外经济贸易　旅游 [M]. 哈尔滨：黑龙江人民出版社，1998.

3. 薛连举 . 哈尔滨人口变迁 [M]. 哈尔滨：黑龙江人民出版社，1998.

4. 李兴汉 . 波罗的海三国 [M]. 北京：社会科学文献出版社，2003.

5. 帕尔默 . 波罗的海史 [M]. 上海：胡志勇，译：东方出版中心，2013.

6.《黑龙江历史档案通览》编委会 . 黑龙江历史档案通览 [M]. 哈尔滨：黑龙江人民出版社，2014.

7. 哈尔滨市方志馆 . 哈尔滨特别市市势年鉴（下）[M]. 哈尔滨：东北林业大学出版社，2014.

8. 哈尔滨市地方志编纂委员会 . 哈尔滨市志 [M]. 哈尔滨：黑龙江人民出版社，1999.

9. 曲伟 . 哈尔滨犹太人图史 [M]. 哈尔滨：黑龙江人民出版社，2015.

10. 曲伟，李述笑 . 哈尔滨犹太简明辞书 [M]. 北京：社会科学文献出版社，2013.

11. 中华民国三十六（1947）年度哈尔滨特别市工商业名簿（三）[Z]. 哈尔滨：哈尔滨特别市工商局，1947.

12. 杜显忠：《在中国哈尔滨第三届边境，地方经济贸易洽谈会领导委员会全体成员会议上的讲话》，中国哈尔滨经济贸易洽谈会办公室编。

13. 中国哈尔滨经济贸易洽谈会办公室 . 车轮的辙印：中国哈尔滨经济贸易洽谈会 1990—2004[M]. 哈尔滨：黑龙江人民出版社，2004.

3.3 Reflections on the History and Culture of "Jews in Harbin"

1. 阿成 . 和上帝一起流浪：犹太人哈尔滨避难记 [M]. 重庆：重庆出版社，2008.

2. 艾书琴 . 黑龙江省社会科学院院史（1960—2010）[M]. 哈尔滨：黑龙江人民出版社，2010.

3. 步平，等 . 东北国际约章汇释（1689—1919 年）[M]. 哈尔滨：黑龙江人民出版社，1987.

4. 余建华 .1882—1914 年犹太复国主义运动初兴阐析：兼谈现代阿犹冲突的起源 [J]. 西亚非洲，1997（4）：37.

肖宪 . 中东国家通史・以色列卷 [J]. 商务印书馆，2001.

5. 参考和引用译者硕士毕业论文《自我解放》和列奥・平斯克的《犹太复国主义思想》，北京师范大学历史学院，2007 年，导师张建华教授。

6. 李述笑，傅明静 . 哈尔滨犹太人人口、国籍和职业构成问题探讨 [J]. 学习与探索，2001（3）：131-136.

曲伟，李述笑 . 哈尔滨犹太人 [M]. 北京：社会科学文献出版社，2004.

李兴盛，等 . 东游日记（外十六种）：上 [M]. 哈尔滨：黑龙江人民出版社，2009.

7. 李述笑 . 哈尔滨历史编年（1896—1949）[M]. 哈尔滨：哈尔滨市人民政府地方志编纂办公室，1986.

8. 陈斯骏，余崇建 . 历史上的犹太国和犹太复国运动 [J]. 世界史研究动态，1984（1）.

9. 东北起大成街，西南止中山路。1915 年，称为"比乐时街"。哈尔滨市人民政府 . 黑龙江省哈尔滨市地名录 [M].[出版地不详]：[出版者不详]，1985.

10. Encyclopedia of Jewish History—Events and Eras of the Jewish People[M].. New York：Facts on File, 1986.

11. 范立君 . 近代关内移民与中国东北社会变迁（1860—1931）[M]. 北京：人民出版社，2007.

12. 葛剑雄 . 中国移民史：第 1 卷 [M]. 福州：福建人民出版社，1997.

13. 黑龙江省地方志编纂委员会 . 黑龙江省志・报业志 [M]. 哈尔滨：黑龙江人民出版社，1993.

14. 黄陵渝 . 犹太教与文化 [M]. 北京：中央民族大学出版社，1999.

15. ROSE J. The Myths of Zionism[M]. London：Pluto Press, 2004.

16. 据《1927、1934、1945 三年哈尔滨市欧美移民人数明细表》记载，1927 年，犹太人 1113 人。李德滨，石方 . 黑龙江移民概要 [M]. 哈尔滨：黑龙江人民出版社，1987.

17. 李兴耕，等 . 风雨浮萍：俄国侨民在中国（1917—1945）[M]. 北京：中央编译出版社，1997.

18. 李兴盛 . 大荒集 [M]. 哈尔滨：黑龙江教育出版社，2009.

李兴盛 . 流人史流人文化与旅游文化 [M]. 哈尔滨：黑龙江人民出版社，2008.

李兴盛 . 流人学的脚步 [M]. 哈尔滨：黑龙江教育出版社，2009.

19. 列宁 . 列宁全集：29 卷 [M]. 北京：人民出版社，1985.

20. 凌国新 . 哈尔滨文史资料：第 19 辑 [M]. 哈尔滨：黑龙江人民出版社，1995.

21. 刘爽 . 哈尔滨犹太侨民史 [M]. 北京：方志出版社，2007.

22. 刘欣欣，刘学清 . 哈尔滨西洋音乐史 [M]. 北京：人民音乐出版社，2002.

23. 马维权 . 黑龙江宗教界忆往：黑龙江文史资料第三十二辑 [M]. 哈尔滨：黑龙江人民出版社，1992.

24. 塞尔茨 . 犹太的思想 [M]. 赵立行，冯玮译，译 . 上海：上海三联书店，1995.

25. 梅力霍夫 . 哈尔滨犹太社区 [J]. 以色列原居中国犹太人协会会刊，1997：44.

罗曼诺娃 . 哈尔滨犹太宗教公会的慈善活动 [M]// 曲伟，考夫曼 . 哈尔滨犹太人的故乡情 . 哈尔滨：黑龙江人民出版社，2005.

26. 辽宁散人 . 滨江尘嚣录 [M]// 李兴盛，等 . 东游日记（外十六种）：（上）. 哈尔滨：黑龙江人民出版社，2009.

27. NOAM M. The Emergence of Zionist Thought[M]. New York: Associated Faculty Press, 1986.

28. 潘光，王健 . 一个半世纪以来的上海犹太人：犹太民族史上的东方一页 [M]. 北京：社会科学文献出版社，2002.

29. STEARNS P N. The Encyclopedia of World History[M]. sixth edition. Cambridge: James Clarke and Cambridge, 2001.

30. MATTER P. Encyclopedia of the Modern East and North Africa. [M]. New York: Macmillan Reference, 2004.

31. 曲伟，考夫曼 . 哈尔滨犹太人的故乡情 [M]. 哈尔滨：黑龙江人民出版社，2005.

32. SELTZER R M. Jewish People, Jewish Thought: The Jewish Experience in History[M]. New York: Macmillan Publishing Co, 1994.

33. 石方，刘爽，高凌 . 哈尔滨俄侨史 [M]. 哈尔滨：黑龙江人民出版社，2003.

34. 石方，高凌 . 传统与变革：哈尔滨近代社会文明转型研究 [M]. 哈尔滨：黑龙江人民出版社，1995.

35. 石方 . 黑龙江区域社会史研究（1912—1931 年）[M]. 哈尔滨：黑龙江人民出版社，2009.

36. 汤亚汀 . 上海犹太社区的音乐生活（1850—1950，1998—2005）[M]. 上海：上海音乐学院出版社，2007. 书中第 32 页，汤亚汀教授把"哈尔滨总会堂"和"哈尔滨新会堂"的照片标注颠倒。这可能受人民美术出版社 2000 年出版的《中国名城百年 · 哈尔滨旧影》（第 71 页）的影响。关于这方面的资料可参见《画说哈尔滨》《老明信片中的黑龙江》《哈尔滨保护建筑》《凝固的乐章——尔滨市保护建筑纵览》《犹太人在哈尔滨》等。

37. 王替夫，金淑梅 . 伪满外交官的回忆：黑龙江文史务料第二十五辑 [M]. 哈尔滨：黑龙江人民出版社，1988.

38. 夏明方，康沛竹 . 20 世纪中国灾变图史（上）[M]. 福州：福建教育出版社 .

39. 中国社会科学院语言研究所词典编辑室 . 现代汉语词典：第 5 版 [M]. 北京：商务印书馆，2006.

40.《新晚报》2010 年 6 月 24 日。

41. 徐新，凌继尧 . 犹太百科全书（修订版）[M]. 上海：上海人民出版社，1998.

42. 徐新 . 犹太百科全书 [M]. 上海：上海人民出版社，1993.

43. 薛连举 . 哈尔滨人口变迁 [M]. 哈尔滨：黑龙江人民出版社，1998.

44. 张铁江 . 揭开哈尔滨犹太人历史之谜：哈尔滨犹太人社区考察研究 [M]. 哈尔滨：黑龙江人民出版社，2004.

45. 卡南 . 卡斯普事件：1932—1945 年发生在哈尔滨的种族冲突和文化冲突 [M]. 尹铁超，孙晗，译 . 哈尔滨：黑龙江人民出版社，2009.

46. 埃班 . 犹太史 [M]. 北京：中国社会科学出版社，1986.

47. 卡特赖特，比迪斯 . 疾病改变历史 [M]. 陈仲丹，周晓政，译 . 济南：山东画报出版社，2004.

48. 卢卡斯 . 以色列现代史 [M]. 杜先菊，彭艳，译 . 北京：商务印书馆，

1997.

49. 曾一智 . 城与人：哈尔滨故事 [M]. 哈尔滨：黑龙江人民出版社，2004.

50. 赵鑫珊 . 上海白俄拉丽莎 [M]. 上海：文汇出版社，2010.

51. 赵永华 . 在华俄文新闻传播活动史（1898—1956）[M]. 北京：中国人民大学出版社，2006.

3.4 Harbin YMCA in Immigrant Society

1. 贾永梅 . 基督教青年会传入中国史实考略 [J]. 史学月刊，2008（2）：19.

2. 彭立红 . 中华基督教青年会与近代中国社会改造 [D]. 广州：暨南大学，2000.

3. 刘子楠 . 中华基督教青年会与中国近代教育 [D]. 福州：福建师范大学，2005.

4. 高志超 . 哈尔滨地下党组织建立初期与基督教青年会 [J]. 哈尔滨史志，1990（1）.

5. 付尚 . 哈尔滨基督教青年会与革命宣传 [M]// 哈尔滨文史资料：第十九辑 . 哈尔滨：黑龙江人民出版社，1995.

6. 哈尔滨市地方志编纂委员会 . 哈尔滨市志・宗教方言 [M]. 哈尔滨：黑龙江人民出版社，1998.

7. 世旭 . 俄国侨民在东北地区的文化活动述评 [D]. 北京：北京语言大学，2004.

8. 赵晓阳 . 基督教青年会在中国：本土和现代的探索 [M]. 北京：社会科学文献出版社，2008.

9. 吴文衔 . 黑龙江考古民族资料译义集（第一辑）[M]. 哈尔滨：北方文物杂志社，1991.

10. 李兴耕，等 . 风雨浮萍：俄国侨民在中国（1917—1945）[M]. 北京：中央编译出版社，1997.

11. 石方，刘爽，高凌 . 哈尔滨俄侨史 [M]. 哈尔滨：黑龙江人民出版社，2003.

12. 中国人民政治协商会议黑龙江省哈尔滨市委员会文史资料研究委员会 . 哈尔滨文史资料：第十九辑 [M]. 哈尔滨：黑龙江人民出版社，1995.

13. 高莽 . 高费的苦难：我和俄罗斯文学 [M]. 郑州：河南文艺出版社，2007.

14. 黑龙江省地方志编纂委员会 . 黑龙江省志・共产党志 [M]. 哈尔滨：黑龙江人民出版社，1996.

15. 纪锦章 . 回忆二三事 [M]// 哈尔滨文史资料第三辑：内部资料 . 哈尔滨 ：

黑龙江人民出版社，1984.

16. 孟庆鹏 . 孙中山文集：下 [M]. 北京：团结出版社，1997.

17. 黑龙江省地方志编纂委员会 . 黑龙江省志 [M]. 哈尔滨：黑龙江人民出版社，1996.

18. 李述笑 . 五卅运动在哈尔滨 [J]. 哈尔滨研究，1984（4）.

19. 孔繁贞 . 哈尔滨妇女协进会成立始末 [M]// 哈尔滨文史资料第二辑 . 哈尔滨：黑龙江人民出版社，1983.

20. 于学蕴，刘琳 . 天津老教堂 [M]. 天津：天津人民出版社，2005.

3.5 On the Business Philosophy of Jews in Harbin

1.《哈尔滨》课题组 . 哈尔滨 [M]. 北京：当代中国出版社，2007.

2. 哈尔滨日本商工会议所：《北满的外国资本及其活动状况》，1936 年，第 26–27 页。

3. 纪凤辉，段光达 . 东方珍珠哈尔滨（上）[M]. 哈尔滨：哈尔滨出版社，1998.

4. 李士良，石方，高凌 . 哈尔滨史略 [M]. 哈尔滨：黑龙江人民出版社，1994.

5. 罗曼诺娃・远东俄中经济关系 [M]. 宿丰林，译 . 哈尔滨：黑龙江科技出版社，1991.

6. 罗曼诺夫 . 俄国在满洲（1892—1906）[M]. 北京：商务印书馆，1977.

7. 张铁江 . 哈尔滨犹太宗教公会的兴衰 [J]. 西伯利亚研究，2007（6）.

8. 张铁江 . 论犹太人在哈尔滨近代经济发展中的地位与作用 [J]. 黑龙江社会科学，2006（6）：31.

Chapter 4 The Role of Important People in the Development Process of Immigrant Society

4.1 New City of Immigrants—"Chicago of the East"

1. 申国政 . 关道设置简要始末 [J]. 黑龙江档案，2006（1）.

何宏 . 哈尔滨铁路交涉总局与滨江关道 [J]. 学理论，2008（11）.

2. 刘伟 . 晚清督抚政治：中央与地方关系研究 [M]. 武汉：湖北教育出版社，2006.

3. 苏建新，李秀梅 . 光绪三十四年度吉林省外务统计表：吉林省档案馆 [J]. 历史档案，2006（1）.

4. 张本政，东北大事记：上卷 [M]. 长春：吉林文史出版社，1987.

9. 哈尔滨档案馆编辑,《哈尔滨经济史料文集》第一卷,1990 年 10 月。

10. 1899 年 5 月 31 日吉林将军延茂与中东铁路总工程师茹格维志签订《吉林铁路交涉局总局章程》。见张本政,东北大事记 . 上卷 [M]. 长春:吉林文史出版社,1987:266.1899 年 10 月 5 日,黑龙江将军恩泽与中东铁路总工程师茹格维志签订《黑龙江铁路交涉局总局章程》。见张本政 . 东北大事记:上卷 [M]. 长春:吉林文史出版社,1987:269.

5. 汪士仁:《吉林交涉汇编》卷三《工类门 · 设立哈尔滨铁路交涉总局章程十条》。

6. 李述笑 . 哈尔滨历史编年 [M]. 哈尔滨:哈尔滨出版社,2000.

7. 吴文衔,张秀兰 . 霍尔瓦特与中东铁路 [M]. 长春:吉林文史出版社,1993.

8. 黑龙江省档案馆 . 黑龙江历史大事记 1900—1911[M]. 哈尔滨:黑龙江人民出版社,1984.

9. 闻衡 . 清末周冕吞文办款案查办始末 [J]. 北方文物,2005(4):15.

10. 徐世昌 . 东三省政略 [M]. 台北:台北文海出版社,1965.

11. 郑长椿 . 中东铁路历史编年 [M]. 哈尔滨:黑龙江人民出版社,1987.

12. 黑龙江省档案馆 . 黑龙江历史大事记 1912—1932[M]. 哈尔滨:黑龙江人民出版社,1984.

13. 尼鲁斯:《中东铁路沿革史》,俄文出版社 1923 年版,第 581 页,转自《霍尔瓦特与中东铁路》,第 135 页。

14. 朱显平 . 帝俄霸占哈尔滨市政的几个问题 [J]. 哈尔滨史志,1986(3):74-90.

15. 详见黑龙江档案馆编《中俄交涉史料汇编 · 中东铁路二》,1984 年版,第 66、67 页。

16. 吕一燃 . 俄国强占拉哈苏苏与中俄交涉 [J]. 中国边疆史地研究,1994(1).

4.2 Study on Administrative Power of Chinese Eastern Railway Affiliated Area

1. 翁同龢 . 翁同龢日记:第 5 册 [M]. 北京:中华书局,1989.

2. 朱有瓛 . 中国近代学制史料:第一辑上册 [M]. 上海:华东师范大学出版社,1983. 内附《光绪二十二年四月堂谕》记载了李鸿谟等出国留学的详细记载。

3. 李朋,高振凌 . 滨江道尹李鸿谟 [J]. 哈尔滨史志,2009(2).

4. 魏声龢 . 增订吉林地理纪要:下卷 [M]. 吉林:吉林吉东印刷社,1931.

5. 李鸿文，张本政 . 东北大事记：上卷 [M]. 长春：吉林文史出版社，1987：483.

6. 薛衔天 . 十月革命与中国收回中东铁路路区主权的斗争 [J]. 近代史研究，1988（4）.

4.3 Li Hongmo (Intendant of Binjiang) and Jilin Railway Negotiation Bureau

1. 孙庆海 . 鄂伦春下山定居 [J]. 世纪桥，2001（2）.

2. 曲守成，于学斌 . 论鄂伦春族定居务农实践中的政府功能：历史的评判与审思 [J]. 黑龙江民族丛刊，1999（4）.

3. 本文作者采访了内蒙古大杨树村领导，出于尊重本人的要求，不刊其名。

4. 萧梅 . 田野的回音：音乐人类学笔记 [M]. 厦门大学出版社，2001.

5. 胡增益 . 鄂伦春语简志 .[M] 北京：民族出版社，1986.

Appendix Ⅱ List of Terms

No.	Pg in ST	Chinese	English
1	3	闯关东	making a living in old northeast China
2	3	清末民初	the Late Qing Dynasty and Early Republic of China
3	3	东清铁路	Dong Qing Railway
4	3	东省铁路	Dong sheng Railway
5	3	中东铁路	Chinese Eastern Railway
6	4	同乡会	Townsmen Association
7	4	直东会馆	Shunzhi and Shandong Guild Hall
8	4	旅哈山东同乡会	Shandong People Association in Harbin
9	4	山东会馆	Shandong Guild Hall
10	5	吉林将军	General of Jilin Ula and Other Places/Jilin General
11	5	阿勒楚喀	Alcuka
12	6	劳动家	Working People
13	7	南满	South Manchuria
14	7	北满	North Manchuria
15	9	四明公馆	Siming Mansion
16	9	会馆文化	Guild Hall Culture
17	12	顺直	Shunzhi District
18	13	滨东同乡会馆	Shandong People Association in Harbin
19	13	滨江厅	A Government Department in Harbin
20	14	交涉局	Negotiation Department
21	14	交涉员	Negotiation Officials
22	18	跑崴子	Undertaking Commercial Activity in Vladivostok
23	18	跑伯力	Undertaking Commercial Activity in Siberia
24	23	京旗回屯	The Jing Bannermen's Reclamation
25	25	招垦政策	Cultivation and Reclamation Policies
26	25	封禁政策	The Prohibition Policy
27	31	京旗移驻	Migration and Station of Jing-banner
28	32	恩养	Supporting the Bannermen with Grace and Provisions/Welfare System of the Eight-banners
29	32	银两	tael of silver
30	34	印子钱	usury
31	35	汉军出旗	the Hans in Manchu Army's Return to the Countryside
32	39	井田	the Hashtag-shaped-field system
33	40	内务府	Imperial Household Department Office

续表

No.	Pg in ST	Chinese	English
34	40	镶红旗	Bordered Red Banner
35	41	养育兵	Reservist for Manchu's Army/Maintaining the Eight-banner Soldiers
36	48	奏疏	Palace memorial
37	56	衙门	Yamun
38	61	梅莽喀	Meimangka
39	62	西沟谷	Sigeohuolo
40	62	霍济墨	Hojimo
41	62	窑集	Yooji
42	62	洼浑	Wahun
43	64	八姓	Jakunhalai
44	71	屯丁	Station Troops Who Open up Uncultivated Land
45	104	阿玛	Ama
46	104	额娘	Eniye
47	111	京旗，京师八旗，驻防八旗	the Jing Banner, Eight Banners of Garrison
48	111	八旗	the Eight Banners
49	112	屯垦	Stationing Troops to Open up Wasteland
50	115	军机处	Grand Council
51	115	红白赏银	reward of silver for weddings and funerals
52	152	十月革命	The October Revolution
53	152	九一八事变	September 18th Incident
54	154	抗日战争	The War of Resistance Against Japanese Aggression
55	154	内战	Civil War
56	154	侨民	Alien
57	155	东北军阀	Northeast Warlord
58	155	满洲国	Manchukuo
59	157	纳粹大屠杀	Nazi Holocaust
60	174	“俄化”政策	the policy of “Russianization”
61	193	阿什肯纳兹犹太人	Ashkenazi Jews
62	192	《关于难民地位的公约》	*Convention Relating to the Status of Refugees*
63	187	《哈尔滨犹太侨民史》	*A History of the Jews in Harbin*
64	188	“河豚计划”	Fugu Plan

续表

No.	Pg in ST	Chinese	English
65	189	卡斯普事件	The Kaspe File
66	193	塞法迪犹太人	Sephardi Jews
67	196	沙皇亚历山大二世	Tsar Alexander Ⅱ
68	193	《上海白俄拉丽莎》	*Shanghai Baie Lalisha*
69	186	《犹太人在哈尔滨》	*The Jews in Harbin*
70	193	《犹太百科全书》	*Encyclopedia Judaica*
71	219	基督教青年会	Young Men's Christian Association
72	239	华俄道胜银行	Sino-Russian Daosheng Bank
73	244	花旗银行	Citibank
74	243	马迭尔宾馆	Modern Hotel
75	239	欧亚大陆桥	Euro-Asia land bridge
76	238	日俄战争	the Russo-Japanese War
77	238	伪满洲国	the puppet Manchukuo
78	238	中东铁路工程局	the Chinese Eastern Railway Engineering Bureau
79	241	乌苏里铁路	Ussuri Railway
80	242	《中俄密约》	*The Sino-Russian Secret Treaty*
81	252	疆吏	frontier official
82	252	商埠	commercial port
83	253	帮办	assistant
84	253	笔贴式	scribe
85	253	文事	literary affairs
86	253	武事	military affairs
87	253	总办	general director
88	254	局夫	civil servant
89	254	局勇	guard
90	254	书识	letter clerk
91	256	清末新政	New Deal period in the Late Qing Dynasty
92	260	关道	Guan Dao/customs office
93	261	关防	guarding the frontier
94	267	租帖	lease
95	269	道尹	intendant
96	269	宣统二年	the second year of Xuantong
97	270	清乡	Clearing-the-country
98	270	通译	translators
99	271	京师同文馆	School of Combined Learning

Appendix Ⅲ Source of Terms

Source of Terms

No.	Terms	Pg. in ST	Chinese	English
1	闯关东	3	“闯关东”是清朝历史上著名的人口迁移行动，广义的“闯关东”是指山海关以内地区的民众出关谋生，狭义上是指从清朝同治年间到中华民国这段历史时期内，关内百姓去关东谋生的历史。我们通常所说的“闯关东”是狭义的。19世纪末，中原地区的人口已经增长到一个饱和的状态，江浙地区早已没有多余的土地，东北则地广人稀，汉人前往关东的现象越来越多。再加上1860年中俄《北京条约》签署，俄国强占中国黑龙江以北、乌苏里江以东的全部领土，东北边疆危机空前强烈。为此，清廷于同年正式开禁放垦。随着禁令的解除，关东地区迎来了大量的人口涌入	“Brave the journey to Northeast” is a famous migration wave of people in the Qing Dynasty. Generally, it refers to people who lived within areas south of the Shanhai Pass going out for a living. To be more exact, it refers to the history of people who lived south of the Shanhai Pass to earn a living to the east of the pass from the reign of Tongzhi in the Qing Dynasty to the Republic of China (1912—1949). The so-called “brave the journey to Northeast” is narrowly defined. At the end of the 19th century, the population in the central plains of China saturated, and there had already been no vacant land in Jiangsu and Zhejiang. Since Northeast had vast land but few people, more and more Han people went there. In addition, due to the *Treaty of Beijing* between the Empire of China and the Russian Empire in 1860, the Russian Empire occupied all the areas north of the Heilongjiang River and east of the Wusuli River by force. As the threat in Northeast was looming large, in the same year the Qing government officially lifted the prohibition on the exploration of those areas, and a large number of people flushed there
2	清末民初	3	清末民初是1900—1912年，这段时期是清朝晚期，民国开端。清末民初在中国历史上处在一个社会激烈动荡的阶段，造成这一社会状况的重要因素是自清王朝实施“闭关锁国”政策后，积贫积弱的中国逐步在科技、经济诸多方面落后于西方国家。这一时期，严酷的专制王朝崩塌，大一统体制宽松，铁板一块的社会在旧与新的拉扯中，门缝透光，窗户渐开，最终门被打开了	“The Late Qing Dynasty and Early Republic of China” existed from 1900 to 1912, the end of the Qing Dynasty and the beginning of the Republic of China. It is a tumultuous period in the history of China. The main reason is that after the Qing government took the policy of “closing its door to the outside world”, China which had already been weak and poor further lagged behind Western countries in many fields such as economy and science. Meanwhile, the draconian despotic regime was collapsing, the system of centralized unification was getting loose, and the clotted society struggled between the old things and the new things—at first, light went in through cracks—finally, the door was opened

续表

No.	Terms	Pg. in ST	Chinese	English
3	中东铁路	3	中日甲午战争爆发，使东西方各殖民列强在远东地区的争夺迅速加剧，尤其是对中国东北权益垂涎已久的沙皇俄国和日本发生了直接的利益冲突。沙俄为了掌控在中国东北的势力范围，全面营建了中东铁路。中东铁路是19世纪末20世纪初中俄双方共同修筑的重要交通性廊道，自俄罗斯远东地区延伸到我国东北地区。人们时常将中东铁路唤为“东清铁路”或“东省铁路”	After the Sino-Japanese War of 1894—1895 broke out, the plunder in the Far East among eastern and western hegemonic imperialist countries accelerated, and the Russian Empire and the Empire of Japan were the biggest rivals for the interests of Northeast. In order to expand its control of Northeast, the Russian Empire comprehensively constructed the Chinese Eastern Railway which acted as an important transport corridor made by the Empire of China and the Russian Empire from the end of 19th century to the beginning of the 20th century. It stretched from the Far East in Russian to Northeast.
4	同乡会	4	同乡会是指同乡之间为联络、交流、互助而自行组建的非营利、不结盟的独立性民间团体。同乡会传统上就是记录乡人在外打拼事业、生活印迹的史证，从同乡宗亲史就能一窥时代演化的图景	Charging no fees and making no alliances, a Townsmen Association is a kind of independent non-governmental organization which is made for the purpose of liaison, communication and help between people from the same area. Usually, it witnessed how townsmen made their careers and lived in other areas, and from the history of relatives in the same area we could see how the periods transformed
5	旅哈山东同乡会	4	哈尔滨山东会馆于1915年由山东同乡会组织成立，馆址位于滨江太古十道街。中东铁路沿线主要的城市几乎都建有山东会馆或同乡会。山东人“闯关东”由来已久，铁路兴起之前他们便在关东地区有着较深的基础，但是也有相当一部分会馆的兴建是在铁路通车之后的	In 1915, Shandong Guild Hall in Harbin was made by Shandong People Association, located in the No.10 Street of Taigu, Binjiang. Along the China Eastern Railway, almost all the main cities had Shandong Guild Halls or Shandong People Associations. It had been a long time since Shandong people “braved the journey to Northeast”, so the business foundation had been laid before the construction of the railway, while quite a few guild halls were made after the railway worked
6	山东会馆	4	随着鲁商实力及影响力的逐渐扩大，山东商帮的脚步也逐渐蔓延至全国各地，鲁商兴建的山东会馆也随之兴起。山东会馆多是客居他乡的山东人在外建立的民间组织，最初是由官员倡导，为举子提供食宿的科举会馆。后商人成为兴建主体，并随着鲁商的足迹而遍布大江南北。最早的山东会馆兴起于北京，原为在北京的山东官员所倡导，是为进京的山东籍学子提供便利的科举试馆	With the enlarging strength and influence of Shandong businessmen, Shandong business groups spread all over the country, and Shandong Guild Halls made by Shandong businessmen mushroomed. Those guild halls were mostly non-governmental organizations made by Shandong people who lived away from their hometown. At first, the construction of such guild halls was proposed by government officers to provide boarding for candidates for the imperial examinations. Later, businessmen became the main builders of the guild halls which spread around the country with the businessmen. The oldest one was made in Beijing, which was originally proposed by a Shandong government officer in Beijing, serving as accommodation for candidates who came to take the imperial examinations in Beijing

续表

No.	Terms	Pg. in ST	Chinese	English
7	吉林将军	5	吉林将军又名“宁古塔将军”，清朝初年，为了加强对黑龙江流域各民族的统治，抵御沙俄的侵略，清政府设立宁古塔将军	General of Jilin Ula and Other Places/Jilin General is also called as General of Ningguta. In the early years of the Qing Dynasty, the government set the General of Ningguta to strengthen its dominance over different peoples along the Heilongjiang River and defend itself against the invasion of the Russian Empire
8	阿勒楚喀	5	阿勒楚喀位于黑龙江省南部，即今阿城镇，清代阿勒楚喀地区归吉林将军管辖。阿勒楚喀副都统衙门既是清代八旗驻防的军事组织，也是清政府在东北地区成立的一个政权机构，管理阿勒楚喀地方，对地区社会的稳定巩固和经济的快速恢复发展都产生了重大影响。宣统元年，裁撤副都统衙门，设阿城县，县名简化为阿城	Alcuka is located in the south of Heilongjiang, namely Acheng Town, which was administered by General of Jilin. The yamen (government office) administered by the assistant military governor of Alcuka was a military organization of the Eight Banners garrisons as well as a political agency of the Qing government in Northeast. It governed that area, playing a significant role in the solid stability of society and the quick growth of economy. During the reign of Xuantong, the yamen was removed, and Alcuka was transformed as Acheng County, Acheng for short
9	劳动家	6	劳动家其实就是指旧时的劳动者，他们是在殖民地或半殖民地从事重体力劳动，收入低下，从事脏且累工作的人（如矿工、车夫、搬运工）	Working people actually means laborers, especially these who did manual labour with low wages in colonized or semi-colonized countries. Their jobs were usually foul and tiring, such as miners, coachmen, porters
10	南满	7	以松辽分水岭为地理界线，此线以南区域称为“南满”。总的来说，南满指辽东半岛，这里曾经属于女真时期的满族聚居区，地处东北南部，皇太极改姓满后，称“东北满洲”。在地理意义上，满洲通常是指今天辽宁、吉林、黑龙江三省的全部，加上内蒙古的东北和外兴安岭以南地区	With the Songliao watershed as the geographical line of demarcation, the area south of the Z-shaped line is called as “South Manchuria”. In general, Southern Manchuria refers to the Liaodong Peninsula which used to be a Manchu ghetto during the Jurchen period, located in the south of Northeast. After the emperor Huangtaiji changed his surname into Man, that area was called as “Northeast Manchuria”, and the place was called as “Southern Manchuria”. Geographically, Manchuria is usually referred to as all the areas of Liaoning, Jilin and Heilongjiang, with the northeastern part of Inner Mongolia and the southern part of the Stanovoy Range

续表

No.	Terms	Pg. in ST	Chinese	English
11	北满	7	以松辽分水岭为地理界线，此线以北区域称为“北满”。东北沦陷初期，伪满洲国仍沿用“东省特别区”称谓。1933年7月1日改称“北满特别区”，管辖西起满洲里、中经哈尔滨、东到绥芬河，以及哈尔滨至长春原中东铁路沿线一带地方（不含哈尔滨市）。1935年12月，伪满决定废止北满特别区，将其原辖区域（除满洲里、海拉尔市外）分别划归邻接市、县、旗。1936年1月1日，北满特别区正式撤销	With the Songliao watershed as the geographical line of demarcation, the area north of the line is called as “North Manchuria”. In the early years when Northeast was occupied by Japanese invaders by force, Manchukuo still used “the Special Area of the East Province” to call that place. On the 1st of July in 1933, it was changed as “the Special Area of Northern Manchuria”, administering areas from Manzhouli City in the west by way of Harbin to Suifenhe City in the east along with areas from Harbin to Changchun where the Chinese Eastern Railway passed (Harbin excluded). In the December of 1935, Manchukuo decided to abolish the special area and dispatch the areas the special area used to administer (except Manzhouli City and Hailar City) to adjacent cities, counties and Banners. On 1st January 1936, the Special Area of Northern Manchuria was officially abolished
12	四明公馆	9	四明公馆又名“宁波会馆”，是由旅沪宁波籍人士在清嘉庆二年（1797年）建成的、带有慈善性质的同乡会馆，嘉庆七年在公所正式成立。公所为上海人民反帝的著名场所。	Si Ming Mansion is also called as “Ningbo Guild Hall”, which was built by people who came from Ningbo in the reign of Jiaqing (1797). It was a guild hall for fellow townsmen from Ningbo in a charitable way, officially opened in the 7th year of the reign of Jiaqing, and it was a famous place where Shanghai people started activities against the imperialist invaders
13	会馆文化	9	会馆是中国明清时期都市中由同乡或同业组成的团体，是旧时代科举制度和工商业活动的产物，是北京一种独特的文化现象。明清两朝定都北京，每三年在京进行一次科考会试，至清光绪三十年（1904年）科举考试废止，已先后在京举行会试201科，全国各地进京应试的举子130多万人次。每科应试有六七千人，再加上一些随行的人员，多达上万人。为方便这些人的食宿，各省及有些府县纷纷在京设立了会馆，专门接待本乡本土的举子。另外，工商各行业为了维护自身的利益，协调关系，联络感情，也建立了一些行业会馆	Guild halls are organizations which were made by fellow townsmen or people of the same occupation in the city during the Ming and Qing Dynasties. They are the result of the imperial examination system and business activities as well as a unique phenomenon in Beijing. In the Ming and Qing Dynasties, Beijing was chosen as the royal capital where the metropolitan examination (one of the imperial examinations) took place every three years. Before the 30th year of the reign (1904) of Guangxu in the Qing Dynasty when the imperial examination system was abandoned, 201 metropolitan examinations had been held in Beijing, and over 1.3 million candidates around the country came to Beijing for the examination. About 6, 000 to 7, 000 people participated in each exam, and with their entourage the total number was about 10, 000. In order to provide boarding to those people, every province and county set guild halls in Beijing for their own candidates. Furthermore, industrial and commercial occupations also built some guild halls to defend their interests, arbitrate relations and contact with each other

续表

No.	Terms	Pg. in ST	Chinese	English
14	顺直	12	顺直为历史地名，相当于今天的河北和天津、北京区域，清代在此设立直隶省和顺天府，此后人们就用“顺直”称呼这一带地区	A name for a place in history, roughly equal to Hebei, Tianjin and Beijing nowadays, where the Qing government set the Shuntian Yamen, the local administrative agency which was directly under the central government. Therefore, it was called as "Shunzhi District" since then
15	滨东同乡会馆	13	“滨”意为哈尔滨，“东”为山东，滨东同乡即在哈尔滨居住的山东同乡众人	The Chinese Character "Bin (滨)" means "Harbin"; "Dong(东)" means "Shandong". "Bin Dong Townsmen" refer to fellow townsmen from Shandong who were living in Harbin
16	滨江厅	13	清末，1907 年 1 月 23 日（清光绪三十二年十二月初十），清廷批准，设置滨江厅，专理“华洋交涉”及“命盗案件”。滨江厅设于傅家店（后改为傅家甸，今属黑龙江省哈尔滨市道外区），就近隶属哈尔滨关道（滨江关道）	At the end of the Qing Dynasty, on 23rd January, 1907 (in the lunar calendar it was 10th December of the 32nd year of the reign of Guangxu), the central government set a government department in Harbin which dealt with "trades between China and other countries" as well as "criminal or civil cases." The office of the department was located in Fujiadian (傅家店 in Chinese, later changed into 傅家甸 which is in Daowai District in Harbin, Heilongjiang), affiliated with the Customs Office of Harbin (the Customs Office of Binjiang)
17	交涉局	14	光绪二十五年（1899 年），清廷设立黑龙江铁路交涉总局，后因庚子之乱而撤局。光绪二十七年（1901 年），黑龙江铁路交涉总局开局，局址设于哈尔滨道里区石头道街。铁路交涉总局的职能是办理“经涉、牵涉东省铁路公司各事”。铁局经费均由东省铁路公司拨发。总办与会办的任命和调动也必须征得东省铁路俄国总监工同意	In the 25th year of the reign of Guangxu (1899), the Qing government set the General Negotiation Department of Heilongjiang Railway which was abandoned because of the Boxer Rebellion. In the 27th year of the reign of Guangxu (1901), the General Negotiation Department of Heilongjiang Railway began to work, which was located in Shitoudao Street in Daoli District in Harbin. It dealt with affairs about "the China Eastern Railway Corporation", and its operating expenses were given by the corporation. Before the decision was made, the nomination and the relocation of the minister and the vice-minister of the department shall be approved by the director of the corporation
18	交涉员	14	交涉员为官名。北洋政府时期因办理与外国交涉事务的需要，于各省省会设有“特派交涉员”，由外交部特派，承外交总长之命办理全省外交行政事务；各通商大埠，亦分设交涉员，称为“外交部某省某埠交涉员”。特派交涉员与各埠交涉员均受该省行政长官的监督。交涉员的官署称为“交涉署”，特派交涉员的交涉署分设四科，掌办总务、交涉、外政、通商各事	The name of a kind of governmental officers. In view of foreign affairs which needed dealing with, the Northern Warlords Government of China appointed "special negotiation officials" in the capital city of every province. The officials were especially sent by the Ministry of Foreign Affairs, attending to foreign affairs of the whole province according to the orders of the General Minister of the Ministry of Foreign Affairs. In major ports, negotiation officials were also appointed as "provincial representatives of the Ministry of Foreign Affairs". The especially sent negotiation officials and negotiation officials from different ports were all supervised by the local governor. Their office was called as "Negotiation Office", and the office of the especially sent negotiation officials had four branches: General Affairs, Negotiation, Foreign Affairs and Trade

续表

No.	Terms	Pg. in ST	Chinese	English
19	跑崴子	18	19世纪初，伴随着“闯关东”的移民大潮，大批关内人前行到海参崴，捕捞垦殖，繁衍生息，经商、做工、种地、放牧、建立各类生产加工小作坊，定居、打鱼、捞海参，长途贩运布匹、日用百货、皮货、日杂、食盐、水产、粮食、首饰等。当年跑崴子主要有两条路径，一是陆路，二是水路。陆路从吉林珲春到海参崴，直线距离不足50千米，冬季赶着马爬犁从珲春出发经过封冻的乌苏里湾，直达海参崴，半天即可到达；夏季赶着马车走大路绕过乌苏里湾，起大早、贪大黑才能到达海参崴。水路从珲春开船，沿红旗河、图们江顺流而下至日本海直奔海参崴，全程300多千米，顺风顺水至少三天两夜，每年5月下旬至10月下旬是海运的黄金季节	At the beginning of the 19th century, with the wave of “braving the journey to Northeast”, numerous people went to Vladivostok. They fished, reclaimed the wilderness and lived there. They went into different careers: business, labour, farming, husbandry, and workshops of different kinds. They fished and caught sea cucumbers as a living, and they also did long-distance trade in textiles, articles of daily use, leather goods, jewelry of gold and silver, groceries, salt, aquaculture, provisions and ornaments. The “undertook commercial activities in Vladivostok” mainly by land or by water. By land, they started from Huichun in Jilin to Vladivostok. The direct distance between the two places is not more than 50 kilometres. In winter, if they set off in Huichun by sleigh on the frozen Wusuli River to Vladivostok, it only took half a day. While in summer, they had to get up before dawn if they wanted to go to Vladivostok by wagon because they needed to make a detour around the Wusuli River. By water, the journey began in Huichun. The ship went down the Hongqi River and the Tumen River to the Sea of Japan. The whole journey is about 300 kilometres, and it took at least three days and two nights to arrive in Vladivostok downwind. The period from the second half of May to the second half of October was the golden season for sea transportation
20	跑伯力	18	根据资料记载，唐朝时期，伯力是黑水都督府勃利州的治所。辽代时，辽国设五国部节度使，治所在伯力，辖黑龙江下游各部。15世纪时，明朝伯力隶属奴儿干都司。清朝时期，伯力成为外东北第一大城市。1858年，俄国侵占中国黑龙江沿岸并在此设军事哨所，将伯力改称为“哈巴罗夫卡”（Хабаровка）。随着居民点的扩大，1883年10月又改为“哈巴罗夫斯克”（Хабаровск）。第二次鸦片战争时，根据1860年《中俄北京条约》，伯力归属俄境	According to historical data, Boli (Khabarovsk) was the capital city of Boli Zhou under the control of Heishui government in the Tang Dynasty. Liao Empire appointed the governor of five provinces and set the office in Boli which governed the lower reaches of the Heilongjiang River in the Liao Dynasty. In the 15th century in the Ming Dynasty, Boli was affiliated with the army and government office of Nu'ergan. In the Qing Dynasty, Boli became the largest city in Outer Northeast. In 1858, the Russian Empire occupied the coastal areas of the Heilongjiang River by force and set military posts here, and the name of city was changed into “Khabarovka” (Хабаровка). As the residential area expanded, the name was changed into “Khabarovsk” (Хабаровск) in the October of 1883. In the Second Opium War, the Sino-Russian Treaty of Peking sorted Boli into the boundary of the Russian Empire

续表

No.	Terms	Pg. in ST	Chinese	English
21	公议会办法大纲	266	公议会办法大纲是俄国强迫清政府签订的夺取中东铁路沿线市镇行政管理权的条款。中东铁路修筑以来，俄国侵占了铁路沿线大片领土。日俄战后，俄国图谋对这一地区的行政管理权。1909年5月10日，清政府和俄国在北京签订该条款，共18条。根据该大纲条款，俄国实际上控制了哈尔滨、满洲里、海拉尔等中东铁路沿线市镇的行政管理权	It is an article imposed on the Qing government by force by the Russian Empire which intended to grab the rights to administer cities and towns along China Eastern Railway. Since the construction of the railway, the Russian Empire had occupied a large part of the territory along the railway. After the Russo-Japanese War, the Russian Empire coveted the administrative rights over that area. On the 10th of May of 1909, the Qing government and the Russian Empire signed that article of 18 items in Beijing. In accordance with the outline, the Russian Empire grabbed the administrative rights of cities and towns along the railway, such as Harbin, Manzhouli and Hailar
22	关道	260	在两次鸦片战争后开放的通商口岸中，大多数以守巡道兼任海关监督，称"关道"。关道的职能主要是海关税收与办理通商口岸交涉事宜，但由于外籍税务司制度的发展，一方面，关道对海关的征税职能旁落，只拥有税收保管权和对常关的征税权；另一方面，关道的通商交涉职能则得到强化。由于关道职能的发挥是在不平等条约的框架下进行的，又不能不受原有体制的限制和督抚的制约，因此关道交涉职能运行中的矛盾也日益凸显，对它的改革也就不可避免。晚清时期，在陆续开放的通商口岸中，出现了一个新的官员群体，这就是海关道。在晚清的文献中，"关道"的称呼越来越广泛	Most of the commercial ports which were opened in the Opium War (1840—1842) needed customs offices to make patrols and supervise trade, and the offices were called as "Guan Dao" (customs offices). The main function of the customs office was to deal with tariffs and negotiations of trade in commercial ports. However, with the development of the system of foreign tax officials, customs offices had less and less power over customs duties, and they could only store the tariffs and tax ordinary ports. On the other hand, the function of trade negotiations was enhanced. Since the operation of the functions was within an unequal framework with unavoidable restraint of the original system and the local governor, the contradictions in the process of operation were increasingly big, and thus a reform was on the way. In the late years of the QIng Dynasty, in the emerging commercial ports a new group of officials appeared: Hai Guan Dao. In the data in the late Qing Dynasty, the word "Guan Dao" was used more and more widely
23	京旗回屯	23	由于八旗人丁，特别是京旗繁衍日众，从康熙中期开始，清廷就已难堪重负，旗人生计便渐成问题。"京旗回屯"即将八旗兵丁回迁至东北屯田	Due to the large population of Bannermen, especially the Bannermen in Beijing, the Qing government had had too much a burden in the middle of the reign of Kangxi, and the redundant population had trouble in earning their bread. The term "the Jing Bannermen's Reclamation" refers to the fact that Bannermen in Beijing were recalled to Northeast to reclaim land

续表

No.	Terms	Pg. in ST	Chinese	English
24	招垦政策	25	招垦，即招民垦种。清制，凡荒地、山场荒地，以及沿江、沿海新涨滩地等，若确无别项出产者，则皆可招民垦种。有的省份招垦荒地时限定亩数。此类经民承垦之官地，应缴租纳科。清初对于东北地区的招垦政策始于顺治八年（1651年），此时只是针对山海关外（辽西地区）进行开放招垦。顺治十年（1653年），开放耕地的范围拓展到辽东，在东北地区实施的招垦政策以御令的形式确定下来。顺治朝颁布的“辽东开垦令”主要是通过授官的方式吸引关外民众，在清初东北地区民生凋敝、田地荒芜、关外流民众多的情况下，招徕民众出关垦荒的政策是符合实际情况的	Cultivation and reclamation policies were policies to recruit people to reclaim land. By the law in the Qing Dynasty, any vacant land, or beaches along the rivers and seas without owners could be reclaimed by people organized by the government. After the land was reclaimed, the people did the reclamation should pay taxes. The policies in Northeast began in the 8th year of the reign of Shunzhi (1651) for the areas north of the Shanhai Pass (namely the Liaoxi area). In the 10th year (1653) the coverage of land extended to the Liaodong area, and the policies in Northeast were determined in the form of the royal order. “The cultivation and reclamation order in Liaodong” in the reign of Shunzhi mainly attracted people north of the Shanhai Pass by the official order. At that time, people in Northeast lived in poverty and the land was barren, so a lot of people moved away. Therefore, the cultivation and reclamation policies then were practical
25	封禁政策	25	康熙中叶以后，关内汉族民人大量涌向东北，造成民人的土地急剧增加。民地在不断扩大，旗地在不断减少。汉族民人的不断涌入，使满汉土地占有的格局发生了明显的变化，威胁着旗人的生计。乾隆五年（1740年），清廷颁布了封禁东北的法令	In the second half of the reign of Kangxi, a large number of people from areas south of the Shanhai Pass flushed into Northeast, causing a sharp rise in the area of the land which belonged to Han people. The area of the land of Han people was on the increase while that of Bannermen on the decrease. The acute change of the land structure between Han people and Bannermen was threatening the living of the later. So, in the 5th year of the reign of Qianlong (1740), the Qing government enacted the Prohibition Policy in Northeast

续表

No.	Terms	Pg. in ST	Chinese	English
26	京旗移驻	31	京旗移驻是清政府的一项国策，调投北京闲散旗人到拉林阿勒楚喀及其周边地区，让他们到满洲族的发祥之地学习农业和练习国语、骑射，恢复本民族旧俗，既能解决旗人生计问题，又可延续国祚，是清代中叶实施的一个有战略意义的大举动。这项决策始于乾隆九年（1744 年），历经乾隆、嘉庆、道光三朝，持续近百载，成为清政府两次重大的由中央向四周地区的移民国策之一。乾隆年间的移驻规模大，人数多，形成了京旗文化的主要组成部分。嘉庆、道光年间的移驻规模虽不及乾隆年间，但其作为清政府京旗移驻国策的延续，对京旗文化的形成和发展也起着不可忽视的历史作用，深入研究嘉庆、道光年间的移驻，对开发京旗文化具有重要的现实意义	"Migration and Station of Jing-banner" was a national policy of the Qing government. It mobilized Bannermen without duties in Beijing to Lalin, Alcuka and adjacent areas. They would learn skills of agriculture and practise the Manchu language and skills of riding and shooting there. It was a strategic action, which was helpful in restoring Manchu customs, providing means of livelihood for Bannermen and sustaining the prosperity of the nation. The decision began in the 9th year of the reign of Qianlong, lasting three reigns of about 300 years, becoming one of the two major migration policies from the central plains to surrounding areas by the Qing government. The wave of migration and station of Jing-banner in the reign of Qianlong was the largest one with the greatest number of population as an important part of Jing-banner culture. The waves of migration and station of Jing-banner in the reigns of Jiaqing and Daoguang were not as large as that in the reign of Qianlong, but as a successor of the migration and station of Jing-banner policy of the Qing government, they also played an indispensable role in shaping and developing Jing-banner culture. So, the research of them is pragmatic in developing Jing-banner culture
27	"恩养"	32	"恩养"是清太祖努尔哈赤创制并实行的一项针对本民族与异民族的"养人"政策，目的在于最大限度地争取政治资源，维护并巩固统治。入关后，清政府对旗人采取了"恩养政策"，然而随着旗人人口的增加与旗丁的奢侈腐化，八旗生计问题日渐成为朝廷的负担和社会的累赘	"En Yang (恩 养 in Chinese)", namely "supporting the Bannermen with grace and provisions / welfare system of the eight Banners", was a policy made by the founder of the Qing Dynasty, Emperor Nurhachi to support Bannermen and people of other nationalities for the purpose of winning political resources to the most and consolidating the monarchy. After Manchu people passed the Shanhai Pass, the Qing government adopted the policy for Bannermen. Nevertheless, as Bannermen's population became increasingly large and they were used to the extravagant and degenerate life, the livelihood problems of them gradually became a burden to the government and society.

续表

No.	Terms	Pg. in ST	Chinese	English
28	汉军出旗	35	乾隆七年（1742年），乾隆皇帝发布了第一道将汉军旗人出旗为民的谕旨。从乾隆皇帝的这一谕旨开始，除了所谓从龙入关的汉军子弟之外，大部分汉军子弟都在出旗之列，无论是京城八旗还是各省驻防八旗，汉军旗人都开始被强令出旗。到乾隆四十四年（1779年）时，除驻防广州的1500名汉军八旗外，其他各地驻防汉军都已经被出旗一空	In the 7th year of the reign of Qianlong, Emperor Qianlong enacted the first royal order that Han Bannermen were removed from the Banners. Since the order, except those Han Bannermen who accompanied the founder of the Qing Dynasty when he passed the Shanhai Pass, most Han Bannermen were removed——no matter they were members of the Eight Banners in Beijing or the Eight Banners in different provinces, they were forced to leave. In the 44th year of the reign of Qianlong, except 1, 500 Han Bannermen who stationed in Guangzhou, other Han Bannermen in different provinces were all expelled from the Banners
29	井田	39	井田是指具有一定规划的方块田，井田制是我国奴隶社会的土地国有制度，西周时盛行。那时，道路和渠道纵横交错，把土地分隔成方块，形状像“井”字，因此称作“井田”。井田属周王所有，分配给奴隶主使用。奴隶主不得买卖和转让井田，还要缴一定的贡赋。奴隶主强迫奴隶集体耕种井田，无偿占有奴隶的劳动成果。从春秋时起，井田制日趋崩溃，逐渐被封建生产关系取代	“Jing Tian” (井田 in Chinese, which means a field in the shape of “井”, a Chinese character) refers to a demarcated square field made of nine smaller squares. The Nine Squares System of Land Ownership / Well Field System was a national land system which was popular in the Western Zhou Dynasty in slave society. The paths and channels for irrigation demarcated the field into squares which made a shape like “井” (Jing, a Chinese character, meaning a well), so the field like that was called as “Jing Tian”. The well fields belonged to the emperor of Zhou and were distributed to masters of slaves. Masters of slaves shall not sell or buy, lend or borrow well fields, and they must pay taxes. They forced slaves to plough the fields in teamwork and took the results of slaves' labour for free. Since the Spring and Autumn Period (770BC-446BC), the Well Field System was collapsing and was finally replaced by the system of enfeoffment

续表

No.	Terms	Pg. in ST	Chinese	English
30	养育兵	41	有清一代，随着八旗人口迅速增加，国家财力受限，加之八旗子弟又渐染奢侈腐化风气，八旗生计问题最终成了清廷的负担和累赘。为此，清廷曾采取过汉军出旗、设立井田、赎回旗地、设立养育兵在内的一系列措施，力图解决八旗生计问题，缓和社会矛盾，但是收效甚微。雍正初年，具有清代八旗基层救助性质的养育兵制正式实施。一直到光绪三十三年（1907 年），养育兵制逐渐为历史所裁汰，在此期间，清廷曾通过各种“补缺”的形式，尽可能扩大养育兵钱粮能惠及的救助范围，虽无法从根本上解决八旗生计问题，但其作为旗人“低保”的历史作用与价值仍是值得肯定的	In the Qing Dynasty, due to the limited funds of the nation and Bannermen's extravagant life, the livelihood of the Bannermen finally became a burden to the Qing government. Therefore, policies such as "the Hans in Manchu army returning to the countryside", the Well Field System, regaining the land and maintaining the Eight-banner soldiers were taken to solve the livelihood problems of the Bannermen and alleviate the contradictions of society, but few results appeared. In the early years of the reign of Yongzheng, the System of Maintaining the Eight-banner Soldiers was officially in practice, for the purpose of helping the grass-root Bannermen. By the 33rd year of the reign of Guangxu (1907), the system was gradually out of date, and during the period the government tried their best to enlarge the coverage of the provisions for the grass-root Bannermen, but it was not able to solve the problem. As a kind of "welfare for those who live on the poverty line", the policy does have something worth valuing historically
31	梅莽喀	61	梅莽喀 (meimangka)，地名，临近地肥，可打井，适合耕种	Meinangka, the name of a place. Its surrounding areas were fertile, which was suitable for making wells and farmlands
32	西沟谷	62	西沟谷（sigeohuolo），地名，临近地肥，可打井，适合耕种	Sigeohuolo, the name of a place. Its surrounding areas were fertile, which was suitable for making wells and farmlands
33	霍济墨	62	霍济墨（hojimo），地名，临近地肥，可打井，适合耕种	Hojimo, the name of a place. Its surrounding areas were fertile, which was suitable for making wells and farmlands
34	窑集	62	窑集（yoojimo），地名，临近地肥，可打井，适合耕种	Yoojimo, the name of a place. Its surrounding areas were fertile, which was suitable for making wells and farmlands
35	洼浑	62	在阿城区料甸街北正红旗屯南边不远处，有一条自东向西流淌的小河，它的名字叫“洼浑河”（满语叫“洼浑毕拉”，汉译是浑浊的臭水河），它是阿什河的二级支流	Not far from the south of the Zhenghongqi Village in Liaodianbei Street in Acheng District runs a stream which flows from east to west. Its name is "Wahun" ("Wahunbila" in the Manchu language, means a dirty river in Chinese), a secondary branch of the Ashihe River

续表

No.	Terms	Pg. in ST	Chinese	English
36	屯丁	71	屯丁是清代人丁的一种。明代，军队按卫所编组，三分守城，七分屯田，谓之“军丁”。清改卫所军丁为屯丁，仍耕种屯田，缴纳田赋；在有漕地区，则负责运送漕粮。初不纳丁银，康熙十三年(1674年)，以三藩乱起，军费开支浩大，始照州县人丁之例，派征丁银。为保证漕粮运输，不使民屯相混，政府令其另立户籍，每五年编审一次。编定册籍，由粮道掌管。如私改户籍，窜入民籍，则按律治罪。雍正二年(1724年)后，无漕地区卫所陆续并入州县，屯丁亦相继改归民籍，唯有漕地区仍保留之，协济漕运，直至清末	A kind of job of adult men in the Qing Dynasty. In the Ming Dynasty, the army was sorted into groups. 30% of the army was to station the city and 70% to open up uncultivated land. The later were called as “Jun Ding” (soldiers who opened up uncultivated land). In the Qing Dynasty, the name was changed into “Tun Ding” (station troops who opened up uncultivated land). Men who were “Tun Ding” still cultivated land and paid taxes. In areas where water transport was available, they also transported goods by water. At first, they didn’t have to pay poll taxes, but in the 13th year of the reign of Kangxi (1674), the Revolt of the Three Feudatories caused vast expenses of the army, which led to poll taxes in every Zhou and county. To supervise the work of the transportation of food by water, the government re-registered them and changed their household registrations for fear that they were mistaken with ordinary people. Their household registrations were checked every five years. The statistics were compiled into a brochure which was in the charge of “Liang Dao” (the Food Office). If anyone of them changed his registration into that of an ordinary person, he shall be punished according to relevant law. After the 2nd year of the reign of Yongzheng (1724), the station troops in areas where water transport was not available were merged into adjacent Zhous and counties. The soldiers changed their household registrations into those of ordinary people as well. In those areas where water transport was available the system still worked until the end of the Qing Dynasty
37	阿玛	104	阿玛是满语父亲的音译，转写为ama，意为“生养自己的人，称为父亲”	Ama is the phonetic translation of the word *father* in Manchu, which is transcribed as “ama”, meaning “the one who gives birth to and raises myself; father”
38	额娘	104	额娘是满族人对侧室、庶母之称。对母亲，满语称eniye。府邸及世家大族讹称“额娘”。满族管“嫡母”称“奶奶”，管“庶母”称“额娘”	E Niang, the name Manchu people call their father’s concubine. Manchu people call their mother “eniye”. Noble people mistakenly used “E Niang”. Manchu people call their father’s wife as “Nai Nai” and call their father’s concubine as “E Niang”

续表

No.	Terms	Pg. in ST	Chinese	English
39	八旗	111	满洲（女真）社会实行八旗制度，丁壮战时皆兵，平时皆民，使其军队具有极强的战斗力。八旗最初源于满洲（女真）人的狩猎组织，是清代旗人的社会生活军事组织形式，也是清代的根本制度。八旗为正黄、正白、正红、正蓝、镶黄、镶白、镶红、镶蓝	Manchu (Jurchen) society performed the Eight Banners System: Adult men were soldiers in wartime, and they were civilians in peacetime, which made the army very efficient in fighting. The Eight Banners came from Manchu (Jurchen) hunting organizations, and then became a form of organization of the Manchu society and military affairs in the Qing Dynasty. It is also the essential system of the dynasty. The Eight Banners are the Plain Yellow Banner, the Plain White Banner, the Plain Red Banner, the Plain Blue Banner, the Bordered Yellow Banner, the Bordered White Banner, the Bordered Red Banner and the Bordered Blue Banner
40	京师八旗	111	“京旗”是清入关后的一个特有名词。清朝定鼎中原以后，八旗官兵分别驻防京城及全国各地，其驻守京城者曰“京师八旗”，或称“驻京八旗”，简称“京旗”；驻防各地者称“驻防八旗”	“The Jing Banner” is a special term appearing after the Qing troops passed the Shanhai Pass. After the Qing Dynasty took control of the nation, the troops of the Eight Banners stationed in Beijing and other places around China, and the troops which stationed in Beijing were called as “the Beijing Eight Banners” or “the Eight Banners Stationing in Beijing”, “the Jing Banner” for short. The troops of the Eight Banners around the country were called as “the Eight Banners Stationing in Other Places”
41	九一八事变	152	九一八事变，又称“奉天事变”“柳条湖事件”，是1931年9月18日日本驻中国东北地区的关东军突然袭击沈阳，以武力侵占东北的事件。九一八事变是由日本蓄意制造并发动的侵华战争，是日本帝国主义企图以武力征服中国的开端，是中国抗日战争的起点，标志着中国局部抗战的开始，揭开了第二次世界大战东方战场的序幕。九一八事变后，中国人民的局部抗战也标志着世界反法西斯战争的起点	The September 18th Incident, also called “the Mukden Incident or the Liutiao Lake Incident”, refers to the incident that the Japanese army in Northeast suddenly stroke Shenyang on 18th September 1931 to occupy Northeast by force. It was made deliberately by Japan and the beginning of the war to invade China by force. From then on, the local combat against the Japanese intruders started, and the battlefield of the Second World War formed. After the incident, Chinese people's resistance against Japan is also the beginning of the World Anti-Fascist War

续表

No.	Terms	Pg. in ST	Chinese	English
42	抗日战争	154	抗日战争，简称“抗战”，是指20世纪中期第二次世界大战中，中国抵抗日本侵略的一场民族性的全面战争。国际上称作“第二次中日战争”“日本侵华战争”。抗战时间从1931年9月18日九一八事变开始算起，至1945年9月2日结束	The War of Resistance Against Japanese Aggression is also called “the War Against Japanese Aggression” for short. It refers to the national whole war of China’s resistance against Japan in the Second World War. In the international perspective, it is called “the Second Sino-Japanese War or the War of Japanese Aggression Against China”. It began on 18th September,1931 and ended on 2nd September 1945
43	侨民	172	凡旅居国外而保留本国国籍的居民，统称为“侨民”	Anyone that lives in a foreign country and keeps his or her own nationality is called “an alien”
44	“河豚计划”	188	“河豚计划”是日本在侵占中国东北后提出的一项计划，希望采取扶植、亲善犹太人的政策，巩固他们在“满洲国”的统治，并影响英美对日的态度	“The Fugu Plan” is a plan proposed by Japan after it invaded Northeast. By supporting and treating Jewish people friendly, it wanted to consolidate its control over “Manchukuo” and change the Britain’s and America’s attitudes towards Japan
45	《关于难民地位的公约》	192	根据《联合国宪章》与《世界人权宣言》确认的人人享有基本权利和自由而不受歧视的原则，为保证难民可以最广泛地行使此项基本权利和自由，并考虑到难民地位问题需要通过国际合作才能得到满意的解决而不致成为国家之间紧张的根源，联合国大会于1951年7月在日内瓦召开了一次各国的全权代表会议，讨论并通过了本公约	Given that solving the problems of the status of refugees needs international cooperation rather than the tensions between nations, according to the principle of the *Charter of the United Nations* and the *Universal Declaration of Human Rights* that everyone enjoys basic rights and freedom and should not be discriminated, the General Assembly of the United Nations held a conference of plenipotentiaries of all the countries around the world in Geneva in the July of 1951 and passed that convention in order that refugees can enjoy the rights of the principle to the most
46	塞法迪人	193	西班牙系犹太人，Sephardi，亦作Sefardi，复数Sephardim或Sefardim。中国台湾地区翻译为“塞法迪犹太人”，中国台湾译法较为恰切，因为西班牙系犹太人并不是指祖先来自西班牙的犹太人，而是指采用西班牙系犹太教礼拜仪式的犹太人	The Spanish Jewish people, Sephardi or Sefardi, Sephardim or Sefardim in the plural form. Taiwan translates them as “塞法迪犹太人” (Sephardim). That translation is more accurate because they don’t refer to the Jewish people whose ancestors came from Spain but the Jewish people who adopt Spanish ways in the religious services of Judaism

续表

No.	Terms	Pg. in ST	Chinese	English
47	阿什肯纳兹犹太人	193	阿什肯纳兹犹太人（Ashkenazi Jews），是指源于中世纪德国莱茵河一带的犹太人后裔（阿什肯纳兹在近代指德国）。其中，很多人自10世纪至19世纪，向东欧迁移。从中世纪到20世纪中叶，他们普遍采用意第绪语或者斯拉夫语作为通用语。其文化和宗教习俗受到周边其他国家的影响	Ashkenazi Jews refer to descendants of Jews who lived in the areas along the Rhine in Germany in the Middle Age (in modern times, Ashkenazi refers to Germany). Many of them moved to Eastern Europe from the 10th century to the 19th century. From the Middle Age to the middle of the 20th century, they generally used Yiddish or Slavic as the daily language, and their culture and religious customs were also influenced by surrounding countries
48	基督教青年会	219	基督教青年会是全球性基督教青年社会服务团体，1844年6月6日由英国商人乔治·威廉创立于英国伦敦。基督教青年会希望通过坚定信仰和推动社会服务活动改善青年人精神生活与社会文化环境。目前，约110个国家有青年会组织，总部设在瑞士日内瓦。中国基督教青年会创建于1895年，其努力目标是发扬基督精神，团结青年同志，养成完美人格，建设完美社会	Young Men's Christian Association is a global Christian group made by young people for social service. It was founded in London, the UK on 6th June 1844 by the British merchant George William. It hopes to improve the spiritual life of young people and social cultures by pious faith and social service. Recently, about 110 countries have its branches, and its headquarters is in Geneva, Switzerland. Young Men's Christian Association of China was founded in 1895. Its goal is to carry forward the spirit of Christianity, unite young comrades and perfect their personalities and the society where we live
49	日俄战争	238	日俄战争是指1904—1905年日本和俄罗斯帝国为争夺朝鲜半岛与中国东北进行的战争	It is the war from 1904 to 1905, where Japan and the Russian Empire battled for the Korean Peninsula and the Northeast of China
50	十月革命	240	俄国十月革命，又称"红色十月""十月起义""布尔什维克革命"，是俄国工人阶级在布尔什维克党领导下联合贫农完成的伟大的社会主义革命，是1917年俄国革命中第二个也是最后的重要阶段。因发生在俄国历法1917年10月25日（1917年11月7日），故称"十月革命"	The October Revolution, also called "the Red Revolution, the October Revolt or the Bolshevik Revolution", is a great socialist revolution made by the Russian working class with the cooperation of poor farming laborers under the leadership of the Bolshevik Party as well as the second and the last of the important stage of the Russian Revolution of 1917. It got the name because it happened on 25th October 1917 in the Russian calendar (7th November 1917 AD)

续表

No.	Terms	Pg. in ST	Chinese	English
51	《中俄密约》	242	《中俄密约》，即俄国与清政府订立的秘密的不平等条约，1896年6月3日（光绪二十二年四月二十二日），沙俄利用中国在中日甲午战争中战败的困境，借口“共同防御”日本，诱迫清政府与俄国在莫斯科签订《中俄密约》	The *Sino-Russian Secret Treaty*, an unequal treaty signed by the Qing government with the Russian Empire secretly. China was defeated in the Sino-Japanese War of 1894—1895. As a result, on the excuse of "defending ourselves from the attack of Japan", the Russian Empire forced the Qing government to sign the *Sino-Russian Secret Treaty* in Moscow on 3rd June 1896 (22nd April of the 22nd year of the reign of Guangxu)
52	衙门	251	旧时称官署为“衙门”，即政权机构的办事场所。衙门的别称是“六扇门”。其实衙门是由“牙门”转化而来的。猛兽的利牙，古时常用来象征武力。“牙门”系古代军事用语，是军旅营门的别称	In ancient China, the governmental office was called as "yamun" where officials worked. The word yamun (衙门 in Chinese) was transformed from "牙门" (牙 means "teeth" in Chinese and 门 means "door" in Chinese). The nickname of yamun is "six doors". The fangs of beasts were often the symbol of force in ancient China. "牙门" is a military term in ancient China, which is another name of the army
53	疆吏	252	疆吏是指守护边疆的官吏。清代称总督、巡抚为“封疆大吏”。简称为“疆吏”	The officials who guard the frontiers. In the Qing Dynasty, Governor-generals and Governors were called as "officials who guarded the frontiers", "frontier officials" for short
54	商埠	252	商埠是指与外国通商的城市，另指商业发达的城市	Cities which do business with foreign countries. The word also refers to prosperous commercial cities
55	帮办	253	清代后期中央或地方临时机构中主管官的副职，一般为总办之副职，其资格略次于会办，称为“帮办”，即帮助办理各项事务之意。北洋政府沿置，设于税务处各股的帮办，相当于帮股长；海关征税部内班职员亦有称“帮办”的，以洋员为主，其地位次于副税务司；外交部各司、铨叙等局亦置帮办，后多由参事兼任；步军统领衙门各科亦置帮办	The assistant position of the director in a temporary agency of the central government or the local government in the late half of the Qing Dynasty, the assistant director which is a little inferior to the director, is called as "帮办" (Bang Ban in Chinese, assistant, meaning the person who helps others to deal with things). The North Warlords Government inherited the system: the assistants in the Tax Bureau of different provinces equaled to the assistant directors; there were assistants in the Customs Office as well, and most of them were foreigners whose positions were a little inferior to the assistant director; the different divisions of the Foreign Department and the Inspection Department also had assistants, and as time passed by the position was undertaken by the Counsellor

续表

No.	Terms	Pg. in ST	Chinese	English
56	笔帖式	253	笔帖式是指清代官府中的低级文书官员，主要职责是翻译、抄写政府文书，管理档案等，它是清代特有的职官。其发展大致经历了满清人关前、满清人关后到乾隆帝、乾隆帝至清朝灭亡3个阶段	Scribes were inferior office officials in the Qing government. Their main jobs were to translate or transcribe official documents and manage files. The official position only existed in the QIng Dynasty. Its development has three stages: before Manchu passing the Shanhai Pass; after Manchu passing the Shanhai Pass until the reign of Qianlong; from the reign of Qianlong to the end of the dynasty
57	文事	253	文事意思为关于文化、教育的事务	Affairs which are related to culture and education
58	武事	253	武事是指与军队或战争有关的事情	Affairs which are related to the army or war
59	总办	253	旧时官职名称。清末新设置官署或办事机构的主管人员称“督办或总办”、副职称“会办”，资格比会办略次的称“帮办”	A kind of government officials in ancient China. In the late years of the Qing Dynasty, the head of the government or the agency was called “the general director”, the assistant position was called as “the assistant director”, and the position inferior to the assistant director was called as “the assistant”
60	局夫	254	旧时公署的公务员	Civil servants in the government in ancient China
61	局勇	254	旧时公署的卫兵。《二十年目睹之怪现状》第六十九回：“人家办公事的地方，如何容得这个样子，便有两个局勇驱赶他”	Guards in the government in ancient China. In the 69th chapter of the Chinese novel *Bizarre Happenings Eye witnessed Over Twenty Years*, “It is a government office. How could they bear that? Then two guards expelled him.
62	书识	254	清代正额书吏之外的一种临时性书吏，称为“书识”（shū zhì）	A kind of temporary scribes besides Zheng'e scribes in the Qing Dynasty, which is called as “shū zhi” (letter clerk)
63	清末新政	256	清末新政又称“庚子新政”“庚子后新政”，民国称“遮羞变法”，香港称“晚清改革”，日本称“光绪新政”，是清朝末年的一场经济和政治体制改革运动，也是中国现代化的重大事件之一	New Deal period in the Late Qing Dynasty, also called as “New Deal in the year Gengzi” or “New Deal after the year Gengzi”. It has different names in different times and areas: “the Make-up Reform” (the Republic of China), “the Late Qing Reform” (Hong Kong), “the New Deal in the Reign of Guangxu” (Japan), which was a reform of economy and politics in the Late Qing Dynasty as well as one of the major events in the history of modernization of China

续表

No.	Terms	Pg. in ST	Chinese	English
64	道员	260	道员（又称“道台”），清代地方官名。根据清代的官阶制度：道员（道台）是省（巡抚、总督）与府（知府）之间的地方长官	Dao Yuan (or Dao Tai), a kind of local officials in the Qing Dynasty. According to the official rank system in the dynasty, Dao Yuan (Dao Tai) is the local official between the province rank (Governor or General Governor) and the Fu rank (magistrate of a prefecture)
65	关防	261	边关防务，就是在边关时的防守。	Guarding the frontier, namely the defending activities while guarding the frontier.
66	租帖	267	中国旧时佃农租种地主土地时订立的契约。其内容包括田地面积及坐落地点，租佃期限，地租种类、数额及交租期限，中人责任等项	The lease signed by the tenant farmer when he or she leased land from the landlord in ancient China. The contents are as follows: the area and the location of the land, the term of the lease, the type of the lease, the sum of rent and the deadline of handing on rent, and the responsibilities of the broker
67	道尹	269	道尹是中华民国时期的官名。民国三年（1914 年）5 月，袁世凯公布省、道、县官制，分一省为数道，全国共 93 道，改各省观察使为道尹，管理所辖各县行政事务，隶属省长。其任用由省民政长官经由国务总理呈请大总统特批。民国十三年（1924 年）6 月，北洋政府内务部通令废道制，裁撤道尹	The intendant is a name for officials in the republic of China. In the May of the 3rd year (1914) of the Republic of China, Yuanshikai released the system of the official ranks of provinces, circuits and counties. A province was divided into numerous circuits, and there was 93 Daos around the country. The inspector of every province was changed into the intendant who governed the administrative affairs of the counties in the province. The intendant was supervised by the Governor of a province. Before it was made, the appointment of the intendant shall be appointed by the President. In the June of the 13th year (1924), the Ministry of Internal Affairs of the North Warlords Government made orders to abolish the system of Dao and removed intendants
68	宣统二年	269	1910 年，宣统（1909—1912 年 2 月）为清朝第十二位、清军入关后第十位皇帝爱新觉罗·溥仪的年号，也是中国封建王朝历史上最后一个年号。光绪三十四年（1908 年），溥仪登基，次年（1909 年），改元“宣统”。寓意“宣告天下王朝大统”，有为王朝统治的正当性辩护之意	The year 1910, Xuantong (1909-the February of 1912) is the name of the reign of the 12th emperor in the Qing Dynasty and the 10th emperor Pu’yi after the Manchu army passed the Shanhai Pass, and it is also the last reign in the history of feudal China. In the 34th year of the reign of Guangxu (1908), Pu’yi acceded, and a year later (1909) he changed the name of the reign into “Xuantong”, which means “the announcement of the unification of the kingdom” to defend the legitimacy of the governance of the dynasty

续表

No.	Terms	Pg. in ST	Chinese	English
69	清乡	270	"清乡运动"是抗日战争时期日本侵略者在华中占领区实行的一种残酷的清剿办法。为强化对华中地区的统治，消灭和驱逐革命力量与抗日武装，使之成为日本侵略军稳固的兵站基地，以达到"确立治安"、恣意奴役和搜刮的目的	"Clearing-the-country" is a cruel way Japanese intruders suppressed people in occupied areas in the War of Resistance against Japanese Aggression. The Japanese intruders' goal was to consolidate their governance over China and eradicate and expel forces to make revolutions and resist the aggression of Japan. By clearing banditry in occupied areas, the Japanese aggressors made those areas as solid military bases to achieve the purpose of "maintaining security of society", slaving people and looting wealth
70	通译	270	光绪元年（1875年）起，于驻外使馆内普设通译官，掌翻译之事	Since the 1st year of the reign of Guangxu (1875), they were translators who worked in embassies in foreign countries to do translation and interpretation
71	京师同文馆	271	京师同文馆是清末第一所官办外语专门学校，于1862年8月24日正式开办，初以培养外语翻译、洋务人才为目的，以外国人为教习，专门培养外文译员，属总理事务衙门。课程开始时只设英文，由英国传教士任教习，后来增设法文、德文、俄文、日文。同治六年（1867年）又添设算学馆，教授天文、算学。该馆附设印书处、翻译处，曾先后编译、出版自然科学及国际法、经济学书籍20余种。此外，还设有化学实验室、博物馆、天文台等。1902年1月（光绪二十七年十二月），并入京师大学堂，改名"京师译学馆"，并于次年开学，仍为外国语言文字专门学校	The School of Combined Learning is the first specialized school of foreign languages made by the government in the late year of the Qing Dynasty. It was officially founded on 24th August 1862 to cultivate translators of foreign languages and talents to deal with foreign affairs. It was affiliated with the yamen of the Prime Minister, hiring foreigners as teachers to cultivate translators and interpreters of foreign languages. At first, there were only English courses taught by British missionaries. Later there were French, German, Russian and Japanese courses. In the 6th year of the reign of Tongzhi the division of mathematics was added, teaching astronomy and arithmetic. The school had the publishing house and the translation department, which edited, translated and published over 20 kinds of books about sciences, international laws and economics. In addition, it had chemistry labs, a museum and an observatory. In the January of 1902 (the December of the 27th year of the reign of Guangxu), it was merged into the Imperial University of Peking, and its name was changed into "the Peking Translation Institute". It opened the next year, still as a specialized school of foreign languages